An Architect of Democracy

Memoirs and Occasional Papers
Association for Diplomatic Studies and Training

In 2003, the Association for Diplomatic Studies and Training (ADST) created the Memoirs and Occasional Papers Series to preserve firsthand accounts and other informed observations on foreign affairs for scholars, journalists, and the general public. Sponsoring publication of the series is one of numerous ways in which ADST, a nonprofit organization founded in 1986, seeks to promote understanding of American diplomacy and those who conduct it. Together with the Foreign Affairs Oral History program and ADST's support for the training of foreign affairs personnel at the State Department's Foreign Service Institute, these efforts constitute the Association's fundamental purposes.

Published and forthcoming by New Academia Publishing

An Architect of Democracy

Building a Mosaic of Peace

James Robert Huntley

Foreword by Brent Scowcroft

Memoirs and Occasional Papers
Association for Diplomatic Studies and Training

 New Academia Publishing, LLC
Washington, DC

New Academia Publishing, LLC
P.O. Box 27420, Washington, DC 20038-7420
www.newacademia.com - info@newacademia.com

To my wife Colleen,
whose support and
understanding have been
indispensable
and
to the memory of
Walt Raymond,
Clarence K. Streit, and
Jean Monnet

Other books by James R. Huntley

The NATO Story (1965, 1968)

Europe and America: The Next Ten Years (1970)

Uniting the Democracies: Institutions of the Emerging Atlantic-Pacific System (1980)

Pax Democratica: A Strategy for the 21st Century (1998, 2001)

Contents

List of Illustrations

Foreword

A number of years ago, during the Cold War, I met a young man with an idea. He believed that two themes which guided American policy since 1945—international community plus democratic governance—should be intertwined and given top billing in the actions of our country and its European and Canadian allies. In this way, said Jim Huntley, we would eventually find the surest and most durable pathway to peace.

Jim had, as a young Foreign Service officer in the 1950s, worked to bring the German people back into the international community. Today, thanks to Jim's work and that of many others, united Germany is a shining and firm example of democracy at work. Jim then spent several more years in government, in Washington and in Europe, helping to shape and spread the key ideas behind the rebuilding of war-torn Europe and the dedication of NATO and other North American commitments to transatlantic security.

Many of us who had served in government in this period shared Jim's sense of purpose; he helped—both while he was in government and later outside it—to quietly but firmly remind Europeans, Americans, and Canadians continually of our common duty to present and succeeding generations to create a sound and lasting framework for a peaceful world. And rhetoric, although at times a necessary foundation for foreign policy, was not enough for Jim. Through his early years in his home state of Washington, he had learned the value of citizens' combining in nongovernmental associations to poke and prod government at all levels into action on burning problems of the time. He applied these ideas to his work in Germany, where he sent hundreds of Germans, young and old, to the United States to see how a modern working (if imperfect) democracy "did it." One ingenious scheme of Jim's was to create "community action teams" in middle-sized German towns and send them to similar communities in America to learn and share ideas.

In the years that followed, Jim spread the idea of "community action" throughout the Atlantic community, spurring top leaders to create an Atlantic Institute, a multinational private think tank that fostered common intellectual work on our many common problems of the Cold War, our responsibilities to the developing countries and the United Nations, and to the foundations for today's worldwide free economy. He urged organizations in the Atlantic world to combine their efforts through a Standing Conference on Atlantic Organizations, and through a series of Mid-Atlantic Clubs in key cities, where opinion leaders, including Americans living in Europe, could share ideas regularly.

In the 1960s, when it became clear that Japan, Australia, and other East Asian countries might join what was now becoming "an Atlantic-Pacific System," Jim wrote books on this and related subjects.

Jim and I became partners in a 1970s effort to set up international seminars for young leaders from the countries of the Organization for Economic Cooperation and Development (OECD). As in so many citizen ventures, this one did not finally take shape until the 1980s, in London, with major financing and direction by Sir David Wills. He was one of the people that Jim had earlier recruited into his growing network of like-minded friends. Today, this 21st Century Trust has an alumni group of many hundreds of young leaders of the world, from many countries.

When Jim became president of the Atlantic Council of the United States, he stimulated his directors to think about new international conceptions and idea-sharing. For example, he conceived the idea of an Atlantic-Pacific group of defense-oriented members of parliament, who met yearly with the U.S. Commander-in-Chief Pacific to share ideas about global security.

In 1984, with Jim's guidance, the University of South Carolina hosted a conference of "Atlantic-Pacific leaders" to review thinking about our growing interconnected world. Once more, with Larry Eagleburger, Hisashi Owada, Lord Carrington, and others (all out of government at the time), we worked on new ideas that later could be tried out. It is no accident that today there is an intergovernmental "Community of Democracies," which was the conception that Jim and his colleagues such as Sam DePalma and John Richardson, plus the indefatigable Walt Raymond, kept pushing, quietly but insistently. The Polish government, with support from Secretary of State Madeleine Albright, in 2000 brought 107 of the world's democracies together to create the Community, a forum of ministers and NGOs which meets biannually to elaborate on Jim's basic ideas: (a) democracies rarely, if ever, make war on one another; (b) when democracies combine for mutual aid (as in the European Union) they attract weak nations to adopt free institutions so that they can join and share common benefits; and finally, (c) it is not enough to simply create more democracies; they must combine and work together to form lasting ties. In this slow but sure way, international law and world peace grow.

And so it went, over the years. Jim and I and others worked together many more times. Walt Raymond, John Richardson, and Jim formed the latest of a string of American democracy/community citizen initiatives, the Council for a Community of Democracies. One of the Council's greatest achievements has been to get the democracies to create a caucus of their members at the United Nations in New York.

Jim Huntley has made an important contribution to the long-term, hard job of fashioning a peaceful world by spreading democracy and building international community. The main ideas he has given will continue to grown an importance with the years.

Here is Jim Huntley's story. I warmly wish him and his ideas well.

Brent Scowcroft
Washington, D.C., 2005

Preface

If it had not been for the Korean War, this work might have been entitled: "A Lifelong Encounter with State Government," or it might have been called "The Autobiography of an American Diplomat," except that that would account for only one decade (to be sure, formative and exciting) in a long life. But for my total engagement in problems of world peace and transatlantic relations, as a result of a year and a half at the old Iron Curtain, the book could have been about "Germans, Europe, and the USA." But I've also had a lot to do with philanthropy and foundations, from the standpoint of both finding money and giving it away. That work was immensely satisfying and I might have chosen to stay with the Ford Foundation indefinitely; in that case, the title could have been, "Thoughts of a Philanthropoid." But the Ford Foundation stopped its major "Atlantic and European" programs in their tracks, so I moved on. And thus the scope of what I have tried to do, under very different auspices at times, has been wider still.

My career has not followed a linear path. Only one thing has given it purpose and direction: The gradual realization that the growth of democracy in the world and a corresponding growth of international institutions that link democracies in common purpose are the surest path I can find towards peace. This then bounded my life's mission. I chose my jobs (occasionally the job chose me) and plotted my course with my life's mission in mind: help democracy grow and use it as the best binding force between nations. Behind the various chronological road stops lie some interesting stories. I think my children and their descendants may be interested in "how Grandpa got the way he is." Also, these thoughts may be of some interest to colleagues and friends who have shared a good deal of my career life, and finally—if any scholar or historian is interested in the just-over-the-horizon work of foundations and nonprofit bodies of all kinds and how they interact with governments and intergovernmental organizations—these chapters may give clues as to the nature of these processes during the Cold War and after.

My half century of archives (I am an inveterate document and correspondence collector) has been transferred in 2005 to the Paul J. Hanna Collection on International Education, part of the Hoover Institution's massive archives on War, Peace, and Revolution in the 20th Century. The Hoover library is located on the Stanford University campus; anyone is welcome to consult its holdings.

The serious reader may also look on my work, including this memoir and my several other books and articles, as a gloss on the evolution of thought about international relations—and particularly my own thought. Beginning with Machiavelli, modern ideas about the interaction of states have revolved around power and how to use it internationally. Seventeenth century thinkers, such as Hobbes and Grotius, wrote seminally about the Leviathan state and international law, respectively, and influenced those who wrote the Treaty of Westphalia, the main foundation until today of the theory and practice of relations between sovereign states. The nineteenth and twentieth centuries saw the flowering of these and other, newer, ideas about nations and how they interact and about the practice of peace and war. Clausewitz, Mahan, Mackinder, and Norman Angell added to the understanding of grand strategy and geopolitics. Angell wrote mainly about the futility of warfare; indeed, he thought in 1911 that war had become so brutal and destructive that it was unthinkable. After the two world wars, the school of "realists" became especially articulate, with Morgenthau, Schwarzenberger, Kissinger, and others articulating theories of the balance of power.

Back in medieval times, another line of thought—that of a regime of peace that could encompass all states—began; a few writers and early peaceniks in the nineteenth and twentieth centuries expanded on these ideas and put forward schemes for a world federal order. The most practical of these was Jean Monnet, whose thought, in a rather pragmatic way, was probably the most instrumental in influencing the gradual unification of Europe. Clarence K. Streit and Lionel Curtis both wrote about larger schemes of international federalism. Woodrow Wilson—the scholar-president—tried to straddle plans that required mergers of sovereignty (particularly in his ideas of the League of Nations), and still nodded in the direction of those who wanted peace but thought sovereignty inviolable.

Early in this new century, President George W. Bush's administration sought—perhaps without fully understanding what they were doing—to impose a modern-style empire on the world. At least that is where they were heading. This brought a backlash in thought as well as diplomacy, with many older and newer thinkers trying to define the needs of a world system caught in the toils of globalization, interdependence, religious conflicts, and the ongoing struggle between democratic regimes and all the others.

My own work has been influenced by all these thinkers and doers—and many more not mentioned. And my life, since childhood, has registered one encounter after another with those who sought to reorganize the world in ways that were sometimes visionary and forward-looking, and with those who sought to run the world in quite undemocratic and (I think) backward and dangerous ways. My own odyssey, set forth in the following pages, is a tour mostly "in the trenches," because I did not work directly in the fashioning of high policy nor is mine a household name. But I did encounter most of the theories about how nations interact, worked out my own, and worked closely with some of the top "movers and shakers." In these memoirs, the reader will find echoes of the leading ideas of the past, plus my own thoughts, which developed as I went along.

For a deeper encounter with my ideas as to the nature of the world we have to live in, and how the international system could be considerably improved, I refer the reader to my most recent book, *Pax Democratica: A Strategy for the 21st Century* (Palgrave Press, London and New York, 2001). Reference to my earlier works can be found in any comprehensive bibliography on international relations, back to the 1960s. Readers are encouraged to consult this book's appendices, which contain statements by U.S. presidents, various authorities, and the author that reflect the state of thought on affairs among the world's democracies over the past fifty years.

Inasmuch as "democracy" is a principal theme of these memoirs, I should like the reader not to confuse my approach to world affairs with the policies of the George W. Bush regime, especially with regard to Iraq. In my view, democracy derives from the consent of the governed; it is homegrown and not externally imposed. As one "architect of democracy," I have not been in the business of exporting democracy but of helping people govern themselves by their own lights, with democratic principles in mind, and encouraging the democratic transformation of international institutions.

Those who cite Germany and Japan as precedents fail to appreciate that democracy had roots in both nations in the early 1930s and before, a significant factor in the success of U.S. and Allied efforts to help restore and improve their democratic institutions and practices. The great majority of their citizens adopted such measures wholeheartedly and without violence, circumstances I have been able to observe firsthand. In the post–World War II period, democracy has flourished elsewhere too, most often when countries were enmeshed in a network of security, economic, and cultural ties with other democracies. Such external linkages have been key to democratic development.

The use of "peace" in the subtitle of these memoirs has been deliberate. It signals that democracy cannot be forced on a people or nation, but that if old and new democracies work in tandem, conditions for peace will be steadily and firmly created.

It is customary for an author to thank those who have helped him along the way. My list, to be properly exhaustive, would include 80 to 90 percent of those whose names appear in these memoirs. I have helped, but also learned from, many people in many countries, some well known, others less so but just as important to me personally and to the mission we have shared. May I here simply thank them all, for years of friendship and for their hard work in our respective and intersecting vineyards.

How does one know when one's work is done? Especially when the character and shape of the work is sometimes as slippery as mercury! A chance conversation here and there, a singular passage in a book or article, or—especially these days—a surprise reference at a Web site or an e-mail out of the blue opens previously unknown doors. At any rate, I have drawn a line under all the debits and credits now, early in the 21st century, set forth a kind of balance sheet, and hope that whoever reads these lines—soon or perhaps many years later—will better understand one important aspect of the great events of our era: the intertwined struggles for democracy and for world peace. For me, they can never be untangled.

Finally, and a bit frivolously, this work could have had a still different title: "A Hitchhiker's Guide to the 20th Century"—inspired by the tongue-in-cheek radio serial "Hitchhiker's Guide to the Galaxy." Much of the time, I was along for the ride when great things happened. I tried to influence events but usually didn't succeed. Sometimes the success came years later, and by then many others had had a hand in the evolution of the Western world, democracy, modern international relations, and all those good things. At any rate, this is the story of one man and how he tried to help.

James Robert Huntley
Sequim USA, 2006

An Architect of Democracy

1
At the Iron Curtain

5 March 1953: *USSR announces that "the heart of the comrade-in-arms and continuer of genius of Lenin's cause, of the wise leader and teacher of the Communist Party and the Soviet Union, has ceased to beat." Stalin, at 73, is dead.*

25 March 1954: *Soviets announce that the German Democratic Republic (East German occupation zone) is given the right to decide "all questions of internal and external policy."*

It was a dark and stormy night . . . well, afternoon . . . April 1954. I stood just feet from the Iron Curtain itself. Two years earlier, back home in America, I had thought the Curtain was something real—like the border between, say, Washington (where I came from) and Idaho—but mainly an abstraction to help understand the Cold War. But no, this Iron Curtain in 1954 was wooden, a fence about eight feet high that ran right through a village, Mödlareuth. On the other side of the fence were the families and friends of people on my side, the West German side. At each end of the wooden fence, the barbed wire started again.

My driver, Hoppe, took me and a visiting colleague from our Bonn embassy right up to the eight-foot fence at a spot where he knew there was a convenient knothole. I looked through, to see a Soviet officer and a companion from the Eastern Zone *Volkspolizei* (People's Police). They had followed our car, riding in theirs, down a rutty country road on the Eastern side; we traveled on a similar road on the Western side. The East Zone officials' car stopped when we did; they had been tracking us since we had approached the border, an hour before, a chasm where the frontier was the Saale River. We had begun looking at them through the borrowed binoculars of a Bavarian border policeman.

Obviously accustomed to shadowing Western officials in their black official cars, the two Easterners, when we got to Mödlareuth, went right to the knothole. In a minute, I was eyeball to eyeball with the Russian officer. He said something in Russian that I couldn't understand, so I turned my eyeball-post over to my diplomatic companion, who spoke Russian.

They exchanged pleasantries ("Nice day, isn't it? What are you doing here? Just looking around," and so on). Total time: three minutes; then the Communist team retired to a small hillock on their side of the village, to scrutinize us from afar, and we continued looking through the crack in the Iron Curtain.

Mödlareuth probably had a population of less than three or four hundred, a typical Thuringian farming village. Here and there on the East side were large banners, on the sides of houses or on billboards, proclaiming Communist "truths" in German. One sign said, "We here in the East stand for Peace and Freedom," another proclaimed, "Adenauer and other false leaders are thugs." It was unsettling but humorous to see the Communists praising the virtues of Communism with means that we in the West were using to advertise, say, Wrigley's chewing gum.

In the weeks and months that followed, I learned a great deal about the two Germanies close up. Just two months before I arrived in Hof an der Saale, where I was to direct a so-called "Amerika Haus" for a year and a half, the Soviet/East German authorities had decided to relax border restrictions a bit. They needed a way in which they could let the tight reins on the inmates of their vast prison seem to slacken for a while, make people in both East and West feel things were improving . . . in short, to let off pent-up steam, and to permit some of their Agitprop operatives to penetrate the border more easily. After all, it had been less than a year since workers in East Berlin had rebelled en masse and Soviet tanks had had to be called in. The bloody suppression had not been good for the Communist side in the propaganda wars.

For some months in 1954, East Germans who the Soviets thought would not bolt once in the West were allowed to enter West Germany for a short period if they had relatives to visit or some important commercial errand. Small, carefully controlled groups of schoolchildren and others could also transit the border for propaganda purposes. Hof was in a strategic position for this new human traffic, just three or four miles into the West after crossing the border, whether by rail or car.

The Hof Amerika Haus was in a small park four blocks from Hof's *Bahnhof* (rail station). Many travelers from the East disembarked in Hof to look around until the next train south; the Amerika Haus was an attraction for many. With a staff of twenty, I maintained a cultural and information center open to anybody; consequently I and my staff—all Germans—met many East Zone travelers. Some were curious and asked a lot of questions; others left quickly, perhaps worrying that some East German undercover agent might see them. One young traveler from Dresden spent three hours with us—half an hour alone with me, much of the rest listening to records; he had never before heard Negro spirituals. He was, he said, quite sure a great majority of East Zoners were against Communism and especially the Russians, but what could they do? He said there had been a notable decline in unemployment in the past year, as workmen were engaged in the new armaments industry. He thought the new East German Army (started as a response to the move towards a new West German force) would be even less reliable than the *Volkspolizei*. He went away with three books about the United States, which our librarian gave him.

A few months later, the East German regime closed virtually all border-crossing stations and began, with a vengeance, to build a permanent wall, all the way from Lübeck on the Baltic to Hof, very near the corner where Czechoslovakia and the eastern and western Germanies met. The Czechs had their own border defenses, but there were precious few Czechs who wanted to flee their Communist-run country by way of Bavaria. In a couple of years after 1945, the Czech government had rudely mistreated Sudeten Germans, killed many, used some as slave labor, and then expelled the remaining Germans from their borderlands. After all, it was the existence of a noisy, brutal Nazi Party in Sudetenland (awarded to the new Czechoslovakia in the treaties of 1919) that had smoothed Hitler's conquest in 1938, first the Sudeten ethnic–German lands, then all of Czechoslovakia itself in March 1939.

The new East German border fortifications, like the later Berlin Wall, were designed not to keep foreigners out, but their own population in. There were wooden guard towers with searchlights every hundred yards or so, high barbedwire fences between them, plowed strips on either side of the wall. The wall was manned by East German People's Police and plentiful attack dogs. Soviet controllers nearby were ever ready to give orders in unusual cases. Such a border complex was only four kilometers down a rutted, single-track country road from the house my family and I lived in. Prior to 1955, there had been many border crossings, east to west, many of them deadly. But people who desperately wanted out were usually able to find a way, sometimes by driving with permission across a checkpoint, and never going back. The border, more porous than usual during the short "happy period" in 1954, was more or less closed after the new fences went up. Still, some brave, inventive Easterners found a way to cross. In early 1955, there was a thrilling incident: Two East German families secretly fashioned a hot-air balloon, with a gondola big enough for seven or eight and *floated* themselves across the fortifications into the free

West! But for average people, the opportunities to escape were increasingly few. It was not until 1989, when the Berlin Wall came down, that the fortifications all along the border collapsed from human and political pressures.

�֎

In 1970, my wife and I drove to Hof to see the border once again. Hof itself was no longer a rather dirty, rundown little industrial town, as it had been when I left in 1955. The Marshall Plan and the German Economic Miracle had wrought their magic. But the East Zone border was much more formidable than when I had last seen it. Wooden guard towers, barbed wire, and plowed strips had been replaced by twelve-foot concrete walls and towers, surrounded on both sides by treeless meadows to provide a free field of fire. It reminded us of the Emperor Hadrian's Wall in Britain, built to keep the murderous Scots and Picts out of what later became England. We left Hof in 1970 depressed, feeling the Cold War could go on for many years more. But how could one know that in less than two decades, the Berlin Wall, and its counterpart along the entire border would tumble down, with the East Germans free at last?

In 1990, yet another visit to the Hof border brought me glorious release: in place of the concrete fortress walls—a hundred-yard portion of which had been left standing as a permanent memorial—ran a nice little brick path, a memorial winding all the way to the Baltic. At the autobahn checkpoint, the tollbooth-like structures where the guards stopped unwanted traffic in either direction had been dismantled, as were the nearby *Volkspolizei* barracks. The four-lane traffic moved smoothly in both directions now; Germany had been reunited under a single, democratic, federal regime.

We hastened on formerly East Zone roads to Mödlareuth, where the wooden wall with the knothole had been; the border was also gone there— and everywhere—and the village people moved back and forth as in olden days. It was obvious, however, that 45 years of neglect and the shriveled fruits of Communist-style central planning had taken their toll. Less than a year of unification had not yet provided time for much change on what had been the eastern side of Mödlareuth; there, all buildings needed paint; some had probably not had a fresh coat since World War II. This corner of former East Germany looked to me as all of Europe had in 1948, when as a student I saw the old Continent for the first time.

Back to the former Hof border and 1990: We drove a bit in what had been the East Zone; the secondary roads were rutted and had no shoulders to speak of, whereas on the Hof (free) side roads and new housing projects and farms showed what some years of a free economy could do. The contrast was amazing. We returned with friends to Nuremberg to spend a couple of days reflecting on the change and what it meant.

A year later, in 1991, I traveled by train from the northwest corner of Franconia to Berlin, on a trajectory I had never tried. Here are a few notes from my journal, typical of all that I saw on the 150-mile trip:

Probstzella, Thuringia, 18 July 1991: [The] railway station looks pitiful, as does the land around it. Some station buildings are very old, and ill painted, a few are newer but ill painted. On the [Western] side of the border a profusion of flowers everywhere. Here, just a few scraggly ones. It is as if time has stood still here, for 45 years. . . .

All coal/steam–driven [industrial] plants . . . all rusty and rundown . . . houses nearly all gray, earth-colored, dark and dreary . . . filthy stucco . . . occasionally, a striking new factory or warehouse of some sort [built by Western capital] . . . juxtaposed with "Peoples' Housing," all like barracks. . . .

[At Leunewerke, south of Halle]: an immense complex of chemical factories—all "dead"—filthy air, decay everywhere.

There were a few brighter spots, but essentially this picture is what 45 years of Soviet-style Communism had brought to the East Germans. (See Chapter 18 for a more detailed account of the fall of Communism and what it means.)

In 1998, three East German professional women, all in their thirties, visited Seattle under Department of State sponsorship. I spent an evening with them, comparing notes on Germany and discovering something of their reactions to life under Communism and the changes that had come after reunification. Two said their opportunities had improved and they were, on the whole, satisfied with the historic merger. Their families had been ordinary ones, getting what they could from the East German educational system, but no family members were affiliated with the Communist party. The third woman, however, was clearly dissatisfied; she had lost an excellent job and had been "bumped" downward socioeconomically after reunification. Her parents had been solid Party members, she too in the youth groups. It seemed apparent to me that this was an obvious case of what had filtered over to us from the East in those years—years I consider more or less lost for the East Germans: if one was a faithful cog in the Communist system, one could expect perks. In George Orwell's famous phrase: "All animals are equal . . . but some are more equal than others."

❊

I had still another view of these matters in 2001, when an old Seattle class-mate and her husband—let's call them "Betty" and "Don"—came from their home in East Berlin for our 60th high-school class reunion. In 1948, when we were all leaving university, they went off to marry and live in the eastern United States. Don was a war veteran but also, since around 1939, a convinced Communist; he planned a U.S. academic career, but found af-ter about ten years that American colleges and universities, at least at that time, wouldn't give tenure to Communists, nor could they be employed at all by some. Don and Betty went to Berlin in 1962, not long after the Wall went up. Don crossed into the Russian sector and asked the East German education ministry for a job teaching English literature. The authorities were delighted; he and Betty spent twenty years in East Berlin; when re-unification came, Don retired. They now divide their time between Berlin and London, where they also have a home.

After our class reunion, they stayed several days with us, discussing all sorts of questions and visiting old haunts of our youth, just south of Seattle. Sometimes we broached topics bordering on politics and interna-tional relations. Don in particular was often quick to defend the former East German regime, the *Deutsche Democratische Republik*. The East's edu-cation system, child care for working mothers, low unemployment, and many other features were superior to those of the West, he maintained. All *our* troubles in the West were still due to the evils of capitalism. At one point I asked Betty what she thought of the many East Germans who had been shot dead trying to cross the Berlin wall; her reply: "It was tragic. It's so unfortunate: it was a good system, but the wrong people were running it."

Finally, the night before their departure, I told Don I had spent a year and a half right at the Iron Curtain; what did he think of any regime that would by force (and often *lethal* force) prevent its citizens from going abroad? Usually articulate and voluble, he simply fell silent. There was no good answer, even from an 80-year-old Communist who still "believed."

[Note: One good source for what happened under Communism, why and how, is in the biographies of Lenin, Stalin, and Trotsky, written in the 1990s by Col. Gen. Dmitri Volkogonov, who was head of the Soviet Army historical archives when the USSR cracked apart in 1991.]

✷

In 1954, when I first stood at the Iron Curtain, I was amazed and deeply troubled. At the time, I was 31 years old, had served in Germany as a Foreign Service officer for 30 months, had visited Berlin (including the Eastern part) and seen a great contrast, but never had I been prepared for the reality of the Iron Curtain as it hit me when I took up duties in rural, backwoods Hof. Here was a real outpost in the Cold War, and every day gave me new insights. In the third chapter, I'll deal with life as I saw it initially in Germany beginning in January 1952. Two further chapters will recount what I did and saw until I left for America with my small family in June 1955. Those years were, for me, a growing up and a broadening time, in ways I never before could have imagined.

Next, perhaps a view on my life prior to 1952 would be helpful. What chain of events led me to the Iron Curtain in 1954?

2
Growing Up and Outward

29 October 1929: *Stocks on Wall Street lose between $10 and $15 billion in value, beginning what is to become the Great Depression.*

March 1939: *Clarence Streit's* Union Now *is published — "A proposal for an Atlantic Union of the Free."*

Roots

My father served in World War I, returned to the Northwest to begin adult life as an accountant, married my mother, and settled down in Tacoma. My mother's parents were Swedes who had come to America around 1880 and made their way to the Northwest by 1890. Grandfather Lars Berquist was a carpenter but never found steady work or good health; he died in 1915. Grandmother Augusta Berquist had been a schoolteacher in a village in southern Sweden; she ran a boarding house in Tacoma to keep Lars and their three daughters afloat in difficult times. After eight years of Logan Grade School in Tacoma, Mother attended a "business college" for a year. With secretarial skills, a knowledge of bookkeeping and what in those days was known as a "comptometer," a primitive calculator, she worked for a large Tacoma department store, then as accountant at a lumber camp, where she met Dad.

Their house is more beautiful today than it was as I remember it from childhood. This is not the case with most of the fifty-odd (yes, count them!) houses and apartments I later lived in. Today, I look out over fields, woods, and the Strait of Juan de Fuca to the north, across which we can see the lights of Victoria, the capital of Canada's westernmost province. The Olympic Mountains begin just five miles to the south. Our present abode is far nicer than any of the others ... the tale, I guess, of many middle-class

Americans who finally settled down in retirement towards the end of the twentieth century. This is where I belong.

My Dad grew up in a small frontier town, Buckley, in the shadow of Mount Rainier. Its inhabitants were loggers and coal miners; Dad said Buckley had seven churches—and eleven saloons! His father was a good accountant but an alcoholic. Grandmother had come west from Kansas to Buckley when only seventeen and had made her way as an expert dressmaker. She couldn't reform old Grandpa Sherman, so divorced him and married Bob Levesque—my stepgrandfather and certainly the best there ever was. He taught me fishing, and fish we did. Born a Catholic, he stopped churchgoing early on. He was the most moral man I ever knew.

Wells, my father, drove a bus for a time after high school, then volunteered for the Army when World War I began. In France in 1918, he was about to go off to Officers' Candidate School when the war ended. He was a fine man, later managing a printed circuit company of his own in the 1960s. I saw too little of him. Dad never talked much about the war, but I remember that one of his favorite expostulations—when he wanted to express a frivolous disdain for something—was "Bushwah!" Later, when I learned to speak French, I realized that he, like thousands of other dough-boys, learned to make fun of something by calling it "bourgeois!"

Tacoma was a sleepy provincial town in the 1920s, but as a seaport and as the home of many immigrants, it had a certain international flavor. One could tell, too, that the frontier of America was not long vanished from the Northwest; Indian squaws sat on Pacific Avenue, selling woven baskets; nearby was a cigar store Indian in front of a smoke shop. Swedes and other Scandinavians made up most of the workforce in Tacoma's thriving lumber mills. A good deal of the vast, virgin Douglas fir and cedar forests in western Washington had been cut, beginning in the 1850s, but plenty of ancient patriarch trees still stood, and the second growth was extensive; a Douglas fir grows four feet in a year! My father left his job as a bank teller in 1927 to join a firm of stockbrokers. Two years later, the Crash came; wiped out, he was lucky to get a good job as credit manager for a large Seattle furniture company. But before we got to Seattle, we had to sell our Tacoma home and live for a year in a pretty rude shack on five acres bordering one of the countless lakes left by the glaciers in and around Puget Sound. To a six-year-old, it was exciting and bred in me a permanent love of forests and mountains. (As the new century began, my wife and I settled on a plot of two acres, surrounded once again by conifers; you can take the boy out of the country, . . . etc.)

Seattle in the 1930s

Seattle was something else in 1930; its growth, vitality, and a raw sense of identity overshadowed that of Tacoma. The two cities had vied for the site of railroad termini in the 1880s and 90s, but Seattle finally won out. Boeing, in the 20s and 30s a fledgling airline as much as an aircraft manufacturer, added to the big-city industrial atmosphere. Steel, trucks, and light manufacturing were add-ons. When we moved to Seattle, in hindsight I can see that in 1930 it was provincial and backwoodsy; Seattle furnaces of the day ran almost exclusively on sawdust from the mills, not coal, as in most of America. The Depression had started. I recall "Hooverville," about a mile square of flatland south of Downtown where the homeless and jobless lived in packing crates and flimsy shacks alongside the railroads.

At age six, I entered Ravenna Grade School to begin my education; today it is the Ravenna retirement home! I kid my oldest Seattle friend, Brewster Denny, that when we are ready for it, we can go to a nursing home in our old elementary school! I had fine teachers, both at Ravenna and later at Highline high school, which I entered in 1937. Some were a bit rough-cut, like Ravenna's Mr. Leonard, gruff and unsmiling, who handled what was called "manual training." With him, I learned to make a wooden spoon and a kite-string spindle. For high school chemistry, my teacher was Ed Greene, who had been a cowboy in Montana; he had a long, scrawny neck on an appropriately long, skinny frame; he managed to stay just ahead of the pupils. We used to see old Greene driving to school in his 1928 Buick sedan, sitting very straight in the saddle, just like old times on the range.

My parents divorced in 1936, so my mother, small brother, and I moved out to a still-rural area south of Seattle proper. The district had a mixed population. Many were truck farmers, mostly Italians and Japanese. Some business and professional people commuted to Seattle. There was just a handful of stores and filling stations and hardware enterprises, otherwise woods, farmers' fields and early suburban development. During World War II, these suburbs of Seattle grew and provided a bedroom for the Boeing workers. Boeing expanded after Pearl Harbor and at one time had more than 100,000 hands making B-17 Flying Fortresses.

I had already had a year's Boy Scout training in Seattle and luckily enlisted in another good troop in our new "hometown," Seahurst. Scouting had a tremendous formative effect on my character, work habits, capacity for leadership. It also laid some mental groundwork for internationalism; in the summer of 1939, I went to Victoria BC with 50 other American Eagle Scouts from the Seattle area, mainly to help line the streets as King George VI and Queen Elizabeth (the Queen Mother, who died at 101 in 2002) rode slowly by in their open limousine. We Americans were on one side of the street, the Canadian Scouts on the other. I held the American flag, a Canadian Scout held their banner. Just before the King passed us, the Canadian opposite me threw down his flag, and the royal car rolled right over it. I was astounded; later, when we bivouacked in a park, I asked a Canadian Scout how this could be done? We American kids had learned that the flag was the highest symbol of the nation, and we should "never let it touch the ground," as was the rule in battle. The Canadian said things were different in the Empire; the sovereign, not the flag, was the highest symbol of nationhood in all the British Dominions and colonies.

Scouting taught me how to set goals, motivate and organize others, and to cherish what we then called the Great Outdoors. Just back of our little home in Seahurst, the cutover areas from earlier logging began, as yet unbuilt with homes or industry. Second-growth trees were coming on strong. Close to our neighborhood the big forests began, filling 25 square miles between us and Seattle. In the summer, a few Scout friends and I would pack our knapsacks with food (my mother thought I should always take beans and porkchops or salt pork) and primitive sleeping bags, or rolls of blankets, which always got wet. Accompanied by two or three dogs, we hiked three miles or so into the dense woods on what probably were old Indian trails. We made camp alongside a creek. Each kid cooked his own meals over a common fire, usually in the rain. We went to sleep, also usually in the rain, when it became dark. This was heaven for a 14-year-old.

After three or four nights, we had usually had enough of trying to build rude shelters, improving the flow of the creek, or making platforms for better sleeping, so we would go home, sodden dogs and all. Later, our whole troop, with great help from fathers, took treks into the Cascade and Olympic Mountains, where Nature was on a grander as well as more dangerous scale. Once, just before the attack on Pearl Harbor, a Scoutmaster and I took 30 boys on a seven-day, 35-mile hike across the Cascades, from west to east, crossing ice-cold rivers and snowy mountain passes. Greatest attention had to be paid to care of the feet; not a few boys burned their boots trying to dry them before a fire. As I look back on these days, I realize how lucky a boy was to be a Scout in the Pacific Northwest; there were few woods and no mountains in that great stretch of flat land between Utah and Kentucky. The Seattle area was made for scouting. As I write, the Boy Scouts of America, a private association, is having a good deal of trouble. It's sad that the organization is targeted by social groups that demand changes in its goals and rules. Also, modern technology, with TV and video games for kids, sometimes make scouting, with its emphasis on experiencing nature firsthand, old hat.

Serendipity led me from the Boy Scouts to the development of a camping/nature program (what would today be called Environmental Education) for most of the schoolchildren of our district; if outdoor experience was a good thing for Boy and Girl Scouts, why not for all kids? This was a new kind of activity for any schools in the nation; only Michigan and a couple of other states were experimenting. The driving force was the vice principal of my high school, Carl Jensen, who still today, in his very retired nineties, is active in this field. We built camps on Washington lakes and eventually took over an old Civilian Conservation Corps (CCC) camp, today a permanent showplace for environmental, on-the-spot education.

Before and after World War II, Carl and other friends and I worked to extend this type of schooling, using the woods and mountains as our classroom. It is sad that, although environmental education programs continue as part of some schools' learning programs, this is not generally so. Nor is camping—as *camping*—of much interest to kids. Families often go "camping" but take their TVs, gas stoves, and the like with them into the woods, surrounded by others doing the same. "Summer camps" today are mostly specialized—science camps, computer camps, sports camps, golf camps, theater camps, soccer camps, religious instruction camps, and so on. Not just—well, *camp* camps!

University and War

I entered the University of Washington in the autumn of 1941. At the turn of the year, we were at war, and most of my college mates enlisted or were soon drafted. My eyes couldn't pass muster for the requirements of the Air Force, Navy, or Army, so I remained at the university for another year, studying Chinese in case it could later be of use (it wasn't). I went to work in 1943 for Pan American Airways, first as a mechanic (at which I was terrible) and later writing and illustrating training manuals. In 1944, the U.S. Navy, which had contracted with Pan Am to haul freight and sailors from Seattle to Alaska, swept up all the available Pan Am personnel and inducted us into the Navy, physical infirmities or no. I was thrilled. I was finally going to sea, to see the world, help directly with the war. But circumstance intervened, and instead of heading for Pearl Harbor and beyond, my orders were changed to assignment with a Naval Air Transport squadron near Seattle. No "join the Navy and see the world" for me. I was put in the VR-5 Squadron personnel office, which was easy work for me, but I made the mistake of taking such a load off the Personnel Officer's shoulders that he consistently refused my requests for transfer to the Aleutians or Southeastern Alaska, or anywhere else.

The war finished, I returned to the university, married, and took a part-time job with the YMCA-YWCA at the university, helping younger students organize various community-service activities and also have fun. As a Y secretary, my companion for a year was a young Naval officer, just discharged, named Ancil Payne. We became fast friends and have engaged over the years in all kinds of mutual skullduggery. Ancil later worked for a member of Congress from our State, and helped me in 1952 to get into the diplomatic service. Ancil helped me again, in the 1970s, when I returned to Seattle and began organizing Committees for a Community of Democracies plus an aborted (sadly) scheme to train young leaders from many countries in Seattle. After a long career heading a string of TV stations and leading all manner of community nonprofits, Ancil passed away in 2004. He was a fitting member of the Greatest Generation.

In 1946 I had contemplated going into what was then called "personnel work"—all the various interest and aptitude tests suggested this, so I made my own "major" (today called by Harvard and others "an area of concentration") at the university to equip me for working with people. I studied psychology, sociology, economics, and a bit of political science. One also had to dabble in the natural sciences, so I learned some geology and, to complete the requirements for a degree, took a course called "home remedies." I couldn't stand the idea of physics or chemistry, so home remedies filled the bill. Congress's G.I. Bill gave my wife and me $120 per month to live on and paid my educational fees; this was supplemented by $130 each month for my work at the YMCA. Not munificent compensation, but enough to squeak by. The GI Bill made possible a leg-up on higher education for millions of demobilized GIs, many of whom would otherwise never have been able to afford it. It greatly enriched our nation.

As I contemplated what my first real job should be, I was asked by old pals in the Highline school district to take a job organizing a recreation program for the whole community. This led soon to a post with Washington State government; his daughters, friends from university days, told Sam Clarke, director of Parks and Recreation, that Jim Huntley knew more than anybody else about group camping! (A considerable lie, but it shows one that connections can be important, no matter how improbable the tie.) Sam hired me, and for nearly four years I cruised my native state of Washington, returning regularly to the capital, Olympia, to develop plans for turning many of the State Parks into facilities where groups—churches, YMCA, Scouts, service clubs for boys and girls, and so on—could have outdoor and camping experience. I soon realized that many of the groups that could use these facilities knew very little about group camping, so I organized a statewide committee to set up standards and training. This became a continuing pattern in my life: see a community need, devise a way to meet it, and persuade responsible people to back programs. I did this later on a national scale, Europe-wide, and, in most aspects of international relations, globally towards the end of my active life.

What I learned about civic activism and community organization began with the Boy Scouts, benefited from the lofty yet practical aims of the YMCA, and was augmented especially by my Statewide work with the so-called County Agents, men and women employed jointly by the United States federal government, the State, and the various counties to advise farmers and others how to grow better crops, but also how to develop kids and make better communities. These programs today have become infinitely more complicated than in the late 1940s; specialists have developed subprograms of all kinds and created their own bureaucratic niches. But the needs of communities and the depth and breadth of the well of goodwill and civic concern that still animate the majority of ordinary people, were made evident to me in ways that later made possible some bold ventures in internationalism.

1930s Internationalism

Now may be a good time to pick up these threads of my early life, to see how internationalism, psychologically and practically, became the main theme of my work as I matured. It all began with World War I.

As I wasn't born until 1923, all I ever knew about the Great War, as it was called until 1939—when the second installment eventuated—was from my father and others who had been American "doughboys," and from books and schools. On every 11 November, we would stop our schoolwork at 11 AM, and join everyone in the country with a moment of silence, to honor the dead of the Great War. Adults wore little paper poppies (of Picardy) in their lapels.

When I was eight or nine years old, the boys in my Seattle neighborhood and I used to play "World War" in our backyards. Ours was especially apt for this, as there was a ready-made trench behind a low concrete retaining wall. The "Germans," or the "Allies," would occupy the trench and the other side would attack, with wooden rifles and machine guns, and our dads' old wartime helmets. I still have a worn book, *The Great War*, published soon after 1919, which fascinated me. I was repulsed by what little I learned of the realities of the war, but at a tender age I was also ruminating often on the question of why supposedly civilized men and countries should do this to one another?

My mother, a devout Christian Scientist, subscribed to the *Christian Science Monitor*, which I began to read regularly. (Finally canceled my subscription around 1995 because I had too much to read and either the *Monitor* or the *International Herald Tribune* would have to go. More on the *Trib* later.) Mother and Dad both had what now seems to me an enlightened (if just a little self-righteous) view of the world: they bought Woodrow Wilson's claim (I think rightly) that we fought to make the world safe for democracy, that the European countries were weary, nationalistic, and somewhat decadent, that the United States could still, and should, make its mark on the world. The new League of Nations was great, but it was a shame that the Senate of the United States would not ratify the Convention. Intelligent people would do what they could nevertheless to eliminate the scourge of war. The new authoritarians who popped up in Italy, South America, later Germany and eastern Europe, were a great danger and needed to be stopped. But how? These were my family's basic beliefs and concerns.

Eleven years of age brought me to a momentous decision: I would start a newspaper and try to get some of these ideas (and others) across to ... whom? Well, I would start with the neighborhood we lived in: nice middle-class families, some with up to seven or eight kids, whose fathers had all been in the War. A clutch of my neighborhood comrades (all boys, of course) agreed we should publish this vehicle for the news of the world, and include local items that would help to draw subscribers. For a year and a half we struggled to produce weekly (more or less) editions of the *Neighborhood News*. I still have some faded copies, produced by "hectograph," the forerunner of the later ditto machine and the Xerox. All one needed was a powder that formed a gelatin when mixed with water, poured into one of Mother's rectangular cake tins, plus an old battered Underwood to produce the "master," copies of which came off the cake tin in batches of about twenty. One then had to stop (if more copies were needed) and type a new master, etc. We had reporters for neighborhood doings, some Seattle news, a little national comment, and a good deal of "news" and commentary on what was happening internationally. This latter was already my meat. I wrote articles excoriating Mussolini, who had just begun his campaign to enslave Abyssinia (now Ethiopia); Bruce Moehring, my pal from the next block and our staff cartoonist, drew a riveting, melodramatic picture of Mussolini himself whipping the poor black Abyssinians. Hitler was just beginning to appear on our youthful radar screens.

The *Neighborhood News* was great fun while it lasted. But Bruce's younger brother Glen, whom I surprisingly met at a lawn party sixty years after all this journalistic circus, told me the main reason that we shut the paper down, very quickly. It seems that Glen wrote a neighborhood chit-chat column; one issue remarked how often Mr. Jones had been seen visiting Mrs. Smith's home, when everybody else was away. Well, this scandal spelled our demise as publishers. Besides, it was that summer, 1936, when my parents split up and Mother, my little brother Ted, and I moved away to Seahurst, in the rural environs of Seattle.

For one year (my 8th grade), Mother put me in a private school, Open Vista, run by a zealous Christian Scientist. Overall, it was a mistake and I went off to public high school the next year. But a major saving grace at Open Vista was Mrs. Eleanor Leonard, teaching French and current events. She was one of around 100 French-speaking young women who went to France in 1917 to man the telephones for General Pershing's and other American Expeditionary Force headquarters. When I met her, Mrs. Leonard was a housewife and part-time teacher, with husband and three children in my age range. However, she had learned things firsthand, and not too far from the Front in wartime France, to which few American women were ever exposed; she had been close up to the councils of a shattering war. She started me out on the French language, which I continued to study in high school and college. But Mrs. Leonard's great impact on my life was exposure to her profound understanding of world affairs. She used the *Christian Science Monitor* as her text, then interpreted what we read together. Mrs. Leonard and the *Monitor* knew what the advent of Adolf Hitler meant; in 1936 the United States stood by when he marched troops into the demilitarized Rhineland, in defiance of the Versailles Treaty. Britain and France stood by, too, the still war-dazed publics and myopic leaders praying that perhaps this would be Hitler's last, as well as his first, territorial demand. "After all," said so many, "it is only right that Germany take its place in the community of nations, and possibly breaking these Treaty bonds was a natural step." But Eleanor Leonard knew differently. Hitler was not so different from Mussolini, just a lot more dangerous. Dictatorships were by their very nature bound to confront the democracies. War could very well be in the offing. Mrs. Leonard helped put meat on the bones of my nascent internationalism, as well as nurturing my love of freedom.

At high school, a couple of years later, I entered a national poster contest on the theme of peace. My poster (which placed respectably but not first) showed a hobnailed jackboot about to tread on a cobra; the legend read "Stamp out War." If only the huge conundrum had been that easy to resolve! By the time I was in my third year of high school, Hitler had struck in Poland and World War II had begun. Virtually all my classmates read *Life* magazine and some read *Time*. We watched, transfixed and revulsed at what was happening in Europe. Many Americans (but not I) believed that this was not America's war, hoping that we could stay neutral and above the fray. I was from the first in the war party, believing that free Europe's cause was also ours, and that to delay would only increase the chances of civilization's adversaries to prevail. Simple but—I still think—true.

I was a member of the school debate team, which traveled to other schools in the area to debate their teams; each year, a national panel produced one issue for discussions all over the country. In the autumn of 1940, Britain stood alone after a year of terrible danger. She had just barely won the Battle of Britain in the air, but had lost a good part of her regular army in the Dunkirk retreat. She was fighting German units already in North Africa. Apart from Polish, Czech, Norwegian, and French units that had escaped the continent to regroup in Britain under Allied command, Europe was in thralldom everywhere except in Iberia. The British dominions overseas came to Britain's aid again, as they had in 1914, but this was enough to tip the balance, at least to buy time. Hitler, in June 1941, opened general warfare with the Soviet Union; his armies advanced steadily. No one knew whether the USSR or Britain could hold out. A remarkable American journalist, Clarence Streit, had written a widely acclaimed but visionary book, *Union Now*, which in 1939, on the eve of the war, called for a federation of the Western democracies that could withstand and vanquish Hitler. The publisher of *Time* and *Life* magazines, Henry Luce, backed Streit and his ideas; soon there were chapters of Streit's opinion-rallying organization, Federal Union, all over the United States.

Those of us who were alert to the German danger nevertheless probably did not know the full dimensions of Britain's plight. Norman Moss in *Nineteen Weeks* (2003) recounts "the most melodramatic words ever spoken in a British cabinet meeting." In the summer of 1940, Churchill told his colleagues: "I am convinced that every one of you would rise up and tear me down from my place if I were for one moment to contemplate parley or surrender. If this long island story of ours is to end at last, let it end only when each of us lies choking in his own blood upon the ground."

In September 1940, in the suburbs of provincial Seattle, I knew nothing of Streit's popular movement but found the national high school debate topic, "Should the United States and Britain form a Federal Union?" (taken from Streit's 1941 updated book) imaginative and timely. My fellow debate team members geared up to discuss the idea of international federal union, in formal debating style, in high schools around Puget Sound. The debate rules meant that we had to change sides often, and debate either the No or the Yes position. That was the first I ever heard of Clarence Streit; the War intervened for me and more than 15 million other young Americans who were "called up." I never thought about Streit's federal concept again until 1952, when I read a book on Europe and America which dealt in part with Streit's ideas. In 1955, returned from Germany, I met Mr. Streit. But the profound results of those literary and personal encounters for me, I'll leave aside for another fifteen years.

⚜

A last note on my roots: My mother and father were quite unalike in many ways, which no doubt precipitated their parting. But they both shared origins and principles which they passed on to me. Neither had much formal education–Mom finished elementary school, plus six months in a "business college"; Dad finished high school, and later took "correspondence courses" in management. But both were highly intelligent, well read for their times, and rock-solid in their values: don't complain about your lot, make the best of it; read everything you can get your hands on, and above all, keep up on current affairs; treat others kindly; work hard, be a builder; obey the Ten Commandments, the Sermon on the Mount, and the Boy Scout law. These guiding ideals were more than enough for me. I did my best and could always hear their wise counsel, long after they were dead.

1
The Hoh Glacier (foreground) and Mount Olympus, highest point in the Olympic National Park. The author and young companions trekked over and around these and other Olympic peaks during the years after World War II, and also planned facilities and programs for youth who would learn their camping and mountain-climbing skills in these surroundings.

ALBRECHT
DÜRER HAUS
NÜRNBERG

2

The home of Albrecht Dürer in Nuremberg, main city of Franconia, where the author lived in 1952–53. This Bavarian province butted up against the East Zone of Germany and Communist Czechoslovakia, as it was then. In 1990 the author visited this border. Like Berlin on 8 November 1989, this area saw the walls surrounding the entire East German Communist experiment tumble down. The dissolution of the Communist empire had begun.

3

This Amerika Haus in the Franconian town of Hof an der Saale was one of about forty such libraries and lecture halls that the U.S. Information Agency established in the early period after World War II as centers of cultural and informational exchange to help the German people learn about modern democracy. The author directed this Amerika Haus in 1954–55.

On a snowy day, a figure strolls past the stately columns of Widener Library.

4
Harvard University's Widener Library, in Cambridge, Massachusetts, where the author did much of his graduate research in 1955–56, between USIA tours of duty.

3
Pearl Harbor Changed Us Forever

14 August 1941: *In Newfoundland, Churchill and Roosevelt issue the "Atlantic Charter," a vision for the world after World War II that led to the development of the United Nations.*

7 December 1941: *Eight U.S. battleships are sunk or badly damaged when Japanese submarines and carrier-based planes attack the U.S. Pacific Fleet at Pearl Harbor. The United States declares war on Japan; Germany declares war on the United States, and the United States on Germany.*

The Japanese Attack

With the stunning news of Pearl Harbor, American life in every respect was turned upside down. My grandparents, mother, brother and I heard the news over the radio as we were eating Sunday lunch. I had just entered the university and the best I could do, given some eyesight problems which kept me out of the military until 1944, was to reevaluate my academic program. I began more study of history and took a course in "intensive Chinese," which began with learning the characters through flip cards. Later I learned that was not the best method for starting out with a foreign language—by the end of World War II, the U.S. Army had revolutionized language studies, so that any native speaker of the language could instruct using immediate conversation, manuals, and records, enabling the student to begin almost at once to make simple conversation. The study of grammar, reading, and writing came later. I learned German in 1952 in this new way, and Japanese in 1974. French, which I learned in school and college by the old pedantic methods, sprouted only later when I was forced to converse.

As a sailor in the U.S. Navy, I had little time to think about any of the underlying factors of the present world predicament. We were almost all fastened on one objective: win the War. As a present for me in 1995, my wife found a 1943 issue of *Look* magazine, *Life's* rival; I was struck by the virtually total dedication on every page of that popular weekly to the war, the homefront, and all that implied. Even the advertisements dealt, if indirectly, with how to save, plant crops, buy war bonds, use all materials carefully, and so on. As I studied the war years later, I learned that more than 15 million U.S. men and a good complement of women were enlisted in the services between 1941 and 1945. That was about four times more than were called to the colors in 1917–18. Perhaps not more than a couple of million of the 15 million actually served in combat, but the scale of mobilization, along with a mammoth civilian effort to supply the troops with the weapons and materials they needed, was indeed without precedent in history, partly because of America's size. But even then the United States, relatively, did not mobilize its economy and manpower as intensively as did Nazi Germany or Japan. Germany was less than half our size and had many fewer resources, while the Japanese had fewer still, yet it was quite possible that they, and not we and the Allies, might have won. It was, as Wellington said after Waterloo, a "near run thing."

Few of us imagined after mid-1942 that America and its allies could lose the war, but historians now tell us that the margin for victory was much smaller than we thought at the time. Great celebrations took place on VE Day (8 May 1945) and VJ Day (2 September 1945). Soon there was foreboding that the United States. could slip into recession, but the pent-up demand for civilian goods, the lack of physical damage in the United States the existence of great new capacity in industry plus plenty of new manpower now demobilized, all combined to produce an unprecedented postwar boom.

Not so, of course, in Europe and Japan. The British had depleted all their resources and finances. The Continent was damaged beyond belief. In 1956, a Harvard professor, teaching me the interaction of forms of government and "national character" on the political behavior of nations, told of his tank battalion entering a German village in 1945 that had been totally flattened by bombardment. As the tanks rolled down its main street, he noticed one chimney still standing, with the surrounding house totally demolished. On the interior mantle of the chimney a little needlework motto still stood. It read *"Hier herrscht Ordnung"* (here order reigns). The German passion for order, in part, had led to the greatest catastrophe for the German people. More of this later.

Postwar Peregrinations

But my thoughts were not running at all in this direction in 1946–50. I was beginning a family, I was concentrating on university study to prepare myself for a career which I thought, in general terms, was pretty well mapped out. As a veteran—a little older than my peers in college classes—and a citizen, I was pretty unhappy with some of the now-glaring inequalities and defects of American society. I thought that through good solid work with youth in their spare time, I could help establish some better norms for growing up in America, and thus for grownups. For a time, around 1948, I toyed with the idea of emigrating to New Zealand, which, perhaps more than any other country at the time, had begun a successful welfare state (no pejorative overtones; it was a necessary new element in Western societies, as has been pretty well shown). I wrote the New Zealand government to inquire and found that they employed youth workers in a responsible framework. But I could not bring myself, nor could my wife, to leave friends and family for the antipodes, perhaps permanently. In hindsight, this was a wise decision. I eventually visited New Zealand, which was lovely and peaceful, but a place other countries would not really accept as a model. New Zealanders feel themselves very much "out in left field," and they still are, protected by U.S. military power and diplomacy.

The closest I got in this period to "going international" was the opportunity to see Europe. In the summer of 1948, when I had finished my studies, my first wife and I set out on a five-month bicycle trip in northwestern Europe. We had saved up a bit, but our budget had to be meager: $150 per month, plus the expense of rail across the United States and a steamer from New York to Southampton and back. We stayed in youth hostels and with farmers for the most part, with cheap hotel or B&B accommodations in big cities. We had studied Swedish to prepare, as I wanted to meet my Swedish cousins and see where my grandparents had grown and trod.

A couple of the legs of the trip involved hoisting the bikes onto trains and traveling third class. Once, in Norway, we already had about 800 miles of biking under our belts but couldn't face pushing the cycles up a steep switch-backed road from the head of the Hardanger Fjord to the top of the plateau, 3,000 feet up, where the great barren and windswept Hardanger Vidda (plateau) starts—so we put the bikes on top of a bus and rode to the top. Again, when ready to leave Denmark for Holland, we found that one could not travel across occupied Germany by bike or foot unless one had family or commercial business in what was then the British Zone. So we entrained for the Netherlands, encountering German customs officials in the process; to me their uniforms looked just like those of Nazis in the movies. (Later this changed; in a couple of decades and after the Western "youth revolution," German postal officials, border guards, train personnel all became much more relaxed, even congenial and "laid back.") The ravages of war still scarred all of Europe, except neutral and—at the time—rather self-satisfied Sweden; buildings and homes everywhere lacked paint, bombed out parts of most big cities were more evident than those untouched. As our train moved slowly across the heathland outside Bremen, a small but poignant incident touched me deeply: a boy of about 12 or 13 was walking by the tracks, only a few feet from the (rather dingy) third-class wagon we sat in. I suddenly had an impulse to throw him an uneaten chocolate bar we had acquired in Denmark. He caught it, waved, and carefully put it in his rucksack. I sensed then, and knew with some certainty later, that German boys like him had precious little to eat, yet I felt that he had probably secreted the treat to take home to share; otherwise he would have stopped right away to devour it. It was a German capacity for self-sacrifice, as well as fierce determination, that helped his countrymen to recover and rebuild from zero.

We biked across the Low Countries into France, just as forlorn a landscape as the rest. In Paris, we rested and sold our bikes, which we had bought in London, then set out to do what pinchpenny tourists did. We stayed in a rundown little hotel on the Left Bank and ate cheaply, but almost everything was cheap in Paris in those days; one dollar bought you a 350-franc meal in a decent restaurant, *escargots* (snails) and all. One day I thought to look up the friend of a Seattle friend, who was living in a cheap rooming house in the rue du Bac. No phone number, so one day around 11 o'clock I simply went looking for the fellow. The concierge indicated he was in his room, on the third floor. I knocked on his door; he yelled "come in!" and there he was in *flagrante delicto* with a cheery, blowsy French gal. I reddened (this sort of thing never having happened before in my sheltered life) and stood in the doorway, stammering out greetings from his friend in Seattle. He said, "Good to see you, and why don't we meet at around seven o'clock in a restaurant?" I agreed; we met them and had a decent meal; never saw them again. But it made me think that suddenly I was in the town where the Bohemian life had begun.

I also looked up a long-lost companion from high school who had started a little nightclub, with modest success, right next to the police precinct in the heart of the Latin quarter. I saw him again in the fifties and sixties with his partner (Leroy had become openly gay); he died very probably of an early case of AIDS. The Left Bank was one of my haunts over the years, as I struggled to understand French life, and to enjoy the passing crowd, not to mention the food. There is nothing like the *Café des Deux Magots* to give one a feel for what it is to be a Parisian intellectual.

At this time, I was not sensitive to world events or even those around me, i.e., not able to put them in a larger context. For example, on Armistice Day, 11 November 1948, we were caught in a huge demonstration of workers on the Champs-Elysées. We cowered in a shop doorway as this turned into a riot; the gendarmerie arrived; several demonstrators were killed when policemen opened fire. This was pretty scary. But I had little understanding of the general peril that pervaded both France and Italy especially.

The *New York Herald Tribune* (Paris edition) contained articles about great social unrest in France, indeed all over Europe, about the beginnings of the Marshall Plan and the Cold War. Communist takeovers in France and Italy were considered quite possible, if not likely, perhaps in other countries as well. Before we arrived in Europe, there had been a Communist coup in Prague, but we didn't think much about the implications. In May, the Russian blockade of Berlin had begun; U.S. and British transports flew in the food and other supplies, even coal, that the 3 million Berliners in the three Western sectors required to survive. This was ongoing all the time we were in Europe, but I never thought too much about it, even less about a possible decades-long struggle to come. In the summer of 1948, I was concentrating on seeing what Europe on the ground was like, making genealogical connections in Sweden, and enjoying a novel kind of life, on the road through fascinating cultures, and spending as little of our tiny stash of cash as possible.

We returned to Seattle, after a great bout of seasickness on the old RMS *Mauretania*, in December 1948. That winter I began my new career as a youth worker, moving for a better job with the State of Washington the next summer. I liked my work and I liked sleepy Olympia. But great changes were in store, unbeknownst to me.

When North Korea poured over the borders into South Korea in June 1950, and President Truman got UN backing, plus some Allied forces, to try to repel the attack, this was a major event in my life—almost like Pearl Harbor. Before that, I had truly thought that after two apocalyptic wars in the 20th century, with incalculable loss of life plus civic and industrial damage, wars—at any rate big ones—were a thing of the past. We had created a United Nations and that would provide the frame for treating the world's ills. By 1945, my Dad's (and Wilson's) war to "make the world safe for democracy" had finally finished its second installment and we could vindicate humanity's 1919 hopes.

But 1950 did not present a rational world. Nor does it today, although things are immeasurably better as the 21st century begins. I had not yet realized that America could not stand aside from the global turmoil, whether we wished it or not. My thoughts turned back two years to 1948, and our departure from Sweden. We had been heading out on bicycle from Småland, the Swedish province I called ancestral home. A cousin had asked me to smuggle out about $700 worth of Swedish currency, for deposit later in a U.S. bank when we got home. "Why, for heaven's sake, do you want to do this?" I implored. Because, Inga Lisa and her husband Gustaf explained, "we think that before too long the Russians are going to march into Europe and this time Sweden will not be spared, so we are going to leave Sweden for America, with our little girl, as soon as we have a bit more money saved up." I thought they were crazy, but finally gave in and carried the kronor in my money belt, all the way through Europe until I could get it safely to the United States.

Now, in the summer of 1950, I began to see why Inga Lisa and Gustaf had felt so imperiled ... and why other Europeans we had met in 1948 had seemed anything but upbeat, in contrast with us ordinary ebullient Americans. A great danger hung over the world, embodied in the Communist assault on South Korea, the victory of the Chinese Communists over Chiang Kai-shek, the Soviet subversion and occupation of Eastern Europe, with the menacing presence of a multimillion-man Soviet army in the middle of the Continent. I felt in my bones that the trouble really was desperate peoples to whom the United States could not readily bring the fruits of modernization, or the means to overcome the desperate heritage of the past. I could not see then the extent to which the world's troubles were exploited and even inspired in many cases, by the Soviets. Dispel the roots of discontent and ignorance, I thought, and the Communist danger would evaporate. Little did I know that a titanic forty-year worldwide struggle had begun.

Back to the Academic Drawing Boards

These realities finally hit me like a ton of bricks. What about chances for the brave new world that we had planned after the Axis surrender in 1945? Here we were, only five years after the end of one cataclysm, with a new war that could grow to major dimensions, and perhaps lead to more wars to come, with everything depending on the United States. President Truman reportedly had a little sign on his desk: "The buck stops here." Yes, and that was now true for all Americans as well.

I thought long and hard and finally decided that I ought to switch careers entirely, stop trying to make American society better—because the challenges (so I thought) were infinitely greater overseas. Another war was upon us, and yet more to come. I should do *something* "international." I wrote countless letters—to the United Nations, UNESCO, and other UN affiliates, and to the Department of State in Washington, telling them in my earnest way that I wanted to be of service. I took the Foreign Service examination, which might lead to a permanent appointment in U.S. diplomacy; I passed the general test but flunked the language exam. Later I would retrieve all this in Germany, and be offered an FSO appointment; that decision came much later.

By the time this process was well under way, our first child, a boy named Mark, was born, but this did not daunt me. I wrote to my old friend Ancil Payne, now an assistant to a congressman in Washington:

I feel quite powerless to be of any value in the present situation, to lend my thinking power, however limited, to the solution of our [international] problem. My present work is, I feel, important from a long-range view as regards the improvement of society here, but I fear the short-range possibilities are making long-range considerations increasingly academic in nature. In short, I am considering doing something more closely related to the international situation.

But letters of this sort were not getting me very far—at least not quickly enough—so I sought out professors at my old university for advice. One in particular, Linden Mander (an Australian-born authority on international institutions) asked me, "Why not resume graduate studies at this university, to better prepare yourself for the kind of career you want?" I bit that bullet, with some trepidation, left my state government job, and returned to academia in September 1951. Professor Mander procured a Carnegie Fellowship to help fill my income gap, and I worked evenings for the Seattle Parks, teaching kids sports. We sold our car to cut expenses and I bought a bicycle for commuting. Our second boy, David, was born in October, and we settled down for what could well be a couple of years more in academe.

Suddenly however, just before Christmas 1951, I received a thunderbolt telegram from the Department of State: "Offer you appointment as Foreign Service Staff Officer, Class 9, $3,700 per year plus quarters, to serve on staff of U.S. High Commission to Germany, effective 10 January 1952. If you accept, travel orders paying expenses you and your family to Germany will be issued. You must be in Washington for orientation beginning 5 January, your family to travel direct to New York. You will meet them in New York for transit by SS *America* to Bremerhaven, for further transfer to Bonn."

This offered an "interim" appointment, which might last only a few years, but it would be a foot in the door of an international career.

Off to Germany, via Our Nation's Capital

This was stunning; one of my many inquiries had hit the mark. It seemed exactly what I wanted—a start in a foreign affairs career—and we went. Winding up affairs in Seattle was not onerous and the prospects were exhilarating, although I had little idea exactly what I would be doing. A second communication informed me that I would be a Youth Affairs Officer; that seemed sensible, given my earlier career, but I still could not imagine what sort of work I would actually do, nor could any colleagues at the university help dispel the uncertainties. The "reeducation" of the Germans was a mystery to 98 percent of the U.S. population.

On the fourth of January 1952, I enplaned for Washington, to spend two weeks with other new Foreign Service officers, learning in a whirlwind of briefings: what would be expected of American diplomats abroad (including "protocol and etiquette"), how embassies and consulates were set up, what the global Communist threat consisted of (extremely informative, scary), what conditions in Germany generally were like, what cultural and information work (for which I was headed) was like, and so on. At this time, I thought a lot of the punctiliousness and formality of diplomatic life was virtually a joke (some of it was, to be sure), but my ultrademocratic, western-born frontier instincts said quietly—if arrogantly—to myself, "This can all change and you can help it do so." I wrote to myself in my diary, "This stuff sticks in my craw." Ah, to be young again and tilt at windmills! How to get important things done, *despite* the bureaucracy and tight framework of diplomacy, became—without my realizing it then—a sort of side-mission of my life.

Meanwhile, I drank in all the discussions and flow of information that came my way, sorting the important stuff for future cogitation. I was taken aback that Foreign Service personnel were expected to cultivate foreign friends and pass on information gleaned to embassy political officers. I learned that American diplomacy was governed chiefly by considerations of "power politics." There was great emphasis on the propaganda efforts—the so-called agitprop of the Communists and our response. I wrote to myself, "I left the lecture [on propaganda] with a deep desire to learn what positive measures we are taking and planning which will go deeper and strive to remove the social and economic ills upon which Communism breeds." In other words, I was terribly idealistic.

Later, some rough corners were knocked off by the realities of diplomatic work, but it would be some years before I could find a good working compromise—between more idealistic ways to conduct international relations and good old tried-and-not-always-so-true power politics. Today, the latter is called "realism," of which Henry Kissinger is still the high priest. More later on Henry and his canon. Meanwhile, back to the meat of what I was learning, as I then understood it.

In 1952, the work of the United States High Commission for Germany (HICOG) was at its peak, with four main tasks, aside from the military challenge of convincing the Soviets that we had the will and firepower, along with our NATO Allies, to resist any armed thrust they might make across the Iron Curtain. Under U.S. High Commissioner John J. McCloy, HICOG's tasks were these: to help the fledgling government of the new Federal Republic of Germany (in effect the French, British, and American occupation zones, comprising all of west Germany) establish itself, nationally and internationally; to present the American people and U.S. foreign policy to the German public objectively; to continue with the reorientation and reeducation of the German people and their institutions, so that they would become full democratic partners in the Atlantic community; and to promote the idea that the best international course for the new federal German government was to become so firmly interlocked within the nascent European and Atlantic institutions that it would never again be an independent threat to the world. All this was done, to some degree, in coordination with the British and French High Commissioners; I was to learn how this might work later, when I was assigned by HICOG to the "field," i.e., Nuremberg.

I had a little free time here and there, to stroll in Washington and to visit the sights. In my diary I noted this:

> Washington is at once quaint, bustling, grandiose, and impressive. It is distinctly a southern town and yet is a very business-like place. The old homes and buildings are productive of a very charming atmosphere. It's like no other city I've ever been in, in that there seems to be no area which is distinctively commercial or industrial—no crowded skyscrapers or jammed warehouses. Everything I've seen so far gives the impression of spaciousness. There are parks everywhere and little bits of lawn abound. Old homes, more than 100 years old, are found often next to large office buildings. Real estate must be an almost totally different kind of profession here.

Some years later I had three long sojourns in Washington—a total of seven years, and still visit often. I have seen the capital become truly "the world's headquarters," with outskirts (often partly urbanized) that bespeak the requirements of globalization and offices that house numerous international organizations as well our own sprawling government, scads of lobbyists and law firms, at least three great universities, fine restaurants, and all manner of think tanks. No more a "sleepy southern city!"

Also in my spare time, at the behest of a Seattle friend, I called on his college buddy, Andrew Scott, who was with the U.S. administration of the Marshall Plan, something entirely new in foreign relations. When had a victor nation like the United States ever offered to help on a massive scale to rebuild its enemies after a disastrous war, and to make whole, insofar as that could be done, its devastated allies, such as France and Britain? Andrew said he spent much of his time working on the plans for a European Army, a project which later ran afoul of the French parliament, but which now, a half century later, is something the EU members say they still want to do.

I called then, too, on Christian Herter, at that time a member of the House of Representatives from Massachusetts; he was an acquaintance of my father's Seattle friend, Fred Baker. I was terribly impressed. In his twenties, during World War I, Chris had been an FSO. He told me of a German Jew, Kurt Hahn. In 1918 Hahn served on the staff of the last Imperial German Chancellor and worked with Herter to bring to an end the Allied blockade that, after the Armistice, was starving the German people. Now in the 1950s he was trying to affect education worldwide with schools that became the models for Outward Bound and the United World Colleges. Little did I know then that in a few years I should be working at a distance with Christian Herter when he was secretary of state (1961–63) on plans for an Atlantic Institute, and still later with his friend Hahn, to give the international college programs a good start! Chris was a good, if not a close, friend, from then until his death.

One of my last lectures at the Department of State was unforgettable. "Coxey" Smith, an anthropologist known for his erudition and his wit, gave his views on getting to know another culture. In doing so, he described American culture for us; one dominant feature was the U.S. propensity to think that "if a problem is a problem more than ten years, somebody plumbered the deal!" I internalized this for my diary: "There cannot be an unsolved problem [for Americans]. We are so used, in our technology, to finding the mechanical answers, that we cannot conceive of a human, social, or philosophical situation which is not amenable to rectification through hard work and proper application of one's cerebral equipment."

At noon on the 19th of January my family and I boarded the SS *America*, then the new pride of the American merchant fleet, in New York. Even though I was pretty low on the State Department's totem pole, all Foreign Service personnel in those days merited First Class and all that went with it; a great contrast from our steerage-like days on the *Mauretania* in 1948. Before long, we were to wake up in Bremerhaven and a new German adventure that changed my life.

4
Deutschland under the Allies

4 April 1949: *NATO Treaty signed, binding twelve member-states to mutual defense in case any one ally is attacked.*

1 November 1952: *On Eniwetok atoll, United States explodes world's first hydrogen bomb; explosion has the light of ten suns.*

A U.S. consul met us in Bremerhaven, took us for a night to the Hotel Bremen, a requisitioned Allied billet. I was told that my orders were now for Frankfurt, not Bonn—the new capital of West Germany. That little city on the Rhine would eventually be U.S. High Commission (HICOG) head-quarters, but not quite yet, apparently. Next day another consular official put us on the best sleeping car the *Bundesbahn* could muster in those days, four of us in a compartment with two uppers and two lowers, wooden paneling and a chamber pot under the small sink. With all this excite-ment, sleep vanished. The next morning the train arrived in the Frankfurt *Hauptbahnhof*, after seven years still not fully emerged from wartime dev-astation. The station's huge cylindrical domes still held few of their glass panels, while all the terminal's innards were drab and colorless. A driving rain came down through the gaps in the roof.

A car and driver from HICOG met the train and whisked us to the Hotel Excelsior. There we parked for three days until we could occupy our new flat in Jakob Leislerstrasse, part of a large apartment complex built by HICOG in the midst of a ruined neighborhood of Second Reich middle-class houses. The small official Mercedes sped past ancient landmarks—towers from the medieval town wall, little makeshift one-story shops that could not hide the mountains of rubble behind them, cobblestone streets that had been hastily repaired. Yet there were numerous signs of recon-struction. The Marshall Plan was gathering steam; hope was in the air.

Our new quarters were modern and spacious, near-luxurious by comparison with German homes we later visited, most of them still makeshift. Twenty years later, a drive through Frankfurt was to show me how our old U.S. "Carl Schurz Siedlung," by then for Army personnel, looked pallid, drab, and old-fashioned compared to the new Frankfurt of the 1970s, with its skyscrapers, modern hotels and street after street of new apartments, plus old mansions, rebuilt. This was the German Economic Miracle, which had only just begun on my first encounter in 1952.

At last we were in Germany, at my duty station. It was a strange, unsettling yet exciting sensation. I had little knowledge of Germany—beyond that provided by American radio and newspapers, a few books, plus what the Department of State had crammed into me in Washington—of what it was like, or of what it might become. Every day brought a new revelation. For me at least, Germany had become the most fascinating country in the world, and—so far—its people an enigma. I would try hard not to measure them by all the stories of the Nazi and wartime periods. Where did the truth about the Germans lie? I spent four years, and many visits in later years, trying to sort out this burning question ... *Furore Teutonicus*, inbred and eradicable? . . . or just some human beings who had been badly burned by history, theirs and others? . . . or a more complex species, in between?

Certain personnel chores, including a job assignment, had to be worked out immediately. I had been told in Washington that I would be assigned to a youth affairs program, but discovered on my first duty day that *that* program had been "phased out," as part of a continuing readjustment and reformatting of the latter-day "reeducation" programs for the new Germany. As the newborn Federal Republic of Germany was now, in the main, sovereign except for a prohibition on a new German army (soon to change) and lingering foreign affairs dependence on Allied decisions, and as this mix was more or less constantly in flux, due to the pressures of the Cold War and changing American responsibilities dictated by domestic conditions in the United States, we were no longer "the Occupation." But we HICOGers were still to help "reorient and reeducate" the German people, helping them to reform their social institutions ... and not just some, but *all*. A few weeks into my new job as an "exchange of persons officer," I learned that yet a new psychological emphasis would be put on recruiting the German nation onto the Allied team, i.e., the exchange of persons program would have a more political, Cold War cast: "getting to know your new Allies." At that time, I didn't realize that decisions at a very high, interallied level would often have drastic, and frequent, consequences on our essentially educational programs, but I would learn over the months and years that the work of the diplomatic service undergoes frequent change, in most places and cases, and that it is always fundamentally political in nature. But I was also to learn, for myself, that the "political" is always a function of underlying cultural and socioeconomic conditions.

On the first of February, I was assigned a "slot": to work under Dr. Ralph Burns, an affable, straight-shooting but tough old professor from Dartmouth. He headed the vast program of intercultural exchanges of Germans and Americans. Many more Germans, headed for anywhere from two months to a year in the United States, were "exchanged" than were Americans. Numerous American specialists of one kind or another spent time in Germany, advising HICOG and the Germans, and learning firsthand of German problems. At this time, Fiscal Year 1952, as government termed the annual budget cycle, called for:

500 German teenagers to the United States, to go to high school and live with American families for a year

500 German university students to matriculate for a year at American colleges

250 German "trainees" (in their twenties, and having begun a career) to the United States for varying periods of academic study and internship (as we would call it today)

300 German "leaders" to various democratic European countries, to share ideas

1250 German "leaders" to spend a few weeks in the United States, learning how we did things—in government at every level, in police work and justice, in youth programs and women's affairs, in the world of journalism, in labor relations, and in the government of universities and the lower schools.

These last two "leader" programs aimed mainly at short-term results, while the teenagers, university students, and trainees were sent to try to broaden the scope and aspirations of young people for the long-term future, so that they could help rebuild the German *polis*. All in all, more than fifty years after these interchanges began (and still continue today, but on a much reduced scale), and after other HICOG "public affairs" programs had—often deeply—affected German society by other means, it is satisfying for an old-timer to go back to Germany in the 21st century and see what a new, hopeful, and thoroughly remodeled country Germany has become. My wife and I made a nostalgic visit to modern Germany in the summer of 2000, noting vast and for the most part salubrious changes. We visited friends just outside Frankfurt who are upper middle class and have done well. Their home was a revelation, with its marble floors, top-class heating system and spacious rooms, compared with the virtual hovels that their equivalents would have occupied in 1952. Germans know how to live well; in 1945 or 1952, one could never have predicted that their lifestyle would become the envy of Europe—or even the United States. More of this later, and of the tremendous new human problems which the reunification of Germany (1990) has occasioned.

Dr. Burns directed a dozen Americans and about 40 German staff in Exchanges, under Dr. Shepard Stone, who ran the entire Public Affairs program for High Commissioner John J. McCloy. I may have seen Stone once or twice in my months in HICOG; I certainly did not get to know him. Little did I realize then that 13 years later I would work closely with him at the Ford Foundation. Stone, a remarkable man who had earned a doctorate in Berlin in the twenties, had given the major impetus and shape to the reorientation of German life under HICOG.

In twelve larger cities in West Germany, such as Munich, Nuremberg, Stuttgart, Mainz, Duesseldorf, and Hamburg, there were HICOG public affairs operations, each with its own regional Exchanges Officer. These women and men carried most of the responsibility for picking out the Germans who were to be sent to America and Europe on "exchange visits," under the general administration of Dr. Burns and his headquarters staff in Frankfurt. I was assigned to the Leaders Program in Dr. Burns's office, initially as a trainee to prepare for full duties. My mentor (as it turned out, for less than two weeks) was Mrs. Ethel Elliott, a sprightly lady in her forties who ran the Leader Program. She was pleasant enough, but also a ball of unceasing mercurial freneticism, quite unfocused in her attempt to grapple with administrative duties which were far beyond her. She was assisted by a German staff of three. My training was to be for two months, after which I would relieve Mrs. Elliott. My first three or four days at her elbow were overwhelming, as I knew so little about either Germany or the kind of work I was to do, in all its myriad detail. Moreover, I knew nothing of the German language. Nonetheless, it took me less than a week to learn that Mrs. Elliott was utterly incompetent—indeed (in my opinion) mentally disturbed—and that her small staff was about half in numbers of what it ought to be.

I asked for a meeting with Dr. Burns and took the bull by the horns: I said I thought that I should take charge of the Leader program at once, rather than waiting two months. The Leader Exchange office had been given the assignment of readying 2500 German leaders (one principal and one alternate for each "slot," who would go if the principal fell out), from all critical walks of life, for their America visits. All had to be done within a few short months. This meant vetting 2500 application forms— "*Fragebogen*"—which in German had a rather ugly connotation, as it had been used extensively in the earlier de-Nazification program. The candidates were proposed to us by various headquarters' Public Affairs divisions dealing with various slices of German life (e.g., Women's Affairs, Religious Affairs, Local Government, Press, and so on), eliminating applicants with too-colored a political past or otherwise unsuitable, getting approval from Washington for each one, then overseeing the preparation in the field offices of each selectee for the visit and arranging transportation. This included my briefing every individual or small group in person, in Frankfurt, just before their departure. It was up to the Department of State in Washington to work out programs and travel arrangements inside the United States, but our office had to approve and, where we thought it necessary, suggest changes. I told Dr. Burns this was something entirely new to me, but that I would do my best. I would need one more American and at least four more Germans to handle all the paperwork and contacts properly. More than anything, this was a job of organization; I was to discover that my earlier work in student government, a State bureaucracy, the YMCA, and even the Boy Scouts, had given me the necessary tools, although in the beginning I could not be sure.

Dr. Burns agreed, relieved Mrs. Elliott immediately, obtained a young (but older than I) vice consul, Robert Forcey, from the Stuttgart Consulate General to assist me, and requested more German help from higher authority. I went on from there. I began German language lessons, each weekday at 8 a.m., then went to my office for long hours, including most weekends. To an absolute neophyte, the Army method of language instruction—learning straight off useful phrases, such as "Where is the train station?"—was excellent. I progressed fast. However, it wasn't until a couple of years later, out in Hof where few spoke English, that I was able to speak with considerable fluency. In the process, I acquired a distinctive *Frankfurter* accent ... not as laughable elsewhere as if I had learned *Bayerisch* or Adenauer's *Kölnisch*.

In the Bureaucratic Wonderland

My initiation into the intricacies and perils of a large U.S. government bureaucracy, as well as my plunge into German life at more or less its political/social core, was all-absorbing, fascinating, sometimes startling. It also gave me a great deal to digest, internalize, assimilate, and grapple with, and in a great hurry. The first three months of this ordeal were extremely demanding, more so than in any earlier job—or most of my later ones. My journal of the time suggests that even though I was but 29 years old and in excellent physical condition, after two months of six- and seven-day work weeks, considerable stress and strain, I began to worry about my health. However, I somehow came to grips with all the obstacles and, with the help of a staff of Germans who on the whole were decent and intelligent (though some were more hard-working than others), plus my invaluable No. 2, Bob Forcey, we did all that had been demanded of us to "implement" our part of the immense (I came to understand later just how immense it was) German exchanges program on schedule and within budget. It took us five months, but we were right on time, and our chosen German Leaders were leaving like clockwork for the United States.

I shall always be grateful to my staff in those demanding months. We gradually became a team, organized by me on American lines with some consideration for German work habits that sometimes seemed odd. Germans have a great capacity for organization, but in those days at least, hierarchical ideas dominated and initiative was rare. The Nazi period and both great wars had, I think, deprived ordinary Germans of any thought but self-preservation. Later, I came to think that this trait might go back as far as the Thirty Years War, when Germany lost a third of its population.

On the whole, Germans exhibited much distrust of each other, even in our small team, plus a cynical disbelief in the proposition that the majority of them, and foreigners as well, were basically good. I however believed this proposition, coming to the job with an unflinching belief in the worth of each individual. Now and then over my lifespan, I have faced a few thoughtless and self-seeking people who could not respond to that philosophy; but on the whole this bent for starting relationships by assuming that every person is essentially good, though they might need some coaxing to bring it out, has stood me in good stead. Mine was an Emersonian position, reinforced by my Christian Science upbringing; by adulthood I couldn't go along with much of Christian Science but some of its basic tenets stuck with me down the years. It is an optimistic faith. And Americans are an optimistic people.

Encountering the German People

These first months in Germany were a fantastic learning time. I began to form views about Germans — some of which later experience helped me to amplify and modify — and their institutions, their "way of life." On the heels of the searing world cataclysm, through the entire Nazi period to the end of World War II, in which I had played a tiny part, it was now thoroughly illuminating for me to see what German life was *really* like on the ground, day-to-day with Germans, both ordinary and extraordinary. Whenever I could grab a Saturday or Sunday free of work, with my little family I drove or rode local streetcars around Frankfurt and beyond, dipping into the flavor of life. Here are excerpts from my journal in the early months of 1952, suggesting some early impressions of the German people:

> The people are full of vitality, relatively strong compared to other Europeans. They are not, definitely not, Supermen, as Hitler would have had them. For every stately blond Nordic [type], there are ten short, stout, mousy-haired average-looking Germans. They are not as attractive, at least not to us, as Americans. Their clothing is much less stylish, their faces and hair much less well kept. They are friendly, but cold to those they do not know. They are industrious, but generally work from a sense of duty rather than from a sense of responsibility. They expect services from their state and are not nearly as concerned as British or Americans about who governs them. They have a strong sense of self-righteousness [that masks] an underlying guilt complex over their part in the [W]ar. Probably the majority of Germans repudiate Hitler, but there is a constant effort to avoid any personal responsibility for the mess their country got itself into, to shift the blame from the Army to Hitler alone, to shift the blame for the concentration camps to the SS, to decry what Hitler did, but to say in the same breath, "But what could *I* do? If I opened my mouth I would have been purged." There are bright spots: some Germans realize the only salvation for Germany is European unity. Some realize that Germany's basic problem is the poor human relations of German to German. Whether this small amount of human yeast [i.e., residues of the Exchanges program] can leaven the whole—encrusted as it is by centuries of custom and historical accident—is the big question.

With the hindsight of half a century, I would stand by the essence of these early views, and only note that fortunately—*most* fortunately for the Germans and the rest of the world—some of these old psychic ghosts have been exorcised by the passage of time and by the hard work and reflection that went into the tasks of "reorientation" and "reeducation," both by the Germans and their Western conquerors. The modern state of affairs in Germany today is comforting; in their political and social attitudes, today's Germans are not so different from other Western peoples. The United States, Britain, and France, who tried to encourage the changes, deserve great credit. But most of the credit goes to the German people, who proved themselves highly adaptable and determined to find an honored place in the world community.

Very probably, the hopeful Germany of today could also not have emerged without the Marshall Plan, which conducted a program, parallel to that of Public Affairs, of businessmen and trade unionists to study modern industry in the U.S. and in other ways helped to modernize the entire west European economy. The ingenious grants and loans of cash and credits provided a great impetus to rebuilding. In 1952 however, the future was still distinctly cloudy, over all of Europe. Most of the then-living German adults and young people had toiled through the war, many since the Weimar period or the beginning of the Nazi hijacking of their desperate State. They, and younger ones to come, today are less and less burdened by their past and deeply committed to live like the rest of the world's democratic peoples. By twenty or thirty years after I first landed in Frankfurt, the German situation had changed dramatically, entirely, and for the better. We are now all part of an "international community" built increasingly on democratic ideals and methods. The world is amazingly, and hopefully, different—with all its still-vexing problems and dangers— than it was fifty years ago. Our growing interdependence bespeaks John Donne's famous words: "Ask not for whom the bell tolls, it tolls for thee."

Reflections, Lessons Learned

Writing memoirs is a time for self-reflection. I learned a great deal in Germany, much of it through an almost unconscious effort to pass on in my work there that which I had learned earlier in my youth. I was consciously keeping a journal (often the entries were made late at night or in the early hours of the morning), yet with their necessarily uneven character, some of my observations remain instructive—at least to me—today, a half century later. In many ways, although through the German experience and thirteen more years living in other European countries, knowing so many Canadians and their country extremely well, spending long periods in Japan and other Far Eastern nations, plus three lengthy "tours of duty" in Washington, D.C.—my basic principles of dealing with others and my relationship with the "world out there" have hardly changed. It is easy for others sometimes to look at my *Who's Who* biography, with frequent changes of station or employer or line of work, and remark facetiously (or perhaps not). . . . "Gosh, you couldn't hold a job!" I think my employers/supervisors on the whole were satisfied with how I approached things (old Ralph Burns said to me, after I had been struggling two months with my new and challenging tasks, "Huntley, in you we found a real nugget."). But on two occasions, years later, I was "fired," and curiously, I believe, because I stuck to my principles.

At the end of March 1952, I reviewed my new experience with Big Government bureaucracy for my journal. I was astounded (but shouldn't have been) at some of the pettiness and power-seeking of many of my fellow bureaucrats, at the widespread propensity to hew strictly to regulations, even if common sense sometimes called for overriding these, and at the prevalent backbiting and intense competition for place. There were also many instances of just plain poor management. These and other glaring (and I'm sure sometimes costly) defects of the system repelled me. Later many of these early impressions were in part corrected and brought into better focus, and I grew to admire and even love the Foreign Service—but my criticisms still apply to a good deal of the human condition as I have encountered it, not just among our nation's diplomats. How our overall system of government—and business management too—can work as well as it does, amazes me. My basic beliefs never changed, but my tolerance, leavened with some wisdom, increased a good deal. Great respect for "the human condition" and its limitations gradually ensued; we must progress despite these.

In Frankfurt in 1952, a situation arose in which one of my superiors questioned not only my actions but my motives. However, I was determined (and in the end exonerated of spurious charges) to press on with what I thought was right regardless. This incident could well have endangered my position, even sending me and my family packing back quite prematurely to the United States. I then wrote in my journal: "[am] glad to stand for what [I know] is right. I have no feelings concerning job security. I'm determined to speak my own mind and exercise independence." Ninety-five percent of the time, this philosophy has paid off over the years: Do the right thing, stand on your principles, let the chips fall where they may; the general good is thus served.

Although I met some remarkable colleagues in my HICOG days (and especially when I went to Nuremberg to work), I became convinced by mid-1952 that on the whole the average American serving in Germany was not as good a representative of the United States as I would have liked to see. The Occupation (1945–49), with the military in charge, on balance had left a bad taste in German mouths. After 1953, I found exceptional Army people, commissioned officers as well as ordinary soldiers, who seven years after the war presented a better microcosm of the American people (probably because of the high proportion of West Point officers and straight-from-American-society draftees, who in those days made up the bulk of the enlisted forces) than were those wartime officers and men who had elected to stay on in Germany after May 1945. The latter were very much a mixed bag, but for the most part they were opportunists, even black marketeers. Some of these immediate postwar officers stayed on as civilians when the Occupation switched to civil government by the High Commission and by the Germans themselves in 1949. I encountered many during my service, especially in Frankfurt. They tended to stay aloof from the German population when they might have "made friends" personally for our country. The Foreign Service (which had its own problems) could do no more than sprinkle its regulars among the vast HICOG staff. This was a time of great flux in American society, even more so in all of Europe, and even more than THAT, in Germany. In my youthful idealism, I thought the United States ought to be able to send abroad a better cross-section of "the American people" who could work and identify with the German people; I wrote "We need the kind of American over here we may not have—one who can teach by example, not by preaching. We have 'em, but will they come?"

One day in the spring of 1952 I was recounting the sources of my frustration to sage old Dr. Burns, who would soon return to the halls of Dartmouth College. Again, from my journal: "[Burns] opined that the Foreign Service was 'a very impersonal, unfeeling organization' . . . and that 'the American people . . . had never before experienced big bureaucracy [until the New Deal and World War II] and now it was apparently with them to stay.'" Burns, quite frankly, became my model of independence-in-spite-of-bureaucratic-straitjackets, although I never saw him again in my life (unfortunately for me).

One further anecdote testifies to Burns's integrity and strong character. One of the HICOG field offices had selected for teenage "exchange" Hilda Speer, the 16-year-old daughter of Hitler's chief architect, Albert Speer. Alone among the Nazi war criminals sentenced at Nuremberg in 1946, Speer did not receive the death sentence, but rather—when this story takes place—was serving a twenty-year sentence in Berlin's Spandau prison. He had some redeeming features and pleaded extenuating circumstances (see his book, *Inside the Third Reich*, 1969). But Speer still was one of those Nazi elites whose connivance and slavishness at a high level buttressed the regime. Nonetheless, the regional exchanges officer who selected Speer's daughter to be among 30 or so of those in her part of Germany to go to American high schools for a year had been advised by her teachers and independent German panels, whose counsel was usually sound, as well as by other Americans in his field office, that Hilda was a real comer, a good student and one who would profit greatly from this year in the United States. Her papers, along with those of about 500 other German kids, were duly vetted by Dr. Burns's staff and sent on to the Department of State, which would arrange for schools and homes stateside.

In Washington, officials who were no doubt more intimidated by still-fresh and widespread political hatred of the Nazis than were we who lived among them and could be more discriminating and understanding, had doubts about Hilda Speer. The 500 teenage exchangees were gathering in Frankfurt to take their flights when a telegram arrived from Washington: "Cannot accept Hilda Speer because of her family background." Apparently the Washington officials were unwilling to face the criticism that might arise in the press or in Congress when her advent became known. Dr. Burns did not hesitate for a minute; he sent the following telegram, quoting the Bible, to the State Department: "If the parents have eaten sour grapes, shall the children's teeth be set on edge? Hilda Speer on next plane." And Hilda went, for a mind-opening year in the U.S. heartland.

I must frankly say that just a few months after my cold bureaucratic shower in HICOG Frankfurt, and despite Dr. Burns's discerning remarks and my unstinting admiration of him, I seriously thought of resigning in frustration and disappointment. Little did I know then that my thoughts about American colleagues would be greatly revalued—upwards—when I encountered a public affairs field staff of extraordinary competence and integrity in Northern Bavaria. On the whole, after ten years in the Foreign Service, I concluded in 1961 that the American people neither understood nor appreciated what their diplomats did for them, amid constant obstacles to healthy family life and frequent exposure to many varieties of danger. Fortunately, I decided in the summer of 1952 not to quit, and was assigned to Nuremberg in September.

Franconians: The Archetype of the "Earnest German People"

Years later, when I read the quoted words above by Lord Clark, the eminent historian of Western culture, I said to myself, "Yes, that *does* typify the great majority ... so earnest that it hurts." Now an opportunity had come to find out for myself what "life out in the provinces" was really like. And the Franconians (the northern Bavarians) proved nothing if not earnest.

When Napoleon was reorganizing Europe in the first decade of the 19th century, he dictated the extinction of many of the dozens upon dozens of German principalities, merging them right and left, quite rationally, he thought. Bismarck carried the process further. The bishoprics of Bamberg and Wuerzburg, the city-state of Nuremberg, and a few other oddments, which constituted together the loose province of Franconia, were assimilated into a kingdom of Bavaria (promoted from a dukedom), which lasted until the end of the first World War. The idea that all Germans are more or less alike, in appearance or in "national character" is an absurdity, and nowhere is this more evident than in modern Bavaria. Oberbayern—Upper Bavaria—ranges from Munich to the mountains in the south and southeast, bordering on Austria, whose mountain culture is similar. The regions around Augsburg and Regensburg, also old principalities, differ from each other and from the mountain Bavarians a good bit. But the differences within Bavaria become somewhat stark when one crosses into Unter-, Mittel-, and Oberfranken, where I became intimately involved with the locals after 1 September 1952, when I was transferred from head-quarters in Frankfurt to a "Public Affairs Field Office" in Nuremberg. My new responsibilities as Exchanges Officer ranged all over the three ad-ministrative districts (*Regierungsbezirke*) of Franconia. In Frankfurt I was largely paper-shuffling, remote from the population. From my office in Nuremberg, and later in Upper Franconia (the Hof assignment described in the opening chapter and in chapter five), I was able to travel a great deal, to learn firsthand about the problems, the character, the aspirations, and the demons that were history's residue in the German "psyche." I learned in those days and later in Hof largely from immersion in German society and from the observations of my American colleagues also "on the ground," and not from government reports or books.

A month elapsed between the time that I arrived in Nuremberg and my family's catching up with me. We were assigned an "expropriated; seized" (*beschlagnahmte*) house on the edge of Nuremberg, just as all my American colleagues and their families in the "field" were housed. Most of these homes had been occupied by Nazi officials of middle-grade (*Gau-leiter* and the like) and at war's end simply been taken over by the occupy-ing Allied armies, for officers' quarters. For one month, until "our" house would be ready, I bunked with a bachelor officer of the Nuremberg Public Affairs staff, Albert Hamilton, in one of these occupied houses, this one cavernous. Ab and I batched, taking turns with the cooking and so on. HI-COG provided a maid to do the housework, in those days earning about $40 per month.

On one of our first congenial evenings together, Ab said, "Here's a book that just came out, and may interest you," and handed me a volume by Dr. Robert Strausz-Hupé, *The Zone of Indifference*. I had never heard of the author, who a few years later I got to know well. Strausz-Hupé was an Austro-Hungarian, of the nobility of the old double-eagled Empire. He had emigrated to the United States in the '20s as a young man, become a stockbroker, later a political scientist of some note. His earlier book *Geo-politics*, a warning of Hitler's plans and methods, had received consider-able acclaim. Now that the Cold War was on, the book I read, and his later ones (especially *Protracted Conflict*), took just as tough and revealing a line with the Communists. The principal message of *The Zone of Indiffer-ence*, however, was not the evils of Communism, but the relationship be-tween Europe and America, which he understood incisively. He detailed the considerable differences between Europeans and Americans (which occasioned the "indifference" of which he wrote), but stated in his last chapter that because our values, our forms of government, and our aims in the world derived from the same roots, we "Atlanticists" on both sides of the great Ocean should move towards a federal union.

This was another of those few intellectual bombshells that fell on me in these years and helped to shape my views of foreign affairs, of Europe, and of the Germans. When Strausz-Hupé, in *The Zone of Indifference*, alluded to Clarence Streit's works, this struck a distant chord: in high school, in the autumn of 1940, I had debated the thesis of Streit's current book of that time, viz. that the United States and Britain should form a federal union. Streit's later work, also building on his prewar volume, urged that the Europeans, the Canadians, the Americans, plus the Australians and New Zealanders, should without delay form a federal union. Streit influenced many important people of his day, including John Foster Dulles (who, when he became Secretary of State, apparently recanted). I was to meet Streit in 1955, and Strausz-Hupé in 1956, to become an intimate friend of both, and to deepen my understanding of this great concept . . . and also, later, to become convinced of how extremely difficult it would be to bring it about. But it has always been a grand, noble plan to which I have attached my life.

Not long after this, I read another prescient book, *Fire in the Ashes*, by Theodore White, giving an expert journalist's account of the visionary yet practical concepts that were bringing about the union of the West European nations. I learned from White's work of the French political genius, Jean Monnet, who was working practically (in ways that Streit did not, nor could not) to convince the leaders of the inner core of Europe—France, Germany, Italy, and the three Benelux states—that to avoid future wars and to survive the Cold War, they must unite their countries. White, and Truman, Marshall and Acheson too, were convinced that the United States had to back this plan unequivocally. Today, in the 21st century, that process of European unification has progressed far, albeit with fits and starts; I would say that a united Europe of more than twenty states in a few years may enjoy a degree of unity, under common institutions, that will be virtually indissoluble. Today it is practically certain, for example, that there can never be another war between Germany and France, nor among their neighbors. In 1952, however, none of this could be taken for granted, nor could the unprecedented defense ties which committed the United States to Europe in 1949—the NATO treaty—and which we in HICOG were spending a great deal of time and money explaining to the Germans—be deemed a "sure thing," much less long-term. But the historic dent in America's traditional peacetime isolation, the meaning for our people of the treaty commitment to Canada and Europe that "an attack on one is an attack on all," made me an enthusiast, and a latter-day Wilsonian . . . with a few modifications as the years passed.

Strausz-Hupé, Streit, White, and later my personal relationships with a number of Allied statesmen and fellow U.S. Foreign Service officers, formed for me the combined beacon of hope—European union and Atlantic unity—that would animate my work with the Germans and later with other Europeans, my own people back home, and, as the world evolved over the past half century, with democratic regimes and democrats all over the world. This was the great vision I needed, and I have never given up working for its realization, by one means or another, in one venue or another. It is slowly coming true, albeit in ways I never in the fifties could have imagined.

A few years ago, the editors of *Who's Who in America* asked me and some of their other biographees, to give them a short paragraph describing our life's work, to tag onto the standard entry of what we had done, and when. I wrote, and still believe:

> For a full life, embrace a worthy cause. Mine is the unity of the democracies. America's most precious asset is its free political system. It can be successfully defended only if we merge our force, our hearts and our fortune with like-minded peoples. Like-mindedness is not simply a gift of history; it must be cultivated. My life's aim has been to forge consensus among the democracies as a prelude to the creation of a free, just, and durable world order.

The seeds of this resolve were planted during my stay in Nuremberg, to be nurtured later in a small town near the East German border, fertilized by concentrated study at Harvard, and grown to maturity in an off-beat career which unfolded in strange ways.

The Nuremberg Public Affairs Operation

I was extremely fortunate to have landed, for my second Foreign Service assignment, in the regional public affairs office in Nuremberg. My colleagues in Nuremberg were quite different, in kind and manner, from most of those I had worked with in Frankfurt. Part of the difference lay in the nature of my assignments, the earlier in a large headquarters bureaucracy which necessarily had to accomplish the bulk of its work on paper, by paper, and with paper, the second involving constant and intimate contact with Germans of every sort. Frankfurt was in large measure "paper-pushing." I had never encountered this kind of bureaucratic morass before, although several years later I would be dumped again into a similar, if much larger, cauldron of officialdom, in Washington, D.C. In contrast to the Frankfurt bureaucrats, with one or two exceptions, the Nuremberg field staff (about fifteen Americans besides myself) were certainly two or three cuts above the average Foreign Service personnel, in terms of their determination to succeed in the difficult job of helping the Germans reorient themselves, in their preparation for the job (although all but one were under 35), in their sheer intelligence, and in the fact that all of them were veterans of the Second World War and — in most cases — had already spent two years in Germany as "Kreis Resident Officers."

The KROs had been recruited in part from some of the best military occupation officers, i.e., those who understood and could work well with Germans at the local level. But the majority of the KROs had been lifted straight out of some of the best American universities, where they had earned degrees (usually at graduate level) in history and international relations. These latter were an outstanding lot; many of them are still among my best friends today, and others have passed on. In the crucial years between 1949 and 1952, when Germany was in the throes of great social, economic and political transformation and uncertainty, these men were each assigned to a German *Landkreis* (county) as advisors to the local German political class. In those years they also had the residual power of making or reversing German decisions at the local level; this changed in 1952 and the HICOG public affairs program largely replaced the KRO system, recruiting most of the KROs to running America Houses — cultural centers — and undertaking other PR jobs, often in the same areas where they had served earlier.

The chief difference between these KROs and the general run of U.S. diplomats and HICOG officers at this time was that the former (1) had only loose ties to the bureaucratic rules and traditions of the diplomatic service; (2) had superb educations as well as military experience, which fitted them well for their German duties; and (3) had been chosen largely on the basis of their idealism and commitment, and the skills to buttress these. Their work is largely unsung, but a true history of those times in Germany must inevitably give them much credit for the tremendous accomplishments of the High Commission. Elite decision-makers such as McCloy and his French and German counterparts — perched together on a mountaintop across the Rhine from Bonn — of course had an historic effect on Germany, Europe, and what they have become today. But without the diligent work of hundreds of savvy young people with a worm's eye perspective on what was happening, "Atlantic" history would certainly not have turned out as it has — the greatest and most positive American (and

Allied) accomplishment in our entire history, certainly in that of the years after World War II. The work of similar Americans, again at ground level, in Japan was comparable in its importance and effect; General MacArthur could never have done what he did without them.

It is inevitable that most of my readers will have had little if any knowledge of what was happening in the heart of Germany, in the provinces, at this particular time. The world is huge and its problems and prospects so varied that a full picture of what went on in Germany—admittedly at the time a major arena in world affairs—at the *local* level receives hardly any attention from historians or journalists, then as well as now, fifty years later. However, to understand fully the world events and challenges of today some knowledge of what was happening locally in Germany is perhaps vital. Indeed, to help illuminate this chapter in history is one of the reasons I have written this book.

Let me describe what these American men (for at that time there were only a few woman Foreign Service officers, and none of them were in the Nuremberg region) were doing, and how I fitted in. In charge in Nuremberg was Lowell Bennett, 34, a former journalist who had parachuted into wartime Berlin and escaped from a Nazi prison. At that time, and still today, I consider Bennett to have been my best boss ever. He gave guidance to all his staff, but—more important—was responsible for tremendously high morale. Bennett overlooked small bending of the rules if it was in the interests of our broad cause; in fact, at times he broke the rules with us because he found the Bonn (by now, Frankfurt HICOG had moved to the little provisional capital of the Federal German Republic on the Rhine) bureaucracy often insufferable.

In my journal of January 1953, I noted:

> We then proceeded to outline for [a visiting officer from another regional office] the Nuremberg theory of Foreign Service administration. If an operating procedure sent down from [Bonn] Headquarters doesn't work, we modify it or replace it. If we don't like policy as it is expressed by Hq., we scream about it. We believe that those who carry out policy are entitled—nay, required—to analyze what they're executing and advise their superiors.

Reading these words today, after some years of experience running organizations in and out of government, makes me shudder, but only slightly. A certain amount of rebelliousness has always been part of the American spirit, and it often works. There were of course limits. Bennett was not so intolerant of headquarters, however, that he would flout its precepts too often or too openly; he often skated on thin ice, but his verve and dash, plus innate intelligence, kept us all out of trouble. He was not crazy about Germans, perhaps because of his unpleasant wartime experiences, but he knew how to cultivate and live alongside them, and urged us to do the same. Under Bennett's guidance, we immersed ourselves in the culture (used in the anthropologist's sense of the term) around us.

Bennett had a deputy and a few Germans in his immediate office in the Krelingstrasse, where our public affairs staff dwarfed that of the resident American consul, who technically was higher on the totem pole. A canny Floridian with great sense, Haynes Mahoney, was information officer; his job, with his cohort Albert Hamilton, was to provide news releases, pamphlets, films and other media materials needed by the rest of us, to explain American culture and foreign policy.

Dr. Martin Ackerman, one of the most engaging, unusual, and adroit Foreign Service people I ever knew, was senior in years to the rest of us (around 45 or 50 at the time, and we thought that was pretty old). Martin spoke half a dozen European languages fluently; his command of French and German was bilingual. (After retiring he taught himself Dutch and Russian.) He saw our job as multicultural, namely that we should treat the Germans as equals and guide them unerringly into a multicultural Europe and Atlantic community, so that they would learn to play their integrated part in the modern world. Martin not only arranged interesting arts and cultural (in the narrower sense) programs for the Franconians, he pulled every string he could, all the way to Washington if necessary, and with the unreserved help of Bennett, to bring big names in American life to Nuremberg for concerts, lectures, and art shows.

Ackerman and Bennett managed to "acquire" the building next to the old Franconian Justice Ministry—where the 1946 Nuremberg war crimes trials had taken place. This had been converted into a prison for top Nazi culprits, but no longer was needed for this. Now we reconverted it into a Multinational Center. Attached to our American offices were French and British cultural officers; HICOG had its counterparts serving in the British and French public affairs offices in *their* "zones" of Germany. (In summer 1945, all Germany was divided into four occupation zones, with the Russians in the east, the British in the north and the Rhineland, the French in the southwest, and the Americans in a swath that went from Frankfurt through southern Germany to include Bavaria.) Martin Ackerman invited our Nuremberg-posted French and British officers to set up their operations in the Multinational Center. He also persuaded the Bavarian *Kultusministerium* (ministry of education and culture) to send its own German representative to an office there, too. And the four worked together to conduct joint programs that would involve nationals from the three Occupiers and from all parts of Germany, equally. The symbolism was frankly fantastic.

The Multinational Center, visible evidence of the breadth and integrative character of the NATO alliance, was one of the most creative and effective devices that the HICOG public affairs program spawned. There were conferences and seminars on every conceivable subject, including student newspapers, child care in different parts of Europe, police methods, local government, the fine arts, theater, and so on. The French Cultural officer brought a Picasso exhibit, the British a team of schoolteachers, the Americans people like Roger Baldwin, the founder of the American Civil Liberties Union. The Center was enormously popular with the Germans, perhaps too popular and too good to last. After barely two years of operation, it closed down. Two factors, I think, influenced the decision: First, our Nuremberg office told Bonn so often how good the Multinational Center was, that the word got back to Washington, which sent over a "consultant" (a nice academic, but with no knowledge of German conditions) to analyze the program and recommend its future. He sent back a glowing report, urging that the Multinational Center should be the model for *all* U.S. cultural centers in *all* of Europe. This might have been a good idea for the long run, but it threatened the then thirty-eight America Houses in Germany and the provincial headquarters, like Nuremberg, for U.S. information and cultural work centers—and the jobs of their incumbents—in the rest of Europe. The inertia of bureaucracy was simply too great, and the multicultural men such as Ackerman too few, to allow this general multiplication. Furthermore, there were strong overtones of American nationalism ("we know what we want for ourselves") in most reactions of the boss-people, i.e., no real Atlantic community spirit.

Second, and just as important, the success of the Multinational Center rivaled the attractiveness of the Nuremberg America House, one of nine in northern Bavaria, under Bennett. At a certain point, Bennett and Bonn had, in good measure, to support a general financial retrenchment. The Multinational Center got the axe, the America House remained. I believe this was the triumph of bureaucracy over an idealistic yet practical concept which sadly turned out to be, as the Brits say, "one-off." On many other occasions in the years that followed, I was to propose similar multinational programs, in most (but not all) cases to be rejected because of jealously guarded national prerogatives, not least those of the United States.

Years later I had a long talk with Paul Nitze, one of the wise men who guided American policy for much of the Cold War period. He was in a reflecting mode, out of government for a time, and gave me a small pamphlet he had written. One sentence has stayed with me: "To my mind, the most serious modification in our national strategy beginning in 1953 was the decision to emphasize that our first aim was to pursue United States national interests and to play down our interest in the construction of a working international order. The moment we began to emphasize that our policy was directed primarily to the pursuit of United States aims and interests, other nations were forced to look more closely to their own narrow interests." I had no inkling of the major changes in U.S. policy going on in 1953, but in hindsight the unwillingness to engage in joint Atlantic cultural programs had its roots in a recrudescence (greatly visible in the Bush II administration) of American nationalism, the spirit of going it alone, an attempt at Pax Americana, as it may turn out.

Months later, after the Nuremberg operation had been dismantled, I had occasion to note in my journal: "Seems as if there are few people here [in Germany] of the calibre of Lowell Bennett—so dedicated, fearless, and live that they make the program tingle with activity and purpose."

Only later did I fully appreciate the historical backdrop for the incomparable Nuremberg experience. This was the official Party City of the Nazis, where every year huge celebrations were held to glorify the creed and its messiah, Herr Hitler. The symbolism was stark, especially if one visited the three successive Party rallying places which Hitler and Speer had constructed: First, a coliseum-shaped round building, then the large field where 100,000 troops could mass in front of Der Fuehrer (this was the usual image in the scary newsreels), and finally an unfinished, one-kilometer square parade ground, now overgrown with weeds but starkly symbolic of what the Fuehrer really wanted. It would have accommodated half a million German troops and uniformed Nazi thugs. In 1952, American GIs played on four baseball fields in the second amphitheatre. We Americans were in the right place, at the right time, to make a difference in history.

McCarthyism and the Foreign Service in Germany

My work in Nuremberg fascinated me. I longed to stay for another "budget cycle," i.e., a year of picking exchangees, sending them off, and then interviewing them when they returned. Unfortunately, however, our Nuremberg offices were abruptly closed in June 1953, after only one and a half years of intense, productive work. This was part of continuing reorganizations—every few months during this period—and all traced back to geopolitically induced changes in U.S. policy, sometimes initiated by new Cold War challenges, or by domestic politics. For us in Germany, while the old focus had been on preparing the Germans for democracy domestically, the new policies concentrated on an international framework within which Germany could rearm safely and European community–building could be accelerated. We continued to do both jobs, instinctively realizing that democracy still would begin at home.

When Senator Joseph McCarthy's supposedly "anti-Communist" skullduggery began in 1953 to cast a pall over politics in Washington, our effort in Germany became a sitting target for "purges" of supposed leftists, and also for incidental cost-cutting by a newly Republican Congress. Almost everyone, including the new Secretary of State, John Foster Dulles, was afraid of Senator McCarthy of Wisconsin. Neither Dulles nor President Eisenhower lifted a finger for more than two years to resist McCarthy's depredations, which were demoralizing the Foreign Service. Dr. James Bryant Conant, just-retired president of Harvard, was named as U.S. ambassador to Bonn and jointly high commissioner succeeding John J. McCloy. (The tripartite High Commission was phased out during Conant's tenure.) Dr. Conant stood up to McCarthy as well as he could in his confirmation hearings before the Senate, but without the full backing—then or later—of the president and the secretary of state, Conant found it difficult, alone, to resist McCarthy's intimidation and personal character assassination of some of Conant's best staff in Germany.

The atmosphere, in fair measure created or at least greatly exacerbated by McCarthy, was laden with charges of "security risk," "former Communist," and "fellow traveler," and—in some cases—"sexual deviant" leveled at quite a number of Foreign Service personnel, most of them senior officers. It was not unusual for the highly intelligent, able sort of person attracted to the diplomatic service in the thirties and forties to have toyed, at least intellectually, with Communism in his formative years. To be at a major university in, say, 1937, would have meant exposure to great national (and international) ferment; many serious (if in hindsight misguided) young people went to Communist-led meetings or joined Communist youth groups and other "fronts" credulously. The Depression had not yet ended (it would actually do so only when massive war production began, sopping up the unemployment which had lain like a cancer in the body politic since 1930). Capitalism was more or less in the dock for many Americans. There was a strong U.S. Socialist party (3 million votes for Norman Thomas in the presidential elections of 1932), which wished to put U.S. production in the hands of the people, but had no violent program in mind. Yet the small but close-knit American Communist Party was different, engaging in what the Soviet masters called "agitprop" with some success, with copious funds and direction from the USSR.

When Hitler and Stalin in August 1939 signed a nonaggression pact, paving the way for Hitler's conquest of Europe, most American support for Soviet Communism—largely that of some intellectuals and labor leaders, as well as idealistic but myopic youth—evaporated quickly. However when Hitler reversed course and attacked the USSR in June 1941, hard-core U.S. Communists tried again, with some success, to rally new and old support for "our brave Russian allies." After Pearl Harbor, the U.S. government and to some extent Hollywood (which rewrote Soviet history on film—"good old Uncle Joe" Stalin was a prime prop) reinforced a superficial pro-Russian attitude among much of the general public. When a nation is fighting for survival, almost any ally is welcome. President Roosevelt and the government encouraged a pro-Russian opinion; seen geopolitically, the Russians were holding down huge German armies which, in 1942, we and the British were not yet ready to engage on the Continent. As the U.S. did for Britain, the President and the Congress gave massive "Lend-Lease" material support to the USSR. When World War II ended, international conditions began to change. At first, it was hoped that the war-winning British-American-Soviet alliance would continue in the spirit of international cooperation to create a better world. But this was not to be.

When in 1947–48 it became obvious that a" Cold War" was beginning, and that Russian intentions towards Europe and the world were anything but benign, the American public turned vigorously anti-Soviet. The U.S. Communist party atrophied quickly. A small hard core remained for a some years, but virtually all those who had adhered as youngsters in the thirties, realizing quickly how they had been duped, jumped off the bandwagon, if their good sense had not caused them to dismount earlier. A few who had flirted with Communism in the 1930s or 1940s had entered the Foreign Service, but hardly any (with the exception of a couple of Soviet "sleepers"—Harry Dexter White and Alger Hiss—and their counterparts in the UK—Burgess, McLean, Philby and, a good deal later, Blunt) retained any sympathy for the Soviets.

Nevertheless, during the McCarthy years, a good many Americans listened to the senator's absurd tales of a government supposedly riddled with Communists and, out of fear, egged on efforts to "purge" the Foreign Service and other key parts of government of its supposed "hundreds" of Leftist infiltrators. During these years, right-wing groups such as the John Birch Society (ancestor of the neo-Nazi and "militia" groups still with us in the 21st century) defended McCarthy's ideas and began a long-term propaganda campaign full of lies and smears quite the equal of the Soviet Agitprop. Finally, in 1956, a courageous Pentagon lawyer named Joseph Welch almost literally took McCarthy apart in full public view, at televised Senate hearings; McCarthy had made a huge mistake by attacking the patriotism of the Army. Edward R. Murrow helped fearlessly, too, in his TV broadcasts. This was a watershed; key government officials and the public finally came to their senses. The real dangers of Communism lay in Soviet activities outside the United States. But the poison of right-wing propaganda lingers on today in the American body politic; I believe such ultraconservatives as Phyllis Schlafly, insisting (for example) that institutions such as the Federal Reserve are Communist or Jewish plots — presumably both — have hurt U.S. public discourse badly over the years. These have sapped the people's trust in government and other public institutions.

Before his downfall, McCarthy had been allowed to run roughshod over the American diplomatic corps and other key arms of the foreign policy establishment. Because there were so many Foreign Service personnel in Germany, McCarthy took great delight in sending his minions, Cohn and Shine, to seek out "spies" among the U.S. High Commission staff, spread out all over western Germany. Fortunately, I never encountered these men, but their work affected mine. In 1954, when I was director of the Amerika Haus in Hof, orders came from our Bonn embassy to remove certain books from our library shelves forthwith. Cohn and Shine had inspected a few of these libraries (there were then around 40 in western Germany) and pronounced certain works as "subversive," either because the subject matter offended them or — more often — because they had been written by alleged Communists or "fellow travelers." I recall reading one of the forbidden books, a life of Tom Paine by Howard Fast, who had had connections with the United States Communist Party at some point. I hadn't heard of Fast before, but I thought the book was excellent and had nothing to do with Communism. But on orders, with gritted teeth, I removed this and a few other books from the Amerika Haus library. Of course, the thought ran through my mind (and those of colleagues in the same boat) that we were doing, in public view, just what Hitler had done in the thirties: "burning" books that were offensive to our ideology. German newspapers got wind of this and made the analogy readily. No fun for us on the front lines of the Cold War. Against American principles. But feelings back home in America, ridiculous in hindsight, had a flip side: the all too real Soviet danger overseas, especially where I was, in a little town called Hof. But that comes a little later.

In 1954, Charles W. Thayer, a respected Russia specialist and at the time consul general in Munich, resigned from the service after strong pressure from McCarthy. Thayer was accused of leftist sentiments and also rumored to have fathered a child out of wedlock in the distant past. Thayer, in the opinion of those serving with him, was an outstanding Foreign Service officer; his removal was highly damaging to morale and detrimental to the conduct of foreign policy.

Not long after this, several young Amerika Haus directors came to Hof for an impromptu unofficial gathering. Our blood was boiling over the Thayer removal and the Cohn and Shine mess, brought on by the pusillanimity of our superiors, right up to President Eisenhower. The head of a major part of the HICOG public affairs operation, Ted Kaghan, had also been hounded out of Germany because of greatly overblown charges by McCarthy. Kaghan had been called before McCarthy's committee in the Senate and had admitted writing some plays with a Communist slant in the '30s, but Secretary Dulles had refused to support him, so he had to go. More than 200 colleagues attended a farewell party for Kaghan in Bonn; it was revealed in the *New York Herald Tribune* that an overzealous embassy security officer had taken down names of those attending!

Our public affairs boss in Munich, Lowell Clucas, had been named by McCarthy in 1954 as one of a number of "fellow travelers" of Communism who should be rooted out. For some months, the head of the new U.S. Information Agency (of which we were now a part) stonewalled McCarthy on Clucas. But, just when we had thought Clucas was safe, USIA's director, Theodore Streibert, came to Munich to tell Clucas that he wanted his resignation, quietly. Clucas, he said, was a potential liability. The situation was this: Clucas, when at college in the 30s, had attended some Communist youth meetings, no more. But this was enough to excite McCarthy and his stooges. Most government departments, including USIA and the Department of State, had hired extra security officers, many of whom were overzealous in trying to hunt down sacrificial lambs. Hardly any were found, but the earlier Alger Hiss and Harry Dexter White cases, whom the passage of time and hard evidence had shown to be genuine hard-core Communist "sleepers," helped to strengthen McCarthy's hand. Now the spurious ousters of Kaghan and Thayer reinforced the sensitivity of both politicians and bureaucrats in Washington. The stage was set for more purges.

Clucas called a staff meeting in Munich to explain that he had decided to resign. A few of us "young Turks" were incensed and decided, at a rump meeting in Hof, to write a joint letter to the *New York Times* and to the secretary of state, accusing Senator McCarthy of fraud, slander, and anything else we could think of. We drafted a slam-bang letter, but prudently, before we sent it off, we felt honor-bound to show it to Mr. Clucas. He thanked us warmly, with tears in his eyes, but said we should let the matter die and that he was resolved to resign quietly, out of concern for his family. We juniors, who had been willing (some might say foolishly) to fall on our swords for Clucas, were sad and sorry. A very nice fellow took Clucas's place, and the work went on.

Interlude: Munich and Frankfurt

Before taking up new duties in Hof (Spring 1954), I had played musical chairs for some months, with temporary assignments brought about by the rapid downsizing of the public affairs operation in Germany. Once there had been about fifty American Houses; soon there would be thirty and then fewer and fewer. From Nuremberg (closed down as a regional office), I was sent to Munich to sub for a colleague on home leave, as regional exchanges officer for Bavaria. Munich was, and remains, enchanting in its mixture of aristocratic haute couture and haute cuisine, with rough and robust alpine peasant music, beer culture, and deeply conservative Catholicism as the dominant cultural undertones. As I had done in Nuremberg, I would oversee the selection and routing to the U.S. of a number of Bavarian "exchangees," chosen for their current or presumed future importance as leaders in various sectors of society.

One of my righthand staffers was an extraordinary woman named Frieda Hoerburger. Her deceased husband had been *Intendant* (director) of Munich's cultural institutions before Hitler. Both he and Frieda, despising Hitler, lay low in the terrible years. In 1945, Friedl (her diminutive) offered to help the American authorities modernize Bavaria and, enjoying tremendous connections (and respect) all over Munich, she introduced me to numerous characters who had an impact on life there. One was an antiques dealer, Herr Hanfstängel, whose brother Putzi—Harvard trained but without political thoughts or convictions—had been Hitler's court jester. Through Friedl, I became a great friend of Dr. Anton Fingerle, the *Stadtschulrat* (superintendent of schools) of Munich; we used to exchange ideas as he helped me to select good teachers and high school kids for "exchange visits." Now and then, Dr. Fingerle would entertain one of my ideas, saying, *"Hmmm . . . lass mich diese Idee in meinem Kopf laufen lassen."* (Well, let me allow that idea to run around in my head for a while.)

Another of Friedl's circle was Robert Borchardt, political editor of the *Süddeutsche Zeitung,* one of the American creations to replace the ideologically corrupt rash of Nazi newspapers. Press reform, consisting of finding capable Germans who had not been polluted by Nazism or had come home from exile to thrust themselves into the middle of the media world as publishers and editors, worked better than almost all the other U.S.- and British-induced changes in German life. Borchardt was an engaging, deeply serious, incisive man with a pessimistic cast of mind. We had long talks about Germany's terrible past and cloudy future. I believe his coldly analytical articles helped Bavarian readers to rethink their situation and, indirectly, to influence the citizenry towards a generally middle-of-the-road, democratic domestic politics and an open foreign policy. But this took some years; in the early 1950s, party political life was chaotic, reflecting the uncertainties, fears, resentments, and anger that still lurked in so many hearts and minds. Today, in the 21st century, German political life is remarkably restrained, pretty sensible, and moderately liberal overall. Even in socially conservative Bavaria, an amazing economy — the most advanced in Germany — has brought a high degree of well-being to ordinary people, reinforced by the social and political reforms brought about under American tutelage and followed up with the national leadership of people such as Adenauer, Erhard, Brandt, Schmidt, and their successors. Robert Borchhardt, and a number of people like him, scattered around Germany's press world, had a vital role in making the key difference.

We were in Munich long enough to see some of the ongoing fun. On *Vaterstag* on a given summer day, husbands and fathers were given leave from home duties to celebrate en masse, without Kinder or wives. One of the most colorful *Vaterstag* stunts, repeated every year, was to load several jerry-built rafts of logs in the mountains near the source of the Isar River with more occupants than a raft should hold, all dressed in *Lederhosen* and wearing furry mountain hats, with several pieces of a mountain brass band and a large keg of beer. These floated down the Isar through Munich, scattering music, beer, and sometimes occupants as they went.

A couple of months later, the *Oktoberfest* took the spotlight (today international). Munich then boasted 72 (!) breweries, each with somebody's favorite brand and sporting a huge tent on the outskirts of town. In each tent, the beer flowed copiously, the oompah bands serenaded without letup, and the well-lubricated clientele inside the tents gradually melted away as the night wore on. Just outside the tents, by late in the evening, one would have to pick his way over and around prostrate, drink-sodden bodies in the meadows, and wonder if all these fellows would make it home. And when it wasn't *Oktoberfest*, habitués could pack the beerhalls in downtown Munich. The most famous was (and remains today) the *Hofbräuhaus*, which began life as the Royal Bavarian Court Brewery. A huge building of four working floors, it entertained the various classes — workers and peasants on the ground floor, lower middle class people on the next, and so on. One night I went to the ground floor, which was the most fun, and asked for a glass of wine — the waiter was pretty huffy: " If you want that, go to the second or third floor! *Hier ist Bier!*" On the ground floor, there were always a few forlorn souls (the equivalent of today's "homeless") standing at the sheet metal sinks where the barmaids would set down the used beer steins (each girl carrying six, eight, or more) for washing and refilling. The forlorn drifters were quick: they darted to as many steins as they could find and swiftly, drunkenly quaffed whatever fluid remained in each!

In September 1952, a playful political officer in Munich's Consulate General wrote — and Consul General Thayer, with tongue in cheek, dispatched to Washington — a report on a "serious matter" before the

Bavarian *Landtag* (state legislature), i.e., servers in the *Hofbräuhaus* were allegedly short-changing patrons. There were public complaints about the excessive foam on hastily filled beer mugs. Prices had not risen, but patrons were getting less value for money. The dispatch writer reminded his readers that the 1848 revolution in Munich "was touched off by a rise in beer prices." The *Kulturkrise,* needless to say, blew over, along with a lot of the foam.

Frankfurt, with Ernst Busch

In the autumn of 1953, I was posted once more to Frankfurt, leaving Munich with a good deal of misgiving, especially as it had given me opportunities to tramp around the Bavarian alps, reminding me of home in the Pacific Northwest. My new Frankfurt job was again as a regional exchanges officer, once more picking out select Germans of every age for an *Amerikareise,* then following up on their return to try to determine whether they (and we) felt their exposure to the United States held the promise of success. One of my great German friends of that time and for many years until I sadly lost track of him, was Ernst Busch, exchanges assistant for our "evaluation" studies. Ernst had been born in Germany but was taken early in life to New Jersey, where he attended public schools until he was thirteen. His parents, pinched by the Depression, decided around 1931 to return to Germany, where Ernst eventually became a Hitler Jugend, like almost every boy his age. In 1939, he was trained as a pilot for the Luftwaffe, then was shot down over England in the Battle of Britain. By this time, German and Italian prisoners were beginning to cram the British countryside, so Ernst was transferred to Canada, where he spent five years as a POW. He had been somewhat—but superficially, he discovered—brainwashed by the Nazis and encountered many still-fierce ones in prisonership. Gradually, as he thought things over, looked at Canadian life, and recalled his pleasures as a child in America, he began to see that citizenship in a democracy meant something—something priceless. Soon after the war ended, he returned to Germany. Because his English was so good and because he was not politically tainted, Ernst was accepted as a "local" by the American military government and assigned to work with a succession of officers and later—under the High Commission—civilian Kreis Resident Officers, to help reeducate his fellow Germans.

When I met him, Ernst had recently left his favorite KRO (a smart, typically "Establishment" Easterner named Rowland Burk) when Burk became director of an Amerika Haus in Darmstadt, south of Frankfurt. Ernst landed a job in the Frankfurt Exchanges office, where he helped me to learn the necessary things about the State of Hesse. He fascinated me. He had imbibed a tremendous—even unrealistic—attachment in his mind to the American *polis* and, having known it somewhat as a boy and having seen firsthand what the diabolical Nazis had done to Germany, Ernst wanted to reform German life, root and branch. He had no patience with old Prussian Junkers, high Protestant churchmen or narrow-minded Catholics who wanted to control the schools, socialist trade unionists with Marxist ideas, stubborn old-school bureaucrats, and all the other "types" that in his view had made the old Germany—the one on which Hitler had built his evil edifice—so (to Ernst) repulsive. Moderate Social Democrats were Ernst's preference politically. He strove mightily, using our tools of America Houses, press reforms, and interchanges of people, to move German institutions in what he felt was the correct direction. He was right, but also rigid. Every presumed failure of some local or national leader, every apparent vestige of old thinking made him despondent. He worried a lot.

Ernst's wife Ilse (the widow of his Luftwaffe pal, killed in combat, and whom Ernst had promised to take care of if the worst happened) was a fine mate and delighted Ernst when she entered local politics, becoming first a city councilor, then a state (*Landtag*) legislator. When I last heard of Ilse, around 1965, she seemed to be a true comer in the Social Democratic party. Tragically, however, Ernst had to leave his job with the Americans (about 1955) when more downsizing made it inevitable, but then could find no suitable employment. He worked as a traveling salesman for several years, then finally I could no longer find him when I would return to Germany.

I had a close relationship with many of the "locals" who worked for me in Frankfurt, Nuremberg, Munich, and later Hof, but none had the sharpness of mind or fierce compassion of an Ernst Busch. Of others who impressed me, there will be more.

In March 1954, I was posted to Hof an der Saale, as director of the Amerika Haus. This was a lucky stroke for me, as it thrust me deep into the far provinces of northern Bavaria, where it was sink or swim for a young American, virtually alone on the border between Communism and freedom, and (fortunately for me) many kilometers from my immediate bosses, stuck in the mammoth Consulate General in Munich.

5
Borderland Stories

October 1954: First Declaration of Atlantic Unity, signed by 244 leading citizens from NATO countries, is released, proposing an Atlantic Assembly.

July 1955: NATO Parliamentarians Conference meets in Paris for the first meeting of legislators from fifteen countries, today known as the Atlantic Assembly.

Was German Militarism Dead and Buried?

From my journal (November 1952): "The SS had a meeting in Mannheim the other day—5000 of their veterans. This shocked me when I read it in the *Nürnberger Nachrichten*. Ex-SS General Remcke harangued them in a manner reminiscent of certain other German demagogues, demanded the release of German war criminals, etc. Perhaps this is deplored by the majority of Germans, but the fact that, within eight years after the crushing German defeat, the organization most symbolic of the depravity of Hitler's government could actually hold an annual meeting is to me a cause for some concern." Later, another newspaper article disclosed an official finding that two-thirds of the current members of the German Foreign Office also had served in the diplomatic service of the Third Reich.

In 1954, after I had moved to Hof, I visited my colleague Jim McDonald in another "border outpost" of the U.S. Information Service, Coburg, where he too directed an Amerika Haus. After supper, McDonald said, "there's a ceremonial *Zapfenstreich und Fachelzug* (trooping of the colors plus a torchlight parade) tonight in the town square; let's go see." Coburg was the fount of crowned heads, including Queen Victoria's consort, Albert, for many countries in Europe during the 19th century. A small jewel of the Middle Ages, its town square, castle, and churches were virtually untouched in recent centuries. In the old monastery was a room where Martin Luther allegedly threw an inkwell at the Devil—wall stains still there.

At this time there was no German army (the new Bundeswehr began formation in 1955), but to augment Bavarian border police, who carried only sidearms, and the regular U.S. Army border patrols, the Americans had urged Adenauer to introduce legislation for the immediate establishment of a Federal German Border Police, a force of 20,000. Hof was a regional headquarters for these troops—because "troops" is what they were. They wore the old field-gray uniforms, jackboots, and bucket helmets of the *Wehrmacht*. On this cold dark evening, they were drawn up in formation in the Coburg town square; suddenly there were urgent drumrolls. Some of their comrades, each carrying a lighted torch, marched into the Square and tossed their torches into a large bonfire. The band played, the colors were presented, the onlookers cheered.

McDonald and I, with the hackles rising on the backs of our collective necks, looked at each other, horrified. McDonald had been an air force officer in World War II, I a navy petty officer. To us, it looked ominously like, say, Bavaria 1922 all over again. Fortunately, this was not to be. When it came into being, the new *Bundeswehr* had been most carefully designed. I learned later, in 1963, from a new German colonel friend that he and about thirty other officers who had served in World War II were determined that things would have to be different. They were chosen by Lt. General Wolf Graf von Baudissin, even more determined than his cohorts that the old Prussian ways would have to be discarded.

Baudissin's group spent more than a year in a secluded cloister in the forests west of the Rhine, then presented a plan to the federal Cabinet and Bundestag. The plan was adopted. It embraced the concept of the "citizen-soldier"; an Ombudsman (independent inspector general to hear complaints from individual soldiers) was put in place; and the old German General Staff—so formidable a power in German life for close to a century—was eliminated. What served for a planning staff was completely integrated into the new international staff—headquarters of NATO's Supreme Allied Command Europe, then still at Rocquencourt outside Paris.

Not long after the new *Bundeswehr* was formed, a staff college for the armed forces was set up under Baudissin, to insure that the new Germany's officers would be educated to serve a modern democratic state. In 1964, I was privileged to be taken on an informal "inspection tour" of the Bundeswehr; the results, in less than a decade, were gratifying. In 1990, a friend in the Seattle area who was a reserve U.S. Army colonel, was called to active duty to help the Bundeswehr absorb officers and noncoms of the former Army of the East German "Democratic" Republic who were considered "reconstructable," weed out the ideologues, and arrange a new scheme of training for the retainees. The emphasis was to be on service within a modern democratic state.

Also in 1990, I was called to a conference in Washington, D.C., convened by the Konrad Adenauer Foundation to discuss how the lessons learned by Americans about integrating a population (the Germans of 1945) into a fully democratic life, might be applied by the Federal Republic in absorbing its new eastern compatriots.

But in 1954 the quiet work of Baudissin and others to insure that Germany would have new armed forces on a totally different model, appropriate to a modern democracy, was unknown to the general public, and even to us junior Foreign Service Officers. The public, both in Germany and in America, was worried that, in the autumn of 1954 after the French *Assemblée Nationale* had torpedoed the idealistic plan for a European Army (largely an attempt at making sure that Germany would never again have an independent military force) and that, once it had been agreed among the Allies, with German assent, a German force would somehow have to be created to augment the thin NATO tripwire along the Iron Curtain, the nascent trends toward European and Atlantic integration—and German democratization—would be halted.

With that as background, witness the scene in my small office at the back of the Amerika Haus Hof, in December 1954, as Herr Bohlmann, the proprietor of a little firm that contracted to keep the Haus windows clean, was ushered in at his request: I found out quickly that he was not there to talk about the contract, but to ask my advice on a delicate personal matter that greatly concerned him. He (and, he said, several friends) had received letters from the *Amt Blank*, the federal German office charged with implementing the plans for a new German army. Herr Bohlmann and other local colleagues had served in the *Wehrmacht*. Bohlmann was drafted in 1939, just after graduation from the German equivalent of high school. He was discharged as a Captain when the war ended. Without vocational or tertiary education, he had little choice but to become a small entrepreneur; the window-washing service now enabled him to raise his family and pay bills, but only just. He felt he was at a career dead-end.

Now Bohlmann had the offer to reenter German military service. In many ways this was for him an attractive prospect, but still he had grave doubts. "Herr Direktor," he said, "I do not want to resume my old rank and profession if the new Army is going to be like the old one. I'm concerned how an army can be appropriate to a democracy. In the old days, when we officers walked down a street, civilians would often step into the gutter to let us pass. We were expected to obey orders from superiors without question, and our underlings were expected to obey us also without question. Are these things right in a democracy? Can you tell me how the American democratic army is run?"

I replied, "I may be able to do better than that; my own personal opinions wouldn't be worth much." Whereupon I phoned my good friend, Lt. Col. Dewitt Armstrong, commander of an armored battalion whose task it was to patrol a key stretch of the East Zone border. I put the question to Dee: Could he bring a couple of officers and an enlisted man or two to meet with these nonplussed Germans? Some who could speak German?

Subsequently, we had several evening meetings in the Amerika Haus. The Germans voiced their concerns and their hazy (often wrong) ideas as to how the military kept its cohesion and did its job in a great democracy such as the United States. One German said he thought that in a democratic army, the various units must surely *elect* their officers and noncoms. Armstrong and colleagues disabused them quickly: The U.S. Army relied on strict obedience, officers were appointed by higher authority, not elected, and so on. After much discussion, we all agreed that what made the Army of the United States (and those of its democratic allies) different from a military run by a dictatorship or autocracy was this: a properly constituted armed force of any kind, in a democracy, was subservient—without question—to the elected government of the nation. On this, there was no question in the United States. Nor in Germany, one might add, after that time.

[Fast forward: At the time of Watergate I thought of this democratic principle. General Alexander Haig was at that time the deputy head of the National Security Council in the White House. At the crucial point when President Nixon's authority was crumbling and he had not yet decided to resign, in many countries it would have seemed natural for a man in Haig's position to phone the Pentagon and ask for, say, the 82nd Airborne Division to be deployed in support of a military coup, to prevent chaos in the body politic. But the principle was clear: the U.S. armed forces remain under elected civilian authority at all times.]

However, in 1950–55 the place of the military was under intense public scrutiny in west Germany. My job gave me an excellent opportunity to sound out opinion in all parts of society. Although the SPD (West German Social Democrats) had passed a national resolution refusing rearmament unless still another attempt had been made to deal with the Russians on a reunification of west and east Germany, that "unless" said a lot for what most Germans thought. At local trade union discussions I attended, a few Communists tried ham-handedly to get workers to come out against rearmament under any circumstances. When the time came, there were enough cool heads around Hof—where I was—and the rest of West Germany—to permit a peaceful political solution. Conscription was introduced, a new *"Bundeswehr"* was constituted, and all went smoothly in democratic fashion. In 1964, when I took my *Bundeswehr* inspection trip at the invitation of the Federal German government, my chief concern was not that there was too much spit and polish and clicking of heels, but the reverse: the new recruits were a good deal more sloppy and lackadaisical than U.S. commanders would have allowed!

Communist Infiltration in the West

In some of my letters and journal entries of the late forties and early fifties, I still retained a common Western view of Communism: it was a misguided effort by woolly idealists, from Lenin on, to bring about broad changes in society by force. But at least its ideals were pointed in the right direction, many of us hoped. Facing Communism and Communists up close in Hof brought about a notable change in my views; I became a card-carrying Cold Warrior. The nurturing of a liberal democratic society—everywhere—was still my own priority, but when the makings of another world conflagration, fuelled mainly by the totally unscrupulous people in the Kremlin, were right there staring me literally in the face, the immediate need to fight the Soviet system and its satellite managers took precedence.

In the mid-1950s, the extent to which the Soviet Agitprop would and could intervene in internal West German affairs became palpably evident to me when, soon after the meetings described above of earnest German veterans and American officers had taken place, Col. Armstrong phoned me. He had had questions from his corps headquarters in Stuttgart: their French Army liaison office had informed them that two Tass (Soviet news bureau) correspondents reported a hotbed of "recrudescent German militarism in Hof." The colonel disabused his corps commander of such ideas, but this illustrated graphically just how omnipresent, as well as baldfaced and lying, the Soviets could be. And also how long their Agitprop tentacles stretched at the time.

During the period of a cross-border lull in 1954, the East Germans did their best to interfere in all manner of public affairs in West Zone areas around Hof. On one occasion, a Hof schoolteacher (patently some kind of Eastern agent) was offering opportunities for university study in the East to Western youngsters who were struggling to get higher education that their families could not afford. They were told that not only could they gain admission to Eastern universities and free tuition, but they would also be given a stipend of DM 100 per month, not much in those days but enough to insure subsistence. There were also cross-border visits of schoolchildren, West to East and vice versa, arranged and paid for by Eastern authorities and tightly controlled by Eastern manipulators.

But after Christmas 1954, Eastern authorities suddenly cracked down, closing the temporarily porous borders and cutting off propaganda visits. The existing wall was then greatly fortified and a more frigid period in the Cold War set in. The Soviets were fighting the political battle against a stronger NATO, including German forces, which loomed up as a result of the failure of the European Defense Community legislation in France, and the "end run" which the NATO countries engineered to bring about West German rearmament in a different way. This succeeded, and the resulting new *Bundeswehr* proved to be an outstanding model for a democracy's army. Our worst fears on both accounts—a Soviet-launched attack (through the Fulda Gap or the Hof Gap, four kilometers from my home) or a new Prussian-style but old-fashioned German military that could devastate Europe again—were subsequently allayed. But in 1954 there was great cause for concern. Would the Germans truly take to democracy as the years went on?

I remembered some words of Ernst Busch, my trusted "local" in Frankfurt, who usually took a very gloomy view of Germany society's prospects, but who was sometimes right. In November 1953, I had recorded in my journal:

> Ernst is not terribly optimistic. He thinks much progress has been made, but he says the Germans, as [a] people, are not yet basically democratic. . . . The troubles are in people's attitudes and only basic education can change this. He is very concerned over arrogance, false pride, the *Beamte* [bureaucratic tenure] system, the reemergence of the nationalistic organizations (the *Stahlhelm*, for example), the difficulty of introducing democratic reforms into the schools. He fears Adenauer, who is a benevolent authoritarian. . . . Our foreign policy, maintains Ernst, has gotten ahead of the evolution of Germany.

German Institutions and "National Character"

When I landed in Germany in January 1952, my knowledge of Germany and the Germans was distinctly rudimentary. During my formative years (1930s to 1950s) my main sources were newspaper articles, *Time* and *Life* magazines, radio (some commentators were exceptionally good, well-informed), the comments of my parents plus a couple of teachers, and one specialty magazine, *The Reporter,* edited by a savvy Italian-American named Max Ascoli, which started up in the late '40s only to expire in the early '60s. Nor had I undertaken much academic study of European history. So I was intellectually ill-prepared for my new job. Yet I was eager to learn and so managed, I think, to come out of four years of intense working and living experiences with Germans to form some useful and probably (looking back on those days) fairly accurate views. Much of what I had learned in Frankfurt, Nuremberg, and Munich while managing exchanges and educational programs gave me some fine insights into the "makeup" of the people. But my "total immersion" in the backwoods and borderland town of Hof and the province of Oberfranken nicely brought everything together. Fortunately, I was still keeping a concentrated journal, which focused largely on impressions wrung out of my daily contact with these people and their institutions. I was seeing them in their home context.

The comments that follow are based mainly on my *Oberfranken* experience, plus insights gained from later academic study and frequent contacts over the many years since with Germans. They are certainly the most fascinating, important, dynamic and potentially dangerous group of people in all of Europe, as they have been since at least 1870. I stress the word "potentially" because, although in my mind as the years tick by I become relatively less concerned with a "German danger" or what has been more broadly called "the German question," there is always the possibility that things can go deeply, seriously wrong in Europe because of Germany. I can therefore still not be 100 percent certain that the *Furore Teutonicus* could never be unleashed again. But this probability becomes more and more remote as the bonds of the European Union and its ties with the United States continue to strengthen (of course with ups and downs) and the forces of globalization and international law bind us all more firmly together, virtually inextricably. A transatlantic or intra-European war as the 21st century begins is highly unlikely, in my view now more or less impossible.

German institutions—not just the skeleton of government, but social institutions such as the business world, trade unions and workers, the media, youth, women's roles in society, the media, religion, the integration (problematical) of immigrants, the educational system, the practice of law, the scientific world, and so on—have undergone major transformations since 1945. I was on the scene when great change was beginning to happen. I and other American thirty-somethings, plunked down in Germany in the early years after World War II, may have had an important—perhaps indispensable—hand in encouraging (and in some cases inducing) healthy change; but the Germans brought about their own recovery—moral, political, social, and economic. Unless the great majority of them had not felt the absolute necessity of transforming their society so that they could rejoin the modern international community, it never could have been done. However, the scope and direction of this transformation might have been very different but for the Americans, British, and French who coached them along and exposed them constantly for some years to new ways of thinking and acting. And most Germans were ready.

Institutions are created and run by people. In the 1940s, there was an intense debate among American academics as to whether or not there was such a thing as "national character," i.e., did the inhabitants of a given country, or nation, exhibit common characteristics of psychological make-up and behavior? The debate, I think, was instigated by those who felt that it was wrong (even in such a blatant recent case as that of "the Germans") to believe that just because individuals had been brought up in a given national culture, they would all exhibit certain traits. Of course such a theory of "national character" doesn't explain much or even hold water universally, but far too often clumps of prejudices have formed which people seek to apply, as a kind of shorthand in dealing with "foreigners," to the detriment of a society as a whole and to the cases of specific individuals. Particularly in modern Europe, or in the United States, does this kind of "stereotyping" work any more, if it ever did? My most heart-wrenching experiences in Germany of the 1950s were to encounter such biases unfairly at work, against the Germans and even among them, as well as on their part against people of other cultures.

Nevertheless, a clutch of predominant cultural traits were certainly shared in the 1950s by a majority of Germans and manifested in a variety of behavior. There were also many regional variations; Bavarians were quite different from Hannoverians, even from next-door Swabians. These disparate national building blocks did not come together out of a benevolent sense of common destiny, but largely through the handiwork of Bismarck's Blood and Iron doctrine, with the way prepared by the Romantic nationalists, such as Fichte, Herder, Ranke, and Arndt, who wrote of *"jenseits der Rhein, wo jeder Franzmann heiset Feind"* (across the Rhine, where every Frenchman is our enemy).

In Germany of the 1950s, there were a lot of strong prejudices, left over from the Nazi regime and earlier times, among hardened old conservatives, youngish veterans, radicals who thought they knew what had gone wrong but had some weird ideas about how to reorganize things, and the school and university populations, still greatly influenced by parents and professors, many of whom were leftovers from the Nazi school system. And there was one major disability, glaring to me but not usually recognizable: the *intellectual* adoption of democratic ways (for us, the greatest fault line in trying to guess which way Germany would go) was far more evident and—for the individual—"operable" in daily life, than was the much more important *emotional* embracing, or internalizing, of a new set of values (the "values of freedom" one might call them) and habits to guide everyday behavior.

The Story of Karl Hellmuth Herschel

The example of Karl Hellmuth Herschel was to me most telling. First mention of Herschel from my journal, 19 January 1953:

> Herr Herschel of Koenigshofen was a guest (advisor) at our conference [of teenagers just returned from U.S. trips]. He is an author and newspaper editor, as well as lecturer, who made the most reasoned, forceful plea for European unity I have yet heard. He said, "Germany has but three alternatives; either it becomes an American colony, a Russian satellite, or it joins Europe." He is the most talented, intelligent, calm, and truly mature man I have met in Germany. If there were 1,000 Herr Herschels, all campaigning for *vereinte Europa*, we should attain our goal swiftly.

The next mention of Herschel is a year and a half later. In the meantime, he had become a good friend, had lectured many times for our public affairs program in various parts of Franconia, and had been sent on a three-month "exchange" trip to the United States (from which he returned happy and ebullient). I had hired him at the Amerika Haus Hof when I realized that I was desperately in need of a sound, reliable No. 2. We had nearly twenty German employees and Karl's oversight proved invaluable. But . . . . . .

Herschel's background was fascinating. The son of a cultured Prussian physician (and a descendant of Sir William Herschel of British astronomical fame), Karl at age 18 had entered the Reichswehr cadet academy in Munich just after World War I, then became an officer, rising gradually to the rank of major when World War II broke out. He was in the Panzer forces that overran Belgium and Holland and at one point was commandant of occupied Bordeaux. There he learned to do marvelous culinary things with mushrooms and said he made a number of French friends. (This was not surprising; when I lived in France in the 1960s, a French butcher in Le Vésinet, where I "homesteaded" for two years, and the owner of a small bourgeois restaurant on the left bank where I liked to eat, both told me of the German friends they had made during the war. One of these Frenchmen was a "slave laborer," who had been billeted in a German home and worked long hours in a munitions factory. The other knew ordinary German soldiers in France, and their families were still close in the 1960s, exchanging regular visits.)

Herschel also commanded Panzers in the Russian campaign, rose to division commander, and later became commandant of the German tank school in Stuttgart. He told me that he had always hated Hitler and worried about what would become of Germany, but like virtually all Germans except the most heroic, he obeyed and did what he was told; like all officers, he was asked in 1933 to give his personal oath to the Fuerher and did so. But by early 1944 he had become convinced that only disaster lay ahead for Germany. He joined the plotters of the 20 July 1944 assassination attempt on Hitler. Assuming the murder had been successful, Karl would have been deputy minister of the interior in a new interim government. Fortunately for him and most of the 3,000 others who had secretly pledged to work in the new regime, his name was not discovered in the plotters' records.

Herschel continued in his command until the war ended. His old home in Wuerzburg, together with his library of 3,000 books, had been destroyed in bombings. His marriage had collapsed under the strains of war. He repaired to the village of Koenigshofen, a few kilometers from the East Zone border, remarried, and pieced together a bare living as editor of the local newspaper, itinerant lecturer, and writer on European affairs.

I discovered after several months that Herschel, as my No. 2, was as loyal and reliable as anyone could possibly be. He was extremely keen on his job, understudying me in efforts to modernize German life and prepare the one million Germans who lived in our "area," Oberfranken, for a future in a united Europe, a strong Atlantic community, and a democracy. He had studied the American Founding Fathers and could give authoritative talks on the Declaration of Independence and the creation of the Constitution. His big hero was Lincoln.

Herschel was extremely valuable to me in making contacts with mayors, county officials, school administrators, and the like all over Oberfranken. He played the cello for relaxation; one day I dropped him off at his home for lunch, then proceeded on to my own repast, plus a little quiet work in the drafty Tower Room. Picking Karl up on the return to the Amerika Haus, I asked, "Did you have a little nap after lunch, Karl?" No, he said, he had dashed off a little sonata for cello! Dvořák was his favorite composer.

He was a voracious reader, brought himself up to speed on every issue that we dealt with, and more. He dedicated himself with all his being to democracy, especially after he had seen the American variety at work. Yet, in "his heart," emotionally, he could not easily shed the old ways of a Prussian officer. He was respected by most of our staff; they all understood *"Gehorsamkeit."* (We would call it the "obedience principle" or the "authority complex.") We had a few German veterans on our staff, and they did not particularly relish Herschel's ways; they had been yelled at too often in the *Wehrmacht*, *"Es wird gemacht!"* (It shall be done!).

But there was never open rebellion. When I discovered Karl's weak spot, I told him as well as I could that an American staff (whether composed in our case of Germans, or not) operated on American principles. We were not the Army, but people who helped the Boss to make decisions and worked collegially. In particular, I had learned in America to be a team member in any enterprise and I treated my Germans that way. Karl learned, but never entirely. And he was invaluable to me. When I left Hof, he stayed on as No. 2 to my successors, and he was invaluable to them, too. But his effect on staff morale had become so burdensome, on balance, that by Christmas 1954, when we held a staff Christmas party, most of us—especially Karl—were at one point terribly embarrassed. A couple of anonymous staff members saw to it that "Santa" gave Karl a special present, which he opened in front of all: It was a little notebook, with a pencil attached, which dangled by a small chain from the third button on the tunic of every top sergeant in the old *Wehrmacht* (and I suppose Bismarck's and Friederich II's armies, too). When the sergeant wanted to cite a soldier for breach of regulations, he would quickly write down the circumstances in his little book, in preparation for demerits. Herschel's face reddened, as did most faces around him. But he got the message: Some of his colleagues thought he personified an old *Oberfeldwebel*, doubly galling for him as he had never been a noncom, having ended the war with a general's command. I know that he redoubled his effort to change after this, but it was not easy for him. Knowing him intimately, incidentally, rounded out my command of German by including some exquisitely fine Prussian curse words!

I thought so much of Karl that some years later, when I was posted from Washington to Brussels in the new U.S. Mission to the new European Communities, I pressed my superiors to arrange a transfer for Karl, a so-called "local employee" of the United States Foreign Service, from Germany to Brussels. This had never been done before but I made the case that Karl's understanding of the projected European union was so great, his command of languages so good (he spoke and read at least five), his devotion to the United States so unlimited, and his efficiency so undoubted, that I needed him. And, with only two other "locals" in his branch of our Brussels public affairs office, Karl was no longer encumbered with staff direction or administration. He served loyally in that office for several years, long after I had gone on to other things, and eventually retired to a little rose garden in Bavaria.

By way of explaining his complex character, not too unusual in Germans of his era, I should flashback to July 1954, when Herschel and Klimt (our program coordinator for the Hof Amerika Haus) took a car trip with me of several hundred miles through northern Bavaria to Frankfurt, Hannover and Tuebingen, for a look at how other America Houses ran their programs. We stopped for a night in Hannoversch-Muenden, where Ernst Busch and his wife Ilse lived. (Busch, the reader will recall, was my No. 2 for a few months in the exchanges office for Hesse; his wife by 1954 was a member of the City Council—a woman who was as modern, liberal, and forward-thinking as her husband, perhaps even more so.) The five of us had a jolly dinner, and then I spent some time alone with Ilse and Ernst, talking about "the reintegration of Western culture," according to my journal:

> Ilse said Herschel's philosophy o.k., fundamentally good ideas
> . . . but he is not "integrated." He is egocentric—sees all situations
> with himself at the center. He told his story of writing to Eisenhower, inviting Piskoe of the [Christian Science] Monitor, going to
> Bonn to see and thank the U.S. powers-that-be. [He had according
> to Ilse] a very immature viewpoint.

Later, I recorded that "Karl told me . . . when he visited the U.S., he realized that the Europeans had failed Europe, not the Americans. You are the real Europeans, he said, you've held the torch high. He is completely disgusted with Germans as a people; sometimes a little frightening, though I must agree with him." Still later, I quote him as saying to me, "Jim, I am convinced that I will eventually die in a Nazi concentration camp." He's very concerned with a "resurgence of the German Curse, nationalism."

As I watched and listened to him over the years, I came to see Karl as a tragic figure, typical of many well-educated, cultured Germans. Goethe has Faust agonizing over his own split personality: "zwei Sehle wohn in meinem Brust" (two souls are at war within my breast). For too many generations—perhaps since the Thirty Years War—the Germans had been disunited, a charnel house for the rest of Europe (a role they then embellished to a fare-thee-well in the 20th century), a fountain of great ideas about man and society in the Enlightenment, and yet the repository of a dark side that tolerated the impossible—even the unspeakable—because of the conviction that Order must come first in the hierarchy of human requirements. Herschel was an eminently good man, a person of ideals that were right, but I believe he looked back on his career and personal life as a failure because, along with most of his countrymen, he knew he should have spoken out, made common cause with other good people, resisted much sooner. He never said this to me in so many words, but I believe this endless brooding went on in the hearts and minds of many contemporary Germans. Karl was a 20th century archetype of what went wrong. But also of what could go right. The gentler, more civil, freedom-loving soul of Germany has, by this new century, pretty well won out. I believe that.

The Slow Conversion to Democratic Ways

Old German national traits lurked in many breasts elsewhere. In the fall of 1954, I stopped by Frankfurt again to chat with Ernst Busch, the "local" who had so idealized American civic ways and, like Herschel, castigated Germans who could not learn. Busch, again like Herschel, saw national-ism as a German curse. Again, from my journal:

> [Ernst's] sister, an American, had visited last summer. Ernst was obviously disappointed. He had not seen her for 22 years [when he and his parents had left her behind, as they returned to Ger-many] and hoped she would be a first-class American, with open eyes and some sort of attitude like his. Instead she turned out to be a German nationalist, who thinks that Germany should stand up for its rights, scuttle the French, team up with the Americans, etc. etc. The same old nationalistic stuff one hears from pretty far right—very hard, cynical with regard to united Europe, etc. Karl [Herschel] has an American cousin who is like this, only worse. I told Ernst "There is just as great a percentage of boneheads per 1000 of population in Europe as in the U.S.; the only difference is that over there somehow the masses are willing to try changes and accept leadership more readily."

Today, when I consider the hamfisted attitudes of my rather bigoted barber (for instance) in my little 21st century country town—and worse, look at the spawning of homegrown "militia" that have distinct Nazi ten-dencies—I wonder if Americans have improved much over the decades. I believe today's Germans in some ways may be ahead of us in their attitudes towards the world. There seems to be no inclination to "go it alone"—to remake the world—in Germany.

One practical problem of the early postwar period was how to fit Ger-mans to carry on intelligent group discussion of knotty civic problems. If there had ever been a common knowledge of parliamentary procedure, it must have been lost during the Hitler period. Just after Christmas 1954 this social lacuna came home to me graphically. These were pre-TV days in Germany; films were still popular. Adult education organizations in the various *Landkreise* (counties) ran *Kulturfilm* programs and the U.S. information services supplied them plentifully with interesting and instructive movies about the United States, Europe, current world problems, and so on. In Bavaria, every *Landkreis* had film operators, supplied with vans and movies by the Americans. It was their job to tour the counties, showing films of our offerings plus a wide selection of their own. Call this "propaganda" if one wishes, yet the themes of our movies were mild and positive compared to the tendentious trash they had been shown in the Nazi period, or that the Communist fronts would provide them with, when they could. For several years, this film program filled a gap in widening the worldviews of ordinary Germans.

I had been asked to provide the conference room of the Hof Amerika Haus for a meeting of an association of those who managed the film programs in all the Bavarian counties. Some of these managers invited me to attend the meeting, which I did. Beforehand, two called on me to explain a particular problem that must be dealt with by the meeting: Two years earlier, the group (an *Arbeitsgemeinschaft*, or informal working group) had been formed on the spur of the moment at a similar meeting in Munich. At that time, they had elected a certain Herr Winkler to the chairmanship. They had had several meetings since that election but now they said a consensus called for ousting Herr Winkler as chairman. He tended to dominate meetings, did not represent them well to authorities, and so on. How could this be done, Herr Direktor? said the delegation, asking me for advice.

I said: What are the election provisions of your constitution or articles of incorporation? Constitution? Articles? Elections? They breathed deeply: We have none; this is a very informal organization. I asked if they had ever provided for a term of office for the chairman. Term of office? they said; none was specified. Winkler assumed that he was to be chairman forever, and they couldn't have that. Cogitating, I observed that until now all they had was an informal, transitory group that they could certainly regularize. My suggestion, to which they vigorously nodded agreement, was this: At a suitable point in their meeting, one of them should ask to be recognized and say something like this: "Herr Winkler, we appreciate all that you have done for us in this interim period. We think that now you must agree with us that our organization has shown its value and that it would be good to set it up more formally and permanently, with a written constitution. I therefore move that we appoint a committee to write such a set of articles, to be discussed and adopted at our next meeting. Then we can have an election for definite terms for a set of officers. We thank you for your interim leadership during our formative period." I said this

would save face for Winkler and enable them to change chairmen gracefully, if gradually.

The dissidents said "fine." All was arranged. When the meeting started, I sat in the back of the room as an observer. One of the revolutionaries
asked to be recognized and then, to my consternation and that of his fellows, began by saying straight off, "Herr Winkler, you have done a *lousy*
job as our chairman! It's time we replaced you. You must step down."
Winkler, who was both smooth and ruthless, managed the whole thing
adroitly, so that no drafting committee was set up, everyone was mortified
(and most embarrassed), and after an hour and a half of rancor the group
went home, quite unhappily, with nothing accomplished, and Winkler
still in charge.

On another occasion, I attended a meeting of a Franconian organization pushing European union. They were enthusiastic at the prospects.
Each of the thirty or so delegates made an impassioned speech of one sort
or another, accompanied by a resounding stamping of feet on the floor in
each case. On such occasions, an American group would have given ap-
plause; this was the German way. That was simply a cultural difference
of no importance. But there were no questions or discussion of points just
made. When a delegate wanted to speak he gave a tiny signal to the chairman, his name was inscribed on a list, and when the time came he or she
gave a speech. This robbed the occasion of any sense of give and take, or
indeed of practicality or coherence. There was little evidence, especially
on the part of the chairman, to summarize the problems as the group saw
them and then agree on a one-two-three set of steps to deal with them, or
how to disagree.

Many other times I noticed the same pattern: a good deal of interaction between chairman and individuals, but no person-to-person sparring
or discussing. No questions from the floor. No striving for consensus. In
short, very little was ever accomplished.

I do not know if this kind of "parliamentary" behavior has changed in
Germany, but I was so concerned, after numerous similar experiences, that
I wrote my superiors in Bonn and suggested that an expert should investigate German patterns and provide a manual of parliamentary procedure
and a guide to conducting discussions, for wide dissemination. Nor was
this only a German trait; I noticed similar "get-me-on-the-record" behavior in many Europe-wide conferences later.

✄

The "authority principle" displayed itself often, notably in deference to
those in charge (*die Obrigkeiten*), and also in the way authorities, even the

most menial bureaucrats, regarded ordinary citizens as beneath them.

One day in Hof I took a couple of hours off to get some exercise, riding my bicycle down a park-path not far from my home. Suddenly, in the middle of some woods, a figure stepped into the path, hand high. "Halt! It is forbidden to ride bicycles on this path. Don't you know this?" No, I said, I hadn't seen any signs, and there was no one else on the path at the time but him and me. "Nevertheless, this is so. I am a Park Warden. You must dismount." His words were all said with a good deal of vehemence and officiousness; I had been accustomed to civil servants in the U.S., but exhibiting calmer, more civil behavior. I was nettled, so I asked, "Do you know who I am?" Negative. So I then said, "I am the Director of the Amerika Haus." What a change came over the little man! *Ach, verzeihung, Herr Direktor! Ich habe nicht gewusst.* (Oh, my apologies, Mr. Director, I didn't know!) Then I let him have it: "It doesn't make any difference *who* I am or what my station, or that I am an American and not a German. You are an employee of the public! The most lowly worker in this town should be accorded the same respect as the *Oberbuergermeister.*" He got the message, but it probably meant to him only "don't cross the Americans."

In those days, one often encountered the same sort of haughtiness in a German bank (whose personnel were treated as *Beamte* — tenured public officials): they were doing *you* a service, and you'd better just be resigned to waiting until they were good and ready to wait on you! Or in the post office, where officiousness was also legion. Or on a train or tram, when the conductor would order anyone around, as he thought necessary.

Years later, my wife and I were training around Europe on Eurailpasses. It so happened that we took a long ride from Ostend in Belgium to Berlin just two days after German reunification officially took place (3 October 1990). We missed the great celebrations, including the stirring 4th movement of Beethoven's 9th in the Berlin Concert Hall, with the Federal president and all manner of officialdom present. (The words of the chorale, "All men shall be brothers . . . " reportedly moved everyone present mightily.) Our train passed from what, until two days earlier, had been West German territory, to the East. West German conductors had punched our tickets several times, with genial informality. (My journal even described them as "a happy-go-lucky and polite lot.") This was far different behavior from that of German conductors in the "old days," when I first knew Germany. But since around 1965, during many visits, I had encountered a big change in the demeanor and behavior of German officialdom; they had become a thoroughly recognizable species of Western democratic man. But on this day in 1990, as the train crossed the border from west to east, a new set of officials and conductors (not one, but two) took over, employees of the as-yet-to-be-integrated East German railways (then

still called the *Deutsche Reichsbahn*). In contrast with their western counterparts, who by this time wore rather scruffy, nondescript uniforms with
soft caps, the eastern conductors still wore smart uniforms and peaked
caps reminiscent of the *Wehrmacht* or SS.

My wife, traveling in the next compartment to mine because we had
not been able to find two seats together, was accosted first by an eastern
conductor when she presented her Eurailpass: "These are no good in the
German Democratic Republic and you will have to buy a double-fare tick-
et now." My wife's German was halting and she was flustered, but understood. She tried to explain that our travel agent in the United States had
said our passes would be good anywhere in Germany. "No matter" said
Herr Conductor, as he loomed over her. Traveling in her compartment
was a young man in a business suit who had a *Bundesbahn* (West German
rail) pass; he interrupted the conductor, identified himself as a member of
the Federal Bundestag, and reminded him that the two halves of Germany
had just been reunited. The conductor capitulated, but not without a little
lecture. We continued on without incident. The contrast had been striking.
Bringing the East Germans, who had known only unbroken authoritarian
rule since 1933, into the fold of a pretty thoroughly democratized, modern
Federal Republic, wasn't easy, and the process is still far from complete.

I recall another revealing incident, in 1952. I had just been posted to
Nuremberg and paid a visit to Wuerzburg to confer with the Rektor (president) of the university. My guide was the head of the Wuerzburg Amerika
Haus, George C. "Curt" Moore. As we motored over to the university,
Curt counseled me to be sure to address the Rektor as *"Ihre Magnifizenz."*
"What kind of a Student Prince affair is this?" I scoffed. Curt, who had
been around these parts longer than I, said, "No kidding. Do it." The Rektor preferred to conduct our interview in German, so I haltingly did so,
asking questions about his experience with students sent to America for
a year of study. He thought that might be OK, but he could not see why
we would send high school pupils. It became clear that he was of the old
school, correct and courteous but not too keen on the Americans. I noticed
a broad scar on his cheeks, two in fact. Later I learned that this was the
sign of having fought a brave "duel" as a student member of a *Korporation*,
an old-time dueling fraternity. The mark of a courageous member was to
have gained such a scar in an encounter with another member. The dueling fraternities were outlawed, probably quite rightly, by the Occupation
authorities soon after 1945. But by 1952, I was told, they were coming back
to prominence. However today I think they are pretty well dead and buried in Germany. It took a long time for Germans to root out some of the
demons of their past.

(Postscript: Fifteen years later, Curt Moore was the outgoing chargé d'affaires in our embassy in Khartoum. A terrorist group stormed an embassy party, took Moore, incoming ambassador Cleo Noel, and a Belgian diplomat to the basement and executed them, as an example to the West. A great shock at the time, this kind of terrorism had only just begun to be prevalent. A great loss to the diplomatic corps, Moore and Noel were exceptional public servants. Their names are included in a list, chiseled in stone, in the lobby of the Department of State, of Foreign Service officers who have given their lives in the line of duty. It is long and heart-rending.)

German child-rearing was a matter of intense interest. A young man whom I had sent on an interchange visit to the United States was fascinated by the contrast between the American and German approaches. He said he liked the "free and natural way of the children in America." Baiting him a little, I asked if he didn't think that American teenagers didn't often abuse their freedom, with behavior bordering on license? He said, "Perhaps, but the odd thing is that when they grow up, they're OK" In the midfifties, this observation squared with my own. But when the sixties arrived, parents and all adults, in the entire West, had to reevaluate the states of childhood and adolescence. More of that later.

To illustrate what occurred in Germany in these early postwar years, the tale of Dr. Walter Stahl and his wife and children may be instructive. Walter, whom I met after my "German tour," was the executive of the German branch of the European Movement. Like me, he was a war veteran, though a bit older. His prewar marriage had dissolved and he remarried. Walter said he and his new wife were determined that any children would be raised in the new, "American" fashion, eschewing the authoritarian patterns of the Prussian past. That was what was wrong with the old Germany, he allowed, and now they and other Germans would set things right. I saw their first child, then about five, at their home and observed how Dr. Spock's and John Dewey's strictures were being played out in a German home; the little girl was coddled and deferred to in ways far beyond the management of my own children. When Sabrina was about ten, Walter and his wife sent her to a famous (some might say notorious) school in England, where children were "given their head" and encouraged to be free of all constraints so that they could develop their little potentials fully. Sabrina was a handful by the time she returned home as a teenager of the sixties. Walter confided in me ruefully, "There's got to be a middle way." Their last child was raised in what they felt was a good compromise between authoritarianism and no-holds-barred let-the-little-things-be-free philosophy. By that time, the whole Western world was looking for some kind of balance—rather unsuccessfully for the most part—in ways of helping the young strive towards maturity. In Germany, on the whole, I think the liberalizing changes were for the better. Walter was right in linking the "failed society" of old Germany with the disaster that befell the land. Because so many thoughtful Germans in Walter's day decided to democratize the quality of their family life, I believe overall progress was enabled. Yet some years later, Walter confided to me that with Sabrina, he and Mona had overdone it. The second daughter was raised in a kind of "middle way."

The cultural "crust" which had to be broken in so many families had been grounded in the Father cult; "*Vatti*" always had the last word, and traditionally his role as a "man" superseded almost any authority that the wife had. An amusing incident which illustrates how men banded together, almost subconsciously, to enforce this principle: On a weekend in 1952, my wife and my fellow Foreign Service officer, Bob Forcey, took our two boys, one about two and a half, the other a bit more than a year old, to visit the castle of the Hohenzollerns in Swabia. Once into its courtyard, I told Bob and my wife to go visit the castle rooms while I managed the boys; we'd later switch roles. I rolled Mark and David around the courtyard in a double-stroller. Two old men were sitting at a table, drinking beer. As we passed them, one asked me, "*Was sind Sie für ein Kindermädchen?*" (What kind of a nanny are you, anyway?) and they both laughed heartily. I had a hard time answering as I laughed back. I had been fed a big diet of Dr. Benjamin Spock and obviously these old duffers wouldn't understand if I tried to tell them!

Three German intellectuals had an inordinate influence on the political thought of the university age youngsters who revolted in the 1960s, not only in Germany but all over Europe and to the nth degree in the United States. One evening in 1953, I was riding a train from Frankfurt to Stuttgart. Opposite, and alone with me in the compartment, was a rather distinguished-looking portly man in a black suit, with a gold watch-chain across his belly. We fell into conversation. His name was Max Horkheimer, he said, and he was Pro-Rektor of the Johann Wolfgang Goethe University in Frankfurt. A German Jew, he had left for America when there was still time, in 1933. Before emigrating, he and Professor Theodor Adorno and other colleagues had begun a new school of social research in Frankfurt, had taken their ideas with them to New York, and there begun all over again. to search for social truths. In their new life, they began what became the New School of Social Research in New York City, which in turn became known as a liberal and inventive new institution for training social scientists. In 1946, he and his colleagues had been invited by the

Department of State to return to Frankfurt and to begin all over again, for the third time. Horkheimer said his mission had been to rebuild his old university. He and I had a pleasant chat, and I met him again in Frankfurt to talk about his ideas, which my journal for December 1953 recounts: "Prof. H says German professors are losing their 'aura' of authority and this is a bad thing. Traditions are falling and with them the automatic respect students used to give professors. It was sort of irrational, he said, but it helped to hold things together. Bad deal, I say."

In view of subsequent events, especially in the sixties and seventies, this conversation proved to be ironic, excruciatingly ironic, to be exact. I knew there was a succession of HICOG grants to keep the university, and especially its school of social research, going, but I paid little attention. However fifteen years later, what the French called *les événements de soixante-huit* (the events of '68) grew like wildfire, spreading from Berkeley to Paris to Frankfurt and farther. One of the intellectual gurus of this movement was Herbert Marcuse; his mentor and probably a deeper, broader thinker was Theodor Adorno, both part of the équipe that had followed Horkheimer to America and back. Marcuse had written a little book that was translated widely and became a bible for the "revolution." In the fifties I read a bit of Adorno's works, though I never heard of Marcuse at the time. If McCarthy and his gumshoes had really wanted to root out one nest of radical thought which later would feed the turmoil among youth in a few years, they would have gone after Horkheimer and company. But McCarthy's crew was not known for its subtlety or intellectual depth. Of the Adorno/Marcuse circle, more later.

It is interesting to note the many ideas, good and bad, which originated in German-speaking lands and were transferred to other countries and continents, and which later migrated back to the country of their birth. The para-Marxism of the Adorno school is one example. Freudian, Jungian, and other schools of psychiatry is another. German ideas about education of young children, beginning with Herder, is yet another. The modern concept of civil service began in Germany, under the Prussian reformer Stein; it migrated to the USA in the 19th century. Now, after all of Germany, under Prussian influence, had instituted a near-military type of public service, Germans and others who had lived in America returned in 1945 to the Fatherland to help create kinder, gentler institutions. The idea of the modern University, with emphasis on research and graduate studies, was copied by many American colleges as a way of furthering knowledge in the 19th century. Many Germans, like Horkheimer and my friend Professor Arnold Bergstraesser of Erlangen and later Freiburg Universities, returned from exile in the United States to lead in the rejuvenation and liberalization of higher education. Bergstraesser was a man of the vital center.

German Transformation: Sociological and Psychological

In Bavaria my American colleagues and I had endless discussions about what had gone wrong in Germany and how to put it right. We agreed that the all-inclusive concept of "German national character" was not a useful way to approach the conundrum, but we did think that there was something one might call "cultural traits" that, while not exclusively German, could be found often in the general population. One of these was the necessity, on the part, of most Germans, to "establish relationships." This applied, in our view, to things both animate and inanimate. Again, from my diary (in December 1952):

> The Germans do not like to have anything disordered or disorganized. This includes offices, grocery stores, forests, fields, backyards and junkyards and—social relationships. The German passion for organization of society is reflected in the near caste system. Each profession has its place in the hierarchy. Once a person is born into a certain "slot," it is difficult to step into a different level. If your father was a farmer, you become a farmer. If you are a waiter 40 years of age, you would not think of entering a factory—you would be sure (if you could get a job) to get no further than sweeping up. It would be unthinkable to begin such a change in career and wind up successfully. Social pressure on such upstarts is flattening.

In 1952, I sent a Herr Loetzen (a lay Catholic functionary) to the United States for a three-month exchange tour. In the process of debriefing him, he observed that Germans seem to have a need to stand apart from one another (confirming my own observations, above, about their need to "establish relationships"). "They are always forming groups," said Loetzen. "They are always finding the problem in a given situation. Their groups always differ 'fundamentally' from one another. One rarely finds a group formed for the purpose of unifying several segments of society—rather than change an established group, a new one must be organized." I saw this often, but this behavior seemed to change a good deal as the Germans found that they, like all Europeans, would have to organize broadly, in what today is called "civil society," i.e., apart from government or business activity, to promote the unity of Europe in cooperation with others.

My colleague Martin Ackerman, striving to help reform the Bavarian education system, worked hard—and successfully—to get the Education Ministry to adopt a more flexible structure that would accommodate what we called "late bloomers." Until the U.S. occupation, it had been virtually impossible for a youngster to enter tertiary education who had failed to pass the necessary exams at age 12 which would send him or her to a *Gymnasium* or *Oberrealschule* for preuniversity training. In adulthood, there was no means for retracing the trajectory to make up for lost years and education. This reinforced class rigidities. But today, although the German system is still less than perfect in this regard, there are much better opportunities for further education, and thus for switching careers. One wonders today, in 21st century America, if we may not be slipping into the same trap as the old German (and also French, British, Japanese, and other supposedly modern school systems) in demanding that our children be "tested" frequently during their elementary and secondary school years, and to let success or failure at, say, age 11 or 15 determine how far one might go later. Social class is one of the great determinants of one's level of educational attainment; but the reverse is also true. No one, including the Germans, seems yet to have solved this set of riddles. But at least there is a good deal more flexibility in the German way of education today than there was, pre-1945.

❧

Time and again, as the years passed, I have noticed the marked transformation that came about as Germany *socially and psychologically* began to reflect the changes that had come earlier *politically*. The people of the new Federal Republic, created in 1949, had, by 1990, well internalized the habits of equality necessary for people of a functioning democracy. Karl Herschel, had he still been alive, would have understood that the "two souls" warring within his breast were now somehow antiquated, passé, and no longer a part of the makeup of younger Germans.

The last time I saw the old man, in his retirement in Bavaria, he continued to inveigh against "the Germans" but at the same time said—and it was evident—that he still loved "Germany." He played some recordings for me—a symphony of Dvořák, a Schubert string quartet, and a recent disk featuring the band of the 7th Grenadier Guards regiment, activated as part of the new Bundeswehr. This latter featured German marches, beginning with the 16th century and ending with the *Grosse Zapfenstreich*, a ceremonial series of evening marches and hymns for honored guests of the military. This ended with the national anthem, *Deutschland über Alles*, resurrected with new words, The tears streamed down the old man's face; he was surely thinking of his early days as a cadet, a *Reichswehr* officer in the old Weimar days of a 100,000-man army, and then of the days he considered—after some years of enduring the growing shame of Hitler—as ultimately degrading. He insisted I take the recording with me; it sits on the shelf with a few others I acquired—men's choruses and children's singing nice old youth movement tunes, later also marching songs. *Lili Marlene*, which British troops in North Africa sang as much as Rommel's opposing army, is among them. Much German music, especially that of Wagner, will always raise the deepest sort of schizophrenic thoughts in *my* breast. (In Hof I got to know Wagner's granddaughter Friedolin, who was probably the only sane descendant of the bunch.) I too love Germany, but I hate what generations of Prussian martinets, nationalistic historians, Bismarck, the German admirals at the cusp of the 20th century, Ludendorff, and finally Hitler himself did to distort good German impulses and reinforce the bad ones.

Sometimes people ask how it was possible for the Germany that loved Mozart and Heine and Schubert to have turned so sour. My own view is that almost *any* people, given the right combination of historic circumstances and demonic leadership, plus a certain apolitical talent for organization, could end up where the Nazis took Germany. The political soul of a people may be likened to the keyboard of a great church organ; heavenly music may flow out of it, or the man at the keyboard may be a demon like Hitler. Germany's organ, for more than a decade, played vile music and its people marched; Hitler knew just how to punch the "right" keys. Civilization, preserved once again in 1945 from perhaps the greatest threat since the Huns, owes its always precarious but still hopeful condition today to some luck (or if you prefer, what the Germans call *"die Hände Gottes"*), plus the heroic efforts of the British, led by the most commanding figure of the 20th century, Churchill, and the Allies. American power—of a determined people with an extraordinary capacity to marshal its power—clinched the outcome, but it was touch and go for a while.

It is a wonder of our preceding century that the Allies won and that civilization was given another chance. In the struggles of today and those to come, we are extraordinarily fortunate to have the now-sensible and democratic people of Germany on our side. And that western civilization as a whole is better integrated and full of purpose (whatever our media feeds us daily) than ever before seems to me an inescapable truth. Events in the Middle East after 11 September 2001 may, however, force our civilization to face new momentous challenges. The future is cloudy.

In June 1955, I left a Germany well on the way to mental, moral, and emotional reconstruction. The fruits were to ripen over the next half century. But the job that I had gone to help with had largely been done by 1955. I am proud of my small contribution. The next big step was to provide such a framework of international integration, within Europe and across the Atlantic, that wars in the West would be a thing of the past. I saw this task as, for me, overriding, but I had much learning and thinking to do before I could understand what my next contribution should be.

Franconian Fun

Not all was serious or fraught with danger in the year and a half in Hof. Some amusing, pleasant times filled the interstices between killings at the border, countering the Soviet Agitprop, or weighing the indeterminate heft of the Germans in a future united Europe and broader, democratic Atlantic community.

Not least of Hof's pleasures was the musical life. From a candlelit December evening in the cathedral, with Bach's *Matthias Passion* inside and deep snow outside, to the Sunday morning trio and quartet concerts in a home open to nonchurchgoers, to the regular provender of plays and operettas in the Hof theater, it was all glorious, and cheap too, to a young Foreign Service family with a meager income. In the spreading around of *Kultur*, it is hard to beat Germany's government-financed schemes. There is something to be said for publicly subsidizing art.

Oskar Faul was one of the most amusing people in Hof, although I'm sure he never thought of himself that way. After meeting him casually at some of the Amerika Haus lectures, he asked for an office visit. Oskar was a short, plump little man of perhaps 50 to 60. I never knew what he had done before or how he had come to Hof, but something in his background made him a true *Original*, as some of the townspeople described him. He brought a large cardboard portemanteau to show me, and slowly unveiled the contents: This consisted of a chart, which Oskar said he had been designing for many years. He had tried to interest historians and educators, but with little success. Perhaps the Herr Direktor would see the true value of his work and help his efforts gain recognition. It might even provide a key to the great problems of the world, averred Oskar.

I was puzzled. The chart was like a pie, with many slices and labels tacked on all over it. Some read "natural science" or "basic philosophy," others referred to history and religion. In other words, what Herr Faul was trying to do was to compose a scheme linking all branches of human effort and knowledge in one dramatic, integrated, intelligible swoop. We talked about it. He felt sure that, if it could be adopted by universities, scientific academies, and governments, it would help mankind to see the interrelatedness of all things and thus contribute to peace. His objective was laudable, but his means incomprehensible. I asked him to leave it with me for a few days, which he did, and I studied it, calling on Karl Herschel and other senior staff members to help me understand it. The long and short of it was that we all recognized Oskar Faul as that not-so-rare species, the educated fool. But my colleagues and I were always kind to him. His efforts were obviously well intended, and I could never be certain that our assessment was right: perhaps I just was not sufficiently learned myself to appreciate him. And still, there are others who pursue Faul's laudable aim—an integrating theory of all knowledge.

Here's where the Oskar story gets interesting. Because of his unusual ideas, I invited him to be a member of the Hof German-American Luncheon Club, along with some school teachers, editors, the *Oberbuergermeister* and the *Buergermeister* (Nos. 1 and 2 in city elected officialdom), three or four American Army officers who were stationed in or near Hof, a Mr. Smith—who I thought at the time must have been in the CIA but never identified himself as more than an American who had returned to Hof to resume a prewar business: selling Turkish carpets!—plus a good sprinkling of educators, trade union leaders and local businessmen. The members met twice a month at the Hotel Strauss and seemed to enjoy trading ideas. Each spoke in his own language, which the others more or less understood. If we needed interpreting, there was Herschel or Klimt.

The Luncheon Club enjoyed about a year of reasonably happy exchanges of views. Some transnational personal friendships resulted. When the time drew near for me to end my tour in Hof, I explained to the Club that Uncle Sam wanted me back in the United States and that I would regret leaving Hof and its nice people. And so on. Unbeknownst to me, the Club officers met shortly after this, according to Herschel, who was present. They said, "Wouldn't it be nice to give Mr. Huntley some nice souvenir of Hof?" After much discussion, Oskar, who I think was Club secretary, said to the others, "Why not a painting of that little wooded ridge near the river, on which Mr. Huntley's villa sits?" This sounded like a wonderful idea, but who—asked the *Oberbuergermeister*—would paint such a picture? And wouldn't it cost a good deal more than the Members could afford? Ah, said Oskar, it just so happens that I know a fine artist right here in Hof who could do it, and I'll find out what it would cost.

Oskar reported back, Herschel later told me, that a fine painting of the house and environs could be had for 60 Deutschemarks (around $15 in those days). He had brought along a sample painting done by the artist, and it seemed decent enough. Everyone agreed this would be a bargain, and authorized Oskar Faul to get the job done as soon as possible.

At my swansong meeting of the Club, I told them how wonderful the townspeople had been, how much my family and I had enjoyed them and the surrounding countryside and town, and I also said appropriate things about the importance of German-American friendship in the uncertain days ahead. The president of the Club, the chief editor of the *Frankenpost*, Herr Poppenberger (who had become a good friend), made some nice remarks and unveiled the picture. It was not a great painting. In fact it was pretty amateurish, but as in so many cases, it was the thought that counted, and it was a nice souvenir. It was shipped with our household goods to the United States.

Some months later, Karl Herschel wrote to me. The painting's anonymous artist, it seemed, had been unmasked: Oskar Faul had asked his wife to do it, and he had pocketed the 60 DM! Some of the Club, Herschel reported, were scandalized, but I believed the affair hilarious, just one of many fond and happy memories.

The Luncheon Club spawned other amusing moments. After lunch in the Hotel Strauss, it was our custom to invite one member, by prearrangement, to speak for half an hour on any subject he liked. A general discussion would then ensue. The new second in command of the Army's Hof Counterintelligence Detachment, a green lieutenant from Salt Lake City, offered to talk on the subject of German-American relations. After a *tour d'horizon* that covered many features of German life, past and present, plus the outlines—as he saw them—of the Cold War and the cloudy prospects offered the German people in these hazardous days, Lt. Sampson avowed that he had come to "the solution" of the German question: Germany should become the 49th state of the Union! (This was before Hawaii and Alaska were granted statehood.) I have often reminisced about this idea: it could never have fit, then or now, for many reasons—not least the unlikelihood that any U.S. Congress would entertain such an outlandish proposal.

But a question that still plagues me today is how the United States might best extend the system of freedom that our people enjoy. After all, we have gradually absorbed, one way or another, some island dependencies such as Puerto Rico, Guam, Hawaii, and the Virgin Islands, all with quite different histories and peoples. Would Cuba's unfolding have taken quite a different course in 1898 had we given it formal associate status, leading to possible statehood, as we did Puerto Rico at the time? The United States, after the original 13 states established their union, expanded westward across the continent by a unique process: The Northwest Ordinances of 1784, 1785, and 1789 provided a settled constitutional path for scantily populated frontier Territories eventually to become full states within the Union. Are not the European Union and NATO taking a not-dissimilar course in the 21st century, with the Baltic States, Slovenia, and others gradually assuming membership in some form of union with politically likeminded, but sometimes very different ethnically, groups of nations? The federal concept, begun (but abandoned early) in The Netherlands and in a more halting way until 1848 by the Swiss cantons, is one of America's political gifts to the world.

A couple of years later, I visited Hof to see the changes, in the course of my new duties promoting European togetherness, based in Washington,

D.C. A faded Hof newspaper clipping quotes "Herr Huntley" the former Amerika Haus director as saying "I think of Hof as my *zweite Heimat*" (my second hometown). I surely felt that way, as I did later about a few other towns. I had no idea that I would become a polyglot/cosmopolitan, but that is what happened. It would not bother me if Lt. Sampson's proposal had been picked up. In fact I recalled some words of Lincoln. The Declaration of Independence, Lincoln declared on the eve of the Civil War, gave liberty "not alone to the people of this country, but hope to the world for all future time. It was that which gave promise that in due time the weights should be lifted from the shoulders of all men."

The Americans did not (as many think) invent democracy, but we virtually did invent working federalism. The successful combination of the two, after the vicissitudes and triumphs of more than two centuries, is certainly *the* unique American contribution to world civilization.

Our nation is still weaving these golden threads into the great tapestry of the brotherhood of man. How this can be done, where and even why, are questions that continue to preoccupy me, from my days in Germany of the fifties to the present. The rest of my life's work has consisted largely in this search for a secure, free, prosperous framework for all of mankind to live in peace.

Coda

In January 1954, Henry Kellerman, a German-American who was the Department of State's backstopper and policy planner for the vast public affairs operation in Germany, spoke to a group of Foreign Service officers. He told of his observations after a three-month tour of Germany; his parting remark was this: On his departure from Bonn, he met with Chancellor Adenauer. *Der Alte* said to him, "Have you noticed the friendliness, even cordiality, which exists everywhere between the German people and the American forces?" Kellerman told Adenauer that there had indeed been some change since he had last visited three years earlier; to what, asked Kellerman, did the chancellor attribute this change? "The largest part has been brought about by the American 'public relations' program." My colleagues and I took heart from his observation; this is what we had been sent to Germany to do, and the chancellor understood that.

Now it was time for me to go home and see what might be done next.

6
Academic Retooling and Alantic Immersion

23 October 1956: *Hungarian Revolt begins with student demonstrations. Soviet troops bloodily suppress revolution.*

30 October 1956: *UK, France, and Israel attack Egypt to "internationalize" Suez Canal, which President Nasser of Egypt had "nationalized."*

Halls of Ivy (September 1955)

"Rupert? This is Sam Beer. There's a fellow named Huntley here who says he talked with you last June. He's a day late for registration as a graduate student here at Harvard. I need to approve his application. He says you told him in June that he shouldn't have any trouble if he was a little late registering, but *I* think he's got only a marginal academic record." There was a pause; Professor Rupert Emerson was probably telling Beer that he thought I was worth Harvard's trouble anyway. Beer acquiesced, appearing slightly disgruntled, then put down the phone and turned to me.

"Professor Beer," said I, "Beg pardon, but I believe I heard you tell Professor Emerson that I had a 'marginal record.' I greatly respect Harvard's standards, but I think if you'll refer to my academic transcript from the University of Washington—there in front of you—you'll see that I graduated Magna cum Laude, was elected to Phi Beta Kappa, and had a grade–point average of something like 3.8. Is that marginal??"

Beer said, "Well, the University of Washington is a marginal institution. I think you'll find our standards here rather higher than theirs. But, we'll take you, and I think you'll find it worth your while."

Ouch! I was then 32 years of age, a family man with two children, had had a respectable wartime stint in the Navy, had already done some graduate study in international relations, had spent three years working for state government out West, had been nearly four years in the Foreign Service in demanding jobs, and now I had been nominated by my parent department, the U.S. Information Agency, for a year's graduate study at government expense—and this man was telling me that I was a "marginal case"?? But I quickly retrieved my aplomb and advised myself to be humble and press on. My career at Harvard had begun on a chastening note, and I had a big challenge ahead. Square One. Do your best, no matter what.

✄

    The background was this. USIA was a new agency, a creation in 1953 of the new Eisenhower administration. A special commission headed by C. D. Jackson and Gordon Gray—both old superbureaucrats and men of the world—had strongly advised the administration to separate the activities that some called "psychological warfare" and others "international information and cultural" efforts from the Department of State. These gears had been shifted for me in Germany without much trouble; there was already a massive public affairs operation there under the High Commission that simply moved under the new USIA's wing, though with a few bureaucratic snafus. (Among these, I learned some years later that my personnel file for the first two years of service in Germany fell between some file cabinets during office moves in Washington; whereas I had been highly and often recommended for promotion by my superiors in Germany, the necessary file of ratings by bosses, commendations, and the like was unavailable for the "promotion panels" that decided such things in Washington, D.C. The missing file was found years later, when it didn't make much difference any more!)

    The élan among the newly minted USIA people was palpable. When I reached Washington on my first home leave, in June 1955, the sense of purpose and mission was evident. Plenty of paper-pushing and bureaucratic infighting (as I was later to learn), but also plenty of earnest leadership at most levels, too. If there was ever a place for idealists in government, USIA in the 1950s was it.

    I had written to Washington from Hof a year earlier to ask if there was any chance for an officer like me, young with some experience but insufficient knowledge for much of the work I could see ahead, to "go back to college." This request seemed to languish until I hit Washington and met the key people directing USIA's activities in Europe, especially the man who would help decide and guide the kind of training he and I thought I needed. This was Benjamin B. Warfield, who had been pulled from the CIA, where he had been assistant director of training, to become head of training for the new USIA. Ben was astute and discerning. In principle, USIA's director for Europe and his colleagues thought a year at a university, studying the European area in some depth, was a good idea, but they were not, as was Ben Warfield, former college presidents or specialists in matching up human raw material with formal study that could benefit both the officer in question, and USIA. However, my Europe-USIA bosses said "in principle, yes," and "find Huntley the right kind of academic program in the right institution." A good deal of the preliminary search was up to me, with Warfield figuratively at my elbow all the way. I was a test case; no USIA people had until then had that kind of assignment.

Accordingly, I visited a few universities while on home leave in June 1955 to see which institutions might fit my plans and the Agency's. Stanford (home of the great Hoover Institution on War and Peace in the 20th century), New York University, and Columbia were high on my list. Ben Warfield said, "Why don't you add Harvard?" So I did. I visited all four universities and had to admit, when I reported back to Ben, that Harvard seemed the most congenial. I wanted to dig deeply into the historical backgrounds of the major European countries, the previous attempts to unite them, the philosophical and intellectual bonds that tied them to the United States, the prospects for military alliances such as NATO—in fact I had more questions in my mind than one man could possibly attempt to satisfy in a lifetime! I put these thoughts and others to academic advisors and heads of departments at the universities on my list. All except Harvard had programs of "West European Area Studies" and should have been ideal for what I wanted. But although Harvard's graduate curriculum was not so structured, its faculty seemed to have more flexibility and more interest in taking on a maverick like myself and exposing him to the human resources of a great university.

After a lot of back and forth on this, Warfield validated my gut feeling about Harvard: I couldn't do better, he thought. He had to admit that as a man who received his B.A. and M.A. from Harvard, in history, he had a built-in bias for Crimson and Gray. But more than that, Ben saw that in many ways I did not fit the template of a suave Foreign Service officer emerging from the Eastern Establishment. In those days, the Foreign Service and many other key positions in the executive branch of the U.S. government were still dominated by these types. Usually old families from New England or New York or Pennsylvania sent their progeny to prep schools such as Andover, then on to Ivy League colleges. Evan Thomas and Walter Isaacson's 1986 book *The Wise Men* tells the story of six members of this Eastern Establishment (John J. McCloy, Dean Acheson, Averell Harriman, George Kennan, Charles Bohlen, and Robert Lovett) who, with a likeminded professional Foreign Service corps, virtually made the foreign policy of the United States during and just after World War II. This bias for the Northeast changed later as the Foreign Service Act of 1946 and U.S. demographic changes brought in a more geographically diverse group. In the 1950s, however, one was still a "leg up" if he (not many women in those days) had come with a Northeastern pedigree, geographical or academic or—usually—both. Over the years, the Foreign Service came to better represent the character of the whole country. But the Eastern ethos and cachet tended to dominate for a long time, and this was no bad thing.

Ben Warfield said, "If you have a Harvard degree, plus some polish that will inevitably come with it, it will help your future career. I recommend Harvard." That was what I chose; how much cachet I derived is an open question, but the learning opportunities, the celebrated Harvard ambience, and—above all—the opportunity to encounter truly great academic personalities (and a few others who, while not famous then or later, were respected practitioners in their fields) were aspects of the experience that sharpened my thought and gave me new concepts to apply to my chosen work.

Some great professors were permanent fixtures at Harvard, some were visiting for a semester or a year. Samuel Beer, the head of the Government Department who had given me difficult moments at registration time, was already renowned as an expert on the British Parliament and politics; I wrote a paper for him entitled "A Case Study in British Foreign Policy Formation: The Western Union and Council of Europe Agreements." In 1999, when I gave a lecture at Harvard, Professor Beer, now in his nineties, was still on campus; I had sent him my 1998 book, *Pax Democratica: A Strategy for the 21st Century*. He invited me for lunch at the Faculty Club to talk about it. Sam was always skeptical, finding the right piercing questions to ask, always boring in for the intellectual kill to make the scholar dig deeper. He was a scholar's delight, and still is. In the Spring of 2002, he was still active, writing a trenchant letter to the editor of *Harvard* magazine about the roots of terrorism after 9/11.

Elites

Crane Brinton, a historian of Western thought and revolution, was another star who gleamed in my firmament. I took his course on Intellectual History of the 18th and 19th Centuries in Europe; when I talked to him of my need to learn about the historic process of amalgamating states into larger units, he suggested a "reading course" (one-on-one), steering me first to his slender volume, *From Many One: The Process of Political Integra-*

tion, the Problem of World Government (1948), the very subject on which I yearned most for enlightenment. His book cited the Roman Empire as one of the most successful and lasting historical attempts to unify a large and disparate group of peoples. Brinton had me read, among many books, *Roman Wall* by "Bryher," a novel that recreated what it must have been like around 50 A.D. to be a Roman official in an outpost of empire, a corner of what we now call Switzerland.

Brinton believed that if a group of societies possessed certain anthropological criteria in common, it could make for their successful amalgamation. These criteria included, for example, a symbol around which the empire or federation could unite, such as a monarch or a flag. Other criteria, such as a common language or a common cultural history, were obvious. But one criterion, which I had never thought of before, fascinated me: the need for a multinational elite, whose members were drawn from all parts of, for instance, the Roman empire. Members of the governing class could easily interact with one another in the empire's army or officialdom or commerce because they had what then passed for a common education: schools that taught Greek and Latin and what might even, in the 19th century, have approximated an English patrician's classical education at Eton and Oxford.

To learn about the role of leaders, Brinton guided me to the works of Gaetano Mosca, a conservative member of the Italian Parliament before World War I and also a discerning political scientist. Mosca wrote about the importance, for any politically integrated nation, of having an educationally well-honed "secondary elite" — analogous to the majors and colonels in an army, who would push ideas up to the generals and then carry out their implementation orders. This element was obviously necessary for any well-integrated state; Brinton reasoned that it was also even more critical if, for example, one were trying to bring about the unification in modern times of Europe, a multistate conception in which I was vitally interested.

This basic thought — that a protofederation's "integrated" elite was the touchstone for success in developing policy and also for carrying it out — began to grow in my mind. It became one of the trilogy of objectives that I sought consistently to serve in my later life — just one example of how I maintained and burnished this idea of a "multinational elite."

In the 1980s, I led a delegation of Americans to see what NATO was about, with its politics in Brussels and its Supreme Headquarters Allied Powers in Europe (SHAPE) in nearby Mons. My thoughts wandered back to Brinton and Mosca when I cornered General Bernard Rogers, at that time Supreme Allied Commander Europe (SACEUR). "General," I asked, just fishing, "how do you like your new job?"

"I'll tell you," he said to me, "I wish I had had this job *before* I became the chief of staff of the U.S. Army. I would have done many things differently."

Over the intervening years, from the fifties to the eighties, I had come to know many top Allied military commanders. Those who contributed most to the Alliance and who worked most effectively with officers from the other Allied countries had been posted at least once, and many more than once, in a command on foreign soil. Probably they had some of the same mental equipment as the Iberian centurion commanding a Roman legion on the Rhine, after a long stint in Dalmatia or Asia Minor. Brinton's multinational elite was already at work, knitting together a modern, farflung world in the throes of willy-nilly integration.

At Harvard and later, I did a good deal of research on multinational elites. One paper in particular dealt with World War II experience at Eisenhower's supreme headquarters in England. Here, American and British officers were mixed together during the planning for the 1944 invasion of Normandy and beyond, with an admixture of French, Polish, Norwegian, and other nationalities. I came to the conclusion that a special personality type was also probably necessary for the metamorphosis of a national type into a multinational one. I've known many people who worked for long periods overseas; the inoculation did not always "take." But without the exposure of international living and education, the personality factor usually did not kick in. I'm still wondering how this process works—and specifically, how we can consciously train multinational leaders. (George W. Bush might have become a different kind of president, for example, if he had spent some time early on, living and working overseas.)

Power Politics vs. Multinational Integration

Carl Friederich was a German who had migrated to Harvard in the thirties and then carried back to Germany, after 1945, his old and new thoughts on future German constitutional arrangements and—even more important—the constitutional configuration of the projected European Communities, including common political and military institutions. While I was at Harvard, he and Professor Paul Freund of the Harvard Law School gave a joint seminar on Federalism; when I heard this, I jumped at the chance to join and was not disappointed. One of the texts was a "how-to-do-it" book (*Studies in Federalism* [1954]) edited by Friederich and Robert Bowie, which they had written expressly for the European and American gurus of the "unite Europe" movement. Bowie, also a Harvard Law professor, had served as general counsel to the U.S. High Commission in Germany and later in many incarnations in Washington. He was serving in Washington during my year at Harvard, but we later met and became friends.

The Friederich-Freund federalism seminar, quite naturally, concentrated on the legal and political problems and prospects for unifying Europe, drawing on political thought in the United States and other federations. The quality of our professors' thought might be indicated by the remark of a fellow student who, one day emerging from the seminar with me, said, "You know, that Paul Freund is my nomination for God!" I could only agree, heartily. Many other Harvard barons, in my mind, qualified for Assistant Deities. The quality of Freund's legal mind, incidentally, put him on several presidential lists in that period for an appointment to the Supreme Court. He never made it, but along with Judge Learned Hand — also passed over — he unqualifiedly merited selection in many minds. Almost always, unfortunately, politics has played a more important role than professional qualifications in such judicial appointments.

Professor Gottfried Haberler, another displaced German, led a seminar on international economics. I needed that exposure too, because understanding the Atlantic or European communities without considerable knowledge of international trade and money was a nonstarter. A high point in this seminar was the appearance, several times, of MIT Professors Paul Samuelson, author of the longest-running text on basic economics, and Charles Kindelberger, one of the architects of the Marshall Plan.

Hans Kohn, probably the most respected student of nationalism of that day, came to Harvard as a visiting professor. I audited some of his lectures and we became fast friends. He agreed to be my mentor for a reading course in the history of French and German nationalism. I was convinced that any viable schemes for European unification would depend in great measure on these two history-bound countries overcoming their bitter distrust, centuries-long feuds, and clashing nationalisms. Dr. Kohn did not disappoint me; I learned especially the various cultural and historical streams of thought that had animated German political behavior over the past two centuries. Although my knowledge of contemporary German life, based on four years in postwar Germany, was perceptive, it lacked the depth that Kohn helped me to acquire. I wrote a paper for him on the prospects for Franco-German reconciliation, at the time a major question.

Kohn was revered for his scholarship, but on leaving City College in New York he received no pension, and so spent the rest of his old age as an itinerant "visiting professor" at top colleges and universities, a year at a time. Lucky students! In the frontispiece of one of his books, he inserted this German motto: *Wozu brauch' Ich Würzeln? Ich habe ja Flügel!* (Why do I need roots, when I have wings?)

His life story, which I learned piecemeal over the next twenty years or so, included birth in an Austrian family of Prague, service in the Czech Legion in World War I (marching all the way from the Eastern Front to Vladivostok and a ship to safety, when the Russian revolution broke out), and academically distinguished careers in England and America. He showed me, through books and long weekly one-on-one discussions, how a rather apolitical and fractured Germany had become a "nation" after the Napoleonic Wars, eschewing the Enlightenment ideals of Goethe and Schiller and embracing the siren songs of nationalist historians such as Ranke and Arndt, translated into action by Bismarck and his Prussian soldiers and bureaucrats. This exposure filled a gaping hole in my understanding of where the Germans had come from, and where they had thought they were going. And the French hardly took second place for chauvinism.

An interesting fallout from my association with Hans Kohn, which went on for many years, was his introducing me to Professor Robert Strausz-Hupé, of the University of Pennsylvania. The latter was visiting Harvard for a couple of days; the three of us talked about the prospects and need for a strong Atlantic community. I was delighted to meet Strausz-Hupé, whose book *The Zone of Indifference* (1952) had opened up the whole idea of a commonalty of interests and values that spanned the Atlantic. I told him that I was headed, in the summer of 1956, for a post in Washington that would deal with European and Atlantic questions. He and Kohn revealed their plans for a ten-day conference, to be held in a year or two, on the intellectual and practical aspects of a North Atlantic community. We agreed that we could help each other. This was a case of kindred minds clicking, an association that did not end for many years. Kohn died in 1971, Strausz-Hupé in 2002, at the ripe old age of 99.

In a lecture course taught by two young professors in tandem, Politics and Governments of Continental Europe, I struggled with the main questions they posed, "Are written constitutions the main influence in determining political behavior?" or "Are national cultural traits the principal determinants?" This was not an either-or matter. One of these young instructors was able to give many concrete examples of determinants; he recounted vividly, for example, how his tank column in World War II had entered Germany near Aachen. Their tanks were grinding their way through a village that had been completely flattened by artillery fire and attacking aircraft. Among the ruins stood a lone chimney, complete with mantelpiece, which had somehow been spared. On the mantel, where old American homes might have displayed a "Home Sweet Home" motto in needlepoint, was the sole remnant of the soul of the family that had lived there, a plaque announcing, *"Hier herscht Ordnung"* (here order reigns). This nicely limned a key feature of German culture which I had noticed so often when I lived there: Order before all things, an iron concept that had forced Germany to its knees in an impossible quest for perfect order—at home, throughout Europe, in the whole world.

Dignitaries on Campus—Past, Present, Future

André Siegfried, the grand old political sociologist of French academe, was also lecturing as a visitor to Harvard. He methodically, with great care and marvelous discernment, dissected the French body politic for his listeners. How is France governed today? What are the roles of the various social constituents of France in present day politics? What of the influence of commerce, industry, women, youth, the universities, demographic changes, and the elite postgraduate schools set up by Napoleon—especially the *École Nationale d'Administration?* A few years later, I was to learn close up of the virtual domination of the bureaucracy, and often of the business world, by the graduates of the *Grandes Écoles*, the *énarques.*

The other Harvard graduate students I met were an interesting lot, but I was so busy, dividing my time between my family, writing numerous papers, and poring over countless books in my basement carrel at the magnificent Widener Library, that I had little time to develop acquaintances. But one whose name in years to come was on everyone's lips everywhere was notable: Henry Kissinger. He and I participated in a graduate student-faculty seminar on national defense, run by an Air Force Brigadier General on leave. What pearls of wisdom we elicited from one another are now lost to my memory, but of course I could never forget Henry. Later, in the sixties, we came to know each other rather well. I was helping to set up the Atlantic Institute, a think tank in Paris. I used to call on Henry at Harvard, and then on his literally next-door office-neighbor Bob Bowie; both gave me useful ideas and guided me to other key people I should be meeting. They always wanted to see me separately, never together. From the late fifties through the sixties, Henry had gotten consistent help from the Ford Foundation for a summer school on international politics, to which sharp young foreigners were invited for exposure to Harvardian ideas about the world.

By the sixties Henry had become known for *Nuclear Weapons and Foreign Policy*, which earned him a niche with Nelson Rockefeller and launched him on a political career. Once, when he was secretary of state and I was secretary of a group of "Mid-Atlantic Clubs" (see Appendix D) in various capitals of the Atlantic world, he made the mistake (as many of us thought at the time) of announcing: "This year [I believe it was 1972] will be the Year of Europe." This implied, to many Europeans, that Kissinger had finally taken time off from the exigencies of Vietnam to "deign" to turn his gaze on the Atlantic Alliance. I asked the secretaries of the Clubs in London, New York, Paris, and Washington to take up at their next membership meetings the question of Kissinger's new motto and to quickly send me a précis of their conclusions. All agreed it was a poor idea—wasn't every year "the year of Europe?" And what would happen when the year was over? I sent off all four accounts to Henry, who thanked me, although not too warmly.

Once, in 1974, when he was out of government, I went to see him in his New York office, to get his backing for another far-out idea of mine: the creation of a large and richly endowed "Atlantic Foundation." He said it was a good idea. As he was to see President Ford the next day, he said he would take it up with him and get back to me. As we exited his office, he saw General Brent Scowcroft waiting for him, and said to me, "You take this up with Brent, too, when you get back to Washington." I was able to say, "I already have," as Brent and I were already plotting together.

Aside from a few words with Kissinger when he spoke in Seattle twice in the following years, I have encountered him only on the intellectual battlefield. I'm sure he doesn't think our "duel" of importance, but I believe our sharply differing views on the world of politics are important to somebody. At least I hope so. Among his prolific writings since retirement, his 1994 book *Diplomacy* stands as the epitome of this difference: Henry is a "realist," with his ideas about how the world of nations runs still grounded in his earliest book, his doctoral dissertation on the Concert of Europe, which ran the Continent, more or less without a major war, for around forty years from 1815. Henry, I believe, has been in love with this idea that a few of the Great Powers could settle the fate of all the others. History gives a lot of support to this claim. The balance of power, and the employment of all the tools of power politics, became his stock in trade. I believe he saw himself as a latter-day Metternich or Castlereagh or Talleyrand, wheeling and dealing in the world's capital, Washington, which in the 20th century overtook Vienna and London.

It was no accident, I am sure, that Kissinger decided on a "Year of Europe," instead of making NATO and the European Communities the continuing centerpieces of American foreign policy. In *Diplomacy*'s index, there are only three or four references to NATO and no more than that for the European Communities or the Council of Europe. And most of these references are to visits that he or President Nixon made to the precincts of those bodies to make speeches. I believe that he failed to make anything like full use of the unprecedented international institutions that grew up during the Cold War, or even to understand their true character.

Curiously, although born not far from Nuremberg, Kissinger's genealogical proximity to Europe never made him a "multinational man," as I believe most of the founders of the post-1945 Atlantic community were. I'm proud to be one, admittedly from mostly a worm's-eye view of affairs. Most observers give Kissinger his due: he was without doubt one of the six or eight most skilful and worldly American secretaries of state. Yet, as I came to understand and to declaim later in my book *Pax Democratica*, he did not succeed in creating a still-stronger architecture of peace based on lasting institutions, as Marshall and Acheson had done.

Early on, in my mountain days in the Cascades and Olympics, I suppose I had the camper's adage engraved on my heart, "Always try to leave the campsite better than you found it." If this should hold true, as an axiom, in diplomacy and politics, we would all be better off. But, as a close friend of mine says, "Republicans can't be happy without some seemingly insoluble problems to solve." Many Democrats, too, I'd say. Clean up your mess.

Henry Kissinger became a celebrity after the fifties. In 1955 a true historical figure of the forties and fifties visited the Harvard campus to give a lecture: Field Marshal Sir Bernard Montgomery, at the time deputy to the Supreme Allied Commander Europe, U.S. General Alfred M. Gruenther. Monty packed the lecture hall, speaking with great competence, and even more demonstrable confidence. In the question period, he was asked, "If Europe were invaded by the Soviet armies, what would you and General Gruenther do?" Without hesitation, Monty replied: "Use nuclear weapons to stop them." Questioner: "Without an OK from Washington or the North Atlantic Council?" "Of course," he answered. This was an off-the-record lecture, without journalists, so no headlines appeared in the newspapers. However, this merely confirmed what so many of us thought: Nuclear war in those days could erupt almost without warning. Wow!

Sharpening a Young Man's Perspectives

In those days, I never heard Kissinger expound on his theories of power politics, but a capable stand-in did so. Daniel Cheever, a young lecturer, goaded a small seminar on Principles of International Politics into revealing our own biases, and then constructively knocked them apart. I must admit that at the time my own preference for an idealistic set of guiding principles rested on two points: (1) the strengthening of the United Nations and its auxiliary agencies was the best hope for mankind; and (2) if we wanted peace, we needed to cultivate "mutual understanding" among and between all peoples. I found, thanks to Cheever, that these were pretty hollow, weak reeds to rely on in the up-front, dog-eat-dog world. There was also a considerable difference between diplomatic tactics—or the short range—and strategy.

Cheever convinced me that the "realist" view of the world was probably the prevailing operative principle of the times, and of virtually all time past. The empires of old and small entities such as the Greek city-states operated in this way. Here are the Athenians, the Bush II superpower of the day, talking to the Melians in 416 B.C, as quoted by Thucydides:

> Of the gods we believe, and of men we know, that by a necessary law of their nature, they rule wherever they can. And it is not as if we were the first to make this law, or to act upon it; we found it existing before, and shall leave it to exist forever after us; all we do is to make use of it, knowing that you and everybody else, having the same power as we have, would do the same as we do.

The great dynasties of Europe, from the Middle Ages to the dawn of modern nationalism in the late 18th century, calculated this way. Through marriages among future monarchs, mercantilist competition, and mostly wars, they strove to gain advantage—overwhelming if possible—for their interests as they saw them. When the French Revolution spawned modern nationalism and the "nation-in-arms," the actors shifted to protocabinets and chief ministers, plus general staffs and, in a few cases, weak early parliaments, but the principles remained the same. "The national interest," once said a friend of mine, "is whatever those in power tell the public that it is." But these mythical and often enduring interests dictated what the "powers" did with their foreign relations. To a considerable extent, this is still the case. But there have been some important recent "amendments" to these immutable "laws" of international politics.

In the new world of post–1945, Cheever and much of the class agreed, there were some powerful new forces: international law, still in adolescence, and universal bodies, most notably, the UN, which represented at that time more a congeries of hopes than a true force; the fledgling institutions of European unity, which in 1955 still elicited more hope than reality, though grounded in powerful common interests and seen as such by Western Europe's component–states of the old Carolingian empire; and NATO, a well–defined joint response mechanism, with political and military institutions of some substance, which the Atlantic powers felt were essential tools with which to meet the challenge of Communism. In 1955, these hopeful signs of a world built on something other than power political interplay among the great nations, were still in their infancy. Now, nearly half a century later, one can see all these trends converging in a post–post Cold War world with infinitely more substance and probable permanence than seemed possible to me in those long-gone Harvard days. Unfortunately, in the Bush II administration, the key bigwigs, including the president, seemed to have let the NATO Alliance and the key multinational institutions drift; these do not seem, in the 21st century, to any longer act as our nation's chief international anchor. The problem does not lie entirely at George W. Bush's door, however; Clinton paved the way in the 1990s, and one can see in hindsight that the nation has drifted away from multilateralism ever since Nixon closed the "Gold Window" in 1970. The struggle between these principles goes on, but there is at least one working alternative now to "power politics," i. e., the law of the jungle.

The argument was never resolved in our Harvard seminar, of course, but Cheever accomplished his purpose, with me at any rate. I began to see that power politics was and probably would be for a long time to come, the chief pillar of the Westphalian international system. The corollary, that if we just had enough "mutual understanding" of the kind I and my colleagues in Germany had been cultivating—with a considerable degree of success, albeit in fertile soil—it was still not enough to turn the tide in any important aspect of international affairs. What I came to see later was that such features as the interchange of persons and the exchange of cultures and ideas were much more important tools than the power–dealers could ever imagine. But this alone, even if we spent millions on it, would not vanquish conflict. It could best be used to buttress the new principle of multilateralism.

Thanks to Professors Brinton and Friederich, with good dollops of Kohn, I also began to understand much more clearly what European institutions might and could do if we could bring about the right sort of "institutional architecture," with the necessary public support. NATO and the vestiges of the Marshall Plan (at that time lodged in a transatlantic economic body called the OEEC) also represented a wider circle within which national interests could be sublimated and joint interests institutionalized for the long pull. This was the "Atlantic community" idea, which Strausz-Hupé's book had first planted in me in 1952, in a cold and rainy Nuremberg autumn, and which ideas had come further to life when I met the author in 1955.

I was beginning to form my own philosophy of international relations. During this concentrated academic year at Harvard, I wrote only three or four times in my journal. But an entry from January 1956 suggests the outlines of my integrating thought. With regard to the world I would later call "like–minded":

[The] kind of relationship which the Atlantic community requires between its members in the years just ahead . . . is a *common devotion* to ideals, principles, institutions, and human welfare. We need to accomplish a reversal of the scale of loyalties of the individual. The world, the Atlantic community, the U.S., Illinois, Peoria, it should read, instead of the reverse. Especially among the creative minority of Western society must we create this new attitude and new devotion.

At the time, I didn't realize what I was getting into nor what opportunities, if any, the future would bring to me, so that I could help realize this ideal.

Now, about fifty years later, I see a good deal of progress in this program of continuing integration, some of it willy-nilly because events brought about response, but also because a goodly number of individuals, including me, have worked to create the web of institutions, the multinational elites, and the general concepts that serve as a scaffolding for a growing world community. However, the great majority of people—even today's "movers and shakers"—in the Atlantic world simply do not realize what we have accomplished together or what it means for the future. (Now, I must hasten to add: "what it *should* mean.")

Little intellectual pathways led away from, and then back to, this central goal; I filed many questions and concepts away for future study. For example, what was "culture," anyway? And what did we mean by "community," especially in an international sense? Diverted to one of these little pathways during my Harvard year, I noted down eleven different definitions of "culture"—most of them, if not all, quite respectable, but used for different purposes. I came away with a correlative idea, which proved to be somewhat new to my bosses in Washington when I got there: All politics is rooted in culture. Different cultures dictate different approaches to international politics. Finding and emphasizing the common elements in several cultures that ought to be cooperating was, for me, the challenge.

While at Harvard, I paid a "duty" visit to Washington; on return I jotted down some thoughts on U.S. foreign policy and its promulgation: "We make a grave error in trying to treat our political problems as [just] political problems. In most instances, our most serious political problems . . . have their roots in social and cultural causes. The gravest social disorders cannot be cured by increasing economic aid or by diplomatic maneuvers. Politics only reflects underlying social strength or weakness."

I wrote these words based mainly on my understanding of Europe of the 1950s, but I believe the same principle applies even more aptly today to American relations with most countries around the world, where the American politicos seem to feel we must sort things out everywhere. Now, in the early 21st century, we have seen that the "loss" of Afghanistan, in 1974 or 1989, whichever date you prefer, is the result not only of failing to see that country's strategic importance in the future, but especially of failing, when things turned sour, to maintain an excellent public and cultural affairs program (which we had in the 1960s) in that country. Perhaps military or economic intervention might have been necessary at some point, but the collapse of the human resources that USIA had invested in and nurtured in that part of the world was, in my opinion, the main and direct cause of Afghanistan's "loss" and the inordinately costly, massive intervention that was required after September 11, 2001. Among other contributing factors, the Clinton administration had willfully acquiesced in the demands of Jesse Helms, chairman of the Senate Foreign Relations Committee in the 1990s, that USIA be abolished and its functions transferred to the Department of State. For reasons to be discussed later, this was a disastrous move, depriving our nation of a slender but sound base in professional personnel who understood Central and South Asia and who had for years cultivated key Arab and other Islamic peoples and who understood the culture of the area in depth.

Also, there had never until 1950 been an international structure called a "Community." But because the European actors who were creating a union dared not call it a "federation" or even a "confederation" (which it now is) at the time, "community" seemed like an unexceptional and attractive term to sell to the European peoples. They yearned collectively to be free but at the same time looked backward at their individual brands of "nationhood" on which they had relied for generations. My time at Harvard gave me useful insights into this and other key questions. In some ways, this European process of supranational integration is now leading the world.

I still had plenty of study ahead, to round out and augment these ideas, but I would be so tied up with the practical, active processes of unification, in different ways, that I would not have a chance until nearly twenty years later—1974 and after—to sit down with time to think, study, and write at length.

Meanwhile, our nation's capital was calling.

7

Into the Jaws of the Bureaucracy

"If I have achieved any good, it has been through patient thought."
Sir Isaac Newton

25 March 1957: *By Treaty of Rome, Belgium, France, Italy, Luxembourg, The Netherlands, West Germany establish the European Economic Community (Common Market) and EURATOM.*

4 October 1957: *USSR launches "Sputnik 1," forerunner of ICBMs, inaugurating a space race between the U.S. and the Soviet Union.*

The National Beehive, Capital of the World

After a brief family vacation on the Atlantic shores, organized by my father, who quite fortuitously lived and worked near Boston at the time, we took off for Washington, D.C. In those days, air conditioning was in its infancy. We found a nice little house to rent just across the D.C. border in Maryland, but with hot, humid air virtually all day and all night long from May well into September. In our modest home, we did manage to invest in an exhaust fan, which replaced some of the fetid indoor air with only slightly better outdoor air at night. My office, at 1778 Pennsylvania Avenue Northwest—two blocks from the White House—was similarly accoutered. Until I was promoted to a slightly higher grade the next winter, only the bosses had window air conditioners. Until air conditioning was perfected and more or less universalized in these eastern climes, Washington was anything but a fit place to conduct the nation's business. But we bureaucrats were expected to carry on the traditions of 150 years, and get things done anyway.

A couple of times during my Harvard year, my superiors in USIA had summoned me to Washington, partly to find out what I was learning that might be of use in their work, and partly to try to figure out what to do with me when I came back "to the fold." My big boss in Bonn, Joseph Phillips, wanted me back in Germany, some spoke of sending me to Paris to work on NATO and European unity problems in the cauldron, while the head USIA honcho for Europe, Bill Clark, noting that I spoke Swedish, thought for a time maybe Finland would be a good assignment. (Shows what the dear fellow knew about Finland! About 10 percent of its population was ethnically Swedish; a number of Finnish Finns spoke Swedish, but trying to operate with Swedish alone would have harmed our program.) In Washington, there were some opportunities, but it was hard for my bosses to pin them down in view of an almost constant reorganization that was going on.

Eventually, my new duties boiled down to these: (1) work with the State Department on the public relations/psychological side of NATO and European unity; (2) feed to our USIA posts in Europe the information they needed about changing developments in these all-European fields; and (3) manage USIA Washington's communications with a few small countries, such as Switzerland, Belgium, Netherlands, Luxembourg and Iceland. For all these purposes, I was the responsible "desk officer." These duties (not all much related to one another) entailed dealing with an inordinate amount of cables, dispatches and letters—both incoming and outgoing. I understand that the volume and rapidity of such communications between Washington and "the field" today is such that neither the Washington bureaucracy nor the officers in the various embassies have anything like enough time to sit back and think. This was my complaint in 1956—how much more of a burden the officers of, say, 2006 must bear, with computers, e-mail, fax machines, and the Internet demanding so much of their attention. And we didn't even have Xerox in 1956! Most of the few documents I have kept from those days are faded carbon copies or mimeographed sheets of poor paper.

As I settled down to work, I looked around at my colleagues. They were not as uniformly idealistic or intelligent or diligent as the Public Affairs crew in and around Nuremberg in 1952–53 had been, but in hindsight I respected these Washington officers. Now, years later, I calculate them to have been generally two cuts above most bureaucrats in Washington and elsewhere. At the time, I deplored the power- and place-seeking, the infighting, which were rife. But as the years went on, and I served in many different institutions, in the United States and abroad, I discovered that for the most part this is a universal and inescapable, if deplorable, facet of all human behavior. One has to learn to deal with this, keep one's backside "covered" (as bureaucrats are incessantly saying), and discount generously for this behavior in determining what constructive things one might realistically hope to accomplish. And a man or woman seeking *only* to realize ideals will be lost without a practical set of defenses (and offenses, when needed) against those who care little or nothing for ideals. But, on balance, these were *very* good people that I worked with in 1950s Washington.

My boss, the assistant director for Europe for USIA, was William Clark; he was connected with the Rockefellers and had been editor of a Philadelphia newspaper. Capital fellow, practical and full of common sense, not much acquainted with European affairs at firsthand but quite capable of seeking and using advice, and of making good decisions, especially regarding personnel, a vital trait. His deputy was Walter Roberts, who became one of Washington's longest-serving bureaucrats and whose positive influence was often decisive in major decisions over the years. Walter came out of Vienna in the Hitler years and had been in Washington ever since. He knew the Washington establishment intimately and was clever at getting things done. He and Bill Clark had two special assistants, one for policy and one for programs. Both were consummate schemers and fixers, types which seemed essential in such rather critical times. Our office collectively was known as IAE.

Walter and I got along well, but this was not true of all who encountered him in those days. Among my catalogue of humor of the times was Walter's attempt to do what he thought was a favor for Dr. Martin Ackerman, my trusted colleague from Nuremberg days. When I got to Washington in 1956, Martin was "wandering the corridors," in bureaucrat-speak. He had returned to DC after landing in Hanoi, only to return almost immediately when our embassy there closed down, the French having suffered their ignominious defeat at the battle of Dien Bien Phu and the colonial war having gone from bad to worse. Consequently, Martin was hoping for an assignment, either in Washington or somewhere in the field. I mentioned this to Walter Roberts, who said, "Oh, I have a great idea for Martin!" and proceeded to seek him out. His "great idea" (which to many officers would have seemed a plum) was duty as the cultural attaché in Walter's hometown, Vienna. "Oh, thanks Walter, but I can't do that. I spent six years in Bavaria and that would just be more of the same." Roberts was incensed, and Martin ended up in the Belgian Congo. To most Viennese, the Bavarians seemed like hopeless peasants.

There were a variety of "desk officers" like myself in IAE, mirroring the organizational patterns in the Department of State. They had usually served in the countries that they "managed" from Washington. If the public affairs officer at our embassy in Paris, for example, needed help from Washington, or wanted to block some mistake he was afraid Washington was making, he might write a "back channels" letter to Earle "Shorty"

Titus, the France Desk officer. Shorty was top of the line in intellect and background, having been in the Foreign Service since the midthirties, serving in both France and Spain. He was not in a more lofty executive capacity because he had no thirst for power nor did he feel he had the qualities of leadership that were required. But every time I wanted the best advice in the place, I went to Shorty. We became fast friends until his passing in his late eighties.

Messrs. Clark and Roberts had two special assistants, one for Policy and one for Programs. Mr. Policy was Ed Schechter, like Roberts a refugee from Vienna, whose task it was to be sure that our office understood what current U.S. policy was on any given day by carrying over the stone tablets from the Department of State. Mr. Programs, John Mowinckel, was a suave hot-shot officer who oversaw how budgets and policies were reflected in what the various "posts" in the embassies were actually doing.

Carrying NATO Water on Both Shoulders

None of the desk officers had much knowledge of NATO or collective European affairs, beyond reading government dispatches and the main newspapers. So for this they turned to me, who had supposedly "brought down the tablets" from Harvard. It was a case of the one-eyed man being king in the land of the blind. I jumped enthusiastically into this breech by keeping company with the key State Department officials who dealt with so-called European regional affairs. I was not in IAE for long before William Nunnaly and Richard Straus, State Department types who were dealing with the public side of NATO matters, invited me into a small circle that was preparing an American response to a highly important set of questions posed to all the NATO governments by the "Three Wise Men" of NATO. Eisenhower, when he was Supreme Allied Commander in Europe (1950–51), had worried greatly about the lack of understanding among the publics of the Alliance countries, both of what NATO was really about, and of their Allies. Without a base of popular support—what one of my military pals called a "we-feeling," it would be difficult for the Alliance to mount and maintain a sufficient conventional deterrent force, or to back the potential use of the nuclear deterrent (if it came to that) over what could be a long and difficult Cold War. Key leaders in Europe agreed with Ike (who by now had become U.S. president), but no one seemed to know what to do about it. Not only did the public fail to comprehend these things, but hardly anyone (even in the bureaucracy) really understood the meaning of "deterrence" —the hard facts of arming oneself with an awful weapon and convincing your opponent that you would use it if you had to, but relying on this fateful equation to insure that no one would ever use nukes.

I was continually searching for ideas, large and small, which might help create a broader, better psychological public climate among the NATO allies. One smaller idea, which got nowhere, was my proposal that all uniformed NATO service personnel should wear a small shoulder patch saying, simply, "NATO-OTAN" (English and French). Several of my colleagues, however, were quick to point out that French troops fighting in Algeria, with this prominent patch, would cause the freedom fighters to identify NATO with the French colonialists, the last thing the United States (and most small NATO countries at any rate), would want. Some years later, after the British, French, Portuguese, Dutch, and Belgians had finally liquidated their overseas empires, the idea might have helped.

As an aside, I must mention here that on returning from Germany to the United States, I had made a point to meet Clarence K. Streit, the *New York Times* correspondent at the League of Nations in Geneva during the '20s and '30s. He was the author of *Union Now* (of which I had heard when in high school, and later in Nuremberg, when I saw Strausz-Hupé's references to it in *The Zone of Indifference*). I was tremendously impressed with Streit and his federal recipe for the Atlantic democracies, and we maintained a cordial tie until his death in 1990. He asked me in 1955 to be the executive director of his interesting nonprofit organization, Federal Union. But I declined (I now think wisely). I also met the publisher of *Life* magazine at this time, Andrew Heiskell, who was also chairman of the American Council on NATO, another U.S. nonprofit that tried to muster public opinion for the Alliance. Heiskell also wanted me to take a job with them, at a good deal more than I was then paid, but I also (again wisely) turned that down, too. Harvard and future assignments to Europe with USIA seemed to me better uses of my time. However, over the years the work of nongovernmental, nonprofit bodies in Europe and other areas (today called "civil society") came to interest me more and more. While in Washington from 1956–58, working on NATO and other European questions, I kept in close touch with people such as Streit and Heiskell and their volunteer cohorts.

These links became more and more important to me as I became deeply involved, in my governmental role, in the future of NATO. I had always believed it should be much more than a military alliance, as putting political flesh on some of its bones would be likely to give its constituent governments and their publics something besides sheer military force to rely on. Also I thought giving NATO a political—and a cultural—side would help to insure its long-term survival, when the Cold War finally would subside. It is interesting that today, at the beginning of the 21st century, when the Cold War is long gone, the constituent nations of NATO have found new ways to interact. The Alliance seemed to be expanding rather than contracting, in membership and in the geography over which its writ runs (at least until the 9/11 crisis, after which some in Washington seemed to want to replace the 21-member (26 in 2005) Alliance with a "Pax Americana"). Whether NATO ties are deepening is a problematical question.

In 1956, the NATO governments were considering the set of conundrums revolving around public support and the Alliance's durability. Looked at from the intergovernmental equations of the midfifties, the key question was this: How could NATO take on a broader cast and a more peaceful role, to complement its obvious power role, probable key to survival of the West in the Cold War? No one knew how long the confrontation with the USSR would last, so the effort by the "Wise Men" to give the North Atlantic Treaty's Article 2 more substance was undertaken.

The Three Wise Men's Exercise

The North Atlantic Treaty, signed in Washington in 1949, was short. The heart of the treaty is Article 5, invoked for the first time following the September 2001 destruction of New York's World Trade Center Towers—ironically committing the Europeans and Canadians to come to the aid of the United States. Article 5 begins as follows: "The Parties agree that an armed attack against one or more of them in Europe or North America shall be considered an attack against them all"—in short, one for all and all for one. A remarkable commitment, especially for the United States, whose leaders never dreamed that *our* country would be the first beneficiary. This firm pledge, however, was the heart of the Allied mutual commitment that helped mightily to keep the Cold War from ever turning hot.

Earlier in the treaty, Article 2 had suggested the promise of bigger things to come. Its text (and the focus of the Three Wise Men in 1956) was this:

> The Parties will contribute toward the further development of peaceful and friendly international relations by strengthening their free institutions, by bringing about a better understanding of the principles upon which these institutions are founded, and by promoting conditions of stability and well-being. They will seek to eliminate conflict in their international economic policies and will encourage economic collaboration between any or all.

This treaty language was pretty heady stuff, if one were to take it literally. I certainly did, and some of the framers had. At the time the treaty was negotiated, the Canadians had made a particular point of insisting that such an Article, capable of expanding broadly NATO's competence in the future, and of demonstrating to populations weary of wars that the treaty's signers had recognized the deepest reasons—lying in shared political values and institutions—that ultimately bound them together. In other words, Article 2 embodies the basic purpose of the Treaty—to defend a way of life.

The North Atlantic Council, composed of all the governments signatory to the Treaty, decided in May 1956 that it was time to give Article 2, stressing NATO's nonmilitary character, prominence. Three "Wise Men" were appointed to lead this effort: Lester B. Pearson of Canada, Halvard Lange of Norway, and the Italian Gaetano Martino, all foreign ministers of their respective countries and all deeply involved in the origins of NATO. They were expected to produce a report with recommendations as to how NATO could give form and substance to the provisions of Article 2. But high-stakes multilateral diplomacy is never as uncomplicated as it might appear; probably at the insistence of the United States (which wanted to know beforehand the kinds of measures that the Wise Men might produce, to avoid catfights in public), the Wise Men decided that as a first step towards preparing their report, they would ask each of NATO's fifteen governments what *they* would like to see proposed. In this way, one might emerge publicly with a sum of composite recommendations, all carefully agreed upon in advance, behind closed doors.

Thus the U.S. government, with the Department of State in the lead, had to muster some proposals, answering a questionnaire from the Wise Men about how to implement Article 2. Thus I was called in as USIA's representative, to work with Nunnaly and his State crew on a report that the secretary of state would "hand over" to the Wise Men—a circuitous trail of causation, but government often works like that.

I took this as a golden opportunity to put forward some of the ideas that had been rolling around in my head since days in Germany and, where they began to come together more coherently, at Harvard. I had written a paper on "Atlantic Cultural Cooperation," which I now—somewhat gingerly—put forward. Some of my colleagues in IAE were less than enthusiastic, but when my big boss, Bill Clark, pronounced it "good," I gave it to my State colleagues. By 10 August 1956, the moment of truth was arriving; the team at State had only three or four days to finish its reply for the Three Wise Men.

I fought hard to get the essence of my proposal incorporated in this reply; Nunnaly was mildly encouraging, although worried about what

Dulles's views would be. My idea admittedly would have required a great deal of expense and added some new bureaucracies, nationally and within NATO. It called for a large-scale NATO program of exchanges of persons and ideas, all tending to help member countries deal better with the strains within their societies. My argument was that this would (a) prepare some of the socially fragile countries (in those days, Italy and France especially) better to resist the lure of Communism; and (b) give people in the NATO countries a more positive view of the Alliance.

It turned out that Dulles didn't understand such things as cultural and information operations, couldn't see how multinational approaches to improving the ways that peoples of the Alliance countries live could be done, or would help. Nunnaly reported to me that when Dulles saw our last draft of the reply to the Three Wise Men, he quickly skimmed its pages and said, "Why not let freedom work for itself?" and slammed the report shut. Nunnaly said Dulles thought that all "cultural activities should be carried on by private groups, that they should be self-sustaining, and that NATO had no business stimulating, subsidizing, or facilitating same" (to quote my journal). Obviously, Mr. Dulles did not know (or did not care) that the United States had been spending millions for some years carrying on its unilateral cultural programs around the world, not to mention the under-the-table support that his brother Allen had been dishing out to many still more offbeat but crucial programs through CIA channels.

My journal further notes: "It is really disquieting to find out sometimes how extraordinarily human these figures in high places can be; they have foibles that may be understandable, but often detrimental to conduct of U.S. affairs." Now, almost half a century later, I can only underline this proposition. When the Bush II administration came to office in January 2001, I have it on good authority that Secretary of State Colin Powell (for whom I have the greatest admiration generally) was queried on the possible reconstitution of a USIA; he reportedly said, "Why? When I was in Vietnam all USIA ever did was produce pamphlets that no one read!" How few of our citizens—even some of our most remarkable leaders— understand the need for the United States to have a trained, dedicated corps of individuals overseas, learning patiently about other cultures and explaining ours. The eleventh of September 2001 brought this need home with a vengeance, although I fear the necessary lessons may not yet have been learned.

Before the Wise Men had completed their report, the extraordinary Suez Affair erupted (31 October 1956). The failure of major NATO powers to consult with each other in advance of such measures was evident to all, so when the Wise Men's report was finally presented to the North Atlantic Council (December 1956), it was heavily weighted on the urgent necessity for more and better political consultation among members. Still, the report bears rereading now, a half century later, to remind one that the founders envisaged more than mutual defense in military terms. A key paragraph recalls:

> The second and long-term aim of NATO: the development of an Atlantic Community whose roots are deeper even than the necessity of common defense. This implies nothing less than the permanent association of the Free Atlantic peoples for the promotion of their greater unity and the protection and the advancement of the interests that, as free democracies, they have in common.

It is interesting to note that, despite all the subsequent transatlantic rows and spats—always magnified by the media—among and between NATO members, this aim, which I consider a main foundation stone for the twentieth century and even more for the new one, has been regularly advanced, and often called forth, through many vicissitudes and trials.

The report did contain a special section on Cultural Cooperation, which was not nearly as forceful or far-reaching as I had hoped, but which nevertheless laid down some principles for greater exchanges of persons, for some common cultural endeavors of the member governments, for supporting the work of nongovernmental organizations (NGOs), and for a few cultural endeavors to be undertaken at the initiative of the NATO staff. This latter provision eventually enabled us, for example, to undertake the production of short films on the cultures of all the NATO countries, translated into all the languages spoken by the member-peoples, and widely distributed for showing in movie theaters, like newsreels or then-popular "short subjects." I was the lead U.S. officer for this project, which became a truly major undertaking: Imagine a film about, say, Italy's people and culture, translated into Icelandic, Danish, Norwegian, English, French, German, Turkish, Greek, and a few other tongues! Just keeping track of who was doing what, and how, and with what monies, kept many people in NATO headquarters and in each member government very busy for many months.

Being young, enthusiastic, and full of idealism, I was disappointed with the seemingly general and insubstantial (I thought) character of the Wise Men's report, especially as it did not reflect (as our own government's recommendations did not) the overarching task that I hoped NATO would take on, viz., a large program to analyze our societies together and see how we could share "best practices" and in the process also create a large group of multinational leaders devoted to the realization of a true Atlantic Community. Over the years, much has nevertheless been accomplished

along these lines, as the countries of the Atlantic group—and others too—
have been thrown together in the development of what may become a
"world civilization."

Some of the superficial or less than salubrious influences (much poor
television and cinema, fast foods, and other facets of "Americanization")
may constitute steps backwards in some people's minds. And through
such media as much-expanded television, cell phones, computers, fax
machines, and the Internet, the "connectedness of peoples" has increased
myriadfold without much effort on the part of governments. On balance,
this general cultural sharing is for the good, in my belief. But I was worried in 1956 about the quality and durability of Atlantic/Western civilization, and I still worry today. Also, the institutional and informal bonds
which hold us together, and which in my view form the core of an eventually democratic world community, while continually strengthening, are
not yet nearly sufficiently strong to constitute an adequate and permanent
foundation—a sturdy community—for world peace. Globalization lacks a
positive sociocultural dimension, and—even more—an adequate political
framework.

I believe now, as I wrote in my journal in 1954, that "the containment
of Communism [or today, any threat to freedom, anywhere] lies above
all—one could almost say only—in the establishment of *healthy societies*
where human needs are being reasonably and progressively met."

In the White House

I had several occasions to attend meetings in the White House of the Icelandic Working Group of the Operations Coordinating Board (OCB), a
very minor cog in a big and complicated enterprise that President Eisenhower, building on his experience in Army staff work, had instituted, and
President Kennedy later scrapped. A National Security Council had been
set up by President Truman to coordinate the views and problems presented by departments of government dealing in one way or another with
foreign political/military matters. This started small, grew large over the
years and today has a major role—sometimes *the* major role—in helping
the President make critical decisions. In many administrations the national security adviser and the secretary of state clash and blood is on the
floor. This was the case with Henry Kissinger, who finally was appointed
to both jobs concurrently. Zbigniew Brzezinski also had problems with
Secretary of State Cyrus Vance.

Eisenhower thought that it was not enough to have the NSC hash out
policy positions for his approval; once that had been done, there should

be a lower-level group to decide how to carry out the various policies. I was on a lower rung of the ladder so, as the Icelandic desk officer for USIA, I would once every couple of weeks trot over to the White House to talk about Iceland's problems and devise schemes to fix them. Iceland was important in those days because it was considered a large "unsinkable aircraft carrier" right in the middle of the North Atlantic, which either we or the USSR would dominate. The United States got there first in World War II, built a large air base, and stationed some troops. Iceland was a small country demographically—at the time with about the population of Tacoma—spread out over a desolate, virtually treeless huge island. Its population lived almost entirely from fishing, with a few cold-zone sheep and small crops thrown in. The United States wanted, under the Marshall Plan, to help its economy grow. Our OCB group spent hours talking about helping to build a cement plant there; plenty of limestone was lying around. We also talked about how to make the Icelanders happy members of NATO. They had no armed forces, so the propaganda job was tricky. I went to Iceland several times and learned a good deal about its history and its literate people—still the biggest consumers of books per capita in the world. I also learned that the sun set at around midnight in the Reykjavik summer. And rose again at 1 a.m.!

In December 1956, shortly after the brief Hungarian Revolution had run its tragic course, Bill Clark asked me to be one of two USIA bodies to be loaned to the White House. Although Secretary Dulles had talked bravely during and after the 1952 election of "rolling back" the Iron Curtain, when the Hungarians—fed up with Soviet rule—overthrew their puppet government in November 1956, the United States (wisely) decided it could not intervene militarily, covertly or otherwise. The Russians put down the revolt bloodily; thousands of Hungarian refugees poured across the border, mainly into neutral Austria. NATO countries offered to settle the refugees, temporarily in camps, then in homes and jobs. Tracy Voorhees, a noted Republican activist and friend of Eisenhower, became the President's Coordinator for Hungarian Relief. Along with General J. Lawton "Lightnin' Joe" Collins as his deputy, he had the job of arranging to receive the 35,000 Hungarians (the U.S. "quota") and arrange for their placement around the United States. State Department personnel interviewed Hungarians in temporary camps in Austria and sent short questionnaires back to Washington with data for those we were to accept. While an airlift began depositing our quota refugees at Camp Kilmer in New Jersey, a computer whiz from the Ford Motor Company set up a huge (for those days) computer operation there to sort out the job experience, family size, physical condition, possible family or other connections in any part of the United States, and so on for each refugee, then match these with offers of jobs and homes from the hundreds of communities who opened their hearts to the dispossessed.

When Clark nominated me to help, he said I would probably be working for General Collins; I tried in vain for several days to connect with the general; a colleague who was to join me reported that the general's staff said he had no office space as yet, but would contact me when he did. I waited a few days, then suddenly was asked for some copies of my biography, to be given to the deputy head of USIA at 10 the next day. As my secretary was slow in typing it, I showed up with the bio at 10:20. Told that the deputy had left for Bolling Field, to join General Collins in a flight to New Jersey, I rushed to the street and grabbed a cab. As I arrived, Collins's plane was warming up; I dashed out, went aboard, and handed our deputy my papers. He said, "Say, as long as you're here, why don't you go along with us? Then you can talk to the general and find out what this is all about." On the flight, General Collins briefed me on the project and hired me on the spot.

On the following day, a Saturday, I joined others in General Collins's new suite of offices on Lafayette Square. The general's executive officer plus some legal beagles and Ugo Carusi, former Commissioner of Immigration, were there. Life was never the same after that day. Collins told us, "I will never criticize you for using your initiative, but I may criticize you if you *don't*!" I worked flat out for him, as his special assistant, for three weeks, until 4 January. We made a second trip to Camp Kilmer, accompanying Vice President Nixon, who made a short, impressive speech to a gathering of all the officials working on the Hungarian program; he had just returned from visiting the camps in Austria. I took minutes, as secretary, of three meetings that day.

As a boss, the general was decisive and demanding, but fair and had a well-organized mind. When the work began to run out, I was to return to USIA, but Tracy Voorhees insisted that I be sent to his office in the White House to help his chief assistant. With an Army master sergeant as my stenotypist-stenographer, I churned out answers to letters for Mr. Voorhees's signature. Never in my life, before or since, have I had a secretary like that sergeant; he sat at my elbow as I dictated several letters, whipped them out in a few minutes while I checked a previous batch for signature, then took more letters. From what was little more than an enlarged clothes closet, we turned out something like 40 to 60 letters each day; a few could follow a form but most required individual treatment and some thought.

Voorhees was a difficult man to work for; he had an incisive lawyer's mind and grasped issues quickly, but had bad work habits. From my journal:

He comes in early, sits down in his big temporary conference room–office and begins to talk with Harry [his general counsel] and me about what needs doing. In the middle of the conversation he will suddenly call for the secretary to place a call to New York or Arizona. Meanwhile, he is interrupting frequently to make a list of things to do on a long yellow pad. When we get a chance, we shove big stacks of letters to sign under his nose. He may shove them right back, declaring he is too busy, and then we have to wait patiently for a chance to repeat the procedure. He picks these letters apart incredibly, chancing on slight grammatical errors, or, really, differences in grammatical usage. He doesn't like my comma punctuation and I don't like my stenographer's, so it really makes for confusion when he finds major differences. He is usually unwilling to let small, inconsequential differences or errors go and requires letters redone four or five times upon occasion. When he finds major differences in interpretation, he may throw down his pencil and make an almost insulting statement about the poor staff work he is getting.

And so on! To think that we were in the middle of an emergency, in the White House, working long hours. But I also found a fine side of Voorhees. Among other things, he got his staff members tickets to Ike's second inaugural parade. I found that I agreed also with most of his political views, meaning he was right in holding them!

One afternoon, when I was exhausted and with little prospect of finishing the stack of work on my desk by day's end, a regular White House staffer urged me to go for a swim in Ike's pool. The president was away, and I was the only swimmer. Ike's pool valet showed me the bathrobe the president used and his shaver. It was great luxury, better than the YMCA pool I frequented when I had time. When Nixon later became president, it was said that he had the pool covered to make it a ballroom. I never got to meet President Eisenhower.

This interlude at 1600 Pennsylvania Avenue, which lasted less than three months, was an eye-opener and a great opportunity. There is a special aura in the White House, no matter which president or party is in power (and I visited a good many times over later years). The departments of government—even the offices of the cabinet secretaries—do not match the White House for awesome quiet, for much better than average food (served by mess-jacketed sailors), for the splendor of decor in the principal rooms and offices. This is perhaps the most history-laden precinct of U.S. government; one feels it deeply.

But at other places within the government, more important decisions (to me, at any rate) were being made, and I hastened back in their direction.

The Atlantic Community and the European Community: Partners or Rivals?

It was difficult in the midfifties for a lower-level young bureaucrat to readily and clearly discern exactly what U.S. foreign policy, in the world and particularly towards Europe, *was*. I looked in vain for basic documents that said such things as "NATO is the bedrock of U.S. foreign policy, and therefore . . . "; or "we hope for this kind of a society to develop in France [or Italy, or Germany], involving a, b, and c, and the U.S. will do what it can to promote these." If one read the host of official documents (on these matters, usually classified), one might be able to pull out the elements of a broad, coordinated policy overall. But, even if there were two or three National Security Council documents (such as the famous NSC-68) that laid down some important fundamental principles, "policy" as we desk officers had to try to express it in our work usually was something that seemed to just ooze out of the bureaucratic walls, or fall occasionally from some big shot's lips. And we were supposed to "know." In other words, I longed for visions, large and small, but always workable.

The truth about European policy in the crucial fifties, in retrospect, seems to be this: Those who knew what they wanted and had plans for how to get it, fell into at least two camps inside the U.S. government: There were the Europeanists and the Atlanticists, promoting their own visions, but the Europeanists became stronger and stronger and, over time, the Atlanticists, weaker. Strange to say, the Europeanists, both in Europe and the United States, were found more *outside* the governments than inside. George Ball, a Wall Street lawyer who encouraged Jean Monnet, the "father of a united Europe," took Monnet's ideas to his friends in successive U.S. administrations, and often embellished them, was the leader of the European cabal. The Ford Foundation played an important role. There was a close-knit group of Foreign Service and other government officers who agreed with Ball and who pushed Monnet's ideas and shaped U.S. policy. One who was most influential was J. Robert Schaetzel, who occupied various key posts over the years, and who, for me (because I came to know him well) epitomized the no-holds-barred united Europe first, close Atlantic ties second — and later — position.

From a close reading of many accounts, and especially Monnet's memoirs, my impression in the fifties, and even more today is that the "united Europe" people wanted a Europe that could rival the United States as a world power. I had to deal with this reality then without understanding the full extent of Ball and Monnet's (and many others') influences. Once that process was complete, the Europeanists felt that the two great democratic powers would and could form a natural "partnership" (as it came to be called when Kennedy formed his administration), and (without anyone saying it), run the world together. (See chapter 8 for a more detailed examination of how this looked two years later, from "the field," in this case, Europe.)

"Partnership" was sometimes called the "two-pillar" theory and by some disgruntled Atlanticists the "dumbbell" concept. Regardless of the metaphors, I never believed in this kind of dichotomous arrangement. Fifty years later, Europe is still not effectively united (although great progress has been made) and, in some ways, transatlantic ties of a truly durable nature have come to be less than they should — or would — have been if a more integrated theory and policy had driven both U.S. and European actions.

When I was posted back to Europe, in the summer of 1958, I traveled extensively to take the temperature of Europe and Europeans. I recall one day seeing several posters in the Lyons region of France, calling on local citizens to vote in an unofficial straw poll for or against a United States of Europe, etc. A clever pro-European federalist named Altiero Spinelli (to whose group USIA gave money) was back of this. He used various cities' voting machinery to try to rally a strong pro-European unity movement. It had a good deal of effect. The poster's supposed appeal to the voters was this: It portrayed two huge blocks of granite, each planted in the ground to suggest absolute immobility, and leaning towards each other. Looming above the stones, one labeled "USA," the other "USSR," was a great, muscular giant, prying the stones apart. The clear implication: Vote for a federal Europe and we can go our own way, and influence both the Cold War contestants impartially, decisively. This was the so-called Third Force concept, a very Gaullist idea, though de Gaulle was in no way a federalist.

In my view then, this kind of overbalance of power thinking could just as easily split Europe away from the United States and wreck NATO as it could reinforce a strong Europe, which would presumably, someday, form a partnership of equals with the United States. Since those days, Atlantic connections have remained reasonably strong; with all its transformative problems, NATO still, at the turn of the new century, seems an essential piece of the international furniture. However, the Third Force or Partnership idea has caused a lot of trouble over the years; while the small countries, such as Denmark, The Netherlands, or Greece, have never seemed keen on a "stand-alone" Europe; the French in particular, and some portion of the Germans (usually to placate the French) were for this concept, as they saw in the Third Force the possibility of remaking a consolidated world power out of Europe, one able to challenge the United States on the international stage.

My conception of the two ideas—Europeanist and Atlanticist—was that they could be mutually reinforcing. In the winter of 1958 I presented this in a graphic way to my USIA bosses (see Appendix A). It showed European and Atlantic arrangements as a series of concentric circles, with the original economic core (the Benelux pact) of a united Europe at the center, the early postwar European defense arrangements as the next surrounding circle, then the Coal and Steel Community (1951), and (then not yet in effect), the European Economic Community and Euratom (1958). In two outer circles were NATO and the planning body for the Marshall Plan, the OEEC. The whole made a big "pizza" with the various pieces made up of the member-countries; some were participants in everything, others in just two or three. It was meant to suggest the unity of the whole endeavor, even though the various circles represented different institutions and degrees of commitment.

My bosses liked this chart so well that they paid for its translation and printing in several different European languages, well distributed by our embassies. As the years went on and both memberships and institutions grew, I added the changes. In my 1998 book, *Pax Democratica*, I included up-to-date charts and futuristic ones as appendices. By 2002 the pattern and number of institutions, plus the continuing burgeoning of putative memberships into the Balkans and Eastern Europe, and even further, made a workable chart increasingly problematic. I never discussed the chart with my State Department peers and I don't know what their reaction was, if any. Maybe the convinced Ball-Monnet "two-pillarists" didn't see the relevance, i.e., that the chart might have shown Europeans that they could have it all. More likely, they didn't care, because their efforts with much of Europe's elite, as well as the American establishment, turned out to be decisive—at least most of the time.

The practical relevance of all this was sharply displayed in 1957, when the Treaty of Rome, creating the European Economic Community (EEC—the Common Market) and Euratom, was signed and ratified by the six key countries. Since the first European Coal and Steel Community (ECSC) had come into being in 1951, the policy-makers at the State Department had made a symbolic gesture to the idea of a united Europe by creating gradually, in effect, a new "embassy" accredited not to a country, but to the multinational ECSC. David K. E. Bruce, a distinguished American who had played key roles in and out of government since the Second World War, was the first to be named ambassador to the ECSC. All the other multilateral efforts, consisting mostly of the continuing transatlantic economic collaboration which had grown out of the Marshall Plan, plus NATO, were concentrated in one special office in Paris. It was called, in the bureaucratic fashion, by the acronym USRO—U.S. Representative to Regional Organizations. At the time, the United States had one Permanent Representative, with the rank of ambassador, to both NATO and OEEC. He also had been tracking all the efforts to unite Europe. USIA's public affairs officer on USRO's staff made no distinction at the time, in terms of budgets or his general programs, between the "Atlantic" and the "European" aspects of his tasks.

By 1957, when it was clear that a more substantial nucleus of the hoped-for united Europe would come into being on 1 July 1958, with the advent of the two new communities in Brussels, a major organizational decision for the U.S. was unavoidable: Would the U.S. representative (with rank of ambassador) to the three communities be moved to Brussels and—in effect—the relationship between the uniting Europe and the existing "Atlantic" bodies, and our representation to them, be severed? The answer was yes; it could hardly have been otherwise when the major political and economic work of the two sets of bodies was becoming clearly separate. This, in effect separating the political-military aspects of our European policies from the most important parts of our political-economic work, I considered then to be a major mistake, and I still do.

But with respect to "public affairs"—the name then for what today is called "public diplomacy" in Washington—would these functions also be separated into two distinct packages, one with the job of tracking developments in European unity, and explaining them, through our information work and cultural relations (as well as in our subsidies to many nongovernmental groups and educational institutions with multinational roles), and the other, the tasks which concentrated on NATO and transatlantic economic relations? Or would our public affairs work continue to be looked at as part of a grand whole? I argued strongly for keeping the Atlantic-wide and European-wide activities together, in one Paris office; my reasoning was twofold. I tried to convince my USIA bosses that psychologically and philosophically, if not institutionally, the two "arenas" of foreign policy were tightly connected, that the making of "Europe" and also of an "Atlantic" community were both integral parts of an eventual reshaping of world politics. Peace by multinational integration, I said, was our overall prime goal, with the corollary furtherance of democracy, a criterion of membership every postwar Western treaty in this field had set forth.

I also insisted that splitting the single budget into two, one part for the public affairs office remaining in Paris, the other for the new office in Brussels, was not cost-effective nor conducive to good coordination. Needless to say, I lost the battle. Among other things, the two U.S. ambassadors—one in Paris, one in Brussels—each wanted his own press attaché. So the split was made, and in the summer of 1958, I was dispatched to Brussels to become deputy public affairs officer for the new U.S. Mission to the European Communities. (More of that in chapter 8; a bit more Washington story must be told first.)

More Atlanticism with the Burgesses

One day in 1957, when these matters, both heady high policy and practical, were being decided, the desk officer for the United Kingdom in our Washington office asked me to meet two of her old friends, W. Randolph Burgess and his wife Helen Morgan Burgess. Burgess had been deputy secretary of the treasury for Eisenhower until the president decided to appoint him as the U.S. representative to both the OEEC and NATO, in Paris. The Burgesses asked for briefings on the character of all the European and Atlantic efforts, with which they would be dealing. I say "they" because Mrs. Burgess was the granddaughter of J. P. Morgan and during World War II had been commandant of the female U.S. Marines; she was a redoubtable, forceful woman, if also kind and thoughtful as a friend. Ambassador Burgess was an intelligent man of parts who had been chairman of the Federal Reserve Bank of New York, once the U.S. representative to the "bankers club" of Basel (the Bank for International Settlements), which made most of the great international monetary decisions between the wars and for some time afterwards. He knew a good deal about financial and economic affairs, but not much about military matters; yet he would have to sit on both councils, the one for coordination of trans-Atlantic economies and the other for conducting the civilian oversight of NATO.

We must have had at least half a dozen meetings in the Burgesses' old Georgetown house, usually for a long teatime. I saw a great deal of the Burgesses, then and later; they were to become strong partisans of the broad Atlantic community idea. I like to think that in this indirect way, I helped to influence some aspects of U.S. policy. Besides, the Burgesses became fascinating friends. I was also beginning to learn the great importance of seeking out the elites who made policy and getting to know them, in all countries of the broad Atlantic scheme.

I clung to my views about the relevance and relationship of the drive for European unification and the parallel, complementary, gradual integration of the Atlantic community. Just before I left Hof in 1955, I had set down my ideas for myself:

More than ever, it becomes clear that we need to supply a Grand Idea which can take the place of European unity hopes for Europeans and serve as something more than the equal of the Communist appeal. The only thing that has the necessary glamour and substance seems to me to be NATO unity. Why try to sell the Europeans on the value of their uniting, alone, when they are so obviously frustrated by tradition, apathy, etc.? Why not offer to do the thing together? Only something as dramatic and far-reaching as this will really do the trick.

The years from 1956 to 2001 were marvelously good to Europe, to the United States, and to Canada. The European unity idea has made better progress than I, in the fifties, thought possible; the Old Continent has above all moved far along economically, with a common currency, the Euro, for most members. The fact that war between France and Germany (and others in Western and Central Europe) now seems virtually impossible is reassuring. But today, as I look at the world in the aftermath of 9/11 in New York and consider problems such as the clash of religious ideologies of many countries in Asia with the West's, and the unbridled power politics in Africa and many other areas, I see that the future I hoped for, for Europe and the United States, is somehow needed on a greater scale, perhaps with other modes of effort, for the entire world. And the future, regrettably, is cloudier than it was. 11 September 2001 may have spelled the beginning of the decline of the Atlantic alliance, rather than a set of new opportunities for "integrators."

I was to expand and clarify these ideas, and continually update them, as a result of my two years in Washington (1956–58). But an immediate spur to reflection was a major conference in Belgium.

The Landmark Bruges Conference

In September 1957, my boss in Washington approved my attending the weeklong Conference on the North Atlantic Community, held in the sleepy medieval town of Bruges, Belgium. This was the culmination of an effort planned by Professors Strausz-Hupé and Kohn, whom I had been helping since Harvard days.

Many prestigious Europeans and Americans were invited, a total of about 80 people from various walks of life who were much involved in the thinking and the making of the "Atlantic community." That cast of characters included such eminent Europeans as Paul-Henri Spaak, a former Belgian prime minister who had become secretary general of NATO; Robert Schuman, former French foreign minister who, with Monnet, had conceived the "Schuman Plan" and brought to fruition the European Coal and Steel Community; Gen. Pierre Billotte, who had been de Gaulle's chief of staff during the war; Dr. Willy Bretscher, editor-in-chief of the *Neue Zürcher Zeitung* and despite the haughty neutrality of his native Switzerland, a ferocious pen-foe of both Hitler and Stalin; George Brown, MP, who later became UK foreign secretary; John Davenport, associate editor of *Fortune* and a strong editorial proponent of an Atlantic federation; Air Marshal Sir Lawrence Darvall, retired commandant of the NATO Defense College; Volney Hurd, chief of the Paris Bureau of the *Christian Science Monitor*; Frøde Jakobsen, MP and leader of the wartime Danish Resistance; Mrs. Mary Lord, U.S. delegate to the UN General Assembly and U.S. representative to the UN Commission on Human Rights; Adriano Olivetti, founder and chairman of the typewriter firm; Dr. Kurt Hahn, founder of progressive schools in Germany (Salem, 1923) and the UK (Gordonstoun, ca. 1935) and in 1957 proponent (with Air Marshal Darvall) of the Atlantic College project (expanded to a network of eight United World Colleges by the end of the twentieth century); Joseph Retinger, a legendary Polish war hero and *éminence grise* of the postwar European Movement; James "Scotty" Reston, then and for many years the most respected *New York Times* columnist and foreign editor; Jacques Rueff, a preeminent economist of his day and, in 1957, a judge in the new European Court; and Jan Tinbergen, renowned Dutch economist and later head of a UN development agency.

Also present were people of less fame, but of equal substance and considerable influence. From the United States, apart from Kohn and Strausz-Hupé, we had Ben Moore, a towering early postwar influence in the Department of State and once head of the office called "Regional Affairs" for Europe; Clarence Streit, who had written the noted *Union Now*; Kenneth Lindsay, an MP from Britain who represented Oxford and Cambridge universities in Parliament (an archaic idea that later evaporated from history); Arne Sejr, a Danish Resistance hero and industrialist; Jacques de Bourbon Busset, distinguished French ambassador and author; Walden Moore, director of the Declaration of Atlantic Unity and a tireless Atlanticist; Walter Elliott, British MP, who had held many ministerial posts and was cofounder of the NATO Parliamentarians Conference; plus four American university presidents: Gaylord Harnwell (Pennsylvania), Raymond B. Allen (California), Harry Gideonse (Brooklyn College), and Colgate Darden (Virginia). Most of these names (and of others at Bruges) showed up in successive efforts to rally publics and politicians and academicians to the support and elaboration of the rather new idea of an Atlantic community.

In the 21st century, one would be lucky to get such a distinguished group together for more than a couple of days; a conference of more than a week, with some festive dinners and trips around fabled Bruges, would not command attention in the fast-paced 21st century. But the leisurely Bruges approach made possible the development of many friendships and informal sharing of ideas, some of which might later have an impact; many actually did. As a U.S. government official, and a young one at that, I did not take an actual part in the official Conference deliberations, but I was present at all the plenaries and many of the working group sessions. What was striking about this conference was that it paid a lot of attention to the shared cultural heritage—as well as the differences—among the North American and European peoples. The conferees rightly understood the importance of central ideas, past and present, in the formation of an essentially common culture, especially the moral values, as well as the political and economic interests, that underlay the post-1945 flowering of international integration, as a force in Europe and across the Atlantic. It is important to note that Swiss and Swedish participants at Bruges were not from NATO countries, but that did not keep them from acting as members of a true community of values and purposes.

The conference came up with several unanimous resolutions that enunciated principles, or made recommendations to their governments and—via the media—to the world in general. A few high points:

"The principles of the Atlantic Community," including "respect for the intrinsic value of the human being" worldwide; affirmation of "the liberty of a morally responsible individual"; respect for tolerance, but not to the extent that tolerance could be carried so far as to destroy the institutions on which it depends; and an admonition to all authorities "to show how the failings of Atlantic civilization are not the result of the application of these principles, but of the departure from them."

In *Education*, the group deplored overspecialization in the universities and urged greater interdisciplinary work, and urged a "judicious unburdening of the curriculum" in secondary schools "in order for the young to have more time for living experience," especially in other countries. Here, the Conference was taking up a concept put forth by Kurt Hahn and Air Marshal Sir Lawrence Darvall for a series of "Atlantic Colleges" in different countries, which eventually came about over a generation. Later, I was deeply involved for a time (see chapter 11). Hahn remarked memorably at the Conference—and often later—that for students "to spend part of their schooldays" abroad "could be immensely fruitful in stimulating that early love of one other country on which a genuine loyalty to the wider community can be founded." How wise was this man! This thought I had found to be true in Germany, when I dispatched teenagers to the United States for

a year in American high schools. It also was confirmed in studies I did
in later years of teenage exchange programs, as well as by the anec-
dotes of many others who studied abroad at stages in their lives that
were both earlier and later than those of the late teenagers on which
Hahn laid his hopes.

An Atlantic Economic Community was proposed, a precursor of the
Organization for Economic Cooperation and Development (1961).
This received further attention at the Atlantic Congress in 1959 (see
chapter 8).

Tensions within the Atlantic Community were discussed at length,
especially those European criticisms of America which were then as-
cribed, among other things, to a European "inferiority complex" in
the face of U.S. economic and technological dominance. In the United
States, the Conference saw a public opinion "critical of the ingrati-
tude of its allies." Only a strengthening of a "sense of [transatlantic]
community" would serve to diminish tensions and misconceptions.
A series of complex and detailed recommendations dealt with a wide
variety of exchanges. How much things have changed! And how little, despite a vastly increased interchange through the media and by
means of a great increase in the work of nongovernmental bodies, the
great bulk of it of value in developing the psychological sinews of
community! In the 21st century, we take each other much more for
granted—even if sometimes too much so.

Considerable attention was given by a special group of the conference to *the Atlantic Community and Totalitarianism*. A socialist and
a trade union conferee presented reasons why "the Communist system was unacceptable to the peoples of the Atlantic Community." The
Conference recommendations in this area recommended no compromise on Atlantic principles; solidarity and the "will to achieve (our
common ideal)" would win out eventually.

A commission on *Underdeveloped Countries* urged more aid (nothing new), but emphasized that increased production alone was an
insufficient aim: social stability and free institutions were equally important. "Access to international markets," involving an increase in
the "willingness of the (Atlantic peoples) to accept over the years a
great volume of imports from the underdeveloped countries, some
of which will be competitive with their own domestic products," was
also a key recommendation. (These ideas were representative of proposals by many subsequent meetings, both private and governmental.
A great deal has been done, but "globalization" and development still
do not always make good partners in the 21st century.)

Attention was also given to *"the adequacy of existing Atlantic*

Community institutions." Recommended: strengthening and giving official status to the NATO Parliamentarians Conference; giving a more political than ambassadorial status to representatives to the North Atlantic Council; allowing some nonmilitary officials and private citizens to attend the NATO Defense College; more funds for the NATO information services; and additional government support, too, for "voluntary associations" that furthered Atlantic goals. (Most, but not all, of this was subsequently done.)

In addition to these proposals, I had a hand in shaping yet another. When the conference had been deliberating for four or five days, I lay awake one night in my rather tatty room in the St. George's Hotel, swatting mosquitoes (legendary predators bred in the ancient and fetid Bruges canals) and musing on what had been going on in this assemblage. The immense scope of the various commissions, the cogency of some of the ideas being floated, and the wonder at how such a variegated group of eighty people could in such a short time fashion some truly important ideas struck me forcibly.

I turned on the single light bulb at the center of the room and set down on a pad some proposals for an "Atlantic Institute," a kind of multinational, private, and independent think tank, within which the kinds of people attending the conference could continue a long-term dialogue, authorize studies of problems affecting joint policies of the Atlantic world, but also more long-range matters. The next morning I showed my jottings to Walden Moore, a genial but quietly formidable New Yorker who turned out to be an extremely influential "Typhoid Mary" in propagating infectious ideas across the Atlantic community. (More of Wally later.)

He and Douglas Robinson, who was then Secretary of the NATO Parliamentarians Conference, both thought the idea was great. Douglas had written to me a few months earlier, reminding me, in a phrase, that something like it, "a Studies Center for the Atlantic Community," had been proposed at the 1953 meeting of the new Atlantic Treaty Association (citizen groups from all NATO countries) at Oxford, and a second reinforcing recommendation adopted by the A.T.A., for presentation to the Three Wise Men, in 1956. My proposal, I think, put a good deal more meat on the bones of these mere slogans. By quietly lobbying the Bruges Conference, a few of us succeeded in getting the idea into the final key recommendations. In fact it took the lead place in the conference report, which set forth these ideas:

The Atlantic Institute should promote "a sense of community" among Atlantic peoples. Its mission should be to revitalize "Western cultural and spiritual values . . . and the social institutions of the Atlantic Community." It would work to "harmonize the long-term interests of the Atlantic Community with those of developing countries." It would act as a focal point "for the Community's cultural response to . . . totalitarianism." Finally, it would devote itself to "[t]he discovery and development of Atlantic leadership adequate to these tasks."

The final resolution also gave attention to the organization and working methods of such an Institute. These, along with the purposes, were to be changed a good deal in the three years which followed, during which the Standing Committee, set up by the Bruges conferees as they departed, would refine the concept and seek funds, eventually to be superseded by the much greater elite firepower generated after the London Atlantic Congress in June 1959. Thanks to my bosses in Washington and later in Brussels, I was able to help guide the effort materially. Nothing could ever have been done, of course, without the unremitting support of many superior people, some of considerable public importance, others working very much behind the scenes. It became my job to mobilize these far-flung human resources. Eventually, in the fall of 1961, an Institute actually began work in Paris. These matters are dealt with in some detail in the two chapters that follow; in September 1957, I could hardly have imagined all this, but I worked, sometimes in a rather vague way, to bring it about. I saw it as a possibly important "engine" for the creation of a durable, many-faceted transatlantic relationship.

Washington: Back to Reality and Opportunity

On returning to Washington from Bruges, I set down my reflections on the Grand Idea which had preoccupied me since my days in Germany. I saw the vision of an entire world, which would probably take a long time coming, built on the solid fundamentals of democracy and community, the two principles emerging out of the European and Atlantic amalgamating processes of the day. Here is my revised vision, as I set it down in my journal in October 1957:

A global view, a sort of Weltanschauung, is really necessary if the idea of an Atlantic Community is to make any sense at all. One World [using a phrase made famous by Wendell Willkie's 1941 book of that title] — a world in which the rule of law is universal — is eventually necessary if we are to avoid global suicide. The UN is not, at least for the time being, susceptible of transformation on this basis because of the Russian program and because of the disparate interests of underdeveloped and developed. We must begin somewhere, nevertheless. Look at the U.S. as sitting at the center, or converging point, of a number of circles, representing communities. There is the American Hemisphere community, the Pacific community with our SEATO allies and Japan, some sort of community represented by the Baghdad Pact, a kind of association with much of Africa, and the very definite Atlantic Community. We cannot stress any one of these to the exclusion of the others. Yet we should get on with the business of consolidating the rule of law, one step at a time, until eventually, in some unforeseeable way, we have it covering the world. The place to begin is where we have begun—the Atlantic Community. Benelux is, historically and geographically, the core. Then we expand to ECSC, the Common Market [EEC], Euratom, Council of Europe, NATO, OEEC, and so on. Only as the component countries are truly capable of democratic government in the Western sense can we really make the ties solid. . . . Volney Hurd [the *Christian Science Monitor*'s correspondent in Paris, who became a close friend] envisages an Atlantic consultative assembly including Morocco, Tunisia, Algeria, Europe, other African territories, North and South America. Why not, as these countries become capable of sophisticated government? . . . The policy of the United States should be gradual, organic union with all countries that are ready.

The reader will encounter later in these pages some permutations and commutations these ideas underwent as the world changed, and as I too changed, and others made their contributions. But essentially these are things that are still at the core of my beliefs as the 21st century begins to unfold. In fact, the global essence of what I hoped for in 1957 began to come together in Warsaw, June 2000, when a large intergovernmental framework (perhaps *too* large, nebulous and unwieldy for an easy beginning), called "The Community of Democracies" (CD), was established, for future elaboration, by a conference of more than 100 foreign ministers. (See chapter 18) The general idea, despite the fact that the conference was virtually ignored by the world's media, was thus registered officially— internationally, a marker was set down. Now it will be important to see what becomes of this idea, which has animated me for half a century.

In November 2002, the intergovernmental CD met again, in Seoul. This time, things had changed a great deal since I wrote down my hopes in 1957 and even since 2000, but the most disappointing change, for me, has been in the attitudes of many of my fellow Americans, reflected rather acutely in the Bush II administration, most of whose leaders seem largely ignorant of the deep currents—one might characterize these as "anthropological," not just political and economic—in other parts of the world. These leaders seem to see everything through a lens of Pax Americana, an American empire, a real dead end, when—with American leadership—we should be striving for a Pax Democratica, the Peace of the Democracies. If there is to be lasting peace, a union of democracies will have to make that peace and preserve it.

It would be unfair to lay the full blame for entertaining imperial ideas on the second Bush administration; these trends in American elite thinking were also exposed in the Clinton era, and before that. An obvious disjuncture arose in the character of the transatlantic ties at the end of the Cold War. The rhetoric of American and European leaders often sounded good, but actions began to be less than indissolubly "Allied" in nature; the near-fiascos in the Balkans, before that the Gulf War (which was not, in effect, a NATO undertaking but something less), and the vacillation in policy towards Russia, are all good examples of the failure of U.S. leaders, first and foremost, to act as if the great bulk of American interests are contained in a policy which serves the composite of all the interests of the democracies of the world. It is especially hard, I think, to get a consensus in Congress for broad policies of reinforcing and expanding community-building among democracies. It is also difficult for Congress, under our system, to support long-range important work on a sustaining basis. More of this later.

The NATO Parliamentarians Conference

In the autumn of 1957, I was made secretary of a committee of members of parliaments of the NATO countries and an aide to U.S. Senator Karl Mundt. This was supposed to be a brief assignment, but I returned to the task each year until 1964. The NATO Parliamentarians Conference (NPC) was the brainchild of a couple of Canadian and British MPs and the young, extremely able Brit, Douglas Robinson. I had met Douglas on a trip to London in 1956; he turned up at the September 1957 Conference in Bruges, where he played an instrumental role behind the scenes, and we plotted continually thereafter for the good of the Atlantic community. The idea of the NPC (later to become a full-fledged interparliamentary organization) was to bring several legislators from each NATO country annually to meet with counterparts. They would deliberate over the condition of Alliance affairs, form committees for "hearings," and submit reports to their parent legislatures. Eventually, the NPC became the North Atlantic Assembly, heard reports from the NATO Secretary General as a matter of right, and became moderately influential with respect to the actions of NATO and its member governments.

It might be interesting to know that the NPC was not created by an official act of governments, or even parliaments. When that route seemed insurmountably difficult, a Canadian Senator, Wishart Robertson, invited a few colleagues from the British Parliament and the U.S. Congress to join him in incorporating a simple nonprofit, private body under British law. In such unobtrusive ways many good things have begun; this is part of the genius of the Atlantic way of life.

In the early years, the NPC got the attention of several top U.S. senators, including Henry M. Jackson of Washington and Jacob Javits of New York. Working with their counterparts, they produced brilliant reports on such matters as nuclear energy and defense coordination. Later, the NPC/NAA deteriorated somewhat, especially as it came under the influence of assertive but inadequate U.S. members of Congress, who used it somewhat as a plaything for their own political benefit. The more able U.S. senators and representatives seldom were named delegates, because people such as Wayne Hays, representative from Ohio, as chairman of the whole conference (who could not be shaken loose once elected), dominated both the selection of delegates and agendas for the meetings.

In 1962, a fine Dutch MP, Col. J. J. Fens, told me privately of an amazing but also humorous instance of Hays's abuse of his position. Hays invited several key NPC delegates, including Fens and others from various NATO countries, to the United States for a tour of his home State, at U.S. taxpayers' expense. The delegates thought this was a good opportunity to visit the vaunted Middle West and "take the temperature" of a part of the U.S. electorate. Once airborne, it became clear that the NPC group were going to "help" Wayne Hays in his current election campaign! They dutifully (albeit fuming quietly) accompanied Hays and were expected at most campaign stops, dinners, and lunches to speak on Hays's behalf.

My assignment with NPC and Senator Mundt (arranged by Douglas Robinson) was to provide the chairman and his Committee on Education and Cultural Affairs with ideas that could perhaps form NATO-oriented proposals for endorsement, and to keep the minutes of the committee. Don Henderson, an aide to Senator Jackson, was consultant to the committee; we worked closely together to try to make a part of NATO's weak civilian programs more effective.

Although at the time it was not easy to see progress from these recurring meetings, I noted over the years that delegates from various parliaments were influenced by our work, and no doubt we by their views. A

kind of consensus began to develop, which undergirded the fragile solidarity of the NATO countries in small but sometimes important ways. My
connections with Senator Mundt became excellent. He was a genial, rather
conservative legislator, but insightful on some positive matters—such as
cosponsorship of the 1947 Smith-Mundt Act, which inaugurated the highly effective U.S. exchange of persons programs of the post-1945 years. He
and I and Henderson collaborated on several important items, such as—
later—NATO support for the Atlantic Institute (see chapters 8 and 9).

A bit of the fun in these assignments was Washington to Paris and
back on Air Force One. Again, service personnel in mess jackets provided
steaks grilled to order. On one such trip in 1964, I learned to know John
Lindsay, then a New York City congressman; he was a bright young star of
the moderate Republicans in those days, but unfortunately his unmemo-
rable term as New York mayor, plus illness, took him out of the national
spotlight early. He was deeply interested in NATO and its problems.

Goodbye to Washington

By early summer 1958, I had been nearly two years in IAE. Bill Clark and
Walter Roberts were looking for just the right assignment for me, taking
into account my considerable acquaintance with the European scene generally, the plans for an expanding European community, and with NATO.
Because of the general bureaucratic split in State Department treatment
of European-unity affairs vs. NATO and Atlantic economic questions, my
bosses had to choose whether I was to go to Paris or Brussels. The latter
seemed wisest, although NATO matters also intrigued me. A USIA "old
hand," John Hamilton, who had managed the joint public affairs office in
Paris, was transferred to the new U.S. Mission to the European Communities in Brussels (called forevermore "USEC"). In fact, this new "embassy
to Europe" had not yet opened; I was the first Foreign Service officer to
arrive there, "at the creation," so to speak.

Before leaving for Brussels, I had lunch with Roy Benoit, USIA's language expert. We had become friends through Ben Warfield, his boss and
my mentor in the Harvard gambit. Roy said, "How's your French?" I answered probably not sufficient, as I was by no means fluent. "Roy," I said,
"I passed the written exam in French for Foreign Service entry." Gently, he
probed. First he picked up a saltcellar and said, "What's that in French?" I
replied haltingly, "Ah, well, if I knew I've forgotten." Same with the pep-
per mill, a fork, and a knife, and so on. Roy replied, "You no doubt know
a lot of diplomatic French, political and economic matters and all that (I
did), but you really need some brushing up on just day-to-day stuff." How

right he was! He recommended what I subsequently did in Brussels: find a good "native speaker" who would simply converse with me a couple times a week. Eventually I learned a fair command of the language, which became essential when we began the push for the Atlantic Institute.

On 30 June 1958, I enplaned for Brussels and another big adventure. The country itself—Belgium—was interesting, but the gradual birth of a united Europe was USEC's main focus.

8

The Unification of Europe and the Ambiguities of Atlanticism

4 November 1958: *Poland proposes its modified plan for East-West agreement on a nuclear-free zone in Central Europe, with unification—and neutralization—of Germany.*

8 January 1959: *Charles de Gaulle takes office as president of France; the National Assembly grants him vast powers; de Gaulle supervises drafting of a new constitution for the Fifth Republic.*

On 1 July 1958, I presented myself at the Brussels Embassy of the United States, met a few people, and began to help the USEC deputy chief of mission, Clarence Birgfeld, the next day to set up quarters for the second U.S. diplomatic mission in Brussels—this one to the European Communities. (Eventually there would be a third U.S. mission in the Belgian capital, this one to NATO, occasioned by de Gaulle's opting out of the NATO mutual defense infrastructure and supranational commands.) Other officers posted to USEC began to trickle in—Bernard "Red" Norwood, the economic officer; Howard Myers, to handle relations with the new European atomic energy agency; and Deane Hinton, to manage political matters. A special crew of nuclear experts, seconded by the U.S. Atomic Energy Agency, had the job of helping Euratom and protecting U.S. interests.

In a week or so, after Birgfeld had secured some quarters for USEC a few blocks from the regular Embassy and not too distant from the buildings where the two new Communities were to be housed, our chief of mission, Ambassador W. Walton Butterworth, arrived. He was a courtly, kind, astute, and experienced top-level diplomat. Had it not been for one egregious mistake for which he took undeserved blame, Ambassador Butterworth would very probably at that time have been an under secretary in the Department of State or ambassador in a prestigious capital. In 1950, however, he—and Secretary of State Dean Acheson—had made the gaffe together, and Butterworth paid the penalty. At that time, Butterworth was assistant secretary for the Far East. From Washington, he covered Korea, as well as the entire arc of countries from Japan to Indonesia. A few weeks before the sudden invasion of South Korea by the Communist armies of the North, Butterworth (based on the intelligence at hand) had assured Acheson that Korea was quiescent and that the American policy of leaving the border between the two Koreas outside of the U.S. ambit of "strategic interests" in the Far Pacific should continue. Secretary Acheson made a public speech to this effect ("Korea is outside our strategic perimeter"), and not long after, the Communists overran most of South Korea (June 1950), changing U.S. policy in the Pacific forever. President Truman and Secretary Acheson had to eat Acheson's words, MacArthur was charged with retrieving the catastrophic situation in South Korea, and the United States was in a major war, the third in the 20th century.

Poor Butterworth (and I never dared ask him his side of these matters) was accused of Communist sympathies and worse by Joe McCarthy and was accordingly demoted in Washington. In the early 1950s, he was made deputy chief of mission in the London embassy. It was considered then and throughout his career that his appointment to a top post, in Washington or at a major embassy abroad, was out of the question, because he could never get confirmed by a Congress either full of enthusiasm for McCarthy's ideas or completely intimidated by them. Thereafter the Department of State continued Butterworth in new assignments dealing with European unity. The U.S. "embassy" for the Coal and Steel Community, set up in 1956 in Luxembourg, did not require congressional approval for its head, and Ambassador Butterworth was appointed chief of mission. In 1958 the two new European Communities, for economics and for atomic matters, in Brussels, were simply added to his brief. He did a splendid job, and was much respected and liked by his staffs in Brussels and Luxembourg.

Butterworth, well supported by a good staff (no excess baggage, as in many of the old embassies), pioneered something truly new in diplomacy: official U.S. representation to an agglomeration of six major European powers, a supranational creature. Under the Treaty of Rome (1957), for example, trade policy for France, Germany, Italy, The Netherlands, Belgium, and Luxembourg was no longer the province of the individual member-states of the European Economic Community. Other nations, including the United States, had to deal with the new European Commission in Brussels on trade matters. There was also a new European Court in Luxembourg to adjudicate intramural industrial and commercial disputes among Communities' governments and firms in the six member countries; this meant that from time to time the court would even have the power to rule on mergers involving U.S. firms! (This has happened, increasingly; by the same token, U.S. courts have ruled on European mergers and other antitrust matters, showing how tangled the skein of transatlantic and indeed global interdependence has become.)

The first head of the European Commission, the German Walter Hallstein, and his European bureaucrats dealt with Butterworth and his American staff on behalf of "Europe." This was unprecedented. The United States, at the highest levels, had decided that eventually there should be, and very well might be, such a supranational unification of European powers and that we could deal with them collectively. We wanted this to happen, and did everything we could to make the new communities work. The United States also needed to protect its trade and other interests as well. Hallstein was treated by USEC as if he were the prime minister of a major government. (This was also true of relations with the companion Commission set up for the new Euratom; eventually all three European communities—including the ECSC—were combined into one.) This was heady stuff, for Hallstein's fellow commissioners and his growing staff of Europeans, who all took oaths *not* to seek permission, advice, or counsel from their governments, but to swear loyalty to the new European Commission alone.

The USEC Public Affairs Office

This was also heady stuff for us, the USEC staff, as history was being made in big ways. We were part of an historic experiment: the possible creation of a new supranational polity. My immediate boss, Public Affairs Officer John Hamilton, and I undertook our job with great seriousness. Hamilton had already established working relationships (from his previous Paris post) with many of the most important nongovernmental organizations that were studying or promoting European unity from many different angles. He and I were to intensify this work, and to arrange subsidies for the groups whose goals, programs, and personnel seemed most likely to affect positively the future of a united Europe. We also were charged with taking the temperature of the European press and publics as regards the process of European unity. I had a tiny staff, composed of Karl Herschel and two fine Flemings who read a dozen European newspapers; each day we cabled a digest of important press accounts to Washington.

The most interesting part of our work revolved around the NGOs— nongovernmental, private bodies—that might influence the process of European unification. The idea of unifying the European states is not new. From the Middle Ages down through the Enlightenment, thinkers have tried to plant the idea, primarily as a means of stopping Europe's unceasing internecine warfare, rife since the Romans, with a respite under Charlemagne. But this was always too visionary an idea for monarchs and church interests. After the two world wars of the twentieth century, however, the concept gained many converts. Woodrow Wilson's League of Nations was an effort—wider than Europe, to be sure—to amalgamate the modern nation-states in pursuit of peace.

In the 1920s, an Austrian aristocrat, Count Richard Coudenhove-Kalergi started a nongovernmental body called *Pan Europa*. It reflected, or perhaps even planted, the idea of a modern European union in the minds of leading cabinet ministers, such as the French prime minister Aristide Briand and his German counterpart, Chancellor Gustave Stresemann. Some feeble efforts to express this concept intergovernmentally had been undertaken by means of treaties full of good intent but little substance and, worse, providing no means of implementation. American secretary of state Frank B. Kellogg had signed one such treaty, the Kellogg-Briand Pact (1928), supposedly outlawing war. Once the Great Depression and the Hitler takeover in Germany had hit Europe, however, such idealistic schemes for developing cordial relations among the great powers and preventing future conflicts fell away.

After 1945, the idea of European union drew fresh breath. Various private schemes proliferated. Count Coudenhove-Kalergi was still on the scene, but his movement for a broad but fuzzy union, encompassing a "Europe from the Atlantic to the Urals" (as de Gaulle was to call it) had minimal effect. And by the 1950s, the idealistic count was old and fading.

The European Federalists

The work of the European federalists was to prove more efficacious in planting the seeds of firmer ideas in public minds, attracting attention, and indirectly pressuring governments. Unfortunately (and this has been the case with many private efforts since those days) the movement broke up into two or three parts. One group, headed by the Italian Altiero Spinelli, was fiery and bold in its approach. Spinelli, a former Communist who had been imprisoned by Mussolini for many years, had had an epiphany in jail. He abandoned his Marxism because he felt, with the time for reading and reflection that prison gave him—plus the hideous realities of the Second World War as it unfolded—that Communist "theology" embodied a false understanding of people's real desires and motives. Capitalism was no longer Spinelli's bugbear; nationalism took that place. He and his group (the Union Européenne des Fédéralistes) put forward the idea of a federal Europe, which, in his view, would make European strife irrelevant and sublimate the rivalries that had riven the old Continent since Charlemagne. Spinelli argued for bold promotional moves, such as convincing mayors and regional authorities around Europe to permit him the use of their electoral machinery for a series of citizens' votes: "Do you favor a federal Europe?" and so on. Spinelli, some years later, was appointed a member of the European Commission; he then had to eat some of his fiery words as he contended with the mundane and sometimes nasty power realities of the unification process, not all of it pristine or virtuous.

Spinelli's more radical federalist movement competed with one or more nongovernmental groups that wanted to proceed more gradually. Dr. Hendrik Brugmans, the Dutch rector of the College of Europe (founded 1950), was one of the gradualists. They recognized the agonizingly slow progress that would be required for the retraining of politicians' and publics' minds to embrace federalism as an ideal, but they did not receive the press that Spinelli's federalists did. John Hamilton and I made some grants to the College of Europe, and also directly to the Association Européenne des Fédéralistes, Hendrik Brugmans's pet NGO. Although the AEF and the UEF had doctrinal fights, on balance the tension provoked positive action.

One spinoff from the Spinelli "go-for-broke" federalists was led by Alexandre Marc, a Frenchman of Russian origin, who emphasized education, holding seminars, courses, and conferences, especially to open the minds and seize the hearts of young people. Since the 1920s Marc had been preaching federalism, a way of life that, in his mind, embraced not only relations among nations, but also those within the neighborhood community and the family. His CIFE organization (Centre International de Formation Européenne) spread all over Europe. With U.S. help, Marc started a particularly effective training mechanism, the College of Federalism, on the Swiss border in northern Italy. Marc was a living example, until his death in his late nineties, for future-oriented young Europeans.

In 1965, Marc and his equally indomitable wife, Suzanne, came to see me soon after I became involved in grant-making at the Ford Foundation. They arrived in New York determined to wring a grant from Ford, now that their friend "Jeem" was there. Both sat across from me, Suzanne speaking English, Alexandre French (although later, at age 70, he taught himself passable English). I tried to explain to the Marcs that the chances of getting a Ford grant for CIFE were essentially nil, that my bosses did not share my enthusiasm for projects such as theirs. Some back-and-forth ensued; then Suzanne leaned across my desk and spoke most earnestly, "But, Jeem, Alexandair *nevair* take *non* for an ansair!" Eventually CIFE received a token grant of $25,000, which no doubt helped. The Marcs simply persisted until my boss, Shepard Stone, said in effect, "Oh, what the hell!"

Here, an amusing footnote to the Marcs and Ford: Alexandre had been in touch with Ford's International Affairs division long before I arrived there. The powers-that-be, not taking Marc and his ideas too seriously, arranged for him to have a dialogue with Stanley Gordon, an ideal foundation gatekeeper who knew how to say no in many, mostly indirect, ways, while avoiding gratuitous enmity for the foundation. On the day described above, when Alexandre and Suzanne had come once again, hats in hand, to ask for money—because they thought their old friend Jim had *his* hands on the purse strings—Alexandre told me of several perplexing encounters over past years with Gordon in Europe and in New York. Marc bluntly asked me, *"Qu'est-ce que c'est, ce Stanley Gordon, ce type de chinois?"* I had to work hard to suppress a smile, let alone laugh. Stanley, who had become a good friend, had a thankless job taking on all the difficult work of shutting Ford's doors gently so that his bosses would be shielded. The confidential, unvarnished advice for someone looking for Ford money would have been: "If they refer you to Gordon, your chances are microscopic, if any!" Alexandre, who was extremely determined and no fool, could rightly have supposed that Gordon was some kind of inscrutable Oriental! And in his inimitable way, he was.

For me, Alexandre Marc—buttressed by his indomitable Suzanne—was a prime example of what one determined individual, pursuing an ideal in practical ways, can do. He saw the special importance of bringing along younger leaders who could (and did) take over active management of CIFE in Marc's later years. He was also, as my research at Harvard had deemed essential, building a "multinational elite" for the future. Together with the College of Europe at Bruges, the CIFE managed to feed a great number of well-prepared, enthusiastic young people into the bureaucracy of the new European Communities—today, the European Union. The great progress of Europe-uniting would not have been possible without these quiet, continuing efforts to educate and form a new kind of European personality.

An interesting historic footnote: In 2003, I came across a book (John Hellman, *The Communitarian Third Way: Alexandre Marc and Ordre Nouveau, 1930–2000*) which placed Marc, Paul-Henri Spaak, François Mitterand, and other young French and Belgians in the thick of interwar battles among Europe's intellectuals to find adequate organizing principles for societies demoralized by the 1914–18 war and the Depression. Interacting with German youth movement leaders—before and during the Hitler years—many men like Marc flirted with fascism out of desperation. World War II cured these trends, and European federalism was part of the cure. I mused on history's tragedies: Marc and others I was to work with in the 1950s and 1960s found new, realistic paths towards a rebirth of liberal democracy and a new hopeful age of federating Europe. The United States was, from 1948, square in the middle of the creation of this new Europe—and I was lucky to have been square in the middle of my country's most noble cause of the era.

The European Movement and the United States

In most European countries, and especially within the Six that formed the three initial Communities, there were private "umbrella" bodies, including the various federalists and educational groups called collectively "the European Movement." This had begun at a huge unofficial "Congress of Europe" in The Hague (1948). Together, they formed an international force of some importance, which both reflected and influenced public opinion. Virtually all the "pro-Europe" NGOs belonged, and there was an attempt—most successful in Germany—to coordinate their activities nationally and spur them all on internationally. Britain was a special case, not yet ready to join the Communities but with especially active NGOs (a traditional British specialty, in all fields from the prevention of cruelty to animals to societies of chartered accountants and beyond); the enthusiasts in the UK did their part, with special efforts under the rubric of "Britain in Europe" campaigns, which finally in 1973 helped mightily to swing the necessary parliamentary votes for entry into the Communities.

CIA undercover subsidies helped the European Movement get started and supported different parts that were well run; the European Youth Campaign was one of these. USIA helped other parts of the movement. For a time, I was USIA's liaison to CIA in these matters.

In 1961, I attended a meeting of all national branches of the European Movement in Munich, with some 600 in attendance. A remarkable thing occurred: about a hundred Spaniards showed up, mostly young entrepreneurs, lawyers, teachers, journalists, and other professionals. These young people stood up repeatedly, to voice two messages: (1) We want to be part of "Europe" and Spain must join. (2) We want democracy.

At that time, Gen. Francisco Franco, the aging Spanish dictator, was still pretty much in charge. (He died in 1975, effectively ending his fascist regime.) When, in 1961, the young Spanish members of their "shadow" European Movement returned home, many were promptly clapped in jail. For the most part, they were released in two or three months, having supposedly been taught their lesson. This showed me how powerful the popular swell in favor of "One Europe" had become, and that even in a dictatorship on the fringes of the Continent, it could not be stopped.

Today's Spain is a thoroughly democratic part of Europe, a member of the European Union, NATO, and other multilateral bodies, and has prospered enormously to boot.

I give some credit for the gradual evolution of Spain into a modern country (after three centuries of relative isolation) to the ordinary people, the workers, who went north to France and beyond in the 1960s to find work. In Paris (1961), my wife and I hired a nice Spanish maid and nanny. One day she asked if it were possible for her father, about to arrive in France, to live in our basement until he found work and a permanent abode. We met the man, a simple carpenter, and decided we must help; he fixed up bare-bones digs in our cellar, did a little garden work, and before too long found a job and a suitable abode for his family. From talking with him, it became obvious to me that such people, coming to northern Europe from Spain, Portugal, Greece, Turkey, and beyond had also been part of the movement towards democracy and community, in other words displaying "European solidarity" in many simple, perhaps inchoate, but still concrete ways. The popular infectiousness of the European idea was palpable. The U.S. government helped knit this popular swell together and gave it institutional "hands and feet." A unified Europe of one sort or another, and perhaps on a slower timetable, depended primarily on the popular recognition that there had to be another way to create an orderly, just, and free European entity, without the devastating wars of the centuries.

An extraordinary academic institution, born in the late 1940s, in Bologna, Italy, also played a crucial part in training future European leaders. It was the brainchild of Professor C. Grove Haines of the Johns Hopkins University, who had been plumped down in Italy at the end of World War II. A historian, Grove understood the vital currents impelling Europe and the Atlantic world towards greater unity. With some funds from the Marshall Plan, and later from USIA and any government agency (including Italian sources) he could convince, Grove set up a graduate school of international affairs in Bologna. About half the students were Americans, getting up-to-date knowledge about Europe from a stellar Euro-American faculty; the other half were Europeans, many of whom in later years would become important figures in their own countries. The influence of men such as Haines—largely unsung—in bringing about our greatly improved international system cannot be overestimated. Long after I left government service, I was able at least twice to "save" the Bologna Center from financial extinction, once with funds from the Ford Foundation and later from USIA again. Now, in the 21st century, the Bologna Center is well established, both in Europe and the United States, as a valued European pillar of Johns Hopkins.

The British were especially creative in spawning nonprofit groups, large and small, which contributed to public enlightenment on both the European and Atlantic fronts. One such initiative that took my fancy early on was the work of John Sewell, a compact little man with owlish glasses and a clipped gray moustache, who parlayed his experience as director of a Workingman's Educational Institute in Exeter, the county town of Devon. Entranced soon after WW II with the twin ideas of European and Atlantic unity (which he always saw as intimately entwined), Sewell recruited some of his fellow educationists to develop TEAM—The European-Atlantic Movement. This was not some farflung massive undertaking with a London headquarters and a great budget. TEAM was run out of John's home in Exeter, entirely the work of volunteers whom John had recruited from his adult education classes. TEAM organized yearly study trips for teachers and others to Luxembourg, Paris, and later Brussels, to familiarize participants on the spot with the work of the new multilateral institutions. John also put on longer summer schools at Oxford, for citizens of every stripe to study more deeply the currents that were bringing countries together. Talk about your shoestring operation! John was not only a great organizer and teacher but a most interesting human being; in 1918, as a British soldier, he was sent to Russia with the ill-fated Allied expedition that had tried to throttle the Bolshevik revolution at birth. As a military photographer he had helped to document history. Once, in 1958, when I visited John's headquarters, he picked me up in his 1932 Austin, as immaculate and shiny as the day he bought it. We helped him with small grants.

Space does not permit me to make a full list of NGOs that USEC subsidized, but one more should be mentioned: the European Center of Culture in Geneva. Its director was the famous French-Swiss author, Denis de Rougemont, who became a good friend. He was the author of numerous important books (one of them was *Love in the Western World*—not, perhaps, what the reader might think it was!), and a founder of the Congress for Cultural Freedom, which played a big role in the Cold War. Through his modest center Denis sponsored initiatives such as a league of European cities, a European civics campaign, and regional commercial networks that flourished at the natural intersections of several European states. An example of the latter was the German Freiburg/Swiss Basle/French Mulhouse triangle. De Rougemont's theory was that such regional connections were more natural than many relationships resting on national origins; today, this "natural geographic unity" theory is a reality—a powerful motor towards "one Europe." De Rougemont was an unusual intellectual, because most do not have his facility for translating good ideas into practical institutions and concrete sociopolitical results. He was both a thinker *and* a doer.

None of these efforts to bring Europe together into a whole could have worked, in my opinion, without the American example from which to learn. The development of U.S. federalism, and especially the making of the Constitution of 1787, were cardinal models on which Europe could both build and innovate. In 2001, when former French President Valéry Giscard d'Estaing became chairman of a European "Constitutional Convention," he pointed out the importance of the 1787 model to the delegates and suggested, somewhat obliquely, that Europe also needed a "Declaration of Independence" — leaving the distinct implication that Europe needed to be less tied to the United States. The new European Constitution was presented to voters and parliaments in 2005. Some states approved, others refused to ratify it. The future of the European amalgamation was again cloudy.

Building Europe's Civil Society

In most European societies, citizens' action groups were not commonplace in the early postwar years. Aside from conventional (mostly religious) charities, few foundations or independent groups were accustomed to mobilizing opinion for good causes (except, of course, for political parties). Britain was the main exception. We Americans, working to help Europe organize itself, were able to show the Europeans in many instances how to set up citizen organizations and foundations and show results. It was exciting work and had to been done most carefully. Later, in 1969, I became a cofounder of the International Standing Conference on Philanthropy, which helped to popularize the idea of foundations, voluntarism, and NGOs — a complex that the late John Gardner called "the independent sector" of society.

During two years in Brussels, John Hamilton and I made more than a million dollars worth of grants to European NGOs. We were careful not to duplicate anything done by the Central Intelligence Agency, which had been in the business of supporting many pro-European groups since the late 1940s, long before USIA was created. For two years in Washington, I had been USIA's liaison with CIA, to be apprised of what subsidies (all confidential at the time) they were giving to groups in Europe. In the process, I had formed a few friendships with CIA officers, some of which lasted for years. The great hullabaloo that erupted in 1965, when some of the U.S. press "blew the cover" of many of these operations, hurting — in some cases, irremediably — the reputations of noted scholars, political figures, and others on both sides of the Atlantic who were thus "exposed" as recipients of "spy agency" money, was a tragic event. But it also showed the great difficulty in giving public funds clandestinely, no matter how worthy the objectives.

USIA, largely through our Brussels and Paris offices, also made some grants to educational and other groups promoting European and Atlantic "togetherness" on a confidential basis. Our purpose, and that of the CIA, in maintaining secrecy, was solely to avoid compromising the European figures involved. One of the most prominent was Professor Raymond Aron, a towering 20th century political sociologist, who was deeply hurt when his participation in the Congress for Cultural Freedom became public. Most unfortunately, I think he had never been told of the connection. In hindsight, maybe the high degree of caution was not needed. Yet I think that if all the grants had been open and public in the delicate atmosphere of those years, many of the good people who had accepted and used the confidential money to good purpose would not have taken part. In the rather grim and uncertain days of the Cold War, our policy at the time— both USIA's and CIA's—was prudent and, in my opinion, extremely effective. This was during years when our Soviet opponents were spending from five to ten times more than we on what they called "agitprop"—propaganda plus political agitation.

During World War II, Churchill had urged Allied clandestine efforts of this kind, saying, "the truth must be protected by a bodyguard of lies." This mentality, perhaps unfortunately, carried over into the conduct of the Cold War by a significant but extremely able group of CIA officers. Fortunately, I don't think that in Marshall Plan Europe, or after, those who doled out the money for clandestine operations of this kind had any lying to do, except for maintaining the secrecy of the source of funds. I believe the full story has yet to be told. The United States did what it had to do and did it well: an unsung success of major proportions.

I continue to believe that the European idea and to some extent the Atlantic idea would have moved a good deal more slowly towards fruition without covert U.S. support. Indeed, it is quite possible that transnational European and Atlantic institutions might not have thrived at all without this help and the practical counsel that went with it. There were in those days no ready sources of funds in European governments or in such tiny foundations as then existed in Europe or among European business groups for bolstering what today is called "civil society." Only in Britain, and to a lesser extent in Germany (where Allied tutelage had helped to bring civil society to life), were societal capabilities available to do these kinds of things, fundamentally political in their impact, but dealing in the international currency of education, culture, and society. I think one must also realize that the geopolitical situation facing the Atlantic Allies in the 1950s and 1960s was a good deal closer to that of the perils of World War II than of a later time. By the 1980s, Communism as an international force had largely been eroded. The struggle was for survival well into the seventies. In the last third of the twentieth century, as some developing countries moved rapidly towards maturity by letting civil society flower, we in the West pioneered the way; and now civil society in the West, on a private basis (sometimes with overt government aid) helps its counterparts in the rest of the world establish this indispensable pillar of democratic society.

In the late 1960s, however, this kind of foreign aid became a serious bone of international contention. Suddenly there were attacks on the CIA's work in postwar Europe: Following the revelations in the magazine *Ramparts*, James Reston wrote several full-page articles for the *New York Times*, detailing further actions he thought had been unsuitable for the intelligence agency to undertake. A good deal of what he said was incorrect and the slant that he and other writers put on these actions seemed designed to denigrate an extremely effective governmental operation of which our citizens could be justly proud, had one been able to lay all the facts before them. I had been privy to a fair share of these "secrets," some the press never learned of. By then at the Ford Foundation, I exchanged several letters with Mr. Reston, deploring the damage being done to many of the staunchest pro-Europeans and pro-Americans in Europe. He finally replied, in his third letter, that maybe the *Times* had gone too far. Years later, 2001 in fact, I read a book by Volker Berghahn, *America and the Intellectual Cold Wars in Europe*, that set the record even straighter. Berghahn's main thrust was to clarify what the Ford Foundation had done (much of which I had *not* known) to bolster the government's work in this then-murky area. Even when I was in government service and later in the Ford Foundation itself, I was not aware of some of the interconnections and patriotic "burden-sharing" Ford and a few other foundations had undertaken. My view today is that both on a private basis and a governmental basis, we Americans can be proud of an overall U.S. effort, which made a great difference in what happened in Europe between 1948 and, say, 1975.

I have no general views of the CIA and its worldwide work; my "need-to-know" was limited to the work of pro-European-unity groups that the "Agency" (as CIA was commonly known) was helping in the 1950s. I'm sure that a great deal of this undertaking in Europe has not yet become generally known, and that is just as well. It is my conviction that the CIA and (lesser) USIA monies used for these purposes were well spent and accounted for. Officers of the CIA of course were a mixed bag (as in any branch of the federal bureaucracy), especially when their covert operations in the 1980s began to follow presidential directives in Latin America under Reagan. Much of this seemed to me, at a distance, badly conceived and even counterproductive, but of these efforts I know no more than the ordinary citizens who read their newspapers. However, as for Europe in the Marshall Plan and "European beginnings" days, the job was extremely well done. And the quality of the CIA officers whom I met at this time was even a cut above that of the general run of USIA people with whom I worked (and they were very good).

Crosscurrents: Atlanticists and Europeanists

Earlier, I've recounted some of the 1950s internecine warfare in the Department of State and other U.S. foreign affairs agencies, pitting the adherents of the George Ball–Monnet concept of an Atlantic Partnership against people such as Will Clayton, under secretary of state under Acheson; John Hickerson, assistant secretary of state for Europe and one of the architects of the NATO treaty; and later Secretary of State Christian Herter. The Atlanticists were inspired by Clarence Streit, with his visionary call for an Atlantic federation (*Union Now*), and by more practical but tougher people outside the executive branch, such as Sen. Estes Kefauver of Tennessee, Gen. William Draper, former Supreme Court Justice Owen Roberts, Henry Luce of *Time* and *Life* magazines, and Elmo Roper, one of the fathers of modern opinion polling.

I believe, to somewhat oversimplify the Europe-related differences and tensions of the time, that the partnership advocates did not want to drag the United States into any kind of tight Atlantic union with Europe (and perhaps Canada and a few others, such as Australia), but instead to concentrate on helping Europe to become a great power on its own. When a united Europe would have become sufficiently self-confident, they believed, it would be time to talk about strong "partnership" links (vaguely defined at the time) with the United States. The essential point of most partnership proponents was that Europe would need time to be sufficiently united and strong to parley with the United States as an equal. Many Europeans liked this idea, especially President de Gaulle, who came to power for the second time in 1958, as I was arriving in Brussels. In his view, the new union of European states would naturally be led by France and, when necessary, could form ties with the USSR to try to counterbalance U.S. power and influence. From time to time over the next few years, he tried to play such a role. An important wing of the European federalists wanted a united Europe to form a "Third Force," between Europe and America (see chapter 5). This could make an amalgamated Europe a great power again, they were convinced, although perhaps in different ways from those envisaged by de Gaulle. The Third Force idea was the old balance-of-power concept in new clothing, but potentially just as pernicious.

I believe that Jean Monnet himself, the revered "Father of Europe," who produced a series of excellent plans for institutionalizing a united Europe—and saw some of them through to birth—was not really a Third Force advocate, as were some of his coterie, American as well as European. Unfortunately, I never met Monnet, but I knew many of his closest associates and talked often with them, and I have read Monnet's memoirs and biographies by others. I'm sure that his admiration for America was genuine and strong. But this was not, I am also convinced, the case with many of his adherents. The Americans among them could not really conceive of the United States as relinquishing some sovereignty (as would be required in any truly durable and effective transatlantic community) and looked on partnership as a way of postponing this. The Europeans in this group were envious of American power and wanted to establish a united Europe that, as a Japanese nationalist of the 1990s expressed it, "can say no to America." I believe the partnership advocates in large measure did not understand fully what they might create, nor the extent to which the failure to complete a strong Atlantic Community would hobble the world internationally, in our present time and beyond. They posited a continuation of benevolent American attitudes towards a uniting Europe; but I and others did not feel we had all that much time to educate our fellow countrymen in the responsibilities of world citizenship, beginning with Atlanticism.

More important, I believed then (as I do now) that Europe would never quite make it to effective unity. Today, in the early years of the third millennium, the core of Europe has a single currency (a boon to those doing cross-border business and to many travelers), effectively a single market, no internal customs and immigration barriers, and many patterns of behavior and powers of its own that draw Europeans more closely together. However, there still is not a single European foreign policy, nor an effective common defense force, nor a common economic and fiscal regime. Inequalities vis-à-vis America rankle Europeans and continue to postpone the "United States of Europe." Part of Europe's trouble lies in today's U.S. governments, which do not make European unification easy in many respects. Of that, more later.

Partnership Ascendant for a While

Within and around the State Department, starting in the Eisenhower years and then during the Kennedy administration, the partnership advocates gradually won the day with the Monnet-Ball propositions. Elsewhere in government, however, the way was not always so clear. General Lauris Norstad, a World War II hero and Ike's close friend, who became NATO's Supreme Commander in Europe (1957–63), saw things differently. He did not want to see a split develop between Europe and America that could affect NATO's solidarity. When the French Assembly shot down the European Defense Community treaty in 1954, the solution found (a looser Western European Union) for bringing in a major German ground force to round out NATO's defenses on the critical eastern front had in fact increased Atlantic solidarity, but somewhat at the expense of the movement towards supranational European political and defense institutions.

Issues involving control of nuclear weapons under changing technological and political conditions seized the attention of Norstad and others. Norstad had a plan for a NATO regional strategic missile force, combining the separate French and British nuclear deterrents, which would represent an important step forward in both Atlantic and European integration. This was countered with a proposal, by the partnership group in the State Department, for a so-called Multilateral Force (MLF) that would have put emphasis on European control of a limited degree of nuclear integration, with atomic weapons based at sea, all within NATO. Neither proposal succeeded; the MLF ideas found most European decision-makers cool. Nor could Norstad, perhaps not fully considering the economical and political consequences of his own plan, prevail.

In 1958, when de Gaulle assumed power for the second time and gave France a new constitution (the Fifth Republic), he was determined to split NATO, if he could, with France leading the European wing, the United States (and perhaps Britain and Canada) managing some sort of overall Atlantic conception. He insisted on calling the United Kingdom and the United States "les Anglo-Saxons," as if the multiethnic United States could ever be characterized based on racial ideology. He decided eventually that he could not win over his then-weak European Communities partners to a French-led European force, nor could he break the determination of the United States to exercise both a substantial amount of American military independence and unchallenged leadership in NATO. General Norstad did not believe in either de Gaulle's or the predominant U.S. view of these matters; he was a genuine Atlanticist who tried to find compromises that would help consolidate both European and Atlantic ties.

Lauris Norstad, whom I came to know well after his retirement, told me that not long after de Gaulle became president of France in 1958, he invited Norstad to dinner. The president asked the supreme allied commander where the American nuclear weapons were stored in France. Norstad replied, he told me, that he had to respect his conflicting responsibilities wearing two hats—commander of U.S. Forces in Europe *and* supreme allied commander for NATO. In the first capacity, he would not be able to divulge the nuclear information to de Gaulle without an OK from Washington, and he could not get that. In his second, NATO capacity, he did not have the power de Gaulle was asking him to exercise. De Gaulle was unhappy. Norstad believed that from that day, *le Général* was determined to get NATO forces and headquarters out of France and France out of the militarily integrated side of NATO. This break eventually came about in 1963, weakening NATO a good deal, but—as it has for more than half a century—the Alliance survived, its strength helping to bring about the USSR's capitulation in the Cold War and, in the 1990s, to find other important tasks that demanded continuing close cooperation among the United States, Canada, and Europe—including the French—at least fitfully.

Another side note to history: Once in 1962 I invited retired French General Jean Valluy to lunch in Paris. He was a staunch Atlanticist, having commanded the NATO central front. I asked him if he knew de Gaulle. "*Mais oui!*" he replied, "We were at St Cyr together." Having gone this far, I gulped and asked, "What do you think of him? "*Il est un bon acteur, mais la pièce est très mauvaise!*" (He's a good actor, but the play he is producing is very bad!). With the French sometimes on the sidelines, NATO solidarity persists. But it is strange that my fellow bureaucrats in Washington, for the most part, could not in the 1950s see a disjuncture between an Atlantic Alliance of Europeans and North Americans and their preferred partnership concept—with a politically and economically united Europe at one end of a dumbbell and the United States at the other end, sorting things out as best they could but with no way to break voting ties or devise a joint policy when one partner demurred. Nor could they seem to understand the major contradiction between an Atlantic-wide integrated political/defense policy and a bifurcated dual set of political-economic arrangements.

I had encountered the partnership idea between 1956 and 1958 in Washington and didn't much like it. I (and some others) greatly preferred the concept of a strongly united Europe at the core of a wider Atlantic community, with a sharing of policies in various fields, accomplished by a multinational elite operating common institutions. I was a minor proponent of a pragmatic policy, which was graphically articulated at the Bruges conference in 1957. The two concepts—Atlanticism and partnership—were argued at some length as to which should take precedence; Frøde Jakobsen, Danish MP and wartime resistance leader, hit this nail smartly on the head: "Let us unite whatever can be united, whenever it can be done, and not worry too much about the symmetries." In Appendix A, I have included some charts that show this process as it happened institutionally, as the new organizations developed over several decades from loosely organized cooperation to a high degree of integration—from a tight nucleus of European powers starting with the Benelux union to a NATO, an OECD bringing Japan, Australia, and New Zealand into the equation, and an OSCE that now involves countries far beyond Europe proper and North America.

In Brussels, I became much better acquainted with J. Robert Schaetzel, the Department of State official who had been such an avid proponent of the Monnet-Ball idea of an Atlantic dumbbell. In fact, in later years I came to believe that Schaetzel was effectively the spider at the center of Monnet's U.S. web, although George Ball and Robert Bowie seemed to be the main ones who laid out the strategy. (More about them later.) Schaetzel had been given a Rockefeller Foundation grant to take a year's sabbatical (1958–59) from his Washington duties (where he had dealt with mainly nuclear energy matters) to see on the ground what would happen when the two new European Communities emerged into the sunlight and to get a sense of what U.S. policy should be for future relations with the growing European amalgamation. He had a desk in USEC but was technically "on sabbatical" and not attached to our mission. However, Ambassador Butterworth and the chiefs of our various divisions regularly consulted Schaetzel. Several years later, he became ambassador to the Communities himself, after guiding the branch of the Bureau of European Affairs in Washington that dealt with regional European matters. He had as much influence, I think, as any single individual in bringing the partnership idea to fruition.

Parenthetically, another young Foreign Service officer, Stanley Cleveland, at the time the political officer for the U.S. embassy in Belgium, just down the street from our USEC offices, was also playing a crucial part in the thinking that helped to mold and advance the Monnet ideas. Cleveland tried hard to convince me that partnership should come first, major Atlantic interconnections later. He (and his two brothers, Harlan and Van) were important players in the postwar development of European policy; Stan in particular was close to Monnet and his coterie. Most unfortunately his diplomatic career was cut short just at the time when he might have made his greatest contributions.

Schaetzel—sometimes with Cleveland and others, sometimes alone—and I had many long conversations, sometimes over lunch of *Waterzooie* or *Carbonnade* and other favorite Belgian dishes. I argued the case for pursuing a strong Atlantic course and a strong European course simultaneously; Bob vigorously took the "two pillar" side, no holds barred. I recall saying to him once, "But suppose in a few years there is a strong United States of Europe (as Monnet had begun to call it) and then the European and American pillars try to pursue common policies toward the rest of the world, to sort out the future together? How do you know that the arrangement won't be as unstable as a two-legged stool?" He was sure our basic interests and Europe's were sufficiently congruent to obviate that kind of impasse, and besides, the European publics and political classes were more inclined to like the "third force" idea, that a Europe equal to the United States could stand up to us or to the USSR, as required. At any rate he was ready to take that chance. Furthermore, he and Cleveland too clearly did not like the idea of a politically strong Atlantic community; I believe now that they were typical of many who simply could not face the implications of some sacrifice of American sovereignty for a greater good, or at least felt that Americans were far from ready for that sort of upheaval (and maybe they were right in this connection).

It is noteworthy that Robert Schaetzel, around 1960, persuaded the Foreign Service Institute (the training arm of Department of State) to feature the European Communities and their relationship to the United States in its curriculum. At that time, it was considered an honor and a privilege for most FSOs to look forward to careers that would deal with the new invention of supranationalism. Unfortunately, when I inquired twenty years later, it seemed that few aspirants for ambassadorships cared about the uniting of Europe, or NATO, that much: most wanted to shoot for an embassy in a major country. Multilateralism as an ideal was fading, or so it then seemed.

Schaetzel and other Europeanists in later years helped to keep the Atlantic Institute afloat (of this, more in the next chapter), but the ways and means for doing this and keeping relevant U.S. foundations and NGOs on board in a common effort were to some extent a bone of contention. Schaetzel, more than any other individual, did a great deal to keep Monnet's ideas alive, as a possible guide to multinational integration on different planes. In the 1980s he formed an American Council for Jean Monnet Studies. Unfortunately, the inevitable demographic changes of our times brought forth little younger leadership for keeping perennially good ideas of the 1940s to 1970s alive and evolving. Schaetzel's Monnet group quietly went out of business. One day, while writing this book, a friend in Washington sent me a short paper Schaetzel had written, calling for a vast new effort, public and private, to bring Europeans and Americans together to share problems and "best practices" of modern democracies for solving them. This, he reasoned, would help the peoples of the North Atlantic region see how much they have in common; perhaps this could help bring us back together. His idea was amazingly like the one I floated to Secretary Dulles in 1956 (see chapter 4) for a broad NATO effort to show our peoples how much we needed each other, not just geopolitically or economically, but in the ramified work of making our societies think and work better and creating better world models.

A conversation I had in London in the early 1960s with Max Kohnstamm, Monnet's right-hand man, illustrates the differing perspectives of Europeanists and Atlanticists, a wholly unnecessary tension, in my view—both then and now; there was a solid middle way, perceived by only a minority of active thinking people. I told Max that inasmuch as the European states and North America considered their defense interests inseparable (this perception remained strong until at least the end of the Cold War), and as both had so much in common in economic and political terms in facing the world, why didn't it make more sense to proceed with a much stronger set of Atlantic arrangements? And, I said, nothing would preclude strengthening the core (a European entity) more quickly than the bonds that tied the whole. However, I argued, the end result should be a very strong Atlantic Community. Max demurred, as I expected, saying (and I quote him nearly verbatim): "If the huge United States were able and willing to break itself up into, say, four independent states, then those states could combine on a more or less equal basis with France, Germany, Italy, and, eventually, Britain." Otherwise, he averred, if an Atlantic union were to comprise all the west European countries, plus a big, already integrated U.S.A., the latter would inevitably swallow up the former. The United States would dominate, just as Prussia had dominated the new German imperial union after 1871.

I argued that because the United States was a full federal democracy (unlike Prussia in the 19th century) and because any successful European or Atlantic union would have to be a federal state, using some parts of the 1787 U.S. constitutional model—with all constituent states having the same number of votes in an upper chamber and representation in a lower chamber on the basis of population—his "model" was a false one. Look at the United States today, I said: Just because California and New York have much more population than other states, neither dominates American politics. Nor has a modern federal Germany produced domination by its larger constituent states.

The Europeanists however came to dominate U.S. policy for years, especially when George Ball left his private law practice to become under secretary of state in the new Kennedy administration (1961). Another factor was equally important in maintaining the cohesion of the Two-Pillar cabal in both Europe and the United States: Jean Monnet, who had pioneered the supranational European Coal and Steel Community, had decided in 1955 that he did not wish to continue as president of the ECSC's High Authority. He said at the time: "[T]he decision to transfer new powers to European institutions depend[s] on parliaments and governments. The stimulus would thus have to come from outside." Shepard Stone, head of the Ford Foundation's international affairs program (and who had been my big boss in Germany and who would be my boss again in 1965, when I joined Ford) believed Monnet was right and thus obtained generous Ford funds to subsidize, for many years, Monnet's new independent, multinational public outreach NGO, the Committee for a United States of Europe. The consequences of these two developments—Monnet's and Kennedy's commitments to a two-pillar transatlantic partnership—were profound.

Monnet's committee was like no NGO ever seen in Europe—or perhaps anywhere else—in its breathtaking concepts and its effectiveness. Monnet's tremendous prestige and proven internationalism (he was a man truly above the fray of any national politics) gave the committee a powerful launch. Ford provided the group with the wherewithal to hire an able multinational staff, people who had worked already with Monnet at the High Authority or earlier in Paris, when Monnet conceived the Schuman Plan. Other Monnet acolytes remained within the secretariats of the ECSC or the two newer Communities in Brussels, often in public information posts, with copious funds for telling the "European story."

The two main things that made the Committee for a United States of Europe work exceedingly well were, however: (1) the private contact work and idea-peddling, mainly done by Monnet himself, among the top political and trade union figures of Europe, enlisting their help; and (2) the continuous strong cooperation of the American establishment (including Stone and Ball), with its tightly knit and sizeable group of Two-Pillar advocates, such as Schaetzel and Robert Bowie, at the heart of the State Department, Henry Owen at the National Security Council, and others at key power centers. Monnet's staff did not conduct a large campaign to convince public opinion; that was done by the prestigious members of his committee individually, and generally by the more populist-oriented European Movement. Indirectly, the Communities' numerous and well-financed information offices helped, as did the U.S. government. Monnet chose the members of his Committee for a United States of Europe carefully, gathering in the top figures from all of Europe's main political parties (not cabinet members, but backbenchers and key opposition leaders, all with great influence), who made the news when they needed to but more importantly kept the governments in line, despite coalition changes. The Committee also included the principal trade union heads, but there were no matching industrialists and bankers; Monnet knew that most of these business elites were in favor of tight European integration anyway; including union heads was aimed at co-opting the Left, and this worked well. With Monnet's guidance and gentle prodding, his committee formed a model, powerful multinational lobby. And Ford Foundation money helped make all this possible.

The task of explaining the detailed ins and outs over two decades of the Europeanist Two-Pillar lobby is not mine; experts have done a much better job than I could. (See especially such books as Monnet's *Memoirs*, François Duchêne's admirable biography of Monnet (1994), and *Eisenhower, Kennedy, and the United States of Europe* by Pascaline Winand (1996). I try merely to give the flavor of how these great currents of history were, to some extent, manipulated by gifted and dedicated people, for a great cause, as seen from the vantage point of a distinctly minor actor, a worm's-eye view by myself.

Monnet's Legacy

In 2000, my wife and I undertook a rail tour of Europe, visiting people and places important in my past. In Paris, we stayed in a private club about 300 yards from the Porte Dauphine. On the corner facade of a noble *Empire*-style building in the Boulevard Flandrin was an historical marker, placed there by Michel Rocard, a recent French prime minister: "In this building, Jean Monnet, with a small staff, conceived and developed the plans for the union of Europe, 1958–1965." Monnet truly deserved every accolade he ever received. His ideas for promoting world peace were formed long before the advent of the European communities, between the two world wars and especially during the second. In May 1940, when he was a French supply attaché in London and the Germans had begun to overrun France, Monnet convinced Winston Churchill to make an historic broadcast to the French: Let us at once create an Anglo-French Union, with a joint cabinet, common citizenship and all that goes with it. This came too late to prevent a complete French collapse and could not be acted upon, but Monnet continued, when he went to Washington as a supply planner later in the war, to lobby for greater unity among the most natural allies, all of the Western democracies. In 1943–45, he floated ideas among the U.S. establishment for a "federation of the West," and when that did not quite fly, he modified his plans to fit emerging perspectives. During this time, he met Clarence Streit, the proponent of an Atlantic federation of democracies. But Monnet came to the conclusion, once the war ended, that one would have to start the nucleus of a world peace system in Europe.

My impression of Monnet continues to be that of someone who, while more than willing to work with whatever leaders and political materials were at hand, never lost sight of his real aim: facilitating the birth of a permanent peace system, based on democracy and gradual federation of the West and eventually the world. This vision, in the beginning years of the 21st century, seems much closer to realization than ever before, despite all fits and starts, ups and downs. Monnet's genius, for me, was his pragmatic approach, doing whatever could be done in a given political situation, but always willing to revise his plans, to broaden or narrow the scope of the proposed participants. This was not the case, however, with most of his cohorts, who concentrated on taking advantage of the short- and medium-term possibilities and who necessarily became locked into ideological rigidities.

The Euro-Atlantic Mafia

I choose these words carefully. In laying out the dichotomy between Europeanists and Atlanticists, I have necessarily simplified matters a good deal. I consider this "great debate" to have been to some extent futile, occasionally destructive, but for the most part one that pushed the Western world willy-nilly towards unity. Most Europeanists worked hard also for a stronger Atlantic set of arrangements; most Atlanticists accepted the European ideal and the Communities in particular as desirable in themselves and worthy of support, perhaps some day on a world scale. With a few exceptions, most of the people I worked with in the intense years 1956–63 (and after) were constructive "Euro-Atlantic citizens." A few examples will suffice.

Soon after arrival in Brussels in 1958, I met Curt Heidenreich, a German military officer who had resigned his commission to work for the new Euratom Commission and later for the combined Communities, in both Ottawa and Washington. Curt had served in the Luftwaffe in World War II. After the war, in a torn-up Germany, he made a career as head of personnel for the U.S. Army's Post Exchange system, the low-cost retail stores at which the American forces and their families bought all kinds of American and foreign goods that were not available in Germany at the time. When the new *Bundeswehr* was formed in 1955, Curt was called to the colors, ending up in Washington with a NATO military planning body, the Standing Group. His contacts with important Americans in the military, the Eisenhower administration, and the Congress developed quickly. He became something of an expert on nuclear warfare and — more important — an expert lobbyist. It was natural that he should be placed, in 1958, at the right hand of those who were guiding Euratom, the new nuclear energy agency (civilian uses only). Curt was delightful, full of ideas, and extremely open-minded. Dialogues with him were more pleasant than those with some of the Euro-ideologues; Curt was able to see clearly the complementarity inherent in the Europeanist and Atlanticist ideas. He was sent to Washington around 1960 to be the first European in the combined Communities office there, then went to Ottawa as the EC's chief of mission/ambassador to the Canadian government. Later, he finished his career heading the EC's Washington office.

A tiny glimpse of Heidenreich's broad vision: One day in 1958 he and I were riding in a Brussels taxi. The USSR had recently launched Sputnik, the first space vehicle, and I expressed concern. The United States had fallen behind. "Don't worry," Curt said to me, "Your country has the brains and drive to overcome their lead and win." It was mettle such as this that fortified many of my Euro-Atlantic compatriots in those chancy days.

In 1970, when I was starting some private "Mid-Atlantic Clubs" in London, Washington, Paris, and other cities, Curt worked closely with my other old friends in Washington to bring these informal discussion/ luncheon groups alive. As he grew older and infirm, Curt never lost his verve or appetite for constructive sharing of ideas; an "old pal" who was truly "an Atlantic man." Not long before he died, he bought an antique Messerschmitt fighter, a Luftwaffe mainstay in World War II. It had been kept in a barn near Gettysburg, Pennsylvania, "rescued" in the North African campaign from a German airfield by a GI who was subsequently wounded and sent home. The GI had convinced the captain of an aircraft carrier, carrying wounded Americans bound for Philadelphia, to ship the Messerschmitt, tied to the flight deck. Once in port, the GI took the plane home, but could never restore it properly. Curt hired some local mechanics and had been preparing to fly the old crate.

Another close friend, a member for years of the Monnet entourage, was a Cambridge don in medieval history, Richard Mayne. He and his first wife, Margot, had met as history students in early postwar Britain and gone on to embrace the cause of European unity. When the European Coal and Steel Community was set up in Luxembourg, Mayne became one of its publicists and later a Monnet strategist. After Monnet resigned as ECSC president, Richard served for a few years in the new European Economic Community (common market) in Brussels, where I met him. In my USEC public affairs role, our activities were quite compatible, indeed complementary. I learned a great deal about the inner workings of the Commission from Richard, he learned about U.S. policy towards Europe from me. We became great friends. Monnet had called Mayne to Paris around 1960, to become part of his tightly knit private team in the Boulevard Flandrin, where the visionary strategies for uniting Europe were under construction. Richard and Margot bought a delightful old cottage outside Paris; my wife and I were to see them often in the early sixties, when I was setting up the Atlantic Institute.

While studying at Cambridge, Mayne wrote a short article laying the Cold War East-West split at the door of the Council of Nicea (787 AD), when the early Christian fathers broke on doctrine, leading to twin late Roman empires and separate churches, one in Byzantium, the other in Rome. Byzantium's inheritor was eventually Russia, Rome's was Charlemagne, and so on. The 1950s border, wrote Richard, between the Soviet empire and Western Europe marked the demarcation (with a couple of geohistorical footnotes necessary, to cover Czechoslovakia and perhaps Poland and Hungary) between modern-day Western cultural-theological-political concepts—which had evolved towards freedom and democracy—and those of the Russian-dominated East. It was an eye-opening intellectual effort; Richard was, in the American parlance of the day, one smart cookie, always with a humorous twinkle in his eye as well.

In the 1970s, when the Euroatlantic theological wars were more or less over—or at least on a very different plane of contention—Richard Mayne was an editor of *Encounter*, a brilliant, UK-based journal (funded, it later developed, by the CIA) devoted mainly to sorting out, quite independently, issues confronting the Western world. I had always been sad that Richard had never spent much time in the United States; I felt it represented a lacuna in his development as a true "Atlantic man," a species representing a synthesis, or at least a broad understanding, of the two great, intertwined cultures of the modern West. He visited Washington and a few other American places now and then, but superficially, in my opinion. He once wrote an article for *Encounter* reporting on impressions drawn from an American trip; I was amused and yet troubled by his final conclusion: He breathed more easily, he said, when his returning plane set down in Europe, because he found that for all its diversity, the Europe struggling towards unity was "culturally" so much more homogeneous than were any similar ties between the United States and Europe. The United States was so "strange" that Richard felt much more at home back in the Old Continent.

I can't recall if I ever told him in person, but my reaction at once was, "Richard, do you really feel that Norway and Greece, for example, or perhaps Portugal and The Netherlands, are more culturally similar than is the United States, as a whole, vis–à–vis the entirety of Europe?" This question has stuck in my mind ever since, never expressed, as Richard and I sadly grew apart to a great extent. To me, the very political, civic, cultural, and religious foundations of the United States are part of the same bedrock of the European heritage. Our society and theirs grew out of common Greco-Roman-Judaic roots. We Americans are as much the inheritors of Anglo-Saxon-Germanic law, Charlemagne's empire, the Renaissance, the Reformation, and (especially) of the Enlightenment, as are the Europeans.

On the cultural and demographic fringes, various parts of Europe and different segments of American society diverge superficially from the dominant Western culture. (These divergences in the year 2005 may be somewhat greater, on both continents, than they were fifty years ago, to be sure, but the thesis still holds true, in my opinion.) On his American tour for *Encounter*, Richard Mayne saw the externals in America's pop culture and rather chaotic patterns of social behavior, whereas I have always looked more deeply for the common Atlantic roots of our political values and civic culture. We all vote for our leaders, and our civil rights are firmly grounded, protected by independent judiciaries.

This little story is important, because it shows how some European intellectuals (in a tradition going back 200 years and more) tend to look down on American popular culture and mistake the externals for the depths. Today, even though, to a great extent, both continents have merged their popular cultures and their commercial/industrial patterns of globalization, Europe's intellectual snobbism and America's disdain for European aristocracy (and for its socialistic, statist trends) persist. However, as global society is testing Samuel Huntington's proposition that the next phase in history will be cataclysmic conflicts between four or five great "civilizations," Mayne's and my argument (largely still in the ether) is pushed onto a much broader plane. Understanding what "the West" and its "civic culture" are, and how important they are, is vital to the survival of even civilization itself.

Another old friend, Raymond Gastil, has written an unpublished essay, "A Single World Civilization" (1993), contending that there are no longer a number of contending civilizations, but in reality one, emerging, *world* civilization. If so, how we understand it, explain it, and give it political and civic content is, for me, the great question of the age. We must find a way to render the much greater differences between, say Islam or China on the one hand, and the West on the other, compatible, mutually reinforcing, and converging. And we must find our own reinforcing ways to express the values of democracy and human rights in our national and international institutions. Otherwise, the world will almost certainly fall into a new set of conflicts, or one more great—and final?—one. I have striven, for almost my entire life, to help my fellow humans on this planet avoid this apocalyptic outcome. The guiding motto should not be, as the second President Bush has said, "Either you are for us or against us," implying, I fear, that the "us" is the United States. I believe the key questions instead should be, how best can we define the bases for harmony among the many cultures of mankind? How best can we define the common interests and goals of mankind and create a democratic, global, and yet diverse political culture?

Life in Brussels in the 1950s

These memoirs in the main concern the intellectual, cultural, political, and—to some extent—historical currents in which I was caught up, certainly without having planned it that way. I could never have dreamed in, say 1938 or even 1948, that by 1958 I would be, in a very junior—but as it turned out in some respects, strategic—position at the heart of Europe and the Atlantic community. But as diplomats also have families and personal lives, I thought I might here provide a little of that flavor of those years.

Not long before we left Washington for Brussels in 1958, my wife gave birth to our third child, Virginia, a daughter. In 1959, another daughter, Jean, was added to the family; her birthplace in a hospital in Uccle, a borough of Brussels, enabled her to choose, when she was 21, whether she wanted to be Belgian or American, a technical fact of life with respect to the children of many American diplomats. Both girls were lucky that we had as maid and handyman a Belgian couple, Lucy and Oskar, who lived in a small cottage on a property we rented in La Hulpe, a leafy Brussels exurb not far from Waterloo. Oskar and Lucy, from the small German-speaking enclave of Eupen-Malmédy in eastern Belgium, were great "supplemental parents" to our kids. Oskar built a rabbit hutch to enliven a corner of our garden, which the little girls particularly enjoyed. Mark and David, then 8 and 6, attended the American International School of Brussels and commuted by swift Belgian rail from La Hulpe station to suburban Boitsfort and back every day. On their train, a singular conductor befriended the boys, giving them old American comic books from 1944 and 1945, which he had gotten from GIs as they liberated Belgium. Good reading matter? My attitude was, as long as the material is relatively harmless, let them read anything and they will gradually develop a literary appetite for better stuff. Proved true, too, in later years.

My heart, since childhood, had always been in the Great Outdoors. Insofar as possible, I gave my boys an opportunity to sample Europe's woods, foothills, and streams. We often went on weekend expeditions in the forests of the Ardennes, where the bloody 1944 Battle of the Bulge took place, and on the Semois River, where Geoffroy de Bouillon, of First Crusade fame, had his castle, now crumbled. The boys acquired a love similar to my own for hiking and camping and the like; their little sisters followed later.

The International School spawned a couple of Little League teams, a juvenile pastime then in its U.S. infancy. Mark and David's grandmother (my mom), visiting for a few months, sewed Irish-green uniforms for them. This was kids' baseball, quite informal and barely organized, as it should be; now, nearly a half century later, the Little Leagues and the Babe Ruth

Leagues (for kids a bit older) have become the pawns of adults. I learned this much later, while living in a Seattle suburb, Bainbridge Island, in the nineties. On a nonprofit board, the local Land Trust, I had to contend with fathers who seemed to want to live their youth over—through their own boys—by creating, as nearly as they could, highly structured baseball leagues that mirrored professional baseball. One man, chairman of Little League on the island, lobbied hard for the planners of a new town park to include four regulation baseball diamonds, viewers' bleachers, night lighting, and "concessionaires' stands" where onlookers could buy hot dogs and other gustatory accoutrements! Most of this fun in my youthful days lay in simply batting the ball around and competing catch-as-catch-can with one's pals. When I was that age, a few boys used to get together on a vacant lot, mark out a rough diamond and, without any adult planning or supervision, undertake our own games.

Boy Scouts? When I was 12 or so, it was a pretty simple, mildly but clearly organized movement for kids who wanted outdoor skills and experience. Scout leaders hoped also to build something called Character. Sometimes we were lucky to get a scoutmaster who knew all the woodlore and other skills to lead us well. But sometimes the scouts had to train the scoutmaster! Often, as in the case of one troop I was in, the rookie scoutmaster eventually turned out to be a fine leader; his grandson much later became an Eagle Scout. But today, I fear that the modern obsession with technological gadgets and a general coarsening of our society (with TV and now the unbridled Internet at the root of it, to a large extent) have managed to dry up the pool of adults who are able and willing to lead kids in the outdoors, and to dry up sadly, as well, the dwindling cohorts of children who still think they might find joy in simple outdoor pursuits.

Childhood isn't what it used to be; my sons were lucky. My daughters too, although they reached adolescence in 1960s California, not always the best place for kids. All four children had enjoyed some fine beginning years in Europe: Belgium, Italy, England, and France for all of them, with a German add-on for the boys before their sisters were born. To learn three European languages, to attend kindergarten or school with European children, and to get to know other cultures at a rudimentary level is a blessing for Foreign Service kids. However, for diplomats posted abroad for long years with their families, there can also be too much of a good thing: children, and sometimes adults too become disconnected from American culture. This is also true of many families whose businesses send them abroad. This is a dilemma and a conundrum which can never be fully resolved. Yet on balance, I think many Foreign Service children, like mine, who now have their own children (and one a grandchild to boot), would say that their European experience was something they

wouldn't have missed. It's a good way to prepare kids for world citizenship, or something like it. As time goes on, I think we shall see more and
more of this growing together of world cultures, and the youth will lead
the way.

An Interlude That Became an Entire Career

I have recounted earlier the 1957 Conference on the North Atlantic Community in Bruges. Until I left Washington in the summer of 1958, with
the positive assent of my USIA superiors, I kept in close touch with the
organizers of that conference, to help them in any way I could to follow
up some of the recommendations that had flowed quite naturally out of
an extraordinary gathering of fertile minds. A couple of those minds were
somewhat more loony than fertile, as will usually be the case with a motley group of intellectuals and educators selected mainly for their deep
common interest in one thing. In our case, this singular thing was the nurturing of a community of values and purpose that spanned the Atlantic.
When I arrived for my new post in Brussels in July 1958, I told my ambassador, Walt Butterworth, about this postconference activity. I said I could
not easily break it off; besides I didn't want to because I saw great benefits
for the things I most believed in: strong ties embracing the entire West.
Ambassador Butterworth could see clearly the connection between my
duties on his staff, supporting the infant European Communities, and the
larger goal of a transatlantic community built around the European effort.
He gave me time to meet with the adherents of the Atlantic movement as
it had grown for the most part out of the Bruges meeting. When I was to be
away more than a few days for any such meetings, my superiors in USIA
and my embassy put me on leave, so that I could act independently.
     Some of my close new European friends were British. It turned out,
and has always been the case, that the relatively tiny but still influential
and pragmatic proponents in Britain of federal international union were,
like the Danish MP Jakobsen, ready to support any amalgamative scheme
that seemed practical and promising. Some of the British banded together,
in 1957 and 1958, with the "background" blessing (plus financial help) of
their government, to plan a major "Atlantic Congress" for 1959. The Congress gathered more than 600 leading people from all the NATO countries,
plus several—such as Sweden and Switzerland—whose governments es-
chewed NATO-flavored intergovernmental connections as damaging to
their neutrality, but who as individuals felt as strongly as any NATO in-
habitant that the long-term future of the West needed, at all costs, to be secured. One of these was Dr. Willy Bretscher, the editor-in-chief of what at

the time was probably Europe's best newspaper, *Die Neue Zürcher Zeitung*. The most outstanding Swede was Professor Nils Andrén, whose study of international security relations centered on NATO. Many of these and other extraordinary people, those still alive at any rate, are still my close and valued friends.

Douglas Robinson, the young federalist and brilliant organizer who had helped give birth to the NATO Parliamentarians Conference in 1954, was at the center of the planning for the Atlantic Congress. I helped Douglas and some of his federalist friends, David Barton and John Leech most especially, to work with other Europeans to bring prominent Americans to the Atlantic Congress and to fashion a conference format that might have a good chance of leading, at least in some cases, to substantial private or intergovernmental actions and improved public understanding of what was at stake in the transatlantic connection.

It was not especially helpful, incidentally, that Her Majesty's Government insisted on introducing at every stage (especially by means of the Congress logo) the idea that what was at issue were indeed three communities, represented by three interlocking circles, the European, the Atlantic, and the Commonwealth. The reader might guess that Britain was shown prominently at the intersection of the three circles as holding together a grand world vision. A major flaw in this conception was that Britain was not, at that time and still today, anywhere near as strong as she was before two world wars bled her dry, nor was she committed to a full part in the European community effort. The UK instead strove traditionally and for too long after 1945 to perform a balancing role, a vocation much out of tune with its modern capabilities or with the realities of world politics. "Great Britain," said Dean Acheson, "has lost an empire and not yet found a role."

At USEC in 1958 and 1959, our staff spent a great deal of its energy trying to torpedo (a strong word, but apt) the British plan for a European Free Trade Area, with which H.M. Government wanted to encircle—and dilute, or even strangle at birth—the new European Communities. The British did not, at this time, wish to apply for membership in the Communities (as they might have done, exercising a good deal of positive, experienced leadership) but at the same time did not wish to see the Communities succeed without them. This was a tangled question, but suffice that in the end the stratagem did not work: a few peripheral countries in Europe joined the British scheme but eventually virtually all of them, including the UK, faced facts and joined what we know today as the European Union.

Rather than a world of intersecting circles, I have always preferred the image of a series of concentric circles, with European union near the center and Atlantic and advanced Pacific nations in the larger circles. But despite the (to me) misleading logo, the Atlantic Congress went on anyway, and did much good. (In Appendix A, I have included a few charts that illustrate my concentric concept.)

Douglas Robinson and I both wanted, above all, to see the Congress give a strong push to the Atlantic Institute idea, as the conferees had conceived it at Bruges. We had enlisted some intelligent and reasonably influential supporters in 1957 and afterwards, but we needed many more if an institute were to come to life. With other Congress planners, we managed to reserve a place in the panoply of twenty-four committees and subcommittees for express consideration of the idea of a major, nongovernmental, nonprofit center of studies for the Atlantic community—what we then and later called the Atlantic Institute. Today it would probably be categorized as a multinational "think tank." We were able to enlist a distinguished Canadian career diplomat who was about to retire, Dana Wilgress, to chair the project's consideration at the Congress and—if the Congress decided to recommend further effort to launch such an institute—to lead the follow-up effort. Wilgress was a remarkable man whose last post was as Canada's ambassador to NATO. So he knew "where the bodies were buried," at least in the Alliance context, and he was about to retire. The rapporteur of the Institute subcommittee was a peppery young Belgian member of parliament, Lucien Radoux, who had been involved in a number of Atlantic NGOs and who had recently been *chef de cabinet* (chief of staff) to Paul-Henri Spaak, the distinguished statesman. Together with Wilgress and with me as secretary to the committee, we formed a good team. Spaak was one of those Europeans—usually from the smaller countries with no pretensions to great power status—who supported both the European and the Atlantic ideas with equal fervor and tenacity, and who saw no contradictions. As Spaak at that time was NATO's secretary general, he could not attend the unofficial Congress, but he nominated Radoux to work implicitly on his behalf, and was himself extremely helpful later.

I crossed the English Channel several times in 1958 and 1959, to give what I could to the Congress planning, always with my ambassador's OK. Then, from 5 to 10 June 1959, I attended the Congress, pulling strings and buttonholing delegates, mainly to advance the cause of the Atlantic Institute. Before plunging into the story of the Institute, which eventually came to life in 1961, let me set the scene for the remarkable Atlantic Congress.

London, June 1959: The Atlantic Congress

The full story of the Congress must be told by someone more conversant than I with the European scene at the time and with the genesis of the idea and the planning. I was a minor participant with a special axe to grind: to bring about a ringing endorsement by 600 eminent citizens from Atlantic countries of the idea of the Atlantic Institute and a resolution instructing the leaders of the Congress to bring it about. This was done, to my great satisfaction (and also amazement). The story of the Institute belongs to the next chapter. First, I want to set the scene for this London gathering, the kinds of people who participated, and what (beyond setting the Institute ball rolling) they accomplished.

In 1948, a 700-strong group of Europeans, similar in stature and influence to those who made the 1959 Congress "zing," came together in The Hague for a Congress of Europe, conferred for some days, and passed a series of resolutions that were eagerly grasped by citizens' groups and political figures around the Continent. Among the distinguished people present, Winston Churchill, Robert Schuman, Alcide de Gasperi, Paul-Henri Spaak, and Konrad Adenauer stood out; all were either past or future prime ministers of their countries. The idea of a "Council of Europe" was floated there, although, when the governments set it up, it proved a weaker institution than the progenitors wished. A number of educational institutions were recommended; the College of Europe in Bruges (where the 1957 North Atlantic Conference was later held) was an important outcome of The Hague Congress. Above all, the many younger people who attended went home and organized—the idea of the European Youth Campaign was one significant result. A couple of years later, French and German student members of the EYC met at a customs post between Strasbourg and Kehl and joyously, symbolically burned all the official French and German border barriers. This made headlines. Today, in the 21st century, people crossing most of Europe's internal borders never stop to show a passport or make a customs declaration.

A number of British federalists, some quite young in 1948, resolved later that a similar congress, with a wider, Atlantic net, should be held in London, to remind Europeans and North Americans of their wider loyalties. The idea of the 1959 London Congress was to chart out the future of NATO and the Atlantic community for the next ten years.

In my musty files is a "Programme for the Opening Ceremony," held on 5 June 1959 in the ancient Westminster Hall next to Parliament. The band of the Welsh Guards was to play from a balcony, starting at 9:20 a.m.; the entry of "the State Trumpeters, the Guards of the Honorable Corps of the Gentlemen-at-Arms, and Her Majesty's Bodyguard," and others beginning at 10:00 a.m. Then, at precisely 10:25 a.m., the "Arrival of Her Majesty the Queen and His Royal Highness the Prince Philip, Duke of Edinburgh," took place "at St. Stephen's entrance."

I was standing near the aisle as the queen, walking first, and Philip striding after her with his hands behind his back, went to the dais from which she was to speak. She was then young and appeared stately and consummately royal; the prince looked bemused as he cast his glance over the audience.

At this time, the leaders of the 600 delegates, including former heads of governments, members of parliaments, NATO officials, and many distinguished citizens, were presented to the queen. Col. J. J. Fens, a member of the Dutch Parliament and president of the NATO Parliamentarians Conference, then spoke a few words. This was followed by Her Majesty's speech. Her address was short, not especially memorable, but carefully crafted by her advisers (and, one suspects, by the Foreign Office) and completely appropriate. This was pomp and circumstance as only the British can contrive; I believe all present were deeply impressed. Thoughts of the two World Wars, of the gathering storm of the Cold War, of all that we had in common rushed through my young head. London was certainly the place to have done this.

After the formal opening, the Congress delegates repaired to Church House across a square to begin work. The Congress cochairmen, Paul van Zeeland of Belgium and Eric Johnston of the United States, did a marvelous job, with the keen help of Douglas Robinson and his staff of volunteers, to keep the meetings running well and on schedule. Johnston was an excellent choice; he had been head of the U.S. Chamber of Commerce and an economic advisor to Vice President Nixon, and at that time headed the Motion Picture Association of America. He hailed from Spokane in my home state; my father had known him, and he became an invaluable supporter of the Atlantic Institute. A newspaper report of the day indicated "the foreign press colleagues were greatly impressed by the lucidity of Mr. Johnston," who was quoted as saying that economic questions needed to take precedence over social ones in trying to help nations develop. (I'm not sure he was right, but the chicken-or-egg debate on development goes on today, more than four decades later.)

For five more days the committees and subcommittees labored and, in the end, presented a series of pretty cogent resolutions for all-Congress consideration. I was so busy lobbying, drafting and redrafting for the subcommittee on the Atlantic Institute that I had little time to concern myself with what others were doing. All delegates had some time for entertainment and social occasions, however; a gala evening (nearly as impressive as the queen's opening ceremony) was held in the great hall at Greenwich, with Royal Marines parading under searchlights on the greensward and another military band playing throughout a sumptuous meal. Diplomatic work at its most glittering and gratifying, I said to myself.

For the most part, Congress groups worked throughout each evening, hammering out resolutions. But one night, when work had overcome their alertness, all were invited to a special, surprise performance in Covent Garden of *My Fair Lady*, just beginning then to enchant audiences. Rex Harrison, Stanley Holloway, and the bright new ingénue Julie Andrews took the stage at 11 p.m., for their *second performance of the evening*. We were all tired, but the cast must have been exhausted; the effect was exhilarating and, again, showed British hospitality at its finest.

On 10 June, a final Congress plenary session produced a useful declaration, enunciating binding principles of the Atlantic community and calling the nations represented to extend their joint responsibilities further in "military, political, economic, social, and scientific fields." In most respects, the declaration continued the impetus of the 1956 NATO Wise Men's report, with a few new ideas floated.

A notable political proposal stated that "national governments should not take major decisions affecting NATO unity without prior consultation." It was understandable that this would have been proposed; egregious examples of this misdemeanor, including the secret Franco-British decision in 1956 to occupy the Suez Canal zone, were fresh in the delegates' minds. But how far from this principle the members of NATO have strayed in more than forty years! In 2001 and beyond, the United States was severely criticized by its allies for "unilateralism" with particular regard to its response to the 11 September 2001 attacks on New York and Washington. Although NATO's mutual defense clause, Article 5, was invoked for the first time by the Allies soon after the attacks, there was no truly multilateral military response (as, for example, in the Kosovo war)—the U.S. government seemed to pick and choose from among the "assets" of the NATO allies those which it deemed supportive of its own homegrown plans. This is not "prior consultation."

Many Atlantic Congress recommendations relating to closer cooperation, consultation, and integration were seemingly taken to heart later by NATO governments, although to attribute such actions mainly to the Congress would require much deeper study of what happened afterwards and more than this author can undertake. However, in two cases at least, rather precise proposals were formulated and were later acted upon, with considerable consequences.

The Congress recommended "[t]hat consideration be given to the possibility of transforming OEEC into an OAEC (Organization for Atlantic Economic Cooperation) in which all Atlantic countries would hold full membership." At the 1957 Bruges Conference on the North Atlantic Community (see chapter 4), one resolution had called for "an Atlantic Economic Community" as a "long-term goal." It was acknowledged that while the nascent European Economic Community (which did not begin operation until mid-1958) should be supported and observed, parallel developments on an Atlantic scale, and eventually "worldwide," should be undertaken. At the time, this seemed to me a proper course to chart: integrate Europe as closely as possible, extend Atlantic integration as soon as possible, and apply the lessons and practices globally, whenever possible. No one in 1958 or 1959 could foresee what would be accomplished by the turn of the century to come, but in many ways this scheme has been followed; the work of the World Trade Organization, the World Bank, the International Monetary Fund, the International Energy Agency, and many other bodies have brought the world much closer together economically. "Globalization" usually refers to the extension of multinational businesses over all continents, but the intergovernmental institutionalization of practices of governments that provide a framework for a world economy, while not complete, makes farflung financial and industrial processes work fairly smoothly. It is perhaps interesting to trace the development of the idea of an OAEC (OECD when it finally was born).

By 1959 it seemed clear to a few well-placed people that effective steps should be taken to promote Atlantic economic integration. One British delegate to the London Congress, David Barton of the UK, already thinking for months about this need, had proposed in 1958 to a loose, international private group of "thinkers and doers" called the Declaration of Atlantic Unity that its members should recommend the creation of an "Organization for Atlantic Economic Cooperation" (OAEC) to the Atlantic Congress when it met the next year. Walden Moore, the indefatigable "behind-the-scenes" man who headed the one-man secretariat for the Declaration group, acted on Barton's suggestion. The signers of the Declaration (close to 200 prominent political, business, and academic leaders from the NATO nations, including such luminaries as former president Harry Truman, future French president Valéry Giscard d'Estaing, Lord Franks and other British leaders, the Canadian prime minister John Diefenbaker, the noted economist Barbara Ward) updated their 1954 "Declaration" repeatedly to express new "Atlantic needs," proposing precise steps to governments. The Declaration group's constantly revised agenda for high-level lobbying was, to my knowledge, a unique operation for an NGO and highly effective.

Walden Moore persuaded his declaration sponsors that they should adopt the idea of an OAEC for flotation at the upcoming London Congress. This was done, in the form of a Petition to the Atlantic Congress, which was then studied, amended, and passed as a resolution by the 600 delegates. When the conferees went home, several of their leaders worked with their governments to fashion plans for a new intergovernmental body, along the lines of the OAEC proposals. In January 1960, the U.S. government, supported by others, proposed the idea of converting the existing OEEC, which had been the principal consulting mechanism by means of which Marshall Plan aid had been extended, into a body that would include Canada and the United States as full members. The new body was called the Organization for Economic Cooperation and Development (OECD), removing the Congress proposal's geographic limitations. This was of great importance in making possible the inclusion of Japan (a few months later) and still other countries far from the Atlantic basin, such as Australia and New Zealand and, in the 1990s, South Korea and Mexico. The OECD has developed into a major but little-known engine for economic ideas and collaboration among what are today known as "the industrial democracies." The international oil crises of the 1970s, for example, could probably not have been met successfully without the OECD; a new subsidiary body, the International Energy Agency, undertook studies and orchestrated joint members' actions that eventually surmounted the challenges, for at least a couple of decades.

It is unlikely that the Atlantic countries would have moved to establish the OECD—certainly not as quickly—without the public and behind-the-scenes pressures generated by the Atlantic Congress, in turn influenced by the Bruges Conference two years earlier, the Declaration of Atlantic Unity's prestigious members, and by individuals such as David Barton, who was creatively thinking ahead on his own. Isaac Newton is reputed to have said, "If I have accomplished any good, it has been through patient thought." Barton dreamed up his idea, which became OECD, sitting alone in his weekend cottage in Bosham, where Harold once waited, with no luck, for William the Conqueror's invasion in 1066, which eventually took place at Hastings.

The Institute Idea Flowers

In a quite different field of activity, the Atlantic Congress produced another set of recommendations that in 1961 eventuated in the establishment of a second body, an Atlantic Institute.

The 1957 Bruges conferees had used these words, among others, to describe what sort of "Studies Center for the Atlantic Community" was needed:

The Conference members agreed that the *basis* for community among the Atlantic peoples is present in their common strategic interests, their economic and social interdependence, and their shared cultural heritage. However a sense of community, which appears essential for sustained, joint political action, exists only among very small minorities within the Atlantic countries. Many important efforts to strengthen the sense of community are now being made, by both private and governmental organizations. These efforts suffer from the absence of a coordinating instrument.

The 1957 Conference "also noted the lack of any single focus for investigation of the urgent problems of the Community." The resolution expressed "the deep concern" shared by participants "that leadership capable of undertaking the common tasks of the Atlantic Community is not being developed." (These points echoed the arguments in my "midnight draft," given to key participants to seek international endorsement for an Institute (see chapter 4).

The final plenary session in Bruges, by unanimous vote, had endorsed the creation of a multinational, private Atlantic Institute and set forth its purposes, a plan of organization, and a recommended set of working methods: to act as a research agent and a clearinghouse for all kinds of research on Atlantic themes; to encourage development of new specialized institutions but also help to prevent duplication of effort; and to inform publics.

The standing committee that had organized the Bruges Conference in 1957 was given the task of further refining these ideas, finding funds, and putting the Atlantic Institute into operation. This daunting task proved to be too much for the steering group. Although a number of important people from academe, business, and politics joined the effort (chaired by Willy Bretscher), several meetings over the coming year and a half brought little in the way of concrete results. I met with the group several times, helped them draft explanatory papers, and organize a plan of fundraising. Again, my ambassador was generous in allowing me to commit time and travel to try to jump-start the Institute. But by early 1959 it had become obvious that more "elite firepower" would be needed to gather endorsements and, especially, to generate hard work by a larger group of eminent people from all key sectors of the Atlantic world, if such a bold and unusual proposal were to take wings. We also needed an office staffed by a professional and the wherewithal to undertake consultation in depth with these eminent people. They, and the money they could call on, would have to be enlisted.

It was decided by the post-Bruges standing group to cast its lot with the upcoming Atlantic Congress. Six or seven times as many people (and in general, even more important people than had gathered in Bruges) would be attending. If we could get the 1959 Congress's endorsement of the Atlantic Institute idea, that might serve as a much more promising jumping-off point.

With help from key Bruges participants and from the Congress organizers in London, I put together a special subcommittee of the Congress, led by Ambassador Dana Wilgress, with Lucien Radoux as rapporteur, to examine the Institute idea and, it was hoped, propose it to the entire assemblage of 600 persons for their endorsement. My ambassador, again, gave me special dispensation to work with the Institute group as its secretary, a task a bit out of the ordinary for a serving diplomat. But no one seemed to mind and I did my job with enthusiasm. Incidentally, I did not ask for, nor did I take, instructions from my government — which left me quite free to act and use my own judgment.

Result: The Congress subcommittee put a lot more meat on the bones of the Atlantic Institute concept handed to it by the Bruges standing committee; it produced a detailed report as to why and how the institute would work; and it requested "the members of the Preparatory Committee [those who had organized and directed the 1959 Congress] to appoint an ad hoc group to carry out without delay" a fuller definition of the structure, tasks, and methods of work of the proposed institute, and "to take any steps it may consider necessary so that the Studies Centre of the Atlantic Community may commence its activities as quickly as possible." This was a crucial point. We needed the most visible (and committed) sort of high-level leadership if the institute were actually to come to life.

A Declaration of London, headlining all the important work done by committees, subgroups, and the plenary of delegates itself was endorsed by all 600 participants on the final day of the Congress, 10 June 1959. Under the heading of cultural recommendations, this short recommendation constituted a mandate for the institute: "that a 'Studies Centre for the Atlantic Community' be set up, to serve as a clearing house and intellectual focus."

The delegates also laid down important principles (as, for example, that "the Atlantic community has a duty to help less developed countries to help themselves") and proposed a number of steps — some concrete, some less so — which should be taken by the members of the Alliance and which, because of the eminence of most of the delegates, could not be ignored by the powers-that-be. This kind of citizen initiative helped to "seed" public opinion indirectly and put before government leaders some ideas they could not afford to ignore.

The full text of the Declaration is included in Appendix B. The full report of Subcommittee A.3, a detailed resolution on the Atlantic Institute, presented to the Congress and adopted by it, is in Appendix D.

On the day after the Atlantic Congress closed, I went to Heathrow Airport to fly home to Brussels. By sheer chance, I sat next to Paul Van Zeeland, twice Belgian prime minister, several times foreign minister, and a prominent banker in Brussels. More important, he had cochaired (with Eric Johnston) the entire Atlantic Congress. Now, he and others on the preparatory committee were charged with bringing the Atlantic Institute to life. I introduced myself, said I had met him in the receiving line at the concluding Congress reception, and was particularly interested in what would happen to the Atlantic Institute proposal. He astonished and delighted me: "Ah! That is something which *must* be done!" I told him of my involvement in the genesis of the Institute idea, that I was attached to the U.S. Mission to the European Communities but hoped very much to help bring about the Institute, insofar as I was able. Before we landed in Brussels, Van Zeeland said to me, "You must come and see me next week in my office, and we'll talk about it." We made a date, which I later confirmed, and on 13 June I was ushered into his private office on the rue de la Régence. This was the beginning of perhaps the greatest adventure of my life.

9
The Atlantic Institute

1 March 1961: *President-elect Kennedy proposes creation of the Peace Corps of the United States. Done by executive order, "devoted to world peace and friendship."*

13 August 1961: *East Germany builds a 28-mile-long, 12-foot-high concrete wall separating East from West Berlin. Kennedy later announces in Berlin: "Ich bin ein Berliner."*

Issues Facing the Atlantic Community, 1960

The peoples of NATO and a few other countries whose governments were politically neutral, such as Sweden, Switzerland, and Austria, but whose people in their hearts and minds were (most of them subconsciously) part of the Atlantic West—what we call the Atlantic community—seemed beleaguered in the late fifties. Although Stalin had died in 1953, the Cold War was still being waged on all fronts. It seemed sometimes, to many in the know and to publics in general, that the West might even lose out to the USSR. Also, when I was serving in Washington in 1957 the Soviets inspired (no doubt directed) the Polish foreign minister Rapacki to put forward officially—and with great propaganda flourish—a plan bearing the minister's name. In essence, if the West had agreed, the Rapacki plan would have brought about German reunification, but only on condition that Germany would become a neutral like Switzerland and leave NATO, thus fracturing the nascent unification of Europe. Ideas like this could be dangerous, especially at a time when the general public, and many intellectuals who should have known better, did not entirely understand what was at stake.

The launching of the first Sputnik in 1957 had been an even more vivid clarion call to action, plain evidence for all to see that the USSR was running ahead to conquer space before the United States could get there.

Those who attended the 1957 Bruges conference were able to articulate these fears and issues. This proved helpful, especially in laying the intellectual underpinnings for the Atlantic Institute. The Bruges concerns were shared by others, in places high and low. But my journals, old clippings, and especially old correspondence that I have kept reflect how unclear most people were about the importance of the historical and philosophical ties that underlay the North Atlantic Treaty. The fact that several countries, such as Turkey and Portugal, were signers of the Treaty but were in the fifties anything but well-functioning democracies made for anomalies that undercut the unity of the West. Nor were the voters and political parties in such countries as France and Italy all that certain about the virtues of democracy, further enfeebling a weak European system, in the view of many, that had not prevented two world wars or much improved the lot of the working populations. The massive Soviet Agitprop machine knew this and played on these fears and uncertainties.

That is why, within officialdom, political circles, and the mass media of the NATO allies, one could sense a palpable concern for the lack of understanding and of general commitment to key principles of Western civic life, indeed of spiritual values, that formed the only fundamental basis for the Atlantic Alliance. While fear of the Soviets was real, a positive belief in the rightness of the Western cause was uncertain. Many serious people saw the dangers, but also the opportunities, of building a solid, broad commitment to the idea of a community that stretched across centuries of history of the fight for freedom, and across the North Atlantic geographically. Such people were more than willing to attend the many gatherings held in these years. The push for European unity was part of the West's response but was not sufficient. The work of the Congress for Cultural Freedom was more than worth the money and effort, but its coterie consisted mainly of intellectuals. Moreover, the CCF dealt with the philosophical issues dividing West from East, as well as the questions that divided Western intellectuals ideologically, and did not specifically or sufficiently link philosophical questions with the vital political and economic questions of the day.

The Bruges conference and the Atlantic Congress of 1959 stand out as landmark efforts to rally relatively large numbers of deeply serious—and in many cases, especially at the London Congress—prestigious and practical people with clout in politics, business, education, diplomacy, and the trade unions. Due to the exceptional organizing abilities of Douglas Robinson, the now-annual NATO Parliamentarians Conference was also seized with the same questions: How could the NATO countries (and their parliaments) meet the crisis of the spirit that characterized the deepest conflicts and searchings within the Alliance? How could the distinctly negative Cold War consciousness be turned on its head to find positive reasons for efforts to unify the West? The work of these two gatherings, above all, turned on practical steps to unite the Atlantic countries' "hearts and minds," as the popular cliché went.

One might sum up the challenge in 1960 by saying that the peoples of Western Europe and North America lacked a sufficient *sense of community* to insure that NATO and other institutional arrangements (including the beginnings of the EC/EU) binding them together would be more than ephemeral. This delicate job was advanced, to a significant extent, by the Atlantic Institute and various other NGOs and governments working together; but today—in the 21st century—one cannot be sure that the feeling of transatlantic community remains sufficiently strong to withstand the several changes of generation and the worldwide pressures, many quite new, that face its peoples. This task has to be done all over again, and in different ways and on a larger scale.

The Declaration of Atlantic Unity had been signed by more than 200 leading statesmen of the NATO countries not then in office but who would in most cases be politically active again later. The Declaration focused the attention of governments on the lack of psychological and practical unity within the NATO world. Walden Moore, the Declaration group's director, was unceasing in his efforts—parallel to those of Douglas Robinson and the Bruges and London conferees—to help bring about the establishment of an Atlantic Institute to address these needs on a broad front.

Earlier in the 1950s, several international meetings had recommended establishment of "Atlantic Studies Centers" and the like, but their calls were hardly clarion. I knew little of these earlier proposals when I awakened with the thunderbolt in Bruges, September 1957. Bruges plus London put meat on the bones of the ideas and set in motion a determined and tenacious effort.

Regrouping Forces to Create an Atlantic Institute

It was against this geopolitical/geopsychological background of the times, and with the relatively new and more powerful influences that had been generated and concentrated at the London Congress firmly in mind, that I returned in mid-June 1959 to my duties at USEC in Brussels. M. Paul van Zeeland had invited me to meet with him as soon as I could; I hastened to do so. Lucien Radoux, the Belgian MP who had performed deftly as the rapporteur of the Atlantic Institute subcommittee in London, joined us in van Zeeland's office at the Banque de Bruxelles, as did the ever-resourceful

Walden Moore, who just "happened" to be in Brussels at the right time. Van Zeeland, Moore, and Radoux asked me if I could act as the "executive secretary" of a new organizing committee which would try to give birth to the Institute, standing on the shoulders (so to speak) of the London and Bruges conferees. I agreed, providing that the request to USIA for my release would come from the organizing committee and not from me.

I must explain that these new (and ultimately successful) efforts did not just spring out of the blue, although van Zeeland's commitment was wholly new, unforeseen, and most fortuitous. During the Bruges conference I had had an inkling that perhaps the Institute project could be the most important thing I could take on, perhaps ever. After the Bruges conference in 1957, I had shared with Robert Strausz-Hupé, Walden Moore, and Douglas Robinson the idea of my becoming a "coordinator" of sorts for the effort. This would require some sort of release from USIA and government duties, perhaps an extended leave of absence. They were all enthusiastic, although I'm not sure the College of Europe crew were keen; the Rector of the College, Hendrik Brugmans, in this case sadly a minimalist, entertained the possibility that Institute-like activities could begin at his College in Bruges and "gradually," with time, eventuate in an independent Institute. Others — in or near Princeton, in Canada, Paris, London, eventually Milan, and elsewhere — hoped that *they* could grab the Institute idea to enhance *their* particular programs and interests. This was probably proof of the catchiness of the Institute idea, but it also made for pressures and counterpressures that sometimes caused considerable difficulties.

Van Zeeland swept all this aside: we would begin anew and independently. We agreed on a plan of action. Van Zeeland was marvelous at this. He had the broad political and international experience of a foreign minister, a prime minister, and a practical banker to animate him. Among other things, he had been the youngest Belgian prime minister of the century, taking office in 1935 at the age of 35.

We first asked a group of academics with practical experience in the wider world of public affairs to draw up a new prospectus for the Atlantic Institute. They met for two days in September 1959, producing a greatly improved statement that built on the work of the Bruges and London conferences, fleshing out a somewhat nebulous idea.

It is worth mentioning the kind of people that we (with the help of Douglas Robinson and Walden Moore) were able to recruit for this effort at delineation:

G. E. G. Catlin, professor of political science at McGill University in Montreal. A noted philosopher and former confidant of FDR, he was a British subject but truly international in his perspectives.

Thomas Searls, head of the British Council, the main arm of the

UK's official, vast cultural exchange programs. He carried weight in the Parliament, the Foreign Office, and among influential private groups.

Frank Munk, professor of political science from Reed College in Portland, Oregon, then on leave as academic advisor to Radio Free Europe in Munich. Frank had fled his native Czechoslovakia in 1939 to settle in the United States. He was later to become the first Research Fellow of the Atlantic Institute and in 1963 a charter member of the Committee on Atlantic Studies, which I later started.

Arnold Bergstraesser, head of political science at Freiburg University and soon to be director of the research institute of the German Association for Foreign Policy. He had left Germany when Hitler came to power, had had a fine career at the University of Chicago, then returned to his native country after WWII. He had helped me organize student exchanges in Nuremberg in 1952–53.

Léo Moulin, professor of political sociology at both the Free University of Brussels and the College of Europe, later at the Sorbonne, and a brilliant man of broad interests. (Among other things, he had written histories of the Jesuits and also of European cuisine.) He was the only holdover on this group from the Bruges conference of 1957.

We immediately sent this group's new improved prospectus to about sixty important people from both sides of the Atlantic and asked them to meet in Brussels on 16–17 October 1959 to form the "Provisional Committee for the Atlantic Institute." The 35 activists who "signed up" consisted mainly of persons who had attended the Atlantic Congress, plus several others that van Zeeland, Radoux, Moore, Robinson, and I thought ought to be involved. A few were vital holdovers from the Bruges Conference (such as Willy Bretscher, Mary Lord, Jacques Rueff, Adolph Schmidt), but for the most part this new cast of activists was composed of fresh recruits, who together thickened and flavored the old mixture appreciably: each informally represented his or her own country, plus either the business community, the trade unions, political forces, or thinkers — some from academia — and other "free-standing intellectuals."

Paul-Henri Spaak, by then secretary-general of NATO, attended and spoke his piece eloquently. An important new face was that of Charles Spofford, who had been America's first permanent representative to NATO's North Atlantic Council. The NATO Parliamentarians were represented by Dutch MP Col. J. J. Fens (who had convened the London Congress), Gen. A. Béthouart of the French Senate, and Dr. Kurt Birrenbach of the Bundestag. Professor Bergstraesser also participated in this meeting; he was to prove an invaluable colleague for the next few years; more than anyone else (except possibly van Zeeland) Bergstraesser knew exactly what the Institute should be, and could be, in all its dimensions. The indispensable Walden Moore was also present, speaking little in the meetings but undertaking his customary catalytic role in the corridors.

The New Provisional Committee Begins Work

Paul van Zeeland was elected chairman of the Provisional Committee; Radoux was made chairman of its steering group, and I was named the steering group's rapporteur. Van Zeeland explained to me that this title would mean much more to Europeans than something like "executive secretary," which was, in those days, the usual Anglo-Saxon nomenclature for the fellow who "pulls it all together." When I would call on foreign ministers and other dignitaries (which I often did), "rapporteur" would give me the right status and entrée. He was right, as in almost everything.

Spofford returned to Washington immediately after the meeting and arranged through the Department of State for USIA to give me up to a year's leave of absence without pay to work on the Institute project. My ambassador agreed to these arrangements and I said goodbye to him and my colleagues in USEC, not without some regret. I was once again a private citizen. I began my leave effective 1 November 1959 and plunged into implementation of the Provisional Committee's plans for the coming six months, including drafts of the all-important budgets for the Institute (income as well as outgo; where would the money come from, and what would we do with it?). Adolph Schmidt, the director of one of the Mellon charities in Pittsburgh, was able to announce that Mellon would provide a year's funds for the preparatory work, including my salary.

I located a tiny Brussels storefront at 20 rue de Commerce for the equivalent of fifty dollars per month rent, borrowed some old furniture from the U.S. Embassy, employed a bilingual secretary, and we began. Between mid-October and May of the following year, our steering committee — with me doing most of the legwork — would (a) obtain endorsements from highly placed figures in the NATO countries; (b) sound out key people to serve on the Institute's eventual governing board; (c) develop illustrative program plans and budgets for the Institute's initial years of operation; and (d) obtain pledges for as much money as possible from a variety of sources, not just American. This was a tall order, but I entered into the project with great enthusiasm; it is amazing what reserves of energy a younger person (I was then 37) can draw on! I saw the Institute as a potentially great engine to help resolve some of the consuming issues of our age, and potentially the best possible vehicle for my own personal contribution of time, effort, and conviction.

Van Zeeland, whom our little Brussels circle always addressed as *Monsieur le Ministre,* was my greatest source of encouragement. When I was not on the road, I would see him nearly every day in his curious, ornate old office at the Banque de Bruxelles, just around the corner from the Royal Palace. His principal ability (among many) was that of cutting through to the heart of any issue and of finding solutions that (according to my journal of the time) "are neat, reasonable, and amazingly satisfactory to all concerned." He also knew how to motivate colleagues. When, a year later, despite a great deal of our work having been accomplished, we still were not able to declare the Atlantic Institute open for business, my journal again records van Zeeland speaking at a meeting of principals:

> "You know, very often the difficulty of what we are trying to do overwhelms me and I become a bit despondent about it. But then, at the end of a busy day, Mr. Radoux and Mr. Huntley come in with fresh ideas and undiminished zeal, and I am strengthened in my conviction. I say, 'if they can go on, so can I!'" Time and again, I have presented problems to [van Zeeland] which seemed to have only two alternative solutions. Again and again, he has found a way to draw the advantages from both courses of action and still accomplish what had to be done. He is never at a loss to state his own opinions, and yet he always listens to others and accepts their advice when it seems wise.

Later, van Zeeland told me personally: "It's a pity you are not Belgian, for if you were, I should never let you go." That's a fine way to make a young man blush and virtually stagger with contentment!

If I had to pick one person without whom the Institute could never have become a reality, it would be Paul van Zeeland. He had immense devotion to the West, great political skills that often turned hopeless meetings into triumphs, and monumental patience. His great dream was that the Institute might become a kind of "Academy of the West," a place where the seasoned minds and older statesmen (like himself, and he would have been perfect) could commune and find touchstones of unity for us all, in many different fields. The Institute turned out to be a somewhat different thing, and different as well from what I had in mind. Perhaps a half dozen truly great minds could have formed the collegial group van Zeeland dreamt of, but although we involved most of them in various ways, we never got this level of concentrated intellectual firepower sufficiently mobilized. Nor did any of our successors at the Institute in the quarter century of its existence.

Perhaps our major stumbling block was power seeking, which I began

to realize in these years is the most common human failing—especially no-
ticeable among elites, and pseudoelites, who yearn to be ever more important. It was not that the great majority of our adherents were not idealistic;
it was simply that place seeking was also a common trait in all but a very
few. In spite of all I could do, I was blindsided often by such behavior and
learned, sadly, a great deal in the process. I also found a truly great mentor
in Paul van Zeeland, who showed me how to navigate around such human obstacles, as well as many others, and who was not concerned with
his own position but solely with the great task at hand.

Within a few weeks of beginning our tasks, I began to realize that
Lucien Radoux was, unfortunately, one of the power seekers and also (for
himself) a money seeker. Undoubtedly, some side conversations (of which
I was not aware) had taken place at the October meeting when we had
formed the Provisional Committee between Schmidt, the source of our
initial funds, van Zeeland, and possibly others. Radoux was named chairman of the Steering Group. He and I began to meet often with van Zeeland
to plan strategy. Radoux indicated that the office he ran (a European Centre for Cultural Exchanges) alongside his parliamentary duties was "at the
disposal of our group." It soon became clear that Radoux would get a fee
from the Provisional Committee's small budget for his work as the Steering Group's chairman, some money to pay a secretary, and a paid post
for a young man named Jean-Claude Baudoux. Most of this *alimentation*
(literally, feeding) of the budget of Radoux's Centre proved quite unnecessary to our work, in fact even hampered it at times. But as I would at that
time have done almost anything to see the Institute project forge ahead, I
did not demur. Of Radoux, my journal recounts: "He's a smooth, even oily
politician, a socialist who appears hardly to believe in his socialism but at
the right time dons it like a cloak."

On later reflection, I believe that van Zeeland wanted fervently to
keep Spaak involved and also stay on his good side with respect to Belgian politics, just in case the two of them should ever play a public Belgian
role again. They were of opposing parties (van Zeeland a Christian Socialist, Spaak a Social Democrat) but had often worked together in coalition
governments, at times with van Zeeland as prime minister and Spaak as
foreign minister, and vice versa. The new twist to this interesting spectacle
of continuing rivalry tempered with carefully calibrated cooperation was
the Institute project. We, and van Zeeland, needed Spaak; Radoux's paid
engagement was the price. And I must say that Radoux himself had a
good deal to contribute to the cause, by way of practical political wisdom
and many useful high-level contacts, everywhere, it seemed. Although he
and I often had disagreements, we stuck together because we both believed in the ultimate goal.

Van Zeeland provided his own contribution to the "staffing muddle" in the person of Jacques Pirenne, the son of the great Belgian historian of the Middle Ages, Henri Pirenne. Middle-aged Jacques, insofar as I could tell, held a sinecure as an economic researcher for the Banque de Bruxelles; van Zeeland, for his own reasons, brought him into many of our deliberations. He was not paid, at least not from our A.I. organizing budget. Nor was this burden much less weighty for me than was the *équipe Radoux*, but I think I won Pirenne over and neutralized most of his sometimes wacky but well-meaning ideas. All this was like pouring sand into a gearbox, but we progressed nonetheless. We were able to find more oil than sand, and eventually clean out the sand. But more was to come, constantly, from fresh sources.

I also learned to know our other great Belgian, Paul-Henri Spaak (although not as well as van Zeeland). He was more famous internationally than van Zeeland; he left the NATO secretary-generalship during our A.I. organizing days and remained one of our first governors. He liked to preface little speeches in English, by telling his listeners, "People say I speak English like Charles Boyer and that I look like Winston Churchill. I only wish it were the other way around!"

Refining the Institute's Mission

The Provisional Committee held its second meeting, to review what had been accomplished and what remained to be done, on 1 and 2 April 1960. I was able to report good progress on many fronts. In the new statement of purpose that Radoux's Steering Committee laid before the parent group, whose job it was to actually bring the Institute into being, the proposed Atlantic Institute was described as "an instrument for concentrating the intellectual resources of the Atlantic countries," in order to

(a) determine the practical applications of the values on which the common civilization of the Atlantic countries is based;

(b) identify and define the critical issues affecting relations among the Atlantic nations and relations between the Atlantic and other nations or groupings;

(c) relate expert knowledge to the solution of these issues and promote relevant applied research;

(d) enlist the sustained attention of influential persons to the development of an Atlantic consensus on such questions; and

(e) anticipate and assist the planning and action of governments and other responsible authorities by virtue of the imaginativeness and soundness of the Institute's recommendations and the strength of its ties to leading sectors of the public.

To emphasize what the Institute was to be, and what it was not to be, the following words were appended: "The Institute is not an agency of mass communication, nor is it the spokesman for any partisan views or special interests. It is dedicated to the independent development of common views which may form the basis for more closely coordinated polices among the Atlantic nations."

Headed by these statements, a prospectus was printed in French and English, and in the summer of 1960 a small action group headed by van Zeeland began formation of the permanent Board of Governors. Legal steps were taken to incorporate the new body. The action group was especially charged with finding a director general (their minutes called for "a man of state") to head the Institute once it could be activated. National representatives were chosen, each with the mission of raising his nation's share of the Institute's first five-year budget. The carefully selected Board of Governors held its first meeting on 12 December 1960.

One month later, the annual meeting of the NATO Parliamentarians Conference adopted the latest of several resolutions urging the Institute on. During the plenary debate, Canadian MP Robert S. MacLellan gave his opinion of the importance and role of the new Institute: "The Atlantic Institute will be a pool of our cultures; it will be an instrument to help us share our legacies of the mind as we share our material wealth. It will stimulate trade in thought among us and other regions. Possibly our future and theirs will depend more on our trade in thought than our trade in ores or manufactured goods."

As one looks at these words at the beginning of the 21st century, one is tempted to view them as prophetic: in the end, the "trade in thought" between the West and other cultures will be decisive, providing it involves the truly valuable philosophical and practical essence of the West, and less its cultural dross.

Before a new board could take actual charge, certain practical steps were necessary. My work was more than cut out for me. Country by country, with the help of a great many kindred and dedicated souls, I built the necessary financial and human infrastructure, using every personal connection available. My job was orchestration.

The Essential German Involvement

On 25 April 1960, I attended a large dinner at the home of Professor Bergstraesser in Freiburg. We had consulted often on the Institute project and he wanted to introduce me to the "the key to German participation," Carl-

Friederich Freiherr (Baron) von Oppenheim. The baron, who headed a prestigious Cologne banking house, had been an intimate and trusted confidant of Chancellor Konard Adenauer ever since *der Alte* was Ober-buergermeister of pre-Hitler Cologne. The baron was also on close terms with Christian Democratic leaders and the captains of German industry. In 1938, as a Jew, he saw clearly where Hitler was heading and left Germany for South America. I learned that his gentile banking partners had protected von Oppenheim's holdings until 1946, when it was safe for him to return to Germany. His bank was again, by 1960, an important power-house in the German economy.

A similar scenario had saved the Hamburg branch of the prestigious Warburg banking family. These events, in which non-Jews helped to save the businesses of their Jewish partners, are largely unrecorded in accounts of the times, yet they show dramatically the decent side of many Germans.

On the evening in question, in Freiburg, Bergstraesser excused himself from the dinner table during "brandy and cigars," motioning von Oppenheim and me to follow him. We entered the professor's study, the two of us sitting in deep easy chairs while Bergstraesser remained standing. A tall and imposing man with an old fraternity dueling scar across his cheek and one eye missing from the Great War, Bergstraesser turned to Oppenheim, literally pointed a finger at him, and announced: "*Herr Baron*, I want you to hear this young man explain one of the most important new projects of this century." I gulped, and then set forth the idea of the Atlantic Institute, and how we and the Organizing Committee were poised on the threshold of bringing the new institution to life. Bergstraesser then said to Oppenheim, "*Herr Baron*, this is something for which we must organize powerful support in Germany. The future of the West is at stake, and this Institute could help immensely. I want you to take the lead in Germany." The baron asked a few questions, to which I responded, with Bergstraesser interposing his comments from time to time. Within a few minutes, the seeds had been planted. The professor suggested we rejoin the party, but not before von Oppenheim had invited me to visit him soon in Cologne.

My every encounter with the baron proved fascinating and productive. A couple of weeks after the Freiburg dinner, I found myself at the Oppenheim Bank, in the shadow of Cologne's war-battered cathedral and close to the Museum of Ancient Roman and Germanic Antiquities. This was to be the first of several memorable visits over the years. I arrived precisely at 8 a.m., was ushered into a private waiting room, and then to a private dining room. Von Oppenheim, an ever-present aide, and the director of the German Council of the European Movement, Dr. Walter

Stahl, entered. We sat at a round breakfast table laden with rolls, cheese and jam, cold cuts, juice, and coffee. Bacon and eggs were served, while Oppenheim contented himself with a Cuban cigar and a large Coca Cola; this breakfast-hour timing and attendant gustatory regime were invariable at all our subsequent meetings but one, a crucial encounter which I shall describe later.

Now, without the quietly intimidating presence of Professor Bergstraesser, the baron took charge and posed questions that had occurred to him since the evening in Freiburg: Who are the people behind this Institute thing? Why do we need it? How will it work? What will it cost? It was obvious that he wanted to hear the basic idea reiterated, to give me a chance to earn his confidence, and to have Dr. Stahl (whom I had met several years earlier) also get the gist of what was going on. It was a successful meeting, leading to still more encounters, and most particularly with Dr. Kurt Birrenbach, head of the Thyssen steel corporation and the Bundestag's foreign affairs committee, who, with van Zeeland, became for me another "hero of the Atlantic Institute."

Eventually, after many months of work and interchange of ideas, we (the German team and I) were ready for the "Big Push" — an evening in November 1961 with the heads of the great German companies and banks and the Federal Republic's foreign minister, Heinrich von Brentano. By that time, Henry Cabot Lodge had become director general–designate of the Institute. In Oppenheim's drawing room, Lodge was able to obtain a firm, substantial German pledge: five years of collective support from Germany's business heads. Lodge charmed those present by leading off in his fluent but very basic German; it turned out that as a child he had had a German *Kindermädchen!* His French, by contrast, was colloquial and excellent.

For me, this had been a fascinating process, methodical and thorough in the usual German way. Once we had received a commitment from the captains of industry and (indirectly) the Federal Republic cabinet, German support never wavered. The Institute could never have seen the light of day without sustained German financial, intellectual, and moral contributions. These continued for 25 years, until the Institute's "untimely death" in 1986. German support delighted the Americans, emboldened the French, and gratified all others, great and small.

Lining up Further Commitments

Armed with first-draft plans for the Institute and a firm prospect of German support, I spun around Europe and North America by train and by air, enlisting prime candidates for the permanent Board of Governors, obtaining pledges of financial support (in return for budget oversight), discussing how the Institute would work, and developing a consensus among key governments and big shots in the private world.

In The Netherlands, Col. Fens introduced me to other parliamentarians and sent me to see top figures in industry; one of the most fascinating was the head of Philips Electronics, who spun a huge globe in his office and talked geopolitics. I also gained the support of Herr de Graaf, head of the largest Dutch bank. Jerome Heldring, editor of the *Rotterdamse Courant*, became a key supporter. The American embassy in The Hague was a goldmine of support and ideas; I had learned to know Patricia Van Delden, the embassy public affairs officer, in the late fifties. A brilliant woman, she had married a Dutchman who folded her into the wartime underground. She was a genuine hero to the Dutch. Perhaps, like only a handful of Resistance veterans, she knew exactly what the stakes were in the Europe of the 1950s and 1960s. Pat pushed me in the direction of the sometimes-skeptical Dutch elite; if I could convince enough of these people (which I did) of the need for an Atlantic Institute, I could convince almost anybody.

France was another matter. De Gaulle had come to power and obtained wholesale revision of the French constitution. Yet his views of the Allies and of NATO had not yet publicly surfaced in full. Old-timers in the Parliament, including Robert Schuman, Maurice Schumann, Michel Debré, and Antoine Pinay, all favored the establishment of the Institute, provided it would be located in Paris! An eminent French adherent to the cause, since the beginnings in Bruges, was Jacques Rueff, a world famous economist and more recently a judge of the new European court in Luxembourg. Some retired French generals were enthusiastic, including Pierre Billote (who favored a full-blown Atlantic federation à la Streit), Antoine Béthouart, and Jean Valluy, former commander of NATO's central front.

A notable recruit from the French economy was Emmanuel Monick, head of the Banque de Paris et des Pays-Bas; with Jean Monnet, he had urged Churchill in May 1940 to propose the still-born Anglo-French Union to the Daladier cabinet. Monick had also written a book with Michel Debré, published clandestinely during World War II, which advocated an Atlantic Union, not unlike Streit's proposals. It is ironic that Debré later became prime minister under de Gaulle's Fifth Republic and turned 180 degrees, at least in public, to the Gaullist "France first" policies that then became fashionable; a close American friend, who was our public affairs officer in Debré's constituency, assured me that privately Debré was much more welcoming to America and its ideas. When the Atlantic Institute was finally set up, in late 1961, de Gaulle's "France first" policy was a major reason why the Institute's governors had agreed unanimously that its seat must be in Paris.

Adriano Olivetti, head of the noted office-equipment firm, was our spearhead in Italy. He had kept the small Bruges-Philadelphia interim committee in business financially for three years and never lost his faith in the Institute idea. Through his top public affairs man in Rome, Paolo Rogers, we obtained money and a pledge of office furniture and typewriters, which we were able to call for when the Institute began its work. Most unfortunately, Olivetti died early in our effort. Another Italian stalwart was Ivan Matteo Lombardo, chairman at the time of the fifteen-nation Atlantic Treaty Association. Professor Gerolamo Bassani, director of the Istituto per gli Studi di Politica Internazionale in Milan, caught a ring on the Atlantic Institute merry-go-round early and helped to enlist other Italians and, for a time, provided interim quarters so that the Institute could start its substantive work.

Without the British, we might never have had an Atlantic Institute. Col. Walter Elliott, an MP who had served as head of several cabinet ministries, helped us in the early days; he was chairman for a time of the NATO Parliamentarians. His untimely death left a British vacuum on our Provisional Committee for the Atlantic Institute; most fortunately, his widow Kay (of the formidable Tennant family) stepped into the colonel's shoes with nary a misstep. She was created a life baroness and could thus serve as one of our supporters in both the NATO Parliamentarians Conference and on our Provisional Committee. A unique source of advice was Lord Salter, who had been in charge of Allied procurement in the First World War and a top official in the Second. Continually supporting our efforts, and joining the initial Board of Governors, was Sir Geoffrey de Freitas, MP, one of the founders of the NATO Parliamentarians Conference.

Later, Sir Gladwyn Jebb—newly created Lord Gladwyn—joined us. He had been UK representative to the UN Security Council and, just as we were forming the Atlantic Institute, retired as ambassador to France. In all of this, Douglas Robinson played a formidable behind-the-scenes role; in each major country one person had to manage Institute affairs "behind the curtain," as the Germans would say. In other words, ministers of governments and other public worthies always required someone hovering in the background, providing them with facts, ideas, clerical facilities, and often reminders. In Germany, Dr. Walter Stahl played this role superbly well. My job was to orchestrate the whole, through these behind-the-scenes sparkplugs and their principals.

The backers in the United States were a formidable team. They included the new secretary of state, Christian Herter (who replaced John Foster Dulles at the latter's death in late 1959), and a great list of former ambassadors and heads of agencies such as the Marshall Plan (most notably William C. Foster, one of the great public servants of the period) and military commanders, including General Lauris Norstad. With the help of some enthusiastic businessmen who joined with Eric Johnston, we were able to orchestrate timely financial support. Mary Pillsbury Lord, appointed by Eisenhower as a U.S. delegate to the United Nations General Assembly and mother of now-retired Ambassador Winston Lord, gave unstintingly of her time and enthusiasm.

We encountered problems getting medium-term U.S. funds (pledges of three to five years), especially from the Ford Foundation; in later years, when I joined the foundation staff and still later, when I was able to read what various key people had put into both private and public print, I was to realize that Ford's Shepard Stone and his associates, including John J. McCloy, the former High Commissioner in Germany and advisor to presidents, had all put most of their available money and effort on Jean Monnet and his ideas. They considered the Atlantic Institute as somewhat of a sideshow, no matter what I and others more highly placed could say. When the Institute finally began its work, Ford made a rather reluctant grant but then proceeded — with others and behind the scenes — to steadily shift the Institute's objectives and program in the direction of supporting a two-pillar Atlantic partnership, which Monnet and his American and European cabal desperately wanted and which I could not forestall. More of this later.

In early 1960, I was preparing for a trip to the United States to gather in more worthies and more pledges of money. On my departure, my "boss" van Zeeland instructed me to try hard to get a letter of endorsement from Vice President Richard Nixon. We both knew that to get Ike's written backing was extremely problematical. The White House under Eisenhower worked much like a general staff: one did not bother the commander-in-chief with small matters. And in the scheme of things, the Institute was still "small pickings." Upon my arrival in New York, Mary Lord (who had been one of Ike's early political supporters) jumped enthusiastically at the idea of a Nixon letter. She immediately tried to telephone Charles McWhorter, Nixon's chief aide (who had been at the London Atlantic Congress). McWhorter reached Mrs. Lord the next day, by which time I had flown to Ottawa and Montreal. My concierge said, "Phone Mrs. Lord in New York"; I did so and learned that McWhorter was more than agreeable. "Could you," Mary said, "sit down right now and draft a letter that would go from the Vice President to M. van Zeeland?" I did so immediately, and sent it by express to Mr. McWhorter.

A few days later, my business in North America done, I returned to Brussels. On entering my tiny goldfish-bowl office fronting on the rue de

Commerce, my secretary, Mlle. le Boeuf, said, "Oh Mr. Huntley, you must go immediately to M. van Zeeland; he wants to see you." So I trotted down to the bank and was ushered into our chairman's office. His face was alight with pleasure as he handed me a letter. "Just look at this!" he said, as I noted the letterhead: "The Vice President, Washington, D.C." It went on to say what a wonderful idea the Institute was, etc., etc.—just what we had wished for. I could see at once that neither McWhorter nor Richard Nixon had changed a single word of the draft I had sent them! Of course I didn't explain this to van Zeeland, who said—still rather excitedly (unusual for him): "Now here's what you do. Please go back to your office and draft a reply for me to Mr. Nixon." So I did. And van Zeeland changed not one iota of *that* letter!

I'm sure that many bureaucrats and emanuenses have encountered such moments. Of many small events like this was the effort to create the Institute made up. Van Zeeland received similar letters of endorsement from such leaders as Hugh Gaitskell, the British Labour Party leader; Joseph Luns, foreign minister of The Netherlands; Lester Pearson of Canada, one of NATO's "founding fathers"; and Adlai Stevenson, who said he would make an exception and serve on A.I.'s board.

One such incident, involving bureaucracy and major figures, centered on Secretary of State Christian Herter. I was on close enough terms to address him as "Dear Chris," but knowing he was extremely busy, I sent my letters (and those of van Zeeland) to Professor William Yandell Elliott, who had attended the 1957 Bruges Conference and was now on leave from Harvard as a special assistant to Secretary Herter. But we had trouble with the professor, who was (1) terribly impressed with his importance in this strategic spot; and (2) imbued with his own rather precise ideas as to how the Atlantic Institute should be set up. After both Bruges and the London Congress, we had sent Bill Elliott plentiful drafts to show how the Institute idea was evolving. He had continually provided us with a stream of comments (increasingly authoritative as he moved into Mr. Herter's office). We seldom had replies from Herter, but Elliott purported to give us the former's observations. This was a problem: Elliott, almost from the moment of Bruges, had insisted that the Atlantic Institute should be the modern counterpart of King Arthur's Knights of the Round Table. His letters were full of imagery that might serve as tenuous links with that distant mythical past and the present day. I believe Professor Elliott envisaged himself as one of the putative knights!

Finally, as the shape of the Institute neared closure, I was able to see Mr. Herter myself. He agreed to become a governor of the Institute, depending on the outcome of the 1960 elections, which Mr. Nixon lost. Herter played an important early role in the Institute, although I was in no position to dissuade him and others not to put together in 1961 a Washington-based NGO, the Atlantic Council of the United States. I could see that this latter effort might eventually compete with the Institute. Ultimately this happened, which is a later—and tragic—story.

Ambassador L. Dana Wilgress, now retired in Ottawa, was my chief counselor in pulling together Canadian memberships, including his own, for the board. In 1961, he sent me to Vancouver, B.C., to interview H. R. Macmillan, the head of the fabled timber empire, Macmillan-Bloedel. Wilgress had let him know beforehand that, above all, I came to ask for money. "H. R." invited me to his gracious home for dinner à deux (he was a widower) and plied me step by step with questions, some of which were not easy to answer ("How do you know this will succeed? What *exactly* are you going to do with money? Why?" and so on: questions that, chicken-or-egg style, might not be answerable until the A.I. was a going concern. As I rose to say my goodbyes, I was sure my mission had failed. As I started to go out the door, H. R. asked, "How much money do you want?" Primed by Wilgress, I said, "$25,000 a year for three years, sir, if that will work." It did, and he became a staunch governor.

All in all (with strategic help now and then from our committed supporters), I contacted about 200 leading citizens of the Atlantic countries within a year. Their ideas, in almost all cases, were folded into our plans and—by a critical mass of such people—pledges of money were given.

As the Institute later began work, the basic documents approved by the Provisional Committee in April 1960 underwent many changes, but they served as a crucial sort of scaffolding: Supporters wanted to know what they were "buying" by giving money and time, and by lending their names.

Creation of the Board of Governors

Van Zeeland and a small group were constituted as the initial governors in the summer of 1960 and instructed to swell their ranks by co-option. Some of the early board members had great hopes for beginning work in Paris by the end of 1960, but this proved unrealistic, especially in view of the long July-August (and sometimes September) vacations of many principals and of the kinds of people who held foundation and corporate purse strings. Therefore, by 12 December 1960, when we held our first regular Board of Governors meeting, everyone wanted to begin work proper, but the full funding we needed to make certain we could survive for a reasonable period of time was not yet in hand.

Professor Gerolamo Bassani then made an impassioned speech to the board: Why don't you go ahead and *begin* the Institute's work right away, as you would like, but do it with a reduced, provisional staff and budget? And place the Institute's temporary headquarters in Milan, in *my* Institute, the ISPI?" Some sleight-of-hand, to which I was again not privy, had gone into this offer. The board agreed. In hindsight and on balance, this was probably a useful step, as it offered to the outside world an illusion (an *optique* as Bassani put it) that we had at least agreed to get under way, and perhaps show some actual substantive, or programmatic, accomplishment. But problems ensued.

The formal legal steps were taken, and in January 1961 the Institute was launched, under French law as an *"institut d'utilité publique"* — the equivalent of charitable, nonprofit status.

The Institute's Potemkin Village Period

Readers will no doubt recall the marvelous set of wood and canvas façades that Catherine the Great's minister Potemkin erected on the banks of the Volga to convince visiting statesmen from Europe, on a drifting voyage down the river, that Catherine had indeed accomplished the feat of creating many new villages for her subjects in a short period of time. The river was large, and the notables' boat never touched land on the wide river, so the sham was perpetrated.

The establishment of our Institute, for its trial voyage, was in most ways a Potemkin sham. To be sure we had a small staff. Bassani was to be interim director-general, a problematical position; Jean-Claude Baudoux (Radoux's minion) and I moved our families from Brussels to Milan or environs; we employed Miss Frances Sutton — just resigned from the U.S. Foreign Service — as our head of administration. With Bassani's often questionable "help," I hired three Italian secretaries, more or less bilingual; I looked for language and secretarial skills. Bassini insisted above all that they also not be *"senza cultura,"* which I took to mean, safely upper middle class in secondary schooling, taste, and dress. We agreed on these hires. The girls all had *cultura*.

We could not handle things without the equivalent of an office boy, so we hired a nice fellow named Luigi, about 60 years of age, who had recently migrated to the north from Sicily and was without work. Luigi told me that in Salerno he had been a tailor, so I gave him a chance to earn some money on the side by ordering a suit from cloth I picked out. It turned out reasonably well and was cheap, but a couple of years later it began to fall apart at the seams; Luigi had saved money with poor thread. But he was a pleasant chap and helped me learn Italian; the *cultura* girls corrected his pronunciation and added to my vocabulary. I was too busy for formal lessons or a regular "native speaker," so I worked with a book, *Italian for Foreigners*, given me by my Paris friends, the Mayneses.

Bassani's quarters were truly beyond imagination to a young American. The ISPI occupied the grand (but not huge) old Palazzo Clerici in the center of bustling Milan, just a few steps from the famed La Scala. The Palazzo had four main floors, all entered from one grand staircase that was built around an old medieval courtyard.

The ground floor consisted of the ever-present guardroom (where visitors registered), a garage or two, and low-level logistics offices, built around the 15th century. Above were the ISPI administrative offices in quarters added in the 16th century; Professor Bassani and ISPI brainpower were concentrated on the 17th century layer; last of all, in a musty set of unheated offices, we, the proto–Atlantic Institute staff, were quartered in the 18th century. But we had our new gift of Olivetti office furniture and typewriters and some heat—in the form of four or five antiquated electric space heaters. My small office had a Rococo ceiling with a smiling cherub; Baudoux had a splendid little chamber with gold-plated walls and lots of mirrors (it was said that it had been the bedroom of Napoleon III during his invasion of Italy). But the crowning glory was the great *Aula*, the room of state. About 150 feet long, its ceiling was a masterpiece by Tiepolo, painted around 1750, depicting the Four Continents (Australia was not yet recognized as a continent on its own). I could pry open one door of my office, and there was Tiepolo's masterwork, with aborigines and allegorical figures of all sorts strung together, and a few odd arms and legs—plus a monkey on a chain—hanging sculpturally out of the edges of the paintings. Even when frigid air encompassed me, I had only to open that door to charge my antiquity juices.

It turned out that neither our quarters nor the efforts of Professor Bassani were without charge (as we had been led to believe). Bassani received his stipend for months; later we were charged rent, too. As the "keeper of the flame" I had begun to learn that backroom political deals were daily bread for Europe's movers and shakers: the Board of Governors wanted a place to "open the Institute for business" and Bassani's offer was the only one on the table. Later, it proved difficult to extricate ourselves from Milan, when we were ready for *real* business in Paris.

Rural Italy, 1961

I brought my family down from Brussels and ensconced them in a crumbling but charming old villa in the village of Cuvio in the Italian sub-Alps,

not far from Lago Maggiore. Once the home of some minor Italian gran-
dee, it rented for a pitifully small sum and plunked us right into the middle of rural life. There were wild forests and mountains just beyond the
edge of town, where Mark and David (10 and 8) ventured with Luigi and
Antonio, brothers who farmed and welcomed company on their woodcut-
ting expeditions, complete with oxcart, which the boys were allowed to
ride. The brothers had one tractor in those days (which Mark and David
were sometimes permitted to drive); most farm tasks were, however, still
done by hand. The boys were home-schooled; their small sisters, Virginia and Jean, roamed the private park attached to the villa, watched over
by Gina or Agnes, who helped out with house chores and babysitting.
In a corner of the park, a previous owner had built a grand swimming
pool surrounded by amusing stone statues. A mountain stream that ran
straight through the pool provided running water, bereft of any warming
mechanism! Quick in and out, and only in summer.

I settled the family in Cuvio because I didn't want to expose them to
Milan's filthy air. Country life was good for them. But it meant that I had
to spend three hours each day on an (also unheated) ancient train, commuting to Milan; that too was an adventure, stopping at all manner of
little towns. Tiring for me, but also fun. I managed to get a good deal of
work done en route.

One night in Cuvio, we had just gone to sleep when a commotion
stirred outside; it sounded like men screaming invectives. I looked out
from a small balcony onto the crossroad, lit by one tiny electric bulb. There
stood the Town Communist and the Town Fascist, hurling drunken curses
at one another and—it seemed to me—about to engage in fisticuffs. This
had gone on long enough, I thought, so I said, in my still rudimentary Italian but in tones as authoritative as possible, "*State tranquilli, per favore!*"
("Be quiet if you please!") The two men stopped, looked up aghast. Then
one pulled off his cap and said, in poor but unmistakable French, "*Regar-
dez-moi, Monsieur! Je suis le vrai type de la rue!*" ("Take a good look at me,
sir! I am a true street type!") I nearly fell off the balcony with suppressed
laughter. Why in French? Although we had met a few townspeople, rumors must have been rife as to our origins, and my Italian did not conceal
my foreignness. Our Ford auto, with Belgian plates, must have suggested
to these worthy denizens that we were Belgians, hence their magnificent
effort at *opéra bouffe*.

I found a little time to prowl the town myself, looking in at a public yet
commercial establishment known as the *Circolo*—the Circle—equivalent
of the town bar in France or a pub in England. In fact it was the only place
where men could go to get away from their wives of an evening. Given the
mild climate, much time was spent under the adjacent plane trees, playing

bocce, the Italian version of *boules* or English lawn bowls. The pubkeeper always tried to shoo everyone out at midnight, but it took the political pair an extra hour or so to get as far as our house, given their inebriated state, and to demonstrate real Italian street life.

I was also able to become a friend of the village priest (and thus further to exercise my Italian). He was a kindly man and sufficiently worldly to look at some of the *Circolo* comings-and-goings with amusement. He helped me understand village life from a new angle; in some ways, he reminded me of the then-popular novels about a village priest and a town Communist mayor: Don Camillo and Peppone. These characters were built into a marvelous French film, in which the great horse-faced French comic Fernandel played the priest, who always found a way to compromise subtly with the mayor for the good of the town. Communism and the Church, in a way that only Italians could invent, managed to coexist in those years. Karl Marx and any non-Italian pope would probably have revolved at a great rate in their graves!

Ten years after our yearlong sojourn in Cuvio, I took David, one of my sons—by this time nineteen—on a nostalgic visit to Cuvio, by way of much of the rest of Europe. Without warning, we knocked on the door of Antonio and Luigi's farmhouse; when the occupants all realized who we were, they were ecstatic, calling *"Ecco, Davide!"* and insisting that we come in for glasses of powerful *Grappa* (something akin to aquavit or Schnapps—every European country has its own version). The farmers proudly showed us their new machinery, which by this time could have been characteristic of a small American farm. They told us how they were now one of only two farming families left in Cuvio; a decade earlier there had been thirty-eight, and now Antonio and Luigi and one other farmer had bought up all the land and so had much bigger, more productive and lucrative farms. "What happened to all the farmers?" I asked. Simple, they had all gone to work in Cuvio's new shoe factory, which we later toured.

This was a striking example for me of how the entire economic and social life of Europe had been changed by the Marshall Plan, and by the intelligent work of Europe's and America's technicians, working together. Between the 1950s and 1970s, European life, and above all its politics, had evolved remarkably. Some things will always stay the same, I suppose, and some parts of Italy (for example) had to struggle many more years to become reasonably prosperous. I was able to see such changes all over Europe in the seventies and eighties and was glad to have played a small part in the transformation.

On the Road Again: Setting the Stage for Emergence of the Think Tank

No one in those days used the expression "think tank" but that's what we were about. All the new governors of the Institute wanted a truly multinational, semischolarly but politically oriented gathering place for the smart economists, political scientists, philosophers, and experienced governmental movers and shakers of the Western world. It was my job to continue to pave the way, by seeking more finances, endorsements from top-flight people, and—most important—increasingly precise ideas as to how the Institute should work, and what its priorities would be.

As soon as we had a working staff in Milan, I again went on my rounds, crisscrossing via planes and trains around Europe and to North America once more. One memorable encounter took place in London. It was a normal English February, with gray skies and chilling fog. My friend Dr. Dee Myers, the U.S. cultural attaché at our London Embassy and a noted American historian in his own right, took me to visit Professor Arnold Toynbee, the great inventor of the "challenge" theory of the rise and fall of civilizations (*A Study of History*). At this point, Toynbee was well into his eighties and wrapped with a shawl; Dee and I joined him around the typical coal fire of those days, our fronts baking and our backs well chilled. (Having been in London on many previous occasions, and knowing this visit might last a while, I had taken the precaution of wearing my long underwear under my business suit.)

Getting Toynbee's blessing for the Atlantic Institute idea could be of great value to us. I began by reminding Toynbee that he had written an extraordinary article not long after the war for Henry Luce's *Life* magazine, in which he likened the Europeans to the ancient Greeks (who couldn't get it together because of their interminable petty squabbles and fixations on internecine power politics), and the Americans to the Romans, who came along to rebuild Greece's polity within the new Empire. Toynbee's article made everything come out just fine, because he saw the Americans as much more benevolent and democratic than the Romans. He foresaw the rejuvenation of the West in the cause of freedom. Toynbee had also put some of these ideas into a later book, *Civilisation on Trial* (1948), in which he looked to a unified Atlantic community to sort things out for the good of mankind. I explained the idea of the Atlantic Institute, inferring that he was one of the spiritual fathers of the idea.

Well, that's all well and good, said Toynbee, and perhaps it will work. But I've been having some doubts about how things are going these days. His wife (a much younger, bright woman whom he had married in later life) spoke up. She had not sat down with us, but was hovering, in a heavy wool sweater, around the backs of our chairs. "Arnold," she said, "you know that you worry about the developing countries, and what the West is doing to them." Toynbee turned his white mane upwards toward her, and responded, "To be sure. That bothers me a good deal." Mrs. Toynbee continued, " Isn't there a danger that if we create still one more Western organization, even if privately based, it will make the underdeveloped nations feel even more that the West is 'ganging up' on them?" As Toynbee nodded his assent, it seemed clear to me that his mental powers were not as before, and that his new wife coached him in ways that were comfortable to him, and to her.

I replied to the Toynbees (as I had become adept at doing, because the question often came up in various places): " We know that the less-developed countries need to make up for decades or centuries of neglect and in many cases for the injustices of colonialism. They require education in modern ideas and methods, infusions of capital and technical assistance in order to catch up with the modern world. But they have little chance of doing so if each Western country tends to go more or less its own way in dealing with them. It is only through a much closer kind of unity in the West that the combined resources necessary to help the rest of the world can be put to work properly." I pointed out that the new OECD, just begun, was formed in large measure to insure that the worldwide problem of development would be tackled by the richer, more developed West, together. (It is ironic that when OECD was formed, the United States was by far the largest giver, per capita, of such aid; today it is one of the least generous, by this measure. The U.S. government had urged OECD's creation in 1960 precisely to try to encourage Japan, especially, to make an appropriate contribution.)

Further meetings in London and elsewhere followed. As the summer of 1961 wore on, the Institute's American governors, with the support of their British counterparts, began a serious effort to recruit Henry Cabot Lodge, the former senator and Nixon's vice presidential running mate in the failed elections of November 1960, as director-general. Lord Gladwyn, already on the Institute's board, was a close friend of Lodge's from their days as representatives to the United Nations and helped to convince the senator that he should take on the job. I conducted Lodge on a tour of key countries, so he could begin to understand what needed to be done and whom he would have to work with. In October, the Policy Committee met with Lodge at NATO headquarters in Paris, to hammer out an agreement. Lodge said he wanted only $1 a year salary, a rental apartment in Paris, and a car and driver; readily done. But the exact nature of the job required a good deal of discussion, as did the reaffirmation of the Board of Governors' intent to site the Institute in Paris. This latter point was unexpectedly contentious, and again as the result of some backroom shenanigans. During this crucial meeting with Lodge, an emissary from the secretary general of NATO, Dirk Stikker, handed me a note: "Mr. Stikker would like to see Mr. Lodge at once in his office." I passed this on to Lodge who, at this moment, was engaged in some delicate negotiations with his prospective employers; he scribbled on the note: "Tell him later," which I conveyed to the emissary. The latter said Stikker couldn't wait, so I told Lodge I would go see the secretary general and explain.

I had little chance. Stikker, who had been Dutch foreign minister and who, along with the secretary general of OECD, had been made an ex officio governor of the Institute, asked why Lodge couldn't come. I told him the Policy Committee had offered Lodge the director general's job and they were deep in discussion. "Mr. Lodge will be happy to see you in about an hour, when the meeting should finish." Stikker exploded. Why had he not had a chance to discuss these matters earlier with Lodge? And why was the board so fixated on Paris as the permanent Institute seat? He—Stikker—had understood that there were already offices in Milan; weren't these good enough? I pointed out that from the time of its first meeting, the board had firmly decided on Paris and that Milan had been only a temporary arrangement during the organizing period. Stikker was furious. Our interview ended. I felt humiliated, as I hardly knew the man and believed he was taking out his annoyance on me, a virtually unknown subaltern.

Later I found out the source of Stikker's displeasure: First, Bassani and most of the Italian governors had quietly been lobbying to keep the Institute in Milan. Second, they knew (which I and most others did not) that Mr. Stikker owned a villa on the shores of Lake Como, near Milan, near that of Adenauer, and that Stikker would soon retire there. As a governor of the Institute—and possibly its future chairman—Stikker could indulge himself with a pleasant hobby in his retirement. If the Institute established itself in Paris, Stikker would have presumably no influence, as his ex officio status would end when he would retire. By the time I returned to the conference table, all had been settled; Lodge merely smiled, Mona Lisa–like, when I told him about the Stikker meeting; he left the SG hanging. This occasioned some unpleasantness, but was no real obstacle in our path.

On 8 November 1961, a press conference was held at the Hôtel de Crillon in Paris to announce Lodge's appointment formally. The *Christian Science Monitor* quoted him as saying: "Our ideals need stating. We have done better on weapons than ideas." In his concept, Lodge told the reporter, the Atlantic Institute would be an "idea factory," a clearinghouse of the best thinking of private Western leaders. All of this was designed to increase cooperation among the nations of the Atlantic Community. The

Paris *Herald Tribune* also quoted Lodge: "The Institute will conduct studies to clarify and suggest solutions to the problems of world society. We plan to sponsor public forums and conferences to encourage discussion of our findings."

Lodge meant what he said; he quickly energized the entire Institute as we set to work. Once he had taken the job, he asked me to engage rooms for our work at the Hotel Crillon; I pointed out that if we could wait perhaps just a few weeks, we would surely find a permanent headquarters to rent. Besides, I said, space at the Crillon will be pretty expensive. But Lodge was firm. He wanted an immediate start; suitable quarters might take longer to find. And besides, he had a nostalgic reason for wanting to a start at the Crillon. "What is that?" I asked. Cabot's grandfather, the first Henry Cabot Lodge, who, as a senior senator, had effectively torpedoed Wilson's plans for a U.S.-led League of Nations, had stayed at the Crillon while visiting the Versailles Conference (1919). "I want to try to make up for the damage that my grandfather did then," declared Cabot. "I want to see the UN and the Atlantic community succeed in really bringing peace to the world." There could hardly have been a better reason. I negotiated the best deal I could with the Crillon management. We got some temporary office furniture from the American Embassy, put our mimeograph machine in a bathtub, and started work with a cadre from Milan and later recruits.

Our new administrative officer, Josephine Carpenter (an American opera singer who had had a decent career in Europe when U.S. opera turned her down), found us a permanent headquarters at 24 quai du 4 septembre, in the Paris suburb of Boulogne. This was an old *maison de campagne* that had once belonged to the notorious General Boulanger, who at a critical point in the 1880s had been looked to by some as a "man on horseback" who could save France from itself. When Cabot Lodge visited the new quarters to register his approval, he said, "Fine. We could even have a *fête champêtre* (festive, elaborate country picnic) out on the grass when better weather comes."

A side drama: Once we knew the new building was ours, I moved quickly to get our Olivetti furniture and typewriters from Milan. Bassani dug in his heels (refusing to accept the decision of the Policy Committee that Paris was final) and would not agree to ship the material. So, I took one of the Italian secretaries to Milan without notice and had her arrange with a local group of movers to pick up the Institute's machines and furniture and alert customs officials at the French border. We met the movers at 6 a.m., long before Bassani and his staff would arrive for work, and spirited the Institute's property away to Paris. Bassani was pretty unhappy. He was "kicked upstairs," from acting director of the Institute staff to a member of the Board of Governors, saving face all round. Even if he could not accept it, placing the Atlantic Institute in Paris made ultimate good sense; at the time Paris was the European capital of the Atlantic community, even if De Gaulle's advent in 1958 had begun to put the status and even the site of NATO headquarters in question. In fact, this was a stronger argument for Paris: until its demise in 1986, the Atlantic Institute's presence in the French capital was frequently noticed in ways that had an impact on French thought that it could not have had if situated in another European country.

The original intention of the Provisional Committee for the Institute was to create one Board of Governors and one executive head, with two coequal offices—one in Paris and one in Washington. But financial realities dictated that one of the two locations for work would have to be sacrificed, and Paris was chosen. This move was realistic but it never satisfied my hope that in all respects the Institute would be a truly multilateral affair. My fears, aroused when we could afford two offices, were realized some time later, when the Americans most interested in the Atlantic community felt they had to have their *own, American* private NGO. This new body, the Atlantic Council of the United States, eventually became a competitor with the Institute, and led to the abandonment of the Institute by many of its backers, mainly Americans. Thus, in a queer way, American chauvinism (today we might say unilateralism) took over "leadership" of what should have been a private mirror of the NATO-OECD-EU nexus. Even when entirely independent of governments, an Atlantic think tank could not work and express itself as a clearly joint affair, with each country roughly represented proportionately in a common plan of work and staffing, if the largest country would not agree to true multilateralism. Nationalism dies hard, not least in my own country, the United States, which I greatly love.

The Atlantic Convention of 1962

At the very outset of the Institute's official existence in Paris, we faced a small digression. A year or so earlier, the U.S. Congress had called for an "Atlantic Convention" to be held in Paris, with delegations (including many lawmakers, but no American members of Congress) from all the NATO countries, to see what steps might be taken to enhance the unity of the Atlantic nations. The convention had grown out of the prodding of Clarence Streit and the efforts of a number of his supporters in the Congress, but its mandate and agenda went more or less directly counter to the formula—Atlantic partnership—that the Kennedy administration had adopted for transatlantic relations. Many distinguished Americans and

Europeans turned up for several days in Paris in January 1962. Lodge was expected to visit with them and observe some of the proceedings, as did I.

After much discussion—and a growing realization on the part of the Canadian and European delegates that without either congressional members or officials of the U.S. administration in attendance—the convention adjourned with nary but a woolly resolution, urging all NATO governments to set up an intergovernmental commission to recommend concrete steps towards creating a "true Atlantic Community." What "true" meant was anybody's guess, but some of the U.S. participants, especially Clarence Streit and the core of the new board of the Atlantic Council of the United States (ACUS), had their own ideas. The board of the Council also contained people such as Dean Acheson who were not keen (at least at that point) to see some sort of Atlantic federation take shape, so for several years there were a series of rather fruitless debates in Washington. Theodore C. Achilles had retired as an ambassador to become a long-serving (without pay) vice chairman of the new ACUS; he never ceased believing in, and working for realization of, Streit's formula of a full-blown federation of the NATO countries, although it was also clear that Achilles expected that the United States would have to run things. This theme will recur in these pages, in various guises, throughout this account of my career.

In principle, I favored a Streit scheme, but I was now sufficiently realistic to believe that it would never come about in the formula Streit and others envisaged. I was content, over the years, to work for a series of more limited concepts for "togetherness," the development of more limited institutions (both governmental and nongovernmental) to put meat on the bones of the concepts and insure their permanence, and—perhaps most important—to gradually develop a "multinational leadership" corps of people in all Atlantic countries (and later all democracies) devoted to ever-closer union and congenial with their counterparts in schemes for working together.

The Atlantic Convention had little impact on the work of the new Atlantic Institute. People such as Pierre Uri, the Institute's new counselor of studies, and others of the "Monnet cadre" rather scoffed at a formula they considered unworkable and an irritant in their search for a "true partnership." The trouble with the Partnership School was that they, including the passionate American adherents, wanted more or less to hold off on strong, encompassing Atlantic- or NATO-wide schemes until a European union of comparable strength to that of the United States was in place. This too, in my opinion, was in the long run unworkable. I was for more pragmatic but continuing steps to unite what could be united, and often around different kinds of themes and problems. Now, back to the work of the Institute as it began.

Henry Cabot Lodge Takes Charge

The first three or four months of 1962 were spent hiring staff, getting moved into the Institute's new home, and moving ahead with several projects. Lodge rightly felt the need to see some of our governors on their home ground, visit with key American ambassadors in Bonn, Brussels, London, and elsewhere, and connect where he could with people who were important for money, policy, or programs.

Of the $350,000 we had available for 1962, slightly less than half came from America and Canada, the rest from Europe; beginning burdens were shared pretty equally. Even the smallest countries did their part; I have a letter from the minister of finance of Luxembourg pledging $1,000 for the first year and $500 each for four subsequent years. De Gaulle's government and most other NATO governments did their part. Soon after we were installed at the Quai du 4 Septembre, a functionary from the Quai d'Orsay called on me to announce that we could count on $10,000 from his ministry of foreign affairs, more later. We were grateful, but my European cynicism, now growing, told me that this was mainly so that no one could say France had not done its official part, and also so that they could get all our progress reports and perhaps try to put a gentle restraining hand on us, if necessary. One of my good Washington friends once said, of the financing of NGOs, "There's no such thing as tainted money; only just 'taint enough of it."

Our first professional appointment was Dr. Pierre Uri to head the Institute's studies. A noted economist and genius with respect to intergovernmental institutions, Pierre had been one of the tiny group of authors of Monnet's "Schuman Plan" (1950) for the coal and steel union of Europe, as well as a co-inventor of the later Common Market and Euratom communities. But it was clear that a place had to be found for him, at the background insistence of Monnet's coterie, both American and European. I rather imagine, but never proved, that his appointment with us was a quid pro quo with the Ford foundation, whose $300,000 three-year pledge was probably founded on a strong injection of its bipolar Europeanist philosophy. In this and in other ways, the cabal was to make sure that the Institute's launch was firmly in the direction—even on the foundation—of the two-pillar theory. This, by the way, left in the dust our original conception of the Atlantic community as much more than an institutional arrangement between the United States and a Europe-in-the-process-of-unification. In the early sixties, the European Communities were clearly unfinished business and involved only six countries. Scandinavia and southern Europe except for Italy were not involved. And if the United States were to be the opposite pillar, there was no place for the Canadians. Finally, countries historically and philosophically part of the Atlantic West's community of thought and ideals, but not in NATO, such as Switzerland or Sweden, were very much on the sidelines.

During the early stages of nurturing the Institute idea, the Bruges steering group in 1958 had met in Zurich and adopted a declaration, which began: "The limits of the Atlantic Community are fixed by attitudes of mind, not by geographic boundaries." Uri persuaded Lodge to let him write a book, *Partnership for Progress*, which emphasized mainly the requirements of European unity, secondly the place of the United States in the Monnet firmament, and whatever else Uri thought important. This was done, and we paid to translate and produce it in several languages. The Atlantic Institute was thus launched on a course that would mainly support the Kennedy (but really Monnet-Ball) concept of Atlantic Partnership, not a broad transatlantic community of nations bound together in a complex web of intergovernmental institutions and less concrete but still very real habits of thought and heart built on a thousand or more years of common history. Uri was a mixed blessing, partly because of his huge ego and fixation on the "partnership" scheme. But he was also extremely able and his reputation, especially in Europe, brought us considerable dividends.

I believe that none of the Institute's governors and other supporters opposed the idea of unifying Europe and building firm U.S. relations with that process. But the large majority had "come aboard" because they saw the Atlantic community as something bigger and broader than that. Henry Cabot Lodge understood this distinction but was powerless to buck the trend; his successors, all retired American ambassadors, were even more inclined to deal with concrete intergovernmental arrangements, and less—if at all—with the broader but more nebulous issues that bound the free nations together. Things such as education, philosophical ties, and social problems faced in common were for the most part left aside. (These qualities I would later come to subsume under the rubric of "like-mindedness.") The result, in the 25 years of its existence, was that the Institute left behind a pretty solid record of good ideas and proposals and analyses, framed as studies that dealt with transatlantic economic and political relations, but not much else.

To me, this has been a disappointment. Yet I thank God for what we and our successors were able, nevertheless, to do. The chief accomplishment, in my view, was that the Institute cast its net widely in seeking collaborators for its studies and in the process helped in crucial ways to solidify important personal relationships across borders, which thereby began to form a solid human community. There is nothing like the feeling one gets if, say, one is in the British Foreign Office and can pick up the phone to call a colleague in, say, Rome and "out of channels" discuss an important matter as friends do. The Atlantic Institute was only one of several bodies—such as Ditchley, Wilton Park, Royaumont, the Salzburg Seminar, or the Villa Serbelloni—that contributed to the building of such a multinational elite. But the Atlantic Institute, for a quarter century, was probably *primus inter pares* among such institutions, not least because at the time it was only one of two or three (along with the International Institute of Strategic Studies in London) that was truly multinational in its purposes, direction, and personnel. It sat at the epicenter of world affairs, acting as a clearinghouse and focal point for the growing community of democracies for a number of crucial years. It closed only three years before the Soviet empire collapsed; it had probably done its main work by then.

This "networking" approach I had learned from Professor Crane Brinton at Harvard, in 1955, and the lesson was never to leave my mind. A "multinational elite" formed on the basis of common democratic interests and the ideals of peace has been forming all these years, and sometimes I have been able to help in strategic ways. The Institute's other projects, and their leaders, thus lined up in the following way early in 1962.

Pierre Uri wrote a key book on partnership, and conducted a study of European policies towards Latin America (again, not so much to do with Atlantic relations as with a united Europe's future).

Marc Ullmann (French) assisted Uri and researched on international monetary questions.

Michael Cullis (British) headed a cultural relations project.

Ladislav Cerych (French, of Czech origin) studied how the West could best aid education in developing countries.

The College of Europe had brought to completion the compilation of an Atlantic Community Bibliography; these were precomputer days and such a compendium helped libraries throughout Europe and North America to see what had already been explored in learned thought.

Professor Frank Munk, the Institute's first Visiting Fellow, in his year with us wrote *Atlantic Dilemma*, a cold, realistic view of forces that were driving the Atlantic countries apart, as well as together.

Professor Elliot Goodman, our second Visiting Fellow, an expert on the USSR, used our resources and others to produce a profound work on de Gaulle and Atlantic affairs.

Finally, it was decided that an early project would be establishment of a "research clearinghouse," continuing the work begun by the Bruges bibliography. A smart, hard–working Naval ensign, Joseph Harned, was employed on his discharge to start this work early in 1963. By the time of his transfer to the Institute's Washington offices in 1966, he had produced several issues of a compendium called *Atlantic Studies* that told subscribers (largely in universities and international organizations) what research was contemplated, under way, and finally published. The later advent of computers and the Internet made this unnecessary, but in the early years it was an invaluable aid in stimulating and focusing needed research on a field few had recognized: the proper study of the Atlantic community.

The Free World's Aims

In addition, Lodge himself initiated and guided a series of conferences and a subsequent booklet on "The Free World's Aims for Humanity." He felt especially strongly about this. As he explained to me: The Soviets, basing their propaganda on Marxist-Leninist dogma, were fairly clear about what they wanted for mankind. But, said Lodge, the West had not formulated its own composite views, or achieved a consensus on what *it* envisaged as the future of humanity, based on principles of freedom. So we convened a few meetings and generated a great deal of correspondence among some of the "best minds" of the day, all in an attempt to arrive at an agreed statement, as Lodge put it, "to tell the world what we of the free nations are really about."

On 24–25 May 1962, two dozen key thinkers and doers who cared a great deal about such matters met. Among the participants were such luminaries as Dr. James Bryant Conant of Harvard; Jean (later Cardinal) Daniélou, head of theology at the University of Paris; Arthur Koestler, former Communist and author of *Darkness at Noon* and other seminal works of the Cold War era; Nuri Eren, a former Turkish diplomat and writer; Harvard's Dr. Milton Katz, once head of the Marshall Plan; Haakon Lie, secretary general of the Norwegian Labor Party; Lord Gladwyn; and Denis de Rougemont, another great author of the time.

The learned men arrived at some generally agreed conclusions, but not on an agreed Declaration (Lodge had hoped for what he called "a second Atlantic Charter"); for it was evident, once the exercise had begun, that the participants represented collectively one of the cardinal (yet also maddening) attributes of free societies: We may all operate on some general (usually unspoken) principles, but how we make use of these, or even express them, is magnificently representative of the wide range of thought—and of a good deal of disagreement around the vital edges—which epitomizes the West itself.

Five participants had each written a draft declaration. Some were admirable and now, forty years later, seem both timely and timeless. One draft, by Haakon Lie, delineated all the right notes about the nature of

Western democracy, preceded by this preface: "For the first time in history, mankind is within reach of a world without hunger or poverty or ignorance. Scientific achievements of unprecedented scale have given humanity the knowledge it needs to establish a new world order."

Lie's ten points then described the good society, concluding with these words: "[Our] long-range goal for all humanity is a world where the peoples of all nations work together peacefully and freely for the good of all. This world order can come into being only when the freedom of nations and the sanctity of individual human rights are secured."

Lie was a most unusual man. Brought up in the hard—and often bloody—realities of early 20th century trade union–employer battles in Norway, he migrated to America in the thirties, learned a great deal about union leadership and its mistakes, and about U.S. politics. He returned to Norway to head the Labor Party after World War II; today, in the 21st century, I have heard that he is still alive, chopping wood and dispensing wisdom from his cottage just outside Oslo.

The conference rapporteur, John K. Jessup of *Life* magazine, volunteered another statement. Among other things, it hit a strong note of interdependence:

> As the citizen is responsible to his neighbor, so is every nation responsible to the community of nations. No nation's sovereignty is absolute in fact, law, or morals. The solidarity of men, born in village and town, matured in the nation, now increasingly expressing itself in regional form, is destined to become the solidarity of mankind.

A goal still prescient and true, but in the 21st century still so far away.

Jessup's draft also set forth attributes of Western democracy that "have enabled our Atlantic nations to tame if not solve two basic problems of man-in-society":

> • Most governments at most times have been either too weak or too strong; but ours strike a tolerable balance because the means of peaceful correction are always at hand.
> • Most societies differ within themselves on what the rate and direction of social change should be; but ours, being free, permit a rich variety of experiments in change, and in refusal to change.

The Atlantic Institute, in convening the conference, had also laid a draft declaration on the table. Its words, short and pithy, were largely Lodge's. It struck a note echoed by other drafts and statements in the conference report: "A sense of brotherhood enjoins us to help the developing countries to raise their standard of living and thus to become ever stronger partners on the road to freedom." Colonialism had "virtually ended," but the conferees could not help but look over their shoulders at the death throes of the Algerian struggle still under way and the vestiges of Western imperialist attitudes that lingered, in the minds of both developing and developed countries.

As the meeting closed, there were common conclusions that the rapporteur dutifully set down. It seemed evident then that trying to state "the free world's aims for humanity" carefully and cogently was beyond the capacity of a few intelligent and well-meaning people, meeting for just two days. Thus a description of an eventual declaration resulted—food for thought and a lot more hard work. But, perhaps unfortunately, this was never followed up. Buried in these "conclusions" is a statement that is, today, more than ever true: "The world is becoming Atlantic." In 1963, there were perhaps two dozen nations that could call themselves democracies. Forty years later, Communism has fallen, there are no more colonies, and more than 80 countries have embraced democracy. To be sure, some of these are tentative, faltering efforts, but the trend has been unmistakable. In terms of forms of societies and governments, even the United Nations today does not hesitate to pronounce the importance of "democratic governance." In this sense, the Atlantic Institute—building on the efforts of the Bruges Conference, the Atlantic Congress, and other bodies—was attempting to articulate a course for "humanity" that has faltered a good deal over the years but that is unmistakably in a direction that the 1963 conferees would have applauded.

I believe Lodge hoped fervently that we could "break the East-West stalemate" of the time with the power of ideas, but that was not to be. However, without the work of A.I. and many other unsung NGOs, the downfall of Communism might have been delayed. Ideas, especially when spread around judiciously, *do* have power.

Henry Cabot Lodge

Our first director-general was an interesting, unusual human being. I got to know him extremely well during our year and a half together. For the sake of future researchers and biographers, I offer the following comments on the man and his way of working.

We got to know each other in late spring 1961, while Cabot (which he preferred to Henry) was deciding whether or not to accept the director-generalship. He invited me to his home, an impressive but not large country manor house in Marblehead, Massachusetts, looking out over the Atlantic. As we walked into the residence, I noted a wall directly in front of me, with twin staircases on each side leading to the main floor. On the wall were perhaps thirty or forty portraits, some small, some large. I asked, "Who are these people?" Cabot proceeded to pick out a half dozen, some dating from the early 18th century and others (including that of his grandfather, the famous senator) more recent. Every one of them, it seemed, was involved in public service of one kind or another, whether in the local county, in the Massachusetts legislature, or on the national stage. Without having to say it, I could understand that public service was in Cabot's very bones. He must have had a comfortable family fortune, but I believe that the idea of joining the business world was the furthest thing from his mind. For a few years, he had been a journalist.

At the time we met, he was 59, twenty years older and vastly more experienced than I. He had served in the Massachusetts government, but had gone on quickly to the U.S. House of Representatives and then the Senate. His career was interrupted by World War II, when he served in the North African campaign. He made clear to me, as we began to spend a lot of time together (much of it on planes and trains), that during that second war and because of his grandfather's stern and ill-fated opposition to Wilson's plans in 1919–22, he had joined in 1947 with Senator Arthur Vandenberg and a few key Republicans in the Senate to accept Secretary of State Dean Acheson's invitation to work in bipartisan harness on the drafts of the North Atlantic Treaty. Historical accounts bear out the contention that Lodge, after only Vandenberg himself, was most influential among congressional Republicans in drafting the treaty and getting it through the Senate (1948–49). He believed profoundly in not only its political importance, but also in its philosophical and historical significance.

President Eisenhower moved Lodge from the Senate to the United Nations, where he distinguished himself as the U.S. permanent representative and in the process became a popular figure. Those who can recall TV news programs of the late 1950s cannot forget the day when Lodge held a press conference at the UN to display a large, wood-carved American eagle that had hung on the wall of the American ambassador's office in Moscow. Lodge pointed to the back of the figure, where a tiny microphone had been surreptitiously placed. This made the point that the Soviets would go to any lengths in their surveillance of high U.S. officials — not quite cricket, as his fellow delegate (from the UK) Sir Gladwyn Jebb would have said. More or less naive about such matters, the average American viewer in those early Cold War days would have agreed, and probably with some vehemence. Cabot's height and good looks, as well as a disarming capacity to say the right thing at the right time, and pithily, also made him popular. So it was understandable that Richard Nixon should choose Cabot as his running mate in the presidential election of 1960. When they lost, that presented the new Board of Governors of the putative Atlantic Institute with an opportunity.

Cabot Lodge was neither a profound thinker nor a scholar, qualities that some of us had hoped for in the first director-general of the Institute. But the consensus of the new board overrode such ideas; they decided that what they wanted was "a Man of State" with instincts that matched theirs for the task at hand, a public figure who could inspire confidence in the Institute's work. I could still today reel off the names of four or five eminent men of the day from the world of education and the universities (Dr. Conant of Harvard would have been one), but in hindsight I think the governors were probably correct in picking Cabot. He had fire in his belly about our mission.

A cat-and-dog fight over his election as DG ensued in the summer of 1961. It pitted a few Machiavellians such as Radoux and Bassani—and latterly Dirk Stikker, head of NATO—against the majority of the board and was something that might have deterred a lesser man than Cabot. But, as described earlier, he was deft and wily in circumnavigating these shoals. My journal's comments on Lodge following his election as DG (November 1961) follow:

> Lodge is an amazing person. I find working for him fascinating. He is a totally different man than any I have ever worked near. A political animal, he is full of understanding for people's drives and motivations and how to make use of them. He is unusually shrewd and wise. There is no political situation in which I think he would come a cropper. On the other hand, he appears often to be superficial and glib; I believe this is mainly the result of his driving desire to make intensely plain to the man in the street what we are about. He is impatient and sometimes impulsive. His impulsiveness makes the two of us a poor pair, perhaps. He is rather spoiled, having never taken orders from anyone, outside of Eisenhower and a few generals at a time when we all were doing it. He is wealthy, but not rich and takes a more independent attitude toward people and situations than anyone I have ever known. His personal philosophy of life is not always admirable, but it is most unusual and gives one pause. He said to me the other day, "I don't see any reason for doing anything but the things I like. When you're my age [59 at the time], you know what you like and there's no reason you should bother doing things you don't like." Consequently, he is extremely difficult about making

appointments and I am the buffer, usually. If he doesn't want to see someone, I have to figure out a polite and reasonable excuse. Good training. It's sometimes difficult for me to shift gears after years in the USIS, where self- sacrifice was the order of the day for 90% of the people involved and no one was important enough to dictate a different policy.

On balance, Cabot was a great asset. Occasionally he faltered, as when we went to Oslo to meet the king and the government and present the Institute to the leading citizens. I had asked Cabot ahead of time if he wanted me to draft a speech for him, but he said, "No, I'll do it myself." At 8 p.m. in the evening, after a day spent at the Foreign Ministry, a large group of around 500—headed by the Crown Prince—gathered in the great hall in the Oslo town square. Cabot was duly introduced and began to say a good many of the right things. But, half an hour after commencing, he stopped. Now was the time to explain how the Institute was at work, what was at stake for his precious Free World (and theirs) and to set the stage for great things to be done by the Norwegians and "their" new Institute in Paris.

But Cabot smiled, ceased talking, thanked everyone, and walked off the stage.

In such a gathering, no one was prepared to ask questions; it wouldn't have been appropriate. And if Cabot had expected any, he did not show it as he smiled diffidently and retreated.

In a different place, with a different audience, and at a different time of day, a short speech might have been appropriate. But this was occurring at a time when all good Norwegians had finished *Kvällsmat*, their evening meal and had settled down for a good academic lecture of not less than an hour.

Cabot went promptly to his hotel. I stood by to greet Norwegians I knew and thank them for coming. The press attaché from the American Embassy, who had done a good deal to publicize Lodge's advent in Oslo, walked up to me, livid. "How could he *do* such a thing?" he exploded. I shrugged my shoulders and asked forgiveness for Cabot. Nothing quite so egregious happened again. I asked myself "why?" and came to this tentative conclusion: (1) He should have let me or someone see his speech–draft early on; and (2) he was probably overtired and had "run out of gas." The latter seems to me in hindsight more important than the former. Cabot looked strong and healthy, but I think he had a delicate constitution and was able to husband his strength by resting frequently and not overdoing. At our many lunches and dinners, he almost invariably asked for grilled filet of sole, a salad, and a glass of light white wine—suggesting that his delicacy was not feigned. I liked him despite this, but I must say that I was glad he had not become vice president and taken over when Nixon stumbled.

In early summer of 1963, Cabot received a telephone call from President Kennedy, who asked him to go, almost at once, to Saigon as U.S. ambassador. Cabot called me in, explained the situation, said he had in no way asked for the appointment, but could not—as a "good soldier"—refuse. Many things he had started were still undone, and yet A.I.'s track record so far had been I think a good one. Within a month, he was back in Washington for briefings and off to Vietnam. As readers familiar with that period (and secret communications unveiled years later) will know, he was almost at once put in the impossible position of having to tell Ngo Dinh Diem that President Kennedy had great confidence in him in his increasingly lousy position, and on the other hand, secretly approving and advising in the conspiracy of the CIA to throw Diem to the wolves of his leading generals, who assassinated him. Some years later, Cabot gave me the gist of his situation when he arrived in Saigon in the summer of 1963. He hated it, he said, but felt duty bound. It is ironic that not long after Cabot told me this, the new president, Lyndon Johnson, sent Lodge back again to Vietnam. On his eventual return to private life, he came dutifully to meetings of the Atlantic Council of the United States in Washington, but—although I have no reason to think it—perhaps he was sorry that he had not stayed in Paris in 1963.

Lodge had many good things going for him, but the best, in my opinion, was his wife Emily. She made a wonderful hostess, seemed to support him well in all he did, and delighted everyone around her. She too helped to launch the fledgling Atlantic Institute.

Winding Up Work in Paris

A few weeks before Kennedy sent Lodge to Vietnam, I had decided to leave Paris. My reasons were intensely personal; an upheaval in my family life began around that time; my wife wanted to return to the United States with our four children; I arranged to follow them. Meanwhile, we sought a suitable person to take over my duties as executive officer of the Institute. Cabot took the advice of some worthies in the State Department and selected a just-retired U.S. ambassador. As I do not wish to unnecessarily besmirch the decent man's reputation, I shall not name him. Suffice to say, he was entirely unsuitable, didn't understand what we were about at the Institute, and may not have cared. He stayed, I think, less than two years.

The first nomination for new director-general was Gen. Alfred Gruenther, retired Supreme Allied Commander Europe. I believe he would have made a wonderful DG, but in the end he decided instead to become head of the American Red Cross.

Cabot was lucky in recruiting Walter "Red" Dowling, at the time our ambassador to Bonn and a man well known in the Foreign Service for his astuteness and diplomatic skills. Red retired in November 1963 and immediately went to Paris to become the Atlantic Institute's director-general. But not all diplomats make good NGO heads; one has constantly to find money, buttonhole experts (good and bad) to participate in programs, and make do with a fully international staff—some of whom didn't know much about diplomatic protocol, administrative backup, and so on. We were a motley group, and that was more or less as we had planned it. However, with a few expert people on the staff, and almost all of them "dedicated," as current parlance put it, Dowling was able to keep the Institute more than afloat for a few years, when his replacement, John W. Tuthill (another retired diplomat), took over.

Dowling was good; Tuthill was amazingly good. But these appointments and those to follow, until the last director-general took over in 1985, were all U.S. career diplomats. I thought this was a mistake; men such as Tuthill, who had been head of the U.S. missions to both OECD and the European Communities and who had abilities beyond those of the usual diplomat, were quite good for the Institute, but for two reasons I counseled against such appointments: (1) I thought that a statesman-politician-scholar, such as Spaak or van Zeeland or Conant, would be more suitable, at least after a string of professional diplomats; and (2) I believed it was a mistake to establish the precedent that the director-general should always be an American. (I had a good Canadian and a couple of Europeans in mind at various times.) But the governors of the Institute wanted the settled pattern as it came to be.

For my part, after a bit of searching in the United States—and mostly on the West Coast, where my wife wanted to settle—I realized that I had invested so much of my moral-spiritual-professional capital in the effort to give rise to the Atlantic Institute, and in a broader sense (for years) to help make the Atlantic community an enduring reality—that I should stick with the Institute, but in Washington as its U.S. representative. (The reader will recall that the original plans for the Institute called for co–equal headquarters in both Paris and Washington.) Those who (in 1961) had started the new Atlantic Council of the United States seemed delighted with this idea, as was Red Dowling, who felt I think that he could trust me to represent the Institute's interests in the United States and Canada, and keep the necessary U.S. money flowing to Paris. We were encouraged around this time by a Ford Foundation decision to grant the Institute $1 million. It seemed that in many respects we were on our way. I believed (and today I think rightly so) that it was the U.S. public and its influential elites who would have to be convinced—even more than the Europeans—that the Atlantic community concept was their main future. So, in November 1963 I took up new duties in Washington.

An Appraisal of the Institute and Its Work

After all these years, it is impossible not to be impressed with the overall content and impact of the Atlantic Institute's work, and more especially with the quality of the governors and management personnel who contributed to its wide-ranging activities. It was twenty-five years, from the Institute's inception in 1961 until its untimely demise in 1986. What did it accomplish? And why did it ultimately close its doors?

Satisfactory answers to these questions await some competent historical research based on such archives as exist, on the testimony of persons closely involved, and on contemporary press accounts. In the year 2000, a young Frenchwoman, Valérie Aubourg, began a study of the work of the NGOs that helped to create private underpinnings for the public efforts to hold the Atlantic community together. I provided Mme. Aubourg with access to my own papers; she met with many people who were active in these efforts and consulted archives in many countries. I am confident that when Mme. Aubourg's work is published, it will be a valuable and probably unique contribution to a little-known aspect of what it took to win the Cold War and to launch the nations on both sides of the Atlantic in the considerable strides achieved. She has provided extremely useful and little-known information, in particular, about the origins and fate of the Atlantic Institute.

A complementary work, by a young Italian woman, Dr. Tiziana Stella, broader in scope but nonetheless valuable and also, to my knowledge, unique, awaits publication as well. Dr. Stella sought to chart the historical development in the United States of what one might call "international federalism" as a goal of a number of nongovernmental thinkers and groups in Europe and America. Her account begins in the 1860s and covers world peace movements after the Civil War, the advent of World Federalism as a "cause," and an analysis of the work of Clarence Streit and others in championing the cause of an Atlantic federation.

I hope that such historical research continues and that, in particular, even more extensive work will be undertaken on the Atlantic Institute and its fate. As a nongovernmental research organization—and stimulator of multinational unity among democracies through its efforts to bring together leaders of thought and action and to create a "community of thought" and a kind of transatlantic spirit of comradeship among them, the Institute was a success. One example of its long-lasting influence was its key role as the incubator of a subsequent spin-off, the Club of Rome, in the early 1970s. Aurelio Peccei, an Institute governor, was the spark plug in rightly assessing environmental problems as the overlooked but next great set of issues that should occupy the West—the chief malefactors in the spoliation of the world's ecology but also the only powers that had the wherewithal, scientific, financial and political, to do something to change course. I'm sure there were many more such initiatives that could be traced to the Institute; it remains for future researchers to ferret these out. (The origins of the Club of Rome initiative were described to me by J. V. Clyne, a Canadian governor of the Institute, in the late 1970s, when the two of us became deeply involved in the efforts to develop still another international NGO, the Consortium for Atlantic-Pacific Affairs (see chapter 16).

It is evident to me that the world situation, and particularly that of the North Atlantic countries, is quite different at the beginning of the 21st century from what it was when I and others took it into our heads to create a think tank and clearinghouse in the 1950s and 1960s. In those days, the United Nations was decidedly weak and often paralyzed by Cold War rivalries; it had to be reinforced by such bodies as NATO, the IMF, the World Bank, the OECD, and the various European organizations then in formation. The problems of underdevelopment in the world have proven more tractable in some ways than we had thought in the 1960s (and the Institute helped to point to steps for practical action, many of which were undertaken by official bodies). However, the stunted economic and political growth in some regions, especially the Middle East and Africa, continues in the 21st century to confound experts. It is encouraging that the United Nations and its associated bodies in many ways have taken a lead in urging those who might be left behind to undertake the necessary social and political transformations. For the first time, a UN secretary-general, Kofi Annan, has spoken forcefully and frequently of democracy as a main answer to the predicaments of less-developed nations. The Atlantic Institute helped to put the spotlight on some of these problems and, in some cases, to offer ingenious solutions. Governments did not always listen, but some did and in some instances relevant policies were adopted. A.I. was a precursor of the now-ubiquitous policy-oriented think tanks.

In its 25 years of existence, the Atlantic Institute issued a blizzard of policy documents, known from 1965 as "The Atlantic Papers." These covered subjects such as ballistic missile defense, the fate of the pound sterling, the future of NATO, the integration of Europe, the reunification of Germany, the development of the Third World, the impact of the oil crisis of 1973, Soviet strategic doctrine, and Western security policy. In 1969, the Board of Governors was broadened to include Japanese and Australian members.

The Cold War ended a decade before the end of the tumultuous 20th century; the Soviet empire crumbled; its various constituents—including Russia (more slowly)—are today finding their way towards close association with the West. In 1961 the *équipe* of the Atlantic Institute could hardly have prophesied the speed and success of the post–Cold War transformation that began in 1989–91. The "free world's aims for humanity" no longer need to be argued, refined, and propagated across the Iron Curtain, as seemed urgent in 1963. In 2000, a new Community of Democracies (CD) was convened by the foreign ministers of 107 governments, who agreed (*mirabile dictu!*) on a statement of the principles of democracy. In 2002 the second meeting of this intergovernmental body, in Seoul, was able to carry the idea of cooperation among democracies, for the sake of building democracy itself, still further. These steps were dim visions of the initial organizers of the Atlantic Institute; now there is a global reality, however fragile. In 2005 the CD met again.

The world economy, for all its vicissitudes, uncertainties, and ups and downs, is in far better shape than in 1961. "Globalization" to be sure has brought downsides, but the upsides represent far more movement towards good outcomes. The promises of much freer trade, of a generally well-functioning world monetary system (with the advent of the Euro as a key element), of more effective international commercial law, of improved (if in many cases still problematical) world environmental and labor standards, the slow but real progress towards better governmental management of economies, all testify to a considerably improved world regime for unleashing the creative powers of humanity.

Most important, the unity of the NATO and OECD countries and the *glacis* of collective public support for the principles and institutions of Western democracy did not crack—as many feared they might—under the strains of the forty-year Cold War. One cannot pretend there are no problems; they exist at every hand, and many are exceedingly dangerous. The long-term effort to contain and defeat "terrorism" (a most difficult movement to define, as well as counteract) will proceed; this was something—at least in its full dimensions—of which the founders of the Atlantic Institute could hardly conceive. NATO, despite the more limited visions of its founders, has begun to take on roles in turbulent parts of the world (such as Afghanistan and Africa) where the UN itself, for various reasons, cannot.

The point is: On balance, the world is much better off today than it was forty and fifty years ago. And I believe the Atlantic Institute played an important, if minor, role as a stimulator and catalyst in bringing about the necessary transformations of community-building and general internationalist thought. I believe the furtherance of many of the Institute's chief goals was an outcome well worth the effort—the investment of time, thought, and money by private individuals who led it over the years.

❈

Why did the Atlantic Institute ultimately come apart? I have a few tentative conclusions on this subject, which I put forward with some hesitation, hoping that others will study these and other hypotheses and develop still more. I believe this is important not least because the whole matter bears on the accomplishments (as well as the lack thereof) of the West in the past half century. One should bear in mind that the Institute was constantly trying, with some success, to identify and work on problems that represented the cutting edge of international relations. Some scholars should study the "Institute project" because the creation and work of the Atlantic Institute provides a good case history of how (and how not) to develop and nurture such an unusual kind of international "think tank." Those attempting some similar nongovernmental, multinational undertaking can possibly learn something by considering this brief interlude in creating unifying tendencies in the West, and with Japan and Australasia as well.

At any rate, here are some very tentative conclusions as to why, in the end I believe the Atlantic Institute "failed":

• Its conception was unusual—a truly independent, multinational research and energizing organization—for which support by an increasingly nationalistic succeeding generation of leaders from all fields of endeavor and from many countries became increasingly difficult. In other words, the world and its coordinates began to change and big issues became less clear and less certain of definition, let alone solution.

• The drive to power, common (as I suggested earlier) to political, economic, and intellectual elites, injured the Institute at critical moments in its life. For example, the Trilateral Commission, begun in the 1970s with goals generally supportive of and congruent with those of the Atlantic Institute, and by equally concerned and well-meaning leaders, but with a slightly different organizing conception, came into competition with the Institute. Efforts were made to amalgamate the two, but the project foundered, in part (it is reported) because of clashes of leaders about who should head the combined body. When this failed, the quest for scarce private monies eventuated in destructive competition.

• One might look also at the advent of the Atlantic Council of the

United States, begun shortly after the Institute and presumably as a parallel and complementary effort, within the main "Atlantic" nations, as an example of how national feeling was able to divert the energies and wellsprings of leadership essential to the success of both enterprises. For example, even though virtually all the extremely able and experienced people who set up and ran the Atlantic Council of the United States believed intellectually, and strongly, in the magnificent goal of Atlantic unity, most of them, in my opinion, believed *emotionally* that "America knows best, and perhaps *is* best." Competition between A. I. and ACUS grew over the years, because it is a lot easier to draft appeals for financial support and to organize studies on international issues if one involves only the people and resources of a single nation than it is to get consensus of a multinational board and staff and supporters in a number of countries. A few directors of the Atlantic Council remained on the Institute board as well over the years and worked hard to find support for the Institute in the United States; but in the end, the evidence of an increasingly nationalistic U.S. bent doomed the Institute as only a (necessarily) partly American body, but one which relied on a proportional sharing of burdens and a common approach to questions. I believe that this remains a critical issue in assessing trends in broad transatlantic (and even U.S.-Canadian) relations at the turn of this new century: **Most leading Americans are still not capable, when the chips are down, of taking off their national blinders and working together with close, like-minded allies in the search for consensus on what our common burdens are, and how we should share them fairly.** This condition obtains, in spades, in NATO and other multinational efforts involving the allied Atlantic democracies, including most private bodies as well as governments.

• The effects of a freshly disordered world in the period 1968–80, and especially the advent of international terrorism were critical. The Vietnam War, in particular, fueled anti-American sentiment in Europe. This, along with the so-called Youth Revolt in all Western societies, the remnants of the French-Algerian war, and the beginnings of international terrorist activity inspired by Palestinian and general Arab frustrations, conspired to create a quite different atmosphere in Paris for a multinational think tank inevitably connected in many minds with NATO as an agent of militarism. In 1974 a terrorist bomb blew off the main facade and wrecked the ground floor precincts of the Institute's headquarters (moved from suburban Boulogne to central Paris on the rue de Longchamp). This damaged records and the Institute's library, the long-term heart of the operation, and necessitated a debilitating move to much less desirable headquarters. It is my belief that this attack was successful in its aim: to hurt materially the morale of those connected with what was (erroneously) seen as a "capitalist" and "imperialist" mainstay. This was the beginning of the end, even if it was not so seen at the time.

• Mismanagement was the straw that broke the camel's back. Although details need not be laid bare here (partly because certain records have been lost and some individuals involved may be alive), suffice it to say that poor financial control and sketchy financial oversight (by the Board) characterized management of the Institute in its last years. Realizing this too late, the Institute's last chairman persuaded the governors that the situation was irretrievable. The Atlantic Institute was suddenly, peremptorily closed down. A search for its archives a few years ago yielded almost nothing; they had been consigned to a financial institution in Paris which, unaccountably, ordered them destroyed soon after the think tank's operations ceased.

• In a new body such as the Institute, the continuing search for funds often precludes, or at least hampers, the search for adequate personnel at all levels. It is difficult, for example, unless one can assure staff of reasonable prospects of job security and benefits. This problem plagues many good NGOs.

• On top of these critical factors, one must perhaps look coldly at the greatly changed world of governments, intergovernmental bodies, and NGOs similar to the Atlantic Institute. Many things the Atlantic Institute had sought to promote were later done by others—often by many others. In 1961, there were relatively few think tanks; by 1986, there were hundreds, all over the Western world. Not many of these were truly multinational in aims or composition, but the substantive output of such groups became enormous and grows apace today. There has been a proliferation of specialized institutes (some very good) dealing with parts of the broad issues with which the Institute concerned itself at the outset: the International Institute of Economics in Washington is one, the International Institute for Strategic Studies in London is another. The advent of computers and the Internet has also made it possible for think tanks and other groups anywhere to quickly share ideas, bibliographies, and the results of research; the Atlantic Institute's "clearinghouse" function is no longer needed.

So, for a variety of reasons, some understandable, some regrettable, the Atlantic Institute closed its doors in 1986. I think, on balance, that it worked nobly and well towards the goals it had set for itself at the outset. It necessarily restricted its scope; in 1972, an impressive little brochure describing the Institute's work, described its purpose as "to assist in solving problems which are common to the Atlantic countries and, to an increasing degree, countries with similar political structures and levels of development." Its quarterly papers, at the time, included those on "Latin

America in Transition," "Stemming World Inflation," and "Europe and America at the Crossroads." Its studies were done by eminent authorities, for the most part, but were narrower in scope than the originators of the Institute had hoped for. Paul van Zeeland and Henry Cabot Lodge, and their peers on the board, had wanted to tackle some fundamental problems in the transatlantic "psyche," so to speak, and to take the lead in stimulating other bodies and individuals to do needed studies. The founders had specifically enjoined their staff and succeeding governors to be a "catalyst for ideas," but this was never achieved to a significant extent. The world changed, and the Institute had tried to change with it, but the underlying deep needs of Western society had either gone further "underground" or had become less important to people, or both.

10
Foundations and Society's Third Sector

January 1963: *De Gaulle vetoes British membership in European Common Market, publicly rejects concept of an "Atlantic community."*

November 1963: *President Kennedy is assassinated in Dallas, Lyndon B. Johnson is sworn in as 36th president of the United States.*

The Atlantic Council of the United States: Washington, D.C., 1963

On Labor Day, 1963, I arrived in Washington for my new assignment, heading the North American office of the Atlantic Institute. The post of director general of the Institute had not been filled when I left Paris; my appointment to Washington had been agreed earlier by Lodge, when still DG, and General Lauris Norstad, then chairman of the Atlantic Council's board.

Lodge's vacated position was first offered to General Alfred Gruenther, a marvelous soldier who had been Eisenhower's chief of staff at NATO and later Supreme Allied Commander Europe himself. He refused and instead became head of the American Red Cross. I got to know Gruenther well and admired him a great deal. It was said that at NATO parade-reviews, Gruenther, as SACEUR, would greet each contingent in its own native language—including Portuguese, Greek, and Turkish—a rare and valuable sensibility.

Ambassador Walter (Red) Dowling was appointed the new director general of the Atlantic Institute at the end of October 1963; he and I met in Washington and developed a good working relationship. I was uncomfortable, however, with my own replacement in Paris and became even more uncomfortable with most of my new associates in Washington. My replacement as A.I. executive officer in Paris was a less able, retired U.S. ambassador, with no background, nor even stomach, for the job—which was to act as chief of staff and energizer, as I had done. In a couple of years he would be replaced by a gifted and able young academic, Gregory Flynn, who proved excellent at understudying a succession of directors general. But until Flynn's advent and that of Ambassador John Tuthill (who replaced Dowling in 1966), and until relations between the Institute and the Atlantic Council of the United States (ACUS) had been rendered more or less stable, the entire enterprise—American and European—was on rocky ground.

General Norstad, chairman of the Atlantic Council and former SACEUR, kept a loose and more or less unholy alliance on the ACUS board of directors (involving Europe-firsters, Atlantic federalists, and pragmatists) from boiling over. The board represented these and other trends in current thinking about foreign affairs. There were always too many directors (more than 40 to start with, and 125 by the time I became president in 1983). Most were distinguished figures in their own right and each expected to be listened to. Some were former cabinet officers; many were retired ambassadors, with some business people and a few academics. About the only thing they all could agree to was that the Atlantic Alliance was a matter of paramount importance to the United States. How the future of Atlantic relations should play out was continually a subject of debate—sometimes rancorous and often inconclusive. My job, in part, was to keep these controversies from affecting the work of the Institute in Paris and to develop a distinct and useful A.I. program in the United States.

This difficult and unwieldy ACUS amalgam did not deter Richard Wallace, who had headed ACUS as director general since its inception in 1961. Nor did it deter a small clique of board members and volunteers in the office from pressing continually for adoption of policies and programs that would point ACUS in the direction of Clarence Streit's dream: a strong federation of Atlantic democracies.

The immediate goal of the "federalists" on the Atlantic Council Board and staff was to prod the Kennedy administration to follow through on the principal resolution of the Atlantic Convention of January 1962. This meeting had been authorized by a Resolution of Congress and financed by a congressional appropriation. Many European MPs took part, with other elites, but no members of Congress did so. Unable to convince the convention that a Streitian federation was the immediate solution to Alliance disunity (and Streit himself was there, pleading eloquently), the American federalists fell back on a "punting" solution. The meeting eventually proposed formation by NATO governments of the Special Governmental Commission to propose measures that would turn the alliance into a "true community." The latter term was doublespeak for a federation. While most governments were decidedly cool, that of the United States was hostile. The Atlantic federal pattern ran contrary to the Atlantic Partnership model of the administration. The "true Atlantic Community" proposal of the federalists had no chance of going anywhere, but the federal clique running the ACUS persisted for two or three years to mouth the mantra. This greatly annoyed old warhorses, such as Dean Acheson and Lauris Norstad, and deflected the council from doing much positive about the state of American political opinion. Precious time was wasted on such infighting.

I favored an Atlantic federation as a long-term aim. But after my experience in Europe and in government, I was convinced that an Atlantic federal union was an entirely unrealistic program goal for any serious citizens group that wanted to influence the policy of the United States. I felt—and still do—that some kind of transatlantic union would eventually result if groups like the Institute and the Council (plus a number of others) would simply work on the practical objectives of mutual understanding and solidarity among the peoples around the North Atlantic, brought about largely through elite/expert dialogues to achieve consensus on specific problems and opportunities facing the NATO and OECD countries and widespread publication of the results. I also believed that the education systems of the Atlantic countries should and could be retooled to make it clear to students at all levels what the real shape and mission of the modern Atlantic community were, mining its especially rich history. My approach was essentially a nonpolitical one, stressing the nurturing of healthy trends in Atlantic societies that could be brought into historical convergence. I adopted the term "social tissue" to describe what we were trying to create; mine was an "applied anthropology" approach. Richard Wallace and his cohort were unrelievedly political, struggling for the "main chance" of quickly converting contemporary Atlantic arrangements into a fullblown federation. They used the Special Governmental Commission as a wedge to stimulate action on a necessarily vast scale. ACUS key personnel reflected this offbeat view.

In addition to Wallace, the council had recently acquired a full-time, unpaid, working vice chairman, just-retired Ambassador Theodore Achilles. He came into the office virtually every day for twenty-five years, until he died in 1987. The Council became his baby. He was the power behind the throne at any given time. Another volunteer was the immensely savvy diplomat Ambassador John (Jack) Hickerson, older and more malleable than Achilles, yet less willing to spend full time at the council. Hickerson and Achilles had been instrumental in the writing and adoption of the North Atlantic Treaty (1949); the Washington newspapers gave their simultaneous retirement from government and their plunge into the ACUS considerable coverage. Both men were admirers of Clarence Streit, as was Will Clayton, a venerable, long-retired cotton merchant from Texas who had served in important subcabinet posts under Presidents Roosevelt and Truman. Clayton has rightly been termed by some historians as the U.S. official most responsible for conceiving and energizing the Marshall Plan in 1947. Clayton, Hickerson, Achilles and I became close friends. Along with Wallace, Achilles was the one who stuck most stubbornly, and longest, to the Special Intergovernmental Commission gambit.

Former secretary of state Christian Herter, also an admirer (but a practical one) of Streit, was the first chairman of the council. Most unfortunately, he died not long after its inception. Dean Acheson, who was also a founder and remained a board member for years, had nothing but contempt for the federalist schemes of the Streit cabal. He spoke for the pragmatists, and the board members always listened, even if some of them didn't like what he told them. My journal shows Acheson, at an ACUS Board meeting in early January 1964, finally asking the federalists in exasperation if the members wanted to be thought of "as people with poor judgment."

During Acheson's retirement from politics and government, I had gone to see him in 1960 to try to get his support for the Atlantic Institute idea; he rather scoffed at it, saying that "citizens' organizations aren't worth the time and effort. The governments will have to do the necessary things." Four years later, I was to hear him tell the board of the Atlantic Council (referring to a heated discussion of policy choices), "These are the kinds of things we should look into in *our* Institute." He became a staunch supporter of both the Institute and the Council. In retirement he also became convinced that governments could do more. In 1957 while attending a private conference in Brussels, he was reported by the press as urging major strengthening of the transatlantic institutional framework.

Buttressed by some lesser lights on the Atlantic Council staff—paid and unpaid—were several old "federalist warhorses" of the Streit stable. They were ready to fall on their swords to push the ACUS towards an unabashedly Streitian federal union. Wallace, a former Capitol Hill assistant to Senator Estes Kefauver of Tennessee (also a Streit enthusiast), was wily, calculating, and Machiavellian; his real intentions and feelings were almost always shielded by a mask of Southern geniality. He and his colleagues, as I saw it, were more than willing to accomplish their agenda "underground," so to speak, and to use the great names on the board, if they could, as a screen for advancing just one view—their own "federation now" conception. The Council consequently put few resources into the huge task of public education. Later, it began forming study groups on policy questions. But in 1964, and for some years after, some of its leadership pursued the "Atlantic federal union will o' the wisp" almost to the exclusion of other more obvious and potentially rewarding tasks.

Some of the voluble Atlantic federalists were either above the fray or outside it, in either case unwilling to engage in political game-playing. One such was Adolph W. Schmidt, head of the A. W. Mellon Charitable Trust in Pittsburgh. An officer in Col. "Wild Bill" Donovan's OSS during World War II, Schmidt had been a conscientious and principled supporter of Clarence Streit and his ideas since the late 1930s. In his foundation post he was able to put funds at the disposal of such ventures as the Bruges conference on the North Atlantic Community (1957) and the Atlantic Congress (1959). He was one of the first to urge creation of the Atlantic Institute and provide some funds for it. Schmidt often argued forcefully at ACUS board meetings for the adoption of a Streitian vision and program; he spoke logically, with a good knowledge of history; but he could not persuade the Achesons or Norstads of this world (who styled themselves "realists") and the many other distinguished diplomats, politicians, and military figures on the board that this should be done. Most were content with the prevailing Kennedy administration's position—that the proper approach to U.S.-European relations emphasized the Europeans' completing their unification, at which time we would form a strong partnership with them and together settle problems of the world. It took years to define such a partnership; but by then it was almost too late and the public concept tepidly, if at all, received.

Both positions—federation or partnership, as readers will have noted earlier in this work—seemed to me unworkable and unwise. In October 1963 when I arrived in Washington to take up my new duties with the Institute, there was obviously little point in tilting at the entrenched positions of the Department of State and the White House on the matter. I felt much of the debate within the ACUS, both formal and behind the scenes, was a waste of time. I wanted some long-term educational and institution-building measures, developed soundly on long-term concepts for Atlantic togetherness. I also believed that major institutions could not be made to work well without a great cadre of multinational leadership spreading across the whole Atlantic world—people who could man positions in the existing international institutions and those to come and season relevant domestic institutions generously. In 1966 I wrote an article for the journal *Orbis* in which I tried to lay the theoretical groundwork for building such leadership. This bore heavily on my Harvard work under Crane Brinton, who pointed me towards the importance of a multinational elite such as that which had held together the far-flung Roman Empire. In my view, the Atlantic community lacked the human infrastructure—the social tissue—to insure its long-term cohesion and durability.

All of this would take time: here it is the 21st century and effective transatlantic unity still slips in and out of our grasp. But the state of transatlantic affairs is immeasurably better than it was in 1963. Gradual historic evolution, plus a lot of pointed programs, both governmental and nongovernmental, brought about long-term institutional and educational changes that mattered. Not least of these changes was the tangled and productive web of business, trade, and banking ties, today called globalization.

Some side remarks on General Lauris Norstad that might illumine the lack, in those days, of a cadre of strong Atlanticists (like him) in key U.S. positions: One day in November 1963, I had a long talk with the general, who had retired as SACEUR in 1962 and taken a top position in American business. From my journal:

> [Norstad] said that while he found President Kennedy a very reasonable man, he got along poorly with Rusk and McNamara [secretaries of State and Defense], found them "insensitive" to European problems. He said he argued heatedly with Rusk, asking him why he did not use the advice of the good people who reported to him from Europe. He also deplored the influence of McGeorge Bundy [the President's National Security Adviser] and his crew. Norstad has a sharp mind, and an incisive way about him, a rather poetic way of expressing himself at times, and a great impatience. He expects that the correct facts are always delivered to him and he makes up his mind on those, rather quickly.

A few months later at a lunch Norstad (again, from my journal): "made a number of enlightening statements about the present *and previous* administrations; substantially, his criticism was this: that we are 'insensitive' to our allies, that we do not trouble ourselves by trying to understand how they will react to what we do, that men such as MacNamara are so absorbed with the technical (and 'engineering', as Kissinger says) aspects of decision-making inside the U.S. that they entirely ignore what the Europeans think, or may think. . . . Norstad has really got a hold of something: the U.S. lacks so much in style and sensitivity in its diplomacy. We have not *Fingerspitzengefühl* (literally, feeling with the tips of your fingers). What to do about it? I don't know. We need a new breed of people."

In terms of the Atlantic Council's interminable policy debates, Norstad had little patience for the advocates of the Streit line (federation) but even less for those who pushed the partnership idea, which had been put forth definitively by President Kennedy in a speech in Philadelphia, 4 July 1963.

The general's views on the transatlantic future generally coincided with my own, and I relished working with him. He, like most other Allied Supreme Commanders, had had to work in tandem daily with military and political leaders of the Alliance countries and thus had a practical sense of what teamwork could and should be. He had seen NATO in all aspects as a practical working entity, and he felt strongly that in his SACEUR position he had to represent *all* Alliance countries' interests. In our own day, one of his successors, General Wesley Clark, found himself hung up in 1999 on the horns of the same dilemma: Only he and the NATO Secretary General were in a position to act and speak for *all* members of the Alliance in conducting the operations in Kosovo. Alliance solidarity, in its full form, is evident only at the most critical times, for example on 15 September 2001, when the NATO Council, for the first time in its history, voted to invoke Article 5 of the NATO Treaty, which obliges all members to come to the aid of any member that has been attacked. In the wake of the World Trade Center Towers and Pentagon destruction, all countries expressed their full solidarity with the people of the United States. Quite untypically, the French newspaper *Le Monde* even headlined an article: "We are all Americans now." Sadly, the Bush administration, while thanking its Allies, asked them *as an Alliance*, for nothing. The subsequent operations in Afghanistan were conducted not by NATO, but by the United States, which picked and chose assets from among the various Allied countries on which it might call. NATO and true multilateralism remained in the background; some top members of Bush's government did not seem to understand or appreciate them at all. NATO was eventually to supply a "stabilization force" in Kabul, but almost too late to do much good. The conduct of the 2003 Iraq War was an even more egregious, even flagrant, example of this pattern of U.S. behavior.

5
In August 1961, the new Board of Governors of the Atlantic Institute appointed Henry Cabot Lodge (former senator and most recently candidate for vice president of the United States) director-

general of the new research institute. Here, the chairman of the board, former Belgian prime minister Paul van Zeeland, discusses Lodge's new duties with him at NATO headquarters in Paris.

6

Cabot Lodge and the author set about finding quarters in Paris to house the At-
lantic Institute in the autumn of 1961. Temporarily, Lodge decided on a suite of
rooms in the famous Hôtel de Crillon. The mimeograph machine was fitted clum-
sily into a bathtub, file cabinets against a graceful fireplace.

7

The private Atlantic Institute was funded, directed, and programmed in a completely multilateral way. Members of the 1961 Executive Committee (left to right): Henry Cabot Lodge, Paul van Zeeland, Baron Friederich Carl von Oppenheim, Jacques Rueff, Eric Johnston, and Professor Gerolamo Bassani.

8

In the late 1970s, the new Trilateral Commission came into being, sharing with the Atlantic Institute the general objective of a more united Atlantic-Pacific community of nations. Several joint board meetings were held to try to effect a merger; these attempts failed. Shown here ca. 1979, left to right: Aurelio Peccei, Dirk Stikker, Sir Frank Roberts, McGeorge Bundy, Sir John Loudon (Trilateral chairman), Emile van Lennep, and John W. Tuthill (director-general of the Atlantic Institute).

Kennedy's Assassination and American Internationalism

I was recovering from a minor operation on the day President Kennedy was assassinated in Dallas in November 1963. The whole country was rendered virtually comatose. I recorded some thoughts: "Probably not since Pearl Harbor, or perhaps since Lincoln's death, have the American people sustained such a shock. Its effects are incalculable, yet the Union is preserved. [At the president's funeral] a prelate read from Kennedy's favorite Bible quotations and from his inaugural address: 'Your old men shall dream dreams, and your young men shall see visions,' and 'where there is no vision, the people perish.'" Historians often say today that, had Kennedy lived, he probably would not have been able to enact the domestic agenda that his successor, Lyndon Johnson, did, especially the Civil Rights Act of 1965. We shall never know. But one thing that has never been recaptured by an American president since Kennedy's untimely death is the sense of wonderment—even awe—with which he was so widely regarded around the world. Kennedy put forth a vision the whole world could—and did—embrace.

A few weeks after the assassination, I saw my old friend Professor Arnold Bergstraesser. He told me that he had been eating in a restaurant in Freiburg, Germany, when news of Kennedy's death suddenly burst forth. "People poured out of the doors of all the shops and restaurants in that street, all of them with pain in their faces and tears on their cheeks." It had only been a few months earlier that Kennedy had stood in front of the Rathaus in Berlin and uttered the famous words, "*Ich bin ein Berliner!*" Despite his linguistic faux pas ("*ein Berliner*" is a jelly doughnut), everyone everywhere got the point: we are solidly one with you Germans!

Kennedy had embraced a strongly pro-Atlantic policy (although I did not agree with his preferred partnership concept). Later revelations about aspects of his private life were to tarnish somewhat the nobility and youthful optimism of his image, yet he had truly caught the imagination of the world. After Kennedy came the escalation of the Vietnam War, Watergate, the Iran-Contra scandal, the Monica Lewinsky affair, and other setbacks that have tended to fuel public cynicism. Tell-all history and the journalistic drive for immediate transparency sometimes cheat us of the fruits of American virtues.

A few days after Kennedy's death, I noted in my journal that the Department of State had begun a long-range training-and-assignment scheme for some of its best Foreign Service officers. Conceived by J. Robert Schaetzel (by far the most imaginative and energetic of the Monnet-Ball group who championed close U.S.-European relations via the partnership pattern), this went far beyond the modest efforts I had made in USIA to further the same goal: a group of topnotch specialists in Atlantic/European affairs who could staff the key positions in and out of Washington that would be one key to keeping the Atlantic community on track, through thick and thin. Some of the best officers were subsequently involved in these two programs and served with distinction over the decade that followed. Unfortunately neither the training nor assignment programs continued when subjected to new vicissitudes that beset transatlantic ties.

Around 1976, I chanced to meet the head of the Foreign Service Institute, the Department of State's training arm. I was told that that the Europe-oriented education courses, the traveling seminars focused on Europe, and—most regrettably—the career planning that sent top people to the new diplomatic missions that dealt with NATO, OECD, the European Communities, and the like had dropped away. Part of the reason was the waning interest on the part of FSOs headed for big things. Instead of looking at ambassadorships to the multinational organizations or to assignments with NATO and OECD staffs, for example, as the ultimate goals of their careers, most had fallen back on the traditional: They wanted above all to become ambassadors to the major national capitals—London, Paris, Bonn, Rome, Tokyo, and so on. So much for thickening the "Atlantic multinational elite," one of the key components of my own long-term plan for gradually putting together a tightly linked group of government officials, military officers, businessmen, labor leaders, and others who would put the common good ahead of even their own national interests. (I was to become extremely wary of the whole concept of national interests, as it would apply to a wholly new set of relationships among mature democracies, and of "like-mindedness" as the indispensable quality of leaders. More on that later.)

The only government-sponsored training institution that tries to instill a multinational perspective in its students is the NATO Defense College, today located in Rome. When Eisenhower was NATO's supreme commander for Europe, he told Air Marshal Sir Lawrence Darvall to begin a college—like the U.S. War College or the Imperial War College—to train field grade officers from all the Alliance countries, plus a few diplomats, in "multinational thinking." Often, the majors, colonels, and naval commanders who finish this six-month course are assigned to a NATO command, where their freshly broadened perspectives can be used and further fed.

The way that NATO commands have operated in the past also requires that staff officers think *first* of their *common* interests and objectives. Naturally, they reflect their own national backgrounds, but they are first and foremost—at least while on NATO duty—the servants of the composite of twenty-six nations that today form NATO. The small NATO civilian staff in Brussels is similarly pointed in the direction of the multinational good. These are true multinational teams, but today thin on the ground.

Not long ago, a friend who spent years in the U.S. diplomatic corps remarked that the members of that important body were expected, in all their actions, to put U.S. national interests—as currently defined—first. Jean Monnet once famously put the alternative course thusly: If there is a problem that requires international action, the participants in the discussion should not sit around the green table, representing their various countries. Instead, they should all sit on one side of the table, and face the problem on the other side.

One might remark that that approach is not possible unless all the participants—and their countrymen—are reasonably like-minded. Traditional diplomatic methods are still required when dealing with the Iraqs, Irans, Nigerias, Sudans, North Koreas, and Burmas of this world. But it is different, or should be, when we are dealing with our close allies.

Is it beyond our capacity as thinking Americans to recognize that our country's policy elite, and its larger pool of concerned citizens, must begin to think *internationally* more than nationally? In other words, should we follow a course (which at the turn of the century the Bush administration seemed inclined to take) of a *Pax Americana*, or instead a *Pax Democratica*—in which our democratic partners would share with us major decisions about reordering the world? In the 21st century so far, the trend that has prevailed and unfortunately strengthened is to say, even to our closest allies: "Here's the problem. Here's how we see it. Here's what needs to be done. Will you please come along?" And often, there is no "please." For allies in this position, the question would then be, "Why should we be asked to share burdens unless we have a share in determining what those burdens are?"

Contrasts: Working in Washington vs. Working in Europe

For me in 1963, working again in an American office had pluses and minuses. It was much easier to get things done, via pliant and intelligent clerks and secretaries, than it had been in the Atlantic Institute offices. Factors such as one language that everyone knew, one set of business procedures rather than the half dozen or more in the Paris workrooms, one basic kind of office machines and equipment and a standard filing system, made daily work much easier at 1616 H Street Northwest (home of ACUS) than it had been at 24, quai du 4 septembre. The American working environment was a comfortable cocoon. Yet I missed the intellectual rapport with (most) colleagues that I had enjoyed at the Institute during its "incubation" period. With a few exceptions, our Paris staff and the Institute's board members had all been recruited from the already multinational-minded (yet tiny) segment of Europe's leaders and the less visible, yet vital, cadre of research specialists, translators, and administrative and clerical types who had to do the daily work. There were very few of these in Washington, even at the Atlantic Council. I also noted at the time, that I missed the gentility and sophistication of Europe. Now, years later, I still do.

On return to my home country in 1963, I was struck by the marked nationalism of most Americans I encountered: retired ambassadors and cabinet secretaries, as well as the administrative strata on which we could call. In all but a few cases, even ambassadors who had played important roles in earth-shaking events like the creation of NATO were quite convinced *intellectually* that Atlantic "togetherness" was essential for our common future. Yet these same people in many instances turned out to be *emotionally* incapable of putting the common good of the Atlantic nations (and the world, for that matter) ahead of what they saw as the U.S. "national interest." Even such a man as T. C. Achilles, who had seen the overriding necessity for the NATO Treaty and pursued it with eventually triumphant intensity, was—when the chips were down—an ardent nationalist who felt that the United States *must* lead, and that others, of necessity, *must* follow.

This was not the spirit that animated the creators of the Atlantic Institute. Because the Board of Governors consisted of a plurality, but not a majority, of Americans, and because the staff and subsidiary bodies such as the A.I. Research Council were also not heavily weighted with Americans, the atmosphere was much different from that of the Atlantic Council. Readers will recall that the progenitors of the Institute had originally called for a common multinational board, with operational offices in both Paris and Washington, both directed by a single director general. But even leaders as fair-minded and devoted to a common Atlantic future, as for example, Christian Herter, believed that a dominating American focus on Atlantic ties was essential. Perhaps they were right, but this Americocentric vision is still, in the early 21st century, the predominant theme among the policy elite of the United States—perhaps even more than it was in the 1960s and 1970s. It is very difficult for us to try to share a common vision with "foreigners," perhaps because it is difficult to find a common American vision in our huge country. I simply do not know, but I ponder this question often.

In the late 1960s, when I lived and worked in New York, I took the occasion to call on one of the greats of the postwar period, Paul Nitze. He was working in a tiny office at an obscure but useful NGO, the Council on Religion and International Affairs. Mr. Nitze had been an architect of NATO, the Marshall Plan, and the containment policies of the Cold War. He had drafted the famed document, NSC-68, which underlay U.S. planning and strategy for decades. When I first met him, he was setting down his reflections on the development of U.S. foreign policy in the early post–World War II years, 1947–54. Here is what he had to say, a characterization I found it hard to gainsay:

> To my mind, the most serious modification in our national strategy beginning in 1953 was the decision to emphasize that our first aim was to pursue United States national interests and to play down our interest in the creation of a working international order. The moment we began to emphasize that our policy was directed to the pursuit of United States aims and interests, other nations were forced to look more closely to their own narrow interests.

And rarely after 1953, in my opinion, have our national sights been raised, as a top priority, in pursuit of the bedrock international interests that, at the very least, the peoples of the mature democracies share. A wise friend, retired after a long career in the Foreign Service, once put it this way to me: "The national interest is whatever those in power say it is in order to get the public to agree with what they want to do." Sadly, for the most part, I believe this still to be true.

I am sure that Nitze's words were not meant to reveal any partisan inclination on his part, for he served a series of administrations, both Republican and Democratic, without reservation, exemplifying the best traditions of bipartisanship. He was always a political appointee, but never the kept man of a particular president or secretary of state or defense. He simply used his vast knowledge and understanding of the way the world works to enliven and deepen the practice of American diplomacy in a crucial period. It's a pity that there are few such men today. The Eastern Establishment is no more and the coterie of political appointees to high foreign policy posts is spread out geographically but also ideologically. Men such as Nitze could never be compared with such partisans as former deputy secretary of defense Paul Wolfowitz or with Henry Kissinger, who attached himself to Richard Nixon's star.

Networking

The months from September through December 1963 were spent largely in networking—renewing old contacts and friendships, developing new ones. I wanted to know which organizations and people were more or less on the same wavelength about building the Atlantic community in a serious way. Included in this network were:

George Franklin, Council on Foreign Relations in New York
Leonard Tennyson and Curt Heidenreich, Washington office of the European Communities
Ralph C. M. Flynt, head of the international education division of the Department of Health, Education, and Welfare
Arnold Wolfers, dean of the Johns Hopkins School of Advanced International Studies
Ellsworth Tompkins, director of the National Association of High School Principals
Shep Stone and Joe Slater, the Ford Foundation
Philip Moseley and W. T. R. Fox, Columbia University
Wm. Cowan, Oceana Press, Dobbs Ferry, New York
Col. Dewitt Clinton Armstrong and Tim Stanley, international policy, the Pentagon
Department of State and U. S. Information Agency officials involved in Atlantic affairs (a dozen or so of each)
Malcolm Hoag, Horst Mendershausen, and others at the RAND Corporation, Los Angeles
Theodore Geiger, National Planning Association
The World Affairs Council of Northern California
Carl Spaeth, professor of law, and other Stanford University faculty
Peter Odegaard, Leslie Lipson, and Seymour Lipset, international studies, University of California, Berkeley
Max Lerner, M.I.T. faculty and *New York Post* columnist
William C. Olson, Congressional Reference Service, Library of Congress
Charles Cerami, international affairs correspondent, *The Kiplinger Letter*
Clarence K. Streit and other Atlantic Federalists
Walden Moore, driving force on the "Declaration of Atlantic Unity"
Robert Strausz-Hupé, Hans Kohn, and Erasmus Kloman, Foreign Policy Research Institute, University of Pennsylvania

Most of these people became lifelong friends. The association with the organizations involved also proved enduring, leading often to common projects of one kind or another.

Around this time I began an extensive card file on people and groups interested in the Atlantic connection. Over the years that followed, I was often able to put good people, good ideas, and good institutions in touch with one another. I began to develop my theory of building concepts, institutions, and leadership as part of the human infrastructure of a vital, growing international community of values and interests. Now, I see these ideas—and the people behind them—in a worldwide context of modernization. Democracy has spread so far that today, in the 21st century, one must speak of a global community of democracies. The Atlantic countries are simply the vital core of something bigger and—one hopes—in the long run even better.

I had begun networking some years earlier, but had not really codified and made use of my contacts, nor analyzed them with any care, before 1963. Returning to my own country and concentrating on the capital, New York, and major centers of learning helped to put my files (anchored in ancient-technology card files) to work for the Atlantic Movement. In January 1965, I wrote that "the most satisfying, and perhaps in the long run most fruitful, work is putting two people from different countries in touch ([and] not necessarily different countries, at that) and watching the intellectual sparks fly." I also began to learn a great deal more about NGOs, which were becoming more and more influential in the conduct of foreign relations at every level. I had instigated the creation of the Atlantic Institute with this role in mind. Now I made up my mind to see that still more special-purpose NGOs were created.

The Committee on Atlantic Studies

At the outset of 1964, I had made a decision: I would work half-time for the Atlantic Institute as its North American representative and half-time for the Atlantic Council, in a carefully calculated effort—designed largely by me—to try to influence trends in American education. Part of this educational work was done in conjunction with some of the leaders in U.S. secondary education, most of it with leaders in undergraduate and graduate international relations studies throughout the United States. The latter goal was served by a new U.S. Committee on Atlantic Studies (CAS), which I founded and which later became transatlantic in scope. However CAS changed its function over the years to something more modest, namely, encouraging research on transatlantic topics. In recent years its meetings have been funded by NATO. Now, after four decades, that CAS still exists is comforting; but its early objective—to influence the curricula of colleges and universities to reflect what the members thought were vital Atlantic realities, historical as well as contemporary—no longer has institutional advocacy. Over the years the CAS must have had some indirect influence on teaching, as its members have continued to be primarily university professors.

The original CAS members, whom I more or less hand-picked while on various forays to university centers, included:

Chairman Eugene V. Rostow, Dean, Yale Law School
Robert R. Bowie, director, Harvard Center for International Affairs
Robert Strausz-Hupé, director, Foreign Policy Research Institute at the University of Pennsylvania
Harold C. Deutsch, professor of history, University of Minnesota
Paul R. Hanna, head of the School of Education, Stanford University
Leslie Lipson, professor of political science, University of California, Berkeley
Philip E. Moseley, professor of international relations, Columbia University
Frank Munk, professor of political science, Reed College
Robert G. Neumann, director of the institute of foreign and international studies, University of California at Los Angeles
Eric Stein, professor of law, University of Michigan
Ellsworth Tompkins, director of the National Association of Secondary School Principals
Benjamin B. Warfield, former president of a New England liberal arts college and retired head of training for USIA
Robert Jordan, professor of political science, George Washington University
Ruth C. Lawson, professor of political science, Mount Holyoke College

At the time virtually all of these persons could be considered eminent in their fields. Most had held important government jobs, usually in the Department of State or in military government in World War II. Most were prolific writers—usually on subjects in one way or another related to the development of the Atlantic and European communities.

Most of them would go on to still more important posts. Rostow, for example, had served with the UN Economic Commission for Europe and returned again to public life in 1967, when he became administrator of the new U.S. Arms Control and Disarmament Agency. He later spent many years lecturing at the National War College. Neumann was appointed U.S. ambassador to Afghanistan in 1966, spent seven fruitful years there, then held other ambassadorial posts. Professor Ruth Lawson's many books concentrated on the practical, structural nuts and bolts of Atlantic and European institutions. Deutsch was the author of several books on the plots against Hitler's life. Frank Munk wrote an important book, *Atlantic Dilemma*, while a one-year research fellow of the Atlantic Institute. Bowie was in and out of government in the postwar years and had an especially profound influence on policy toward Germany and on the efforts to create a European federal system. Lipson's book, *The Democratic Civilization*, is a classic of political philosophy. Hanna was a profound thinker in the field of educational curricula; his theories of educating schoolchildren in a "progressive widening of circles of community"—beginning with first grade and continuing through high school—were influential.

And so it went; each member had much relevant experience in the various components of the emerging field of Atlantic studies, plus considerable influence within their own colleges and universities. Most of them had had significant government, or intergovernmental, experience. We depended on each other, as a team, to try to stimulate a new focus in American academia (with spillover into the lower schools) on a field that we all agreed had been neglected: Atlantic studies. How was this done?

We organized four faculty seminars in little more than a year—for colleges in and near the District of Columbia, the New York area, the Connecticut Valley, and the San Francisco Bay area (Stanford and UC-Berkeley)—to bring together other interested academics. In many cases, these included deans and college presidents, as well as professors and researchers. The seminars explored the whole idea of "Atlantic Studies," to inventory what various curricula already contained and how more coherent academic programs might be developed. At the undergraduate level and often required for graduation were a series of courses on Western civilization. Even in 1964, these courses were under assault by academics favoring more specialization—usually in the direction of European studies and studies relating to the developing world. Such European studies often omitted the important Atlantic implications and connections.

Another project of my Washington office was the effort to create an Atlantic bibliographical service to give scholars and others periodic access to new works in the field of Atlantic Studies. In one committee initiative, I worked with the Congressional Reference Service of the Library of Congress and with new efforts at cross-documentation at the University of Minnesota. A faded clipping from the *New York Times*, of 24 January 1965, refers in one line to the possible application of "new computer techniques" to such challenges. Beyond my brief exposure to what computers could do during the 1956 Hungarian Revolution to help settle refugees in the United States, my academic colleagues and I had no conception of what these machines might later accomplish. In Paris the Atlantic Institute established a bibliographical service, with an update published twice a year on new books in the Atlantic field, research work in progress, and plans for publications. *Atlantic Studies* appeared for several years, was said to be helpful to scholars and publishers in North America and Europe, and finally was discontinued when other means of contacts among scholars were developed, notably the Pentagon-sponsored AMPARTS program, grandfather of today's Internet. In 1965, the best we could do was a good old-fashioned, cross-indexed 3x5 card file, fed by questionnaires to a growing network. Even IBM punch cards were deemed too costly at the time.

Today the expenses for CAS and its various activities seem ridiculously low: $35,000 or so for the entire 1965 year. In those days academics seemed to have more time; with the help of small travel stipends, they were able to attend a two- or three-day meeting in Washington or Berkeley, involving up to twenty participants. Today, the costs are so much greater, and the time busy professors and other specialists can afford to spend on such peripheral activities is much less. We were fortunate three and four decades ago to get important thinkers to stop and focus on big ideas.

At the beginning of 1965, our committee had great plans: a colloquium with our European counterparts in Paris; an inventory of American colleges' Study Abroad programs (and an attempt to help shape them); a program of grants on Atlantic Studies sponsored by the U.S. Office of Education; an intense survey on selected campuses of Atlantic Studies curricular trends; an exchange of State Department officials with professors of Atlantic studies; and a review of the Fulbright program and how it might be improved, from our committee's perspective. The *Journal of the National Association of High School Principals* also put out a special edition concentrating on the Atlantic community, which I coedited.

Working the Third Sector and Other Delights

In addition to these CAS activities, I was involved in a good many other projects: the recasting and distribution of an Atlantic Institute study, *Common Policy-Making in a Nuclear Age* (something that in the 21st century might elicit either a "ho hum" or an "omigod!"); planning Institute studies on capital investment in Atlantic countries and on EEC relations with Latin America; promotion of an Institute book on problems of aid to education in developing countries; the framing of a study—leading to action, as it turned out—on the transformation of the NATO Parliamentarians Conference into a full-blown (officially sanctioned) Atlantic Parliamentary Assembly; and an attempt on my part to spur the creation of a new private Atlantic Foundation.

The foundation idea was something I nursed along in one way or another for years. Such a Third Sector body was eventually created, but with only modest funds, by Theodore C. Achilles, who gave some of his own capital to the effort. Although this foundation could never do more than make small grants to the Atlantic Council at critical times, even that was helpful. The term "Third Sector" was coined by John Gardner, a great foundation executive, to encompass all efforts in a society that were not commercial or governmental, notably the work of foundations and voluntary organizations. By 2000, Third Sector activity had become a vital force in the United States and, more recently as "civil society," was becoming emblematic of democratic societies.

In spring 1965, I suddenly received an invitation from the German government to join a group of American journalists for two weeks of observing the new German army, the *Bundeswehr*, firsthand. My friend, Col. Horst Krueger, a former liaison officer in Washington, led the tour, which was a real eye-opener. We visited with officers and independent-minded enlisted men at many bases, viewed tank maneuvers, saw the first version of the vertical takeoff Harrier jet emerge like a phantom out of a copse on a war-games field, and discussed the character of the new forces in Bonn. I came away with the firm impression that this was no reincarnation of Hitler's *Wehrmacht*, nor even of the Kaiser's old army or the interwar *Reichswehr*, but a genuinely civilian-controlled force appropriate to a democratic nation. Nothing changed my view that Germany's military contribution to NATO has been genuine and strong—and that there are no militarists, rightists, or neo-Nazis among the top leadership. Col. Krueger, incidentally, had been one of a small group of former World War II officers who spent a year in a remote monastery in the Eiffel Mountains planning a firmly civilian-controlled new German military. I was delighted to think that our 1955 informal seminars of German and American officers in Hof had perhaps helped a little.

I also continued my work as secretary of the NATO Parliamentarians cultural and information committee in helping to educate the members (including the chairman, Senator Karl Mundt) about the realities facing the Atlantic community.

My involvement in all this activity—some in train, some in the planning stages—was suddenly interrupted in 1965 by an offer to join the Ford Foundation. My old boss from Germany, Shepard Stone (whom I hardly knew during German days, but who ran the entire reeducation and reorientation program there), invited me to become one of his associates in the International Affairs Program at Ford. Although my work as head of the new Atlantic Institute office in Washington had begun well, with a number of good projects under way and many more planned, I could hardly say no to Stone. Always the optimist, I felt this was an opportunity

I simply could not refuse. I might possibly accomplish a great deal more for the Atlantic community with Ford's millions behind me than I ever could in an obscure office in Washington, scrabbling for slim resources. I accepted and began work in New York on 1 May 1965.

Ford Foundation: A Prime World Mover

New York! I had visited briefly over the years, but now, to live there! I found the city exciting, possibly the most cosmopolitan and culturally rich of all great cities, on a par at least with Paris and London. I rented a tiny fourth-floor walkup on East 72nd Street, a very modest abode sandwiched in between the rich. I walked to work every day through Central Park and into the canyons of Fifth Avenue. I had such a heavy workload (vetting and weighing an endless flow of grant applications) that I didn't have much time for social or cultural life; but I did meet interesting people and relished the aura of the city. Its decline began shortly after I left New York in 1967, to be reborn in the 1990s under Mayor Rudolph Giuliani. Great cities have their ups and downs, but in 1965 New York was a great place.

And to work for what was then the greatest philanthropy, the Ford Foundation! During my USIA years, I had had a lot to do with parceling out money to "pro-Europe" and "pro-Atlantic'" groups. Now, within Ford's International Affairs Program, the scope and funding possibilities were much larger, or so it seemed. I had not yet realized how restricted the opportunities were despite the foundation's great wealth, because of the myriad demands on its resources.

Shepard Stone headed International Affairs (IA). His right-hand man, Joe Slater, who had also held high posts in postwar Germany, salted the IA program constantly with a rush of fertile ideas and a critical intelligence. From early in IA's existence, Stanley Gordon had been given the job of gatekeeper — fending off supplicants whose projects did not interest Stone or Slater but who could not be denied a polite interview. Moselle Kimbler, who had worked for Stone in Germany, was the sparkling executive secretary of the office. She kept the paper flowing and everyone's morale burnished and deftly handled a steady stream of consultants to staff out specialized grant requests. A recent law school graduate, Richard Catelano, was also on hand to lend sharp wits to the endless and often complex reviews. Secretaries were many (no desktop computers in those days) and amiable. It was a fine place to work. It was also replete, in and out of our office, with some prickly personalities and not-so-obvious pitfalls. Working to help people such as Jean Monnet and his Paris staff, or the American and European intellectuals who came through our revolving door, or remaining cognizant of the rarefied atmosphere of a thoroughly distinguished and demanding Board of Trustees kept one dancing on one's toes.

One of my first assignments was to compile a history of the Ford Foundation's International Affairs Program, beginning in the 1950s and ending with grants made and planned at the end of 1965. Stone and Slater felt this would be needed in internal turf battles at the foundation; they later proved right, although the impact of the report was not what we had hoped. Undertaking this research helped me to understand rather quickly what Ford had done in my area of competence and also to understand much better than I had before the ramifications of the Atlantic idea world-wide. This, and my new assignments to winnow out the good projects from the chaff and recommend grants (in about 10 percent of the cases that came across my desk), gave me in two years an unparalleled oppor-tunity to see what was going on in Europe, North America, and Japan, to advance learning and indirectly mold intellectual resources in this area so vital to world progress. My work also enabled me to gently promote a few projects I thought would be especially fruitful if funded adequately.

Now, in the 21st century, my views now tempered by 35 more years of experience, I leaf through this IA report and am once again amazed at the scope, acuity, and impact of what Ford had done. The total amount of grants made by the IA office in the period 1952–65 amounted to somewhat over $125 million—close to $1 billion in 2005 dollars. Much of this went to projects and institutions that in myriad ways stood a good chance of strengthening transatlantic bonds and freeing the institutions and people promoting Europe's unification from insignificance or, worse, dependence on what governments wanted them to do—or not do. Although in close touch with our government, Stone never hesitated to fund activities and individuals whose impact would be more far-reaching, daring, or different than what the government would have endorsed. We were also entirely free from pressures from the business world, even the Ford Motor Com-pany itself. It was this independence, and the uses of Ford's money that in turn made the recipients more independent, that was the great glory of the foundation. It soon became clear to me, reinforced in recent years by having had access to accounts of the times that have surfaced, that Stone's operation was not as independent or secure within the Ford Foundation as he, or his staff, might have hoped. But that is another story. For a decade and a half, Ford's IA program had, I believe, an enormous impact on what happened within Europe and between the two sides of the Atlantic.

Stone was a remarkable man. The son of a Jewish tailor from Lithuania who settled in Hanover, New Hampshire, Shep, as everyone called him, was a bright lad and an avid scholar. His family sacrificed a great deal to further his education. With his father's help and his own hard-charging efforts, he was enrolled at Dartmouth College, where he built on his scholarship and academic contacts to equip himself to study abroad. His father insisted that he should do graduate work in Germany—in his opinion the best at the time. Thus Shep spent two years during the pre-Hitler years at the University of Berlin, earning his doctorate and finding his wife, Charlotte— "Musi" to Shep and close friends. An extraordinarily gregarious man, and one with an eye always on the main chance, culturally and professionally, Stone built a network of contacts in Germany that lasted through the Hitler years, World War II, and the postwar period. Some of his friends and acquaintances fell by the wayside over the years, but many did not. He had a remarkable network, eventually including all of Europe.

Stone worked for the *New York Times* in the thirties and early forties, writing about foreign affairs. When the United States entered the war, Stone joined up and followed the U.S. armies into Europe as an intelligence specialist and a civil affairs officer. He was able to put his many German contacts to work for American aims under the Occupation, most especially in the de-Nazification and reorganization of the West German press. But by 1947 he had become increasingly frustrated with the army's way of reorienting the German people, as the government directives required. He returned to New York for two years as the deputy editor of the *New York Times* Sunday magazine. When John J. McCloy, one of the greats of American foreign policy in the postwar period, was named U.S. high commissioner for Germany in 1949, he enlisted Stone as one of his right-hand men, to be in charge of the entire German reorientation and reeducation. McCloy's staff, and Stone's very large "substaff," were recruited from the regular Foreign Service, from private life, and from the universities. A few were hangovers from the military occupation, many of them able, some not. Many, like me young veterans who had managed to complete their BAs and MAs in international studies after the war, were in most cases extremely keen and able to contribute.

It had been in 1952 that I, brand new and still wet behind my Far Western ears, was sent to Frankfurt to join Stone's staff, at a very low spot on his totem pole. I met him only fleetingly then but felt his presence continuously, in the directives issued by his office that guided my immediate boss, Ralph Burns, head of the vast exchange of persons program. He also figured in the High Commission staff's "jungle telegraph"—gossip and rumors about what was supposedly going on, or planned, in the rarefied atmosphere of the precincts of McCloy and Stone. They both returned to the United States a few months after I arrived in Germany, but their fingerprints were all over the practical steps that had been planned and were now undertaken to complete our democratizing mission.

242 An Architect of Democracy

So I had known a good deal of who Shep Stone was and what he thought, even though I was not in 1952 a key member of his top team. As the years pass, I believe I understand, increasingly, what his early experience and later tenure in Germany meant to the accomplishment of American and Allied goals in that deeply troubled country.

Ford and the Congress for Cultural Freedom

Once, when I worked for Stone at Ford, I urged him to commission a study on the work of his High Commission office under McCloy in setting the stage for the reintegration of Germany into the world community of free nations. He demurred. "No matter how we would arrange it," he said, "it would seem self-serving on my part." So the definitive biography of Shepard Stone remains to be put before the world. Völker Berghahn did a part of this job, using Stone's career as a framework, in *America and the Intellectual Cold Wars in Europe*, which largely recounted the triumphs and vicissitudes of the Congress for Cultural Freedom. This fifteen-year effort, begun and largely financed by the CIA, was a response to the massive onslaughts of the Soviet cultural propaganda machine in Europe. Realizing the critical importance of the intellectual elite of Europe to the outcome of the Cold War as it began to develop, the Soviets held great conferences of every left-leaning scholar and writer (including as many Americans as they could co-opt) to set up sturdy links with Russians and East Europeans of comparable stature. The Jean-Paul Sartres of the cryptopolitical scene, from about 1948 to the early 1970s, were prime targets (and usually willing ones) for Communist cultural mobilization.

My CIA contacts in the 1950s didn't tell me much about the Congress for Cultural Freedom; I wasn't much interested in or involved with the literati. But Shepard Stone was, especially during his years in early postwar Germany. Stone and a few of the European-oriented Ford Foundation board members understood this situation and the stakes in the world of ideas. Over the fifties and sixties, Ford made a number of grants to the Congress, to supplement what the CIA was doing. I was not personally involved, but I believe that this situation caused a good deal of turmoil in certain circles within the Foundation. In 1965, a series of astounding (and quite inaccurate) articles appeared in a leftish counterculture magazine called *Ramparts*, published in San Francisco. This managed to rip the cover off a good many nongovernmental efforts, including the Congress, backed clandestinely by the CIA in the preceding 10 to 15 years. I knew, from inside knowledge gained in 1956–58 during my USIA days in Washington, that these accounts were for the most part fragmentary, terribly slanted, and grossly inaccurate. The CIA was sometimes discovered by a hungry press to have backed something it shouldn't have, which was thus deemed to have failed, but the successes, which to my knowledge far outweighed the mistakes, would never be recounted.

In 1965, James Reston of the *New York Times* wrote five full-page articles on the subject in an attempt to be more evenhanded. But he too further perpetuated inaccuracies and misperceptions, as mentioned earlier.

In particular, I thought that *Ramparts* and the *Times* hurt U.S. foreign policy considerably by making public the CIA funding of the French and Italian non-Communist trade unions. This had been undertaken in partnership with the AFL-CIO, and largely through an extraordinary labor unionist named Irving Brown, based in Paris, and the former Communist Jay Lovestone of New York. Lovestone had broken with the party in the 1930s and knew what had to be done, and how, to wrest control of the labor movements in Europe from the hands of the Communists. I had come to know Lovestone pretty well in 1963–65, during my Atlanticist days in Washington, when he was a board member of the Atlantic Council of the United States. He never told me anything about the European union struggle, but I grew to like him and found his biography, which I read years later, fascinating.

The key American in the Congress for Cultural Freedom was Executive Director Mike Josselson. In the waning days of the Congress, and sadly of Josselson himself (ill with cancer), I met him at his home in Geneva at the behest of Stone. After Josselson died a few months later and largely because of the press revelations about the Congress, it was disowned by the CIA, given a few terminal grants to keep on publishing some of its excellent journals, such as *Preuves* in France, *Der Monat* in Germany, and *Survey* (on East-West affairs) and *Encounter* in the UK. So the Ford Foundation stepped into the breach, with funds to keep it going for a while. The Congress was renamed and in the summer of 1967, Stone resigned from the Ford Foundation to head the International Congress for Cultural Freedom in Paris, where I visited him a couple of years later. He had done his best with it, but the revelations that men of great stature, such as Raymond Aron and Ignazio Silone, had been involved in a clandestine venture caused many of them to resign from the Congress.

Although I was never party to these under-the-table activities, I knew enough about the European situation in those days, and about how U.S. policy had been fighting a cultural cold war tooth and nail for some years, to realize that much was at stake. Somehow, with even more surprising revelations surfacing since 1991 about parallel Soviet Agitprop activities —some dating back to the 1920s—the United States and its allies emerged on top. Virtually the sole reason the CIA funded organizations such as the

Congress for Cultural Freedom secretly was to protect the often-eminent figures who headed them. Based on what I knew then and much that I learned later, the substance and effect of what was done was wholly admirable, even praiseworthy. The basic problem was that in the 1940s and '50s, one could not rely on private funds—foundations, corporate funders, and so on—to take on programs of such size, duration, and scope. The role of the Ford Foundation and a few other large U.S. foundations, such as Rockefeller, in this kind of activity was substantial in the case of the Congress for Cultural Freedom; but even Ford could not have taken publicly an exposed position of such magnitude. And one had to have frequented certain corridors of government (as Stone and McCloy had done) to see the relative importance of doing things of this kind, and of taking the necessary risks.

Building Atlantic Bridges

As far as I was concerned, my two years at Ford were a golden opportunity to help the Atlantic cause along. Thirty-plus years later, Berghahn's book made it seem as if the Ford Foundation, and Stone in particular, were primarily involved in those years with fighting the cultural cold wars to defeat the Soviet cultural offensive. I find this a distorted picture of what went on. In my first Ford assignment, writing the fifteen-year history of Ford's international affairs grants, the Congress for Cultural Freedom played but a small role, perhaps crucial, but dwarfed by the truly vast array of funding done with other objectives in mind. Its European and Atlantic "action programs" involved political and social objectives, as distinct from grants—many of them large—by other branches of the foundation that were developing European academic capabilities in fields of learning where we thought the United States had been forging ahead in the perilous interwar and wartime years. Whether American pioneering in the social sciences (in particular) was really what Europe's groves of academe needed in the postwar years can be argued both ways, but it was a challenge, and the more progressive figures in Europe could see that. These scholarship-building programs were not generally the writ of Stone's International Affairs programs. IA did put out large sums for programs that involved academicians, such as the creation of the Free University of Berlin. Academic figures certainly figured in IA funding; but IA was oriented primarily towards a general strengthening of European and transatlantic elites in ways that would affect the cohesion of the Western world, with primarily political aims and results.

Accordingly, one finds in the IA history I drafted, such off-the-wall grants as $1 million to the Athens Center of Ekistics (a fancy word for urban settlements); many substantial grants to launch and sustain the London-based International Institute for Strategic Studies (Slater's idea and today a reliable fixture in the world of independent thought about defense and security); funds for the origination and underwriting for the Pugwash talks between Western and Soviet scientists; the funding of Columbia University's American Assembly, which for years has gotten important people together to discuss major world issues; and funding for the building of both a library and an international school for the United Nations. It also granted $875,000 to M.I.T. for a four-year study to determine "what information and ideas reach various kinds of people in foreign countries, the channels by which information and ideas are conveyed, and the effect which psychological, institutional, political, economic, and philosophical factors have on the ways in which people interpret, and react to, the information and ideas." I never knew the outcome of the latter research, although Professor Daniel Lerner used some of the findings in his pioneering study of why the efforts to launch the European Defense Community (1952–54) came to naught. This was all pretty heady stuff.

The IA program recognized—before most pundits did—the growing place of Japan in the international firmament. Among several pioneering grants to Japanese intellectuals and institutions was one to set up the Japan Center for International Exchanges, which today occupies a major place in the work of NGOs in Japan and worldwide. A young Japanese, Tadashi Yamamoto, spawned the JCIE with Ford's help. Yamamoto's work has almost singlehandedly broadened and deepened the philanthropic and NGO field, or civil society, in long-isolated Japan.

The Public Gap in Understanding World Affairs

My own hand in grant-making was tested in the cases of American world affairs councils in various large cities, which one day in 1965 Stone suggested I explore. Earlier, the foundation had made sizable grants to the Foreign Policy Association of New York, a national body that pioneered, with Ford's money, the Great Decisions programs around the country. These involved local citizens' groups studying a different set of world issues each year, for example population, arms control, European integration, human rights, and trade policies, with FPA providing the agenda and a syllabus. World Affairs Councils and other adult education programs have often featured Great Decisions over the years. But our new IA idea was to help local World Affairs Councils become substantial players, if they seemed to have the prerequisites.

I took on this job of exploration and goal-making with zest, as I had long felt that the great body of intelligent, reasonably well-educated people of the United States had not had enough exposure to the character and shape of the world outside our borders, nor the opportunities to get involved in world affairs. The gap in understanding between the kinds of Americans, Europeans, and Canadians who were deeply involved in world affairs—distinct minorities in all countries—and the great general public had appeared to me to be formidable, whether seen from Europe or within the United States itself. And in the United States, because of our geographic and historic isolation, and the lack of a tradition of involving elites (broadly defined) in the management of our foreign relations, this gap was more like an abyss. The lacunae in knowledge and understanding varied a great deal from region to region; the Northeast and Middle Atlantic States perforce nurtured a liberal "Eastern Establishment" from the early days of the nation. New York in 1965 was yet again wholly different in character from other main American cities. Together with Bostonian and Philadelphian movers and shakers, the New York stockbrokers, lawyers, business moguls, publicists, journalists, and academicians had pretty much run the foreign affairs of the United States for 170 years. Even in these places the superelite, such as Acheson, Dulles, or Harriman, were set off from most local civic leaders.

This applied to the Foreign Service, although the demographics of leadership in foreign policy began to change gradually after World War II, when young people like myself from other parts of the United States began to get deeply involved in American interests overseas. Except for New York City—and to a lesser extent, Philadelphia, Boston, and the Ivy League colleges—the group of thinking Americans well versed in the challenges of foreign affairs, and who could influence their thinking co-citizens, was tiny. And the trickle-down theory of opinion formation was not necessarily working well in the sixties. Television news, a few documentaries, and the emphasis on foreign area studies in some of the bigger and better universities were beginning to change this equation, but the effect was not yet clear. The effect on the great American voting public left a pretty thin veneer of comprehension, if any, in the minds of the citizenry in general. Shep Stone and Joe Slater, my bosses, seemed to understand this problem in an instinctive sort of way. Stone considered himself an integral part of the liberal Eastern Establishment; Slater aspired too, with some success. But they were both smart enough to see that the country's course abroad could not be assured by continuing to rely on a few eastern-spawned "Wise Men." Among other factors, the growth of television provided many citizens with a vast new exposure to foreign affairs, which hardly provided effective understanding, let alone wisdom, about what was actually going on abroad and what U.S. interests were. (Today, I believe this gap may be worse than in 1966.)

My new remit, along with shepherding a lot of other unrelated grants to the point of decision, was to see what the World Affairs Councils around the country were doing and whether or not some judicious infusion of funds could help them reach more key people in their regions, and reach them more effectively. Looking back on what we had at that time, and what the councils and other key NGOs active in adult education in world affairs are now able to do, I think Ford made a difference. I started this aspect of my work critically, but with an article of faith that something worthwhile might be done.

Accordingly, I crisscrossed the country, from Boston to Minneapolis, from Cleveland and Cincinnati to Dallas, and up and down the west coast, talking with the executives and boards of world affairs councils that seemed worth the trouble. I found a few that were competently led and that were already doing innovative things to reach adults who had finished their formal education but entertained a serious interest in foreign affairs. Ultimately, we made grants, at my recommendation, to the councils of Northern California, based in San Francisco, Portland, Oregon, Cincinnati, Minneapolis-Minnesota, and Philadelphia. Somewhere between $25,000 and $100,000 went to each of them. Over the years I have followed most of these councils and their executives and can see that most made excellent use of the Ford infusions.

I spent a good deal of time in Boston, assessing its council. With an especially rich endowment of expertise at Harvard, M. I. T., Boston University, Tufts, and other important academic institutions at hand, the Boston World Affairs Council was profiting from these fine resources and using new techniques to attract keen citizens—particularly younger ones—to its programs. By constructing grants correctly, and conditioning Ford money on certain other forward steps, we could and usually did, make a difference in such cases. In my judgment, Boston qualified.

Shortly after McGeorge Bundy arrived at Ford as our new president, I forwarded to him a recommendation for my newest WAC grant of around $90,000 to Boston. Once Stone and Slater had approved such proposals, they would automatically go to the president of the foundation before he presented them to the board of trustees. The previous president's approval for this sort of thing had been more or less automatic. Bundy's predecessor, Dr. Henry Heald, had been a reasonably good manager, adept at moving paper, keeping channels straight, and maintaining accountability while giving his executives considerable leeway. This time the grant was returned from new President Bundy marked "disapproved"—no reason given, just dead on arrival. I asked Stone if I could go see Bundy; in particular I was surprised because Bundy was a Bostonian and a top-grade member of the Harvard "academocracy" who presumably knew his home base.

My visit with Bundy was short, its content astounding. "Mr. Bundy," I said, "I note that you have turned down this grant request for the Boston World Affairs Council. Could you tell me why?" He sat back, gazing at me square-jawed and owlishly through thick lenses, and intoned, "Because my father, in the early thirties, was the secretary of the Foreign Policy Association of Boston, and all they ever did was to meet monthly, have lunch, and listen to some pundit talk about things international. I don't think supporting that kind of thing is a wise expenditure of Ford's money." Trying not to look thunderstruck, I argued back, as diplomatically as I could. "Well, sir. That was more than thirty years ago and things have changed considerably, in Boston and elsewhere. The potential audience for serious discussion of international affairs is much greater; the national and regional intellectual resources to help bodies such as the Boston Council are much greater and more available, and their programs a great deal more ingenious and effective than you seem to think." I then told him about some of the innovative things the Boston Council had started, such as long weekend retreats for young couples seriously interested in foreign relations, but to no avail. I later wrote to myself: "This man has a mind like a steel trap, but he closes it too quickly."

McGeorge Bundy in effect then closed down Shep Stone's entire International Affairs operation. He made it clear that he felt the foundation's priorities should be domestic affairs, plus developing countries and higher education. Accordingly, he gave $1 million each to Cambridge and Oxford Universities; later, grants to Europe (but usually of a different sort from IA's) were resumed. Parenthetically, Bundy's priorities reflected those of the country as a whole: the rather new realization that what was then called the Third World deserved a good deal more attention and a concomitant deemphasis on Europe and the Atlantic. (Why our government and our people are not capable of riding more than one or two foreign policy horses at once, I'll never understand.) However, the lingering Cold War kept what I came to call the *over*developed world on our national front burner. But the emphasis on helping Europe unite and on knitting together a stronger Atlantic community—long-range ideas of fundamental, long-term importance—was greatly reduced, by Ford and other foundations, as well as by the U.S. government. This remains true at the beginning of the 21st century: in fighting the Afghan/al-Qaida war and pursuing Saddam Hussein, the nation turned its attention away from nurturing close ties with our half brothers and sisters in Europe. Many foundations, think tanks, and other NGOs did the same.

Fortunately, before Bundy took over I had already engineered a grant to the national Foreign Policy Association to provide a high-level full-time consultant for their staff, whose job it would be to ride circuit to the World Affairs Councils the country over and advise—free of charge—on how to beef up their operations, fund-raising, programs, and so on. I had formed a solid three-way partnership with Samuel Hayes, head of the FPA, and Joseph Johnson, then head of the Carnegie Endowment for International Peace. Sam hired an extraordinary former Foreign Service officer of Polish extraction, Zygmunt Nagorski, who performed marvelously, with his finger constantly on the pulse of all the regions of the country and the steaming cauldron of it all, Washington, D.C. I was also able at this time to engineer a partnership between Ford and the Carnegie Endowment for International Peace; our efforts to improve public understanding of international affairs resulted in a fruitful division of labor. Joe Johnson, Carnegie's president, was a fine old ex-diplomat who had succeeded the notorious Alger Hiss. The Carnegie Endowment had continued doing quiet, painstaking work under Johnson, thanks to the foresight of Andrew Carnegie, who set it up at the turn of the 20th century to pioneer in the search for peace—a new idea at that time. Joe Johnson's assistant, Dr. Charles Patrick, worked with me on the nuts and bolts of world affairs education; Charlie became a lifelong friend and coconspirator in many subsequent good endeavors.

One amusing aspect of working for a huge, incredibly wealthy foundation was the effect it sometimes had on one's acquaintances. From 1957 to 1961, for example, Professor William Yandell Elliott of Harvard had been party to the Euro-American efforts to launch the Atlantic Institute. A noted economist, Elliott was an expansive southern gentleman who spoke in flowery, vintage rhetoric. His conception of a model Atlantic Institute was remote from mine (and from most of those working for its establishment): he insisted that our proposed multilateral think tank should be a reincarnation of the Arthurian Knights of the Round Table—updated somewhat to be sure. I think he saw himself as one of the knights. His national influence increased substantially when he became an assistant to Under Secretary of State (later Secretary) Christian Herter. For about two years most of my correspondence about the Institute with Herter was funneled through Bill Elliott, who would write, "The Secretary has asked me to tell you . . . " I suspected that often the responses were Bill's own, not Herter's. I went to see Herter myself, collared him for membership on the Institute's board when he was about to leave public office, and got his personal—indeed enthusiastic—OK to our plans. Having been sidelined, Elliott was furious and henceforth wanted nothing more to do with me. On the theory that "you can't win 'em all," I dropped him from our inner circle; but that was not the end of the story.

One evening in June 1965, when I had begun working for the Ford Foundation, I attended a meeting of the Foreign Policy Research Institute (FPRI) in Philadelphia, of which I was still a fellow. Strausz-Hupé had me writing a paper on multinational elites for FPRI. Across the room at a reception Professor Bill Elliott and I spotted each other. Having no hard feelings, I went over and shook his hand. He could not avoid me and asked, rather coolly, what I was doing these days. When I told him I was a program officer at Ford, his demeanor changed at once. "Oh my goodness! I'm now at American University and you *must* come down [to Washington] to see what we are doing!" I readily agreed and later had a lunch at Elliott's new university with a dozen of his colleagues, who I'm sure were all angling for Ford grants. Elliott fell all over himself; it was embarrassing. He thought perhaps I could help arrange a Ford grant to one of his current projects. It didn't work out that way; among other things I had too little influence in the area of his interest. But I must confess I was amused by this (and a number of similar incidents) and had to keep reminding myself, "It's the *money* they want, not your beautiful friendship!" But I did note that some of my Ford colleagues were unable to separate their true popularity from their inflated sense of self-importance.

It is interesting now, in the 21st century, to speculate on how adult understanding of foreign affairs might have been much more broadened and improved if Ford's program of grant giving to World Affairs Councils and like bodies had been sustained long-term. Maybe voters today would be better informed — and led.

The Far Right

The uses of the terms "right" and "left" in characterizing politics always suggest a linear alignment on a horizontal spectrum, showing far right and far left at opposite ends, with ordinary conservatives, centrists and liberals arrayed between them. But when I was in Germany I began to think of a different image. The more I studied and saw the workings and effects of Nazism, Fascism, and Communism, the more I began to feel that they had a great deal in common: their alleged ends — ultranationalism and race purity on the right, and the brotherhood of the world proletariat on the left — might be articulated differently, but the methods they used and the general results of these methods were similar. In short, they were all totalitarian states, attempting total control over their subjects. This similarity has since been adumbrated exhaustively by many observers. Those who thought they were promoting the antithesis of Communism by embracing Fascism were pretty much in the same operational boat: the ends, in both cases, justifying the same inhuman means. Stalin and Hitler were natural pals, who fell out over the spoils of their 1939 pact.

At Ford, back in my own country after some years abroad, and being exposed to homegrown American politics—especially as I got out into the far reaches of the United States to observe bodies such as World Affairs Councils—I had good opportunity to view both political extremes at work and to see the results of a great deal of ignorance and misguided thinking.

A less than innocent (in hindsight ominous) far right skein of circumstance came to my attention while scouting the country for opportunities to help world affairs education. In 1966, I was in Cincinnati, working out the terms of a grant with Bill Messner, director of the local World Affairs Council. We met with Neal McElroy, chairman of Procter and Gamble, who had been Ike's secretary of defense and was now Messner's council chairman. McElroy and Messner told me that a few months earlier, a raucous, unruly crowd of right-wingers had interrupted a ceremony arranged annually by the World Affairs Council to celebrate United Nations Day by raising both the U.S. and the UN flags in the town square. These people led a campaign to denigrate the UN as involving a loss of American sovereignty and therefore dangerous to all our national ideals and identity, and the sanctity of our Constitution. Messner expanded on this pattern of thought after we left McElroy (who, like Ike, was a moderate, rational Republican). Messner gave me books and pamphlets issued by what turned out to be a nationally organized and well-funded movement by the extreme right. I began my own collection of their works and of clippings and more detailed studies about the movement. It occupies a considerable space in my archives—right next to material on the far left. Interestingly, many of the right-wing books and pamphlets were written by Phyllis Schlaffly, who must by now be well into her nonage, still at work.

I have never managed the time to investigate thoroughly the far-flung evidence of the machinations—and they were, and remain, just that—of the considerable right-wing network of pseudointellectuals and eager publicists. But I have learned enough about them and their kind over forty years to know that they should not be taken lightly. Neither should their ideas be ignored, however attractively formulated and readily available they may be. I am convinced that out of such groups as the John Birch Society in the 1940s and '50s and many other kindred front organizations a modern form of neofascist thought has taken root in American and other Western societies. This material—often so puerile that it makes an intelligent person with a modicum of knowledge about the history of politics, gag—has been stuffed into the airwaves and pages of our media in considerable quantity. The raw untruths these thought currents spew forth are usually emitted in unadulterated output at the outset and then translated, often by clever thought manipulators, into forms that seem at best innocuous and at worst, dangerous. In the 1960s, much of this stuff was subsidized by New England industrialist John Welch.

One example: A widely circulated 1960s paperback, *None Dare Call it Conspiracy*, is an attack on the U.S. Federal Reserve system (and other branches of government), citing bogus documents (usually from some other equally spurious publication) as reference points, complete with footnotes, to make the reader believe that its "sources" are reputable. The little book tries to convince the reader that the Federal Reserve is not really a government agency, citing its unusual form of governance—a federation of a number of regional Federal Reserve banks that are "independent" and "out of control" of the citizenry. The book further stated that the Fed is the source of Communist infiltration and, at the same time, controlled entirely by big business, which answers to no one; and that the real powers behind this system, who manipulate Americas' banks and the economic life of the nation, are people such as the Rockefellers and a small cabal of shadowy figures, mostly Jews. Another 1960s book of this ilk entitled *America: Listen!* advances "proof" that the Kennedys and other important families conned us into scurrilous and dangerous foreign adventures, and so on.

More recent books, such as the *Turner Diaries* purportedly show the reader how any sort of left-wing liberal movements and theories are conspiracies that undermine our free way of life. The so-called militias composed mainly of self-appointed armed zealots of the right are an excrescence of this tendency. They team up with the manipulators who have manufactured an entire body of spurious doctrine claiming that any and all Americans should have guns for their own protection and to be ready when it becomes necessary to start another American Revolution to free ourselves from intrusive, excessively liberal government. Any measure to require the registration of guns is denounced with the words: "The first thing Hitler did when he came to power was to confiscate all guns, house to house." We cannot allow that to happen, say the militiamen, the neo-Nazis, and the gun zealots, ignoring Supreme Court decisions over the years. Both the Court and the gun lobby cite the Second Amendment to the Federal Constitution to support their decisions and arguments. What does the Second Amendment say? "A well-regulated militia being necessary to the security of a free State, the right of the people to keep and bear arms shall not be infringed."

A fair-minded, balanced person would see this in the historical context of the Revolution of 1776 and the early decades of the United States, when the colonies could and often did call on their able-bodied citizens—as part of the militia, i.e., all able-bodied citizens bound by reason of their civic duty as members of the whole body politic—to help throw out the British or fight the Indians, or defend the territories on the western frontier. Anyone has the right (and by implication, the duty) to bear arms when the state or nation is threatened, if called. This is the origin of the National Guard and other lawful volunteer units called upon in later years, as needed, to buttress the regular armed services. I point this out not to lay out all the arguments on both sides, which are basically simple though long and tedious, but to give an example of how one growing stream of right-wing propaganda has lent itself, as part of a larger, veritable flood of counterfeit theories that have enlivened and greatly troubled many in the United States. Such demagogues as radio's Rush Limbaugh clutter the airwaves, over the country with this and other highly skewed versions of past and current political life.

In the last two decades, this chorus has been joined by doomsayers of the religious right—many of them fundamentalist self-styled Christian intellectuals, who rely heavily on reminders of prophesies from the Book of Revelation. One well-read author of this camp is Tim LaHaye, who insists that those who do not agree with the tenets of his ideology are not only liberals but humanists. By definition all humanists are atheists, pro-abortion, and espouse the theory of evolution (*Mind Seige*, 2002). They also oppose progressive taxation.

The net effect of this flood, in my opinion, has been to gradually undermine the trust and faith of many ordinary citizens, often not at all aware of how these bogus ideas have been inserted into a great deal of modern political, civic, and recently, religious discourse. Among other things, they have undermined belief in those who develop, formulate, and give effect to foreign policy, and to government in general. One result was the 1995 destruction of the federal building in Oklahoma City by two militia foot soldiers with warped minds.

Lobbies of the left, before, during, and after World War II, also spewed out remarkably similar, populist theories and proposals that poisoned the well of civic confidence, not only in the United States, but worldwide. The large part of the funds to support such campaigns came from the Soviet Union. But in the West, much of the money for rightist campaigns came from some misguided wealthy philanthropists and misanthropists who helped poison the well of civilized argument and civic discourse that must underlie effective self-government. During the 1960s and 1970s a recrudescence of leftist propaganda appeared at the far end of the spectrum, implicitly embracing the idea that the students, workers, and other groupings "disenfranchised by the system" were entitled to use violent and other extralegal means aimed at the overthrow of duly constituted government. In the 21st century, emerging groups of this sort included "eco-anarchist" movements and anti-internationalist recrudescences, as misguided people seek to disrupt such international conferences as the World Trade Organization and the Group of Seven.

There is no doubt that in any democracy, searching criticism of what government does, or does not do, is not only allowed but essential. The freedom of the press is one of the bedrocks of our system. So are the freedoms of assembly and of speech. Especially in the United States, the tradition of expressing doubt in civic discourse is long-standing and honorable. If citizens are fed up with the two main political parties for example, they may form new parties or engage in their own information campaigns. But in the arena of public discourse, charlatans and mountebanks are almost always shown up for what they are. The democratic system works, often imperfectly, sometimes painfully slowly. Citizens know that liberty is preserved only by constant vigilance. But there is a wide chasm between the rough-and-tumble of normal politics and the insidious, covert methods of those who would take advantage of their constitutional liberties to subvert the system that sustains these liberties. The advent of al-Qaeda and similar ideological terrorist groups simply raises the international stakes tremendously. But reason and reason's discourse are the only real defense we have against error, and self-government is possible, in the end, only if it is grounded in that reason.

This rather long tangent from the central threads of my story was launched in order to make the point that the propagandistic attacks of both left and right (currently, more of the right) have tended to insidiously erode much of the energy and civic objectivity of our electorate. I became aware of the nature and extent of these attacks in the United States while studying the work of World Affairs Councils and similar bodies in the 1960s. My central conclusion at that time was, and still is today, that only objective, full, and fair education, in all forms and levels, is the main hope of those who would undergird not only our American system but that of the world as well. We must not look to superficial fixes but must support continuing, balanced, and well-funded, up-to-date education at all levels about and for the world and our place in it.

We have not yet come to grips with this truth and mobilized fully for balanced, continuing intelligent world leadership. Because of the rapidly increasing interdependence of nations (globalization is today's fashionable term), this major educational task must be given the necessary attention and means it deserves. This was a major new understanding, for me, which I carried away from my two short years in the engine room of the Ford Foundation.

Major Contributions of the Ford Foundation's International Program in the Sixties

A young Columbia University professor who often dashed in and out of Stone's offices in the mid-sixties, Zbigniew Brzezinski, took a sabbatical in Japan with money provided by Ford. The resulting book, *The Fragile Blossom*, became a nonfiction best seller and in an important way helped to alter the course of history. When the founders of the Atlantic Institute put their new organization together in 1960–61, we had taken note of the accession of Japan to the OECD, recognizing the country's growing importance to the increasingly global economy and its potential for a share of world leadership. Japan entered post–World War II society as an enigma that changed shape three or four times before the end of the century. Brzezinski, an expert on the Soviet Union and the Cold War, took time out to try to learn for himself the full dimensions of this Japanese emergence. The title of his book was curious to some, as by 1965 many political pundits were picturing a once-again mighty Japan—certainly to be respected and even feared. Brzezinski's book struck the right balance: Japan was indeed showing one path to industrial greatness, but its new society—nurtured by MacArthur's occupation—was nonetheless to some extent uncertain, tenuous, and perhaps brittle. "Fragile," in hindsight, was exactly the right word: increasingly in the 1970s and, to some, ominously in the 1980s, Japan seemed like an unstoppable economic juggernaut, with new industrial methods and attitudes that might well sweep away the North Atlantic lead. By the 1990s, the upward Japanese trend had ground to a halt. Today, at the outset of the 21st century, a ten-year recession showed signs of ending.

Brzezinski studied Japan carefully and sensed its potential but also the flaws of its unique and fragile society. Acting on his new knowledge and sense of history, he persuaded David Rockefeller and a few other farsighted business and political leaders of the Eastern Establishment to create a new and rather different NGO: the Trilateral Commission. This influential force for new thinking and good developments nonetheless became enmeshed for a time in the cabals of both the far right and far left. The Trilateral concept was to form a three-pronged forum representing the newly uniting Europe, Japan, and the United States. The symmetric symbolism was compromised a bit when the founders remembered that Canada too had a strong interest in the common Trilateral agenda—so the U.S. leg was redubbed North America and Canadians were invited. Each of the three components opened small offices in Paris, Tokyo, and New York. Each appointed a chairman of its realm (David Rockefeller for many years serving the North American side, with a Canadian deputy,

Mitchell Sharp), and recruited 30 to 40 leaders from industry, finance, politics, academia, and the ranks of retired diplomats. The creators of the Trilateral Commission did their jobs with great care. Initially under Brzezinski's leadership as director, for many years they were able to raise ideas, expressed through tripartite expert papers on issues crucial to the industrial democracies and discussed in detail with a view to achieving consensus at annual meetings of the full body. Its influence on governmental policy and that of bodies such as the European Union, the OECD, and the later G-7 became considerable. To me, this proved the great value of leadership networks, working without the constraints of government and largely without pressures from industry or other quarters, in attacking intellectually some of the knotty problems that other institutions could not or would not confront. Some years later, in the early seventies, the North American director George Franklin (an old ally from Atlantic Institute days) asked me for nominations for Trilateral membership. I suggested T. A. Wilson, then CEO of Boeing, and Jimmy Carter, the Georgia governor whose name had begun appearing in the national press. Carter, I am told, broadened his view of the world considerably through Trilateral exposure.

The Trilateral Commission, out ahead for many years in helping to create a multinational consensus, deserves considerable credit for its fearless work. Today, with other major forces—such as Latin America, East Asian "tigers," and a new proto-democratic Russia—the uniqueness of Trilateralism has faded. But Brzezinski's ideas and Rockefeller's leadership, from 1966 onwards, showed the validity of the concept. The Ford Foundation deserves great credit for bankrolling Brzezinski and the commission initially.

The Trilateral Commission was for years grossly mischaracterized and vilified by its left and right radical critics, who saw it as an insidious and shadowy conspiracy of Big Business and entrenched politicians to run the world as they saw fit. The truth was different: The growing interdependence of the economically and politically most dynamic nations of the world community—from whom, incidentally, any forward movement in aiding the developing countries or in gradually overcoming the Soviet threat peacefully would have to come—was made operative in considerable measure by the existence of citizen-inspired bodies such as the Trilateral Commission, as well as the Atlantic Institute (which included Japanese, Australians, and New Zealanders on its board from early days), and the Bilderberg group. Public opinion was helped to see the new facts of international life by such bodies and, when some of its members entered politics, government, or diplomacy, they found nongovernment leadership networks on which they could rely to get things done. The idea of such groups gave me much additional grist for my theories about multinational elites; a paper I wrote on the subject in 1966 dealt with this phenomenon, among others. One could not hope to knit together the essential intergovernmental frameworks for a transnational community which has since become worldwide without such informal bodies—today's civil society—to buttress and extend what governments and internationally oriented education could do.

One of the glories of the global democratic community, such as it now is, lies in the work of such nonprofit, nongovernmental bodies.

In another sphere, I was approached while at Ford in 1966 by a group of young politicians (ages around twenty-five to thirty) from both major U.S. political parties. They dubbed themselves American Young Political Leaders and wanted financial support so that they could help organize transatlantic meetings and visits with their counterparts in other NATO countries. One was the Republican treasurer of a New England state, another an assistant to a Democratic congressman, and so on. I engineered a small Ford Foundation grant that turned out to be the beginning of the Atlantic Association of Young Political Leaders (AAYPL), which for many years served to prepare these young people for leadership as they matured. Peter Corterier, for example, was soon to serve in the Bundestag and, in the seventies, as a very young deputy to the foreign minister. Corterier had joined the Social Democratic party as a teenager and until his retirement from the German parliament, led the fight in his party for a pro-NATO foreign policy, which with some of the more traditionally radical young leftists was not always popular. He later became the secretary general of the North Atlantic Assembly—the intergovernmental body that I and others had helped create out of the originally private association of MPs from NATO countries. Thus better multilateral institutions and the nurturing of internationally minded political figures began, in the fifties, sixties, and seventies, to thicken the skein of transatlantic ties that have held together the various public and private bodies and interpersonal networks.

A contemporary of Corterier was a rising young British member of the Labour Party and cofounder of the AAYPL, Alan Lee Williams. He shared Corterier's and my views about NATO and the overriding importance in general of the transatlantic relationship. Williams, like Corterier, had to fight fiercely within his party to preserve the substance of the NATO link for the UK and to downplay the peace-at-any-price leftist movements of the sixties through the eighties. Williams also became a junior minister in the British cabinet, but was forced out of his party by a left-wing Labour surge of pacifism in the eighties. Peter, Alan, and I have remained close friends over the ensuing four decades, working together on the creation of still other transatlantic NGOs.

The Atlantic Association of Young Political Leaders was but one aspect of a general program to strengthen transatlantic leadership that began with the Ford Foundation. Shep Stone, Joe Slater and I saw an increasing need to prepare younger people for roles in society and government, the "successor generation" who would take over from the World War II leaders as they retired from the scene. The Atlantic Council also recognized this need and started a series of seminars for young leaders from the North Atlantic countries and Japan. The ACUS also picked up on the Japan theme from the Trilateral leaders and—to some extent—myself, by initiating a series of Japanese-American studies on common energy problems, touched off by the 1970s' worldwide oil crises.

Just as the Trilateral Commission and other senior bodies reflected the need for nurturing multilateral leadership, so did the AAYPL and other groups that came to Ford for help. In 1965 Ford also began its own program to equip the successor generation for leadership roles by bringing several score Europeans, individually, to the United States for traveling fellowships to view U.S. institutions at work and to further build a transatlantic network.

International Education

I had been in Germany for about a year in 1953 when, in the middle of a conference, I recorded this in my journal: "Why wouldn't the universities of Europe be a good place to start the United Europe in practice? If they could all be Europeanized, it might be a great step toward real unity in Europe. If faculties were truly European and not national, if curricula were more or less common, *if students were accepted anywhere in Europe,* we might break down national barriers."

Most of this turned out to be pie in the sky, although a small College of Europe (see chapter 8) had been started, then unbeknownst to me; and a good deal later, the embryo of a European University—at graduate and research level—was begun just outside Florence. But the phrase I italicized above eventually came to something. While I was at Ford, an imaginative Oxford professor named Alec Peterson called on me. He put forth the idea of what he called an International Baccalaureate (IB), or common secondary school leaving certificate, that would be accepted as having satisfied academic requirements for entry into any university, anywhere. The IB, as it has come to be known, would be based on a single curriculum, carefully designed to cover the basic liberal arts and sciences that all capable 18-year-olds, anywhere, would be expected to know. I traveled to Oxford and then Geneva (where a small group of Peterson's colleagues were already at work), and returned to New York. My bosses could see the point; the IB could presage a gradual revolution in international education. We made the first of several grants. Today, the IB is taught in top high schools in 104 countries around the world, and their students are granted entry, commensurately, to a large, and growing number of universities.

At around the same time, I learned of a previous Ford grant to a related project: the Atlantic College in Wales. At the 1957 Bruges Conference on the North Atlantic Community, I had met the creators of Atlantic College, the distinguished German educator Kurt Hahn and an equally distinguished retired British air marshal, Sir Lawrence Darvall. Along with the many interesting ideas that filled our ears in Bruges, this one had especially caught my attention: to bring youngsters 16 to 19 years of age from many different countries to study together in the last two years of secondary school, and also give them a taste of social service; the Atlantic College in Wales—the pilot school for a worldwide system—specialized in performing Coast Guard functions in the Irish Sea, saving lives on several occasions. At its inception, the Atlantic College, though pretty thoroughly British in its sponsorship and guiding ideas, heard about Alec Peterson's International Baccalaureate and grabbed it. In 1967, I was to become deeply involved in the Atlantic College project. This and the IB were important markers in what I hoped would lead to a great many educational institutions, at every level, providing an international focus to education, leavening the world with potential leaders who saw things from a more-than-national perspective. There are today ten such United World Colleges.

A 2002 series of articles in London's *Financial Times* recounted adoption of the IB by 42 schools in Britain; with a broad-based curriculum different from England's vaunted yet highly specialized A-level exams, many top-grade independent schools in the UK are moving to the IB. In the United States, some high schools have adopted the IB and many universities around the world will accept the IB as the equivalent of conventional entrance exams. For the IB to be adopted generally it will take many more years beyond the first forty. Yet the fact that the IB is in use in schools in 104 countries is significant. I'm proud that I had a small hand in pushing the International Baccalaureate on its way; it could well be a precursor of a significant educational reform that will prepare students for what Wendell Willkie in 1941 called One World.

The Ford Foundation: An Appraisal

I was fortunate during the Ford years to become acquainted with many figures like Professor Alec Peterson who were instrumental in creating influential institutions and programs that tended to leaven the world's forward thinking in strategic ways. Dr. Ernst van der Beugel, for example, the Dutch international civil servant who created the Bilderberg Group, was one such figure. I had met him in Atlantic Institute days and now was to see him frequently consulting with Shepard Stone—a Bilderberg member and also one of van der Beugel's supporters, with Ford Foundation grants. Bilderberg has been a much less obtrusive organization than the Trilateral Commission or the Atlantic Institute and has been attacked for its secrecy. It brought together influential figures from both sides of the Atlantic to review common problems but never issued communiqués or published conclusions or proposals for action. Its membership lists were not in the public domain. I knew enough through Ford's paperwork and my connections with van der Beugel to feel that it was a thoroughly worthwhile way for those who make or influence policy to meet informally for a thorough clearing of the mental decks. It fit well into the set of convictions that I had begun to form while at Harvard with Professor Crane Brinton: if one wants to create a functioning community of nations, then a critical mass of multinational-thinking leaders is a prime prerequisite. If one were to list the factors that helped make the Euro-Atlantic community function well in the last half century, then surely bodies such as the Trilateral Commission, Bilderberg, the Atlantic Institute, the Atlantic Treaty Association, the Atlantic Association of Young Political Leaders, the North Atlantic Assembly, and the NATO Defense College would all have contributed in significant ways. If thinking publics today have empathy for the problems and interests of societies beyond their own, then it is these kinds of high-level but also highly educational fora that must share some of the credit.

Events contrived to catapult me from the Ford Foundation into the lower age ranges of this pattern of multinational education. When I began to see, in late 1966, that McGeorge Bundy's Ford Foundation was most probably not going to provide a framework for positive grant-giving that I could subscribe to, I began to think of other options. So did my bosses, Shep Stone and Joe Slater. By mid-1967 we had all left and the foundation's programs and monies were turned in other directions—not toward aims I disapproved of (for the most part), but towards funding opportunities that were not high on my personal agenda. Bundy's priorities, for example, included some efforts to influence domestic political outcomes, for good ends to be sure (financing black voter registration in Gary, Indiana, was one such), but I was still—and always—focused on preventing World War III and building peace through the gradual interlocking of like-minded nations and peoples.

One day in late 1966, I was suddenly inspired to write to Kurt Hahn, the father of the Atlantic College project and—quite diffidently—volunteer my services. Hahn, in a quick reply I cherish, wrote back: "If Jim Huntley did not exist, he would have to be invented." I had visited the pilot college in Wales three months earlier, with further Ford Foundation grants in mind. I was immensely impressed with what had been accomplished in creating the pilot and had begun to think about the considerable impact this idea could have, if institutionalized and replicated worldwide. Kurt Hahn and David Wills—the chief funder of the enterprise—decided they wanted me to help lay the foundations for a worldwide system of such schools and made me an offer. In fact, being as yet only 44 and burning with desire to make a strong impact for good on the world, I was bowled over by the opportunities that such an enterprise offered.

An excerpt from my journal shows vividly that I saw no other way as potentially productive for using my talents and engaging my motivation:

> [After receiving Hahn's letter] I have tried to go to sleep tonight without success, because I am burning with ideas . . . ideas of how to translate this idea of a new kind of international education into concrete reality with a scale of operations sufficiently vast to make a real impact. . . . [Here followed a list of colleagues from several countries whom I would hope to recruit for faculty and administration.] A whole string of new textbooks can be written . . . a new approach to citizens' rights and duties in the last half of the twentieth century. We can affect international university exchanges. We can influence the reshaping of secondary school curricula.

In short, I was on fire with the idea.

I was appointed by the Atlantic Colleges on Christmas Eve, 1966 as their secretary general. The job was described as duplicating several times over the first College in Wales; the second was to be in Germany, the others in France, the United States, Canada, and elsewhere. I wrote, again in my journal: "I have taken the job because it affords the best opportunity I know of—not only the best available—to develop young leaders who will be internationally oriented."

It took several months to disengage at the Ford Foundation; I cleaned up a lot of grant applications and helped prepare the International Affairs Program for shutdown. In the process, I tried to take stock of what my whirlwind career at Ford had taught me. Following are some reflections.

• There is a "philanthropy market" analogous to but not the same as financial and commercial markets. NGOs, nonprofits, and foundations are all part of this market, which John Gardner called "the Independent Sector" and others "the 3rd sector"—that is, bodies formed to serve the public good but not part of either government or the business world. While independent sector organizations must be well managed, their goals and methods differ from the two other sectors.

• Foundations, at least some of them, are pretty good at starting things that seem to have promise, but foundation careerists like to think of these ventures as getting projects or new organizations off the ground until "other sources of funds" take over. The problem, and today matters are much worse, is that many well-intentioned efforts go belly up because the philanthropy market doesn't lean in their direction. Foundations should think twice about starting good things if there is no other market force to take over; if, despite a review of the market, the project is still one that needs doing, the foundation should be prepared to underwrite the effort for a long time, or endow it and let it run on its own. (Ford did this in its early days, by creating "spinoffs" such as the Fund for the Republic.)

• The foundation process usually ends up being run by a bunch of dilettantes or hobbyists who are continuously looking for nonprofits that match their proclivities, or for NGO entrepreneurs with ideas about a better world that fit nicely with their own, rather than inviting applications that serve broad, specified goals that the foundation's board and management have agreed on. A certain amount of cronyism is inevitable, yet doors should always be open to people with little reputation but with great ideas. Helping inexperienced nonprofit "entrepreneurs" acquire management know-how and community-building skills could receive a lot more attention than it does.

• By 2002, and after having been on the begging side of the independent sector table since 1960—trying to give good ideas "hands and feet" (as old Professor Elliott used to say)—I believed that most contemporary foundations now fail to understand the need of all nonprofits for funds to defray overheads and basic costs. Too many grant-makers assume that such expenditures should somehow be found outside the scope of their grant funds, which they believed should only be used for direct "project" costs. This has become a maddening feature of modern philanthropic life.

• Today, there are probably too many foundations. Many existing ones are the playthings of boards and staff who exist to serve the founders' narrow goals (often political or ideological). Too many founders do not understand the broad social goals that philanthropy, in the true sense of the word, is meant to serve. There is room for many new foundations of a broad, balanced sort; all too often, however, some rich benefactor finds it much easier to dispense his or her surplus fortune in large block grants to a university or some other large institution for, say, new buildings that cost millions. The operating funds to staff such buildings are often starved by opaque foundations, whether the institution is taxpayer-funded or privately supported, and the human side of philanthropy suffers.

(This latter tendency, which some philanthropoids call the "edifice complex," was nowhere more poignantly displayed than when the Ford Foundation board members decided to spend a great many millions to erect a new headquarters that was an architectural showpiece but an economic flop. I even wrote a protesting memo at the time of the project's conception, arguing that the foundation would be better off downsizing into a large warehouse so that more funds would be available for grants. Interested readers may wander into Ford headquarters at 320 East 43rd street in New York to see for themselves: One-fourth of the space is given over to a magnificent atrium/tropical garden. The doorknobs on the offices rank with those in the grandest palaces anywhere. Sad to say, after most foundations suffered substantial losses on the stockmarkets of the late sixties, Ford had to cut back its staff. Much of the new building was then rented to others.)

I still believe all of the above. But the reverse side of the coin—and much more important in the overall scheme of things—is the magnificence of the overall effort to improve societies by means of private endeavor, usually selfless and without an eye to commercial gain. In the next chapter, I'll explore this tremendously hopeful form of human endeavor from a broader, more international perspective.

Weaving the Web: Friends and Others Encountered

Living in the Big Apple for a couple of years was an exhilarating experience. More than Paris or London, New York at the time had become the place where most cultural and intellectual currents of the 20th century intersected. It was close to Harvard, Yale, Princeton, Columbia, and other leading colleges with coveys of learned men and women, in particular the many refugees from Europe who leavened the vital life of their universities and of New York. Ford employed many consultants from among these and many other pinpoints of thought around the East Coast. I became close to many of them, such as Professor Joe LaPalombara, a Yale political scientist who shared many of my perspectives on Europe and on the Ford Foundation and who broadened my knowledge.

One who became a close friend was Istvan Szent-Miklosy, a refugee from Communist Hungary who had struggled in his fifties for his PhD at Columbia and was now teaching international relations with an enlightened but realistic hard edge. He wrote a book on the Atlantic Movement, largely based on the work of Walden Moore, sparkplug of the 1954 Declaration of Atlantic Unity. The Declaration had become a tiny but well-sustained organization (largely Moore and his elite backers) moving governments and transatlantic multinational bodies to foster togetherness in ways they probably wouldn't have done without gentle prodding and pushing of the Declaration. Around Moore and Szent-Miklosy was a tight little group of professors who shared transatlantic interests. William Fox and his wife Annette were Columbia-based political scientists who chronicled intergovernmental links between the Atlantic democracies and helped chart the way ahead. Philip Moseley, Colombia professor of Soviet studies, whose broad perceptions and practical work in helping refugees such as Szent-Miklosy find their way in American academia, was another of my cofounders of the Committee on Atlantic Studies. His ideas fed into my own understandings of the intellectual roots of the Cold War and the West's response.

George Franklin, long the executive director of the Council on Foreign Relations, became a lifelong friend, buttressing the close relationship we had formed in Atlantic Institute days. The Council in the 1960s was a smaller organization than it is today. Many one-shot teams of learned and experienced scholars were called in; one such group authored an eight-volume series (financed by Ford) on the future of the Atlantic community. Books on defense (by then-obscure Henry Kissinger), trade, the nascent European communities, and the all-important American-European nexus poured out of George Franklin's workshop. Today many of these works seem dated, yet in 1966 they provided usually trenchant and informed grist for the mills of public policy. The Council on Foreign Relation's chief economist in those days was William Diebold, whose thinking had helped me during the formation of the Atlantic Institute and whose seminal book *Trade and Payments in Western Europe* had laid the groundwork for a great deal of progress in dealing with the future of transatlantic cooperation at a time when Europe was struggling to recover.

�֎

I found time (by rising at 5 a.m. for several months) to write *The NATO Story,* a small book commissioned by NATO itself and translated into several languages for use in Alliance secondary schools. Later, I wrote a pamphlet for NATO on its civilian programs in environmental and social collaboration (the Committee on the Challenges of Modern Society), which broadened NATO's writ beyond strictly military matters. NATO, for example, sparked a program for cleaning up air pollution in Ankara (in the sixties one of the foulest atmospheres in the NATO area), drawing on British and other experience. Writing for NATO put me back in touch with some of its top international civil servants, extraordinary men and women, at all levels, who served the ideals of the Atlantic community during these tempestuous and dangerous decades. Such multinational institutions as NATO, the EU, OECD, and many others not only serve substantive purposes in strengthening the international fabric of cooperation; as a by-product they also educate, and often mark indelibly, public servants who can think outside the box of national interests and see the common aims, plus the common ways and means, toward a much larger community-in-the-making.

Of these ventures in writing, and a long article in *Orbis* on multinational leadership, I noted in my journal in 1965: "I am in the middle of a small book I have contracted to do ... on NATO. It is torture, not because I don't like to write, but because I simply find it painful to write. I sit down and stare and then write—badly—for a little while, then get hungry or thirsty and knock off for a bit. Then read what I've written and feel like tearing it up, but stifle that thought with the idea that it can all be corrected before the next draft. One or two pages an hour is a pretty good pace. Thank God I don't have to do it for a living." Amen to that, even today, forty years later! Computers have changed a good deal of the writing process, but the human brain hasn't changed. It's still hard going, at least for me.

As I put my affairs in order in 1967 and prepared to leave New York and Ford, I believed I had accomplished a good deal (though not as much as I had hoped); that I had learned much about the pitfalls and benefits of philanthropy; that I had been able to separate my own sense of personal worth from the often hypocritical praise that supplicants inevitably shower on philanthropoids whose favors they crave; and that I had worked with people, inside and outside the foundation, who could be at once brilliant, stimulating, and visionary but also vain, self-serving, inefficient with priorities and time allocation, and poor managers. Yet the balance of these connections had certainly been to the good. Working for the Ford Foundation had been a sobering but also stimulating experience I was glad to have had—but glad to leave.

11

The Mother Country and the Atlantic Colleges

4 December 1967: *The North Atlantic Council adopts the "Harmel Report" outlining new tasks for the Atlantic Alliance.*

Prelude to a Major Challenge

In the summer of 1966, a new opportunity to pursue one of my major goals—the development of a "multinational elite" to lead a better future world—suddenly began to open to me. I was sent by the Ford Foundation on a longish mission to Europe to evaluate some programs we had already funded, to talk with applicants who had asked for FF funds, and to see if there were new areas of opportunity we should consider backing.

My trip began in Scandinavia. The Ford Board of Trustees had decided (with some reluctance but at the insistence of one strong-minded trustee) that someone should see whether or not the foundation was missing bets in the Nordic countries. We all agreed that this part of the world, at least at that time, was probably the most peaceful, contented, prosperous, and egalitarian. A few FF grants had been given to Nordic individuals in many fields, but none to institutions. To form a coherent picture of the area as it might relate further to Ford, I toured Scandinavia for a month and talked with many individual grantees and other recommended sources. I had a delightful time, needless to say, but came away with two conclusions: (1) There wasn't much the foundation could do with grants to organizations there that would outweigh opportunities and needs in other parts of the world; and (2) the smaller countries of Scandinavia (Finland, Denmark, and Norway) all had a serious resentment complex concerning the Swedes. After long discussions I found that—in terms of general public opinion—Sweden was more or less in the same position with respect to the rest of Scandinavia that the United States was to Europe: It was twice as populous as any of its close neighbors and much more prosperous (at that time) than they. It had been lucky not to have been occupied by the Germans (or in the case of the Finns, the Russians) and had thus not suffered much, comparatively, from World War II. The other Scandinavians were envious of the Swedes. But this state of affairs did not overly affect the healthy degree to which the Nordic countries would and did cooperate closely in facing common problems. It was simply an interesting fact of Scandinavian life. I also took the opportunity to say hello to a few Swedish cousins in Stockholm and the province of Småland. I duly reported these and other observations to the Ford Foundation board and proceeded to two or three other destinations in Europe for similar talks.

I was not prepared for what I found in England, and this is the fateful beginning of the "Mother Country" story. In 1963, the Ford Foundation had made a grant of $140,000 to the Atlantic College in Wales. I was instructed to visit the college, talk with the principals in the project, report back as to whether the money had been well spent, and comment on a new request for $1 million that the college trustees had put to Ford.

I had first learned of the Atlantic College project in 1957 at the Bruges Conference on the North Atlantic Community, where I had met the college founders, Dr. Kurt Hahn and Air Marshal Sir Lawrance Darvall. Later, when I was running the Atlantic Institute's Washington office (1963–65), these and others representing the college had again drawn my interest during their visits to the United States to ask for help of various kinds. I thought the principles on which they had started the project were sound, even exciting:

(1) Boys aged 16 to 18 (and later girls), coming from many different countries and selected for qualities of intelligence, scholarship, potential for leadership, and receptivity to new ideas, could benefit greatly from being educated in a multinational environment.

(2) Physical and social challenges would be built into the curriculum of the college in order to inculcate a sense of service to the community, in its micro- and macro-aspects. In tested British fashion, this was thought (quite soundly, I felt) to build character and a strong sense of mutual responsibility to one's fellow humans.

(3) The chosen age group represented the best time in the lives of emerging young adults in which international idealism, human fellow feeling, and loyalty to a wider community could be instilled. University student exchanges had typically engaged young men and women in their twenties who, for the most part, had already been molded emotionally through educational experiences—formal and informal—in their home countries; it was almost too late for most of them to feel like fully "international citizens." I had found

this especially true in my work with German and American teenage exchangees, as compared to those at university level. If the reader would think back on his or her university days, when the opening up of a great new intellectual world seemed to make him or her an instant authority on most matters on which parents and all older people seemed simply not "up to date," it may be easy to grasp this point. In other words, the intellect and emotions of a teenager are more malleable and impressionable than those of undergraduates or graduates in their twenties. (There are of course more risks in betting on the future capacities of seventeen-year-olds.)

(4) Kurt Hahn believed that a youngster of 16 to 18, if studying and becoming a part of the community in a country other than his own, would develop "a love for one foreign country on which a love of all mankind could be based." I believe he was right. This remains the chief rationale (for me) of all international teenage exchange programs. If the right kids are chosen, such an experience is a highly effective way to nurture internationalists—an even more desperate world need in the new century.

Sir Lawrance Darvall (who became a great friend) subscribed to these principles. His experience had been based on the assignment Eisenhower gave him in 1951, when Ike was NATO's first Supreme Allied Commander, namely, to create a NATO staff college for midlevel career military officers of the NATO countries. (This NATO Defense College is still going strong in Rome after more than a half century turning out cadres of multinational-minded officers.) Sir Lawrance saw what a difference a half-year course spent on strategic and other military and geopolitical questions made in the minds and attitudes of most of these colonels, majors, and lieutenant commanders, studying together. Indeed, I feel confident that NATO's military staff planning, preparedness, and actual operations over the years, requiring mixes of troops and officers from nineteen countries (twenty-six since the 2002 accession of new central and eastern European countries to NATO) has been a prime element in the cohesion and effectiveness of the organization. A few diplomats are always thrown into the mix, but their exposure is probably not as mindset changing as those of military people.

At any rate Sir Lawrance and Dr. Hahn thus made an admirable team for the early years of the Atlantic College. Sadly, Sir Lawrance was more or less shunted away from leadership of the project in the midsixties, which depressed him greatly and later disconcerted me when I came to work in England.

I had heard nothing of the Atlantic College, beyond the brief 1957 encounter with the idea at Bruges, until 1964, when I was serving as the

Atlantic Institute's North American director in Washington. Dr. Hahn and other backers of the college—which had opened its doors just two years earlier—came on a sweeping tour of North America. I arranged a dinner for them with prominent Americans tied in with the Atlantic Institute and Council, as well as many other appointments with educators and foundation officials.

Hahn was particularly troubled on this visit that he could not see Christian Herter, who was bedridden in Massachusetts with what proved to be a terminal illness. Herter and Hahn had become close friends when Herter was a young Foreign Service officer posted to Berlin in 1915. When America entered the war in spring 1917, the U.S. legation was closed, and Herter was sent to Switzerland. Hahn in 1918 was the secretary to Prince Max of Baden, the last chancellor of Imperial Germany. The Armistice of November 1918 resulted in upheavals all over Germany, including a brief Communist republic in Bavaria. Demobilized troops rioted in Berlin, and some joined the *Freikorps*—right-wing private armies who fought the Bolsheviks and others in Eastern Europe. These later faded into the new "100,000-man Reichswehr" that the Versailles Treaty allotted to the new German Republic; others became Hitler's brown-shirted bully-boy Storm Troopers.

Soon after the 1918 Armistice, the Kaiser abdicated and fled to The Netherlands, where he lived a long life chopping wood and reflecting (no doubt dyspeptically) on what had happened to his Second Reich. Kaiser Wilhelm died in 1945; one wonders what he thought of the little Austrian corporal who had, with a vengeance, realized Wilhelm's most extreme visions and then brought the temple down upon all Germans and Europe.

In the short interval between the 1918 Armistice and the proclamation of the new Weimar Republic, Prince Max was still the acting head of government. Masses of Europeans were starving, in the German case critically so because the effective Allied naval blockade had prevented food and all other materials from entering Germany after 1917. With the war over, Hahn—with the blessing of his boss, Prince Max—found a German biplane and pilot who flew him to Berne to see Herter. Herter did not require much pleading to get his own ambassador to cable the government in Washington and make a strong case for ending the Allied food blockade. It had been prolonged largely because the French High Command feared that unless the pressure were kept on Germany, she might break the Armistice and resume the war. Kurt Hahn thought that his flight to Berne and the urgent message of distress to Washington had played a major role in lifting the Allied blockade. He delighted in telling the story—a tall, lanky Hahn in an ill-fitting pilot's cap and goggles behind an aviator piloting an old "crate" typical of the fighter planes of World War I, braving wind and clouds and rain. The imagery was priceless and reinforced Hahn's lifelong friendship with a man who became a top Republican legislator and later still, secretary of state.

Such relationships between sometime foes were not unusual during the interwar and post-1945 years; one of my great friends in the sixties was a former Luftwaffe pilot. I am sure that such ties were one good reason the Allied and German leaders of goodwill, who later rose to important positions, together supported so thoroughly any reasonable idea that might prevent the onslaught of yet another major war. Though such pre-1914 or pre-1939 ties failed to stave off the Second World War, the memories of those still alive after 1945 helped a good deal, I am sure, to embolden statesmen to take an entirely different tack to try to ensure peace. Partly based on such personal relationships, major initiatives such as the Marshall Plan and NATO were able to flourish quickly. Hahn and Darvall and their colleagues in the "Atlantic College project" sought to reestablish the equivalent of such ties among those they hoped would form a substantial corps of future world leaders.

Catapulting from New York to London

In the summer of 1966, I returned from my visit to the Atlantic College with the strong feeling that Ford should make a second major grant to the college project so that it could begin to multiply these innovative institutions. I made the case but was turned down, in part because some Ford people thought that, as the Atlantic College was the creation largely of a group of British aristocrats (partly true, but what did that matter?), they could jolly well find the money without Ford's help. I am inclined to think that it was not the array of aristocrats but the array of the *wrong* aristocrats, not the kind that Slater and Stone liked to cultivate, that scotched the project. Before Bundy took over from Henry Heald as Ford's CEO, the latter also expressed exactly this sentiment. My feeling of being out of place at the Ford Foundation was reinforced. Also, within two years, a stock market plunge had greatly reduced Ford's capital and that of virtually all American philanthropies.

One bright August afternoon in 1966, climbing over old rock walls in the Connecticut countryside, I told my bride-to-be, Colleen (my first marriage having most unfortunately crumbled in 1964), that I now saw a bright new possible future in helping launch a string of Atlantic Colleges that could help change the world in a modest but effective way. I evoked Mr. Chips and asked Colleen how she would like to become a stepmother "twice removed" to a bunch of boys from different countries? She accepted my proposal.

On the heels of my Connecticut epiphany, I wrote Kurt Hahn in August 1966 and asked him what he thought of the idea of my helping to fully internationalize and disseminate the Atlantic College idea. His response was immediate and enthusiastic. David Wills, the principal benefactor of the Atlantic College, whom I had gotten to know during my English visit, concurred with Hahn and they began to make arrangements for me to work for their enterprise. In May 1967, Colleen and I married, leaving soon after for England and my new post as secretary general of the Atlantic Colleges.

Largely as a result of Bundy's arrival to take the helm at Ford, Shep Stone's International Affairs department was heading for breakup. Shep left for Paris in the winter to become head of a revitalized Congress for Cultural Freedom (renamed the "International Association for Cultural Freedom"); Joe Slater took over at Ford from Shep, but later in 1967 himself left to head two or three promising nongovernmental bodies and foundations simultaneously. He wryly termed himself "the world's first nonprofit conglomerate."

On the first of February 1967, I too bailed out of Bundy's boat and began my work with the Atlantic College project, first in New York, organizing a U.S. National Commission for the Atlantic Colleges and laying the ground for fund-raising in America. I was exhilarated at the prospect, which (as I wrote in my journal) was "a thing I have been preparing myself for, for years." I envisioned a string of such colleges around the world, and thought of people whom I had known who would make excellent headmasters, board members and so on, to staff a major movement. I thought that a whole string of new textbooks might be written for the curricula, including "Civics, a new approach to citizens' rights and duties" in the last half of the century. Indeed, I thought of how we might, by example, and by spreading the new International Baccalaureate (just then being introduced at the first Atlantic College in Wales), affect university curricula and stimulate international exchanges. "The possibilities are nearly endless," I concluded.

I would learn later that there were distinct limitations on the influence I could bring to bear, yet I am pleased to say that the overall vision I had in mind in 1966, for a group of such colleges around the world, plus a suitable international structure for overall responsibility and guidance of a string of Colleges, had indeed been realized by the end of the 20th century. My major contribution in the late sixties would be to convince the British backers to fully "internationalize" the hazily defined but mainly window-dressing governing council, streamline the governance of the whole, and prepare the idea for long-term realization. But it would take more than a quarter century to do this. My contribution ended up like the OSS officer in 1943 who, let's say, is parachuted in to organize a unit of the French Resistance, has met only a couple of the principals (and only fleetingly), and has to deal quickly and decisively to reach an objective. I was not prepared for the pitfalls and obstacles that are inevitable in such a project, small at the start but with great potential, international in design and intent but—in 1967—parochial and nationalistic in its execution.

As my negotiations with the Atlantic College project began, some colleagues at Ford wanted to keep me on after the demise of Stone's empire and told me that Bundy himself was interested in this. But I believed I couldn't see eye-to-eye with Bundy, who had shot down the first major Ford program I considered my own—upgrading world affairs education for American adults. A Town Hall program in Los Angeles was also interested in me, but the Atlantic Colleges beckoned enticingly—building the Atlantic community had become my consuming, lifelong mission, and the colleges promised a direct contribution. Before I buttoned up arrangements with the college, however, I first told Bundy of my intentions, and he wished me well. I stayed on in New York for several months to put together the structure and personnel of a U.S. Commission for the Atlantic Colleges.

I called on old friends and new in New York and nearby to help out. Samuel Reber, who had been McCloy's deputy high commissioner in Germany and was now retired, knew the Eastern Establishment well and offered his voluntary services. Joan Kan, who had been Meredith Willson's emanuensis when he wrote *The Music Man*, took over as office manager, and we began to set up quarters in a tiny, claptrap office loaned to us by the Council on Religion and International Affairs, whose director was a close friend. We engaged, as a valued consultant, Sandy Allport, the U.S. fund-raiser for an American school in Athens.

Malcolm Muir, a courtly New Yorker of 75 years, was chosen by Hahn and Wills as the chairman of the U.S. Commission for the Atlantic Colleges. I began to work with Malcolm (the retired CEO of *Newsweek* magazine) in the spring of 1967 but soon discovered that, no matter what assets his marvelous connections and experienced mind brought to the project, he was not quite the right fellow. We were always on friendly terms, but it seemed hard for him to grasp the vast potential of the project. He seemed unable, perhaps because of advancing age, to plunge into the enterprise with the same certainty and verve that I (more than thirty years his junior) possessed then and saw as essential. For the commission, I enlisted my old friend George Franklin (executive director of the Council on Foreign Relations at the time) and retired general Cortlandt van Schuyler, who had once been Ike's chief of staff; my journal indicates that "Cort is a do-it-now type who doesn't ask obstructive questions."

My appointment, terms of reference, and general objectives had been made final, through negotiations by letter and cable with Kurt Hahn, David Wills, the main financial sponsor of the Colleges, and Sir George Schuster, the chairman of the board, and—as I later discovered—in charge of almost everything. I understood that my mission was to prepare the project for internationalization and the advent of new colleges and lay the groundwork for extensive operations. I proposed that I arrive in London in June 1967, to take up duties in an office there, spending the intervening time in the United States, organizing local committees, the National Commission, and finding the necessary personnel. I was to discover later that words on paper did not always mean what I thought they meant, and that I had taken on what proved to be an impossible task. However, I do not think I could have seen all this clearly at the time; I had dealt mainly with Wills and Hahn and knew that the three of us believed firmly in the same goals and modus operandi. I also found, a good deal later, that I had been employed, in the minds of some of the other leaders of the project, on the strength of their belief that I would inevitably bring great bags of dollars with me from the Ford Foundation and other U.S. sources. There were thus false hopes and aims on both sides that, more or less from the start, doomed my involvement. But I began work with a light heart, oblivious to these currents. Ironically, what I believed had to be done to make the program solid, eventually *was* done, after I had departed!

Early in February 1967, I took a quick two-week trip to England and Germany, to confer with some of the principals in the program and to speak with authoritative figures on the German scene. (Our first new college was to be in Germany.) It was agreed that Colleen and I would sail for England on 15 June to take up residence and offices in London.

While in Germany, David Wills and I called on the British ambassador to Bonn, Sir Frank Roberts, who took great interest in the project and provided good advice. (Frank and I were later, after his retirement, to become close friends and co-conspirators in good Atlantic works.) I learned that some of the key British actors (including the headmaster of the first Atlantic College in Wales, who was a retired rear admiral) wanted to site a future German college on the sea, so that they could include coast guard rescue work as the core of the "adventure–social action curriculum." This would be carrying on the first college's version of community service plus somewhat "dangerous living" that challenged its first students well. However, Kurt Hahn and a few other keenly interested Germans plumped instead for a college in or near the Alps, where the community-action challenge would call for mountain rescue teams. Later, this became a real bone of contention among the main backers of the college in Wales and—as in many later imbroglios—found me in the middle. This issue later involved pitting some north Germans (from Hamburg, for example) against some south Germans (from Bavaria). My own preference was for the mountains, as a new kind of demonstration program for still more colleges to come, but in the main I tried to put forth the idea that a good solid German committee should *first* be founded, and only then make that kind of decision itself. The admiral, and others, however, wanted to make the site decision before German participation was thoroughly organized, in effect, presenting them with a fait accompli.

Despite this little encounter, I still had at the time only an inkling of the kinds of internal dissension and bickering that would continually bedevil the project principals in the UK. I began to learn that impressive nonprofit projects such as the colleges would nearly always attract able and distinguished figures who could not enjoy complete retirement, but who (probably subconsciously in most cases) yearned once again for importance and — pardon the expression, but it's the only one that fits — power and control. A sad state of affairs, but very human. Once I got to London at a nice little office David Wills had arranged for me, at 1 Mecklenburgh Square, near the legendary Bloomsbury, I began to confront this phenomenon face to face, and increasingly often.

As Colleen and I sailed for Southampton in June 1967, I found time to enter in my journal the strong feelings that motivated me then; this is how I saw the new enterprise:

> Do I expect too much of the Atlantic Colleges? I hope not — if we can indeed begin to turn out a small but sure stream of young, able, dedicated internationalists, maybe one essential ingredient for a durable peace system will eventually be at hand: the human component for new institutions of regional and world government. If we can get the very top people, in a few years, to see it this way, then adequate support will always be at hand.

London in 1967

In the great capital, we found a nice bed and breakfast as temporary "digs," and I began work in the London office. This was envisaged as a kind of headquarters for the eventual chain of colleges, but at the time, it was mainly the focus of fund-raising and the securing of scholarships to the first college. It took me time to separate these immediate functions from the broader (and to me more important) international scheme. I had my eye on the long range, as I am wont to do.

Four of us occupied these offices: Valerie, a secretary or "p.a." (personal assistant) for me, and much of the time for two members of the Atlantic College board, Sir Eric Berthoud and Lord Hankey. They represented an unsuitable anomaly (in my opinion)—members of a governing board who had also been engaged, with paid honoraria, to do what were essentially high-level staff jobs, namely, travel to Europe and elsewhere to organize scholarship committees whose job it was to find top-notch boys to send to the college and the funds to get them there. This was intricate work; both of them did it very well, as both were former ambassadors. However, I soon learned that they also served as the core of the "London office committee" of the College Governing Board, which had been given the remit to watch the new secretary general's operations and keep him in line. So I was fated to struggle with an unworkable set of organizational relationships—a situation I loathed and had always been careful in the past to avoid. I was secretary general of the Atlantic Colleges (of which so far only one existed); the executive officer of an international council that was then only a sham; and in a broad sense the person responsible for coordinating the overseas missions of two of my superiors from the board, who in turn were actually part of the "steering committee" instructed to keep an eye on me! I was clearly not to be the master in what should become my "own house," with clear, broad responsibilities to an international, overall governing body still to be created.

These unsatisfactory, nebulous organizational arrangements were the construct—I soon found—favored by the "chairman of everything," Sir George Schuster, at that time in his nineties but determined to keep all affairs firmly in his hands. He particularly resisted my efforts to create a sound structure for the expansion ahead. Sir George worked from his ancient family seat in Oxfordshire; I received a daily stream of letters and instructions from him, although he constantly insisted that I was respon-sible to the "London Office Committee," not to him. The old adage "no man can serve two masters" certainly applied; but nothing was to change until a year later, when I had finally given up. Before abandoning my post in June 1968, however, I made it very clear what I thought all the college powers-that-be should do by way of sound organization, personnel as-signments, and management. Miraculously, after I departed, they did ex-actly what I had long recommended. But this is ahead of the story, which I lay out because it demonstrates many of the great difficulties that face professedly international organizations that nevertheless depend greatly on retired volunteers (in the case of Sir George, *éminence grise*) to do execu-tive work beyond the scope of their policy-making duties as board direc-tors or governors. Sir George loved what he was doing, and he used his vast experience and skills in ways that tactically helped the college survive and, later, prosper. But there was no room in his retirement plans (he had once been finance minister of the Sudan) for someone such as me. We later came to a complete impasse. It was, I later realized, the "King Lear syndrome."

With my London Office colleague Robin Hankey I got on extremely well. He was the son of the redoubtable Sir Maurice Hankey, secretary to the Cabinet during World War I, and also to the British delegation to the Versailles Conference in 1919. Robin had been ambassador to the young OECD and had a good feel for the multinational dimension.

With Sir Eric Berthoud, however, I had plenty of problems. Again, my journal at the time had this to say:

> One of my problems will be the British [themselves]. They are remarkable people, steady as a rock and fundamentally as sound as any on earth. But many are cautious and short-sighted. Sir Eric Berthoud is a prime example: splendid tactician but no mind for strategy at all ... Also, they can be — perhaps unconsciously — nationalistic in their desire to hold onto and dominate an international enterprise. [For me] to keep any single nation from being dominant in this will be *tough*, but that will be one measure of success.

The third, but by no means less consequential, member of London Office was Valerie, a later-thirties spinster who was fast and efficient but with paranoid and Mussolini-like tendencies, plus a distinct dislike for Americans — and most assuredly me. One day I was puttering around the office in Valerie's absence, looking for a file. I opened a drawer in the filing cabinet and there was a revolver! On V's return, I confronted her; this, she said, was her target pistol. An MI6 friend had seen her shoot and advised her to practice regularly. I instructed her to remove it from our premises.

As they say, I had a "learning experience" to come, and I did my best. But along with the "parachuting in" analogy, I found one still more apt: that of the Yankee in Mark Twain's *A Connecticut Yankee in King Arthur's Court*. Twain's 14th century English nobles and aristocrats were quite unprepared for the newcomer. He, however "modernized" them and their warfare, despite much resistance, before returning to the 19th century and New England. I ran into the same attitudes with many of the Atlantic College board and staff — for some I was like a stranger from another planet, while others (thank God) welcomed my dynamic, kind, but clearcut and sometimes bold ways. In a year and a half, I managed to leave an imprint that appears to have lasted years — especially in convincing most of the recalcitrants that if they tried to have a fully worldwide enterprise, they could not have it managed by a British-dominated board. Other countries—notably the United States—wouldn't go for it. In the long run, I think I helped to set a true course for the future. The eventual creation of almost a dozen Atlantic Colleges (now United World Colleges) by the beginning of the 21st century, all over the globe, shows that the principals did finally get it right. But getting to "launch" broke crockery.

Living in the Mother Country

When Colleen and I arrived in London on 20 June 1967, I set off almost immediately to the Continent to work on the German college project. We had talked about the respective virtues of renting a flat in London as against living in the exurbs and commuting to the office. Our mind was finally made up when yet another member of the Huntley family also "parachuted in" unexpectedly. My seventeen-year-old son Mark in California had become a hot potato for his mother to handle. We had talked about the possibility of his signing up for the Atlantic College, but suddenly she decided on her own to send him to London, announced only by a telegram with his flight number and time of arrival, just a day before he flew in. Colleen picked him up at Heathrow airport and as soon as I returned from the Continent, we changed our plans. It would definitely be the "exurbs" for us now, as a family of three.

Years before, I had visited and liked Guildford, a small town in County Surrey. So we three set out to look it over. Upshot: we bought a "cottage" on the brow of the North Downs, overlooking Guildford, the river Wey and the Surrey Weald, farm and forest lands that lay in the gap between the North and South Downs. The downs are really "ups"—a line of east-west running hills marking off London parts to the north and coastal resorts and towns below the South Downs. Beech Lane, a little cul de sac where we settled, was a godsend. Our neighbors were an interesting mix and most friendly; the town, with its direct rail connection to London, was close, just half a mile by walking path or car, and the quiet was deafening. We lived there for seven pleasant years.

A word about English housing: In 1967, the brick house we bought was just ten years old, built by the town butcher. (We later learned that butchers held a special place of honor in England's small towns; many became mayors.) "Treetops," as the house was called, had a splendid small but sweeping garden, a wrought iron gate, and a grove of beech trees on one side and at the bottom of our garden. Through our neighbors we found an old gardener, Ted, who gradually revealed that he had come from a fairly important family out in the West Country. His parents had tossed him out when he became difficult, and he fended for himself. He lived in a garden shed on the property of nearby neighbors and knew a lot about gardens and life. Ted eventually drifted off, to be replaced by an off-duty fireman, Bill, who learned some gardening from us and whose brother, also a Ted, finally took over the garden and learned from Colleen to paint in oils. We still have one of his works, a sprightly view of the Guildford town hall and the High Street, which Dickens once called, "the prettiest high street in all of England." Near the Town Hall was a venerable hotel, The Angel, which boasted a basement bistro from the 14th century; upper stories had been added, century by century. There was a resident ghost, often seen in his early 19th century uniform.

"Treetops" (every English country house, no matter how modest, has to have a name), despite its newness, boasted only what the estate agent ("realtor" to Americans) called "background central heating." No problem at all, Madam: you just stoke this little coal furnace in the kitchen twice a day, turn on the radiators (in the hallway, plus one each in the dining room and living room, and a heated towel rack in the bathroom). Even summer operation of this (to us) primitive system, which left the two bedrooms entirely unheated, proved unsatisfactory, so we phoned Shell Oil Co., British Gas, and a more modern coal dealer to get some literature on the installation of their types of system. We had thought they would send us materials on the cost and other virtues of their particular fuels, but all we got from them were three or four pages devoted 80 percent to convincing us that central heating would be good for us, for anybody. After we installed a North Sea gas system, with plenty of radiators, visiting Brits would often remark on how "quaint you Americans are, with your ideas about plenty of warmth in every corner!" If you had been brought up in drafty old houses and boarding schools with cold showers and coal grates in the bedrooms, you might even have been taught to believe that "central heating" wasn't really good for you! (We learned later that the Houses of Parliament had burned down in 1834 as a result of a defect in the newfangled central heating! Could it be that from this historic incident stemmed the British abomination of central heating??)

Guildford, the county seat of Surrey, was truly a marvelous little market town. In the small city park were the ruins of a castle built by bad King John on Roman ruins, abutting a rose garden and a bowling green of tightly clipped, emerald green grass. I once asked the groundskeeper, "However does one get such a magnificent lawn?" His reply: "Well, sir, one prepares a completely flat piece of ground, rolls it well to make it compact, applies fertilizer and the right sort of grass seed, and then just keeps at it for four hundred years or so." A true metaphor for much of English life: just start out, let things grow, don't plan or change too much, and all will come right in time.

Next to the park was Traylen's, known widely as the finest antiquarian bookshop outside of London. One did not walk into Traylen's through a big front door. This one sported a buzzer, so that only those whom the trade knew were reputable, or at least who looked as if they were, were let in. Mr. Baker, the manager, was a kindly fellow who always managed to find just what we were looking for, and not at an exorbitant price. My wife once bought an aging, slightly tattered copy of John Adams's *History of the Principal Republics of the World,* printed in London in 1794. Unfortunately, Traylen's had only Adams's volume 1, but it is of the greatest interest to one who, like me, searches constantly for thoughts on America's origins. Mrs. Huntley asked Mr. Baker to please wrap it up and send it to Treetops; it was to be a gift to me. Mr. Baker not only sent it on, but included a little bookplate pasted on the inside cover, with his calligraphic hand noting: "To Mr. Huntley from Mrs. Huntley, on their wedding anniversary, 1971."

Everything at Traylen's was carefully catalogued and shelved; Baker or his assistants could put their hands instantly on almost anything one was looking for; usually they had it or could get it quickly. For the more adventurous booklover, Thorpe's bookshop, around the corner and up the High Street, was a great magnet. It was four rickety stories high, with winding staircases in every imaginable corner, and with very little rhyme or reason for shelving books; some were not on shelves at all. On the first landing of the staircase leading upwards, there was always a higgledy-piggledy pile of books, three feet or so high, which challenged the intruder to at least pick at its edges. One day Colleen walked in hoping to find a copy of Lloyd Douglas's *Magnificent Obsession;* in the very first such corner pile of totally miscellaneous tomes, she found her copy, well used, staring out at her from the mass! Thorpe's premises were housed in what appeared to be an early 19th century shop, with the words "Constitution Hall" in bold letters outside the top story. When it rained hard, large tins were set out strategically to catch drips from the leaky roof.

There was a modest but fine tailor in Guildford, who made two suits for me; they never wore out, but in later years seemed to get somewhat smaller than originally! One dresses differently for work and for recreation in England than back home: I learned early on that in London offices, one simply did not wear anything but a black or dark blue tailored suit, possibly with pinstripes, but no more decorative or colorful. I was even able—finally—to wear a bowler hat I had bought in 1958 at Willoughby's on the rue Royale in Paris. I learned where to buy the best shoes (Church's, in Old Bond Street), to wear sober neckties, and the whole kit. However, I could never adhere to the London (or countryside Sunday luncheon) dress code completely; I always insisted on wearing, now and then, an

American tweed jacket and colorful slacks, just to emphasize my independence. Friends and acquaintances could never pigeonhole Colleen and me; as Americans we were classless, and that was a great advantage. We made friends with people of all types, and grew to love England.

Across from us on Beech Lane lived Joe and Joelle Morgan He was head of personnel for England's largest supermarket chain, she was a young Frenchwoman (a grandmother at 35). On one side of us lived a nice professional family, and two doors from them the St. George Careys, casually and modestly uppercrust. In between these two was Winnie's modest cottage; she had worked for great families as a housekeeper and in her retirement they had seen to it that she was properly housed in a pleasant little place in a nice upper-middle-class lane.

To our north lived Ruth and Geoff Cornwell (always pronounced, "Cornwool"). Geoff was the retired Gold Principal of the Bank of England. He explained how, whenever he or other colleagues had an errand near Threadneedle Street that involved a visit to another bank (let's say), they would always put on a top hat and frock coat, almost Edwardian. At the end of World War II, Geoff had the adventure of his life: The Third Reich had hidden much of its gold bullion at the bottom of a deep lake in the Bavarian Alps. The British Army, with divers, was sent to retrieve what they could, but Geoff, representing the national Bank of England, had to go along (probably without his top hat) to make sure all the gold bars were properly accounted for, stored for shipment, and so on. A film of the adventure was made some years later. Geoff and Ruth delighted in taking us on car trips around the countryside, especially when the annual competition for "the Best Kept Village in Surrey" was under way. Geoff was often one of the judges, and also loved keeping visual records of this and other county events with his Leica.

Just beyond the Cornwells lived a retired banker, whom we learned to know a bit and whose piano we bought. But the Cornwells, I believe on a class-conscious basis, never were close to this neighbor, who had been merely a vice president of the branch of a nationwide but very middle-class bank. When I told Geoff Cornwell once that David Wills had arranged a checking account for us at Glynn Mills, in London, he was visibly impressed: "Well, that's where much of the Royal Family and other aristocracy keep their money!" I didn't much care, being amused, but every time I went in to Glynn Mills for business, I thought of the hilarious scene in Mary Poppins where a group of nonagenarians, surrounded by cobwebs, operated a supposedly solvent but very old bank, quite out of Dickens. Highly polished brass on Glyn Mills's big front door, gleaming walnut counters and dividing barriers, high ceilings with dim old lamps, marble floors, and located on Whitehall, just around the corner from the New

Admiralty Building (new in 1922, completed—as C. Northcote Parkinson delights in revealing in his marvelous spoof of government, *Parkinson's Law*—on the very day that the keel for the last dreadnought of the once mighty British Navy was being laid down).

If the reader wishes to study something quintessentially English, start with London clubs. These are the places where a great deal of the nation's serious business is conducted, over tea, a glass of sherry, or a meal. There were in the 1960s forty or fifty such establishments, which could be classified by a sociologist into political, specialty, academic-intellectual, strictly social, military/naval, and others. It was not so easy to join most of them. One had to be sponsored by members and fit the template. I managed to gain a London perch in two of them. The English Speaking Union was easy to join, especially if one were from the States. In the early 1970s I also joined the National Liberal Club through the "backdoor," so to speak. In the mid-19th century, when the Liberals were riding high, this was a good place to hang out with one's likeminded friends. The premises were close to the Thames Embankment, Downing Street, and Parliament. When I joined, the Liberals were struggling for survival, as was the club. They got a small new lease on life by becoming home to "the Europe Club" and that is how I was gathered into the musty fold. The building was cavernous and run down, with poor heating under vast ceilings, a billiard room about the size of a kids' baseball field, an interesting library (as all clubs had), a huge picture of Winston Churchill (a Liberal from 1904, when he deserted the Conservatives, to 1924, when he rejoined them), and great halls, fit for a medieval baron, where one could have coffee or tea and plot with one's friends.

The club was a fine place for me to meet friends and associates, although the leather-covered chairs, in a century of wear, had sprung leaks of horsehair and occasionally of springs. But if one wants to do serious business in London, one has to have a club. And often newcomers or other people who don't especially fit, must be judged by the members as to their "clubableness." I had belonged to the Cercle Interallié in Paris (started by Marshal Foch, Sir Douglas Haig, and General John J. Pershing during the first World War). Later I was pleased to be invited into Washington's Cosmos Club, and found a second home at the old Rainier Club in Seattle (nothing fusty about the latter). But British clubs, although some have merged and others fallen by the wayside in a more frenetic age, are still the model for "gentlemanly culture" the world round.

We had some good laughs in England, often at ourselves, at other times at the English, but the incidents that brought these on were almost always good-natured and so typical. Living out in the country, but quite accessible to London, we were hosts to a great number of friends from all over England, Europe, and—often—America. Until 1974, the year we moved from England back to the United States, home and country life in the UK was idyllic.

I was charged in 1972 by an American research organization to do a social and economic study of England and its prospects; I thought these pretty bleak. In the beginning of our final year in the UK, there was visible evidence of the social and economic rot that had set in. Poor Edward Heath, then prime minister, could not manage the great coal strike of the winter of 1973–74, which just about shut the country down. Our electricity was often off, the trains ran chaotically, and life was fretful, to say the least. Heath was defeated by the Labour Party, but neither Wilson nor Callaghan, the next two prime ministers, could break the trade unions' grip on the British economy. That was finally done by the Iron Lady, Margaret Thatcher, in 1979. Much as I dislike Baroness Thatcher (in a political sort of way—I never met her), I have to give her credit for turning England around economically. The Communist Coal Union leader, Arthur Scargill, was finally brought down, and new management and industrial styles began to take root. And old banks, like Glynn Mills, began a symbolic round of mergers with others, presaging a new age.

A Visit to Sir George's Country Seat

One more comment on English country living: Not long after we had settled in Guildford, Colleen and I were invited to visit Sir George and Lady Schuster, in the Oxfordshire countryside. Their home, Nether Worton, in Middle Barton, Oxfordshire, was in large part a gem from the Middle Ages; U-shaped, entirely of ancient stone, with mullioned windows and many chimneys, it was not large but nevertheless copious in the interior. The "reception rooms"—the drawing room, the dining room, and library—were at the bottom of the U, and the wings were for sleeping, guests, kitchens and servants. We took the train to Didecote, where Lady Schuster, a tiny gray-haired but vigorous old lady in her eighties, met us at the station. She was driving a large Bentley and, when prodded to tell about the car, indicated that it was really just a Rolls Royce (true) but with a different radiator and without that "silly winged victory" atop it, which would simply have added another £1,000 to the cost, "to no purpose at all." The country roads, as so often, were narrow and hedged on both sides; as Lady Schuster careened through the hedgerows, we gulped invisibly, and then were thoroughly frightened when suddenly a hayrick, with a cloth-capped driver and a team of old Clydesdales suddenly loomed in the road. Lady Schuster saw the impediment and the driver of the team saw her, almost simultaneously; he controlled his horses and pulled as far off the road as he could get them; she slowed only a bit, sounded the "claxon" and swerved left, and they passed each other with only inches to spare.

Once inside Nether Worton, we met Sir George and were all four served tea (it was just 4:30) and engaged in moderately jolly conversation, which at one point turned to central heating. It was autumn and a chill was in the air, and in their parlor, too. I was glad that my wife and I had worn tweedy suits. Lady Schuster I think noted our discomfort and explained their particular type of heating: There were radiators everywhere, heated by electricity. But the warming current entered them only late in the evening. They were "storage heaters," devouring electricity (at a cheaper rate) during the night. In the morning, one then turned some switches and enjoyed warmth for the better part of the day from the stored current. However, the noble lady explained, by 4 or 5 p.m. most of the heat had gone out of them and the evenings were therefore "a bit cool."

Sir George was obviously a rich man, with a large estate and at least one grand car. How he and his lady could bear to suffer such a heating arrangement in the cool months was more than I could understand. But, after we had spent seven years in the UK, we began to understand that this, like so many other things, was quite bearable "because everybody does it."

Reminds me of a fine story in a little book called *The English Gentleman.* The Londoner visits his country squire friend (in a small village not unlike Middle Barton). The two walk down the village street. The London friend asks the Squire, "Bob, when you go out like this, why do you wear that shabby old tweed coat and flannel trousers? You know you don't have to be content with that." The Squire answers: "But it's all right, here everybody knows me." Some weeks later, Squire visits London, where he and Londoner are walking down fashionable Picadilly Lane. Londoner notices that Squire is wearing the same nearly threadbare get-up in which he had been dressed down in his village. Obvious question, "Now you explained down in your village why you dressed like that, but why in heaven's name do you do so up here in London?" "Ah," said the Squire, "because up here, *no* one knows me!"

Some years later, I paid one of many visits to the countryseat of a very wealthy friend, known for his good works. It was, again, teatime and dusk was coming on. My host was dressed in the shabbiest tweed jacket I think I had *ever* seen, just like the proverbial Squire. The elbows had been leather-patched, but the lining was obviously leaking out of the sleeves and the left outside breast pocket was literally *hanging* by only a few threads. When my friend rose to close the drapes on the drawing room windows (partly to insure more warmth), I noticed that although these had once been lined with fine silk, the silk itself was now greatly beleaguered, literally hanging down in shreds behind the heavy drapes.

But never mind. Such idiosyncrasies are fun. These were remarkable people, Schuster in a worldly and class-conscious sense, my friend in every good sense of the word. Fine clothes and home accoutrements are terribly important to the British upper classes, but only in their place. And one had to learn that to appreciate and understand them.

Crisis in the London Office

When I was setting up a New York office and preparing to go to England in the spring of 1967, I first became aware of a transatlantic difference of views about the future of the colleges and about what, specifically, I could do to help. From my experience at the Ford Foundation and USIA, I had learned that no matter how good an idea for nonprofit activity one has, nothing will avail (and no money will flow in) unless there is an *appropriate structure and the right people to run it*. From quick visits to the college in 1966 and early 1967, and through much written and face-to-face contact with the principals, this question of "institutional architecture" of a putatively international nonprofit enterprise, plus the manning of the key volunteer and staff positions, was still an open question for some. I discounted some of this, figuring that I could bring about a consensus when I got to London. I was fairly confident, because the two founders of the College, Kurt Hahn and Sir Lawrance Darvall, and the chief financial backer, David Wills, all held what I considered to be the right (and only) vision for the future of the enterprise, that is, to have organizational goals, structures, and personnel that would lead to the creation of a whole string of Atlantic Colleges. Without this clear vision and a consensus on what had to be done to realize it, mere lip service to "international education" would not suffice. I tried hard to give administrative and executive voice to this vision, but the weight of the entire old Empire fell on me.

Part of my optimism stemmed from my experience in guiding the creation of the Atlantic Institute. But I failed to see the significance of the new role I was expected to play in Britain: the alien parachuted in from outer space to try to reconcile views within a project that had been already a decade in the making. And the key players—all British—were split as to what they wanted and how to get it. And I really did not know most of the players.

So, when I had arrived in London and begun work seriously, I gradually realized that the job of consensus building in the right direction would be a much more difficult and lengthy process than I had imagined. I discovered, for example, that Air Marshal Sir Lawrance Darvall, who had conceived and led the project in partnership with Kurt Hahn, was being shunted away from leadership. In American terms, he was kicked upstairs to head a "Council" that was supposed to be international in composition, but whose purpose and activity would remain strictly on paper until after I had left.

I got to know Sir Lawrance extremely well; he and Lady Darvall lived across the river Wey from us in Guildford. We spent hours talking about the Atlantic Colleges, but he was by then—1967—a man without influence or power. Sir George Schuster, in effect, had taken over management of the whole. The two knights were different people: Sir George had an excellent administrative grasp and excelled in all the details of doing what a number of us were supposed to do. He did it well and retained control remarkably. Sir Lawrance was a different sort: a high-ranking Royal Air Force commander, who was used to outlining broad goals to a staff and then getting their input and action without too much "nannying." It was later said that Lawrance's health made the switch necessary (before I arrived in England), but I am inclined to think that his mind and ways of working were not compatible with those of Sir George, and one or the other had to go. That is speculation, but the truth is that the two knights were more or less incompatible and one was eased out.

As noted earlier, Sir George had set up a London Office Committee, supposedly a branch of the governing body of St. Donat's (the old Welsh castle that housed the first Atlantic College), but actually a device to make sure that the new boy, Huntley, did what Sir George wanted. His instructions, however, did not always come through the committee, but sometimes direct to me. I began to wonder whom I was actually working for and through what channels. After the first meeting of the London Committee, I discerned a great general reluctance to give up British domination of the whole enterprise, no matter what one said in propaganda for overseas consumption and no matter what sort of organizational setup was on paper. I had come to England on the understanding that my functions were threefold: To help create and energize non-British support for the colleges, to plan and bring about a series of colleges, and to help find money. But at the first meeting of the London Committee, it became clear that (1) I was the main component of the international fig leaf that everyone agreed was necessary—but only "eventually"—and an American in a sea of British bosses; (2) I would have as part of my responsibility the oversight of soliciting for foreign scholarships to the existing—and future—college; and (3) I was expected, in particular, to bring plenty of American dollars to the enterprise. And soon I found that Sir George also wanted me to take over the raising of funds in Britain, a task that was more or less fictional, because he really wanted to do it himself. Talk about cleft sticks!

This first L.O.C. meeting, like almost all subsequent ones, dealt hardly at all with the question of a master international plan, with a timeline of objectives, or a discussion of governing bodies and staff responsibilities. I noted in my journal: "Thus the British penchant for wanting to back slowly into anything important. Infuriating and not a very successful [or promising] way to pursue something important in the modern world."

The German Atlantic College

The question of creating a German Atlantic College, which practically everyone said they believed should be the next step in internationalization, became a prime example, for me at any rate, of how the Brits involved had trouble in reaching a consensus on timing, German involvement, and siting and supporting a college in West Germany. This was one of the countries in which I had had more experience of the kind needed—plus a great many more useful contacts—than did most of my colleagues. They did know a number of aristocratic and notable Germans, but we needed a German Organizing Committee to bring together the right "get-it-done" people who could soon take over the entire job, with some guidance and coordination from the London principals. However, it became clear after a few months of wandering around Germany—often with one or two British "minders" with me (some were a great help, others just a brake on progress)—that the admiral-headmaster at St. Donat's had, as noted earlier, a fixed idea of where the German College should be located and how it would work. But Sir George and other key leaders disagreed about the siting and also about whether to follow a quick or languid timetable for its establishment.

The point was often made that financial operation of the Atlantic College–Wales should be completely sound on a long-term basis before starting a German college. This clashed with the view of those—especially Kurt Hahn—who felt that for overpowering psychological and geopolitical reasons, a German college should be established as quickly as possible. Germany was still in an uncertain position in the Western political firmament; creating a new type of upper-secondary, totally international type of education would help give heart to those, in Germany and abroad, who wanted Germany pointed firmly in a Western direction and completely engaged in a visionary and yet practical social-cultural enterprise.

As noted, the admiral insisted that the German college be located on the sea so that the St. Donat's pattern of ocean-rescue teams could be duplicated. Some Germans we consulted (some who became members of an Organizing Committee for the German College) were of two minds on the matter of site. (It was of course completely premature to be locating a suitable site and then handing it to the Germans involved as a fait accompli.) Two or three of us went to north Germany nevertheless to inspect a small number of possible sites, talking to local officials, asking about how an Atlantic College sea-rescue program could be integrated with German coast guard services, and so on. The Island of Sylt, a summer resort area in the North Sea, was one possibility—but it was far from any urban or intellectual centers, proved to have little land available, and could be reached only by sea or rail, with no bridges for cars. We also considered Cuxhaven, a smallish seaport west of Bremen, but it too had disadvantages. The truth was that postwar West Germany, deprived of its entire prewar Baltic coast, now "owned" only its old North Sea coast and a few islands—the choices for a German sea–college were thus greatly limited.

Kurt Hahn insisted that we should also look at the possibility of a mountain rescue service location, which of course would put the College on the edge of the Alps, near Austrian and Swiss borders. Again, we started inquiries with government and education officials in the area, looked at one quite suitable location; but without the leadership or even the imprimatur of a German Organizing Committee, there wasn't a decision and there would not be an effective one for some years to come.

As of today, at the beginning of the 21st century, there still is no Atlantic College in Germany. This can be explained partly in terms of a strange but understandable German timidity, following on the heels of a catastrophic war started by Hitler, to assert itself, even on a nongovernmental basis. (That has changed a good deal of course since the 1960s.) However, the Atlantic College project (as it was then called, but is today the United World Colleges) was stymied basically because it was not turned over to responsible Germans at an early date. Personalities in Britain, many with a rather odd feeling that particularly pervaded the British upper classes in those days, simply wished to dominate the whole affair, not just in Britain but overseas. And I think many of those most closely involved did not even recognize this propensity, a major source of their drive to shine with an admittedly marvelous project. This is old-fashioned stuff, and I must admit that even in my own country, earlier and particularly in these early days of a new century, a neoimperialistic view of the world is found at many levels and quarters. It is unilateralism, one way or another.

There is, most unfortunately, still a paucity of world leaders on both private and public stages, nearly everywhere, who can step away from the parochial psychological constraints of their national backgrounds and social environments to embrace true, balanced partnership with other countries and peoples. Most of us Euro-North Americans know how to conduct ourselves in a modern democracy, as voters and so on, but when it comes to understanding "overseas" and the concerns of other countries, and knowing how to be good listeners and forge common ties and joint action to solve otherwise intractable common problems, large and small, we in America are at the back of the class for not having learned our lessons. But the British, in the 1960s, were in general not much further ahead.

It is fortunate that after I left the Atlantic Colleges in the summer of 1968, I stayed on in England, working with other groups of extraordinary British people on projects that were much more satisfying from this "international teamwork" point of view. Sir Lawrance Darvall, Kurt Hahn, and Sir David Wills understood these international truths.

Götterdämmerung ... more or less

By November of 1967, it became clear that the headmaster of Atlantic College, the admiral, disliked me intensely and felt I was trying to displace him as the head of everything. This was not at all true, but it didn't matter. It turned out that the admiral had "spies" in London—especially the gun-toting Valerie and a young fellow from the chartered accountants (certified public accountants in the United States) who commuted from London to the college to oversee the books. These two reported back every morsel of derogatory information about me they could manufacture to the admiral, who disclosed these bits to Sir George Schuster on a regular basis.

Sir George had me and Valerie busy creating long lists of companies in the UK, some American, most British. (I wrote a note on the Hoover vacuum company, describing it as an American firm; Valerie protested, "Oh, but that is a *British* company!!" Pretty good public relations strategy for an American corporation that for half a century had practically monopolized the vacuum cleaner business in the UK!)

Sir George now expected me to make raising funds—and especially in the UK—my first priority. I protested that until we had a functioning balance in nationalities within an active international council of overall policy makers, this could not be done properly. I also knew, that even if we had settled all organizational and institutional factors satisfactorily, a person in my place—the executive officer of "whatever"—should never go personally to ask for funds. Instead, he would help the notables on his board to make the appeals in person. This was simply good professional fund-raising practice, but not yet standard in Britain.

Sir George, I gradually discovered, was handling a great deal of the "appeal" (British term) for money on his own, right from Nether Worton, where he had a secretary. He sent copies of these appeals to Valerie, who was expected to keep "score," and I was supposed to be responsible for Valerie; but neither she nor Sir George took care that I was "in the loop." So evolves impossibility. Besides, the idea that an American who had lived in the UK for only a few months could go out into the British business and foundation world and make a credible case alone was ludicrous. It gradually became an untenable situation, like something out of *H.M.S. Pinafore*.

I also had problems on the other side of the Big Pond; Malcolm Muir, chairman of the U.S. Commission for the Atlantic Colleges (set up the right way; I had made sure), was not as responsive on moving the new apparatus in America as I had hoped. Malcolm was the choice of dear old Hahn and Wills (a transatlantic "old-boy network"), a perfectly marvelous man, but not—at age 78—a strong, energetic leader. Nor was our amazingly prescient and experienced secretary of the U.S. Commission, Sam Reber, who was also retired and not exactly burning with energy. Both of them believed wholeheartedly in what we were trying to do, but they seemed at times overcome by the obstacles they saw. We had formed committees in several major American cities, whose job at this stage was mainly to recruit some really top boys to attend Atlantic College in Wales. I had handpicked most of the chairmen of these local committees, and we did accomplish an uptake in U.S. enrollment. But the general atmosphere for fund-raising in America had suddenly gone quite sour—for reasons quite extraneous to our educational project—so that, despite their desire to move ahead, Malcolm and Sam and some around them were finding it difficult. My subtlety and patience were, in any event, not yet sufficiently developed to cope with this series of major challenges on both sides of the Atlantic. And, to be fair to the U.S. leadership, the challenges they were facing had magnified considerably, in the space of less than a year. Among other things, the U.S. economy, including the stock market, had taken a steep downturn. This in turn affected most philanthropies.

I wondered how it might have been in the old days of the Wild West or in ancient Rome, when skillful riders were able to stand atop a whole team of horses and manage to win the race, let alone remain upright!

Assessment of the Situation in the United States

I spent about a month in the United States in late spring 1968 and wrote a memo for my British colleagues on return. This amplifies a good deal the new difficulties that were upon us in getting the major American support, in all respects, that everyone agreed we needed. To help set the scene for the major social upheavals that were to make the late sixties and seventies one of the more eventful, and sad, periods of the late 20th century, here are some of the factors I noted as responsible for the U.S. "national mood" as I then saw it, with the assassination of Dr. Martin Luther King a major contributing factor:

1. An increasing pessimism, deep "troubling of the soul" of many Americans, and a sharp rise in tempers over the seemingly endless war in Vietnam.
2. A general uneasiness with respect to the national and international economic scene (the full impact of the gold crisis and the impact of U.S. balance of payments difficulties have not as yet produced a general recognition of the truly perilous situation).
3. Alarm at the widespread race riots, the sharp increase in crime in some cities, the heightened tendency to political radicalization in dealing with racial issues, and the magnitude of the tasks the nation faces if the roots of Negro unrest are to be successfully dealt with. . . . The U.S. establishment is rapidly shifting a major part of the resources, material and financial, of the nation to deal with the urban crisis, of which the Negro problem is rightly recognized to be only a part.
4. A visible trend to isolationism in international affairs, public and private.
5. A diversion of not only funds but highly skilled manpower from the international to the domestic front is evident; to illustrate, one of our best San Francisco committee members, Dr. Brooks, is unable to turn his great talents to our work because, as vice provost of Stanford University, he is totally occupied with the student revolt.

In assessing the consequences, I noted that "it has been most difficult to attract money [in the U.S.] for any aspect of [our College] project for at least 18 months; the difficulties and the prospects are now even worse, one might say abysmal." Both government and the private nonprofit sector, I wrote, are involved in a "general and decisive swing away from international to domestic affairs." Our local committees reported great difficulty in raising funds; "as with national philanthropic sources, the money is being diverted to the cities." (McGeorge Bundy, apparently sensing these trends even earlier, had left the Johnson cabinet for the presidency of the Ford Foundation and was pushing funds toward the many problem cities.) Few new international projects were able "to get off the ground." I concluded that the outlook for the U.S. Commission for the Atlantic Colleges could be counted on, for the next few years, to provide a few good students each year and perhaps maintain one American teacher at St. Donat's, but little more.

This assessment, deeply pessimistic, added to the weaknesses of the U.S. Commission noted earlier. I told my British colleagues that they should not "hope to rely on the U.S. for capital projects or operating grants to St. Donat's, for aid to [our] London office, or for assistance to a German college project," at least in the near- or midterm.

My memorandum went to Lord Mountbatten, who had just become overall chairman of the Council (which later became increasingly international in composition, as I had so strongly recommended), to Sir George Schuster, to the London Office Committee (technically still my supervisors), and to the headmaster in Wales. None of them were pleased at the news, although reading the London newspapers, a good deal of the U.S. situation was clear to see. In the minds of some, if I was not able to raise money in the United States or England, what good was I?

It was time for me to move on; Sir George had, I think, decided this several weeks, if not months, earlier. I too saw no future with the Colleges, sad as that was to me. I felt I had been asked to do the impossible in a short time, without an adequate organizational structure and clear lines of authority and responsibility. I wrote a confidential "valedictory" memo for the London Office Committee on 15 June 1968; here are some of my conclusions and recommendations, sufficient to keep their eyes propped open: "The expansion program and even overseas supporting activities centered on but one College cannot be successful if St. Donat's itself is not in good health. At present it is not. . . . There will probably be a [college] financial crisis in 1969, but it cannot be properly surmounted unless the College is reformed managerially."

Pulling no punches, I recommended replacement of the headmaster, which occurred not long after my departure. I also recommended reform of the curriculum:

In his two years at Atlantic College, each student should become familiar with such modern issues and fields as . . . cultural anthropology, esp. concepts of racial differences and the relative effects of heredity and environment. . . . Sociology, especially the nature of the Western technological/urban revolution. . . . Psychology, including some behavioral concepts, the nature of individual differences, some psychiatric theory, some rudimentary pathology. Political science, . . . philosophy and theory, parliamentary and constitutional government, modern political trends, and studies of democracy, communism, socialism, fascism, capitalism. . . . International relations—power politics—world peace—international cooperation and institutions—and the crisis of modernization. Economics, world trade [and finance], economic communities, overseas aid, etc. Religion and philosophy.

I acknowledged that "knowledge of such a vast scope, imparted to 16–18-year-olds in a really short space of time" would necessarily be superficial, "and there would be great gaps, but *some* exposure to these great issues and principles is better than *no* exposure at all." Today I still believe that all secondary schools should strive to impart elements of this body of knowledge to all students, especially to the gifted ones on whom so much of the world's future depends. (It is good to note that the International Baccalaureate (initially funded by the Ford Foundation) is now the core curriculum for all the subsequent colleges and for many top-level schools around the world.)

I urged that a majority of the members of the council (the international fig leaf) should be non-British—"otherwise, as a mainly British body, its very existence negates its professed goal, a truly international education." I also recommended that the council "alone should be responsible for expansion policy and operations . . . and that it should be wholly differentiated and distinct from the St. Donat's Governing Body. . . . [The council] should issue charters to all Colleges . . . and withdraw these if overall policies and agreed standards are not adhered to." Furthermore, the majority of teachers at St. Donat's were British, hardly creating the international image one would hope for.

I also recommended reform of the London Office, plus a detailed program for expansion of the college system into key countries.

�֍

This was a fascinating, if sometimes quite difficult, period in my life. I felt that my personal opinion of the way the college project had been run was correct; in a conversation with an American employed by McKinsey, the big U.S. consulting firm, in London, my general appreciation was confirmed. Most of McKinsey's business in Britain was with British, not American firms. The "biggest problem" the UK firms have: "They are overloaded with committees and boards that are involved in decision-making. This makes decisions come slowly and usually produces poor decisions. They are always lowest-common-denominator" (my journal). I told David Wills of this conversation and mentioned Kurt Hahn's remark to me that "Germans have no committee sense." I started to say, but David finished my sentence, "The British have too much of it."

Also, the British, throughout their history, have a penchant for letting everything grow organizationally "like Topsy." When Lord Mountbatten, in April 1968, signed on as supremo, most of us thought he would replace Sir George Schuster (who had replaced Sir Lawrance Darvall). But Sir George remained at the helm, like the shoguns in ancient Japan, who stayed in the shadow of the emperor but retained the reins of power. Sir George had obviously, from early in 1968, been laying a "paper trail" that would eventuate in my departure. I saw it coming and stepped down on 1 July 1968, still fascinated with the Atlantic College idea and hopeful that it would eventually work its way to educational prominence. But, it was not to be on *my* watch. Some years later, after a similar encounter with retired people of advanced age, with impressive résumés and a continuing drive for power and control, I came to call the problem that had defeated me at Atlantic College the "King Lear Syndrome."

I attributed the difficulties that contributed to making my departure inevitable to the following:

• Sir George's advanced age, which in his case spelled great inflexibility.
• Bad organization and manning, which would have to be corrected before serious fund-raising could proceed. The project's image was too "British."
• The headmaster's animosity to me, and his poor management of the college.
• Divided opinion on the Council as to how quickly to move on a German college (with the timid members at that time in the ascendancy).
• Some clerical help who could not be trusted and who "poisoned the well," with well-aimed but distorted and untrue tales about me, with the project's principals.

In March 1968, I had written to David Wills: "I cannot effectively raise money (or instigate the raising of money) for an enterprise that is poorly organized and managed."

It was a source of satisfaction in later years to learn from Sir David Wills that my key recommendations had eventually been accepted, the Council had been restructured, Mountbatten had done a good PR job of putting the Colleges on the map, Sir George and the headmaster had both departed from the scene, and although there would always be problems of one kind or another, the whole enterprise was finally destined to take off. I am proud to have been a small cog in the wheels for a few years and to have helped set an effective course for the future. A fine man, Robert

Blackburn, who had been deputy headmaster at St. Donat's, took my place in the London Office, and I went on to other things. Now, in the 21st century, there are ten United World Colleges dotted around the world.

Years later, in mulling over my substantive success (in charting out a path of change) against my background as a youngish American, I realized that these could not have been reconciled. Most—but not all—of the aristocratic/upper crust Brits with whom I worked (and to whom I was responsible) could not understand that my devotion—indeed sense of duty—to the project, as I had understood it and as those who engaged me, mainly Hahn and Wills, had conceived it, overrode the obstacles that presented themselves. I came from the Far West, my father and I were self-made men, starting from humble circumstances only a few years after the closing of the frontier. I could not be classified on a British scale of class, education, or family background. I felt myself the equal of my British coworkers in this particular vineyard, most of whom were used to deference. I cherished my independence. When I felt strongly that our common project required a different perspective, I made this as clear as I could (diplomatically); but culturally I was always at a disadvantage, even though eventually all the important things I had proposed were done. Sometimes, in numerous organizational milieux, I felt it necessary to shatter some china. For some Brits, this kind of behavior is quite impolite, if not unforgivable. But that, in part, is how I learned, and also how I was able at times to bring about progress in important undertakings.

12
Atlantic Jack of All Trades

27 January 1973: *The Treaty of Paris ends the Vietnam War with a call for all U.S. forces to leave Vietnam and a cease-fire between North and South.*

October 1973: *Oil prices rise to nearly eight times the previous year's, prompting the first oil crisis. Frightened consumers bid wildly for OPEC oil. A repeat crisis in 1978 causes recession and leads to the establishment of OECD's international energy agency.*

Another Chapter in the Building of the Atlantic Community

After a great deal of thought and consultation with a few friends in Britain and America, my wife and I decided to stay on in our home in Guildford. I would work from there, finding work from several sources as opportunities arose, and generating a good deal of it myself. My little book on NATO, written for schools in 1965, needed a revised edition, so I began with that. In August 1968, my friends at the Atlantic Council of the United States asked me to write a book for them, which eventually appeared under the title, *Europe and America: The Next Ten Years*. The Council wanted a definitive work on the contemporary situation of the Atlantic community and the prospects and problems it faced. I found this work difficult but extremely satisfying. I traveled to Brussels and other European capitals, as well as to the United States and Canada, to gather information and perspective. The book covered everything—security questions, the transatlantic economy, overseas banking, social matters affecting most Atlantic nations in common, and cultural relationships.

About an author's task, I had this to confide to my journal:

Writing is hard and demanding, because it depends so very much on self-discipline. Some days I think I am getting nowhere and doing worthless work; other days I am delighted and wonder at what I have written. Tonight I said to Colleen: "Writing is like mining. You begin to strike a lode and you dig deeper and deeper. You never knew until you began whether or not you would get anything and often you are surprised that it came out of *you*."

I suppose many writers share such feelings about their work. In the 21st century it is still, for me, basically the same process, after having written four books and countless articles. One friend in London, a fine writer and observer of the international scene, contended that he thought a great deal about what he was going to write, then sat down with a yellow legal pad, wrote down what came to him, and never made any revisions! What a rare gift!

In mid-April 1969, I sent the Europe-America manuscript to my friends at the Atlantic Council in Washington. Later, I went to see them, and we made extensive revisions. One of the great retired denizens of the capital, the vice chairman of ACUS and one of my old "Atlantic" comrades, W. Randolph Burgess, was drafted to coauthor the book with me; he made many good additions and suggestions. Finally it was published by a New York firm, Walker and Co. Randy's name, plus a good deal of his experience as a former chairman of the Federal Reserve Bank of New York and undersecretary of the Treasury, undoubtedly helped sell the book.

Meanwhile, I was thinking of how I could pull together a living and a career out of transatlantic freelancing, consulting, and writing, the type of career with practically no guidelines. My father helped out; his working years in southern California had ended, and he had made a little money. I floated ideas with friends in England and with others abroad. Some of the projects—some remunerative, some not—that I settled on over the next five years involved trying to help "build" the Atlantic community. Although the scope of my work would change later, I never deviated from my drive in this direction: spreading democracy and unifying democracies. Later, I enlarged my interests and my work to embrace what I called the "Atlantic-Pacific System" and—toward the end of the 20th century—the growth of democracy the world over. The knitting together of a global Community of Democracies took institutional, intergovernmental form in 2000. But these broader concepts were only gestating while I was in England; my emphasis from 1969 to 1974 was on building organizations and mutual understanding among the peoples of the Atlantic world, viz., adherents of NATO and the OECD, Western Europe and North America.

Wilton Park

A British institution to which I paid a lot of attention was Wilton Park, where I visited often from 1958 to 1989 and got to know sharp people from the Western democracies, and to understand our common problems better. Wilton Park's genesis was fascinating: Near the end of World War II, Churchill reportedly called together a few advisers to say, "We have several hundred thousand German prisoners still in Britain. Some of them, once they go home, will be able to play a role in the refashioning of their country. Pick out those who are young, bright, and not hopelessly nazified, and create a program to prepare them for democracy and for going home."

A bright, expansive don at Oxford, Dr. Heinz Koeppler, who had fled Germany when Hitler came to power, had the institutional answer. Churchill approved. Koeppler and a small staff of educators and administrators took over a large country manor house at Wilton Park, Beaconsfield, west of London, and asked the commandants of prison camps to screen out the best men and send them there. Each prisoner was given free range of the house and grounds. They listened to lectures from prominent Brits about the world they had seen only through the prism of Hitler's propaganda, and talked and studied for several months. Koeppler acquired a good library, reflecting mainly 20th century thought on the human condition—including some of the books Hitler had burned. A stream of new recruits kept coming, and eventually some 4,000 "enlightened" Germans were ready to go back to their country and work in a framework of freedom.

The program continued for a few years after the war. In 1951, its scope was enlarged to bring intellectual and community leaders from first NATO and later, OECD countries to the program. Wilton Park (using the name still, but having transferred its site to another old country manor, Wiston House near Steyning, in east Sussex) became a unique and shining fixture of British foreign relations—"jealously independent in spirit" (as one of its histories stated) and in the conduct of its debates, even though financed by the Foreign Office. One of Wilton Park's staff wrote of its work: "We are determinedly generalist in spirit. We seek to combat narrow specialisation, widen horizons, stretch minds and dent prejudices. . . . We work by cross-fertilisation and the interaction of people's opinions, background and personal experience."

And so Wilton Park has done, for more than fifty years.

Its work has continued into the 21st century and boasts literally thousands of alumni who have had their perspectives and knowledge enlarged by contact with multinational groups at Wilton Park. I led off discussions there several times in the fifties, and more so after we had moved to England in the sixties. In the 1980s I was invited twice again, in 1989 to shed light on U.S. public opinion as it focused on NATO and related defense matters. One of the conferees was Gebhardt von Moltke, then director for U.S. affairs in the ministry of foreign affairs in Bonn. Gebhardt was a descendent of the famous military family whose prominence began with Bismarck's field marshal in the wars for Prussian dominance in the mid–19th century. A thoroughly sensible chap, Gebhardt and others (like my later friend, Baron von Richthofen, nephew of the famous World War I flying ace) showed how the modern generation has thoroughly evolved, within famous old German families, with strong ties to the modern West and democracy.

The warden of Wilton Park (as Dr. Sir Heinz Koeppler was styled) became a great friend, along with his staff; we collaborated on many projects. The British did this kind of thing exceedingly well. With the assistance of Koeppler, the well-organized and commanding Prussian (who nonetheless encouraged completely open discussion), the institution could be considered one of Britain's great postwar successes in what is today called "public diplomacy." An American professor, Loyal Gould of Baylor University, once wrote of Koeppler's work with German prisoners: "I gained a new respect for Koeppler . . . for his ability to judge character, to select people who could become democrats if only they knew what democracy meant."

I was most impressed to meet former German prisoner-students of Wilton Park, who returned again and again—many after reaching high office in German life—because they revered Koeppler and thought of Wilton Park as the beginning of their new lives amid the chaos born of war. Many alumni became our fast friends; a schoolteacher from Lausanne, a German colonel in the Bundeswehr, a Brit who had lived in Indonesia as a young man and been imprisoned by the Japanese, an American TV commentator, and a wonderful Turkish professor of history were among these. Many such ties among "old boys" of Wilton Park persist for years, with alumni associations in the United States, Canada, and the European countries.

When Sir Heinz retired in 1977, he wisely (no King Lear syndrome here!) moved to a professorship at Baylor University in Texas, where his expansive ways seemed to fit the Texan character extremely well. Two years later, he died prematurely of a massive heart attack, and the university established the Heinz Koeppler Institute in his memory. The announcement called Koeppler "the first and most instrumental keeper of the British idea to encourage democratic institutions in post World War II Germany." I believe he quite deserved this accolade; he had worked for a half century as "keeper."

The British ambassador to Paris held a reception when Sir Heinz retired. The president of the Republic, Antoine Pinay, and many other notables attended. An account in *Le Figaro* praising Sir Heinz said, in part: "This man, who has contributed to fashioning the intellectual climate of the Europe of today, has always had the gift of exemplary simplicity and clarity in his analysis of the problems of our time, qualities that are reflected in the way in which the famous *Who's Who* describes Heinz Koeppler's favourite pastime, 'diminishing jargon.'"

I had discovered many independent international programs over the years; the best were most often run by the Brits and all of them, together, have created one major branch of a vast network of personal, private interconnections that have sustained good transatlantic relations—and sometimes helped to repair them—over many decades. I was determined to create more such networks, and this became part of my self-appointed "mission" while in England and after. I nominated key people from many countries for Wilton Park conferences.

The Mid-Atlantic Clubs

Through Sir Lawrance Darvall I got to know H. W. (Walter) Lessing, an extraordinary English citizen of German birth. He and Sir Lawrance were deeply involved in the creation of a "Britain in Europe" campaign, with a "Europe House," to educate Brits as to the need for their nation to become a member of the Common Market (Britain finally joined in 1973). Walter, a Jew from Bamberg (near where I had worked in Bavaria), was in hospital in 1933, tending a broken leg from skiing, when he heard that Hitler had become chancellor. More clearly than most German Jews, he felt he knew exactly what this meant; he got some crutches and a few belongings together and fled immediately to Paris. From there he landed in Cairo, went into business, and married a lovely Italian whose family had lived in Egypt for years. After World War II, Walter migrated to London and never left, continuing with successful business ventures and dabbling on the fringes of politics. He supported efforts to involve Germans in multinational NGOs and, in his late years, endowed a Center for British Studies at his old university in Bamberg.

Lessing and I found that we shared the same strong feelings about improving transatlantic links. My experience with the Hof German-American Luncheon Club (1954–55) and with an informal lunch group concentrated on Atlantic affairs (1963–65) in Washington suggested launching something similar but better in London. The idea eventually became a string of Mid-Atlantic Clubs (MACs) around the Atlantic world. Walter's agile mind caught the concept quickly. Together we recruited about fifty "movers and shakers" from the London area in 1970, to meet privately for lunch each month for off-the-record discussions of hot transatlantic issues. Our rule was this: not more than half the members could be British; the others were chosen from among the diplomats, businessmen, political parties, journalists, trade union leaders, and scholars from other OECD countries resident in London. Sir Derek Ezra, then chairman of the British National Coal Board (later Lord Ezra), became the M.A.C. chairman followed by Sir Kenneth Younger. Lessing was vice chairman (later chairman) and I was secretary. I made a précis of each discussion for private circulation to all members of all clubs; these records, however, never attributed remarks to any speaker by name.

Later, Walter and I were emboldened to help likeminded persons in New York, Washington, Brussels, Paris, San Francisco, and Bonn (other cities followed still later) to found similar, loosely organized but congenial and more or less likeminded groups. It was understood that if a member of one club were to be transferred to another city in the "network," he or she could join the club there; in this sense, MACs were like Rotary Clubs. Cozy relationships developed among members; fellow feeling was particularly strong within each club, but we were never able put the meat on the bones of interclub ties as we had hoped; each club eventually took on its own special existence. Many MACs still exist. These groups have had the considerable advantage of low-cost operations; by contrast, most international conferences cost a lot of money to mount, especially for travel, bed, and board for out-of-country participants. The virtue of the Mid–Atlantic Clubs was that there were no travel costs; each member paid for his/her own lunch. The premises were in most cases given free (the National Coal Board conference room in London, an old men's club in Brussels, the Cercle Interallié in Paris, the University Club of New York).

Members of most of our MACs were influential people whose contributions to an overall "transatlantic consensus" were not negligible. The "discussion openers" (we did not call them lecturers or speakers) were usually prestigious government, diplomatic, business, academic, or other leaders who, as well as tossing out fresh ideas, sometimes learned something from their conferees.

Once, in 1972, we decided on an unusual joint project for the first three clubs then in existence. President Nixon's national security adviser Henry Kissinger, whose talents had been virtually consumed in a narrow focus on the Vietnam War for some years, had finally concluded a shaky peace with the North Vietnamese. He then announced to the world that 1972–73 was to be the "Year of Europe." This was supposed to make the (truly) neglected Europeans feel good. The three MACs each held a meeting within a particular month, discussed Kissinger's "Year of Europe" idea, and sent summaries of their discussions to me (I was then secretary of the network of clubs). I sent the three accounts (which made fascinating reading) to Henry, with a cover précis. Although the conclusions of the clubs were not identical, all agreed that Henry's "Year of Europe" idea was either not a very good one or at best irrelevant—the essence for all clubs, on both sides of the Atlantic was that "*every* year should be the Year of Europe." Kissinger replied, after the usual courtesies: "The analysis of your three discussions regarding my 'Atlantic Charter' speech had very interesting comments. The things you have mentioned are not uniformly encouraging." He wished me "luck with the Network of Mid-Atlantic Clubs" and signed his regards.

When I left England in 1974 to join the Battelle Research Institute in Seattle, I helped friends there to organize an "Atlantic-Pacific Club," as part of the MAC network. My Foreign Service pal Robert Brand, who in the mid-seventies was U.S. consul general in Melbourne, persuaded Australian friends and a group of foreign residents to start the "Pacific Institute" there. The former Canadian consul general in New York, Bruce Rankin, was a member of the Big Apple's MAC; when he was posted as ambassador to Japan, he tried to form a Mid-Atlantic/Pacific Club in Tokyo, alas, without success. Nick Campbell, who as head of Standard Oil for Europe and a founding member of the MAC London, was transferred to New York and provided strategic help in founding the Mid-Atlantic Club there. And so it went.

Walter Lessing, over ninety and spry at the beginning of the 21st century, is still the active Pater Familias of the Mid-Atlantic enterprise. Such groups, perhaps with modifications, could provide an important element in binding together like-minded leaders in like-minded countries though with a greater geographic spread.

The Standing Conference of Atlantic Organizations

Through the Atlantic College project, I had become a friend of Sir Frank Roberts, in 1967 Her Britannic Majesty's ambassador in Bonn and about to leave the service. British diplomats in those days were obliged to retire at the early age of sixty; most took subsequent positions as directors of corporations or heads of charities. Frank was for years on the board of the Lever company, but had time for other pursuits. I persuaded him to help me "float" yet another transatlantic NGO, which we called The Standing Conference of Atlantic Organizations (SCAO). To rally the right people and plot a course, we held a small conference in March 1973 at the Rockefeller Foundation's study center on Lake Como, attended by the heads of most of the important nongovernmental bodies dealing with transatlantic matters. We were lucky to have with us Manlio Brosio, who had just stepped down as one of NATO's most effective secretaries general, plus Jean Rey, the Belgian chairman of the Commission of the European Communities. Together we put together a body that met annually for many years thereafter, to try to agree on a general program of action that all could embrace, in various ways, to help educate publics in the NATO and OECD countries as to the stakes they had in the health of the Atlantic community. We were trying to emulate what I had seen done in the fifties with the European Movement; we had to be content however with very little money for joint efforts and none for the various constituent groups, which each had to find on its own. For several years SCAO headquarters published a quarterly newsletter, which let its member-organizations know what the other groups were doing.

I was secretary to SCAO during my time in England, then handed over to an American in Paris, Johnson Garrett, who in turn passed it on to a German, Inge Haag, resident in London, in 1978; finally, the "sparkplug" of SCAO for many years was Alan Lee Williams, a sometime Labour MP who ran the Atlantic Council of the Atlantic Kingdom. The chairman succeeding Sir Frank was the former German MP and once secretary general of the Atlantic Assembly, Dr. Peter Corterier. But Sir Frank Roberts continued as chairman of SCAO and as an active participant in NGO work for more than a quarter century after his retirement; he passed away in 1998 at the age of ninety.

Over the years, SCAO became less a coordinating body and more an opportunity for "old Atlantic hands"—leaders of various NGOs and academics, plus former officials from NATO and its constituent governments—to inform themselves about current policy issues and share views. After initial funding from the German Marshall Fund of the United States ran out, NATO traditionally footed most of the bill for SCAO conferences. SCAO's metamorphosis was not exactly what I originally had in mind, but it's still useful in maintaining an important network of influentials. In 2000 Colleen and I attended a SCAO annual meeting near Monopoli, a town founded by ancient Greeks on the Adriatic coast of Italy. The meeting was enlivened by a group of Italian students who demanded answers to searching questions of the day. There was nearly a riot! But an astute chairman calmed them. Democracy at work, and good exposure for the gray heads used to doing their work quietly, even if sometimes with blinkers.

Footnote: In 1996, the Euro-Atlantic Club and the Hungarian Atlantic Club, both of Budapest, asked to become members of SCAO and also to host one of its annual conferences. At least until the early years of the 21st century, opinion polls and media reports all seemed to confirm that the ex-members of the Warsaw Pact in Eastern Europe were even more concerned with becoming members of NATO than with joining the EU—confirming an emotional attachment to the United States that reflected their insecurities and their defense needs, as well as a clearer understanding (I believe) that the U.S.A. was the paramount champion of freedom in the world. Whether these attitudes would remain after the attenuation of Alliance ties surrounding the 2002 decision to invade Iraq remained to be seen.

The Admirable British

The key players in both the Mid–Atlantic Clubs and the SCAO were for years mainly British people who took the missions seriously, and who doggedly kept things going on a shoestring, when necessary. Aside from some early U.S. foundation grants in piddling amounts, plus a few small contributions from NATO and from U.S. and other companies operating in Europe, these operations were nurtured and kept alive mainly by good English souls. I was able, through these and other ventures, to see the other side of British gifts for organizing and administering "charities"—the English nomenclature for NGOs and nonprofits—quite different from those aristocracy–ridden interminable committees and ego-salving efforts that characterized the Atlantic College effort in the early years.

Although I worried for years that British industry would never get the economy properly off the ground (that would require Margaret Thatcher and a virtual revolution in trade unions and industry to pull off later), I came away from the UK in 1974 with an extraordinarily good overall impression of the steadfastness, respect for law, mastery of rhetoric, adherence to principle, and reliability of the British people.

One interesting comment on the British and their economy: In 1969 I attended a Wilton Park conference at which the economy became a central bone of contention. Some of us from countries outside Britain wondered why economic growth in the UK lagged so much behind, say, the United States, Germany, and even France at the time. The warden of Wilton Park, Heinz Koeppler, opined that "social" growth was more important to the British than GNP. One Englishman said, "A rise in GNP also means a rise in GNG (gross national garbage)!" This raised a question still in my mind: How do we (in the "overdeveloped" countries), preserve the true quality of life, the civilities, the social caring, the noble endeavors, the pursuit of good values, when major aspects of our consumer economies seem so often to tug us away from these important attributes of a good society?

Question still unanswered—but it also seems true that if economic growth lags, people suffer—no matter what the general economic level of their country may be. To some extent, the admirable stoicism-in-the-face-of-adversity of the British had, it seemed to me, a flip side. In 1971, there was a postal strike, not at all uncommon. The standard response of the man and woman in the street was: "Well, we can't give in to them; but it's surprising how well we can manage without the post; I guess we can stick it out longer." It really did take Thatcher, in the late 1970s and '80s to turn this attitude around and help people to say, "We won't put up with this hijacking of the whole from one sector of society."

I was especially impressed by the smoothness (by comparison with American practice) of the operation of the law and of local government. In both the United States and the United Kingdom I have over the years gotten embroiled in property and land-planning questions. These are remarkably easier and more clearcut matters in England. An example: A man named Disley, who lived below the hill on which our house in Guildford was situated, applied to build a small multistory apartment building on his property. The Guildford Town Council turned down Disley's application on grounds that his project did not come within the scope of the city planning requirements (we would say "zoning"). We and all our close neighbors received a letter from the Ministry of Housing in London saying that Disley had appealed his case to them and that on 17 February 1969, a hearing would be held in the Guildford town council chambers. We attended. Disley, his architect, and his lawyer all had full opportunity to explain their plans—complete with tackboards and flip charts—to Her Majesty's hearing examiner. All attending the hearing had their opportunity to react. At the end of the morning, the examiner asked if he could visit the properties that might be affected, and he and two specialists came to Treetops that afternoon. We explained how Disley's venture would impact the aspect (substantially) from our house; the examiner actually viewed the prospect from our home, and from other homes nearby. Two weeks later, we all received a communication from the Ministry of Housing, saying that Disley's appeal had been carefully reviewed and the town council's original ruling would stand. No more fuss, no court battles, no never-ending hearings. Disley had had his "day in court," as had we, and the matter was settled. In comparable American cases, often the whole thing would be dragged out interminably—as we found to our bitter regret later on several occasions, in our home state of Washington. British laws, procedures, and public common sense have conspired to make such incidents much more manageable, and more quickly.

Those fine British qualities had gotten them through World War II, when others thought all was lost. And they made it possible for Britain to play a continuing strong role in the transatlantic alliance—at times when many thought *that* too was lost. Neither the home front nor the worldview have been ignored in the course of British experience in the 20th century. Occasional failings, such as the general unwillingness in the 1930s to believe that Hitler would eventually have to be put down by force, are common to most democracies. One has only to visit Churchill's wartime air–raid bunker in London to be reminded of the recovery of Britain from interwar doldrums, and of its steely resolve and tenacity, which eventually won out.

Odds and Ends of a Career

Besides the work described above, I found myself involved in bits and pieces of transatlantic soldering together of institutions and people. For example, in 1970 I shepherded a group of half a dozen American university presidents around Europe so they could compare notes with their peers on problems of higher education, and—at that time especially—the shape of the "youth revolution."

I often lectured for two American firms, Esso (later Exxon) and IBM, on the impact of European unification and Atlantic cooperation; my audiences were always international, for both companies made a policy of recruiting local nationals to man their overseas headquarters. Esso's multinational leadership was especially impressive; they thought nothing of transferring Italian managers to England or French managers to Norway, or eventually to headquarters in New York. IBM tried to man its operations in various countries with leaders from the nations in question. IBM managers, in those days, all dressed like their counterparts in America: dark suits, white shirts, and ties, and had generally similar personality templates. All were interesting, and often one found a kindred spirit, looking at the transatlantic scene from a different perspective, but arriving at conclusions quite similar to mine.

I wrote a running commentary on European efforts to deal with the environment, the pregnant new item on the world agenda, for the old *Saturday Review* of New York. I also managed another writing job, preparing articles on international affairs for a bulletin of the Atlantic Information Centre for Teachers. This was another of those extraordinary, unsung efforts by the British to reach out to all branches of society with positive messages about the world. It was run by Dr. Otto Pick, a Brit of Czech origin who had made a professorial career of note, later becoming vice chancellor of the University of Surrey. Once the Cold War ended, Pick returned to Prague to teach and, for a time, was deputy foreign minister in the new democratic government. In the 1970s, Otto had two "right-hand men" at the Teachers' Centre in London: one was a young, suave, and savvy Conservative MP, Julian Crtichley, who wrote discerningly about foreign matters; the other was John Eppstein, one of the founding grandfathers of what one might call "the Atlantic movement." In NATO's earliest years, Eppstein, who—in 18th century gentlemanly style—kept his handkerchief stuffed up his sleeve and used snuff, saw to it that all the NATO countries founded NATO citizens' support committees. He also knew what the teaching profession, in particular, needed by way of an international dimension and useful teaching materials.

One could not fail to mention John Sewell, a proper, crotchety, but extremely canny and public-spirited man who ran TEAM—"the European-Atlantic Movement." This consisted of a one-man show, supported by phalanxes of retired school people—all volunteers—to bring home to British teachers, by means of conferences and study trips to the Continent, the crucial importance of NATO, the European Communities, and OECD. TEAM put out an indispensable guide to organizations. Sewell was a valuable product and educational leader of the Workingmen's Education Association, one of those incredible, ubiquitous nongovernmental groups that help to knit together the strong—if somewhat class-ridden—civilization that is England.

I worked closely with these and other groups, lecturing constantly and trying to help all of them with their organization and programs, and sometimes with finding resources. Some of this I did for pittances, much of it for nothing.

The North Atlantic Assembly commissioned me in 1969 to conduct a study of "the Implications of Student Unrest" in the Atlantic world. I traveled extensively to interview educational and other authorities in various countries to try to understand the roots, the symptoms, and the prognosis of this international phenomenon. I came to the conclusion that it represented a major upheaval in Western society, and some of its manifestations—such as widespread drug use, a general mood of nihilism, and the makings of an anarchic movement—boded ill. I believed, and still do, that our young people need to better understand the values and benefits of our "civic culture." I also found strong evidence that major transnational organizing was funded by the Soviets; they did not create the large movement, but rode and helped to propel its wave, as they so often did when any opportunity to plague Western society came up. In the 1970s and 1980s, the Agitprop was still very much at work

A group of young leaders (increasingly coming to be known as "the successor generation") asked my help in organizing a series of conferences for their new NGO, EURNAC (the European-North American Conference)

in 1970. An older and more prestigious group of graybeards, all involved in policy-making, enlisted me to help put together in 1973 a "Europe-America Conference" in Amsterdam. These and many other meetings of all kinds of groups occupied me a good deal. I also helped the staff director of the Trilateral Commission-in-formation, George Franklin of New York, to launch that eventually most important NGO. As the years went on, I was saddened when efforts to merge the Trilateral Commission and the Atlantic Institute failed; they were truly complementary institutions of some importance and together could have multiplied their influence considerably.

Constantly I was on the road, lecturing on Europe and transatlantic relations: to universities all over Europe and the United States, teachers conferences, trade union bodies, the Committees on Foreign Relations all over the United States, world affairs councils, political groups, business executives, and others.

In September 1969, I attended a conference on philanthropy in Evian that led to the creation of INTERPHIL—the International Standing Conference on Philanthropy. I was one of its founders and wrote "A Draft Charter for Modern Philanthropy" (see Appendix E), which was widely circulated in Europe and North America. My experience with the Ford Foundation and with NGOs and charities of many kinds stood me in good stead. At that time on the continent of Europe, there were hardly any foundations or private charities of note, aside from religion-related bodies, although the British might be said to have invented the idea of foundations and of independent, nongovernmental organizations. INTERPHIL gave impetus to many new groups, especially foundations, and paved the way, in part, for the wide range of NGOs today devoted to bettering conditions in the developing societies, as well as in the former Soviet Union and its satellites since the late 1980s. In 1986, the Committee of Ministers of the Council of Europe approved an INTERPHIL initiative of great potential importance: the adoption of the "European Convention on the Recognition of the Legal Personality of International Non-Governmental Organisations," to which most European governments eventually subscribed. INTERPHIL's central idea was to emphasize the importance of private initiatives for public purposes—not everything should be left to governments. By the 21st century, this general world movement had been renamed "civil society"; its development has run more or less concurrently with the growth of democracy.

At the founding conference in Evian, I met Frank Wells, an interesting American about my age who had lived in Britain since the war and was carrying on the work of his father and grandfather before him, viz. a "fund-raising" business for NGOs. His grandfather had developed a standard template for helping churches in the Middle West raise money.

Frank's dad ("Colonel Wells") had moved operations to England after World War II, and now Frank was carrying on. Frank and the Colonel had begun with grandpa's formula for churches, something entirely new for the English clergy and laity, but it worked and made money. Then Frank branched out and in 1971 asked my help. As a consultant, I made a plan for raising money for a new UK private trust for the Derbyshire town of Ironbridge, where the modern making of iron and its industrial uses had first begun in the 18th century. The whole town, in effect, became a museum. Such work was a little offbase for me (no political relationship to the Atlantic community), but it provided a fascinating glimpse, once more, of how the UK establishment did things, and how (sometimes) one could persuade them to try the modern world's ways.

In 1972, I was invited by Dr. Roy Pryce of the new University of Sussex to coteach a graduate seminar with him on the origins and results of the Marshall Plan. This experience gave me further insight into British academic life, so different in an exciting new institution from what I had encountered at Oxford and Cambridge, and it thrust me once more into the middle of the small but influential "European elite" of Britain.

One unusual venture deserves separate comment. In 1968, I was the principal author of a confidential report presented to President-elect Nixon by the Atlantic Council of the United States. The ACUS sent me a copy of Nixon's subsequent address on the 20th NATO anniversary, in which he used some of the ideas in my report! This document—plus a useful visit to Pat Moynihan, then a Nixon aide in the White House—also appears to have contributed to a subsequent new NATO program, the Committee on the Challenges of Modern Society (CCMS) another attempt (continuing into the new century) to show NATO countries that the Alliance could be of benefit in more than military and security matters. A few years later, I wrote a report for NATO, detailing CCMS progress, for example, the sharing of pollution mitigation technologies. Around this time, I also enlisted the vice chairman of the Atlantic Council, Ambassador Ted Achilles, in a visit to James Webb, the first director of NASA, to try to convince him that a major place for Europeans ought to be found within the space exploration effort; years later this was done to some extent, but—in the usual fashion—the United States has simply invited other countries on an ad hoc basis to "help out" now and then. A thoroughly integrated, multinational "Euro-American" space effort could have enhanced Atlantic unity considerably in the 1970s, but unfortunately the great majority of American leaders remain nationalist in their outlook—even though they might deny it. As the World War II generation moved off the scene in the '70s and '80s, this pronounced reversion to nationalism became almost inexorable—in 2002–3, it became an article of faith of President George W. Bush and most of his entourage that the Europeans, while nice enough, no longer deserved the kind of close U.S. collaboration that, while sometimes honored in the breach, had been a strong conviction of earlier U.S. administrations. Unheeding bluntness and unilateralism reversed a half century of transatlantic institution-building, with unfortunate consequences for Atlantic unity, and perhaps for the future of the world itself.

The foregoing provides a fair sampling of my most important ventures from 1969 to 1974. As I look back on it, I was constantly trying to reinforce the ties of like-mindedness that link the democratic Atlantic peoples together and pave the way for the worldwide growth of democracy. The international structures put together in the post-1945 period have in most cases been organized around modern principles of representative government and the political values of freedom, requiring a certain degree among the participating peoples of like-mindedness, of mutual understanding. This could not be said of the United Nations, because it has aspired to universal membership, which has meant that many governments run by despots and dictators take part and do not share the like minds of the democracies. But even the UN—and its dynamic and visionary secretary general, Kofi Annan—has become more and more concerned with the protection of human rights and the development of responsible, democratic governance. In the new century there has even been established a call for a Caucus of the Democracies at the UN; the Council for a Community of Democracies (an NGO I helped to foster) urged this course, among others, which would create new structures to bind together democracies worldwide.

An entirely new kind of career (but without dropping the reins of the old one) eventuated in a serendipitous involvement with America's premier scientific and technological think tank—the largely unknown Battelle Memorial Institute. My early ties with Battelle (1971–74) began with a few odd consulting jobs while I was still in England and evolved into a full-time ten-year assignment with the Institute at its study center in Seattle. After seven years in England, Colleen and I headed back to the United States and home in the summer of 1974.

In the fall of 1971, I had perhaps vaguely foreseen this turn of events. Colleen and I enjoyed living in England immensely. We even thought of spending the rest of our lives there. I found it slightly galling that I paid British "rates" (property taxes) and income tax, yet had no electoral voice. I was not always happy with our Tory MP from Guildford, David Howell (later Lord Howell), yet I had no part in his elections nor those of others.

Our homeland, America, tugged us in the other direction. I wrote in my journal:

> Rural Dorset [where we were vacationing] on the seacoast is marvelous. Still very rural and relatively unspoiled. Good weather, lots of blackberries [my downfall since childhood], old houses to visit, beaches, downs to walk on, old pubs to eat in. We liked it. Today I wondered, suppose that an American college, or Battelle, to take two examples, offered me a job in the States. What would be my reaction? I don't know. I like what I'm doing, I like Guildford, I like England. But often I think it would be nice to be back home again.

13
The Knowledge Industry

think tank: A research institute or other organization providing advice and ideas on national or commercial problems; an
interdisciplinary group of specialist consultants.

Oxford English Dictionary, 1986

Fostering Science and General Knowledge

In 1972, when I first encountered a major scientific think tank, the Battelle
Memorial Institute (BMI), there were not many around in the United States
or in Europe. The Stanford Research Institute in Menlo Park, California,
was a post-1945 creation that was, in effect, selling the research capabilities
of Stanford University faculty (and others) around the world. Stanford
had turned to BMI for help in conceptualizing its semi-independent think
tank. In New Jersey the Bell Laboratories had been created to do basic
research on a broad basis early in the 20th century; its discoveries were
proprietary to the Bell System. By 1915 there were about 100 scientific
laboratories, each owned by a business and devoted mainly to routine,
repetitive testing. During World War II, scientific research progressed by
leaps and bounds, in the UK as well; almost all these wartime efforts were
government-funded.

In the social sciences and related public policy fields, independent
nonprofit research centers began to grow, if more slowly. In 1910, Andrew Carnegie gave $10 million to set up the Carnegie Endowment for
International Peace. Later, the venerable Brookings Institution in Washington, D.C., was created to study public policy questions. Immediately
after World War I, a handful of independent national foreign affairs study
groups, such as the Council on Foreign Relations in New York and the
Royal Institute of International Affairs in London, were founded. More
followed in the wake of World War II, but there were no multinational

foreign policy think tanks until the creation of the Atlantic Institute in the 1960s. By the early 21st century, there were literally hundreds—possibly thousands—of think tanks, many working on policy issues that affected government. Some of these were independent and issue-centered, such as the Center for Strategic and International Studies in Washington, D.C. Even more had "political coloration," having been founded with monies from businessmen or philanthropies ranging across the political spectrum. The American Enterprise Institute (mildly right-wing) and the Cato Institute (libertarian) are contemporary examples.

Especially in the field of science and technology, and later with the addition of the social sciences and other branches of knowledge, the Battelle Memorial Institute (BMI) remains the world's largest and oldest independent, not-for-profit think tank. But it is amazing how few people know about BMI, possibly because its headquarters is in the Midwest (Ohio), or because its operations are worldwide, or possibly because the bulk of its work is in the scientific/ technological/engineering fields. It was to this unlikely behemoth (probably more than 9,000 employees by 2000), that I gravitated, beginning in 1972. Again, as so often in my life, serendipity was very much at work.

Battelle Memorial Institute

The Battelle Memorial Institute was endowed in 1923 by a bachelor tycoon in Columbus, Ohio, named Gordon Battelle, who willed his fortune to it. In its early years it was virtually the only institution—anywhere—of its kind. Battelle's father had amassed a fortune making steel and dabbling in other metals in the years following the Civil War. In World War I, Gordon had perceived how science and technological development could be pursued in purposeful ways to win a war, sometimes with added dividends useful for civilian purposes. He passed away in his forties, his mother a couple of years later, and together the Battelles left an endowment of about $3.5 million to found a not-for-profit research institute devoted to "putting science and technology at the service of mankind."

At some universities, a few corporations and occasionally private endowments had created research laboratories, either for profit or to expand scientific knowledge. But Gordon Battelle's bequest had a curious twist: He specified that the new institute would sell its research services to any corporation or other body on a fee-for-service basis. This meant that the sponsoring body would pay Battelle's costs, including overheads and a modest surplus in return for its study of an agreed problem. If Battelle were successful in "discovering" and making practical a machine or process that the buyer of its services could use, all were satisfied. Sometimes the open-ended research did not produce usable results, but Battelle would be paid anyway under agreed conditions—such as periodic benchmarks for assessment of the work it had done. Sometimes the work would stop before useful results were obtained; often it continued to the mutual benefit of BMI and the sponsors.

The Battelle Institute was a not-for-profit corporation—a "charity" under U.S. and ancient Anglo-Saxon law. There were and are no Battelle shareholders and no profits, only a self-perpetuating board of directors pledged to abide by the donors' strictures in a charter approved by the State of Ohio. BMI became operational in 1925, beginning its work with a small staff of researchers. It could have lived off its endowment, as so many academic laboratories do, and perhaps made some useful discoveries; but Gordon Battelle had stipulated (wisely, it turned out) that the Institute was, in effect, to sell its services—and make charitable gifts from surpluses that accrued to this essentially business arrangement. This highly original pattern turned out to be one that paved the way for growth and change in sometimes-spectacular fashion, not simply at Battelle but in society generally.

Parenthetically, some of Battelle's leaders have resisted calling BMI a "think tank," wishing to stress its work as applied research leading to practical action. But personally I cannot see how this definition falls outside commonly accepted usage.

Sometimes, BMI and an inventor, such as Chester Carlson, an obscure lawyer and chemist from Rochester, New York, would agree that if Battelle could give an idea a practical, commercial application, the inventor would share any revenues that ensued. In Carlson's case, the rewards to Battelle were eventually enormous. Carlson had developed a chemical process in the late 1930s that would enable documents to be copied with far better accuracy and speed than the mimeograph, "ditto," or other duplicating processes used in offices throughout the world. He knew the scientific theory behind his discovery, made some copies with a chemical solution, reportedly in a bathtub, but could not devise a machine to make the process usable. Carlson's idea, with Battelle inventing the necessary technology, eventually became Xerox, the first and most noted of this type of copier. "Xerox" by 1960 became not only the name of a machine essential to almost any office, but a generic verb as well: "Please xerox 20 copies of this, Miss Jones."

Battelle and Carlson had agreed, when Battelle's engineers began their work, that they would split any royalties—40 percent to Carlson, 60 percent to Battelle—resulting from the commercial exploitation of a successful copy machine over a period of years. Battelle and Carlson bought a near-extinct company called Haloid and began production. Haloid later became Xerox. Still later, the royalty arrangements were modified and Battelle became a Xerox stockholder, with additional rights.

Xerox machines swamped world markets in the late 1950s and 1960s, and Battelle accrued earnings of several hundred million dollars, all of which—under the terms of Gordon's will—would be spent by Battelle's board on "charitable objects." Battelle's officers and directors in these years used the Xerox surpluses to build research facilities in several places around the world and, in many cases, to sponsor in-house research, initiated on its own, on a wide variety of topics that seemed of possible utility to society. Much of this work had to do with probing scientific and technological frontiers, including defense and national security questions; some of it was pointed at work in the social sciences, broadly defined, that might benefit mankind. This effort in the social sciences—and in the management of BMI itself—was my point of entry into the organization, beginning around 1972. The tax and legal implications of this ingenious, and potentially rewarding (in both the monetary and the public service sense), Xerox money machine eventually led to court battles around 1975, recounted in chapter 14.

By the 1970s, Battelle had nearly 7,000 employees, busy at major laboratories in Columbus, Richland, Washington, Frankfurt, Germany, and Geneva, Switzerland, and at a number of smaller facilities. In the early 21st century, it continued to expand into new fields. Today it manages several of the federal U.S. government's nuclear research laboratories and installations, including the famed Oak Ridge. The bulk of its current work—but not all—is devoted to the natural sciences, technology, and engineering. For instance, Battelle's management of the National Laboratory in Richland—which since the 1940s has concentrated mainly on the development of nuclear energy, for both peaceful and defense purposes—has led naturally to a concern for the growth and containment of Weapons of Mass Destruction (WMD). Early in the 21st century, Battelle scientists, at the direction of the U.S. Department of Energy (contracting agent for the Richland lab), began a new program of R&D to develop ideas for how WMD could be controlled internationally, in partnership with the University of Washington. Thus Battelle once again "backed into" a socially and politically important area of research.

British-based Consultant to Battelle

In 1971, while Colleen and I were still living in England; Battelle employed me on a consulting contract to study its plans for possible creation of laboratories in Britain and also to give opinions on the operation of its existing laboratories in Europe, in Frankfurt, and in Geneva. My reports and consultations led, beginning in 1974, to ten years of work in Seattle as a Fellow of the Battelle Memorial Institute. In BMI's Seattle research center I had a wonderful opportunity to work on problems that had fascinated me since my years in Germany, viz., how to construct a viable international peace system based on the core of the Atlantic community countries and eventually incorporating other democracies, some in east Asia. In some detail, here is how it all happened, another instance of how my abilities and interests would sometimes coincide crucially with those of others. It came, again, as a result of "keeping one's eyes and ears open."

On 22 February 1971, I had a visit from an exceptional young man, Don Evans, a staff assistant to the CEO of the Battelle Memorial Institute, Dr. Sherwood Fawcett. A year earlier, I had been in Seattle, visiting relatives and friends, lecturing, and buttoning up some Atlantic projects that reached around the United States. Friends told me that an old colleague from the Ford Foundation, Matt Cullen, was working at Battelle's Seattle research lab, near my old alma mater, the University of Washington. I looked Matt up; he said he was writing on international affairs with a Battelle stipend. He explained that the Seattle lab was unusual: with money earned largely from Xerox, Battelle had built a splendid small research facility for social scientists, legal experts, "paper and pencil" natural scientists, and "public policy" types. "Fellows" were appointed (usually for a year) to pursue their interests there. They promised to share the fruits of their research with Battelle and to interact with other scholars in interdisciplinary studies bearing on real social, economic, or political problems of the day. A kind of think tank for studies of the future, as Matt put it. I said "Matt, keep me informed," and left, my mind occupied with so many other things that I virtually forgot Battelle until 1971, when Evans turned up on my English doorstep.

It turned out that Matt had urged Dr. Fawcett, BMI's CEO, to make use of me in studies of the future of Battelle itself, especially in expansion of its overseas research activity. Evans and I discussed that I "might help Battelle to restructure the whole Institute." My journal quotes Evans: Battelle suffered from a "total lack of public image, an overseas expansion without forethought, and [was searching] for a role and goals that would fit their size and power and bring the public and the political powers along with them." One of Evans's first assignments with Battelle had been to create a Korean Institute of Science and Technology. I remain to this day greatly impressed with Don Evans, and especially so as I later spent nearly two years working closely with him. I told him I was interested, especially inasmuch as I had begun to wonder how to juggle all the balls in front of me in a way that would keep the family afloat, let me pursue my "Atlantic goals," and allow me to work on practical and constructive things.

Tidying Up My British Days

As I was pondering the possibility of this major career change (or interlude), an old British friend, retired Royal Navy Commander Hugh Mulleneux, phoned from Kent. (Hugh, among other things, had been on the deck of the USS *Missouri* for the Japanese surrender in 1945 and had vowed a future career as a volunteer totally devoted to peace.) He asked if I would agree to serve on the executive board of the British Atlantic Committee, the counterpart of the Atlantic Council of the United States and of similar private, nonprofit groups in every NATO country. This was the first time that a foreigner had been asked to serve on one of these national committees; I asked Hugh if they were sure they wanted a non-Brit. He replied, "Not in general, but you're different." For me, the chance to serve on the British Atlantic Committee was an extraordinary tribute and opportunity; I willingly agreed.

Joining the board entailed, among other things, an invitation in August 1971 to the 30th anniversary of the historic meeting between Churchill and Roosevelt in Placentia Bay, Newfoundland, that resulted in the great Atlantic Charter. The 1971 meeting was chaired by Churchill's grandson, Winston Spencer Churchill, also an MP, and featured historic films and personal accounts, mostly by Royal Navy men and diplomats who had been present.

Now, more than three decades later, I am still extremely close to these old British friends (many, alas, now dead) and find that such friendships, grounded in common devotion to great principles, never die. I wrote in my journal (1971): "This shows how Americans overseas can become important to the indigenous Atlantic movements; [I] recognized [a] new pattern, not only of overseas investment, but of overseas public involvement." A few days later, I wrote a thumbnail sketch of myself, as I thought I was then (and still am, I believe):

> I am a radical—not comparable with today's perhaps, but nonetheless a radical. I condemn the fools of the Far Left, the asses of the Old Right, and the impotent liberals who stand helpless in the middle. We need a new political alliance of decent people, to preserve the good in the old values and perhaps add some new ones, to root out corruption and make our public life square with our professed ideals.

I had been speaking to youth groups around Europe, to business executives and sometimes to political and transnational groups. I wrote, "I'm
really on fire with the potentialities [of these youth]. They desperately
want ideals and goals and leadership. Is it possible to forge some kind
of transnational, nonpartisan coalition to work for good in all Western
societies? The 'Atlantic movement' is not enough unless it includes this
component." And today, more than three decades later, I still hold this
central thought.

Thinking about My Roots

While still at Treetops, our Guildford home, I spent long hours with Battelle president and CEO Dr. Sherwood Fawcett and his staff assistant,
Don Evans, advising them especially on the possibilities of establishing a
Battelle Laboratory in the UK. They had a small office in London, which
stirred up contract research opportunities for the large Battelle labs in the
United States, Germany, and Geneva. Fawcett's question for me—and his
mandate to Evans—was to lay out the pros and cons for spending a considerable amount of Battelle's capital on the creation of a British lab.

Don and I spent hours talking to various experts in London and
around the country, reading voluminous reports—some government,
some private, some scholarly—on Britain and its prospects in the last
quarter of the 20th century. I wrote a largely historical-social-economic
treatise of appraisal, as a backdrop to a decision. Don Evans looked at the
more practical side of costs and markets for contract research. After a year
or so, we both came to the conclusion that this was not the time to mount
such a Battelle venture. In the process, I had come to learn a great deal
about Battelle and much more about Britain. My conclusions were very
much conditioned on the likely effects of the impending (January 1973)
adhesion of the United Kingdom to the European Communities (later the
EU). If Britain had a chance to modernize, it would be because it accepted
many new ideas—and above all the reality of intense business competition—from its new partners on the Continent, and from continuing U.S.
influence.

A footnote on British attitudes: A few days before leaving for the United States, in June 1974, I was seated in our garden, dictating part of a book
on *Managing Across Cultures* (never finished) when the next-door neighbor,
Doreen Simmons, brought over some tea. We talked about England, and
Doreen surprised me when she said that the country was "inefficient."
But, even more surprising, she "liked it that way. If people strove too hard
to be efficient, they would lose something!" Is one quality emphasized at

the expense of the other? A big conundrum for our entire civilization.

Some years later, I found an invaluable history of British industrial development and entrepreneurial character, seen from a cultural anthropologist's view, in Martin Wiener's 1981 volume, *English Culture and the Decline of the Industrial Spirit, 1850–1980*. Wiener wrote, more or less underscoring my own earlier observations: "The political elite [of England] . . . both desired and feared technical advance and economic growth." It was partly because of these long-term discouraging trends that Evans and I eventually recommended against a Battelle lab in the UK. It took Maggie Thatcher in the 1980s and Tony Blair in the 1990s to energize Britain to turn the needed corner; whether these changes (with both good and bad results) will be lasting remains to be seen. At any rate, by 2005, the UK was a far different place than in 1970.

Preparing for a New Post

In May 1973, I had spent a few days at Battelle's Columbus headquarters to learn how these scientists and engineers spent their time, what their "corporate culture" consisted of, and to make contacts for my current and future work. At a dinner for the Association of Nuclear Physicists, Dr. Sherwood Fawcett suddenly leaned over and asked me out of the blue, "Would you have any objection to moving back to the U.S.?" I said no, not in principle; we had always been prepared to return for the right job. Then Sherwood said, "Would you consider living and working again in Seattle?" I replied "Yes, for the right job." He said no more, nor did I, for some months. But of course, Colleen and I began immediately to weigh the possibilities and consequences. The opportunity to return home, not just to the United States, but home to the Pacific Northwest, added further luster to the projected move.

In September 1973, I again visited Battelle-Columbus. Fawcett offered me a three-year appointment (later extended to ten years) as a Fellow of the Institute, based at the Seattle research center. I had told Sherwood of my new interest in East Asia, and particularly Japan, in connection with extending the old Atlantic community into the Pacific, which I had begun to foresee. He said that involved a good deal of study and would help Battelle in its search for new research markets. So Japan-watching became one of my assignments, in addition to helping Fawcett and his close associates in charting out Battelle's future, not least overseas.

So great was the opportunity of acquiring new knowledge, broadening my horizons, and working in a quite different atmosphere than ever before—*and* continuing to work practically on developing the "social tissue" of a developing community of democratic peoples (which Dr. Fawcett accepted readily)—that I accepted without qualms. The next ten months were spent in preparation for new vistas.

A First Glimpse of Japan

On the way back to England, I stopped in New York to see my old Ford Foundation associate, Joe Slater, then president of the Aspen Institute for Humanistic Studies (as well as, simultaneously, president of both the Anderson Foundation and the Salk Institute in San Diego). I told Joe of my coming new position with Battelle and of the opportunity to explore and understand the Far East. Joe said, "How would you and Colleen like to go to Japan?" I said, of course, some time. Joe said, "No I mean next week." I gulped; and we said yes! It transpired that Aspen was sending one of its periodic traveling seminar groups to Japan for an intense immersion in the culture; one couple (out of about a dozen) had registered but suddenly dropped out. Joe had two airline tickets in his hands, which he offered to Colleen and me, along with most of the additional costs; Battelle agreed to foot the remainder.

On 30 September we arrived in Japan (after a one-day stop in San Francisco, in part to buy raincoats for a more chilly fall climate), to begin our pleasant but intensive three-week labors. Our seminar group met key Japanese industrialists, educators, artists, government officials, journalists, the American ambassador, and some of his staff. We delved into Japanese cuisine—some quite modern, some traditional—and learned in the process to eat strange foods, including tiny crabs eaten whole, shells and all, sea urchins, seaweed, and delicious, marbled steaks from Kobe cattle, fed beer, pampered, and massaged daily. Tempura—vegetables and seafood deep-fried in a delicate batter— became our favorite, with sashimi, raw but very fresh fish, a close second.

Out of Tokyo, we visited the ancient capital of Nara, the Middle-Ages capital Kyoto, and an idyllic lakeside resort at Hakone—a station on the old Tokaido Road, nestled near the foot of Fujiyama (Mount Fuji). In a tiny museum, with all captions only in Japanese, we noted a page from a treatise on the way of the Samurai (a caste more or less analogous to European knighthood in the Middle Ages). On this page was a fascinating but repulsive (to us) diagram: a human body with dotted lines indicating how a resolute Samurai might best slash it apart with his razor-sharp sword, much as a master butcher would matter-of-factly diagram the slaughter of a heifer. There were plenty of splendid antique swords around to let the viewer know exactly what tools would have been employed. Shivers climbed my spine, as they would on some later occasions, most notably in the ghastly barren centers of Hiroshima and Nagaski.

In chapter 15, I'll have more to say about Japan, especially about the prospects for the momentous relationship between Japan and the West. In the early seventies, "Japan" was on the lips of all international business-men, economic futurists, and students of international relations— a colos-sus, as many then predicted. Herman Kahn's flamboyant book of 1970, *The Emerging Japanese Superstate,* as well as Ezra Vogel's later *Japan as Number One,* are good examples. Kahn is dead; and one does not hear much today of Professor Vogel's ideas. In hindsight, one sees how deep economic and social currents in a major country such as Japan can wreck the predictions of the most confident futurists or scaremongers.

I was mesmerized by Japan for the next decade myself, though I al-ways left room for the unexpected and also for the inevitable downsides (or upsides, depending on how one looked at the Japanese challenge to the West). My chief concern on my first trip to Nippon was not, however, to limn the dimensions of the growing colossus, but to try to discover what points there could be in the convergence of the Western and Japa-nese ways of life. In other words, was Japan becoming an integrated part of the Western world, and the Atlantic community in particular? (For a time, I called it "the extended Atlantic system.") Many surprises and this fascinating minicareer characterized the next few years of my life.

An excerpt from my journal, 3 October 1973, reveals questions that be-gan to recur frequently on this eye-opening travel seminar, on later trips, and in the digestion of what would become a sizable Japan library of my own:

> Hannelore Schulhof, a German-American [member of our Aspen party] thinks Japan is more like Europe than America to her. Bar-bara McLoughlin, a radio station owner from Aspen, thinks Ja-pan is more familiar to her than Europe! Conclusion: Hannelore identifies with traditionalism in Japan, Barbara with modernity. Yet the overall question still remains: Can the West work with the Japanese, in the things that count?

These and other questions helped me to get Japan into focus.

The leader of our seminar group, and our chief filter and interpreter for elements of Japanese life, was an early-retired American businessman, John Powers, with an elegant Japanese wife, Mikako. He had become en-thusiastic about both Japan and the Aspen Institute's mission and meth-ods. Following standard Aspen procedure from its tested seminars, which tried to broaden American businessmen's views of life through study of history's great thinkers, Powers felt that we seminarians should seek a new door to "self-improvement" through our concentrated confrontation with Japan and Japanese thinking. (I think, but was never sure, that Powers was a convert to Zen Buddhism.) After a day of exposure to, for example, lectures on the nature of the Japanese language, a visit to a 15th century establishment that still teaches Japanese the art of making and drinking tea with elaborate ceremony, and a memorable dialogue with the electrifying (yes!) master of a Zen monastery, the seminarians would eat supper and then engage in Powers's idea of postmortem "interpretation" — a good way to cap off a stimulating day. However, Powers insisted on using the Socratic method (constant probing questions by the leader). This might have worked well if the seminar were collectively seeking a truth from, let's say, the works of Aristotle, but it worked less well when we attempted to shed light collectively on what we had learned — however superficially — about Japan, ancient and modern, in the previous twenty-four hours. Powers thought I should be seeking "self-enlightenment," while I was looking to understand modern Japan and its place in the international firmament. I managed nevertheless to acquire many of the insights I sought.

Perhaps this clash of "teacher-student" goals (microcosmic vs. macrocosmic) might be extrapolated to the age-old contest between those (usually religionists) who believe that if only the circle of true believers could be steadily widened through enlightenment, individual by individual, the sum goodness of humankind would eventually turn some future collective corner and thereafter all would be well. I responded (in my journal during this 1973 trip to Japan): "Maybe, but in our lifetimes, we shall never know, or even make a difference [in the state of the world] by religious conversions. Whereas I believe that we *can* prepare a foundation [i.e., through structural changes] for relative world peace and stability, with peoples and countries 'doing their own thing' without much interference. . . . This is particularly attractive to disoriented young Westerners. But there appears to be no set of ethical principles attached — each works out his own."

This represents an ever-present east-west dichotomy, but one also inherent within virtually all societies, which has bedeviled humankind throughout the centuries. Within Japan, the contrast of the Buddhist way of life, which counsels stoicism and self-awareness, remaining oblivious to the surrounding turmoil, with a more Western ethic, which concentrates on reaching out to others and developing communities of thought and action, provides a modern conundrum of paramount importance. I chose during my life to emphasize the second course, building structures of community "staffed" by enlightened groups. Within such structures, people can be free to develop their individuality and, if they want it, goodness. In the present day, many Christian fundamentalists (and others) have seemed to give up on reforming the "big picture" and have concentrated on making better individuals. The theory, I believe, is that if you can convert enough individuals to goodness, the macrocosm will *eventually* take care of itself. The stoic Marcus Aurelius might have made a good Zen Buddhist—if he had known about it.

My journal view in 1973 of the possible value of Zen thought to me lay in the emphasis on clearing one's thoughts periodically and at crucial times: "mental clearance sale—everything must go!" Then, usually, one would be more ready for change.

This first encounter with Japan was also notable in that we made fast friends of several Japanese and Westerners; chief among these was Robert Borden—a Canadian industrialist—and his wife Sally; John Emmerson, a retired Japan specialist and diplomat, whose understandings of Japan (to which he had returned many times in his life) were deeper, broader, and quite different from those of Powers; Sen Nishiyama, an American-born *Nisei* who returned to Japan just before World War II broke out, fought (most reluctantly) with the Imperial Army, and later became interpreter for Edwin O. Reischauer and other American ambassadors.

I would return to Japan many times over the next fifteen years, usually on behalf of Battelle, sometimes on a sponsored lecture tour. As the new century began, Western media tended to disregard Japan; it no longer loomed as a threat to the United States but as an object of pity, or at least complacency. Japan had lost its "steam" in more than a decade of recession. I believe today—and I think this has been my view from the time I first became seized with this still-enigmatic people—that the truth lies somewhere in between. Democratic Japan is a vital link between East and West, with much to learn but also much to teach. It is no accident that Japan is a member of the exclusive G-7 "club" of big, rich democracies. We shall hear more, good and perhaps not so good, from the Japanese people in the future. Much of the outcome depends on U.S. and European leaders, who ignore or take Japan for granted at their peril.

Meanwhile, my task from 1973 to 1983 was to try to get Japan and its business and technological culture into focus for the benefit of my new masters, the top leadership of Battelle. And I was to try to act as an interpreter of Battelle's managers to the Japanese. In the end, I felt I could literally write a book with a two-way theme, but a short monograph in 1976 was as far as I got. (My head remains stuffed with material for meaty monographs, let alone books, never written!) Suffice to say, in 2006 I remain in love with Japan and its people, but I want further to unravel their enigmatic culture and values, often strange to Westerners. Democracy is the precious, chief value that binds us together, ever more firmly; it is the set of principles and processes, often applied quite differently, by means of which both peoples have learned to manage their kaleidoscopic free societies.

Battelle's Future Prospects and Strategic Planning

Back in Guildford after the whirlwind Japan trip in the fall of 1973, I began to concentrate again on Sherwood Fawcett's desire for my advice, preparing for our transfer to Seattle in the following summer. Gradually, Sherwood and I became good friends. My experience had been so different from his that I believe my service as an advisor proved valuable. He had difficulty, he explained to me, with Battelle's operations in its Frankfurt and Geneva laboratories. Furthermore, he had broad, expansive plans for Battelle's future. Based on its recent success, with U.S. government aid, in establishing the independent Korean Institute for Science and Technology, a Battelle "copycat," and with the European labs that predated Dr. Fawcett's ascendance to BMI's top job, he still felt that he and his executives in Columbus lacked a comprehensive, reasoned perspective on the world generally.

He was in a quandary as to how, exactly, to develop the right relationships with his European outriggers. The Geneva laboratory was run by a headstrong, hard-charging Swiss scientist who seemed to delight in letting his clients in Europe (and occasionally some in the United States) think that he was in charge of the entire "global" Battelle! The Geneva lab tried, sometimes with painful success, to operate independently of the Columbus headquarters. Its staff was entirely multinational, a real plus for Battelle. But the midwestern nuclear physicist Fawcett's inquiring, slightly diffident, fact-based approach to his CEO duties, and especially to Europeans (with whom he had had little experience), clashed with his Geneva director's flamboyant, multilingual, worldly-wise personality. I never met the Swiss gentleman, but worked later with many of his staff and was able, I think, to counsel Fawcett and his U.S. executives on interactions with the often-strange Europeans.

The Frankfurt laboratory was different from Geneva's. Established in the fifties at the recommendation of the Marshall Plan and the U.S. High Commission for Germany—which saw the need to import some American scientific and technical know-how to a Germany in transition to the modern world of the West—the Frankfurt lab's 800 employees were all German. By 1974, a transition in Frankfurt's leadership brought in a new director, a German researcher, whose scientific credentials were excellent, but whose leadership qualities seemed insufficient to motivate and build a large yet cohesive team of natural and social scientists for modern Germany. The director was a pleasant man but seemed to doubt his own abilities, even though he had served a "management apprenticeship" in Columbus and had been chosen, as Dr. Fawcett's protégé, for the top Frankfurt job. In addition to these personality problems, Frankfurt's competitive position in the contract research field was soon to be undermined by the appearance of several new special-purpose scientific laboratories working along the lines of the Battelle model and heavily subsidized by the federal German government.

Dr. Fawcett talked to me, frankly and at length, about these European dilemmas. He asked for my advice, but it was more than two years before he sent me on a confidential fact-finding mission to both labs. Gradually, after I had established myself in Seattle in mid-1974, I was called upon to participate in some multilab research projects that made it easy to conduct a confidential inquiry into the running of both labs. My earlier diplomatic career and my exposure to high European politics had prepared me for just such a role; among other things my ability to converse with my European colleagues in their native languages and to take subtle account of the cultures that had formed them were useful tools. Many opened up to me who would have not done so with Americans not "acculturated" to European ways. The Swiss director, fortunately for Battelle, was replaced by a most congenial Swiss-German, Dr. Valentin Stingelin, before I began inquiries in Geneva. With the German director, the case proved less fortunate: I came to the conclusion early on that the Frankfurt lab was irremediably headed downhill unless he could be replaced; eventually that was done, but too late in the game. And the "unfair" competition with German government–subsidized labs, also beginning to undertake contract research with German industry, probably made the eventual demise of Battelle's Frankfurt lab inevitable anyway.

From watching a large, unique multinational organization such as Battelle at work, I gained a good deal more insight, sometimes rather uncertainly and imperfectly, as to how difficult it is to mount what should be a truly joint endeavor by people of various nationalities, in several different countries. Battelle made a bold start in this direction when it opened Battelle-Frankfurt in 1952, at the height of the Marshall Plan, when contract research did not exist in Germany. In the same year, Battelle opened its internationally staffed laboratory in Geneva, perhaps the most truly multinational facility Battelle operated; its researchers were picked from virtually all European countries and the United States. The Americans in charge of overall Battelle operations seemed, for the most part, unable to cope with the problems and prospects of "foreign" operations; the difficulty of attempting to fit their already established patterns into a foreign

environment to meet largely American needs gradually became insuper-
able. It was probably asking too much of Battelle's U.S. leadership (all of
whom had had distinguished careers in science but few of whom had
studied or worked abroad, or knew European languages) to accommodate themselves easily to European ways, especially when there seemed
to be little comparable effort on the part of most key European staff to
meet the Americans halfway.

The leading Germans at Frankfurt in 1974 were for the most part "very
German" and had come from academia and sometimes industry. In the
beginning they were of a generation that had had to come to terms with
modern Europe, the world, and an American Battelle when their work
habits and attitudes had already been pretty well set in a prewar mold.
Gradually, younger men, trained in academia after 1945—sometimes in
the United States—began to take over, but by the time they had risen to
top leadership posts, the German economic pattern and methods of work,
plus substantial intervention by a new federal German government, had
so changed the conditions for Battelle's kind of work in Germany that it
was too late. Perhaps, if Battelle-Frankfurt could have been led by a group
of hyphenated American-German scientists, who were not only leaders
in scientific and engineering fields but also men with experience in meld-
ing international staffs together, the laboratory might have had a better
chance of adjusting and prevailing. However, most of the corporate leaders of Battelle from the 1950s to the 1980s, while men of great intelligence,
integrity, goodwill, and high intellectual attainments, did not also possess
the skills—unusual in most other fields of work as well—necessary to lead
multinational teams of engineers and scientists.

The same might be said of the conditions at Battelle's Geneva laboratory. It had also begun work at a time when contract research was little
known, if at all, throughout Europe; they had a virtually open field for
finding sponsored research. The first director of Battelle-Geneva, being
Swiss, was almost by definition capable of managing multinational teams
of scientists. He had left Battelle by the time I began work with the Institute, so I never met him. Unfortunately—along with many of his staff
from a variety of countries—he looked down on the American provincials
who, however, were responsible for continuing support of the Geneva operations, even when later they could no longer be financially sustained.
Again, a truly "Atlantic" team of top managers was destined not to spring
from the earth. Battelle was forced to close down both its Frankfurt and
Geneva laboratories in the 1980s. Noble experiments they may have been,
but both were fated to rise and fall with changing conditions and the paucity of European scientists and technicians who could understand each
other, in every sense of the word, and also work effectively in teams led by

American scientist-managers, who had just begun to learn European ways of thinking and acting.

Americans and Europeans have been able to jointly manage some great multinational business firms, such as Standard Oil, Dupont, and IBM, and did especially well in the operation of NATO's supreme command headquarters in France and later Belgium. Men such as Eisenhower, Gruenther, and Norstad, accompanied at NATO by American officers chosen in part for their international savoir faire and knowledge of languages, set a pattern that has been continued more or less to the present day. An enterprise as vast as the defense of the "Free World," calling on the resources of the United States and other key military establishments, could—and did—consciously foster a multinationally minded core of leadership, virtually down to regimental levels. The early institution of a NATO Defense College, to give field grade officers from all Allied countries an opportunity to study international security and "war game" together was a powerful tool in forming a unique NATO command esprit de corps. Given the intricacies of Battelle's line of work, however, and the more limited resources at its command, it was asking too much for it to "breed" quickly the kind of professional individuals from the world of science who could switch national mindsets at will, and in fact become "multinational men"—precisely the kind of men and women who are more than ever needed today, in the era of globalization.

Weighing Anchor for America

After seven years in Britain, including unusual opportunities to breathe the air and dip into the cultures of all of Western Europe, it was now time for us to pack up and head back to my own *Heimat*—a German term with no precise English equivalent. It means the place where one was born and raised and to which one is always, immutably bound. Many Americans don't have such a feeling about their "roots," but I did, and still do. The Pacific Northwest was of capital importance to my life, even when I wasn't domiciled there. I relished the idea of returning to Seattle, the city in which I was raised, to the salty sea air, great conifer forests, glacier-clad mountains, and the people who were mine. I had never completely fit in any other place; even the historic, power-oriented Eastern seaboard did not completely contain my kind of people. And now I was to see whether or not I would still "fit in" with my roots. Today, three decades after returning to America, I find that I'm happy, but that a part of me will be forever "European," too. And maybe just a little bit "Japanese" as well. I am a fervent American patriot, but not a nationalist; my work and my natural inclinations have steered me into a cosmopolitan, world-embracing frame of mind.

When it came time to pack up Colleen's and my belongings for shipment to Seattle, we asked friends at the American embassy in London for suggested moving firms. One particularly acute woman said, "Oh, the ones you want without question are Turners!" After several dozen international moves already, large and small, I had experienced both good and atrocious moving firms. Some were old fashioned: a careful old Belgian transfer company packed EVERYTHING in straw, stowed in wooden crates hand-made on the spot. Years later, a respected firm of movers in Seattle, headed by an old friend, expected to pack us up for Washington, D.C., suddenly were called on to make an emergency move for a large company on the same day we had scheduled. Not wanting to welsh on their commitment to us, they recruited a "pick-up" crew from the Tacoma dockyards—men with strong backs but neither the packing experience nor, apparently, the required set of ethics. Result: awful scratches on valuable furniture, plus (much worse) the theft of several paintings that we valued greatly.

But in 1974, from Guildford in England to Seattle in the northwest corner of the Lower 48: Ah! that was something different. The British movers came with stellar credentials. Their most recent move had been the packing and forwarding of the birds-egg and butterfly collections of a noted duke, who had willed these to the British Museum. Everything had gone superbly; the BM, the Victoria and Albert Museum, and other great museums always used Turner. When the packers started, we noted that they wrapped EACH single item in butcher-paper, carefully secured and packed tightly with still more such paper. On the appointed day, a moving truck appeared at our door; we watched the packing operations carefully and—as the crew chief closed, locked, and sealed our containerful—signed off. Imagine our delight when, two months later, we were ready to receive our goods in a new-bought house on the shores of Lake Washington, and in the presence of U.S. Customs officials and representatives of the receiving firm in Seattle, cut the customs seal and subsequently found everything intact and unbroken. Toward the end of the Guildford packing, a British packer had found a lone paper clip; it turned up in Seattle, carefully wrapped, all alone, in one of the firm's standard-sized butcher papers!

Not long before we left Guildford, word came that Karl Herschel, the stout old Prussian officer who had helped me democratize Bavarians and further the unification of Europe, had in his retirement passed away suddenly. I felt crushed, and compelled to enter the following in my journal:

> I can hear the heavenly brass band now, playing *Alte Kameraden* [a favorite German marching song, which Karl loved and which was also used often by British military bands]. And St. Peter will be asking to hear Karl's cello music. What a fine but tortured old man! He bore all the burdens of Germany and Europe on his conscience. No patience. Not always understanding. But *how* he wanted what was good and right! Colleen never met him. I shall miss him.

The reader may recall chapter 5, in which I recounted Herschel's tale. A few months before his passing, when I visited him and his wife in a small provincial town in Bavaria, he had asked me to listen to some Dvořák (his favorite composer) on records. Then, before I left, he gave me a 1960 recording by the Bundeswehr brass band, with old German military music from the past 400 years. He was totally conflicted, between his pride in the old Prussian army and the "fiend" Hitler, to whom he and countless Reichswehr officers had felt compelled to swear personal fealty in 1933. I could not possibly understand Europe or Germany as well as I believe I do without the friendship of Herschel and many other Europeans who had lived through the bulk of the catastrophic 20th century.

Leaving England meant leaving many friends and interesting projects. I found people to replace me as secretary of the burgeoning network of Mid-Atlantic Clubs and as secretary of the Standing Conference of Atlantic Organizations. With sadness I resigned from the British Atlantic Committee. There were last meetings and celebratory dinners. My German, French, British, and other European friends were as kind as they could be; but it was nevertheless wrenching for Colleen and me. I shall always have two homes—America and "Old Europe" (as Donald Rumsfeld so disdainfully called it in 2003), which is actually far on the way to becoming a "New Europe."

Jagoe's car-hire service, with its uniformed drivers and small but immaculate Rovers, drove us away to Heathrow Airport. "One door closes, another door opens," said my percipient wife then, and several times after that, over the years. And it always turned out that way.

14
The Far East and the World in the Mid-Seventies

9 September 1976: *Mao Zedong, the major actor in the development of the People's Republic of China, dies of Parkinson's disease, and the more progressive Deng Xiaoping succeeds him.*

1 February 1979: *The Ayatollah Khomeini returns to Iran from France to direct a growing revolution, which succeeds in overthrowing the shah, enabling Khomeini to take power. In November 1979 the U.S. Embassy in Tehran is seized and sixty-six Americans are taken hostage.*

Landing in Seattle

On the evening of 15 July 1974, Colleen and I arrived in Seattle after a nine-hour flight from London. With the help of Battelle Seattle Research Center (BSRC) and friends, we had arranged to rent the home of a University of Washington law professor and his wife until we could buy our own. We looked forward to blessed sleep and a quiet next day, having asked our numerous relatives to come and see us *after* a rest. But no, about thirty of them turned up at the airport and accompanied us to our new digs for a party! It was good to see my mother, my brother and his family, and various assorted cousins and *their* families, despite our grogginess.

Finally asleep, Colleen suddenly awoke at about 2 a.m., unable to breathe. Trying out the new emergency services, I quickly dialed 911 and within minutes two firemen, dressed in helmets and other firefighting garb, rushed upstairs and into the bedroom. They quickly diagnosed "hyperventilation" (of which we had never heard) and instructed my wife to exhale into a paper sack and then inhale the same air to recapture CO_2. (Hyperventilation involves too *much* oxygen, rather than the reverse. Odd!) By the time the Medic 1 team arrived five minutes later, Colleen was feeling better. To confirm their diagnosis and see if any treatment were necessary, the Medic boys took us to the nearby University Hospital emergency room for a double-check. We then slept comfortably. It was good to be introduced to the new 911 services and to Seattle's Medic 1 teams, which we were told were first in the nation.

I reported to BSRC the next day, met the staff, discussed logistics and secretarial arrangements, checked out the computers (of what would seem today an archaic vintage), looked over the reference library, and so on.

BSRC premises were idyllic, built a few years earlier on land that belonged to the University of Washington, two miles distant. A main study center building, had spacious rooms in one wing for each of a dozen or so research fellows and offices across a corridor for the secretarial staff. Another wing contained the administrators, who arranged conferences and ministered to the logistical wants of the fellows. Connecting these two wings was a third, containing the library. Separate buildings held space for conferences, motel-like apartments for conferees or shorter-term resident research fellows, and a commodious dining facility, with its own kitchen and space that could be arranged in various ways for meals large and small. Another building housed one of Battelle's contract research operations—social scientists working on studies commissioned by various entities, mainly government. In the middle of the manicured, shaded grounds was a long, winding duck pond, with a Japanese-style bridge and picnic tables for sunlit days when staff might want to eat outdoors.

All in all, this complex occupied twenty acres, situated on the edge of an older but prestigious community of homes called Laurelhurst. The upper-crust inhabitants of Laurelhurst were by and large keen on having a group of quiet "scientists" acting as a partial buffer to commercial areas and the large university, with its sometimes raucous students. In the 1990s when Battelle tried to sell the research complex, unholy hell was raised by the Laurelhursters: most of them wanted no part of a possible college campus or any sort of commercial enterprise nearby. Ultimately, some entrepreneurs bought BSRC with the idea of turning it into an assisted-living compound for senior citizens, not exactly Laurelhurst's ideal either. Around the turn of the new century, Battelle leased the premises back for more of its own research! But this is getting way ahead of the story. Physically, BSRC was a marvelous place for serious work, and the support staff were excellent.

Girding Loins for a New Run at World Order

The advent of the intergovernmental OECD (Organization for Economic Cooperation and Development) in 1960 had coincided with the creation of the independent Atlantic Institute, whose founders, anticipating an ever-increasing thrust of Japan onto the world stage, included among the Institute's Board of Governors some private-sector Japanese leaders and retired diplomats. The later Trilateral Commission specifically made Japan one of its three co-equal legs. When Randy Burgess and I published *Europe and America: The Next Ten Years* in 1970, the momentous reality of Japan had begun ever more forcefully to loom on my horizon. While still living in the UK, I tried to meet as many Japanese as possible—usually diplomats—who sometimes joined the London Mid-Atlantic Club. The press in Europe and the United States bulged with stories of how Japanese automobiles and other consumer products were giving Western carmakers a run for their money. Some astute Western observers predicted a new "Japanese danger" (see Herman Kahn, *The Year 2000* and *The Coming Japanese Superstate*), complete with powerful armed forces and neoimperial aspirations. Others confined their predictions to the advent of a Japanese "economic giant" but "geopolitical dwarf."

Now, at the beginning of a new century, Japan's urge to play a part in world politics has continued to develop—even if still diffidently—while its relative economic preeminence has sadly shrunk in the wake of a decade of low economic growth and deflation/depression. My own 21st century view is that in the sixties to the eighties, the West overestimated Japan's ability to continue its powerful forward thrust, but that in the late nineties and now the new century, we would be fools to believe that Japan, contrariwise, would wallow indefinitely in economic doldrums and political uncertainty. There will be a secure and appropriate place for Japan in world councils, counting on a cyclical economic upswing and a growing need to engage in world political-military security issues. As of 2005, the signs were already there. The decision of the Japanese Diet to send troops or naval forces both to the Gulf War of 1991 and to the later Iraq conflict (including major financial commitments) bespeaks a quiet, growing, positive willingness to engage in responsible endeavors of the international community.

However, in 1974, when I was appointed a BSRC fellow, everyone was simultaneously bullish and apprehensive about Japan's future. World War II was little more than a generation away in Western memories. Although the changes in Japanese society since 1945 had been tremendous, uncertainty lingered. Was it possible that unpredictable world events could conspire to cause a kind of "social regression" among these new Eastern partners of the West? And what kind of a partnership was this now globe-girdling "Atlantic-Pacific arrangement" to be, in any event? What was it that the United States and its traditional Western allies were asking the Japanese to commit themselves to? How were the changing currents in the West itself—and especially in Europe—affecting the global scene (and thus Japan as well)? After much consultation with colleagues in Seattle and especially in New York, Washington, D.C., and Europe, I determined that Japan and her interaction with the West were of capital importance, but insufficient for the studies I was proposing. The investigations and the various likely outcomes would necessarily have to encompass all of the "overdeveloped" countries (as I half-humorously began to refer to them in my lectures) and their important interactions, plus their collective impacts on their own societies and on the rest of the world. Stirring in my mind was the concept of an eventual worldwide "community of democracies," but at the time I thought that using that term and positing a global vision would be a bit too much to bite off. So I concentrated then on what at that time I called "the Atlantic-Pacific System."

Among other things, I quickly began to prepare myself for extensive on-the-spot inquiries in Japan by studying the Japanese language. By the time Colleen and I took our first Battelle trip to Japan in the spring of 1976, I was sufficiently equipped linguistically to ask directions, make pleasantries, order meals and train tickets, and so on. I could not spare the time to learn to read Japanese—and especially not the written *Kanji* (characters borrowed from the Chinese), or even the two simpler, but still demanding, substitute alphabets. But my oral command, at least in the 1970s and 1980s, enabled me to get around on my own. My interlocutors on serious subjects in Japan almost always spoke passable English, so I "made out" without great trouble.

I was fortunate that Battelle CEO Sherwood Fawcett agreed to put extra resources at my disposal. In addition to *Carla Kewley*, a recent University of Washington graduate in the French language as a principal secretary, the others who became part of the team for Battelle's Core Program in Advanced International Systems, were:

> *Martha Darling*, whom I had met through friends at the OECD and worked with in Europe in young leader programs. Martha was a graduate of Reed College, known for its free-thinking products; an MA from the Woodrow Wilson School at Princeton, and a doctoral candidate. Martha was quick, good with people, and a great help. She later left Battelle to become a White House Fellow and much else.
>
> *Dr. Raymond D. Gastil*, a Battelle Fellow whose office was next to mine and who became a lifelong friend. Ray was a Harvard product, from BA to PhD, a noted anthropologist, and adept with economics, sociology, political science, and history—a real polymath. He published books and papers while at Battelle, notably one on the cultural regions of the United States. He had worked for several years with Herman

Kahn at the Hudson Institute and taught at the University of Oregon. His doctoral thesis had been on Iran; he was also a German specialist and had done extensive work on geopolitics. A member of the Board of Freedom House in New York, in the early seventies he invented the annual compilation of the volume known as *Freedom in the World*, which assessed (and still does) the state of political liberties and civil rights in all countries and territories of the world. Ray is today one of the great experts on democracy—what it is and how it develops. His advice on assessing the prospects for "progress" in the world (he even wrote a book on progress itself) was invaluable for my work during the two years we were together at Battelle.

Dr. Toshio Nishi, a Japanese graduate of Gakuin University who had come to the University of Washington for his advanced degrees. Toshio was our sounding board on things Japanese; I enlisted him and Martha on a study, "The Eye of the Beholder: Japanese and Western Images of One Another." He subsequently became a fellow of the Hoover Institution at Stanford, where he wrote a controversial but illuminating study of MacArthur's impact on Japan, from the point of view of the son of a Samurai. Later, Toshio labored on a novel involving the clash of American and Japanese civilizations and values and returned to Japan as a professor at a major university. As a prime example, within himself, of the "warring spirits" in the breasts of his countrymen and the processes of Westernization at work, Toshio nevertheless possessed a genial personality plus excellent powers of analysis. He too was invaluable to our team.

By October 1975, together with these team members and calling on large pools of advice from friends and colleagues in many places, I had put together a paper on our core program of studies, outlining several proposed investigations. The first project eventually evolved into my book, *Uniting the Democracies: Institutions of the Emerging Atlantic-Pacific System* (New York University Press, 1980). Our second project, on Western and Japanese images of one another, never reached publication but Martha's and Toshio's research, plus my own visits to Japan, offered much material for a short monograph on the subject of what Japan and the West had to learn from one another. We also produced materials for an Atlantic-Pacific bibliography, augmenting what had been done at the Atlantic Institute in Paris. All of our team members gave lectures and participated in conferences, some sponsored by Battelle itself, within our newly defined field of Atlantic-Pacific studies. We were also available for frequent consultations with staff from Battelle's many laboratories and helped, I think, to broaden the outlooks of some natural scientists and engineers who were struggling

to comprehend and come to grips with foreign cultures and the geopolitical and geoeconomic worlds.

The 1975 paper "The Battelle Core Program on Advanced International
Studies" was a kind of road map for a whole series of questions and
research topics important for the general direction in which some of us
(some beyond Battelle) believed the world was heading or, in some cases,
should be heading. I make no apologies for broadening the strict role of a
social scientist who poses hypotheses and then lets the chips objectively
fall where they may. (There are in fact very few such academic animals
around; all but the least senior usually have working hypotheses that
they define and defend, consciously or unconsciously.) I had an "axe to
grind." Since 1952, I had been convinced that the Western world (by 1975
defined to include Japan and other developed and potentially developed
countries in the Pacific) would, one way or another, have to achieve much
greater unity of purpose and action than heretofore, if the inevitable
world problems and crises ahead were to be successfully dealt with.
I never purposely skewed facts or statistics to fit this broad goal, but I
tried constantly—and still do—to make a case that is rarely made or, if
made, heard. Policy-makers, opinion-molders, and the general public in
the major overdeveloped countries still do not understand sufficiently the
concept, let alone the realities, of international interdependence and the
growth of democracy and what these require of us—especially the richest,
most powerful, and most "advanced" countries. This group certainly
includes Japan.

Our Core Program was not constructed casually or lightly. I consulted with numerous experts in North America, Europe, and, later, Japan
and built their ideas into my own evolving concept and that of our BSRC
staff. By 1975, Jim McDonald, an old colleague from German days in the
early fifties, had retired from the Foreign Service and was appointed by
Dr. Fawcett to administer BSRC. This enabled me to spend more time on
my studies and less on the various representational and administrative
tasks I had perforce to be involved in. McDonald's advice with respect
to our conception of the Core Program, and of how to carry it out, was
of exceptional value; we were a team, as we had been more than twenty
years earlier. After ten years more, we both retired from Battelle, I in 1983
and Jim in 1984.

Battelle Faces Serious Problems

Not too many months after I settled down at BSRC, Sherwood Fawcett—in
one of our many discussions of Battelle's broad future—confided in me that

the Institute confronted two new and grave legal problems that might seriously compromise its financial future, especially the considerable funds it had earned through having helped materially to develop technologies such as Xerox. It had used these to open up new areas of knowledge (the studies I planned being one).

In 1975, Battelle's disposable "surplus" capital was around $500 million. A judge in Franklin County Superior Court of Ohio, where Battelle had begun its nonprofit life, was seeking to further his impending reelection campaign. Reading Gordon Battelle's 1923 will, the judge concluded that Battelle over the years had not followed Gordon's strictures to "distribute surpluses to charity" and particularly the 25 percent of such surpluses that were supposed to be spent in central Ohio itself. No one could argue about the 25 percent requirement, although the eventual disposition of these monies involved a far greater number of charities (including educational institutions and research institutes, some of which had to be created on the spot) and far larger sums than any comparable small region could readily absorb. But about the remaining 75 percent I felt there was a strong case to be made that Battelle, by investing in many fields of basic research was already contributing to "charitable" purposes, under existing law, which include the advancement of science. Such research included studies of a "free floating" nature—like mine of the Atlantic-Pacific, and not commissioned by any other entity than Battelle itself. I argued that Battelle was certainly, under established law, such a charitable endeavor. But the Franklin County judge did not see it this way, and Dr. Fawcett was loath to see Battelle's lawyers use that argument. So Battelle had to "give away" millions of its patrimony to educational and other endeavors around the world, and in fairly short order.

Also, for abstruse legal reasons which I cannot paraphrase, the Internal Revenue Service also wanted its "cut" of Battelle's millions; it ruled that Battelle was *not* a not-for-profit body and therefore owed back income tax over several years on its "earnings." (In 2003, the IRS reversed itself, Battelle again became a not-for-profit institution, but the government, to my knowledge, never rebated the substantial taxes the Institute had paid over the intervening quarter century).

These events necessitated serious changes in Battelle's own forward research and educational programs. I was necessarily involved in a small way, as was Jim McDonald, in bigger, budgetary questions. Whereas in the summer of 1974 when I arrived at BSRC, a substantial team of scholars from various places and disciplines were gathering for a year's interdisciplinary study on the important new question whether court proceedings around the nation should be televised, after 1975 and later years such open-ended "proactive" Battelle-financed studies were sharply curtailed.

Soon those of us who were on longer-than-one-year appointments, found our Battelle masters, with reason, insisting that we too take on projects on contract with outside bodies to earn our keep, so to speak.

Helping Build Seattle and the Northwest

McDonald and I, given our Foreign Service experience and the need for Battelle to become more of a force in the Seattle community, felt it our duty to involve ourselves in the civic, educational, and artistic life of the still-provincial Northwest. Jim served on the board of the Seattle Opera and other civic groups; I joined the board of the local World Affairs Council and the complementary Committee on Foreign Relations. We both worked with various parts of the University of Washington (especially its just-retired formidable president, Dr. Charles Odegaard), where our knowledge might help and whose resources Battelle might tap. We encouraged Seattle leaders to envisage a central role for the Northwest in developing an "Atlantic-Pacific Community" — Seattle was geographically its convenient center, just 8000 miles west of London and 8000 miles east of Tokyo.

In 1977, after trying hard with a conscientious but underpowered board of the World Affairs Council to beef up what was then a rather scrappy program of community education, I arranged a small Battelle grant to bring the directors of three of the best World Affairs Councils in the nation to Seattle for a week, to study our council, its program, personnel, and organization, and suggest how it might better relate to other community institutions, especially the university. The expert team spent a week independently looking over our scene and produced a fine report advising the Seattle Council what it would have to do to become a real power in the community and state. With a few other Council directors, I engineered a series of decisions, some of them wrenching, such as gracefully thanking the entrenched volunteer president of the Council for his efforts and replacing him with a part-time, later full-time, paid professional CEO.

Within two or three years, the Council took off and, with a few brief lapses now and then, has steadily progressed. Throughout this exercise I became aware of an unpleasant but, in some situations, essential quirk in my own modest chart of abilities: I can often sense where organizations are failing to meet their potential and why; and — if a major shakeup in leadership, staff, and board is needed — I can engineer that in ways that release the potential of an otherwise handicapped group. In 1971, I had been able in Geneva to help the new INTERPHIL replace a quite ineffective board chairman and thus clear the decks for major contributions to the nascent world of modern European philanthropy. Years later, after I retired from Battelle and began a new but short career running the Atlantic Council of the United States, I reorganized management structure and habits, got the Council's Board to redefine its mission, and pruned the staff of ineffectual individuals. However, for this necessarily unsettling brand of activism, I was put out to pasture prematurely! (See chapter 16 for a sad but fascinating tale.) Bulls in china shops sometimes face unpleasant consequences, even when some crockery obviously needs clear-the-decks destruction.

McDonald and I, and our wives, became members of the Council on Washington State's Future, a loosely organized body put together by Governor (later Senator) Dan Evans. This group met for dinner three or four times a year at BSRC to discuss major issues facing the State of Washington. Jim McDonald and I both formed lasting friendships with business executives, attorneys, labor leaders, civic catalysts, mayors, and educators who formed this council. Land-use planning, educational issues, and the Northwest's place in the world economy were among the subjects we studied and debated.

In 1975, George Taylor, a just-retired former pre–World War II professor of mine, and Jim McDonald worked together to create the Washington Council on International Trade, which became a regional powerhouse and a model for what other states have since done. Under the council's aegis, business, government, and labor executives have trekked to Washington, D.C., annually, to discuss trade issues with our congressional delegates, and sometimes to foreign lands such as China, the object in the 1980s of a hilarious and useful group visit. Among other things the council operates an annual summer school for social science teachers, to help them understand world trade and its domestic and political backgrounds. I contributed to this with an analysis of international organizations important to the world economy.

The Ford Motor Company Study

In the winter of 1974–75, Battelle contracted with Henry Ford II for a study of nothing less than "the future of the Company." Together with seven other Battelle researchers, each from a different field of expertise (propulsion, federal taxation and energy policy, manufacturing, organization and management, and so on), I put together a futuristic view of European markets and operating conditions for Ford's manufacturing. On 8 April 1975, the Battelle team foregathered at Dearborn, Michigan, to present our findings to Ford's top executives. Ford's corporate planning executive showed us the conference room in which we would perform: roughly 30 by 60 feet in size, with recessed ceiling lights, a massive horseshoe-shaped hardwood table with about forty red, upholstered plush chairs around it; a red carpet and pink ceiling encompassed all. A very large projection screen and other audio-visual aids were at one end of the room. Chairman Henry Ford II sat at the other end, flanked by a vice chairman, Phil Caldwell, and company president, Lee Iacocca. A set of command buttons seemed to grow out of the floor by the chairman's seat.

The company planner who briefed us in advance pointed out that Mr. Ford disliked large gatherings, so would we mind sitting off-stage in the projection room and come out only when it was the turn of each to present his findings? Our team leader, Ron Hamilton, would remain in the conference room throughout the entire proceedings, cueing each of us when to appear before the Emperor (so Ford seemed!). We all sat on some hastily rustled and rather uncomfortable chairs in a projection room, watching the proceedings on television until each was summoned.

When it became time for me to present my findings on Europe, I combed my hair, brushed off my blue mohair suit, and strode, as nonchalantly but also as commandingly as I could, into the presence of the Almighty, and took a seat at the horseshoe table. Mr. Ford and his associates had had an opportunity to review all our written reports in advance, so I—like my colleagues—simply reviewed our conclusions, made a few comments, and let the questions fly. One of Ford's courtiers wanted to know what we (I) thought of the prospects for possible large Ford investments in Portugal or Spain. I managed to describe the serious political risks (as neither Iberian country had yet thrown off their dictators' yokes), but pointed out some hopeful signs that both societies were already preparing for the transition that was sure to come—for example, a new generation of eager young leaders, keen on both democracy and "joining Europe." Although I thought a Ford investment might be a mistake—at the very least premature—I avoided saying so. Mr. Ford said, "Well, our board just okayed a $1 billion investment in Spain, so I hope we were right." Fortunately, the planning executive said later that I had handled my inquisition in a "classic manner." (I did not tell Mr. Ford that I had worked indirectly for him at the Ford Foundation.) The day went well; Mr. Ford told us at the end of the day that "my confidence level has risen as a result of our talks." This was certainly good enough.

I noticed—and the significance of this did not dawn on me until some years later, when events at the Ford Motor Company thrust Iacocca into the national limelight—that at several times during our presentations, when President Iacocca intervened to ask a question or make an observation, Henry II put him down, curtly: "That's enough, Lee." No wonder

Iacocca soon deserted Ford to become head of Chrysler; he appeared a quite unhappy man in Dearborn.

Much of the credit for the success of this venture must go to Ron Hamilton, a Battelle economist and management specialist, who on several occasions showed brilliance in the way he orchestrated teams of this kind to serve industry. In this lay one of Battelle's great strengths: its capacity for putting together groups of just the right specialists to provide a rounded and incisive view of a complicated set of interlinked problems. This was to be shown in a still more complex Battelle exercise in 1979–80. Again, Hamilton, teamed with an outstanding Battelle-Frankfurt management expert, Klaus Staehle, put together multinational teams of experts that collectively might provide a rounded picture of "The World in the 1980s," and sell a series of specialized studies to a number of companies, which would then have proprietary rights to the results and the right to quiz our various experts in greater depth. This necessitated a team visit to Houston at one point; it was my first experience in that great (but to me, soulless) business capital of the Texan domain.

The World in the 1980s: The BASICS Studies

Ron Hamilton, with Dr. Fawcett's support, invited me into this predictive exercise, which would involve BMI's major laboratories in the United States and the two big labs in Europe, Frankfurt and Geneva. This was a much more complex — and breathtaking — undertaking than our labors for the Ford Motor Company. The Battelle team included experts on world energy, world trade, key technologies for the future, the U.S. economy as affected by likely political, social, and technological change, and the European Community in the 1980s. My job, in a sense, was to synthesize all these studies into a sixth, overarching study — my own view of world politics in the 1980s. My wide-ranging investigative trips, interviews with all kinds of specialists in the United States and elsewhere, my long periods living abroad (five European countries over seventeen years), plus my reading since joining Battelle, had given me the general background necessary for a global look ahead into the coming decade. But the study's clients and my colleagues wanted answers, or at least informed guidelines to many other pointed questions. Everyone involved wanted to know, for example, how the Cold War would evolve over the next decade, whether or not the ties between the Atlantic allies would weaken or strengthen, how China would develop and what impact this might have on the world political situation, the effect of developments in the Islamic world, the cohesion of the advanced democracies, and so on. The entire program was entitled "BASICS."

Some background for this futurism: By the spring of 1975, I had up-dated some old "circle charts" that I had begun constructing in 1956 (and used extensively in public information activities in Europe); these showed the progressive, almost inevitable, knitting together, by means of various multinational institutions, of the OECD countries, the developed democ-racies. These formed the core of my *World Politics in the 1980s* study for BASICS. Thenceforth I was to reissue the charts every few years for many purposes (see Appendix A); they were incorporated in my 1980 book, *Uniting the Democracies,* and again in the 1998 and 2001 versions of *Pax Democratica.* The last chart appeared in 2004, after the substantial enlarge-ment of NATO and the EU. What happens institutionally to link the de-veloped democracies, it has been my belief over fifty years, affects world outcomes more critically than any other major development.

The circle charts were used at the National Defense University in the 1970s and later by colleagues at various universities, and at NATO and an independent group in Brussels that monitors international institution building. At the outset of the new century, I was still showing these dia-grams to colleagues and students at the University of Washington and elsewhere.

My method of proceeding with the 1980 World Politics study was this: I conceived of the world geopolitical situation as a "multi-ring circus," with major events taking place more or less within each of eight "criti-cal arenas." I identified these arenas and 66 discrete "descriptors" — fac-tors that might influence developments in the arenas and on each other, sometimes reciprocally, sometimes in a one-way direction — and, with the strategic help of computers, "massaged" them in various ways. The trick was to identify which factors were truly important (sometimes using find-ings from the companion BASICS studies) and then, employing complex graphics, to see what a total world picture would look like. Keeping these "descriptors" and "arenas" of conflict and/or cohesion in mind, and with a lot of help from my colleagues and their relevant research, I managed to construct three alternate scenarios for the world (no minuscule view here!) and how it might be expected to develop under different conditions in the 1980s.

By 1990, when I took a look back at what we had wrought, I felt good about this crystal gazing of a decade earlier. Here is World Scenario A, which we predicted would be most likely to eventuate.

Good Luck, Low Risks, Modest Gains: Improved international co-operation in trade, money, and energy, plus moderation in Third World, prepare way for steady if moderate economic expansion from 1985. West reinvigorates alliances, redresses balance with

USSR, whose economic weaknesses show. Small wars and turmoil in some developing countries, but diplomacy wins out. EC [European Community] exceeds 12 members. World economic growth around 4 percent.

We gave this scenario a 50 percent chance of likelihood, by comparison with 20 percent probability for Scenario B ("Gloom and Doom") and 30 percent for Scenario C ("Strong Economy, Restive Middle East"). There were bits of Scenarios B and C in the actual outcome (looking back, especially from a 21st century vantage point), but I believe our preferred scenario, by 1990, had held up reasonably well.

The only major development that I (and the great majority of prognosticators of the day) failed to predict was the dissolution of the Soviet empire in 1989–91. Virtually all Sovietologists and political scientists, diplomats, and the "intelligence community," believed that the Soviet Union and Communism would not last forever, but very few thought the end would come so soon, or so bloodlessly. 8 November 1989 was the day the Berlin Wall fell, signaling the disintegration of the entire Soviet empire within less than two years.

I have often thought that to construct retroactively our Map of World Issues and Forces, illustrating how the turbulent and dynamic globe looked in "snapshots" taken periodically in the past, might show futurists and others more clearly, or at least more suggestively, how things change and how, in many cases, they stay the same.

One might look at the BASICS Scenarios for the 1980s and say, "Well, intuition and a good background in these matters would probably have yielded pretty much the same results, with a good deal less work." However, I strongly disagree. It was the application of techniques of systems analysis and the use of computers to crosscheck the interactions of the various factors and the arenas of conflict that made the study much more integrated and plausible than it would otherwise have been. The whole exercise, consuming the better part of six full months of my work (plus a good deal by others), greatly enlarged my own horizons and made me look for key developments that I might otherwise never have seen or understood. For this alone, I thank the Battelle Memorial Institute and my valued colleagues of those days for the mind-broadening opportunity it afforded me.

Among other things, I was introduced to a significant use of computers and systems thinking by some of my colleagues in the 1980s BASICS study: how the "cross-impact analysis" of the many factors I had determined would constitute "vectors" of change or might affect other factors. Rolling these around in my own head—and seeing what collided with what, how, and where—was one of my own ad hoc methods, but some of my systems-trained colleagues convinced me that the rigorous, "leave no stone unturned" way of looking at *all* the factors *together* in matrix fashion was a productive thing to do. It probably would never have occurred to me, for instance, to estimate the impact that the advent of a common EC foreign policy (proposed in the 1970s but never fully realized, even by the outset of the 21st century) could have in important ways on the cohesion of the Soviet bloc in the 1980s. However, going through this exercise showed me how systematic quantification, fed into a computer in the right way, could lead to significant new insights, or at least force me to think in ways I hadn't considered.

I profited a great deal from my years at Battelle, but this BASICS exercise, which demanded that I learn a great deal more about the world and what was happening to it, topped all expectations. The exposure to the rigors of systems analysis, using computers, was one of the major factors that made it possible for me, as the years went on, to often cut through to the heart of matters that seemed obscure to the ordinary observer. I also learned a great deal more about the value of assessing probabilities of several outcomes or impacts, which all might be plausible but some more likely than others to eventuate. More proof, for me, that the human mind is more than the sum of its parts. Or that sometimes, several human minds working together can produce insights that no single one of them could come up with or that would trump the different minds involved. Three plus three might, in some cases, equal seven, or even eight.

I still do not pretend to be a world expert in these matters, but I do believe I see the world much more "whole" than many, and certainly much more so than I did before Battelle. Science and system, my Battelle work suggested, have a good deal to learn from humanists and the "social sciences" (which are still anything but sciences), but the reverse is just as true. To my two top bosses at Battelle, Sherwood Fawcett and Ron Paul, I owe a very great deal for providing me with such enriching experiences.

Japan, the Far East, and the Atlantic System

I spent a large part of my time in 1974–76 learning as much as I could from books, journals, and resident experts at the University of Washington and other American colleges about Japan and its interaction, past and present, with the West. I had marvelous interviews, for example, with Professor Richard Storry of Oxford and with Professor Edwin O. Reischauer, Harvard's premier expert on Japan and earlier our ambassador in Tokyo. Much of this was in preparation for a major trip to the Western Pacific in 1976, armed with questions the answers to which, I hoped, would help me to see better the outlines of the Atlantic-Pacific System that I believed was in the making. Japan was the main focus. In 1976 my wife and I were to spend two months in that country, trying to intensify and clarify the impressions of our 1973 three-week Aspen "traveling seminar," recounted in the previous chapter. My theory was that although one can gain a great deal of insight into the nature and international role of a nation by reading and consulting experts (and I did), nothing beats time on the ground and intense contact with the locals. Even the flavors and fragrances, and the looks on peoples' faces, can add a great deal to cultural learning, in the broadest sense.

Feeling that Japan's future and, to an important extent, that of the United States, were bound up intimately with that of other countries in East Asia, we devoted the first part of our 1976 journey to New Zealand, Australia, Indonesia, Singapore, Malaysia, the Philippines, and Taiwan. We omitted China and South Korea (in hindsight perhaps a mistake), but we couldn't see everything. Besides, in 1976 China was in the throes of the Great Cultural Revolution (1966–1976); travel there would be difficult, and useful contacts limited, if available at all. At the time, South Korea, although modernizing economically, was still under dictatorial rule; there would be little opportunity (I judged) to see with any accuracy through the surrounding mists.

On 25 February 1976, Colleen and I took off from Seattle for a great, if sometimes frustrating and often confusing, adventure which on balance turned out to be most illuminating. Colleen came along to take notes, on occasion to interview women with useful insights, and to add her acute observations to mine. It was essential to make the absolute most of our short but intensive sojourns; the following account reflects the core of what we learned.

�֎

May 1976: First port of call was **Honolulu**, where the evidence of Japanese influence was pervasive, especially in politics, education, and tourism. During its existence as a state, Hawaii has voted largely Democratic and sent mostly Japanese Americans to Congress and its state house. Key Japanese traits—sense of duty, diligence, and determination—rub off on other Hawaiians, and Japanese-Hawaiians are in turn changed. Here also was our first impression beyond the continental United States of the Chinese diaspora, which tended to dominate banking and many other businesses. The Portuguese (I noted in my journal) "are the Poles of Hawaii—the butt of most of the racial jokes. Caucasians are [and in the 21st century remain] outnumbered. The native Hawaiians struggle to retain their identity, with the aid of a massive Trust set up by law under the will of a 19th century native princess."

My main target for illumination was the East-West Center, attached to the University of Hawaii and set up by Congress at the instigation of Lyndon Johnson. Consecrated to promoting pan-Pacific visions and understanding, it supplements the powerful but quietly influential presence of CINCPAC (headquarters of Commander-in-Chief Pacific), where a full admiral and his staff provide broadly defined security oversight of America's interests around the Pacific Basin. My retired USIA friend, Cliff Forster, was then living in Hawaii and provided, then and later the astute observations of someone born of U.S. missionaries in Japan who had made the most of his bicultural attributes in both the military and diplomacy. Cliff saw the interdependent Atlantic-Pacific system much as I did; we clicked.

The East-West Center in Honolulu has acted as a collecting point for scholars and other experts from Pacific countries. Dr. Everett Kleinjans, the president of the center, was a noted Japanologist who had lived in Nippon for many years. We talked about how, curiously, Japanese do a rather poor job overall of speaking English. Kleinjans thought this may be rooted in Japanese culture's "shame syndrome" (a phenomenon described by Ruth Benedict in her seminal 1944 book *The Chrysanthemum and the Sword*, which she wrote as a guide for American postwar occupiers of Japan) as contrasted with the "guilt cultures" of most Western countries. The Japanese, said Kleinjans, fear to "open their mouths," believing they will mispronounce or misuse the foreign tongue and thus bring shame on themselves and their teachers. (I had no such inhibitions trying out my rudimentary Japanese; my efforts on the whole were next to miserable, but I was determined.)

At the East-West Center I first learned of Japan's demographic problem — at the time the birthrate stood at 1.0, barely replacement level. The result (seen now a quarter century later) has been a growing population bulge of senior citizens, now tending to live longer and to be cared for by an ever-diminishing cadre of workers. Japan was merely the first of a large number of industrialized democracies to experience this brake on social and economic progress. The phenomenon explains part, if not all, of Japan's excruciating economic dilemma today, whereas in 1976, many Western observers believed and feared that Japan's rapid economic growth would permit her, in a few years, to outpace all others in the race for the top. An interesting young Japanese researcher in the East-West Center's Population Institute explained these trends to us, pointing out that the Japanese economy was quickly shifting its labor-intensive industries to low-wage countries, copying the growing American practice, today called global outsourcing.

Daniel Lerner, an M.I.T. political scientist, was studying Pacific communication problems at the East-West Center. I had met Dan years earlier, when he was completing his landmark study of the ultimately unsuccessful effort to create a European Defense Community. Dan was the only center scholar I met who understood what I was about: trying to determine the possibilities for a Pacific community built on the common security and economic interests of democracies in the region, and relating this to the Atlantic community within an Atlantic-Pacific system. Most center scholars I spoke with —and above all Dr. Kleinjans—had little sympathy for either an Atlantic or Pacific community, much less an amalgamation of these. Dr. Kleinjans. said that in the view of such countries as Indonesia, this kind of community would "simply be the carnivores combining again." In the eyes of Asians, he said, "Europe is virtually already as united as China—which has one people, one culture, virtually one language," and is a continuing danger to the East.

In short, students of Asia (or other continents outside Europe and North America) generally have no sympathy for the great European war-prevention scheme that finally stilled the damaging intramural conflicts of the great powers over the last half of the 20th century. I took it as one of my tasks to encourage, if I could, a greater understanding in Europe of Asia-Pacific cultures and the reverse in the Pacific countries. The United States, in my hypothesis, stood as the vital link between the two. Some developments since the 1970s, such as the Asia-Pacific Economic Cooperation forum, have put a little meat on this fragile Pacific Rim intellectual skeleton. However there are still great gulfs: between East Asians and Americans, between Europeans and East Asians, between America and Europe-Africa linkages, and so on. The world remains round, but a holistic view of this earth and its interlocking problems and opportunities is still remarkably lacking among policy-makers and influentials.

Strangely, successive CINCPACs or SACEURs (Commanders-in-Chief Pacific and Supreme Allied Commanders Europe) have been the best-placed leaders in our interconnected world to understand such linkages, suggest ways of dealing with them, and provide vital continuity. Two who stand out are retired Admiral William Crowe, CINCPAC in the eighties and later ambassador to Great Britain, and SACEUR General Wesley Clark, who led NATO's war in Kosovo and who is reported to have said he had more trouble getting decisions out of the Pentagon than out of the NATO Council of (then) nineteen nations.

I left Honolulu wondering why our civilian systems could not find and groom comparable nonmilitary leaders for civilian problems, plus a civil structure comparable to NATO and our Pacific ties. I still wonder, in 2006.

❉

New Zealand was our next stop, for two weeks of roaming the vast (considering its minuscule population) two-island nation and observing its inhabitants. The latter, nicknamed Kiwis, for the most part are no doubt among the friendliest and most hospitable people on earth, but also among those whose minds and culture seemed most closed to the outside. Things have no doubt changed since 1976, but the geographic isolation of this people still, I believe, makes them think that they can leave the big things in the world to their Aussie neighbors and especially to their faraway American friends, as their small population means their contributions to global problems are more or less marginal. So why worry?

This of course is less than fair to the Kiwis, considering New Zealand's sacrifices in two world wars, her decent contributions to overseas development aid over the years, her respectable record in support of the UN, and the fact that she does not dump her own domestic problems on the world's doorstep. New Zealand, along with Australia, sent forces to the Vietnam War. Yet, the absence of New Zealand troops from many recent UN peacekeeping operations (including the dangerous peacemaking and peacekeeping operations in East Timor, Afghanistan, and Iraq) makes one wonder.

There is also the matter of New Zealand's virtual withdrawal from the ANZUS (Australia-New Zealand-U.S.) security treaty of 1951. In 1986, the New Zealand government decided to prohibit any port calls in their country by U.S. naval vessels that could not be certified as containing no nuclear weapons or nuclear propulsion systems. Quite naturally, the United States refused, on grounds that classifying its warships as nuclear or nonnuclear would give aid and comfort to potential enemies. In 1989, the New Zealand prime minister declared the ANZUS Treaty a "dead letter." (At this point, the Cold War was still very much a reality and the potential menace of China a serious concern.) All these things lay in the future at the time of our 1976 visit. My mind was concentrated at least twice, however, by glimpses into New Zealand's past: (1) at Auckland's national war museum, where we saw a brass plaque in a most prominent place, commemorating the Battle of the Coral Sea (1942) and thanking the Americans for deliverance; and (2) a small but impressive war memorial in the cemetery of Queenstown, a tiny resort city in a parched area on the South Island, which read: "For King and Country: 1914–18, 1939–45," followed by the names of about fifty young men who had fallen far from home.

These were poignant reminders of how New Zealanders felt deep gratitude (at one time, anyway) to the U.S. Navy for turning back the Imperial Japanese Navy in its drive south in the beginning days of World

War II, and its reverence for young lives snuffed out in distant battles for the British Empire. (There was, I learned, a habit among New Zealanders of referring to trips to Britain as "going home.") But time and generational change can greatly alter perceptions. The world—especially the post–Cold War world and the advent of positive and humanitarian elements on which New Zealand can and does put its own small emphasis—has apparently, in the view of New Zealanders, brought them a happy cocoon existence. They tend to let the Australians and especially the United States (sometimes NATO) do the nasty work of world-policing and deterring enemies—an understandable, but not necessarily commendable, attitude. Like Sweden, Switzerland, and Austria, the New Zealanders are, sad to say, freeloaders in the free world's security system. By 2005, I came to qualify this view, however, as the Bush II administration had begun what looked like a drive for a Pax Americana, instead of a Pax Democratica in which all would share burdens and benefits proportionately.

We spent a pleasant, memorable evening in Wellington, New Zealand's hilly little capital, at the home of George Laking, former ambassador to the United States, and his wife. They invited his son and daughter-in-law, plus Sir John and Lady Marshall. Sir John was a former prime minister and still at the time a power in New Zealand politics. I took an informal poll: The oldsters agreed that their future lay with America and the OECD grouping, that security arrangements might be improved but were essential, and that the Japanese deserved a wary attitude. Young Laking couldn't quite see the "security bit"; "who threatens us?" he said. He was more open to Japanese ties in economic and political terms. But, as often in other countries, these elite opinions seemed not to reflect most other views we encountered. New Zealanders appeared in 1976 generally not simply ignorant of such questions and the wider world, but positively disinterested.

My journal recorded my bottom-line impression of New Zealanders: "NZers are friendly, yes, but not too interested in outsiders. They are a very happy, insular, sports-and-recreation-oriented people with little time to think or care about the outside world. A humane society, yes. But a very remote one, perforce."

❃

Australia, New Zealand's closest neighbor (800 miles to the west), provided a startling contrast to our previous port of call. We based ourselves in Melbourne, at that time nearly two million in population and ever a rival of more commercial, dynamic, elbowing Sydney. Bob Brand, the U.S. consul general in Melbourne, and his wife Jo, old friends from our days in England, gave us a royal tour, introduced us to an interesting cross-section of the region's elite, and provided backdrop for animated discussions on what this part of the world is all about and how it relates to the rest. Bob has always been one of America's greatest enthusiasts for the "togetherness" of the Western democracies. Around the dinner table, we jointly (and a little giddily) coined an acronym to signify what this process of amalgamation was all about: we called the OECD group, in security, economic, and cultural terms, "WOMBAT" This was a play on the name of one of Australia's eye-opening marsupials, the harmless, steady little wombat—which Jo and Colleen found entrancing at the Melbourne zoo. After all, Jo said, kangaroos get all the press but the wombats move ahead, slowly but determinedly, to make their way. WOMBAT, our little joke, came to mean: Western Oriental Movement for Bringing it All Together. The "oriental" indicated that Japan was a full member of this community, and that probably others in the Far East would join up in time. (This was certainly true of South Korea, which in the midnineties joined the OECD. Others, such as Singapore or Malaysia, could be in line.)

In 2003, Brand (now a professor emeritus at Penn State) and I were chatting on the phone, as we often did over the years, about the state of the world. I told him that Henry Kissinger had been appointed chair of a Council on Foreign Relations (New York) panel to study the future of transatlantic relations; I also said that I wondered if Henry would take sufficiently into account the value of the extensive array of intergovernmental (and some supranational) organizations which have, over 50 years, enshrined and facilitated the cross-Atlantic, cross-Pacific, and intra-European ties. Bob reminded me that once, when he was stationed in Melbourne, Kissinger stopped over on a long trip. Asked by a reporter if he planned a more extensive visit to Australia, the secretary of state shot back, "But Australia isn't on the way to anywhere!" On this—and a good many other things—Henry and I haven't seen eye-to-eye. But now, in the early 21st century, I'm pretty sure we agree that a "drift to empire" is not a viable course for the United States.

After several visits to Australia, and steady coaching by Brand (as he coached the entire National Defense University when later on its staff), I came to appreciate the vital importance of the sixth continent. It is the closest reliable Western outpost to the vital "sea-lanes of communication" between the United States, the Far East, and the Indian Ocean. If, for example, the Straits of Malacca were closed to first–world shipping, Australia commands both alternate routes. Bob Brand urged the Australian government to move its one aircraft carrier and much of its fleet to its west coast, near Perth, to reflect its vital concern for the opening to South Asia, the great Indian Ocean beyond, and the Middle East. (This has largely been done.)

I found Australians, in and out of government, in the universities and think tanks and in the business world, increasingly cognizant of such geopolitical truths and of their interdependence with the rest of the world. With Brand's continuing attention, he and I later would launch the Pacific Institute in Melbourne—a Far Eastern outrigger of the chain of Mid-Atlantic Clubs and a possible counterpart to the Atlantic Institute in Paris. A quarter century later, Bob reported to me that our faithful chief organizers of the Pacific Institute, Alfred Brooks and Martin Holme, continued their work. This bespeaks an entirely different public and elite attitude than I found in New Zealand: a recognition of the interdependence of the world's democracies and the role of far-off Australia in a global drive for peace, stability, the international rule of law, and economic well-being. The New Zealanders were picky and choosy; for the Australians, our interlocking futures spread across the board.

Although one could see important differences between Australian and New Zealand perceptions of international politics, it was fair, at least on my first visit Down Under, to say also that many intelligent, educated Australians found the idea of an OECD grouping based on interdependence a bit hard to comprehend and, at the very least, novel. I spoke to several clubs and academic groups on these concepts; only with time, and the gentle but persistent prodding of Brand and others, did the WOMBAT concept begin to come through. Australia, in these respects, has come of age in the late 20th and early 21st centuries. Australian troops have been found in peacekeeping and peacemaking missions in Africa, Kosovo, Afghanistan, Iraq, the Solomon Islands, and most especially in East Timor (1999–2001). There, Australia took the lead in bringing stability and a new start to an indigestible bit of Indonesia that had been brutalized by that large and fitful nation.

"Australasia" (a term disliked by both Aussies and New Zealanders) is simply a microcosm of one aspect of the European security equation. In the longer run, it is virtually impossible to expect countries such as New Zealand or even some main NATO allies to eagerly share a "burden" of defense (such as in Iraq in 2003 and after), whose dimensions they have had no hand in defining. Despite a close, structured economic community between New Zealand and Australia, plus military staff consultations, the two are not sufficiently close to permit a balanced regime of decision-sharing and proportional burden-sharing as part of a global—or even re-gional—security scheme. (In 2006, in Brussels and Washington, there was talk—finally—of expanding the Atlantic alliance formally to the Pacific.)

I found a congenial community of intellect in **Sydney** and **Canberra**, Australia's capital, as I had in Melbourne. Members of Parliament proved especially cordial and open-minded, as did foreign office people. No doubt I was steered to those who might share my concerns and insights, but I nevertheless came away with a strong feeling that Australians were people who could discern large truths and lead when they saw the need and opportunity. Sir John Crawford, one of the most interesting people in Canberra, and Sakuro Okita, a remarkable former minister of foreign affairs from Japan, put together the Pacific Forum on an informal basis (but underwritten by governments). Recognizing the growing interdependence of the Pacific Rim countries and their interdependence, in turn, with the developed Western world, these efforts paved the way for the later Asia-Pacific Economic Cooperation meetings, made formally intergovernmental in the midnineties.

Later, a kind of American diplomatic "mafia"made up of three retired consuls general—Brand, Robert Foulon (who had been Brand's counterpart in Perth), and Norman Hannah, an especially astute and serious man who ran regional American affairs from the consulate general in Sydney, enabled the early volunteer Committees for a Community of Democracies (1979–86, described in chapter 16) to establish close ties with an equally remarkable group of Australians. How fortunate we have been, on both nongovernmental and intergovernmental levels, to have gathered such a grouping of people who were both visionaries and doers to grasp what in 2000 became a new global movement, the Community of Democracies, a creation of more than 100 governments, with citizens' groups alongside them. That gets ahead of our story, although the seeds—at least many of them—may hark back to my 1976 Pacific tour.

I recorded my take on Sydney on this 1976 visit in my journal:

Wandered over the very historical "Rocks" today. Oldest bit is the ramparts of the 1804 fort, some houses and pubs almost as old. Mixture of many things British (older architecture, flags, the way meat is cut and displayed in butcher shops, the way many things, e.g., toilets, work primitively) and American—a superfluity of our TV shows, some clothing styles, huge new skyscrapers. Sydney on a working day is jammed with life, sidewalks overflowing, buying and selling; doing, doing. A good, vital place.

On 16 March, I spoke to a seminar at the University of New South Wales. Professor Julius Stone, Australia's grand old man of international law, was present and chatted with me in his office later. He called my lecture on interdependence of the OECD group "a revelation—it was like walking from the dense jungle into a sunlit clearing." (How could I not like Stone immensely—and instantly?) He urged me to talk to Professor Richard Gardner of Columbia University about my ideas (which I later did; Gardner was a charter member of the Mid-Atlantic Club of New York). Stone went on to say that the United States should press hard for reform of the UN—give the "spoliators" something to think about. Stone remained an important ally until his death a few years later.

In 1980 I returned to Australia for a second visit, and later for a third. I had an introduction to Peter Coleman, a bright MP, who invited me to speak to the Quadrant Group of Sydney, composed of 25 or so national movers and shakers. Several were members of Parliament, one was an Australian Supreme Court justice, and others were publishers, academics, and intellectuals of various sorts, some of recent European origin. It was a lively group, interested in the wide world outside, even beyond Asia, and I stayed in touch with them for several years. The Quadrant people published a magazine with that title, somewhat similar to *Encounter* in the UK and *Preuves* in France—all had been subsidized by the Congress for Cultural Freedom (see chapter 10), largely a creation of the C.I.A. When C.I.A. funding was withdrawn, *Quadrant* continued publishing; it had obviously struck a chord with a critical mass of influentials. Peter Coleman later wrote a fascinating book about the Congress for Cultural Freedom.

I was to return again, and yet again, to tighten up the links with the newly born Australian Committee for a Community of Democracies. John Wheeldon, an editor of *The Age* and a former Labour MP, and Jim Carleton, a cabinet minister in Tory governments, were the chief energizers of the counterpart of a series of such groups in South America, Europe, East Asia, Canada, Africa, and the United States. The Australians were hard driving, exceedingly intelligent colleagues in this general adventure.

✄

After a 2,000-mile flight from Sydney to **Indonesia** on 18 March, traversing the immense trackless desert that is the largely uninhabited central wasteland of Australia, we touched down in **Bali** for a four-day rest. When today one says "Bali" the horror of the terrorist bombing of 2003 comes at once to mind. But in 1976, Bali was a peaceful island (in every sense) of lush tropic beauty and friendly languid people, just beginning to be appreciated by Western tourists, and enjoying a culture distinctly its own—in this sense hardly a part of Indonesia.

We engaged a car and driver and a guide-interpreter, Mr. Masna, for a day, to take us to the renowned volcano, Kintamani, whose rim towered 5,500 feet above the verdant Bali countryside and whose crater was of stunning size, at least a mile across. Masna—whose command of English, French, German, and Japanese was both commendable and shaky—arranged beforehand (without consulting us) to stop at four artisans' and artists' shops along the way, to watch woodcarvers, silversmiths, painters, and weavers at work. We were kindly but persistently assaulted by the proprietors, who most certainly had promised commissions to Masna if we could be brought to take their bait. Masna and they were visibly disappointed when we, on a miserly scale, bought only one thing: an appealing wooden frog which, after some years out of Bali's humid climate, now displays increasingly large cracks. On the return trip, Masna spoke only when spoken to, and the driver accelerated with unseemly haste and some risk to our necks. For them, we had not been a good bet.

The countryside of Bali is lush, with all manner of tropical crops, lots of warmth, and no visible water problems. The farms are like hanging gardens, with the proverbial rice terraces spilling over hillsides and gorges. The population is dense, seemingly well fed and happy; a few beggars approached our car, but with dignity. Masna said a boy selling several dragonflies impaled on a stick was "sick." A dozen or more gamins assailed us to buy crude sculptures, beads, postcards—anything. An old man outside our restaurant, who said he was a "gardener at a famous temple," had stacks of coins before him on a stone wall and asked quite frankly for a contribution for himself. A boy of no more than 12, among a group of copper artisans, hammered away determinedly on a small anvil. Women, old and young, walked along the roads with stately carriage, bearing heavy headloads (no hands). An ant heap of men and women were busy on the approaches to a new bridge, at either end of which stood traditional monster-statues to frighten evil spirits.

Along the way to the volcano, we passed a sizable villa, surrounded by palms of various sorts and gardens leading down to a pool of water. Our guide told us that Sukarno, Indonesia's first president after Independence in 1949, had stayed here and had seen a beautiful maiden in the pool; she was summoned to him, so local legend said, for purposes that do not require elucidation. (Such legends are found around the world. A few miles east of Guildford, where we had lived in England, was a " Silent Pool," where King John of Magna Carta fame was hunting and chanced on a naked girl in a sylvan stream. As he stared, local myth has it, she was so covered with shame that *she* drowned herself.)

On the next day, we saw an exotic but interminable Barong play. Barong is a good spirit who fights with evil spirits. Both try to ensnare an adolescent named Sanewa. Our guide explained that the play is based on Hindu theology, the principal religion of Bali. "There are both good and evil spirits in the world," he said, and "they balance out over time, so there is no point in worrying; accept your fate and take your chances."

The people of Bali seemed poor but amazingly dignified. We saw slums, but nothing like the misery, filth, and penury that were to assault us in **Jakarta**, our next stop. Except for some officials and intellectuals we encountered, there was little human dignity on offer in Indonesia's sprawling capital. This was our first encounter with true Third World underdevelopment, an experience that simply cannot be shared or appreciated without being there.

(One New York day in 1966, I walked down an especially trashy block of Park Avenue, where it circles around Grand Central Station, with Charlie McVicker, an old-time Ford Foundation staffer who had served in India and Indonesia. I said, "Charlie, doesn't all this trash and dirt bother you?" Flash-like he replied, "Not at all. I love really *filthy* countries—this isn't at all filthy! It's just dirty.")

Jakarta was, for the most part, extremely filthy. After barely three days in Indonesia, the filth, the dense smog, the ramshackle buildings, the pitiful flea markets (where one could buy used suitcases—exceedingly used) got to us. There were traces of grandeur in some pockets of fading Dutch colonial architecture, some palatially wide avenues that reminded me of the road from Den Haag to Scheveningen. The Dutch built extensive canals in Java, to transport spices to the seacoast, but since 1949 most had silted up and become breeding places for mosquitoes. The residences of notables, the posh clubs, the fancy hotels and department stores, the public offices were all surrounded by high fences and armed guards. Between the islands of grandeur and the boulevards were connecting lanes, rutted, crooked, teeming with humanity. We learned that many of the inhabitants (six million in 1976) of Jakarta have no dwelling and sleep each evening wherever they can. Water is short in Jakarta; there were water-sellers everywhere who walk or ride the streets to sell supposedly uncontaminated water. In the evening, the streets of the dilapidated areas come alive with small commerce of all sorts: little canvas awnings sheltering four or five seats for a minirestaurant; vendors of sweets, fruits, and Chiclet chewing gum, whose potential customers are assaulted by small boys; and newspapers and magazines, each vendor offering only a pitiful handful.

One evening, our embassy had arranged for me to lecture a group at the home of former foreign minister Subardjo. Nearby, we passed a boy of twelve or thirteen sitting dazedly on a dirt sidewalk, too out of it to even beg. Sick? Very poor? Hungry? Drugged? Perhaps all of these things. Then the guards opened the heavy gates and we entered a glittering residence to mix with the top classes. The vast gulf between the two was dramatic; it made us almost sick. I can't recall what I told some of Jakarta's elites, but their questions were intelligent and friendly. I could only think back to 1958, when I had been reading the secret cables in Washington from our ambassador in Jakarta. At that time, I had little notion of what underdevelopment really meant—what it felt like—but as Sukarno was then dictator and gradually handing government over to Communists, I bought the idea, then current that if Communists secured Indonesia, Vietnam would then be caught in a tremendous vise between Indonesia and China. In those days, the "domino effect" seemed quite plausible.

By the time of our visit in 1976, General Suharto had long since ousted Sukarno, and I was told that economic conditions were gradually improving. One factor in the economy had remained constant, however: graft and corruption, small-scale and large, still permeated Indonesian life. A driver's license cost 3,000 rupiahs, officially but 50,000 slipped under the official's pack of cigarettes brought one instantly to the head of the queue. Government red tape, a businessman told me, was wrapped around every act facing the small entrepreneur; the Dutch had simply reinforced these native tendencies, never letting the native people learn to decide for themselves, let alone train them to govern or exercise some civil rights. It had been only worse under Japanese occupation.

Of an evening in Jakarta, it was impossible to look out from our tenth-story hotel room over a vast sea of hard-pressed people and their miles of shacks, punctuated here and there by a verdant, fenced private park or a couple of skyscrapers, and wonder, "What will they ever do?" and, more fundamentally, "How can it all work?" And yet, it does work, somehow, a quarter century later. We were terribly depressed, although people who knew India told us that the Indonesians were on the whole much less impoverished than the Indians.

In 1998, Suharto in turn was overthrown, and a period of turmoil set in. Finally, through two reasonably fair elections, it was Sukarno's daughter, Megawatti Sukarnoputri, who replaced Suharto, the man who had overthrown her father! Later, a seemingly able general replaced her. Because of its vast population, ethnic rivalries, growing Muslim-Christian hatreds, and political instability, vast Indonesia remains a major question mark. In the early 21s century, the prospects for good government and economic development seem at least hopeful. Democracy has real, if delicate, roots.

❈

Hitler would have loved **Singapore**: *ein Volk, ein Land, ein Fuehrer!* That's perhaps a little hard on the people of Singapore and their leader for forty-plus years, Lee Kuan Yew, but order above all pervades here, at the considerable cost of freedom. In 1976, we were amazed. No crime, no obvious dissension, contented people, clean streets, lovely gardens, no rats, no poverty. Singapore was, and I believe still is, one of the finest cities in the world. How? Why? Essentially, because the "father of his country" Lee Kuan Yew had a good British education, took carefully what he wanted of Western systems, created a rather benevolent but still one-party state, and laid down the law his way. He dominated a small populace (around five million) in one quite manageable city-state. He infused a brilliant reading of modern economics with Confucianism, exuded charm and English manners abroad, and befuddled the West's pouncing TV chattering classes for decades.

But it takes only a few days in Singapore, plus a close reading of what goes on there, to reach a conclusion: This is what docile, obedient Chinese Confucians can do if they have a manageable task of government and the right leader to tell them how. As I wrote in 1976, "Lee Kuan Yew is like Oliver Cromwell . . . a martinet, puritan, and authoritarian."

There has been a little change since 1976, but even Lee Kuan Yew is still senior minister, in charge behind the scenes, and a gently repressive government remains. Yet hope remains based on a gradual liberalizing trend.

Singaporean snippets soaked up along the way:

• Don't chew gum, and above all don't spit it onto the pavement; heavy fines ensue.

• Don't bring in marijuana or other drugs—if you do, you're destined for a hefty jail sentence (tough, like Turkey's, only much cleaner quarters) and probably 10, 20 or more lashes.

• Visitors entering Singapore with longish, hippy-style hair had it all cut off at the airport, or were sent straight home.

• On a bus tour, the guide pointed out the prison where hundreds of British prisoners of war were incarcerated after the Japanese lightning conquest of Malaya in 1942. Q: "How many prisoners are in there today?" A. "Seven."

• There are income tax deductions for garden expenses. Results: a garden city, and we should try it!

• There were but two or three members of Parliament from parties other than Lee Kuan Yew's—clearly window dressing.

• If you are a resident reporter for, say, the *International Herald Tribune* or the *Economist*, be prepared to see articles that you write deemed offensive by the Singapore government and the offending issues confiscated before they hit the newsstands. And prepare your editors and publishers for lengthy libel suits by His Eminence.

Singapore, we became convinced, is a city-state with no original culture (using the term anthropologically). Although the majority of the populace are Chinese, Singapore is not a Chinese city. Nor is it a British city, even though it seems so in many ways—with British-style uniforms, traffic systems, signage, imperial-red letter boxes, and so on. Can one create a wholly new culture? Singapore is trying.

For all its marvelous living conditions (for poor as well as for wealthy), beauty, modern facilities, and a splendid sense of order, Singapore is no democracy. But it is a good example of what one strong leader and a tiny made-to-order postcolonial state can do in a world of jungle politics and lousy economics in so many places. Lee Kuan Yew has seemed as if he would live forever. Nearly fifty years of the Great Man's rule has given his immaculate city vitality, riches, and an equitable distribution of wealth that the rest of Asia, with the possible exception of Japan, does not yet know. As a kind of insurance policy, Lee Kuan Yew also gave his people a treaty with the United States, providing us with a base to replace lost berthing privileges at Cam Ranh Bay in Vietnam. But is Singapore a model for anybody? Can it last? Can it liberalize?

✼

Toward the end of March 1976, we found ourselves in **Manila**. Comparisons with Singapore and Malaysia were inevitable. Again: for clues to the vibrancy of the Philippines' economy, look for the overseas Chinese.

There are a good many Chinese in the Philippines, but not in such proportions as in Indonesia or Malaysia and certainly not as in Singapore. This is a primarily Malay land, with overlays of four centuries of Spanish Catholic colonialism and then half a century of eventually benign American tutelage—but colonialism nonetheless. Perhaps it was a mistake for the United States to assume, after Dewey took Manila, that "the little brown brothers" (as Taft called them) were unready for modern government and economic life. One could ask: "Might it still not have been better to give the Filipinos independence once the Spanish had been thrown out?" But Teddy Roosevelt's government thought not, and perhaps he was wrong. At the time of our visit, and for some time to come, the authoritarian Ferdinand Marcos was in control. He was no Lee Kuan Yew, but in fairness to the Philippines and its people, the large population is cast over 17,000 islands sprawling in a vast area of the South China Sea and hard to govern. At the time of our visit, the Muslim insurrections were only just beginning, to continue into the 21st century's war on terrorism and to bedevil succeeding Philippine administrations, some relatively effective and efficient, but all reasonably democratic by Southeast Asian standards, all afflicted by corruption infusing the elites.

In 1976, Manila seemed large, ramshackle, and resembling physically its 1900–46 colonial foster parent, the United States, both in the grandeur of its 1930s-vintage public buildings and in its depressing suburban strip developments. Here and there were dignified old Spanish buildings, of great character and beauty. Beyond the great boulevards were tiny streets teeming with Asian life. All over Manila were unsightly telephone and electricity poles; when I remarked to our host (Kjell Aarnes, an amiable Norwegian I had known in graduate school, in 1976 a UN administrator) that some of the poles might well be buried, he suggested that the government could not risk burying them. They fear that "unsavory elements might rip the [precious] cables out of the ground, to some unsavory end." However, one could note various signs of progress; for example, the birth rate had fallen from 3.8 to 2.7 in the previous year. Things did not seem to work as well as in Singapore, but the Filipinos seemed nonetheless light years ahead of the Indonesians.

Kjell, my wry Norwegian friend, predicted that Malaysia would follow Thailand into the Communist camp in five to ten years. The problem, he opined, was not direct attack but subversion "à la Vietnam." (I noted in my diary that, "Zimmerly of the U.S. Embassy says Thailand has the countersubversion know-how, the troops and equipment, all U.S.-trained to suppress rebellion, but he thinks that neither the king nor any government has the will to resist. Now they have sent U.S. troops home, it seems the domino theory will work itself out. Kjell believes only the Pacific community concept will prove viable—any mainland area is untenable.")

❊

Another short stop in the kaleidoscopic tour, a dramatic contrast with Indonesia, **Malaysia** had plenty of everything and not too many people. Its capital, **Kuala Lumpur**, was a gorgeous city, built on and around hills, with a halfway decent government and a seemingly contented people. But there was dissension in this heaven, chiefly ethnic-demographic—45 percent of the people were Malays, 40 percent "overseas" Chinese (the entrepreneurial mainstays of most southeast Asian economies), the rest Indians and other leftover imperial transplants. The Malays—barely—had the upper hand and were trying to force "Malayism" on the Chinese. This seemed stupid at the time, but I gather that the policy has been more or less successful, with plenty of "affirmative action" to give the Malays a leg up on the good jobs and decent education. In my 25 March 1976 journal, I wrote:

The Chinese are the cleverer and the quicker, and by far the better businessmen. The Malays feel inferior and seek to legislate not just parity but dominion in all aspects of Malaysian life. School exam results are all listed in the newspapers; the Chinese excel, far out of proportion to their neighbors, and this too rankles. But after the Chinese party recently won an election, they made the mistake of celebrating too blatantly—rubbing it in. There were bloody riots.

During our 1976 stop in Kuala Lumpur, in the local newspaper a Malaysian director described her new production of *Hamlet* as being really about the awful fate of dying childless. This was a major problem at that time for Malays, who constituted a precarious majority and feared being overwhelmed, economically and demographically, by the bustling overseas Chinese.

Islam was even then an important factor in Malaysia's ethnic-religious cleavage. I noted this too in my journal: "[The Malays] are religious fanatics (Muslim) and charge everyone taxes to support their mosques. One very smart young Malay in the Foreign Office said that most of their leaders do not have a 'world historical view' but rather only the one of Islam. This leads to mistakes [he said], sometimes grave ones, in both perception and execution." In the intervening quarter century since our visit to Southeast Asia, the Muslim fundamentalists in Malaysia, Indonesia, and the Philippines have made considerable strides in cultivating the sociopolitical ground to foment much greater internecine strife and terrorism. The 2002 bombing by Muslim terrorists of a nightclub in Bali (whose population is almost entirely Hindu, and most of whose visitors are Western), the destruction of an American hotel and many of its occupants in Jakarta in 2003, and the continuing Islamic insurgency and terrorist acts in the Philippines put a quite different cast on not only Asian, but also global, affairs in the early 21st century.

Malaya was a British colony (Malaysia after 1963, when Singapore was separated from Malaya and both given independence) to which the colonial overlords had brought rubber trees, thus insuring—along with Charles Goodyear's invention of vulcanization—that Malaysia would have an industrial future. One hundred years earlier, the capital Kuala Lumpur was a village; by 1976 it had become a city of great modernity and beauty. Life in this capital smacked of all the latest: handsome government-built housing, attractive shopping complexes, and imports from everywhere, (I wrote then) "architecture which puts Seattle to shame." The British did better by Malaysia than the Americans did by the Philippines. The country has great mineral wealth; I added a sober note in my diary: "[Malaysia's] future should be bright, but its long coastline, open to infiltration from Indo-China, is an invitation to constant [Communist] subversive efforts." As the United States had withdrawn entirely from South Vietnam barely a year earlier, it seemed to us (and others) in 1976 that all of southeast Asia was precariously open to Communist penetration and takeover, by one means or another, in the years that lay immediately ahead.

One more puzzle-piece supporting this judgment was the opinion of Bill Knapp, a boyhood friend from Seattle, who in 1976 was ALCAN's representative in Kuala Lumpur and who, by reason of long experience in the Far East and considerable study, was something of an expert on China and the adjacent region. Bill was convinced that China would eventually displace the United States in East Asia, and that Japan would become China's satellite.

The glittering crown jewel of Britain's latter-day colonies (about the only one left by April 1976 that amounted to more than an unself-sustaining dot on the globe), **Hong Kong** was breathtaking. China originally ceded this land, plus Kowloon, to Britain, then "leased" it for 100 years in 1897. As we flew in, the colony's main island was ablaze with light from seemingly countless skyscrapers around the glittering harbor. We reveled in its modern center, lively with order and commerce. In the last quarter of the 20th century the undisputed financial center of East Asia, British Hong Kong was nonetheless indisputably Chinese, perhaps (although we didn't know it then) a foretaste of what the reborn Shanghai would become twenty-five years later. But aside from the wealth and show in the colony's center, the reverse side of Hong Kong became quickly evident.

As we left the colony proper on our second day and drove to the border with mainland China, another, less pleasant part of Hong Kong revealed itself. Sweatshop factories and myriad little shops and stalls lined roads and harbor. Drab but decent-looking and crowded mass housing abounded, as did the rural slums the nearer one got to the "Bamboo Curtain" separating us from Red China. In this borderland area, on both sides, crowded farms appeared untidy, hodge-podge, and distastefully unpleasant in appearance. Nor did the few solid, massive new houses built by a few obviously prosperous families relieve this poverty. The lack of taste—high walls, garish colors, and uninteresting shapes—to us was nigh unspeakable. It is interesting to note that a few years later, when it became apparent to the wealthy Chinese of Hong Kong that Britain's hold (and their presence) in the colony was doomed, a great many moved to Vancouver, British Columbia, where they promptly bought expensive older houses in the leafy suburbs. There they began immediately to tear down these nice old residences and build—to the limits of the shady lots—vast extended-family compounds that stuck out even more garishly in the New World than in the far eastern corner of the Old. We were often told that Chinese "liked crowding"; these later Canadian developments verified another small piece of "overseas" China as a cultural puzzle.

As I visited British Hong Kong officials, the American consul general Charles Cross (later a great friend when he retired in Seattle), and various business and banking people, other puzzle pieces began to slip into place. Not many Hong Kongers appeared to be sitting on the edge of the all-too-possible volcanic eruption that the 1997 handover, from Britain's governor-general Chris Patten to China's Deng Xiaoping, peaceably or otherwise, could have easily brought with it.

In 1976, Chuck Cross's main job, apart from helping U.S. businessmen or tourists who might need it, was to monitor—with a sizable staff—what was going on in Red China. Deng had started a tentative quasi-capitalistic rehabilitation of China's economy. He seemed much more stable and sensible than Mao, yet the prevailing political system was still Communist Party to the core. No one in those days could predict which way China would turn. No one foresaw the Tiananmen Square upheaval (which caused anxious moments for Hong Kong), but many thought upheaval of some kind or other was in the cards. And most of these liberalizing but disruptive forces have surely not spent themselves as the new century unfolds.

A cultural note: Before leaving Hong Kong, Colleen and I reserved dinner places at the Chiu Chow Restaurant, which had been recommended strongly by Seattle friends. They said it would be "authentic Chinese." It was noted for its steamed crab. What happened on that rainy night as we stepped out of a taxi, is worth quoting from my diary:

> On arrival, the bulky Chinese proprietor looked at us in surprise [as if we were unexpected], sent us upstairs (as we were obviously not regular clients, who all seemed Chinese). Decor was drab, seamy—Art Deco woodwork, weak lights. At half a dozen tables sat Chinese families or couples, reasonably well dressed. Only one young waiter spoke English (and that only scantily). With good cheer, he managed to advise us and take our order. The crab was fair, the "Delux Vegetables" tasteless, the spring rolls greasy. Halfway through, I dropped one chopstick. I signaled an older Chinese waiter, who was apparently a kind of supervisor on that floor, but his face reddened and he ignored us. A waiter brought new chopsticks, but then another brought us both fork and spoon. (Was it his compassion?—or had the old Chinese decided to make an example of these barbarians who could use civilized utensils only clumsily?)
>
> Near the end of the meal, the young mother at the table next to us picked up her two-year-old and moved about ten feet away, where there was a tin potty [fixed to a precarious rack]. The little

boy urinated and they returned to continue eating. On the wall was a sign, "No spitting!" We hurried out as quickly as we could, our heads full of speculation on cultural differences!

Although the physical changes from 1976 to 2000 and beyond do not seem as great as those in other states of East Asia, the political evolution (if one can call it that) in Hong Kong today seems startling. When I first visited in 1976 (and on several subsequent trips), Hong Kong was much more a Chinese city than Singapore, yet it was ruled by Britain with a light hand as a Crown Colony. Although I have not returned since Hong Kong was returned to Chinese sovereignty (1997), I have an uneasy feeling that at some point the government in Beijing will make an important misstep, and the goose that lay the golden eggs for the entire Far East for two generations will collapse. I hope that I am wrong, but in 2006 the fragility of the great metropolis that has symbolized what enormously free enterprise, ruled under essentially British law with wellsprings of Chinese entrepreneurship and Western investment, seems from a distance even more attenuated than it was in 1976.

Most observers in 1976 knew that somehow, sometime fairly soon, Britain would have to turn over the reins to Beijing. The new post-Mao Communist overlords seemed smart enough to leave the golden goose quietly alone. But in 2003 the strains of trying to integrate an essentially modern (Hong Kong) Chinese society—especially one possessing great wealth and built on British concepts of the rule of law and civil rights—apparently became too great. All seemed at least workable so long as there remained some kind of dynamic balance within the quasi-democratic body that "governed" Hong Kong under the fragile arrangements agreed to by Margaret Thatcher's government and that of Deng Xiaoping— that strange entity that neither party intended as a permanent solution to be ruled by a local business tycoon chosen by Beijing to work its political will.

But in the early 21st century, with a post-Stalinist, post-Deng (but still very authoritarian) kleptocracy developing a new China with a modern free enterprise economy, the jury is still out. From the point of view of China's Communist Party and People's Army leadership, the struggle to assimilate the immensely valuable but politically cancerous Hong Kong regime is a tremendous but necessary gamble. Chris Patten, Britain's last governor general of Hong Kong, deftly building in a few short years on the Colony's existing British rule of law and civil rights regime, left Beijing a Trojan horse in the form of a voting populace that demands full government accountability—fair and free elections to a representative Hong Kong local parliament.

The seeds of democracy, thus planted, will be difficult to kill. Can there evolve instead a gradual and peaceful merging of a much more advanced Hong Kong with a Beijing regime under increasing pressures from political ferment in a burgeoning capitalist economy? Can both the countryside and the new middle classes be contained? Will China's balance be weighed for freedom? In alternative scenarios, China could break up into warring parts, or become more rigid, fascist, aggressive, but capitalist—Hitler did it, after all.

Yet China's emergence into the modern globalized economy, especially its recent admittance to the World Trade Organization, entailing acceptance of Western-conceived rules of international commerce, will be a test case. This involvement may be too much for China's rickety political structure to assimilate before a political explosion occurs. Or can modern systems of protected civil rights, independent judiciary, and political liberties mature in time? A hundred years ago, Sun Yat-sen, China's father of democracy, thought so. One can only hope that China's future will prove benign, and that Chris Patten and Margaret Thatcher's gamble will win out.

❦

Our last stop in East Asia before turning to the *pièce de résistance*, Japan, was the great disputed offshore island, **Taiwan**.

Given the unsettled transition on the Chinese mainland, I had elected not to try to visit there. China thirty years ago was too big and unsettled a mass for me to swallow. Having seen a good deal of the "overseas" Chinese in most of Southeast Asia, I elected instead for a short visit to Taiwan, which I also thought might somehow, along with Hong Kong, point the way as time went on for the huge population on the mainland. At the very least, Taiwan was a "bone in the craw" of the People's Republic and a major strategic flashpoint between United States and Chinese interests, and remains so today. Later, Taiwan was one of the potential major crisis points that I had to deal with in the Battelle Study "World Politics in the 1980s," and much later in my book *Pax Democratica: A Strategy for the 21st Century.*

In early April 1976, landing in **Taipei** gave us the unmistakable feeling that finally we were in China. Contrasted with Singapore, Indonesia, Malaysia, the Philippines, and even Hong Kong, Taipei's streets and buildings *looked* Chinese, and the majority of people we encountered spoke only Chinese. There were some miniskyscrapers, but none like those we saw in Singapore and Hong Kong. Streets were wide and well paved; traffic was horrendous. People on these streets looked prosperous. Schoolchildren all wore uniforms. We were told that in the countryside there was also little poverty. Taipei's air pollution was considerable. In my diary, I opined, "I believe in respect of the general condition of the populace [Taiwan] is a cut above Hong Kong."

As Americans, we felt very welcome. In 1976, Taiwan was anthropologically still China, not an outpost of overseas Chinese.

We splurged in Taipei, staying at the Grand Hotel, the most imposing hostelry of our trip and probably of the entire Far East at the time. Its 12 to 15 stories stood on a verdant hillside, garish to Western eyes but nonetheless imposing in its vibrant red imperial Chinese architecture and sweeping tile roofs. The Grand was massive, but the large luxuriant woods surrounding it gave it needed scale. The rooms were cavernous yet spare and tasteful, each with a private balcony overlooking the teeming city. Each guest on arrival was immediately assigned a "houseboy," whose only job was to see that one's clothes, shoes, and quarters were always immaculate and that one's every wish would be immediately satisfied. Not since my early days in postwar Germany, when the High Commission provided all of us "occupation" families with maids, had I felt the same discomfort of a typical American frontier type at being "served."

The economic growth and improving social conditions in Taiwan were phenomenal, but I recorded that "the political plight of the country is pitiable." Free of fighting the grinding civil war of the thirties and forties, the Kuomintang performed in Taiwan much better than it ever did on the mainland, with an ever-rising standard of living. But by 1976, Taiwan was virtually a noncountry internationally; this, coupled with the still–iron hand of the Kuomintang over all political development, gave a fragile, tentative character to life around us. At Soochow University, for instance, Professor Liang told me that he could no longer get the full range of UN documents for his work; the UN and most of its affiliates were intimidated by mainland China, abetted with reluctance by the United States (which later agreed to the "one China" formula), into recognizing only the Communist government in Beijing. The latter still considers Taiwan only a province of China. When we visited, the Kuomintang government was still insisting that it would eventually "take back" the whole of mainland China.

At supper, Professor Liang, then 70, gave us his background. He had been a diplomat in the Chinese Embassy in London in World War II. He had served as a legal officer at the UN from 1946 to 1965, and at the League of Nations before the second great war. In Geneva, he had known Clarence Streit, my venerable friend who had projected a federal union of the Atlantic democracies. Liang was as much a "citizen of the Atlantic Community as anyone I know," I wrote in my notes, "and here, now, he is so isolated. I find it appalling." And I still do. Taiwan has managed to over-come its isolation in many respects over the years, but the strain on the new (and democratic) leadership of the country remains great. The more independent and politically Western Taiwan becomes, the more the rulers in Beijing fume and rage.

After long talks with people at the U.S. "cultural institute" (the face-saving term for an embassy, a term we couldn't use then, nor even today) and a few more Chinese scholars and newspapermen, I came to the con-clusion that the only solution for Taiwan was (1) a thoroughly democratic regime, replacing the aging Kuomintang leaders; (2) eventual indepen-dence; and (3) giving up the ridiculous Kuomintang dogma that it was the rightful government of China, and would someday retake the mainland.

The first condition has been realized, possibly beyond the hopes of any Taiwan and China watchers of the 1970s. The Kuomintang is no lon-ger the only — or even the dominant — political party, and representative institutions today characterize a free society.

The second condition, independence, seems still very far away. Even if justice demands it, international politics utterly deny it.

The third of my conditions — the realistic abandonment by Taiwan of the Kuomintang doctrine that the whole of China will someday be in its grasp—has taken place quietly, as a result of the growth of democracy and the replacement of the old leaders by a new modern elite, more of local Taiwanese extraction than of transplanted mainland Chinese. Taiwan now has a working multiparty system.

In the new 21st century, a move by mainland China to "regain its lost province" seems a remote possibility, yet still not unthinkable. The status quo is preserved largely because the United States reasserts, whenever necessary, its determination not to allow "reunification" by force. The Sev-enth Fleet remains a powerful deterrent. Furthermore, there is a good deal of traffic between the two Chinas today, much of it commercial and some tourist. For the near future, China's emergence as a more modern society, with a humming internationalized economy and a growing middle class, does not seem to foretell an impending power grab for Taiwan. But I still ache for Taiwan's people, a vast number of whom are pariahs in their own land. Quietly, the United States and the West have worked to find a place, however informal, for representatives of Taiwan in the less formal yet still important councils of the world. In 2003, Taiwan's government hosted the first of a series of meetings of parliamentarians from Pacific Rim democ-racies. This suggests that tiny Taiwan can be a beacon for the growth of Asian democracy.

After this brief visit, we were off to our primary objective, Japan, the nation that had ruled Taiwan (as Formosa) for the first half of the 20th century and which many thought might come to rule—or at least share with the United States—the world economy and the security of East Asia. This, our second, visit would be by far the longest and most memorable. I returned several times to Japan, in the 1970s and 1980s, so that the observations that follow must be taken as an overview after long periods of intensive, study. I have now become a routine—if rather more sketchy—"Japan Watcher."

The foregoing "snapshots" of key Far Eastern places and nations in 1976, with reflections on political and economic development pressures, illuminate the context for my growth in understanding of the world. The overriding reality in 1976 was still the Cold War. I believed—and remain convinced—that good governance based on democratic principles and a steady tightening of links among democracies are the twin answers, in the long run, to a Pax Democratica in a much more peaceful world.

15
Japan and the Atlantic-Pacific System

8 June 1982: *U.S. President Ronald Reagan addresses the British Parliament in an historic speech on democracy, noting a "global campaign for democracy now gathering force."*

The Future Is Not Always What You Fear It Might Be

It is interesting, from a vantage point thirty years later, to observe what has actually gone on in East Asia. In 1976, it was not difficult to project liberal quantities of impending doom on numerous fronts, but this is not what has happened. As I returned over the next few years, especially to Japan and Australia, and as I stayed in touch with East Asia watchers (and do-ers) among my American and foreign friends, I began to see hopeful signs. Except for Japan in the decade of the 1990s, there has been surprising, even startling, economic and political progress in the Atlantic-Pacific system. During this period the word "democracy" has become a worldwide slogan expressing more and more insistently what most people want, and what most of those in the Far East are gradually acquiring. The growth of GDP in most places, including China, has forged ahead—albeit with some setbacks in the late 1990s.

These positive changes have come about in part because the usually muted encouragement of the United States and others to form partnerships for constructive purposes has worked well. In Australia and Japan, in particular, I became aware in 1976 of something eventually to be called APEC—the Asia-Pacific Economic Cooperation forum. The product of original thinking by Sir Jack Crawford of Australia and retired Saburo Okita, one of Japan's best postwar foreign ministers, APEC eventually became a full-fledged intergovernmental organization that has helped to lower trade barriers around the Pacific Rim—including western South America—and arrange intercultural and governmental exchanges and cooperation on a broad scale. At APEC's fifth interministerial conference, held in Seattle in the fall of 1993, after formal deliberations President Clinton and government heads of seventeen countries repaired for an informal American Indian–style dinner on an island in Puget Sound. Only the Chinese president, Jiang Zemin, wore a Western business suit and tie (no more Mao jackets); the rest sported their newly acquired northwestern lumberjack woolen shirts! APEC was meant, in part, to insure that Canada, the United States, and key Latin American countries with Pacific coasts would meld with their Far Eastern counterparts in a vast, hopeful—if still essentially visionary—free trade area. At the 2003 APEC summit meeting of twenty-one countries in Bali, all summiteers observed the local dress code, Thai silk jackets.

Even more important than APEC, at least so far, was the advent in 1967 of ASEAN, the Association of Southeast Asian Nations, which brought together all the developing states of Southeast Asia. Its geographic borders stop short of Australia and New Zealand to the south, and also exclude China, Japan, and the two Koreas to the north. From its inception, ASEAN's leaders have put aside their more or less obvious political differences and commonalities (most today are democracies, fairly stable or still emerging) in favor of economic goals and loose cultural ties. Not wanting to appear as satellites, future or emerging, of Communist China, but also not wishing to seem an anti-Communist bloc, the ASEAN countries have welcomed such obvious nondemocracies as Laos, Vietnam, and especially Burma (Myanmar) into their ranks. Preoccupation by the larger international community with the problem of post-hypercommunist Cambodia—when finally admitted—has also posed puzzles for ASEAN. Democracy is not yet strong enough in most of these countries to act as ASEAN's fundamental cement. But the trend is hopeful; like-mindedness, at least in the economic sense—is growing. Early in the 21st century, ASEAN found ways to include China in its discussions and various initiatives, as the Bush administration, Brazil, and others sought closer trade links in various parts of the Western Hemisphere.

On the whole, such regional fora in East Asia have found their place in developing patterns of cooperation, in some cases among potential or earlier enemies. The United Nations, with its stuttering yet continuing nation-building project in Cambodia and the quiet but effective work of its affiliate, the Asian Development Bank (where Japan plays a leading role), have helped to create a much more hopeful outlook for all of East Asia. This continuous economic emergence of East Asia was slowed but not halted in the 1990s, during perilous times of near-meltdown in Europe, America, and Japan. The East Asian economies and most of the region's political systems show remarkable resilience and hopeful signs. In the early years of the new century, Islamist terrorism has introduced a new note of uncertainty and fear into the East Asian political mix.

Regional security structures, although they present a rather crazy-quilt pattern, also help to reinforce political, economic, and cultural ties in this huge, variegated region. A major linchpin of all this has been, in large measure, the result of constant intelligent attention by the American military in the area, mainly centered on CINCPAC, the headquarters of the Commander-in-Chief Pacific, at Pearl Harbor. A series of extremely astute and well-informed U.S. admirals have carried the burden of what in effect is a proconsular role. Admirals William Crowe and Dennis Blair come immediately to mind, although others have also been quietly effective in constantly tending military-to-military and (more important) military-to-political ties around the vast Pacific. American diplomatic missions in the area remain vital, but CINCPACs have a broader responsibility and sometimes greater regional influence, in contrast to country-based ambassadors. The United States has been most fortunate, and the Congress farsighted, to see to it that military and naval officers reaching high command have been picked, with few exceptions, from the finest candidates and educated commensurately. As in the stabilization and positive evolution of Europe, with American supreme commanders, the results in the Pacific region have on the whole been extraordinarily constructive; these top admirals and generals have often spoken for the Atlantic and Pacific alliance countries, as well as for Washington.

Japan in the Scheme of Things

For all these reasons and more, conditions today in East Asia are a good deal more hopeful than they appeared in 1976, to an outsider quickly looking in. Two major exceptions can be cited. The situation on the Korean peninsula carries with it in the 21st century the strong possibility of a nuclear war, which seemed only a remote possibility in 1976. And Japan, the media-target world powerhouse of the 1970s, has lagged behind its then-hopeful trajectory. Because I bypassed South Korea on my various Far Eastern trips in the 1970s and 1980s, not foreseeing its amazing economic rise nor its emergence as a modern, substantial democratic state, nor the new virulence of the iron dictatorship to its north, I hesitate to comment on the security outcome there. (In early 2006, news journals recorded a fascinating proposal by NATO's secretary general and SACEUR to form a new Atlantic-Pacific NATO that would include Japan, South Korea, Australia, and New Zealand.)

It was to study Japan's culture, its people and their institutions as a whole, that my wife and I spent two months in the island state in 1976.

And I returned several times over the following ten years, representing Battelle's interests and always visiting those Japanese (and foreign expatriates) who seemed instrumental as observers or actors in impelling the modern evolution of Japanese society. We made sure to study appropriate geographic nodes in order to put the past into better perspective. Here, for example, I was able to say, is the spot where St. Francis Xavier first set foot on Japanese soil at Kagoshima in 1549. And here, not far away, is where a few enterprising Brits built a nail factory, the first modern industrial establishment in Japan in a little stone building still standing, not long after Commodore Perry's "opening."

I have drawn the following account from my journals and personal archives, notes by my wife Colleen, and reports prepared for Battelle. In the 1970s, my bosses were especially keen to know how best to connect with Japanese companies, research organizations, government, and universities, in an attempt to achieve a combined Japanese-American effort that might broaden knowledge generally and lead to industrial and commercial advances. And I compelled myself to learn, in addition, as much as I could about Asia's giant (and to gain a rudimentary knowledge of its language) in order to get Japan within my sights as a leader in the developing Atlantic-Pacific System, as I then saw the long-term focus of my personal career interest.

In the previous chapter, I described the places we touched on our East Asian journey. From 23 February 1976, we progressed from Australasia northward through Indonesia, Singapore, Malaysia, the Philippines, Hong Kong, and Taiwan. The last two months of our trip we spent in Japan.

Teeming Tokyo

On 5 April 1976 we landed at Tokyo's new Narita airport, some fifty winding miles from the capital across a distinctively rural area. Narita airport remained incomplete for nearly two decades to follow, because a determined group of farmers and environmentalists physically blocked the construction of a vital third runway. General MacArthur's regime had given Japan a modern democratic constitution, and the laws and practices to go with it. But in the seventies and eighties, the Japanese government lacked the conventional powers of land condemnation (eminent domain, as we know it) and the necessary political will to push the project through, basing virtually all social decisions on patient consensus-building. (Strange how a people who ruled most of East Asia with an iron hand during World War II could today be so hesitant; but I learned that traditional decision-making in the normal course of Japanese history usually required a long period of consensus-building before dramatic decisions could be made.)

Meanwhile, "green" activists and farmers around Narita enjoyed the powers of civil society, including civil disobedience, that MacArthur had given *them!* (The governing Liberal Democratic Party also needed their votes.) This was only one of the many social conundrums we observed and puzzled over as we tried to understand modern Japan.

This damp, cloudy Monday was not a propitious day to begin our affair with **Tokyo**. The soggy capital's satellite cities and suburbs seemed endless as our taxi driver wound his way towards the metropolis and our destination, the International House of Tokyo. Because of the airport impasse, high-speed train service to Narita would take some years to replace the car or bus on endless, winding secondary roads, over small bridges and grade crossings. Rain poured down, and somehow the ubiquitous blue-tile roofs seemed depressing, an initial bit of culture clash. Our driver seemed sullen at first, but gradually changed his demeanor as I tried out my small-talk Japanese; at the end of the trip he was obviously grateful for a generous tip—which taxi occupants (or any recipients of service) are not supposed to give.

The taxi, incidentally, was decked with freshly washed window curtains and the driver wore white gloves; this was virtually *de rigueur* everywhere. And our cab, like others, was a top-of-the-line Toyota Cedric; we thought perhaps it hadn't been exported to the United States because the curious name wouldn't go over, or because (at that time) it couldn't compete with Cadillacs and Lincolns. Twenty years later, Toyota surpassed virtually all comers—foreign or Japanese—with Cedric's replacement, the Lexus. Today, we cherish ours.

Soon after World War II, John D. Rockefeller III, carrying on the family philanthropic legacy and exercising his own long cultural love affair with Japan, presented Tokyo with a unique institution, right in the classy Roppongi district. In rather un-Japanese fashion (for the 1950s) he put together a board of directors, mainly Japanese, to help plan and then manage an International House. It was intended to offer spare but tasteful accommodations for foreign scholars while they pursued their studies of Japan. It offered small but adequate and soothing sleeping quarters in Japanese "less-is-more" style but with Western beds and fixtures; a quite decent dining room and food; a reference library; conference rooms; and a small but enchanting Japanese garden. Given the teeming urban surroundings, I-House (as everyone called it) was a surprisingly quiet hideaway. John D had had a great idea, magnificently executed, which met our needs on this and later occasions and which has certainly furthered Japanese-Western cultural and intellectual rapprochement powerfully.

Throughout the years, as I returned many times to I-House, the staff were invariably kind, thoughtful, and cheerful. Not the least of their duties was to prepare for every occupant leaving for other parts of the big city a little slip with directions in Japanese for the taxi driver—always including a small, hand-drawn map! We soon learned that Tokyo was so large and spread out, with such a crazy-quilt pattern of streets left over from the days of myriad medieval villages and a system of house numbering that defied Western conventions and logic, that a well-instructed taxi driver was almost invariably a must—unless one could go directly by subway to a well-known major center and could decipher the subway map! In Tokyo, these and major station signs and downtown streets also included the necessary words in Romaji, or Roman alphabet.

To situate I-House, Roppongi district was a good choice. It was not a commercial or industrial center, but mainly a residential area for small but often tasteful individual homes and small apartment houses (again, many blue roofs!), with a convenient subway stop and some small shops. Just up the street from I-House was a small tempura restaurant, where one watched the delicate frying of seafood and vegetables, each one ordered separately, prepared before one's eyes. This, and a Roppongi coffeehouse (pre-Starbucks and not to be confused with the Bulgarian Coffee House on Roppongi's main drag!) were our frequent haunts for sustenance when we wanted a substitute for I-House's sparse though more than adequate Western menu. Among other things, I-House could give us a recognizable breakfast, or even a decent hamburger. "Western" was standard fare in the great hotels and small, in and out of Tokyo, but one could also order Japanese breakfast—not at all recognizable to a Westerner: bean soup, shredded lettuce over cold rice, with raw egg on top and pickles on the side. Accustomed as I became over the years to Japanese cuisine, I drew the line at classic breakfast.

Double-Barreled Culture Shock

With the usual eight hours of jet lag, plus the new sights and sounds and cultural differences to surmount, not to mention the distinct limits of my language skills, the immediate challenge of coping sometimes led me to near despair—and even more so after we'd left Tokyo, which leaned in a cosmopolitan direction. We had visited Japan three years earlier with the three-week traveling Aspen Seminar, but on that occasion all logistics, programming, and scheduling problems were expertly managed for our group. In a sense, in 1973 we had simply basked in Japanese culture as it was laid before us by experts for twenty-one days, with time enough to compare notes with our fellow travelers. (The English have a good term—"cosseted"—for such treatment.) In April of 1976, however, we were our own minders and trip planners, carving out every visit and connection with the people and the culture on our own. It is, for example, still hard to imagine that I found my own way around the cavernous Tokyo rail station, sometimes with immense "language slippage," to buy Bullet Train and steamboat tickets for remote islands, but somehow did it. I-House helped a good deal to fill this gap; but once out of Tokyo, we were strictly on our own.

To try to convey the double impact of what anthropologists call "culture shock" as applied in Japan, let me quote from my journals of the time:

> I feel lost when I go out [of International House] alone, like coming out of the cocoon. This sense of "lostness" must afflict all Western travelers to Japan, unless they have human guides and interpreters, or are themselves fluent [in the language]. Many Japanese speak a little English—and quite a few a lot. But the barriers are nevertheless great and many.
>
> Also, whether one is Japanese or foreign, the pressures of life in Tokyo are great. So many people are packed in this small space that it is easy to feel claustrophobic. Sidewalks in the Roppongi quarter, for example, are tiny in width. There is barely enough room for two people [abreast]; one is constantly stopping or stepping aside, or back of one's partner, to let others pass. After a while, it becomes a strain. Or take paper clips: they are two-thirds the size of ours.
>
> The vastness of America is truly wonderful—it makes people *think* big as well. The Japanese, Tadashi [one of my longtime Japanese friends] says, think of their country as "weak and small." How foolish! They do not understand the nature of wealth. (Years later, I am still convinced true wealth is mainly a matter of brains and hearts, and of expansive souls and daring, which not always but sometimes pay off.)

To the Provinces in Search of Japan

In advance of our trip, I had amassed a rather formidable (for me) list of people and institutions I wanted to visit. These notes had been culled from American and other Western specialists, and also from among the most important people we had encountered in 1973. Some I saw soon after arriving in Tokyo, but others were saved for a second round of Tokyo visits two months hence, close to the end of our long trip.

Osaka, our next stop, is Japan's Chicago, dull gray and smoggy. Stepping into the street outside our hotel, the dense air pollution was so palpable we could "feel" the particles and soon returned to our air-conditioned room. The river near the hotel was filthy. "No wonder," I wrote, "the well-to-do Japanese enjoy going abroad." In Osaka, as in Tokyo, one often saw Japanese in the streets and subways wearing white hospital masks. In the wake of international environmental protection treaties, especially since the 1997 Kyoto Treaty, it is likely that pollution problems (much more urgent-seeming than those of Americans) have been abated somewhat in Japan. Perhaps the problem lies partly in the Japanese mindset. Time after time, we would explore some exquisite, small private park, such as one in Kyoto where we visited the descendants of a family that had taught the tea ceremony to visitors, in the same house, for 500 years. Their tea pavilion was immaculate, polished and dignified, yet minuscule. Through the open doors one could see the carefully trimmed trees of all hues, the cultivated mosses, and the contrived brook. But outside the high wooden walls, on an ordinary street and just outside the teahouse gate, lay a startling amount of trash, just plain urban flotsam and jetsam, randomly distributed all the way to the filling station on the corner.

On a later occasion, we took local buses to a glistening white beach just outside Fukuoka; being Pacific Coast beach buffs, we wanted to see a Japanese beach. No bathers were there, nor lifeguards nor little coastal refreshment stands—just beautiful sand, strewn with all manner of plastic containers, rotting raiments, and just plain garbage. We gazed in wonderment and went back to lodgings quickly.

Private life in Japan is an art; care of public space seems not to be an individual's felt duty. The urban landscape, and the rural one as well, is thus often a good deal less pleasing than one would expect.

We took ship from Osaka to Kobe, and thence to the island of **Shodo-Shima**. The little town was literally constructed on rock and crags. A road linked a few inns and shops, bowered with traditional cherry trees in blossom along the way, some modest farmhouses and a few terraced rice fields, but the slopes of the mountainous rock island, and of many others throughout the Inland Sea, were by and large too steep for cultivation or even habitation. In other parts of western and northern Japan we saw constant evidence of the meticulous work of hundreds of years of unremitting labor by the inhabitants. This still left much of Japan uninhabitable.

When much of the population were farmers, well before World War II, one could imagine the sense of hopelessness that must have induced so many peasants to leave for America, or to follow military leaders who wanted more land in Korea, China, and other parts of East Asia. By our day, after MacArthur, mightily changed world economic conditions, and the extension of the Marshall Plan to Japan, new opportunities for a fresh industrial start had opened up. Japan's future had been radically changed, in thought and in practice, and its people given hope. Like Hitler, the Japanese militarists of the 1930s had also wanted *Lebensraum*, and in the early 20th century probably deserved it much more than the Germans. The world, with its vast inequities and problems of all kinds, works better in the 21st century; even in 1976 it was hard to imagine a pre-1945 Japan, but we did and could understand, though not sympathize, with those who had sought to take over East Asia by force; they were only doing what the Western imperialists had done. Today, thankfully, Japan has formed a fruitful partnership with the United States and the West.

En route to **Fukuoka-Kokura**, our destination for a one-month stay, we spent a night on an execrable small steamship, somewhat dirty and untidy but with excellent views out the porthole to more islands. This mildly unsettling experience was leavened by a morning stop at the island of **Matsuyama**, complete with a grand medieval castle, surrounded by cherry trees in bloom. We saw, on Matsuyama and later, many medieval Japanese castles. These had been copied from European models as interpreted by some of the European monks and traders who came to Japan in the late Middle Ages, and by a few Japanese who somehow got to Europe and back. (Yes, around 1400, a subject of the emperor actually made his way to Rome and back.) By now, I had seen castles of every variety in Europe but none had prepared me for the exquisite, detailed stonework of Japan's, whose 500-year-old walls were without mortar and whose stones were chipped and hewed to fit *exactly* against the surfaces of neighboring stones. I don't mean just fitted nicely, I mean *precisely*. One could hardly insert a penknife between any two rocks. In the overall system, each rock-wall surface held its neighbors together in an interlocking whole, sometimes a quarter mile in length and half a hundred yards high. By comparison, most of Europe's stone fortresses, not to mention the American frontier "forts," look ham-handed and slapdash. Something went on in the mind of the Japanese builder that was alien to his average Western counterpart: perhaps the amazing isolation of the Japanese archipelago over centuries made the difference, or the preoccupation of Japanese craftsmen with detail and perfection of form and function. This highlighted something of a great gulf between artisanship and art in the West; in Japan they were seamlessly fused, and remain so today.

Often a jarring historical disconnect arose in such places. In the courtyard of Matsuyama castle, surrounded by flowering cherries and walking up clean-swept, perfect cobblestoned ramps towards the handcrafted wooden towers, we were assaulted by incongruous frontier American music from a loudspeaker in the castle keep: tunes such as "Turkey in the Straw," "Home on the Range," and "Camptown Races"! What a curious mélange of East and West, of old and new, and especially of cultural diversity is this modern Japan! It is not East any longer, but it is also most definitely not West. Japanese acceptance and extremely selective incorporation of Western cultural artifacts of all kinds are amazing, sometimes incomprehensible.

We encountered another example of cultural misappropriation a week or two later. As we wandered through a Fukuoka town park, a life-size Greek-style statue suddenly flanked the path. On its pedestal was the word *Demeter* in English, not Greek or Japanese! We later asked one of our anthropological interlocutors (he and the others didn't know that was their function) how it got there. "Ah, so! Well, that was left over from a whole lot of sculptures of Greek gods erected here during the XVIII Olympic Games (1964)." Why Demeter, and only he? Answer: "Somebody just liked him, I suppose."

Another attempt to please (whom?) with a blend of cultures arose when one of the staff at I-House, Usui-san, labored mightily with a Tokyo travel bureau to find just the right *Ryokan*, or authentic Japanese country inn, for us in Matsuyama. Many friends had told us that we must experience *Ryokan*. On our 1973 Japan visit, we noted that one part of a grand Western-style hotel in the country had been given over to a graft of this modern excrescence onto an authentic *Ryokan*. A true *Ryokan* had only *tatami* mats for beds, polished wooden walls and floors (on such floors one had always to walk unshod), a deep wooden bathtub in the form of a cube with wooden buckets for cold and hot water, a tiny shrinelike alcove containing a small Buddhist statue or a simple naturistic object, always accompanied by a scroll with a small poem or aphorism in *Kanji* characters; plus toilets on the old Turkish model—a hole in the floor with a flushing mechanism. (On Bullet Trains built for the 21st century, incidentally, each car possessed two distinct kinds of toilets: one on the Japanese (and old Turkish) public model, with two small pedestals for the feet and a hole in between, and a separate Western-model water closet in another room.) The *Ryokan* also provided authentic Japanese cuisine, different but for the most part delightful for the Westerner, who probably by the 1970s had tasted *Sushi* and *Sashimi* at home, at least in major cities.

Imagine our surprise when our taxi rolled up to our *Ryokan* in Matsuyama. It turned out to be a rather horrible, and quite disconcerting, mélange between an old inn and the worst of the West. Let my journal tell the rest:

Our toothy, tiny *Ama* [mother, guardian, houselady] greeted us at the door of our room, to which we were escorted by four (no less) men and women who carried all our baggage. (They had stood at the entrance of the hotel as we descended from our taxi; all bowed in greeting.) Our *Ama* bade us sit down; she gave us hot washcloths to clean hands and face, and then poured tea. She asked when we wanted dinner (in our room), gave us each two kimonos, showed us the TV and well-stocked fridge, then vanished.

[T]he entrance to our chambers was concrete, with small rocks embedded. This was to simulate the "outdoors." At this level, we must leave our shoes. We stepped up four inches, in stocking feet into the apartment. There was a sink alcove, a room with Japanese-style (but porcelain, not wooden) deep [square] tub, and a separate toilet room. The toilet seat [not the lid] had a cover made of terrycloth (are these laundered after every guest?) and two red slippers, each marked "Room 208, W.C.," to be worn only in the toilet.

Our sleeping room had ten tatamis [a tatami mat is always the same size, about four by six feet]. There was a *tokonomah* alcove, but instead of a nice ideographic scroll, there was a garish Western nude and some tired flowers. The TV had four cost-free channels, and 4 more coin-operated ones. The wallpaper was peeling here and there; the top of the toilet [tank] was broken; renovation was long overdue.

Between our sleeping room and the windows/walls to the outside was a long, narrow room with two Western-style armchairs, a soiled green rug and a small table. Our view therefrom looked out on another garish hotel.

My purpose here has not been to criticize accommodations in a small, not-so-flourishing country hotel where the effort was unmistakably to please both Western and Japanese guests, but to show how the desire of this part of the East to accommodate the West, plus a certain kind of Japanese guest who might want "modern," but rather to stress the sometimes unsettling way in which Japan—at least at that time—was trying to be *both* its old cultural self and emerge as a new modern Japan, with cultural grafts it thought would get that message across unmistakably to the world.

In a much larger sense, this is both Japan's secret—its continuing "differentness" plus its selective modernization—and the global reality against which its whole economy and society bump up against continually. It has succeeded, in a century and a half, in virtually squaring this circle of cultural accommodation in ways that neither the Shogun's emissaries—

waiting in amazement and growing fear on the beach in Tokyo (then Edo) bay—nor Commodore Matthew Perry (1854) could have forecast. In the early 21st century, as Japan's economy and its political weight in the world seem again to be evolving from the uneasy stasis of a decade, the same questions are posed anew: Is Japan becoming a fully recognizable part of "the modern West"? Or will it always be a singular cultural construct, never quite "fitting in" and yet powerfully and unmistakably a partner of the Occident as it plows forward into the future? On this and subsequent trips we never quite arrived at satisfactory answers, but we learned empirically a good deal more about the phenomena that were central to the question.

Fukuoka in 1976

In anticipation of our trip, I had spoken at length with one of my closest and most astute Foreign Service friends, Arthur Hoffman, about how to acquire some deeper insights into Japan than would the ordinary tourist. I wanted to do in two months—plus one trip before and several after this 1976 sojourn—what had taken me seventeen years of living in different parts of Europe, insofar as possible. Arthur had lived in Japan twice, once in 1946 during the MacArthur occupation and again in the late fifties, helping to ease the Japanese into democracy and providing an "American window to the world" by running a U.S. information center on Japan's big southern island, Kyushu, at the city of **Fukuoka** (population around 1 million). Arthur had also had a long stint in Germany (where I first met him) and assignments in Czechoslovakia and at NATO, the OECD, and the U.S. mission to the new European Communities. He had spent a few months in 1975 at our Battelle Center in Seattle as a visiting scholar, working on a manuscript, and had returned once again briefly, heading a multicountry journalists' group touring the United States.

After some cogitation, Art said, "What you ought to do is go to a largish Japanese city and spend some weeks. Don't just rely on impressions of Tokyo, nor on fleeting ones of small towns and institutions. Get the *feel* of a place that is not the usual haunt of the tourist; I suggest Fukuoka, and I'll arrange something in advance for you." This was wise. We followed his suggestion and plumbed some anthropological depths in a very short period of time—not enough to make me any kind of Japanese expert, but sufficiently long and intensive to give me some cultural, economic, and political coordinates I never could have gotten from books or long chats with Western "experts." It helps to have lived in other societies and to have learned something about cultural observation. A lot of little things, seemingly unimportant in themselves, begin, like a mosaic, to gradually form a large coherent picture.

Art sent letters to the U.S. cultural center in Fukuoka, still existing more or less as it had when he ran it nearly two decades earlier. After all the introductions, the director during our visit, Jonathan Silverman, put us in the hands of Ito-san, an experienced and sympathetic chief "local" (as the indigenous employees of American diplomatic establishments all over the world were then known), who helped us chart our days in Fukuoka and surroundings. For a month, we met Japanese of varying stations and occupations who could tell us something to fit into our "cultural mosaic" of their country. Here are some samples:

• I had a long talk with a forty-year-old professor of constitutional law, who was gloomy about Japan's future and believed the country could turn Fascist. The problem, he said, is generational—neither the young nor the old believe in democracy and could well be manipulated by unscrupulous politicians. (Note: In Tokyo—but not Fukuoka—large dark vans, topped with loudspeakers, pop up all over the city, blaring martial "patriotic" music and ultraright-wing slogans, startling to the outsider, but few [locals] seem to pay any attention.) After thirty more years since our 1976 visit, I believe the fascist-militarist danger is not great, although—as in Europe—one can never be certain what social or economic upheaval, or a loosening of ties to the United States and other key developed democracies, might bring.

• We visited Shotukuji Temple, where the Japanese version of Zen Buddhism started. Nearby was a small city museum commemorating the two abortive Mongol invasions of the 13th century, which both made landfall on the beaches of Fukuoka. Dioramas and archeologists' finds of armor, helmets, and the like made history come modestly alive. Both incursions failed, unlike William's historic cross-Channel adventure in 1066. The occasional museum commentary told us that here the word *Kamikazi* was born—a "divine wind" which blew one Mongol invasion fleet off course and saved Japan—hence the 1944 mustering of Japanese pilots ready to sacrifice their lives in "divine wind" suicide attacks on American ships. Apart from a few reciprocal Chinese-Japanese visits in the 7th century, it appears that the Mongol attempts, a few lengthy visits by Western missionaries, and a strictly contained Dutch merchant presence on a small island in Nagasaki harbor, in the 16th and 17th centuries were all the foreign contact that the Shoguns would permit until Perry "opened" Japan in 1853–54. There is no other example of any consequence of a major country with a highly evolved civilization that so successfully resisted the cultural incursions of other civilizations, peaceful or otherwise. The early Chinese contact, it is true, had a crucial impact on the life of Japan, most notably Japan's adoption of the Chinese *Kanji* ideographs to write down their own (very different) language, always with their own Japanese twisting.

• We paid a visit to a local bank to change some traveler's checks and open a temporary account. It reminded us of the similar layout and "customer processing" of German banks of those days. Space for customers was small, for bureaucrats large. Bureaucrats, all in uniform, sat in rows facing the public, but took their own time about responding. The ones handling my modest request let *me* know they were doing *me* a big favor by letting me open an account! Hirasawa-san, the consular local who accompanied me, explained that the purpose of requiring the women employees to wear their unprepossessing uniforms was to eliminate "competitive dressing," which might embarrass some employees and perhaps some women customers! (At another time, I learned an old Japanese adage: "The nail that stands up on a crowded board gets hammered down!")

• We visited Nishitakatsuji-san, chief priest of the Tenman Shinto shrine at **Dazifu**. His ancestor, Sugawara Michizani, founded the shrine in 900 A.D. and was later deified. So Nishitakatsuji-san is the descendant of a god? (A Japanese friend said later: "More like a saint.") He had attended Harvard Divinity School, spoke excellent English, but seemed to see his function as carrying on the family function; the shrine was visited by thousands from all over Japan, mainly in the spring. Parents would buy a little paper prayer, wrapped in ribbon, and tie it to a tree at the shrine. Each was praying for success for his son or daughter in upcoming and crucial secondary school leaving exams. If one does not pass this exam, it means no university and much shame to the family. There are cramming schools everywhere to help students prepare, especially if they have failed once or twice. Each year, sizeable numbers who can't make it commit suicide. Nishitakatsuji-san's job was to ease this arduous process for families. We were in no hurry, nor was he, but when I tried to gain further insight into Shinto with probing questions about philosophy and comparative religion, there were no real answers—only smiles. Later, after a good many such encounters, and a good deal of reading, I came to a conclusion best expressed straight from my journal of the day spent at this shrine:

Cannot escape impression that the Japanese are a *super-ficial nation*. They do not delve. There is little interest in or study of philosophy. They are open to outside influences, but only of a certain kind, and/or to a certain depth. Technical things and styles sweep over them like a flood [Pierre Cardin scarves, as one example at the time]; they absorb, adapt, amend. But they are rarely touched deeply by these outside ideas, e.g., Christianity. "Just pile on another [cultural] layer" seems to be the general happy attitude. Perhaps they are so impervious because they were isolated for so long, and because their traditions are unbroken [at least] back to the beginning of the Christian era. Perhaps they are the oldest nation? (No, Persia is older, and so is China—but otherwise probably so).

• We flew to **Kagoshima**, Kyushu's southernmost city, for a long chat with Hatanaka-san, president of MBC-TV, one of Japan's most important television companies. Our long route to Kagoshima from the airport lay through miles of azaleas, planted carefully along the road. This southern portion of Kyushu is extraordinary for its lush vegetation, many mountains, and seaviews, plus active volcanoes, one just four miles across a strait. No wonder Kagoshima's Italian sister city is Naples! Hatanaka-san, a courtly old gentleman of perhaps 70 years, spent a great deal of money sending 15 local teenagers, every year for ten years, to the United States for a year in a U.S. high school. He showed remarkable affection for America, but little understanding of Europe. He looked at my "circle charts" (Appendix A) showing the progress of international institutions, then said, "I have always thought of Europe as just a collection of disparate countries, always at odds with one another!" He told me that it was a lot easier to attract girls for his school year in the United States because the boys "fear if they take a year 'out' they will fall behind their cohort as it moves to university." Time and again I was to hear the same complaint— from U.S. as well as Japanese teenage exchange programmers. (And strangely, the same was often said by those trying to arrange for young French men to visit abroad or participate in international seminars and the like; it is perhaps a built-in, mainly subconscious desire not to have one's cultural virginity assailed! Signs of two of the world's most watertight, impervious cultures.)

Fukuoka, for us, was not without its lighter side. Strolling down a street, there was a little cafe named in English, "Tea and Snack: The Passion." Elsewhere, another called "Original Cabin Snack." (Whose cabin? Uncle Tom's?) On a litterbin: "Keep Beautiful City." We saw a cocktail lounge named simply "Joy," and billboards for a candy bar called "Yell!" plus ads for "Salt" toothpaste and "Barona Sausage." In a large department store, the Women's Department bore a large sign: "We're Jeaning Company, Wrangler!" (Readers should keep in mind that there were plenty of young American sailors and soldiers to whom Japanese vendors wished to minister; the misuse of foreign languages is standard all over the world—and perhaps most often in the United States,)

Still more fractured "Englishese": TV ads for a male deodorant called "Mandom" (a corruption of "kingdom"?), replete with shots of Charles Bronson (his images, incidentally, were plastered all over Southeast Asia at the time); and a big Fukuoka billboard, advertising something unfathomable, but headlined "Tradition with GUTS!"

All over Fukuoka, there are crowds, crowds, crowds, and people appear to thrive on it. I noted in my diary: "The Japanese seem to be *claustrophiles.*"

One of our priceless memories is of a little Fukuoka hole-in-the-wall restaurant with the Japanese name, "Sometimes Clear, Sometimes Cloudy." This made a lot of sense in view of its menu, which was not written down, was potluck, and changed each day. There were no other foreigners but us. The habitués seemed glad to see us, with lively conversations held in their broken command of our language, and ours of theirs. We visited several times, and on the last evening, the manager gave Colleen a small, beautiful bowl, in characteristically rough Japanese style. Many such homely, earthy objects are made purposefully with asymmetrical earthen shapes, very different from Chinese pottery, always perfectly shaped to approach heaven.

Now and then we tired of Japanese fare in Fukuoka, and were lucky to find a Shakey's Pizza with a young Japanese baker who said his name was Chris and later came to visit us in Seattle. Shakey's offered entertainment—a lone banjo player, who plunked out a few Stephen Foster airs. Nearby was a Colonel Sanders Chicken outlet, unmistakable for the full-size effigy of the Colonel out front (like an old cigar-store Indian) with all his features intact—except that he had almond-shaped, slanted eyes. Our choices for junk food were several, once we had added a McDonalds. Most of the time, however, we ate what the locals ate, and for the most part enjoyed it.

Before leaving Fukoaka, we took a side trip to see a large steel plant, the Yawata Works at **Kita-kyushu**, the island's major industrial city. I had advised that my wife would accompany me, which seemed to disconcert the welcoming committee. But they gave us both white hard hats when we arrived and carried on. A managing director and the head of personnel and labor relations were standing on the steps of the administration building. At their side were three members of the works council (the trade union). We all went inside to a conference room to talk first about labor-management relations. The cooperative attitude, with both labor and management talking to us together, and answering all my questions about strikes ("never have them; we cooperate"), or changes in production ("we always discuss them together and all work for the good of the company"), were impressive. Then all five took us on a tour of the works. I had never before been in a steel mill, anywhere; looking into the molten steel in the retorts was like a glimpse into the mouth of Hell.

Nagasaki

It would have been as easy to go to Hiroshima, but we chose **Nagasaki** to look at the secondmost (and last) atom-bombed city in the world. The rest of Nagasaki's history was much more interesting; and besides, like almost everyone else in the West, we knew Hiroshima's 1945 history and were properly subdued even without seeing it. Nagasaki had a small memorial Peace Park, with all the gruesome statistics set forth. Rebuilding had been well done. We proceeded to older historical sites.

Deshima, a small island connected to Nagaski's inner harbor, was leased to the Dutch East India Company with the right to serve as Japan's sole export-import center, from 1641 to not long before Commodore Perry opened Japan, 208 years later. The Dutch Factor (superintendent) was allowed once a year to go to Edo (later Tokyo) to pay his respects to the Shogun; otherwise, the Dutch never stepped off their island. Japanese merchants did practically all the offloading and onloading with Deshima. This was a strange arrangement, but typical of the efforts of the Shoguns to isolate the country after the Catholic missionaries were, yes, expunged. After the Franciscans had been tolerated from 1549, when Xavier first arrived, to 1597, Shogun Hideyoshi, fed up with what he ultimately believed were political subversives, crucified 26 monks and some Japanese converts in the middle of Nagasaki.

We visited Nagasaki's large Catholic church, built around the time of the imperial Meiji Restoration. There we heard the tale of the 1597 crucifixion and another story from one of the priests (an Italian). It seemed that on the day in 1865 of the consecration of the new church, a group of modestly dressed peasants approached the officiating priests after the mass. They revealed themselves as descendants of 16th century Christians who had fled to remote islands and practiced Christianity clandestinely ever since. Now they could come into the open because the emperor had restored religious toleration, marked in Nagasaki by the opening of the new church.

These simple Christians said their families had practiced church rituals in secret, celebrating communion for example by performing it symbolically during the daily tea ceremony and by hiding their rosaries.

Once the Catholics had supposedly been completely expelled, the Shoguns decided early in the 17th century to rely for their sole link with the outside world on Dutch Protestant merchants, who profited considerably with their trade monopoly at Deshima and were not interested in converting anybody—just profits, thank you. Through this tiny funnel passed not only trade goods of all kinds, but a clandestine, growing stream of knowledge. Even before the Perry opening, would-be Japanese students of Western modernity learned all they could from friendly Dutchmen at Deshima, often while working there as servants. Eventually, these scholarly openings to the West came to be known by the Japanese as Dutch studies. It was incumbent on inquisitive Japanese to first learn the Dutch language, which they assumed was the speech of the entire West! There are scholarly artifacts of this "Dutch period" in some Japanese libraries and museums. In a minor way at least, Japan was able to make a start on learning about the outside world well before Perry's coming.

After Perry's few-holds-barred opening of 1853–54, an explosion of knowledge began, with Japan eagerly (if sometimes forebodingly in the view of the authorities) soaking up what the outside had to teach them. Beginning in the 1850s a good deal of the early Western contact was fostered in Nagasaki and nearby areas by European entrepreneurs—at first mainly the English. We saw the home of one of these, Thomas Blake Glover, on a Nagasaki hillside. Nearby was an old Japanese house, with a balcony overlooking Nagasaki harbor, which was advertised as the "home of Lieutenant Pinkerton and Chocho-san," the star-crossed lovers of Puccini's romantic opera, *Madama Butterfly*! No matter the fraudulence of this tourist trap, we loved it!

We took a small steamer from Nagasaki to **Kashimae**, to visit the islands where Christianity had supposedly thrived in secret. As the little ship pulled away from the dock, steamship company employees at dockside unveiled paper streamers bearing good luck *Kanji*, as passengers held the shipboard streamer ends as long as they could. As a loudspeaker blared "Auld Lang Syne"(!) we stood on deck and waved; all waved back, long after the streamers had sunk into the water. Strangely touching, if also incongruous. A group of our shipboard companions consisted of about two dozen Japanese men taking a characteristic "stag" holiday, without their wives, from jobs in their common workplace. This was the usual practice. Each "salaryman" (white collar worker) had his camera and often his bottle of beer. Not raucous, just excited on an outing, which—we were told—incidentally helped to reinforce company spirit.

Filtered through mist and weak sunshine, these islands, more than any other Japanese geography we saw, conjured up Japan as foreigners imagine it. There may have been as many as 99 of them, with twisted trees on tumbled rock shores and a few small fishing villages. In the most remote places, even a few small Christian churches had survived the intolerance period. We spent the night in what seemed a most authentic *ryokan*, with no nods this time to supposed Western tastes. We slept on futons before feasting on a true Japanese evening meal (no substitutions): a wooden tray, with indentations for rice and many kinds of seafood, all raw. There were the familiar *sushi* and *sashimi* (raw fish wrapped in rice and seaweed, and raw fish alone), sea urchin, sea cucumber, small clams, and whole baby crabs, which one ate raw, shell and all, somewhat like munching popcorn—all washed down with *sake*, of course.

Kobe and Kyoto

We now made our way up the east coast of Japan's main island. A brief stop at Himeji Castle, perhaps Japan's largest and most perfect medieval fortress, complete with almost excessively fine craftsmanship—obliterating all European counterparts I had ever seen for sheer loving care and artistic exuberance and flair. If Japan had had a Rococo period, this might have been where it started.

We lunched near **Kobe** with Her Britannic Majesty's Consul General Russell Greenwood and his wife. He was a droll fellow and full of knowledge of Japan, having lived in the country for years. Approaching retirement, she wanted to go back to the Mother Country, but Russell had his doubts; he would be content to live in Kyoto and teach English.

If one chose Japan to settle in, then for many like the consul general, **Kyoto** would be the place. It was Japan's medieval capital; the nearby site of the ancient beginnings at Nara was only historic, not so charming. It is said that the U.S. Army Air Corps had plans to bomb Kyoto in World War II, which would have obliterated its lovely old bamboo-and-paper structures, but Secretary of War Henry Stimson intervened. He had seen prewar Kyoto and did not want to be responsible for its destruction. (In the same way, Assistant Secretary of War John McCloy had put Bavaria's jewel-like medieval town, Rothenburg-ob-der-Tauber, off-limits to Patton's Third Army near the end of the war—the tanks and artillery were commanded to envelop but not touch the old walled city and move on.)

In a corner of Kyoto is an unusual enclave, Doshisha University. Its head, Otis Cary, was living out his days—as had his father and grandfather before him—in a carbon copy of a hall at Amherst College in

Massachusetts. Doshisha is one of several such American institutions of higher learning with religious roots, established in the 19th century. Cary and his fine family all spoke perfect American English, but it was obvious that culturally these generous people were neither fish nor fowl. Cary's life was admirable, his long service to Japanese-American understanding outstanding, but there seemed to be a price: though *bicultural,* in reality he seemed to be of *neither* culture. As a longtime student and practitioner of intercultural relations, I see this as a problem to which there really is no good answer.

In Seattle, my Japanese tutor had been a fine young man, Takada-san, who, fortuitously for us, lived in Kyoto in 1976. He became our guide, especially to Buddhist temples. Kiyumizu Temple provided a splendid view from the hills around Kyoto, but the real jewel of all such temples in Japan, we were told, was Ginkakuji (Golden Temple). Sitting next to a quiet pond full of water lilies, it was covered with gold leaf. A similar "Silver Temple" is nearby. The most startling Buddhist structure of all, however, was the old monastery on Mount Hiei. Eight hundred years ago the resident Tendai monks would muster in front of their chapter house for repeated swoops down into Kyoto to loot and burn and . . . whatever. Finally, the same Hideyoshi who crucified the Catholic monks had again had enough. He exterminated every last one of the Tendai around 1600 A.D. In the 20th century, Hiei boasted the most majestic scenery we were ever to see in Japan. Kyoto and its surroundings are many times thus blessed.

To finish the day, Takada-san took us to a drafty little teahouse for tempura and soba noodles, and then to a geisha show in the heart of Kyoto, where the all-girl (some pretty old at that) company mounted a play-and-dance skit that was a good deal more fun than Kabuki theater we had seen in Tokyo.

The following day, we resumed our trip to Tokyo, stopping near Kyoto to talk with the head of a university think tank, Junji Tanaka, and later some gentlemen of the Kansai Economic Federation. (Kansai is the overall name for the great industrial-commercial region surrounding the great centers of Kobe and Osaka.). Sakamoto-san and Ueno-san did all the talking (in good English); they were extremely articulate about Japan's problems, straightforward, and well informed. There was none of the "inscrutable East"; they called a spade a spade and were even willing to talk about defense problems. I liked them; they were hard-boiled, tough, concerned, and smart realists. Though not optimistic, they seemed to want the right things. These were the kind of infrequently encountered Japanese with whom I could most readily connect. Before and after this chat I found a good deal of the inscrutability that frustrates foreign observers. Some of one's interlocutors are keen to please, so one never is sure what they really think. Others simply smile, listen politely, and hesitate to reveal their own views at all.

Occasionally, one gets a brisk and unsettling brush-off. Several years later, after several trips to Japan, I had alerted the Mitsubishi Institute in Tokyo of my pending arrival from Seattle, and of my wish (for a third time) to talk Battelle business. We were hoping for some sort of partnership with the Institute to exploit an obviously big, if not yet very open, market for company-funded research projects (unleashing trained researchers to try to solve industrial problems). Although I had met with some of Mitsubishi's key people a few times, and always in impressive surroundings (sometimes like Henry Ford II's boardroom, two years earlier, in Dearborn), on this occasion, they arranged a new rendezvous: a most unimpressive little suite of offices (like the cubicles in Dilbert), made to wait half an hour, and then ushered into a pen only slightly larger than the others to visit with one of the "gaijin-handlers." (*Gaijin*, literally, means "barbarians.") These are people employed by every important institution in Japan—they always speak at least passable English, know how to make polite conversation, and show foreigners things they might like to see. But on this occasion, it was an immediate signal: Forget any immediate Battelle-Mitsubishi future. Someone, somewhere had decided this new kind of venture wasn't for them, so they turned off their spigot of pleasantries! All is not always what it seems, especially in Japanese business culture. Some research partnerships for Battelle did eventuate some years later, but the chief barrier was always the Japanese belief that they would rather obtain a license for some proven technology than take the risk of financing some creative research that might prove fruitless.

Again in the Imperial City

On 10 May, we returned to Tokyo for the remaining three weeks of our Japan visit. In Fukuoka, we had no trouble with taxis, but the vast size of Tokyo again provided a real challenge. Having spun around London for seven years, I was used to taxi drivers who had taken a stringent test on London geography before acquiring their special licenses. One could tell a cabbie, "Bank of England," "Victoria and Albert Museum," "Hayward Heath, Kenmore House," "the Reform Club," or almost any destination, and he would go straight there (meaning the shortest route through the mostly medieval street pattern, complicated by tortuous one-way streets). If a London address were in a hidden Mews or back street, the cabbie might consult his little book of maps, but these men never skipped a beat. Conditions were more or less the same in any major European city (although French taxi drivers were sometimes Algerian, white Russian, Romanian, or Guadalupean). But Tokyo? It seemed as if every migrant to the capital from any provincial town had immediately secured a spot cabdriving and tried to learn on the job. The nice little hand-drawn maps on tiny slips of paper that I-House provided in *Kanji* supposedly contained ironclad directions for the driver.

However, my first day of interviews back in the capital required three cab trips, and every cabbie got lost! The destinations in two cases were huge skyscrapers in well-known commercial quarters; both drivers nonetheless seemed puzzled by the I-House direction slips, turned them around every which way. We drove around aimlessly, until I insisted we stop and ask a passerby. My second driver did not know where the Tokyo *Hiru-ton* (Hilton hotel!) was and I-House had presumed any cabbie would know. I pulled out my standard but very basic Tourist's map of Tokyo, with the Hilton plainly shown in *romaji* (English phonetic characters) and pronounced by me in good Japanese. But the cabbie couldn't read these and finally asked other cabbies. So it continued, near the end of the day, in locating Sofia University as well. I finally abandoned the cab and found the university on foot, returning alone to Roppongi and I-House, my superannuated driver having proved unable to read the little map at all! Apparently neither the old Imperial Army nor the new schools provided courses in map-reading! Tokyo is a great city, fascinating but also frustrating. After two weeks and a number of fruitful interviews, we were more than ready to fly home.

What did I learn in this extended visit in Japan? One might characterize the lessons under two headings: I met a few fascinating characters, some of whom remained good friends and interlocutors for years. Others left a strong but sour taste in my mouth. Through them and in more general observations, I came to some general conclusions about Japan and the rest of the world.

⁂

Dr. Masamichi Inoki, civilian commandant of the Japanese officer-training college in Yokosuka, was a political scientist, a German specialist, and a social democrat—in other words a civilian in a military job, training cadets for all three armed services. Why had he been appointed (around 1952)? Because General MacArthur, at the beginning of the Korean War, determined that, despite Japan's celebrated "no-war, never" constitution, a sizeable Japan Defense Force was urgently needed to insure homeland defense, if it came to that. Within a few weeks of the beginning of war in June 1950, the South Korean Army and the U.S. forces in Korea had been pushed back to a small perimeter of defense in southeastern Korea, with no certainty that they could recover and retake Korea. For several years to come, the possibility of an American defeat, and a consequent "opening of Japan" to Communist conquerors, could not be discounted. The Japanese government acquiesced readily and searched for former Imperial Army officers who might staff the new forces; few without the old military-imperialist leanings were available. For the combined cadet school, it seemed crucial to find someone untainted with old ideas. Inoki, by then known as a superior student of geopolitics, got the job.

Inoki-*sensei* (*sensei* being the term for a distinguished academic and teacher) filled the bill admirably and put the College on the right track from its beginning. As a young man in the 1930s, he had followed his father's advice and studied German language and philosophy. Following World War I, his father believed that Germany would be the best model for Japan's future, insisting, for example, in 1927 that the Kaiser would be returned from exile to reign again. So Max (as Inoki asked me to call him) learned German and studied the *Reich*, its people and ideas, but never had the chance to visit there. During his university years, he became a socialist, thus, to the militarists, posing something of a danger. When World War II began, he was not trusted with a military commission and spent the war doing odd research tasks—on steel and on Germany—for the Mitsubishi Research Institute under contract to the Imperial Army. In 1944, the General Staff ordered Inoki to make an estimate of "how long Germany could hold out" soon after the Allied campaigns in North Africa and follow-up landings in Sicily and Italy. Inoki and a few colleagues studied what fragmentary information they had (in some measure, from an old edition of the *Encylopaedia Britannica*), then offered their conclusion,—"probably no longer than the end of 1944." They were fired—this is not what the warlords wanted to hear. In the event, Hitler staved off capitulation for several extra months, until May 1945, because of the Herculean surprise in the Ardennes, when an entire new German army of boys, old men, and a couple of SS divisions broke through to disrupt Allied timetables and exact sizeable casualties.

In the summer of 1945, a staff officer in white gloves drove up to Inoki's house with a belated check for his services and a sheaf of highly secret papers relating to his research, which he was asked to keep. Inoki declined. By that time, he said, he weighed but 37 kilos (a bit over 100 pounds) and was so weak from malnutrition "that I could not even climb stairs." When we discussed the atomic bomb, he said, "It was a terrible thing and it killed a quarter million people very quickly. But it was far better [for the Americans] to use it, because otherwise our emperor and our leaders would never have capitulated. Not only would many more

American lives have been lost, but millions of Japanese would have starved to death" or been killed trying to defend Japan's landing zones. (After reading reams of postwar debates and documents, I have come to the same conclusion.)

After World War II, Inoki-*sensei* joined the new Japanese Socialist Party, but later dropped out when he was unable to find anyone who would accept his dues. He settled for the Social Democrats, a quite respectable group like the British Labour Party, but with not much influence.

In a four-hour lunch-plus-long-talk, Inoki and I agreed on everything. "We are in the West," he said. He was keen on my idea of a Pacific Defense Treaty like NATO, and an Atlantic-Pacific community. As I sat there, I began to feel that Inoki was, in a sense, an incarnation of my old friend, Professor Hans Kohn, whose unflagging belief in the Liberal West was such a source of strength to me. Max and I remained friends for years, until I lost track of him in his dotage.

Dr. Jiro Tokuyama, the top defense specialist of the Nomura Research Institute and at the time a columnist for *Newsweek*, was of a different color. When I laid out my case for a Pacific mutual defense pact, including Japan, he told me "Why do you need allies for this? The Russians do it with only puppets. You should be able to do so, too." He said it was definitely in the U.S. national interest to have troop, planes, and ships in Japan and elsewhere in the Far East, so why should others (such as Japan) do more to help the common defense? The United States would have to do it anyway, he intimated. In my diary I noted: "I found this invidious. On reflection, I think he was taunting me. But it is a prevalent view, even in the U.S." Now, more than a quarter century later, it is fortunate that he was wrong. Japan has helped the common defense in the Pacific and globally—Japanese Navy units in the first Gulf War, some specialized troops and $5 billion cash in 2003 for Iraq. But our defense arrangement is still an unequal one, especially as Japan is not obligated to come to our defense if we are attacked. This is one of the origins of my later aphorism on Allied defense: How can an Ally be expected to share a burden, when it has had no hand in determining what that burden is?

Dr. Tokuyama was not exactly my cup of tea—green or otherwise—but at least he helped me to realize the complexities of many Japanese minds and the prevalence of profound belief in the dog-eat-dog Westphalian theories of sovereignty and power politics, still, in the early 21st century, the straitjacket of world politics. When he later visited Seattle, we had more productive talks; nothing beats consistent or repeated dialogue.

Masamoto Yashiro, the president of Esso Japan, was a dynamic man of early middle age with whom I found a near-perfect consonance of views: a world free trader, broad in his understanding of virtually every part of the world, encouraging in his view of the need for a Pacific NATO. He had served at Standard Oil (not yet EXXON) headquarters in New York, knew the top executives well, as I did at the time. As we talked, I harked back to my experience a decade earlier lecturing to midlevel Esso executives from all over Europe; it had been remarkable to me how varied in ethnic and educational backgrounds they had been, and yet how they worked and thought together with remarkable smoothness. Yashiro-san was definitely a prototype of the multinational leader that I felt we badly needed, in government, in education, in the corporate world, and elsewhere if the newer world emerging was to work right. Sadly, I later lost track of Yashiro, who at the time told me he was probably headed back to New York soon for a top executive job.

Sen Nishiyama, a truly unique and remarkable individual, was an accident of history. His parents were first generation Japanese, who settled in Salt Lake City, Utah, where Sen was born around 1918. He attended elementary school, joined the Boy Scouts, played baseball—in short, began to grow up American. But in the midthirties, Sen's parents decided to take the family back to Japan, where Sen landed just in time to be conscripted into the Imperial Army. I didn't learn much about his wartime experiences, except that he was lucky to have been made an interpreter and to have avoided combat. In the American occupation, Sen became an interpreter for MacArthur's staff and for many years was an invaluable local employee. His background and personality fitted him uniquely to be a go-between for the two cultures, not just a purveyor of linguistic meanings. When President Kennedy appointed Professor Edwin O. Reischauer, the noted Japan scholar of Harvard, ambassador to Japan, Reischauer made Sen Nishiyama his personal assistant. When we met Sen, he had retired, worked for a Japanese company, and kept his role as interpreter of Japan to America and vice versa, along with an active role in the International (nondenominational) Church of Tokyo. Sen was greatly valued by the Japanese for his objective understanding of "the Americans." When inquiring people from the USA such as I looked him up, he was equally willing, indeed keen, to help us learn the essentials about Japan.

�֍

Hisashi Owada is perhaps Japan's top professional diplomat of the post-war era, and now, in retirement, distinguished also for something he did little to bring about: he is the father of the young lady who married the Crown Prince of Japan in 1993 and gave birth to the likely heir to the Imperial Throne. (I say "likely" because no woman has ever been Japan's monarch. In 2002 there were sad newspaper stories about the Crown Princess's inability to produce a son and continuing debate about the possibility of a change of tradition.)

Owada was posted to several Japanese embassies in Europe, including the mission to the OECD, and to the United States. He was especially valuable to his country, and to ours, for his deep commitment to learning everything he could about the United States and its people. These efforts included leave to study at Harvard Law School and later to teach there. I did not meet him until 1984, when we attended a conference on "The Western Community" at the University of South Carolina and became good friends. Like Inoki-*sensei* and my other close Japanese friends, Hisashi and I shared important convictions on the need to encourage democracy worldwide, freer trade, the defense of the Atlantic-Pacific community of likeminded peoples, and the cultivation of leaders who shared ultimate values about the future of a liberal international regime. He has been truly one of the makers of the modern postwar world. After retirement, Owada-san became the head of Japan's (research) institute of international affairs and later a Justice of the World Court in The Hague.

✖

Kenichi Yanagi was Japan's consul general in Seattle, where I first met him soon after our 1976 trip to his country. We became good friends. He seemed to value my consuming interest in Japan and strove mightily to leave a positive mark on Seattle, which he did. One day, Yanagi asked me for a "confidential lunch"—just the two of us—to talk about something he felt was "extremely important." I wondered what the subject might be—trade matters, Japanese investments in the United States, defense questions? It turned out that he wanted my sincere opinion on the question "Would Japan ever be a democracy?" He had heard lectures by me and others on the subject of democracy in the world, and now I was on the spot. He seemed deeply troubled about the future of his own country, recognizing Japanese idiosyncrasies that appeared to impair Japan's fledgling democratic order. I think I reassured him by telling him, first, that *I* had distinct doubts about the future of democracy in the United States or almost anywhere, and that it would always be a delicate and fragile component of any modern society that practiced it. That did not satisfy Yanagi, as he knew Japan was "different" and said so. Again, I believe I reassured him, based on my overpowering desire to have learned all I could about his country, by saying that while Japan's practice of democracy was in many respects unlike ours, I believed the Japanese had made remarkable progress and that the stability of their system was probably no longer in doubt. And, a quarter century after that conversation, I feel the same way, only more so. When last I saw Yanagi—another remarkable man—on a later visit to Tokyo, he headed Japan's Overseas Aid Agency.

✂

Tadashi Yamamoto was an old friend from my Ford Foundation days, when Shepard Stone's office helped him realize a great vision—to establish the Japan Center for International Exchanges, which has acted for more than forty years as *the* key place for arranging all manner of nongovernmental interpersonal and interinstitutional arrangements with foreigners. Tadashi, a dedicated Christian, had attended college in the United States not long after World War II and caught the "bug" of what today is called "civil society," composed of nongovernmental organizations and foundations practicing the habits of liberal democracy. Tadashi's JCIE has, among other things, acted as the Japanese anchor for the Trilateral Commission and has made a name for itself worldwide.

In 2002 I phoned Tadashi on behalf of friends in Washington who were helping to organize the forum of NGOs that was to meet in Seoul in November of that year, alongside the foreign ministers from the Community of Democracy countries. I asked Tadashi for names and addresses of civil society leaders in Japan who should be invited. Sadly—and surprisingly—he told me, "Jim, if you want Japanese or other East Asians to attend, you had better send somebody over here in person to meet some key people and explain the context. Frankly, there is a great deal of resentment and misunderstanding of your government's perceived unilateralism right now, and it will take more than simple letters of invitation to convince most knowledgeable people out here." There was no change in Tadashi's and my cordial relations, but it was evident that despite the great efforts of both governments and private bodies over the years, the course of Japanese-American relations was at that time at least, a rocky one. Nonetheless, the great importance of Tadashi's work over many years can hardly be overestimated.

❋

Many other interesting and distinguished Japanese came my way in these years. These included a Japanese couple who had produced a number of bilingual dictionaries, two young entrepreneurs who showed expansive international traits, several serious scholars who in various ways deepened my understanding of their country and of international affairs, and more humble people who graced our paths—not least Waichiro Nakashima ("Nakky"), the college friend of a Seattle friend of ours and an engineer at the Honda factory in Sayama City. Nakky took us under his wing to show us "the peoples' Japan" on outings to favored places, such as the Great Buddha of Kamakura.

Just before our departure from Tokyo for home, I received a telephone call from Professor Nakahara of Tokyo University, whom I had met through the graces of a professorial friend in Seattle and with whom I had had a halting (because neither of us spoke the language of the other well) but sensitive and instructive chat. Nakahara-*sensei* called to say that he remembered we were to leave on this day, that he wished us "bon voyage" and that he regretted his duties at his university prevented him from seeing us off personally. This was more than ordinary courtesy, as I hadn't thought either of us had made a strong mark on the other—given our one, rather disjointed, meeting. However, this and similar incidents made clear an endearing Japanese principle—more strongly held than by Americans I think—that "the friend of my friend is my friend, too." A year later, I met a Tokyo diplomatic acquaintance, Fuji-san, at Harvard; after a long private discussion on his hopes and fears for Japan, he invited me to call him by his first name, Hiroki. "All my friends call me Jim," I said. We smiled, and I was very touched. I wouldn't want to live in Japan for a long time—too strange and difficult an environment. To most Westerners, Japan seems a crazy, upside-down, frustrating, problematical, and occasionally infuriating society. One of my Battelle colleagues dismissed the Japanese: "Oh, they're just economic animals." But America and most of "abroad" must seem equally difficult to the Japanese. On the other hand, as we packed to leave Japan, I wrote: "I cannot help *liking* the Japanese. They and their ways are infectious. I have great respect and affection and admiration for this people, and great hope for them, and for us, if we Americans can but measure up to the challenge" of working in harness with them to make a better world.

Taking Stock: Tentative Conclusions about Japan and Its Place in the World

In 1976, I formed some tentative conclusions about Japan and its people. Years later, after several more visits there and meeting Japanese often in international milieu, and after much additional reading and interchange with scholarly and diplomatic Western experts on Japan, I find I have modified my views substantially. Here are some conclusions, optimistically updated:

1. Japan feels vulnerable. Most Japanese I met told me that "their country is weak and small," and there was a widespread anxiety that the prosperity, stability, and growth of the sixties and seventies were somehow too good to last. In this they were correct, as the headlong growth stopped in the late eighties. However, I believe that the qualities and causes that now seem to be restarting their economic engine, lie mostly in Japanese minds and attitudes, which in turn have retarded necessary change in the institutions of government and business. In 2003, a stage of Japanese regeneration appeared to have begun, based in part on a restructured electoral system that has enabled an energetic prime minister, Junichiro Koizumi, to rein in the destructive factionalism of his LDP party and the domineering role of the top civil servants in a government of short-term cabinets.

2. A strong sense of insecurity persists, despite the continuing development of strong defense forces. There is fear—at times at least—that the United States under certain circumstances might not honor its nuclear guarantee. In a region prone to volatility, unpredictability, and instability, the U.S. alliance remains absolutely essential. At the outset of the 21st century, this situation appears to have stabilized a good deal, and mutual trust is greater. The big dangers for Japan (and the United States) now lie in dangerous trends in North Korea and in the future path of the Chinese.

3. The Japanese feel they are unique—Asian, yet different from other Asians, but not Western, despite all the accoutrements, a modern, democratic and highly industrialized people. This has led now and then to an identity crisis: "What have we to give the world beyond Toyotas and Sonys?" This question was answered in some measure in the 1970s and 1980s; more searching in an expansive period that seems to be on its way in the new century will provide further confidence.

4. Japanese leaders are proud that others increasingly accept their country as a major power. To be members of the OECD, the G-7 and

G-8, APEC, and other important international organs is a great honor, yet as a leader in its region and internationally, Japan is still "coming of age." Japan's support of coalition efforts in both Iraq wars—1990 and 2003—was a clear indication of an increasingly two-way street with others for Japan, and of growing international maturity.

5. High levels of literacy and education, a strong group ethic, and the homogeneity of the population have made for extraordinary economic gains, which—with pauses as with every other nation—will continue. The key Japanese "secret" is perhaps the successful transfer of feudal loyalties and village cohesion, beginning with the Meiji Restoration, to a modern urban setting and industrial culture. Japanese workers are intensely proud and highly motivated. The major industrial problem to be resolved is how to cope with the demographic challenge of low birth rates and increasing longevity, with the resulting probability that in a few years every two Japanese workers will have to support one old age pensioner. Other highly industrialized countries in Europe and later the United States are facing the same situation, in a bit longer time frame than Japan.

6. The old idea that the Japanese are no more than good industrial spies and copiers of Western technology should be discarded. Their capacity for innovation, impaired somewhat by their cumbersome language (hard to adapt to computers, for example) and by their political rigidities, is nonetheless virtually unlimited. The impenetrability of the language for foreigners, incidentally, cuts both ways: it is a major obstacle to *our* understanding what *they* are doing, or expecting.

7. A healthy rate of economic growth can be expected in Japan over the long term, but the images of "Japan as Number One" or of "Japan, the sick economy of Asia" are both inappropriate. Japan is, more and more, becoming a "normal" country.

8. Despite their general inscrutability and politeness, the Japanese can be a volatile people. Economically they can be plungers, as in global and domestic real estate markets in the eighties. Socially they are occasionally prone to emotional outbursts when their almost infinite patience runs out, or sometimes, for example, when they are joining colleagues in drinking bouts away from home. The Japanese political system is not repressive, but the social system is innately, if subtly, so.

9. An overwhelming majority of the Japanese people appear to have accepted liberal parliamentary democracy and made it their own, in Japan's own way. This is the healthy situation domestically; yet in my several visits I could detect no special or widespread awareness that democratic values and institutions constitute something impor-

tant that the Japanese share with other parliamentary democracies, or which are important to nurture in presently nondemocratic societies. This may be changing.

10. Japanese abroad are not especially liked. Their social structure and value systems are probably, on balance, a tremendous asset to Japan domestically but, in some important ways, a serious liability in the country's foreign relations.

11. A healthy majority of Japanese leaders in various fields seem to recognize the congruence of basic interests among the advanced democracies. But at the beginning of the new century, I must register a caveat, based largely on the 2002 telephone conversation I had with my friend Tadashi Yamamoto. It is evident that the governments and the people of both Japan and the United States need to pay increasing and constant attention to their broad relationships at every level. We have invested too much time in intellectual partnerships, in nurturing our common economic, political, and defense interests, to simply take these assets for granted.

12. It is a serious error, common to most Western visitors to Japan, to assume that Japan is a Westernized country. Many external features of the society are visibly Western, at least in form. However, Japan's *receptivity* to foreign ways is a good deal greater than its capacity for *digesting* them. Most of the basic values underlying Japanese culture are still thoroughly and fundamentally Japanese. It is extremely easy for some foreign observers to fall into the trap of thinking this gap unbridgeable, whereas in truth a great deal of Japanese life is culturally compatible with the West. However the differences can also cause excruciating, embarrassing, and sometimes difficult problems for both Japanese and Westerners, seriously hampering communication and understanding.

13. This intercultural problem remains the chief obstacle to achieving smooth, productive working relations across the board between Japanese and Westerners. Gradually—but only very gradually—the friction points are eroding; much patience and goodwill on both sides remain essential. The more that both Japanese and Westerners can live and work or study in one another's society, the more our Atlantic-Pacific system and the wider world of democracies will flourish. If the Westerner digs a little deeply in Japan, he will find the Japanese people thoughtful and kind, painstaking in their consideration for "serious" foreigners, open, receptive, and responsive. But it takes effort; the development of such personal sympathies and emotional attachments is the first, essential step in acquiring and maintaining a sense of community with another culture, especially that of Japan.

400   An Architect of Democracy

Japan in the Larger International Community

It is my conviction—greatly reinforced by numerous trips to the Far East and by contact with many Japanese, especially—that two contemporary points of view, common in high places, are dangerously wrong: (1) that it would be quite sufficient to go on with our earlier projects for European and Atlantic communities and, as necessary, involve the Japanese only as "associates" rather than full partners in an Atlantic-Pacific system; or (2) that the Euratlantic framework is now passé, as a dangerous number of both Americans and Europeans seem to think, typifying the two extremes of U.S. "unilateralism" versus a European "multipolar world." For Europeans, this seems to mean a balancing act in which such major "power centers" as China, Japan, and Russia join Europe to square off against each other or, in various combinations, against American hegemony, perceived as increasingly tangible and dangerous. For many Americans, another alternative means putting our "chips" on a new, alternative community of Pacific Rim nations.

In my opinion, neither is a good solution. On the east coast of the United States, the first view tends to get a greater hearing, while the second predominates on the west coast.

Since the end of the Cold War, the "West" (which in the 21st century usually includes Japan, South Korea, Australia, and New Zealand, together with Europe, Canada, the United States, and a few others) has become a less coherent concept. The breakup of the Soviet empire has put other geopolitical factors into play. The economic lassitude of Japan in the nineties tended to encourage many to discount its future—most probably in error, as recent indicators show. China's development has greatly increased consideration of Japan's likely growing role in east Asia. The nuclear nonproliferation problem, concentrated for Japan and her neighbors on dangerous developments in North Korea, greatly increases the uncertainty and potential volatility in the area. The problem of international terrorism, so apparent after 9/11, has not seemed to touch Japan directly in the new century, as it did in the great youth revolution of the sixties and seventies. However, it seems patently in Japan's interest to join the global coalition to dismantle the main terrorist networks. Her leaders seem to recognize this and quietly have been of great help.

In view of these and other international pressures, including those arising from a much more interdependent world, it will be necessary to redevelop new concepts that will bring the constructive energies of Japan, as well as those of other wealthy and reasonably mature countries, jointly into play, to make interdependence still more real and workable.

To redirect this grouping of powerful modern nations and retool a leading concept for them, a fresh set of goals has been bubbling to the surface over the past few years, building on two world trends: (1) the adherence of more and more nations to the principles and practices of democracy; and (2) the growth of international cooperation—in some cases integration—among nations, both worldwide and regionally, in large part is a result of "globalization." This can only be guided and brought within a tighter regime of international law, not stopped. Both multipolarity and American hegemony are illusions. These self-evident truths, as I saw them in the 1970s and 1980s, became more and more visible, despite occasional countertrends, as the 21st century opened.

In the final chapters, I shall try to explain how these conclusions have been reached and what some of us have tried to do to help build new, durable global and regional institutions and ideas to give "hands and feet" (as that crotchety old Professor Elliott of Harvard used to say to me, forty years ago) to international interdependence. There must be a central place for modern Japan in such a scheme. My next big set of tasks had to do with designing an adequate scheme and charting historically how we of the Atlantic-Pacific system have come as far as we have.

16
The Atlantic-Pacific System

10 June 1983: *Congress passes bipartisan legislation funding, and indirectly establishing, the nongovernmental National Endowment for Democracy, which President Reagan signs into law on 22 November 1983.*

Battelle and Public Service

We returned to Seattle in June 1976, exhausted but full of ideas. Most of the people I had seen and institutions I had explored in the Far East were later to be of direct value to my bosses in the Battelle Memorial Institute. Some were to serve as key contacts in Battelle's world of science and technology; others appeared in my general appraisals of the Far East and my views on the future evolution of where trends and events were taking us worldwide. I gave several seminars for Battelle colleagues on my Far Eastern travels and on the concept of an Atlantic-Pacific Community. Chapter 13 recounts the central points of my service to Battelle; I was available to its top officers at any time and was often asked for advice and counsel with respect to BMI's interaction with matters foreign and international.

It was extraordinary that Battelle provided me and some others the time and tools to do this work; in a small way it was perhaps reminiscent of the support the Medicis gave to artists and thinkers of the Renaissance and modern philanthropists such as Andrew Carnegie provided to science and the study of international relations. Battelle's top officers in the 1970s and 1980s were extraordinary individuals, all the more so for being natural scientists and engineers with a broad concept of the value of exploring all fields of human concern for the general good.

The University of Washington, my old alma mater, was a special resource, a well of knowledge from which I could draw, and a home for like-minded knowledge seekers with whom I could share ideas.

Several professors were playing with concepts that impinged on my own worldview. One in particular, George Modelski, organized an interuniversity seminar of scholars stretching from British Columbia to Oregon, interested in world peace and democracy. George himself was especially interested in long, five-hundred-year "cycles" of democratic development around the world. I also continued my involvement with the local Northwest civic scene, and especially with officials, nonprofits, and business executives concerned with what was happening—and what might happen—overseas to affect their work and lives.

This chapter traces how my thoughts and concerns expanded from 1974 to 1983, and my efforts—through extensive writing, networking with scholars, specialists and leaders far and wide, counseling to governments (especially our own), and organizing work in the realm of nongovernmental organizations—to benefit what I saw at the time as a growing but still pretty fragile and nebulous Atlantic-Pacific system. Above all, I wanted to help make constructive things happen, to contribute to a more durable and far-reaching association of like-minded nations.

Plans for the Future

To build on all that had gone before in my career, beginning in 1952 with the Foreign Service, incorporating the building of the European and Atlantic communities and adding a new perspective on the Pacific dimension, was not a simple matter. But, all-encompassing as this then seemed, I determined on some goals and some practical steps that governments ought to take toward such an expanded democratic community of nations, and towards which I would try to nudge key leaders.

Ultimately, my three months of exploration in East Asia resulted in a new idea for me, a global community composed exclusively of democracies, which a quarter century later the Clinton administration, in the person of Secretary of State Madeleine Albright, pounced on and today continues to grow. Others had no doubt begun to formulate a similar conclusion without direct help from me; but perhaps I floated the thought over the intervening years in ways that finally caught fire concretely, at a high level.

In 1975–80, it took me a great deal of conceptualizing (some might call it dreaming), before I got this set of ideas into proper perspective, at least for myself. My thinking went through several stages: Around 1973, while still in England, I first began to elaborate and embroider some of my thoughts about an Atlantic-Pacific community. These had in part impelled me to join the Battelle staff so I could flesh out the new concepts. The case for incorporating Japan, Australia, and newer democracies in the Far East I set forth in a book, *Uniting the Democracies* (1980). In the eighties and early nineties, the concept broadened again to a worldwide community of democracies; I put these updated thoughts into another book, *Pax Democratica: A Strategy for the 21st Century* (1998, revised 2001). This evolution in my thinking was greatly influenced by interaction with a number of people from several countries, including my own, in conferences, correspondence, networking, one-on-one discussions, and the organization of new, special purpose nonprofits.

As I wrote and talked to people in these years, I recalled often what Cabot Lodge used to say to me when we faced some challenge and I asked him for guidance: "How do I know what I think until I hear what I say?" And then he would launch into a soliloquy that broadened into a discussion and helped crystallize his thought. Literally, he talked himself into the outlines of a solution, or at least a sensible position for an intellectual attack. For me, Cabot's maxim became, "How do I know what I think until I see what I write?"

In the late seventies, it seemed to me that if I were to help reconstruct world architecture, I could best concentrate on three elements of a broad plan for bringing about change, and especially better integration of the democratic nations:

> *Concepts,* basic ideas that, if implemented, might make a positive difference in international outcomes.
>
> *Institutions,* which would always be needed to put concepts to work and insure that any new course in world affairs would outlast its pioneers. (Jean Monnet, the "father of a united Europe," often repeated his adage, "Without institutions, these efforts do not last.")
>
> *Personnel,* top leaders and especially the next level down of key personnel (using a military analogy: generals plus colonels and majors), who could staff the new institutions with dedication and competence, a corps of like-minded leadership. (This harked back to my work at Harvard with Professor Crane Brinton in 1956. In 1966 I published a monograph in *Orbis* applying these ideas to the strengthening of NATO.)

The first element of such a three-pronged effort, *concepts,* involved a question that first had to be answered for the sake of many contemporary leaders and the general public: "Why do we need a new effort at improved world order?"

Another set of questions, leading to the matter of *institutions,* was, "What sort of international architecture, embodying these new concepts, do we have already and how did it evolve? Is this a foundation on which to build future development?" Still further, "What sorts of societies and cultures were able to produce what we have so far, and why?" I had long felt that democracies—at least fairly well-developed ones—had an edge in putting together the basic elements of an effective international order. (Though personally hampered by the lack of a classical liberal education, this empirical reasoning eventually led me in the 1990s to study especially the works of Immanuel Kant.) By 1976, especially in Europe, it was clear that the touchstone of effective management of international interdependence rested in good measure on the relatively common and compatible characteristics of the integrating powers' systems of governance and the political thought that underlay them. Long conversations with my next-door colleague at Battelle, Raymond Gastil, helped clarify many questions, especially about democracy. Gastil was then, and no doubt remains today, one of the world's great experts on democracy. His propinquity in 1975–77, and that of several other interesting scholars, was of great help in adding to my knowledge of the components of a serviceable concept for managing the international system that I was trying to develop.

The institutions rubric called for a great deal of research. I had read many books and had collected copious articles about international law, international and supranational bodies, plus my notes on personal experience, but there was still a lot to learn. I returned to Europe many times in these years, to consult with people who were building and operating the new European communities (later combined into the European Union). The Council of Europe, the OECD, and NATO also deserved special attention. Were these and other new institutions adequate for the demands of the long-term future, let alone the challenges of the seventies and eighties? This preoccupation also required, among other things, assembling a considerable new library of books, journals, clippings, and directories that I still maintain. Above all, I was further impelled—to a large extent by my long talks with Bob Brand when in Melbourne (1976)—to further refine the "circle charts" I had invented in the fifties to show the progress of institution-building among the Western democracies (see Appendix A). These graphics helped me better understand and share with others what these combinations of states—by the seventies becoming not just European and Atlantic, but also Atlantic-Pacific—were trying to do together that they could not *adequately* accomplish alone. Brand, in his later retirement and teaching at the National Defense and Pennsylvania State universities, helped to improve the charts. Colonel Joe Bulger, a retired Air Force officer possessing great facility with computers, helped me to make the charts visually commanding.

I had some of these charts, in draft form, with me on my 1976 trip to the Far East and sometimes showed them to experts for their comments. The insights gained on that three-month sojourn enabled me to improve and expand the scope of the charts (see Appendix A), which others often found instructive. Some were later published by the North Atlantic Treaty Organization in its monthly *NATO Review* and also by an international association in Brussels whose journals and directories dealt entirely with international organization.

Finally, the question of *leadership* received a lot of my attention in these years. It became sometimes impossible to separate questions of personnel from those that dealt with institutions—both so often went together. In the process of creating or redesigning institutions, one inevitably ran up against the question: "Who is going to establish and staff these structures? Which people in governments and private life will be sufficiently informed and interested to ensure their support in building the institutions?" Conversely, I would often think about how to educate leaders, both current and budding, in ways that would help them run new organizations and practice new methods: "What new skills and perspectives would leaders of the future need? How could the 'national blinders' (which had so often doomed far-reaching international efforts) be overcome? Could one actually cultivate like-mindedness?" (For a more extensive discussion of these three principles the reader may consult Appendix E.)

In 1976–77, a number of my Battelle colleagues, plus an important cast of characters in the Pacific Northwest and Western Canada, made a valiant but ultimately unsuccessful attempt to launch what could have been a major contribution to the solution of the "successor generation" problem of insuring a seamless emergence of a fresh and even larger supply of like-minded leaders. The Western "youth revolution," which began in 1964 and gathered steam throughout the 1970s, left many indelible calling cards in history for subsequent generations to sort out. Twenty-five years later, by the early 21st century, much of what many consider a general degradation of civility—and in some cases of civilization itself—had its roots in the sixties and seventies, and in the failure of more mature people, essentially the World War II generation, to understand the gravity of our situation and the ultimately pernicious influences that were at work. University presidents and faculties, political authorities, and the leaders of churches and other vital institutions of modern society by and large faltered in their attempts to contain the deleterious effects and to turn youthful energies and enthusiasms into major efforts to create better societies and a progressing world. On balance, my view of this movement was a negative one.

On the occasion of the 1980 assassination of John Lennon, who might be typified as one of the leaders of this youth revolution, I wrote my 20-year-old daughter, in part:

[A] lot of [this] unrest, the neuroticism, the psychopathic behavior, and the splintering of value systems (all symptoms of social disintegration at a fairly serious stage) can be attributed to the impact of modern technology on tradition-bound societies. . . . The breakdown of religious values and institutions, the trashy character of many peoples' "recreation," the growth in crime and violence, the aimlessness of so many peoples' lives, the instant communication between the bulk of the world's peoples [and this a decade before the advent of the Internet and e-mail!], and the near-instant travel possibilities—all that and more is staggering too. The average person in the West is assaulted from all sides by the attractions and delusions of the consumer society, the fantastic technological possibilities for doing things people never thought of before, and by the problems of the entire world [again, this, long before CNN and the Internet]. It's no wonder a lot of people are shaken up, unsure of what to believe, ready to put their faith blindly into something or somebody.

This tumult extended from the University of California–Berkeley campus to the Free University of Berlin and the Sorbonne, points east and west of these, and even south to Latin America and west to Japan—incidentally also the world's most flagrant overconsumers of energy. In 1973 and 1979, a substantial majority of the world's oil producers, gathered in OPEC, boosted prices, and tried to hold the West to ransom, largely in an effort to pressure Israel. This, in turn, weakened the United States and its allies economically when they were still busy, after thirty years, trying to contain the expansionist Soviet Union. Sad to say, the faltering leadership of President Jimmy Carter (probably the best *ex*-president the United States has ever had) in trying to cope with a fractured world also contributed mightily to a sense of malaise, even fear and confusion, around the world. Carter's most egregious foreign policy failure was probably the ignominious, botched helicopter mission to attempt the extraction of American embassy hostages in Tehran; the world over, the United States looked as if it had clay feet. (In 2003, the Bush administration's forceful policy of intervention in Iraq, without the help of key allies, had the opposite effect, sadly symbolizing a presumed drive for "Pax Americana.")

The emerging Atlantic-Pacific system, the engine which at the time was the main flywheel in making the whole world work, was thus in the late seventies in bad shape. I have cited but two outstanding examples— the disaffection of youth and the oil-power squeeze—in a relatively long list.

A good deal of my time in those Battelle years, 1974–83, was spent not only in trying to define these ideas for a better world order but also in helping personally to create some nongovernmental (and in a few cases, governmental) organizations that could push the process along and expand the human network I had begun to develop two decades earlier. Serendipity led me, during and soon after the 1976 East Asian trip, to conceive of one such organizational effort, the Consortium for Atlantic-Pacific Affairs (CAPA), which combined all three elements of my long-range plan.

The Consortium for Atlantic-Pacific Affairs

As I prepared to spend three months in East Asia, a memo I wrote to my Battelle colleagues sketched the outlines of an ambitious plan we were later to dub CAPA, the Consortium for Atlantic-Pacific Affairs. I thought of this new institution as something along the lines of the Atlantic Institute in Paris, which I and others had kick-started in the late fifties and early sixties—more or less a comparable think tank for the Pacific Rim plus Atlantic countries, concentrating on the common problems of Europe, North America and the democracies of East Asia and the training of younger scholars in the process. The memo served as one tentative guide for my study tour spanning three months in the spring of 1976. I would take soundings in the Far East on the desirability and feasibility of the rather ambitious idea.

On my travels I began to see more clearly the needs of the East Asian countries, particularly Japan, and of the United States. The emphasis in a CAPA plan, I came to believe—and a good many colleagues were to agree—should be more on helping to enlarge the scope and depth of understanding of younger leaders from the twenty-four OECD countries especially, who were in urgent need collectively of new perspectives to make our interdependence still more operable. The personal ties formed among such young CAPA leaders would be expected to flourish, providing eventually a human network of real consequence. We would be very much in the business of preparing the emerging generation that would eventually replace that of World War II.

I talked about these ideas in Japan, Australia, and most of the other countries we visited in the spring of 1976 and returned with a general blessing (and an improved concept) for the CAPA plans. But in order to convince Battelle to "float" such a plan, it was necessary to achieve some kind of consensus among the older leaders in several key countries, including Europe and Japan; they would necessarily have to combine forces to shape the plans for the new institution in detail and find the financial means to launch it. Above all, the readiness and commitment of key Americans—especially our foundations—would be essential to success. But we would also have to know that their funding counterparts in other key countries would do *their* part. This required extensive soundings abroad, a process I had now begun, while juggling my other "projects," such as a book on the nature of the "expanded Atlantic system" and the retooling of the World Affairs Council of Seattle.

In the fall of 1976, I tested the waters for CAPA in New York and Washington, D.C., and also swung through Ottawa and Calgary. In the U.S. capital, a number of my friends in strategic places rallied to the cause. At this time, I was especially delighted to recruit Lt. Gen. Brent Scowcroft, who later became the national security adviser to President George H. W. Bush. Scowcroft had taught international politics for some years at the Air Force Academy and immediately saw the point of CAPA. He became a member of the CAPA Provisional Committee, which evolved into the Board of Directors.

It was not generally difficult to attract key American leaders in diplomacy and business to the CAPA cause. But it *was* difficult for them to imagine how to finance such a major and somewhat visionary project, especially in the far Northwest. Sad to say, by April 1977 (after I had begun a preliminary search for funds in the Seattle area), I confided to my diary: "Northwesterners are stingy." Most were also provincial. It took a leap of faith and vision to back such an idea and to see even their own home ground as the base for a world-oriented institution and to open their purses for an ambitious plan that might help shape the future. Nevertheless, several company heads and a few private individuals gave willingly. Most Northwest donors, however, made only small, tentative contributions for a feasibility study, not wanting to disappoint Seattle's "old boys' network," which we took great pains to recruit.

A quarter century later, I would have to amend my view of the limited philanthropic instincts and vision of my fellow Northwesterners somewhat. Today, many of those with new "dot.com" money, as well as some companies and individuals with "old money," are getting the hang of philanthropy; but today's contributions aim largely at local needs or at pet causes such as the environment or—as in the case of the splendidly endowed new $26 billion Gates Foundation—at a broad, obvious, and uncontroversial global need such as world health. The need for a much-strengthened international structure (sometimes requiring a largely mythical, yet widely perceived, "sacrifice of national sovereignty") calls for a degree of bold globally aimed entrepreneurship that few business and other leaders seem unable or unwilling to venture. This remains especially true outside the traditionally international Northeast, and to some extent among leaders in California and Texas; the nation's philanthropic institutions, with few exceptions, require a general retooling for the 21st century.

So far, twenty-first-century philanthropy generally seems to have little place in it for broad visions like those of John J. McCloy and Shepard Stone in the old Ford Foundation. The major foundations today have become a good deal more bureaucratized, less under the guidance of corporate boards, which also lack the wisdom and experience of McCloy types, and more under control of their midlevel academically oriented staffs. These younger philanthropoids tend to emerge from a fractured academia, armed with narrowly defined hypotheses (usually a result of their doctoral dissertations) about the ills of society, global or national. Just as there has been an overspecialization of knowledge in general, this overspecification of foundations' guidelines has done considerable damage to the life of nongovernmental groups with imagination. From the 1950s to the 1970s, foundations and especially the bellwether Ford set broad guidelines and then judged applications for money on their merits. Not so in 2006; today's foundations generally lay down narrow and precise guidelines. Woe to applicants who seek general support for expansive programs that deal with large ideas.

The Canadians, especially in the West, proved in 1976 and again years later to be at least a partial exception to this narrow philanthropic view. We were lucky to find some of them interested in the CAPA project. In 1976 Ottawa, there was some measure of enthusiasm for CAPA (including in the U.S. embassy—doubters in one office and keen proponents just next door), with the temperature improving as I proceeded westward through the provinces. In Alberta, my old Calgary friend Bob Borden took me to Edmonton to see Sandy Mactaggart, Bob's financier friend, and thence to the premier of Alberta, Don Lougheed. Mactaggart and Lougheed, egged on by Bob, were keen on what we wanted to do. We began to lay plans for a Canadian-American-led CAPA leadership training program, with western Canada joining Seattlites in ventures at two centers, one in Banff, where a new business school was a-borning, the other in Seattle at the Battelle campus. Sandy and Bob both generously supplied important start-up grants to the project.

At this time, we also tweaked the interest of a major Calgary foundation, the Devonian, which offered CAPA a tantalizing prospect: $800,000 if we could raise at least as much in the United States. In February and March 1977, I returned to Alberta and British Columbia to take more soundings; about this time, we in Seattle were gleeful to receive top-level support from Jack Clyne, a former B.C. Supreme Court justice and later head of the biggest Canadian timber company, Macmillan-Bloedell. He had also been a governor of the Atlantic Institute, my old Paris creation (and thus was trained in thinking multilaterally). Once Jack Clyne was recruited, we could hardly keep him still, nor did we want to; he knew practically everybody who was anybody in Canada and in New York, including David Rockefeller, whom he importuned for CAPA.

In December 1976, I had been invited back to Japan by NIRA, a major "futures" research organization, to give a paper at a Tokyo conference. I took the opportunity to talk with key Tokyo leaders (some of whom I had met earlier) to ascertain potential interest in CAPA. To this end we gathered four Japanese of international bent and two Americans living in Tokyo for a meeting at the International House. As usual, Mikio Kato, I-House's program manager, was his inestimable self, organizing, preparing, and following up the conclave. Kato-san and I continued to work together amicably for many years. CAPA was eventually able to count on an impressive group of Japanese industrialists, academicians, and diplomats. A special Seattle-Tokyo Committee was formed and later met in Seattle. From this group we recruited top Japanese for our eventual board of directors, including former foreign minister Saburo Okita, who had initiated what eventually became APEC, the intergovernmental Pacific Rim economic "ginger group." A vice president of Seattle's Rainier Bank, Clarence Hulford, was lent to us for two years; he had extensive business contacts in Japan and was of great help. Unfortunately, this high-level Japanese interest in CAPA never inspired financial contributions; Japanese philanthropy was still in its infancy.

Jim McDonald, Battelle's Seattle campus administrator, and I meanwhile worked hard to create a Seattle Committee for CAPA. Our prize adherent, and eventual chairman of CAPA's board, was Eddie Carlson, who was more or less at the time "Mr. Seattle" and near the pinnacle of a career of civic and business leadership. In early adulthood, Carlson, a "hometown boy," had been managing secretary of Seattle's premier men's club, the Rainier Club. He had worked with Seattle's movers and shakers; and, when an opportunity arose to run a major new Seattle hotel, young Eddie was ready. This hostelry eventually grew into the chain of Westin Hotels around the world. From this spot, Carlson was a natural in 1978 to be tapped to head United Air Lines. Every Seattle man and woman business or civic leader knew and respected Eddie. He put his heart into CAPA, helped us to recruit key Seattle people, and provided sound, practical ideas as to just how CAPA should recruit its "students" and what it should attempt to do with them. He also took time from his busy schedule to actually beard national leaders in their dens for CAPA.

A vignette shows Carlson displaying the homespun Northwest traits that could captivate foreign leaders. Early in 1977 we had a meeting in

Seattle of Japanese and Seattle leaders to explore the CAPA idea. One participant was Ambassador Shizuo Saito, who had been consul general in Seattle some years earlier. Eddie walked up to the ambassador, saying, "Welcome home, Dan!" Most Japanese liked nothing better than not only to be accepted in the West but thought of as "family."

Probably the most influential and productive CAPA recruit, after Eddie, was Dr. Charles E. Odegaard, who had just retired from the presidency of the University of Washington and was considered by many, then and later, as the best chief executive the university ever had. The "UDub" (as community wags had begun to call it), then probably one of the top ten in the United States, was my alma mater. I was enthusiastic about Odegaard and took pride in corralling him. He knew personally the key characters in the U.S. and European higher education scene and grounded his thoughts and ideas in his chosen academic field, the history of Europe in the Middle Ages. He related this historical knowledge to a masterful synthesis of transatlantic events right up to the present. Charles was, among other things, a member of the much-maligned but strategically important "Bohemian Grove" brotherhood, which gathered major public figures from the West Coast (and occasionally from other parts of the United States and abroad) for an annual one-week "campout" in California's redwoods. A great deal of wisdom in public affairs emerged from this network over the years. Odegaard was able to get direct entree for CAPA to many important people whom we might not otherwise have been able to approach. He was eloquent in explaining CAPA's educational and global political aims.

In the weeks before Christmas 1977, I visited several European countries to try to gauge the degree of warmth and conviction that a CAPA program for young leaders might elicit. Many of my interviews and unplanned encounters were depressing. These were the days of the Baader-Meinhof Gang in Germany and the Red Brigades in Italy, piled on top of the momentous problems for the entire West—indeed the whole world—by the 1973–74 energy crisis and by the unabated vicissitudes of the Cold War. Add to this the disastrous Vietnam War, and it seemed at times that Western society was itself in danger of coming apart. Fortunately, the great majority of my European friends and colleagues were still alive and busy; visiting them was a great comfort.

Here are a few excerpts from my diaries of the time, illustrating the depth of these many comradeships, but also the perilous and unsettling nature of the times:

(Brussels) To the Palais d'Egmont for a North Atlantic Assembly reception. Geoffrey de Freitas, as president, [headed] the receiving line with Belgian Foreign Minister Van Elslande, and Helen de

Freitas, whom I hadn't seen for about 5 years. Dinner then with John Vernon [longtime deputy head of NATO information] and Art Hoffman [public affairs officer in the United States Mission to the European Communities]; all is so smooth; we have been at this so many years together; our aims and our associations are so similar and all are congenial. This *is* the social tissue of community, stretching back 25 years.

(December 1977) Rome is marvelous. . . . Yet there is a sense of impending doom, bigger than Italy. How could one nurtured and protected by the Pacific Northwest ever sense this? The problems all seem manageable [if one is] out there. We are skating along, however, on the seat of our civilizational pants, careering down the icy slopes, and no one knows the end. . . . A rough, depressing time. My courage falters.

Germany hardly gives one greater comfort, although it can hardly be said to be afflicted with the unraveling effect sensed in Italy. The [Baader-Meinhof] terror in Germany makes everybody edgy and life seems so infinitely fragile—at least the civilized kind of democratic, free enterprise society so laboriously constructed since 1945. One could plunge Far Right again if the present regime can't maintain an acceptable level of law and order.

I had a lot of faith and optimism until recent months. Now I fear that the economic and social strains of the last decade are beginning to tell. The onslaught of the barbarians—the counterculture and the nihilists and anarchists, the mishandling of Vietnam, the oil crisis, the inability of Europe to exorcise the demons of class and hate, the indecision and deepening recession: it all makes a most unpleasant picture. Worried.

At the beginning of the 21st century, these old woes, so very real at the time, now seem remote and largely digested, if imperfectly, by Western societies. The end of the Cold War, the reintegration of another lost generation of youth (at great cost) back into society's fabric, the disappearance of Communism as an institutionalized threat, the staving off, if only temporarily, of the energy crises, the rocky spread of democratic governance, the half-flowering of an unprecedented unity and internal peace in Europe: all this makes one wonder why, in the seventies, there was such a sense of uncertainty and foreboding. However, this far into the new century, there are again substantial if somewhat different grounds for pessimism and a new, general apprehension.

Perhaps because of all that happened to the world's engine—the West—in the past couple of centuries, and the substantial progress in ordering global affairs, there remains, more than ever, an overpowering need for many institutions, such as CAPA hoped to be, for fashioning a forward-looking consensus among tomorrow's leaders. The absolutely essential like-mindedness among our societies needs to grow. But bound up by our distorted and disjointed array of national perspectives on the world and quarreling over petty matters (such as whether or when to throttle a tyrant, as in Iraq), we may be unable to cope with a still-menacing future. In the new century, this is truer than it was in the late seventies.

Back to CAPA's story, it was perhaps instructive to again try to answer Lenin's incisive question (regardless of the source, it has always seemed *the* question of the age): "What is to be done?"

Getting Organized. In 1978, the Provisional Committee for CAPA, composed now of two dozen or so of the most acute minds and visionary, energetic people the West could produce, went into action. I had secured largely positive (often enthusiastic) responses from more than 300 luminaries whom I had interviewed in the 24 OECD countries. A Curriculum Conference was convened, producing some precise recommendations as to how CAPA would work, whom it would attract, what it would ask of them, and what sorts of results one could reasonably expect. We aimed high—the core of the curriculum would consist of three-month seminars (including travel and briefings in Europe, the United States, and Japan) designed to highlight the main problems facing world leadership. We anticipated a glittering array of "men and women of the world" from academia, government, business, and labor as guides and tutors, interpreters in the broadest sense; we actually lined some of them up, contingent on funding. We arranged twin "anchors" for CAPA, in Seattle/the Northwest and in the province of Alberta. The brains and the practiced leadership were at hand, but a stumbling block remained.

Money. Our financial plans, carefully done, projected a "student body" of around thirty every three months, with tuition fees paid largely by their firms or parent institutions, sometimes by means of scholarships. For CAPA's first five years or so, through the planning, start-up, and full-operation phases, we projected a need for $2.5 million. Battelle could provide the home facilities. With a lot of help from individual members of the Provisional Committee in Europe, North America, Japan, and Australia, I spent several months scouring the world of foundations, wealthy individuals, and other institutions that might be expected to contribute. We were driven in large part by the "challenge grant" of the Devonian Foundation of Alberta, which required matching. Devonian's money was based on a 19th century coal empire. The latest heir to the founding family, Don Harvie, and his board were in the process of giving away all the foundation's money and CAPA was a congenial target. Dangling this carrot in front of American philanthropies and financiers plus Europe's likely sources of funds, I made the rounds.

At length, we had pledges of something like $1.2 million in hand (two-thirds of it Devonian's) but we could never get beyond that. Local Seattle sources for this kind of thing, mainly rich families and big companies, were less than generous; there were a number of gifts for the planning period of five to ten thousand dollars each, and in a couple of cases, twenty-five thousand promised, but never enough to make a big difference. (This was more than a decade before the dot.coms took off and made Seattle, for a time at least, worthy of the name of a second Silicon Valley, with a number of young millionaires starting foundations.) But in the eastern United States, we could never break new ground. Sources such as the Rockefellers, the new MacArthur Foundation, Ford, and the various Carnegie funds, in declining all gave us more or less the same two answers: (1) there were already quite a number of nonprofit institutions around who were doing "more or less" what we proposed (and if not already doing it, could possibly be "retooled" in new ways); and (2) the damning response that "something that ambitious could not possibly be carried off by the American and Canadian northwest." In short, because there was nothing like this north of California or West of the Mississippi, there was no reason to believe that the power of leadership *we* could muster was sufficient.

General Scowcroft, an enthusiastic provisional committee member, went with me to Chicago to see the leaders of the new MacArthur Foundation. We were, I think, persuasive and methodical, but some uncertainty in a new foundation, plus the opinions of the east coast Establishment as filtered back, doomed that ploy. The president of MacArthur, Jack Corbally, was keen on CAPA and later recommended to his board that we be given a $1.5 million grant—but his masters turned him down.

With Eddie Carlson, then the new chairman of United Air Lines, I sought Henry Kissinger's personal support in the latter's Washington office. Kissinger knew me from Harvard and Atlantic Institute days; Carlson was already a known figure in the top CEO firmament of the United States. We wanted Henry to join our future board of directors, and to help in corralling some east coast money. But he courteously begged off on both counts. More than two decades later, I now believe that Henry's unwillingness to throw his weight into this spur for multilateralism was grounded in his innate belief that the system of the most powerful nation-states dominating international politics would remain relatively intact for centuries to come. In his 1994 book *Diplomacy* and other writings, he made his position crystal clear: the Atlantic system ought to work smoothly, but for him NATO, the European communities, and other such bodies were mainly just useful fora to serve the national interests of the United States.

✂

CAPA's Leadership. Jack Clyne, our Canadian cochairman, knew most of the elites in his own country, as well as many in ours. He was backed up by a formidable Vancouver personality, Robert Bonner, who headed BC Hydro. Bob, fired and sobered by his World War II experiences in the 51st Highlanders, declared with fervor: "Never again! We've got to lay the foundations for a lasting peace *now!*" Beyond the Devonian challenge, we had some invaluable up-front seed money without strings from two modern Alberta energy and land tycoons, Bob Borden and Sandy Mactaggart.

Jack Clyne wrote an appeal to his friend David Rockefeller, the founder of the Trilateral Commission. We had an excellent backdoor approach to David as well, through his college classmate and relative-by-marriage, George Franklin, who had run the New York Council on Foreign Relations for years and had been my friend since the early days of the Atlantic Institute. When the Trilateral Commission was formed (1973), George was chosen as its executive. But neither the direct approach to David, nor George's personal involvement (he was a member of the CAPA Board), could move David Rockefeller. In answering Clyne's entreaties, he noted "that the persons who attended the [CAPA provisional committee] meeting were almost all from the Pacific Northwest. The center would perhaps be of maximum value for your area, and I am not certain that without some record of accomplishment it could draw participants from some of the centers in the East or from foreign countries." He thought existing organizations could more or less do the job CAPA envisaged, he said. In various ways, this point of view could be defended (although weakly), but CAPA was determined to be a truly multinational, and not just U.S., enterprise, spanning in its direction and program the entire swath of industrial democracies, at the time from Bonn to Tokyo and Australia, via the Pacific Northwest. Rockefeller presented us with a Catch-22 situation, which we were often to encounter: Unless and until we could prove our worth over a few years of operation, we could not expect to gain the start-up help we needed to "prove our worth." But how were we to get the money to even launch the program?

✖

The Speedboat King and the Dacron Tycoon. There were several brief but prodigious efforts undertaken during CAPA's "twilight period" to try to garner major support in the form of multimillion-dollar grants. Two are worthy of mention, as they showed the reluctance of most CAPA supporters to give up on what they thought was a splendid idea. One involved Norway and Japan, the other Italy and Canada. In hindsight, these seem now, a quarter century later, more curious and even hilarious than ever. In the early eighties the prospects seemed nonetheless to glitter.

One of our CAPA enthusiasts was Tim Grewe, a stellar, youngish editor of *Verdensgang*, Oslo's most important newspaper. Tim, one of my old-time friends from NATO days, had been personal secretary for years to Halvard Lange (longtime Norwegian foreign minister) and thoroughly immersed, through Lange, in the creation of the North Atlantic Treaty itself. In the late seventies, Norway had begun to develop aggressively the North Sea's newly discovered oil deposits. This led to new contacts in the world of affairs far afield, for Norway: One of these was the prospect of joint ventures with a highly visible Japanese financier, Sasakawa. The latter had built a vast financial empire in his own country, based on highly lucrative earnings from laying hold of, and selling, vast amounts of Japanese war surplus items in the early years after 1945. Sasakawa later ran up an even larger fortune from his sponsorship of motorboat racing, plus gambling proceeds in this new industry. Conventional Japanese industrial and financial figures, and most of Japan's media, looked askance at a man whose fortune had been amassed out of Japan's defeat, plus a second nest egg derived from a rather tasteless, if innovative, activity based on maniacal public gambling instincts.

When the CAPA Provisional Committee heard Grewe suggest Sasakawa as a CAPA "target," the Committee, with some enthusiasm, gave Grewe "a hunting license" (a term common to both Americans and Canadians of the still rather wild Northwest frontier) to probe the possibilities on his own. After some months, Grewe's probe foundered; his report: CAPA might lose much essential Japanese moral support, from government as well as industry and academia, if we were to found our enterprise initially on such a distasteful source. So we bombed, reluctantly, with Sasakawa-san. Later, some retired diplomats and businessmen found the appropriate formula for accepting Sasakawa's money, without strings or too much opprobrium, for an independent U.S. foundation that has promoted Japanese-American concourse with useful conferences and scholarly studies.

✻

The other tenuous hope for really big money—just possibly dwarfing the Devonian offer—came through Alberta acquaintances of a fabulously wealthy Italian industrialist, Felice Guarducci. In the 1950s, this gentleman had secured for his small textile company near Florence the sole license for Italy to manufacture textiles out of Dacron, the synthetic whose qualities eclipsed those of nylon. Guarducci told me: "I was walking down Fifth Avenue in New York and in a shop window saw this gorgeous, brilliantly white sweater and said, 'I must have that.'" Signor Guarducci obtained the Dacron license and built up his empire quickly, dominating the Italian market and engaging in some export as well. By the 1970s, Guarducci was not only rich but prominent, a likely target for the Red Brigades and other murderous Italian anarchists who were spreading terror by their seemingly random attacks on big industrialists and—worse—their families. Children were kidnapped and murdered or mutilated if not ransomed, business figures themselves suffered "kneecapping" and, for some, ultimate death. The idea of the terrorists, like counterpart groups in the United States and other parts of Europe, was to intimidate and disrupt the forces of order by scaring the wits out of Big Business and the politicians.

Guarducci determined to send his entire family off to Edmonton, in backwoods Canada untouched by such murderous antics (2,000 miles distant from a short-lived spree of terrorists pursuing *Québec libre*), to live and finish their schooling. One of our staunch Alberta supporters of CAPA, Sandy Mactaggart, phoned to tell me the Guarducci story and to ask my help for Signor Guarducci's seventeen-year-old son Fabio. The eldest son, Fabio was looked on by his father as his successor in running his vast multinational empire. Papa wanted Fabio, who had just finished high school in Edmonton, to go to Harvard and could I help? Sandy intimated that if I could successfully bring this off, Signor Guarducci might make a very substantial contribution to CAPA. My reaction: "If the father wants to help us, now or eventually, that would be very nice. But I want no part of a quid pro quo. I'll see if we can counsel the father and son and find a spot for him in higher education." Sandy agreed, and with his proper British background of integrity said the two deals were obviously to be "unlinked." But we of CAPA had at least wistful hopes.

I arranged for the son, Fabio, to meet me in Minneapolis for a long weekend. I enlisted Jack Edie, a prominent Minnesota educator, to sit down with us for long talks in a hotel. Jack and I quickly ascertained that although Fabio was bright enough, his poor mastery of English would never get him into Harvard or any comparable college. We also felt, even more importantly, that Fabio would need to have a much better idea of his career goals (or responsibilities, if he were later to take over the Dacron company) and, more broadly, of what he wanted to get out of life and a university education. These were new ideas for Fabio, who had understandably never thought much about his future. In other words, Jack Edie, as a superior headmaster of a renowned school and I, as a man who had run some international schools and seen a good deal of the world, counseled the young man. Fabio also visited our country home on Puget Sound a few weeks later, for more talks about the world and his future place in it, and how to prepare.

As it turned out, a small New England liberal arts college with whose president I was acquainted was unable to take Fabio on, largely for language reasons. Edie and I advised Fabio to study English intensively and, meanwhile, to probe the University of Alberta in his adopted "hometown," Edmonton. Eventually that university opened its doors to Fabio. One day, four years later, my wife and I received a phone call from an ecstatic Fabio: "Mr. Huntley! I just graduated from the U. of Alberta, and I earned all A's!!" We were delighted for him. We never heard from him again.

Meanwhile, not long after our counseling sessions with Fabio had set him on his course, Papa Guarducci expressed what he thought was appropriate thanks for the guidance by inviting me to his home in Prato, near Florence.

In early December 1979 I was in Frankfurt, talking CAPA and collecting materials for my next book, *Uniting the Democracies*. Somehow, Felice Guarducci tracked me down at the Deutsche Bank and asked if I was busy the next weekend? No, I said, but I had to go to London for meetings on the Monday, and thence back to Seattle, but I had a couple of days free. "Good!" said Guarducci, "Fly down to Florence and spend the weekend with me!"

Thus I was a cosseted guest in Guarducci's Prato villa. On the Friday evening, we drove to a vineyard near Siena for a raucous dinner with Guarducci's friends, some business associates and Italian nobility of various sorts, plus their wives and/or mistresses. Marvelous wine, food equally so. We left the Ducca di San Clemente, our host, in a somnolent alcoholic haze and drove back to Prato. On Saturday, Felice took me to Florence to visit museums and take tea with another of his aristocratic friends. At 7 a.m. the next day, Guarducci roused me to dress quickly, as we were expected on a prearranged boar hunt. I had protested that I didn't hunt but said I'd be pleased to come along. What an experience! Literally unforgettable.

Imagine a drizzly, foggy Sunday morning in the Tuscan countryside, with Guarducci weaving his way down winding country roads to a huge, wild holding, surrounded by high walls, with one entrance leading to a large farmhouse. The estate and its 9,000 hectares (about 15,000 acres) was leased by yet another Ducca, whose friend Guarducci and the latter's companions could hunt in this preserve any time they wished. We pulled up at the kitchen door of the gatehouse. Inside were three peasant wives, presiding over huge soup pots and pans of sauces. Guarducci took a large spoon and tasted the contents of each receptacle, suggesting a little more of this or that be added, and so on. We jumped back into his station wagon, plunged down a tiny lane for a half mile and pulled up at a small cottage. This was Guarducci's "hunting lodge," with a couple of beds, a tiny sitting room, and a large closet. From this, Guarducci extracted several hunting attires that he thought I would find useful for the day; I chose an Austrian *Loden-Mantel* and hat to match. Guarducci got his guns out and checked them over. We popped back into his wagon.

Aside from watching a very large boar meet its doom, the highlight of this escapade came with the midday repast. We reached this target by narrow lanes through scrub woods, passing some pheasant pens, and finally pulling up at a hexagonal wooden lodge. It consisted of just one large room, with open windows—no glass, but wooden shutters that were open to the elements, despite the wind and rain, a blazing fire in a fireplace, and a cook shed tacked on at the back. The same peasant ladies we met at the gatehouse had meanwhile transported the dinner with them to the lodge: roasted meats, vegetables, and plenty of wine; our host from the previous night, the Ducca, had brought that. But first was *grappa*—the concentrated Italian version of schnapps, brandvin, or gin—distilled from grapes. Then wines and the dinner. I'm not much of a drinker, but I watched the others enjoy the fruits of San Clemente's vineyard; some seemed not to have ended their party of the night before, but simply kept on topping up. The fire roared and the weather outside, although mild, was blustery. During the dinner and after, I noticed that the farmwives were leaving their shed-kitchen with huge plates of food, bound for a manger about fifty feet from the hexagon house. In the stable, tables were spread and a lively assortment of local types—peasant farmers, a couple of professional hunters, tradesmen, and artisans from nearby villages and towns—gathered. After they had consumed their meals, and we ours, these beaters and part-time game wardens—about thirty of them—flocked over to our hut and hung into the room over the four open window sills. It was time to plan the grand strategy of the boar hunt.

It was marvelous to see Italian provincial democracy—albeit flavored somewhat with a big dash of feudalism—in action: the businessmen and nobles gave their opinions (sometimes clouded by stupor) as to where the boar was most likely to be on that day, and what hunt tactics should be used. The townspeople and peasants had their own ideas and expressed these freely—which parties of hunters should go where and which groups of beaters should position themselves, and where, to drive the prey. Most weight seemed to be given to the opinions of a grisly oldster who hung just inside the door. The discussion seemed to consume close to an hour but was getting no place. Then Signor Guarducci took firm hold of the meeting: "We've heard lots of opinions, and good ones they were too. But it's time to make decisions: Now, Paolo, you and so-and-so, take your jeep and go to the western edge of the forest; Ducca, you and Antonio follow, but to the eastern edge; Giorgio (a marchese), you manage a group to the north," and so on. The beaters then knew where they should congregate, and when to start. It was all planned in a few minutes, and everyone set out for their appointed stations.

No wonder Italian industry and finance do so well, despite weak and changing governments in Rome! They give proper deference to the rich and aristocratic, yet the lower classes have their say as to plans. And the hard-charging upper middle class had the final say. I hoped that it usually worked this way in other milieus besides hunting.

Guarducci and I drove off for some minutes and parked near an indistinct crossroads in the mesquite (or so the plants seemed). We got out of the wagon, Guarducci with his gun, and waited. We could hear the voices and noise of the beaters in the far distance, sometimes closer, sometimes farther away. Then all was quite still. Suddenly, Guarducci cried, "There! There she is!" and a huge mother boar, with a little one alongside, came running down the road towards us. Guarducci raised his gun and fired twice; I was petrified, wondering if I had come to this backwoods of Italy for my own premature end. But the mother was also frightened—thank Heaven!—and suddenly veered off into the woods, about 50 yards from us, never to be seen again (that day, at any rate). We both thanked *la Divinità*. In a few minutes, a jeep came careering down the woodland road, draped across its hood was a huge male boar, tusks gleaming and quite dead. The proud hunters emerged to accept our congratulations; they said the beast would weigh around 250 kilos (570 pounds)!

Guarducci drove me back to his little hunting lodge. We hung up my borrowed togs. Then he said, "I am *so* tired (read: overcome by excitement and perhaps extra drink) that I simply have to sleep now. I've arranged for two of my companions to take you to Pisa so you can catch your plane to London." Of course I was delighted, and more so when his hunting friends showed up: A butcher and a barber from Pisa who, as beaters, had been indispensable to the aristocrats and tycoons who shot the day's boar. We three had a jolly time at the air terminal, with the aberrant leaning Tower nearby. I gave them both espresso at a bar and we recounted the hunt, as each of us saw—and embroidered—it.

Nearly a year later, in September 1980, Felice Guarducci rang me again and invited Colleen and me to spend two weeks at his villas in Prato and on the Mediterranean, an offer we readily accepted. No Guarduccis were present, only a butler and maid in Prato who prepared all meals, and a splendid housekeeper at the seaside, who again ministered to our comfort. Felice left a little Fiat for us to use; among other places we visited were the "Tuscan Manhattan," studded with medieval tower-homes of the grandees of San Gimignano, and later Siena. We paid a call on a Guarducci daughter and her husband in Fiesole, just outside Florence, and visited the great museums and churches of our favorite Italian city. We were most grateful.

So ended contact with Signor Guarducci. He had shown his gratitude munificently for helping his son—two weeks in his villas plus the unforgettable boar hunt—and felt that was sufficient. There never had been a quid pro quo arrangement, although Sandy and I had both kept Guarducci informed about CAPA and had oh-so-indirectly implied that he might want to help. So it often is with fund-raising, a usually harrowing, cliff-hanging experience for the luckless "social entrepreneurs" (as a recent Harvard graduate has termed them in his book of the same name) who want to change things.

CAPA Flames Out, but Is Reborn

In July 1982, after three years of intensive planning and organization, plus two more of sporadic seeking for big breakthroughs, the Provisional Committee for CAPA held a last meeting and wrapped up its books. We had a peerless international board, a program that a great many people of importance thought was ingenious and needed. One cannot however sustain such a search for launch mechanisms and wherewithal indefinitely. Most precisely the lack of funds finally did CAPA in, as a protoinstitution.

But the story fortunately doesn't quite end here. In 1985, I helped the University of South Carolina put on a conference, "The Future of the Western Community," which brought together a stellar cast, including some of those who had helped to nurture the ill-fated CAPA. George H. W. Bush, then vice president, spoke. Conferees included Lord Carrington, the former British foreign secretary, Lawrence Eagleburger and Brent Scowcroft, later to figure prominently in Bush's presidential administration. The conference made some policy recommendations to governments and the private sector; one was to create a new foundation, or several in various countries, which would collect and disburse funds to nonprofit groups that incubated imaginative projects to link the West together more closely.

Sir David Wills, a quiet but most effective and generous British philanthropist, was one of the CAPA believers present at the South Carolina gathering. Earlier in 1985, David had told me that he was going to think over the "foundation idea," and he did. The South Carolina conference (with a resolution on the importance of new, targeted foundations) reinforced his conviction. Two years later, after he failed to attract other monied figures in Europe (and sometimes elsewhere too—he asked the Sultan of Brunei for a cool billion or so, but in vain), he created a new grant-making foundation, beginning modestly with a single project: a new NGO in London that one might call CAPA II, with aims and methods very like those of the original CAPA. By the beginning of the new millennium, David's group, the 21st Century Trust, had shepherded well over 1,000 young leaders through the thickets of international politics in its well-fashioned seminars.

So CAPA didn't die, but was resurrected and given new hands and feet, and money, to suit the times in the late 1980s. Chris Patten, the energetic foreign affairs commissioner for the European Union, became the new millennium chairman of the Trust, and a group of prestigious trustees has given enthusiastic backing. Sir David passed away in 2000, secure in the knowledge that through the Trust and his other main creations, the Ditchley center for established transatlantic leaders' conferences and the Atlantic (later United World) Colleges, he had done a great deal to build the social tissue of a future strong community of democracies.

So, the CAPA idea lives on, through an increasingly broad and strong network of 21st century alumni from around the world. I never imagined that the CAPA idea would be realized in this way, but there is immense satisfaction in knowing that eventually it materialized. By 2003, when the transatlantic connection began to experience dangerous and possibly fatal tensions, to me there was an obvious need for a dozen or so centers, built on the foundations of CAPA, the 21st Century Trust, Ditchley, and—on the official level—the NATO Defense College.

The Evolution of the Committees for a Community of Democracies

If dates and times of this accounting of the late seventies and eighties sometimes puzzle or confuse the reader, that is because I was involved in several projects—not always closely linked—at the same time, or during overlapping periods. My book *Uniting the Democracies: Institutions of the Emerging Atlantic-Pacific System* was published in 1980 and led to a number of articles and speaking engagements, plus various nonprofit efforts to see its principles eventually established in the policies of the "overde-veloped" countries. In 1975, I had testified before Congress in favor of a bill to begin the federation of these nations. I had continued to help the Mid-Atlantic Clubs proliferate; new groups were started in Melbourne (1976), Seattle (1977), and San Francisco (1979). They joined a network of such clubs in London, Brussels, New York, Washington, D.C., Bonn, and Paris. Some of these eventually fell away, but most were still in business a quarter century later.

From October 1976, I was for some years a member of the Board of Directors of Federal Union, the nonprofit educational (and lobbying) group started by Clarence Streit in the 1940s. Federal Union changed its name in 1982 to Association to Unite the Democracies (AUD), taken from the title of my new book and meant to express the mission sanctified by a majority of the members at the time, that the course towards lasting Atlantic-Pacific unity had actually begun (through such bodies as the G-7, NATO, and OECD) but would have to be pursued by more pragmatic and gradualist means. A full-blown Atlantic federation was simply no longer in the cards, although Streit's great idea animated many initiatives with more than just a whiff of "federal union." NATO was one; the continental European Union—coupled with the idea of an Atlantic Partnership—was another. The U.S. Congress, in 1962, had provided funds for calling a convention of prominent Atlanticists, whose mountain of effort resulted not in a clarion call for a federation but a series of tepid proposals that excited neither governments nor publics; JFK's administration had a different plan (see chapter 8). A similar effort to launch, by interparliamentary means, an Atlantic Federal Union foundered before Congress could vote the monies. Streit's imaginative idea had become at once too extreme and passé. (It is interesting that in 2005, after bruising board battles, the Streit Council for Atlantic Union was formed to again serve the grand idea.)

In the years that I worked actively for Streit's concept as one of his board (1976–94), I became gradually disaffected, partly because of its increasing implausibility, but more because the small organization fell into the hands of unscrupulous and self-seeking individuals unworthy of Streit's and many other good souls' ideals. It is sad that NGOs with originally laudable ideas often wear themselves out in this way. Just as I had supported the early plans of the European federalists, I supported Atlantic federalists, too, because I felt that groups with idealistic goals—however outlandish these might seem to many—paved the way for more powerful NGOs with more modest and practical programs; their members could say implicitly to publics and governments: "Those federal idealists want the moon, we are ready to settle for half of it." In Europe, for example, Jean Monnet's pragmatic way—starting with a Coal and Steel Community in 1951 and moving on gradually to still more European "communities," and then later a "union," was able in part to progress because Monnet and his advocates could say, "Let's do this bit by bit instead," abjuring the "all or nothing" approach.

By the turn of the new century, it had become safer to talk about a "federal" Europe precisely because the founders of the 1950s had not insisted on one all-embracing scheme, all at once, but had indeed progressed, step by step, more than halfway towards their ultimate goal. In 2002–3, the former French president Valéry Giscard d'Estaing chaired a European "constitutional convention," just as the European Union was about to welcome the former Soviet Union's East European satellites into its membership. In 2005, the idea of a European Constitution foundered, but no doubt will again be launched, if in altered form.

Pushing and Pulling the United States Government

On 30 October 1982, the *Sankei Shimbun*, a leading Tokyo daily, reported on a conference of defense experts and political leaders. The meeting called for formation of exactly what Bob Brand and I had proposed in 1976: a Pacific alliance of Japan, Australia, Canada, New Zealand, and the United States—a counterpart of NATO. This gave Bob and me great satisfaction and hope that further organizing efforts would bear fruit. Two years later, although such an alliance never was formally put together, I was able to initiate a series of informal annual conferences of members of Congress and of parliaments from these Pacific/East Asian countries, together with defense officials and parliamentary counterparts from NATO countries, under the aegis of the Commander in Chief of U.S. Pacific forces in Pearl Harbor. We called this the Atlantic-Pacific Forum. Our aim was to show the Pacific democracies and some of the Atlantic ones just how intertwined their security interests were. After a few years, the project was suspended.

My old friend (from Hungarian Revolution days), Walt Raymond, joined the National Security Council staff under the new (1981) Reagan administration. Walt had a long history of stimulating and protecting the growth of democratic governments and citizens' movements; he had had a quiet but distinguished career in the CIA. In view of the damage done by the 1964 *Ramparts* revelations, Walt had decided to resign from the Agency and try, at a very high level—the White House itself—to create a new, large, publicly funded but privately incorporated body (something the Brits call a Quango, for quasi-nongovernmental organization) that could undertake a global effort, through grants and completely in the open, to sustain weak democratic governments and help create new ones. From his perch at the National Security Council, he was eventually successful in achieving his goal—the new National Endowment for Democracy (NED), by securing the strong support of both parties in Congress and President Reagan. NED, which celebrated its 20th anniversary in 2003, has done a wonderful job of helping spread democracy.

And sometimes my constant efforts inside the Washington Beltway (we in the State of Washington called the District of Columbia "the other Washington") would pay off. In my journal on 8 April 1982 I noted:

> Bob Brand has called, from State. Undersecretary [Lawrence S.] Eagleburger has been asking for "ideas" that could be floated by the President during his trip to Europe this coming summer. Eagleburger used the word "democracy" and alluded to its importance vis-à-vis our allies. Brand gave him the full load of CCD [Council for a Community of Democracy] ideas. The National Security Council staff poured some cold water on it, *but the President liked it.* The tide seems to be running in our direction, at least for the time being.

Later, Walt Raymond gave me more details about the genesis of an extraordinary speech delivered by President Reagan to the British Parliament (8 June 1982), in which he proposed a common objective for the Western countries: "to foster the infrastructure of democracy, the system of a free press, unions, political parties, universities, which allows a people to choose their own way to develop their own culture, to reconcile their own differences through peaceful means." Reagan noted the great efforts of the German "political foundations" to do this, intimated that the United States would soon undertake new efforts (the National Endowment for Democracy embodied this public mission.) The president urged other nations to do the same. Not long after this, Parliament authorized establishment of the parallel Westminster Foundation quango, and in the intervening years several other NATO and OECD governments have done likewise. (See Appendix F for further excerpts.)

Mark Palmer, my friend and fellow board member of the Council for a Community of Democracies (an NGO launched in 1999), was the principal author of Reagan's Westminster speech. In 1982 he was a young Foreign Service officer, later became ambassador to Hungary in the critical years 1989–91. In his retirement he wrote a 2003 book, *The Real Axis of Evil*, which set forth his ideas on how to "retire" the world's remaining 45 dictators over the next quarter century. This was somewhat controversial, but sparked a healthy public dialogue.

Walt Raymond and the Promotion of Democracy

With a nod from Battelle, I spent a good deal of time in 1982–83 help-ing Walt Raymond conceptualize the NED and shepherd it through the governmental and nongovernmental thickets of resistance, which at times were fierce. Here my experience with the reeducation of the Germans, a good deal of grant-making to European NGOs through USIA, and the Ford Foundation's many efforts to further democratic development, helped a good deal. Among other things I critiqued some of the president's draft speeches and budget documents for submission to Congress. I also lob-bied some key members of Congress whom I knew. My own part was minor compared to Walt's efforts and those of key members of Congress, such as Representative Dante Fascell, but I am proud to have had a small hand. And Battelle's gift of my time (and that of a few of my Battelle col-leagues) was certainly a public-service contribution, if largely unnoticed.

Then undersecretary for political affairs in the State Department, Lawrence Eagleburger, had a major hand in guiding the development of what was first called "President Reagan's Project Democracy." I had met Eagleburger in the early seventies, when he was political counselor at the U.S. Mission to NATO in Brussels, but not seen or heard from him since. Fate was to throw us together in various unforeseen ways over the next decade and a half.

In 1983 Walt Raymond and I had felt some satisfaction when the first part of our "plan" for democracy, NED, was created. It was also to play a small but important role in launching the second objective of the plan (and one which has taken much longer), namely, the uniting of the de-mocracies as a new way of conducting international relations. But for the bipartisan NED, that particular role could not, in the Beltway atmosphere (at any time) be more than tangential and only mildly supportive—mainly by providing funds for small conferences to share ideas about how the democracies could and should work together. These meetings planted im-portant seeds that would bear fruit only twenty years later. Walt Raymond passed away suddenly in early 2003, after heroic efforts in and out of gov-ernment to conceive and nurture institutions that would make the "de-mocracy enterprise" permanent. The Bush I administration carried on the thrust; the Clintonites professed pro-democracy leanings, but until Mad-eleine Albright pushed in 1999 for the Community of Democracies (see Appendix I), little that was concrete or lasting was done. Young George W. Bush had some radical new ideas about spreading democracy when his administration came to power in 2001. In 2005, the Council of the EU and the United States issued a ringing summit declaration of their intent to promote democracy worldwide at the head of their common agenda (see Appendix J).

Walt Raymond spent the last fifteen years of his life working the NGO network to stimulate government from the outside by using alliances of important people and educating those less important. He led former members of Congress (under their own alumni association) to Cuba to try to encourage a more sensible policy towards that country, as Castro's years were inevitably waning. In 1985–90, Walt worked with me, through the University of South Carolina and by other means, in the attempt to construct a new private foundation with ample funds to help the plethora of private bodies struggling to promote democracy and—especially— closer ties among democracies. This pot of money however was not to be, as private individuals of wealth and existing foundations who might have helped could not see the need. Walt also, virtually single-handed, helped Slovakian democrats establish a "storefront" Democracy Institute in Bratislava (ca. 1994–95).

In 1999 Walt Raymond became president of a reincarnated CCD—this time a Council for a Community of Democracies, to replace the old CCDs; Robert Hunter, Clinton's retired ambassador to NATO, was elected chairman of CCD. Clinton's secretary of state Madeleine Albright, in that same year of 1999, seized on our idea and ran with it. To see an intergovernmental community of more than 100 democracies actually established in 2000 was the crowning achievement of Walt's long career (and perhaps of my own); he lived long enough for the members of the "unite the democracies" movement to see a weak but still very real Community of Democracies (CD) inaugurated in Warsaw, and then to go on to a second major meeting—co-opting the Department of State in the new "no-nonsense" Bush II administration—in 2002, in Seoul. This was no mean achievement.

Walt's work and mine and that of a group of strategic thinkers on "the outside" (most of whom at one time or another had been on the "inside") is carried on by the new CCD, which led the effort, behind the scenes, to prepare comparably for the third CD conference of democratic governments, with a parallel conference of NGOs, in Santiago, Chile, in 2005. Bush's secretary of state, Colin Powell, was convinced by our CCD and by his undersecretary for global affairs, Paula Dobriansky, that the administration should continue U.S. participation in the Community of Democracies—no mean achievement, either for CCD or for Powell. However, by the beginning of 2005, the pitfalls of Bush's major effort—trying to impose democracy by military means on Iraq, a country with virtually no experience with democracy—seemed obvious, substantially negating most of whatever American goodwill and sincerity that had been earned in the Middle East over the years. Pro-democracy efforts in Afghanistan fared better than in Iraq, but it appeared that insufficient resources were not committed by the United States or its allies to insure stability there. As the new century wears on, the time is ripe for new and better approaches to democracy-building and achieving mutual understanding with the Arab world. Perhaps the 2005 initiatives by the EU and the United States can do this.

❋

On Christmas Eve 1986, Walt Raymond was wondering rather abjectly if his efforts thus far had really been of much use. (The new NED was in those days constantly under partisan attack from all sides and the bureaucratic infighting in government was leading to even more pitiful dead ends.) I wrote him a few words of encouragement, repeating what Lincoln had said, just prior to the Civil War, of the Declaration of Independence, that it gave liberty "not alone to the people of this country, but hope to the world for all future time. It was that which gave promise that in due time the weights should be lifted from the shoulders of all men."

Virtually all Americans would today roundly applaud Lincoln, but it is important to recognize that a national debate has swirled since our nation's beginnings as to *how* this might be done—as an active part of our policy, or simply a passive notion as to our own responsibilities as a model. Woodrow Wilson's legacy of democratic internationalism has given rise to fresh debates at the outset of the 21st century; some claimed that the Nixon-Reagan-Bush I governments had been "realists" and that the Bush II people were reclaiming Wilsonian idealism. This was a misguided notion, damaging and obfuscating the international integrationist heritage of Wilson, but this sort of debate, largely over semantics rather than the realities of an only partly democratic world, diverted the attention of people who want a better world order.

Committees for a Community of Democracies: In Search of Concepts and Backing

In the 1970s and early 1980s, from my Battelle base, I poured all the catalytic effort I could into trying to help fashion a workable concept that would unite the democracies to establish a permanent peace and to promote democracy itself. A new product of serendipity came to hand in December 1979.

What was then called the CCD, for short—and still is now, in its later 1999 incarnation—was conceived at a cocktail party in the Washington, D.C., home of Bob Brand, my Foreign Service buddy who had become the deputy assistant secretary of state for Far Eastern–Pacific affairs. Also munching and imbibing that evening was a retired Foreign Service pal of Bob's, Robert Foulon. Amid the usual Beltway chatter, Foulon and I tucked ourselves into a corner and started talking about serious things, especially the inadequate structure of current world politics, in particular the lack of attention to democracy-building as one of the main components of a new world peace structure. Bob had served in Germany in the Marshall Plan days and in several weak countries in Africa and felt that the more advanced, democratic nations of the West should strengthen their own links (such as EU and NATO) but use these as steppingstones towards a global combination of democracies.

We talked with Brand and a few other friends, including one of Streit's disappointed Federal Unionists, Richard Olson (who had been staff aide to Congressmen Morris Udall and Jim Wright, Speaker of the House at that time), and to William Olson (no relation to Dick), my old Rockefeller Foundation buddy from New York days, now dean of the School of International Service at American University in Washington. Mixing people with diverse backgrounds but ultimately congenial goals, I found, almost always produced electricity.

Foulon, a good drafter, put some of our guiding ideas on paper and thus began a series of meetings (the first committee, in Washington, met on 5 November 1979; in Seattle we established an outrigger a year later—a kind of trial regional support system for the parent group.) A series of such committees in several countries strove for consensus within their ranks and among their counterparts. These groups eventually embraced the globe, which added more and more people wielding different kinds of influence. They were united by experience and conviction in the cause of an International Community of Democracies. For a couple of years, I was chairman of the first, informal core group with an almost phantom "headquarters" in Washington, D.C. In 1983 I passed the chairmanship to Dean Olson, who in turn was succeeded in 1985 by the very solid former assistant secretary of state Samuel De Palma. Sam was retired and, using his formidable experience with the UN, NATO, and the Washington corridors of power, steered the committee into a series of influential conferences around the world. These began spewing out plans and proposals that could be thrust into the right hands within key governments and parliaments. The United States CCD in Washington was not in charge of the much larger and far-flung group of committees—they sprang up even in places such as Mauritius, Perth, Bonn, Montreal, and Tokyo—but instead served as a central point of communication, more or less like the hub of a wagon wheel, with CCDs in many places in touch directly with any other CCD or with all. We found great enthusiasm in all continents, with the possible exception of the Middle East—then, as today, a tough nut to crack. Former ambassador David Popper was later to succeed De Palma as CCD-DC chairman.

At first, in 1979 and 1980, we called this scheme the Committees of Correspondence, after the famous groups of reformers and radicals in the capitals of the original thirteen American colonies who informed, inspired, and goaded one another to action during the pre-Revolutionary years. But this was an 18th century American rubric that didn't quite seem to fit 20th century needs or ears, so we renamed our groups the Committees for a Community of Democracies. We then proceeded to enlist friends and colleagues from parliaments, the media, business, and academia in other countries, asking them to also form such committees. Then, in 1982, we began to bring them together for a series of international meetings.

The Washington, D.C., CCD never had funds to finance a proper central office or to pay staff. The committee's members—many former diplomats, some academicians, and others who believed fervently in the idea— all worked as volunteers. There was a D.C. office of sorts, run by one of our members for the U.S.-Netherlands Bicentennial Committee, that we were able to use as CCD's mailing address. Weekly, a group of ten or twelve of our CCD members would meet over "brown bag" lunches at a big conference table, to chart out future steps. Usually, these involved the creation of new CCDs abroad, plus regional and global gatherings to spread the idea. At the time, I was still in Seattle, but visited the Beltway often and with Battelle's encouragement used some of its facilities to make CCD hum, in a modest way. Members each gave what they could to defray postage and administrative costs. This original CCD was my idea of what a true NGO could and should be, at least in its formative years: unpaid, self-propelled citizens combining to further a common civic purpose, even doing the "grunt work" themselves. Such a group cannot remain permanent, but it's a good way to start.

From 1983 to 1987 the new National Endowment for Democracy doled out a few grants to CCD—never enough to let us create a permanent core structure with paid help, but sufficient for arranging conferences with like-minded people in various parts of the world who were seeking partners in supporting greater cooperation among democracies. The U.S. Information Agency also gave some help. The second CCD (of many) was the creation of a London group, composed in large part by my old friends there; they helped immeasurably to push the big idea of a global community of democracies along. Behind the scenes, Walt Raymond at the NSC was a strong proponent of what we were trying to do; under another hat, we even succeeded with Walt's help to get a rather enthusiastic letter of support from President Reagan.

I was reminded in those days of the Belgian national motto: *C'est l'union qui fait la force* (In unity there is power). CCD tried to fashion the pieces of unity that eventually could be combined and tested internationally, meaning intergovernmentally. Secretary Albright's 2000 meeting of the first Community of Democracies was probably the most important of CCD's indirect accomplishments.

In November 1982 our British Committee held a small conference in London that launched the International Association of Committees for a Community of Democracies. There were delegates from the United States, Germany, France, and The Netherlands. They elected me international chairman, and proceeded to have a spirited but genial argument as to our main purpose: Was it to consolidate the half-built edifice of cooperation among OECD and NATO countries? Or was it to aim for a global grouping, including many more democracies, some only just begun, others with serious troubles? We decided we should try to bring about both schemes. There was also the question of whether we were primarily a group that wanted to promote democracy itself, or a group that felt a peace system could best be created by democratic nations and peoples, growing together. At the turn of the 21st century, these questions were still with us, and with the nations.

CCD adopted the Declaration of London of 7 November 1982 (see Appendix G for the text). At various times the media took lackluster note, from different angles, of the idea.

One of our most enthusiastic and learned CCD members was Robert K. Olson, who produced, as a backdrop for the London conference, the *Reader on Democracy and Community*. Delegates had copies, but even Battelle's most fancy xerox machines could not produce enough to spread them more widely. Olson's compendium laid out the historical origins, the common security and economic interests, the serious proposals for closer transatlantic ties (beginning with Admiral Mahan and Norman Angell), the half-finished structures for cooperation, and the obligations of the developed world to the developing. We tried to get the *Reader* published, but didn't have the administrative wherewithal to take on such a task and stick with it. For those who still have copies, it is a valuable and fairly comprehensive compilation of source material up to the 1980s.

Our 1982 Declaration had an interesting influence on German politics, too. A longtime supporter of Clarence Streit's ideas, Rudolf Wagner of Munich, liked the more pragmatic thrust and inclusiveness of CCD's new program. He managed to get the Bavarian annual convention of the Christian Socialists to adopt a two-pronged resolution (October 1984) on foreign affairs, calling for equal emphasis on completing European unification and pushing for a "closer union of Free Nations." Wagner was proud to bring me personally a copy of this declaration. Later, Klaus de Vries, a Dutch MP, told me that my book, *Uniting the Democracies,* and the later London Declaration had had an impact on the foreign policy of The Netherlands.

I don't think I could prove it, but I strongly believe that today, more than two decades later, the formation of an actual intergovernmental organization called the Community of Democracies, which in 2000 brought together in Warsaw more than 100 democratic member governments, can be traced in substantial part to the volunteer spadework of the original Committees for a Community of Democracies, begun in 1979 and spreading widely after that. These modest groups fashioned the term "Community of Democracies," produced a stream of useful action papers and concept papers exploring the idea, and spread these to limited segments of publics and governments for several years. I would estimate that at least 800 to 1,000 individuals in around 40 countries were seriously touched and involved in this modest movement over the two decades that followed.

By early 1999, the terms and general outlines of the CD concept had drifted around Washington sufficiently that Secretary Madeleine Albright, for example, when asked by the *Los Angeles Times* (17 January 1999) what she might consider her most important goal, to be achieved during her term of office, said, "The 21st century . . . ought to be the century of democracy. . . . We're going to be putting an awful lot more emphasis on organizing the democracies, working with them . . . so that they can work with each other better." One of her aides, according to the article, referred to the proposed organization as a "club of democracies."

But this is getting ahead of the story. In 1982, events were set in train that would take me, for the third time in my life, to Washington, D.C. Many of the projects outlined above were continued—some by means other than the founders had envisaged—and I managed to get deeply involved in ways I had not imagined. This became more or less the story of my life, with glances both backward and forward: broaching and nurturing ideas, serendipity, and careful catalytic action.

17
Back to the Beltway: 1983 and Beyond

November 1986: *The Iran-Contra scandal breaks in Washington—the Reagan administration is accused of illegally funneling arms to Nicaraguan rebels in contravention of express congressional prohibition, using funds derived from the sale of arms to Iran.*

A Short, Fascinating, Transformative, Tumultuous Career Episode: 1983-85

By the spring of 1982, I had begun to feel career stirrings. Battelle had given me ample opportunity to try various paths to influence the public, our government, and others—a major book, monographs, the founding of CAPA and the CCDs, the effort to shape the new bipartisan National Endowment for Democracy, many lectures around the developed world. I had also given back to Battelle in the form of future studies, for which I had written appraisals of regional and world politics, the "anthropology" of various mature nations, and especially management appraisals concerning Battelle's big multinational laboratories in Europe. By the early 1980s I felt pressures for a change hard to resist.

Part of my frustration lay rather precisely in my hip and back joints. In August 1983, I would need a fresh substitute for the left hip joint replaced in 1979 (using primitive technology, it turned out), plus two more such operations in 1989 and 1990. These I could not foresee in 1982, but the pain problems and general debilitation continued unabated and I longed for rest and recuperation. But osteoarthritis is not something that allows for much R&R; it is a chronic, not an acute, condition. It has its ups and downs, most of which cannot be forecast or avoided, only ameliorated, sometimes. These pains (plus the enervation of painkillers) produced a continuing malaise. For a normal and otherwise active person, this was a substantial drag on productivity. Years earlier I had set a hectic pace

for myself. Making an all-out attack—with as many others as I could enlist—on some of the chief ills of our civilization, was my lot in life, and I
was zealous in my efforts, despite my infirmities, to keep the ball rolling.
Most of the time my successes exceeded my defeats.

In June 1982, exhaustion overcame me, and my doctor ordered me to
stop all travel and take a month's complete rest. Some of my projects lay
in suspension, most to be continued or later revived, largely because the
human network that had animated them remained more or less intact.
The deep beliefs and steadfast qualities of such people—all over Europe
and North America, in Japan and Australia—kept the concepts (and to an
important extent, the process) of community-building going. Sometimes,
however, especially in the eighties and much of the nineties, the chosen
vehicles lagged or were snuffed out, usually for simple lack of money.

Meanwhile, the Battelle Memorial Institute, whose leaders saw my
overall output as useful to them and as a worthwhile form of public service, were feeling the financial pinch acutely, surprisingly to me, and
even more so to them. By the 1980s, Battelle's federal tax problems (the
Internal Revenue Service insisted they pay more taxes than the ordinary
not-for-profit organization, because they were "in business") finally gave
way to a substantial drain on capital. As noted earlier, the machinations
of an elected judge in Franklin County, Ohio, where Gordon Battelle had
written his 1923 will, backed the corporate leaders into a political corner.
Again, they acquiesced and more capital flowed out of the till. This meant
that the generous program of public service—largely research on community problems—would have to be cut back severely, altering the scope
and objectives of the Seattle research center. More money would have to
be generated through conferences that financed themselves, for instance,
and by the remaining Research Fellows, like myself, seeking out contracts
for whatever research could match the needs of companies, governments,
or other entities with our own capabilities. Some of this contract research
I managed to scare up, but the search and the skewing of my own work
in the direction of moneymaking rather than public service were uncon-
genial to me.

So I began to think about other institutions in which I might find a
good home for my international community-building instincts. As on a
few previous occasions, I elected not to follow the dictates of some large
institution that would divert my attention from what I saw as some of the
world's greatest needs. I wanted to follow in the footsteps of such men as
Jean Monnet, behind-the-scenes animator of the predecessors to today's
European Union, and of Clarence K. Streit, whose principles on Atlantic
federal unity were far in advance of political leaders of the day but which
were nevertheless incorporated in some of the most powerful post-1945

institutions, such as NATO. I was no Monnet or Streit. Times were different from the early decades after 1940, when they had done their main work, and my methods were different. But I still felt a sense of mission—to carry out the preservation and further development of the international democratic community.

As one last throw of the dice, with Battelle and U.S. Information Agency support, I undertook a survey of nongovernmental bodies small and large that were trying in their different ways to promote the "togetherness" of the Atlantic-Pacific world. In 1982 Battelle chairman Sherwood Fawcett told me to "take as much time as you can" to make this survey; he and I both hoped it would help indirectly to create the makings of an Atlantic-Pacific Movement so that the various NGOs could see they were not alone. By the summer of 1983, the work was done: not simply a catalog of who was doing what, but also an analysis of why most such bodies were needed, what their problems were (mostly financial), and to some extent an examination of the ways they could multiply their efforts by cooperating with other organizations. No one had done this kind of analysis before, and to my knowledge no one has since. The three-volume survey was widely praised for its helpfulness and would be used later as an argument to fill the many funding gaps.

The Atlantic Council of the United States

The Atlantic Council of the United States, as noted in chapter 9, had been created in 1962 by Dean Acheson, Christian Herter, and other retired greats of the early postwar period to marshal the experience and intellectual resources of American leaders who, like themselves, wanted to preserve and extend the accomplishments of the Atlantic community. They brought together people who had concentrated on promoting the Atlantic Alliance (the American Committee on NATO), those who formed the U.S. contingent supporting the then-new Atlantic Institute, and a broader grouping—an Atlantic Council initiated by Secretary of State Herter as he left office in 1961. This grouping wanted to collect economic as well and military and political elites to spur the development of a tighter community with many functions. The combined organization was dubbed the Atlantic Council of the United States (ACUS) and set up offices in a building close to the White House. The initial board of directors comprised more than 50 important people; within ten years its membership had swelled to 120.

An initial task of the ACUS was to try to spur the new Kennedy administration to act on the recommendations of the Atlantic Convention of

1962, set up by Congress with its own appropriation (see chapter 9). The chief proposal of the Convention was to create, with America's allies, an Intergovernmental Commission that would survey institutional and other factors binding the Atlantic countries together and make proposals for reforms and changes that would result in the creation of "a true Atlantic Community." This may or may not have been a great or timely idea, but the new ACUS was unable to convince the Department of State or the new President, John F. Kennedy, that it was worth pursuing. Following the advice of George Ball and other top members of his administration, Kennedy had resolved on a quite different course, that of advancing a "two-pillar Atlantic partnership" between the still unfinished European community and the United States. Despite this concept's many defects, certain of JFK's key advisers were zealots and relentlessly set his and succeeding administrations on this course.

The leaders of the new ACUS, Acheson, Herter and others, were divided. Most felt the transoceanic partnership was at best premature; others were keen to torpedo the idea if they could and put in its place a virtual federation of the entire membership of NATO and OECD. Some of the latter were gradualists; others—like Will Clayton, who had been a father of the Marshall Plan, and Adolph Schmidt, a distinguished Pittsburgh banker who had backed the ideas of Clarence Streit's powerful 1939 book, *Union Now*—were keen federalists and in a hurry. A third group wanted to concentrate principally on preserving the military and political ties embodied in the NATO treaty, with concentration on the vital tasks of the Cold War.

The second group—the federalists—had an advantage: the director-general and CEO of the new ACUS, Richard J. Wallace, was an ex-newspaperman who had been an aide to Senator Estes J. Kefauver of Tennessee. Kefauver was Clarence Streit's chief proponent in the Congress, and Wallace, in determined but genteel Southern ways, was to push ACUS to espouse Streit's federal ideas. He was soon joined by two strong federalists who had just retired from the Department of State after long, distinguished diplomatic careers, Ambassadors John F. Hickerson and Theodore C. Achilles. Hickerson, a crusty and polished old Texan, had been assistant secretary of state when the North Atlantic Treaty had been conceived. Achilles was one of the treaty's principal drafters. Both were convinced that Streit's federal plan was a good one—in fact, the *only* one—and were resolved to do all they could to bring it about, now as private citizens. Both became members of the ACUS board. Within a few years, Achilles would become an all-powerful vice chairman of the Council, a post he held until his death in 1985. For nearly twenty years, he had his own office with ACUS and was the power behind the throne, deftly and determinedly pulling the strings. No matter who occupied the titular executive post of ACUS director general, (later termed president), Achilles guarded the real executive authority for himself, although he had no executive responsibilities. This became a major problem.

The Atlantic Council gradually became an important force in Washington, despite the inability of the federalist zealots to convince either the various administrations or a working majority in Congress to buy the Streit concept. In the early days, from 1963 to 1965, I was the Atlantic Institute's office head in Washington and worked out of the same office with both the ACUS and AI programs. I took a more sociological than political approach, spurring Achilles and others to begin special transatlantic seminars for the successor generation, already in the process of replacing those who had won World War II and created NATO and the Marshall Plan. At the Council's request, Council Vice Chairman W. Randolph Burgess and I, from my home in England, wrote a book, *Europe and America: The Next Ten Years* (1970). The book had a modest success, but—like most such ventures—was no best seller.

I would pop into Washington now and then to consult with Burgess, Achilles, and others and sometimes dropped ideas that a current administration might want to adopt. In 1970, for example, I went with Achilles to see NASA Administrator James Webb. We tried to persuade him to envisage an Atlantic rather than a solely U.S. space program, but Webb and those who would have to decide were too nationalistic to contemplate such an approach. I had better luck in 1974, when Joe Harned, the ever-faithful No. 2 of the Council's staff and I called on Patrick Moynihan, a special assistant at the time to President Nixon, and persuaded him to propose a new set of tasks for NATO, outside the military realm and intended to show European and North American publics that the Alliance was more than just a conventional security treaty. This gave birth to what was called the Challenges of Modern Society program. Environmental and city planning experts from all the NATO countries would demonstrate in a series of studies what the sharing of practical ideas about local government, social problems, and the newly fashionable ecological syndrome could do to improve the lot of ordinary people. It turned out to be a modest success; I wrote a little book about it for NATO a few years later, translated into all the Alliance's languages.

During this period, I also helped produce the ACUS pamphlet on Summits, such as the new round of G-7 meetings. What should they aim at? What should they try to tackle? How could their work best be followed up?

A Time for Choice

In December 1982, Colleen and I attended a 10th Anniversary Gala of the Mid-Atlantic Club of New York, a glittering occasion. This particular M.A.C. was the jewel in the crown of the movement that Walter Lessing and I had started in 1970 in London. We were also invited to Washington quite specially for a meeting of the Board of Directors of the Atlantic Council, of which I had just been made a member; this was a special honor for me and I was most appreciative. (Zbigniew Brzezinski and former president Gerald Ford were elected at the same time.)

Ted Achilles also wanted a long private talk with Colleen and me. A couple of months earlier, he had broached an idea, then quite amazing to me, that he wanted to pursue: Ted had asked if I would like to move to Washington for the next few years and become the CEO of the Atlantic Council of the United States. At that time, I was approaching my 60th birthday and was quite happy in my native Northwest. Since our return to Seattle in 1974, I had found my work with Battelle fruitful and challenging, although—as explained earlier—I felt in my bones it was time for a change. But I honestly did not envisage leaving Seattle; I had thought of independent scholarship and writing or of joining a university or another major institution in the area. By now, I was a sort of futurist and that field seemed promising too.

Ted's proposal—and he lobbied hard with Colleen and me—was a virtual thunderbolt. On the one hand, the step seemed a logical progression from all that I had done earlier, a chance to work with the nation's elites to fashion some new institutions and programs for a changing future that would bring the industrial democracies ever closer. I knew I was a good administrator and could do the job; most of the staff and many of the other board members knew me well, and management seemed to pose no important problems. But I had lived twice before in Washington DC (1956–58 and 1963–65) and found the climate abhorrent. Some people can manage to adjust to the hot, humid, pressure-cooker summers of the District of Columbia and to its abominable and quirkily changeable winter weather; but others find the climate a true burden. I was one of the latter. Northwest weather, while often gloomy and moist from the late fall well into spring, was always supportable, indeed bracing. Half the year was a positive delight. The Seattle climate was not unlike that of London, or the rest of northwestern Europe, and I had always felt at home in these places. But Washington? Yet again?

I was not sure I wanted to work inside the Beltway, as it was now so conveniently called after the huge interstate highway had ringed the District of Columbia and more or less circumscribed the arena where all the politicking and lobbying, and the reporting of these, would take place. Also, most of our children were in the Seattle area and others nearby; grandchildren had begun to come along, and we were keen to be near them.

However, Ted Achilles implored us to think it over. He explained that he and the genial director general, Francis Wilcox (who had been a powerhouse on Capitol Hill as chief of staff of the Senate Foreign Relations Committee, and later dean of the Johns Hopkins School of Advanced International Studies) were both past retirement age, Ted explained, and wanted to drop the executive burdens they had been carrying for years. Ted's wonderful wife, Marian, whom Colleen and I both loved, also urged us: she wanted Ted more at home and relaxed in his later years (Ted was then nearing 80.)

I asked Ted then, and again in the months that followed, "Do you really intend to retire and not be directly involved in the executive direction of affairs?" (I had had enough by this time of having created boards of directors, served as executive, and been a member of many other boards to know that the running of affairs depended on a clear system that married top executive responsibility with authority—the "chain of command" in military terms. A good NGO board made policy, the CEO carried it out, and a good one proposed policies to the board. A major institution (such as ACUS certainly was) needed to give its CEO plenty of latitude and make the policy-execution nexus crystal clear. We told Ted that we would think this over carefully and get back to him. He and Marian again said how keen they were to have us in Washington, saying I was just "the right man" for the job.

�֎

Back home in Seattle and at Port Ludlow, Colleen and I wrestled with what would be a major change. We not only had to think of what the "other Washington" and my new responsibilities would be like, but of what the shift would mean for our future in the Northwest—because we surely would come back, perhaps in five years, for real retirement—and we would have to think about Colleen's mother, who lived in an apartment in our second home in Port Ludlow and would not want to come to D.C. with us, about disposing of a condo in Seattle, and about leaving all our many friends and family in the area for an extended time.

However, this was an opportunity for what Colleen and I saw as a possible crowning achievement in my lifetime of public service. The chance to use virtually all the skills and knowledge that I had accumulated about world affairs and about how to run NGOs won us over. Early in 1983, I phoned Ted Achilles and said I would do it. The usual exchange of letters took place. I would have to be elected formally as president (rather than director general), in effect with more powers than Wilcox had had and replacing both him and Achilles. I told him I would do the job for no more than five years. The Council's board elected me president, unanimously, in the spring, and I was to take office on 1 September 1983. Accordingly, I gave Battelle my formal notice; my boss Sherwood Fawcett (who had become a member of the ACUS board a few years earlier) was all for this step. We both saw it as progress, as we shared the big ideas about the world, many of which had been worked out during my years with Battelle and with their help.

Further exchange of letters took place that summer with Ted, in which I asked him again, point-blank, if he really meant to retire fully from executive responsibilities, and to which he answered yes, though somewhat unconvincingly. I told him what I expected to do and how I intended to use my authority; he said, "You'll be the boss." I think in his head he meant this, but in his heart he had doubts. The Atlantic Council had been his life for eighteen years. He had also helped mightily to finance its operations; as a privately wealthy man, he often provided 15 to 20 percent of the Council's budget. He had a foundation for the purpose (which I had induced him to start in the 1970s) and we both expected his grants to continue. Meanwhile, we had sold our condo in Seattle, arranged to rent our second home at Port Ludlow to dear friends so that Colleen's mother could continue there in her separate apartment. We set a firm date for my retirement from Battelle; the Northwest bridges had been burned.

We canvassed places to rent in the Washington area and settled on a spacious new apartment on the outskirts of Alexandria, Virginia—not far from Mount Vernon and other national shrines. We arranged for our effects to be picked up at Port Ludlow at the end of August and delivered to Alexandria on the day we would arrive there to take delivery. But nature intervened.

The Best Laid Plans . . .

The night before the movers were to converge on Port Ludlow, my arthritis had been flaring up for several days and I was feeling poorly. As I tried to sleep that night, I heard noises on our dock (our home was on a small hill just up from a salt water bay) and jumped out of bed to see what was going on. I thought (and later believed this to have been an hallucination induced by a painkiller) that I saw a man fishing from our dock! I ran to an exterior door and towards the dock, only to collapse with shooting pains in my left (operated) hip. With my wife's help I staggered back into bed. Morning found me in no shape to help supervise movers, let alone climb into an automobile and drive 3,000 miles. I simply could not walk. The upshot: Colleen watched the movers load, while my brother drove me to the Swedish Hospital in Seattle, where I had my second hip-replacement operation on the same joint as in 1979. In a few days Colleen flew to Alexandria to meet the movers from the Northwest. With the help of trusted Beltway friends, she installed our effects in the new apartment, turned the key, and returned to Seattle just in time to care for me as I exited the hospital with another new hip! This time, it was a "total hip replacement" and not just a partial one. I would have to spend three months or more recuperating before I could travel. In my diary I noted: "One advantage of a big operation is that it makes you cherish life anew."

The Atlantic Council was informed of this change in plans; I would start work on 1 January 1984 rather than earlier; they could adjust while I convalesced out West.

Two good friends, now my tenants, were scheduled to move into our Port Ludlow home on the day after my entry into the hospital, complicating matters further. We phoned good friends in England and arranged to rent the condominium they had just bought, across Port Ludlow bay from us, so that I could recuperate there for the rest of the year. That worked very nicely; as we were near home for this *pénible* period. (This French word, meaning "unhappy, depressing," expresses exactly how I felt.)

We duly arrived in Alexandria in mid-December, to be confronted with a ferocious snow and ice storm that lasted several days. I was able nonetheless to get to the ACUS office in Washington for long talks with Achilles, Wilcox, and my soon-to-be No. 2, Joe Harned. Just before Christmas, Ambassador Kenneth Rush, then chairman of the ACUS board, asked me to lunch in the City Tavern, in Georgetown. I did not know him well and welcomed the opportunity to chat *unter vier Augen* (under only four eyes—yours and mine), as the Germans charmingly say. Rush explained in confidence that my job was to change "the atmosphere and culture" at the ACUS dramatically. It had been run, he said, in a rather casual, slipshod fashion; what we needed was to "institutionalize" things so that it would become a proper, effective organization, ready for the long term. He said I was to have full power, responsibility, and authority as CEO. This was fine with me, and I confirmed all this in a letter to him, recounting our conversation. However, it soon became clear that neither Achilles nor Wilcox wanted to accept this arrangement.

The night before the changeover, Rush invited two dozen close ACUS associates and wives to a black-tie "retirement party" for Ted Achilles and Fran Wilcox at the quaint brownstone on "Eye" Street, the Alibi Club. It is so exclusive that—at least at that time—membership was limited to about 100. At dinner's end, Ambassador Rush gave a nice speech, toasting Ted and Fran for their selfless devotion and wishing them bon voyage. Responding, Achilles thanked Rush and the board, but said, "Oh, I'll be right back on the job tomorrow morning!" This was *Donnerwetter*, a real shocker, again as the Germans would say.

✄

At my first staff meeting the next morning, I began by sharing my sense of mission with my staff of twenty colleagues:

> When the history of this century is written, the movement for an Atlantic community and for a larger partnership of all democratic nations will probably be seen as one of the two or three great developments in human affairs. Whether this will have been abortive, or will have become *the* major trend in international relations in the twenty-first century, depends in some measure on *us*—the staff of the Atlantic Council of the United States.

Achilles insisted on being present at this meeting, and when I had finished, told everyone that he wanted to turn over the reins to me "gradually." I was taken aback but said nothing. The next day, Wilcox told me that he too wanted "to stay on" and wanted his old office, which I planned to take over. I gently disabused him and arranged for a small office for him, out of eyeshot and earshot. I was not about to accept the appearance of control without the substance, nor vice versa. It soon became clear why this had to be my position.

I found the Council offices a pigpen, both literally and figuratively. Visitors to the Council faced antiquated, dingy facilities, a poor public face for a supposedly important national institution. I quickly arranged for complete cleaning and painting and also ordered a new set of modern telephones to replace a 1960s set that had only three outside lines for a staff of twenty and little facility for intercommunication. We moved our best furniture into the foyer, placed so that a proper receptionist greeted visitors. These were relatively small things, but essential to present the right "public face." I was quite determined.

On my first day on the job, Joe Harned informed me that the Council had only enough funds to operate for three months. Nor was there any money in the pipeline. By 1 April we would be bankrupt, with no funds to pay bills or meet payrolls. I requested the chairman to appoint a special committee (without my predecessors) to investigate the situation, and also immediately asked board member Raymond Shafer, former governor of Pennsylvania, to arrange a cost-free consulting arrangement with Coopers Lybrand, the national accounting firm with which he was connected. They cooperated magnificently, arranging a quick audit of the books and an appraisal, and made recommendations for reorganizing our budgeting, accounting, and money management. They also looked at staff duties overall and suggested useful changes. At their recommendation, I immediately replaced our part-time accountant and later had to replace two more staff members who could not overcome their alcoholism. One secretary had piles of files under her desk, rather than in cabinets, and could barely find room for her feet; moving furniture and painting provided the excuse for dealing with that. I began an audit of staff responsibilities, cut a few and reassigned some others. The board's investigative committee okayed all these actions and provided a few more constructive thoughts. Messrs. Achilles and Wilcox were obviously not too happy with this process, but they knew as well as I that it was essential.

It is fair to say that, had I known of the parlous financial situation of ACUS, I probably would not have taken the job; apparently I had been selected in large measure to raise funds and—although my predecessors would not admit it—to first straighten out the management and organizational mess they had (perhaps unwittingly) gotten me into. Once in the job however, I had to clean these Augean stables; I felt that I had been hired under false pretenses. This was a personal as well as a professional tragedy.

Ted Achilles and Fran Wilcox had been dear friends of mine for years, but I had to either swim or sink in the detritus they had created. One small illustration: On my first or second day in the office, Wilcox came and said he wanted to show me how he had controlled expenditures; he had a little 3-by-5 card in his hand, with the months of the year down the left side and two columns to the right; one of these showed money he expected to spend, the other, money he expected to come in. When one began to overshoot the other, he explained, he would worry.

Another, greater, problem involved office space. Since its inception, the Council had acted as provider of free offices to retired diplomats, specialists on Atlantic affairs. In some cases, this was entirely warranted, as many of these "club members" were among the world's true experts on questions such as trade and payments, the OECD, Europe, and important aspects of NATO. Though their help was vital, it cost money for office space that sat empty when they were home or on vacation. And in some cases, these offices were simply a home away from home for retirees who didn't want to spend all day every day with their wives. The place was much more an old men's club than a suite of busy and productive offices.

By the year 1984, the Atlantic Council of the United States had become like an old Southern plantation after the Civil War, with worn furnishings and a feeble welcome for visitors, peopled by relatives and holdovers from antebellum days. I changed the physical character of the place, ordered new equipment where essential, and gently persuaded some of the obvious hangers-on, over time, to retire, at least from our free premises.

My deputy, Joe Harned, and I meanwhile went on the road urgently to elicit new grants from some of the Council's old backers and to clean up the deficit before we went bust. We were greeted like old friends, but the foundations or individuals were not always forthcoming. I was particularly disappointed by the reaction of a clutch of Mellon family foundations (Carthage, the Scaife Foundation, the A. W. Mellon Charitable Trust among them). One of the retiring heads, who had been most helpful during the early days of the Council and the Atlantic Institute, told us that the "atmosphere had changed" and their funding priorities were now somewhat different. I couldn't comprehend this until a few weeks later, when, to help with fund-raising, we hired a smart young college graduate whose family quite incidentally was connected with Pittsburgh and the Mellons. After making some discreet inquiries at my request, she informed us that some of the younger Mellons (especially young Richard Mellon Scaife, who headed a new, very large charitable trust for the families) did not approve of NATO at all. Writing more than two decades later, it is interesting to note that this particular Scaife is frequently cited as the dispenser of much largesse to distinctly right-wing causes.

But we did manage to dig our way out of the financial hole in time. Before the new grants could come in, I found it necessary to telephone Achilles, then in Florida for a winter vacation, and ask for an urgent temporary bailout with a grant of $75,000 from his North Atlantic Foundation. Every year he had given money, though grudgingly unless the program was his own idea. He found the necessity of using this grant (no problem with supply on his side; the capital was there) as general purpose funds to erase a deficit and buy time embarrassing and uncongenial to him, but we literally had no choice. I think Ambassador Ted intensely disliked my phone call and the trenchant memo that followed—but I had no alternative. And, after all, he was the one who implored me to come to Washington and who had also presided over past uncontrolled spending that occasioned my desperate call.

The board's special committee reported to the entire board on 20 March, indicating all that was in train. The directors approved what the Committee and I had done, including the program reviews then under way.

Accomplishment

By the end of 1984, the Council was well out of debt and the supply of money was steady. We had also had a series of board working groups to look into every aspect of the Council's management and program, which they did with enthusiasm. I intended to make our directors feel fresh momentum—and believe I succeeded. I was particularly keen to look at new vistas for the Council, which had acquired the reputation of simply a pro-NATO claque, with a few additional interests, such as Japanese-U.S. nuclear energy cooperation. I proposed a series of studies to the board to actively support the idea of an Atlantic-Pacific community, looking towards the future. We arranged, for example, for an Atlantic-Pacific Caucus to begin annual meetings in Pearl Harbor, under the tutelage of CINCPAC, bringing together members of parliaments from democracies around both oceans to study global security challenges.

The Atlantic Treaty Association—a kind of umbrella group that, since 1954, had brought together the various citizens' organizations supporting NATO—held its annual meeting in Toronto in 1984. Until then, the ATA had been a weak, even pitiful little body that arranged such annual conclaves but did little else. I knew what could be done with an energetic executive and a little travel money to counsel with these various national bodies, coax them to do better, use their imagination, and in the process help them to reach their publics and get good things accomplished—rather than simply offering a place on a letterhead to people whose time was past. I thus proposed replacing ATA's secretary-general (a genial but lazy fellow) with an active just-retired French ambassador who was keen on NATO and vastly more experienced.

The chairmen and executives of all fifteen ATA bodies had a side meeting in Toronto and elected my candidate and approved a bigger program and function for his office; but they could not find the necessary additional funds. I suggested that all return to their capitals and seek to increase their respective shares of the modestly expanded budget. I further offered to approach one or two American foundations for a few thousand dollars so that the new ATA secretary general of ATA could begin immediately to show what could be done with modest new funds. Imagine my amazement when my own chairman, Ambassador Rush, cut me off, in front of my international colleagues: "Jim," said Rush, "I don't want you to do that. If there are any extra funds around, we'll need them ourselves for the Atlantic Council."

How to Twist in the Wind

This was a harbinger of something unpleasant that began increasingly to poison the air my staff and I were breathing. This was the same chairman who only ten months earlier had told me, confidentially, that my mission was to sweep away the cobwebs and "institutionalize" the operation. Among other things, Ambassador Rush had been Nixon's envoy to Germany and then deputy secretary of state; he knew the ins and outs of NATO as well as anyone. For him to take such a narrowly national tack, and embarrass me in front of our peers, was most distasteful.

Shortly before Thanksgiving 1984, as I was entertaining a visitor in my office, Rush poked his head around the doorway and, with no attempt to excuse himself to my visitor, abruptly asked, "Jim, could you come out here for a minute?" I exited and said, "What's up?" He took me around a corner to Achilles' office and said, "The Executive Committee [of the Board] has decided not to nominate you for another term as president." I was thunderstruck, more so than I had been two years earlier when Achilles implored me to take the new job. One year only? During which I had transformed the management, financing, staffing, vision, and program of the Council?

I knew that at several times in the past year, I had incurred the displeasure of Achilles and Wilcox. I always told them of any important steps I was taking, but when the matter at hand was clearly of an executive or administrative character, I did not ask their permission. I observed formal channels, asking the chairman or the Executive Committee for their OK on matters that came within board province. In hindsight, I may have moved too quickly in some matters and had not deferred to Achilles when he—but not I—thought he should have a decisive say. For example, the offices had not been repainted for twenty years, and the original contract with our landlords provided for regular repainting at their expense, not ours. My decision to have the painting done was unsettling to Achilles. And he rebelled at the new telephones, which cost $9,000 but were essential. In short, he had been used to running the Council in almost all its aspects before I arrived, and Wilcox had done his bidding. Achilles had been used to exerting his authority untrammeled but without the responsibility required of an elected or appointed executive. I had happened along just as the Council faced bankruptcy, but with a complacency on the part of my predecessors and boss, the chairman, that to me had been alarming. Because Ambassador Ted was never one to confront a situation or a colleague directly but simply held in any reservations he had, swallowed hard, and let his feelings fester, I had misjudged him. When he could stand it no longer, and realized that the executive authority had been seeping away from him, he simply asked the chairman to call the Executive Committee of the Board—without me, a Board and Committee officer, present—and demanded that they fire me. And he did all this without ever giving me a warning or asking for a man-to-man talk.

The Beltway Old Boys' (and Girls') Network

Put yourself in the position of these (for the most part, quite distinguished) men and women—former members of Congress or the diplomatic corps, ex-cabinet secretaries, in some cases top generals and admirals, and so on. They were used to meeting quarterly for often interesting ACUS debates on foreign policy, perhaps to perfunctorily approve budgets and ratify a few program activities. They were pleased to be doing in a private setting with their peers some of what they had done in government—at least in terms of prestige and mutual esteem. Occasionally, great public servants would be asked to chair the preparation of an important set of Council recommendations for the Department of State or the president. (Many of these were meaty, with much wisdom, and occasionally effected important changes.) Those few who were at all intimate with the Council's financial situation knew tacitly that Achilles' North Atlantic Foundation would always come to the rescue if there were shortfalls. In short, Ted Achilles, on the surface genial and (all would agree) most knowledgeable about government and NATO and our milieu, had the directors of the Atlantic Council in his pocket.

A further factor was at work: the Beltway Old Boys' Network. With a few notable exceptions, the members of the board were people who had had distinguished careers—a few in business, but most in government. Even some who were properly retired, often from politically appointed positions, depended, tacitly but firmly, on fellow board members for their status, including possible future appointments to a new cabinet or presidential commission or the like. The 125 members of the board represented the foreign policy elite of the nation. If the three or four members of the Executive Committee who had known me for years had put their backs up and faced down Ambassadors Rush and Achilles, that might have ended their Beltway standing, or perhaps brought about the collapse of the Council itself. In short, the ACUS was an extraordinary gathering of mostly extraordinary public servants who, in their later lives, had become valued Beltway pundits.

I protested and was granted a hearing with the Executive Committee, where I set forth in great detail what had been accomplished by the Council under my administration of just one year. I brought in letters from important people and proof of the helpfulness of our programs, but none of this availed. My "accusers" remained silent, and the chairman of the Committee had no choice but to take a vote, which went against me. It was then that I finally faced reality: The unspoken and unwritten conditions of my employment were unknown to me when I took the job, namely, to keep Ted Achilles busy and content in his old age. (Ironically, both he and Wilcox died within two years of my departure; sad, because despite everything that had transpired, both had been good, trusted friends. *King Lear* has something to say about all this.)

The "constitutional" authority for this separation was the Council's changed by-laws, adopted early in 1983 when I was not present, that provided for an *elected* President whose term would be for *one year* (like all other officers of the corporation). I had foolishly overlooked this. It was thus formally proper for the Executive Committee to decide "not to propose me for reelection" at the following month's annual Board meeting. But their action was unprecedented and ethically wanting: Ted Achilles had pleaded with me to leave my home in Washington State to spend "five years" (as he always said) as his and Fran's replacement. I had sold an apartment, rented another home, made a lot of inconvenient family arrangements, left a good position with an internationally known research institution in Seattle, and more or less burned my civic bridges in that city. I had always planned to return to the Northwest in retirement after five years of public service that I had regarded as a duty to the country, however inconvenient.

Lesson number 1 from this experience: Read the constitution under which you are to serve, so that you can think fully about your formal position. And lesson number 2: Above all, understand the financial position fully, in advance.

The full Board of Directors met in December 1984 to hear reports on my year's stewardship and to elect 1985 officers. The chairman, vice chairman, and other officers were duly reelected, but after a few evasive words from the chairman, Lt. General George Seignious was nominated for president. I bore no ill will towards the general, who was an honorable man (he had said to me, after the earlier meeting in which I was forcibly "retired" and the Executive Committee decided to nominate him in my stead, "Jim, I want you to know I did not covet your job," and I always have believed him). Seignious proved to be a competent executive and did well by the Council for several years; I was later able to help and advise him, and he me.

At this "day of the long knives" Board meeting, I asked for time and repeated what I had told the executive committee. As directly and politely as I could, I said I had staved off Council bankruptcy and other impending disasters but had not realized that I was not to retain the necessary full executive authority. A few board members spoke on my behalf and pointedly resigned then and there in protest. A few more did so later. Brzezinski wrote a scathing letter to Rush, which his secretary inadvertently sent a copy of to me! I received several fine letters from other members who "deeply regretted" my parting. Lawrence Eagleburger, then a board member, was not present at the meeting. When I saw him a few weeks later, he expressed his "disgust" with the board and said he would not stand for reelection as a director. He and I were to enjoy a cordial, mutually supportive relationship for years.

After the board meeting, as several members came to shake my hand, Eugene Rostow, my old friend of more than two decades and a member of the Executive Committee, asked if we couldn't have a quiet lunch together. In 1963, I had persuaded Gene, then dean of the Yale Law School, to help me form a national Committee on Atlantic Studies to spur reform of university curricula. We sought more emphasis on the modern elements of Western civilization — political, military, economic, and cultural — that would help students to appreciate the heritage and responsibilities that were theirs. Gene and I had worked together beautifully, and I was always honored to know him. At the Cosmos Club, I told him how I felt about my precipitate removal, including a derisive offer of three months "goodbye" pay, with no relocation expenses, and he sympathized. During lunch, I arranged a telephone call with my lawyer Arthur Barnett in Seattle, whom I had engaged to represent me if necessary in a fight for adequate severance arrangements. I wanted Gene, himself an eminent lawyer, to get the picture from another attorney. They talked first about the forcible removal of the Japanese from the West Coast in 1942, which Arthur had fought all the way to the Supreme Court, and Gene was fascinated. It didn't hurt for Rostow to know what kind of lawyer was pressing *my* case. The two were equals in civic conscience and knowledge of the 1942 breach of the Constitution, and both deplored what had then happened. (In 1942 Barnett argued the case of a young Japanese American who had refused removal to a concentration camp before the Supreme Court; he lost the case but was vindicated when the Court amazingly reversed itself half a century later!)

Gene came back to the table obviously impressed with Arthur, who eventually got me a decent settlement from the Council. He gave me a note that his wife Edna, a dear friend, had written to me that morning, saying she was mortified and sadder than she could say that my brilliant work at the Council had come to this. Gene said there was nothing that others or I could do. "But, Jim, you have to realize, this is Washington and things are different here. One day you can be doing nicely in your office and the next, poof! You're out! It's just the way things are here."

A few weeks earlier, President Reagan had summarily removed Gene Rostow from his post as director of the Arms Control and Disarmament Agency. About that time, Gene also broke his foot—two simultaneously ignominious incidents. But, said he, "I just took it for another example of the ways of the Beltway." I told him I understood "serving at the pleasure of the president of the United States" and the attendant vulnerability, but it seemed to me that the job I had held at ACUS was a nongovernmental, professional post, so why the board's lack of conscience? "Ah, that's just Washington," he said. "In a high-powered organization such as ACUS everyone understands that you would be vulnerable, even if your removal were not justified by the facts." He smiled that toothy smile that so engaged me, and I shrugged.

Lesson 3: Don't underestimate the power of the Beltway establishment to protect their collective behinds and close ranks within any organization, political or parapolitical, where they come together, where egos collide, and has-beens (or wannabes) scramble for attention.

I was in a parapolitical position and didn't know it! The Council gave David Acheson, a Washington lawyer and son of the venerable Dean (by then deceased), the job of working out a settlement with my lawyer and me. The conciliation and fair outcome were largely due to a small board committee appointed by Rush, composed of General Andrew Goodpaster, U. Alexis Johnson, and Tim Stanley. Goodpaster had been Eisenhower's cabinet secretary and later Supreme Allied Commander Europe (and my nomination for God, as a Harvard classmate had said of Professor Paul Freund); Alex Johnson was one of the State Department professional greats; and Tim Stanley had been a pal since Harvard days and had started his own NGO to study the problems of the developing world.

Lesson 4: Don't try to live and work inside the Beltway if you can help it! Colleen hung a sign on my typewriter at home: "Mental clearance sale! Everything must go!!!" Great girl! Great idea!

(Note for other Beltwayfarers: The above remarks are a personal allergic reaction, which may bear no resemblance to the experience of others who have settled in Washington, D.C., during and after long careers in government service or in think tanks and NGOs of various kinds. I was lucky in that my ties with Home (the Pacific Northwest) remained virtually as strong as those during my long years of government, foundation, and NGO service on the east coast. Many, Foreign Service officers in particular, are not so fortunate—their early and long careers, oscillating between Washington and everywhere possible in the rest of the world, has made the nation's capital, at least after some years, their real and virtually only Home. It's a great place to live if (a) you can stand the weather; and (b) you are not dependent on it for most of your psychic sustenance.)

One Door Closes, Others Open

The year 1985 opened with a great void. What were we now to do? Our first impulse was to return straightaway to home-state Washington, for invigoration from the climate, friends, and congenial atmosphere. I had no desire to find another executive position inside the Beltway. Opportunities for consulting work suggested themselves, however; I might engage some clients and in a year or two move back home, taking the clients along if I could. That is exactly what happened, and soon I had more consulting business than I could easily handle. I bought my first Macintosh computer, which in effect allowed me to operate for the most part without clerical help; and to change the operation of interpersonal "networking" dramatically. Colleen filled the clerical gaps. I wrote in my journal: "Learning to use my new computer—a fantastic addition to one's *life*, not just work life!"

Old friends at USIA heard I was available and engaged me for two projects. One was a USIA survey for the Congress of a unique teenage exchange program. A few years earlier, the U.S. Congress and the Federal German Bundestag had agreed on an annual exchange of 100 teenagers from each country to attend secondary schools in the other. It was an unprecedented idea, in parliamentary terms, and expressed vibrantly the close ties between the two nations. At about this time, the chairman of the Christian Democratic Party, Walter Leisler Kiep, in a speech to American colleagues in New York, had expressed this closeness well: "Germany has two constitutions: one is our Basic Law, adopted in 1949; the other is our unwritten alliance with the United States of America."

Congress had appropriated the necessary funds and mandated the program's management to USIA, which had all the necessary machinery, including close contacts with the nongovernmental entities that accepted the teenagers for U.S. placement and ties with those administering the program in Germany. There, the Bundestag had opened a special office that arranged for the selection of Germany's young participants and for the placement of the American teenagers in German homes and schools. The scheme had been neatly arranged and continued for many years. Just as I became free of my ACUS ties, the Congress decided it wanted an independent appraisal of how the program worked—in both directions. I was a natural choice, in major part because I had helped to run such teenage exchange programs in the fifties, from Germany.

There followed a fascinating series of interviews in the Federal Republic and the United States, some with the heads of the various NGOs involved, others with teachers, school administrators, and parents of both "receiving" and "sending" families. I also met a number of the teenagers

454   An Architect of Democracy

themselves—sometimes in small groups after they had returned to their hometowns, sometimes individually while they were still attending the foreign school. I found that for the most part the program worked well, and the results—in terms of broader and richer attitudes by all involved— were substantial. I found some anomalies, a few mistakes, and a lack of follow-through, but for the most part the governmental and programming organizations on both sides were doing a good job. In only one case, that of an NGO that had become the personal fiefdom of the now-aging man who had started it and was now making a hash of it, did I feel it necessary to intervene, very privately and delicately, to explain to some key board members what was wrong. It seemed that most were aware of the situation and my intervention was only the catalyst for the private thoughts they already entertained. This happened often in my career.

Lesson learned: The attention of an outside consultant with no axes to grind can be of considerable importance to an organization that needs impartial outside intervention to provide fresh perspectives and an objective analysis of "what's wrong and how it might be fixed."

Another lesson learned: Often over the years, and not just in 1985, nongovernmental, nonprofit organizations suffer from a common organizational defect. Their constitutions, articles of incorporation, by-laws or what have you often omit a crucial provision, namely, that every member of the board of directors should be serving a finite term (for some groups, two years, for others, three, or more). It may be wise to stipulate that a particularly helpful director could be nominated again after an interval of, say, a year. Or reelection for one second term could be optional. But most directors will have done their duty and given their best in one term of office. The lack of such a provision sometimes makes the delicate removal of some board members who have overstayed their welcome virtually impossible. Inclusion of such a term-limits rule makes it possible for the entire board to thank the retiring member profusely while making way for an invigorating replacement and, even more important, preventing domination by individuals or cliques.

I made one important suggestion for the Bundestag and congressional members who oversaw the program, namely, that they form a small joint commission to guide it on a permanent basis. I believe this was especially important to insure continuity of stewardship, as otherwise individual parliamentary members can clasp hands onto such a long-term exercise and never let go. In other cases, the vagaries of parliamentary politics can be such that a member can suddenly be removed electorally, and the search for his or her replacement may eventuate in later mistakes. I'm glad to say that this was done and the program continues—in the 21st century—as one small but solid contribution to the foundation of mutual understanding between two key Atlantic allies, at a time when such non-political anchors ("the bonds of social tissue" one colleague called them) are more important than ever.

Time after time, I have met or heard of Germans, some extremely important and some less so, who as youngsters or as people of position spent weeks or a year in the United States on our exchange of persons grants. The Fulbright program for graduate students and professors is only the best-known of these many private and public ventures; the Rhodes scholarships are another. As in all human endeavors there is the occasional misfire—the selection was a wrong one, or the program flawed, or both. But in the large majority of cases (and not just with Germans), I remain convinced that money spent this way, sending Americans abroad to learn and bringing foreigners to our country, gets us the biggest bang for the buck of almost any federal expenditure.

Helmut Schmidt was one of the great success stories of such exchange programs. Alas, the same cannot be said of Jacques Chirac, who apparently enjoyed his year at an Indiana college, jerking sodas on the side, but failing in the end to let this experience temper some unnecessarily harsh rhetorical bombs lobbed at the Americans in 2002–4. Obversely, it has seemed to me that George "Dubya" Bush glaringly exposed his lack of understanding or care for Europeans in general during the same tense period; he apparently never learned lessons that a longish sojourn as a young man in France or Germany, for example, could have helped to temper some of his Texan bombast and Yale arrogance. If I could earmark future leaders with some certainty, I would insist that they all study abroad and live with foreign families at some point between 16 and 25 years of age. Failing that kind of prescience, I propose that the best late adolescents be "exchanged" to provide the constant leavening of character and attitudes that those who will later influence or direct others will require. Such interchange programs are also of great value for emerging and mature leaders. Rudyard Kipling spoke trenchantly on the value of exposure to other cultures: "What knows he of England who only England knows?"

As a byproduct of the Congress-Bundestag assignment, I was able to take a fresh look, in some depth, at the German national mood and psyche. From my journal (October 1985):

> Germans are not exactly the same as 30 years ago—less deferential to Americans (always want to talk German on *their* turf), also more *Angst* -filled, especially the younger ones. But there is a democratic solidity, a fair stability which makes me think that *this* time they have got it right. Nevertheless, their youth—some of them—can arouse fear. *Wohin?* [Where are we headed?] We

[Americans] *must* keep them bound to the West and to us; and are
we up to it?

Today, two decades later, if I were to ask again, "Are *we* up to it?" I
would have to answer a good deal less optimistically. In the new century,
it is evident that some of the close ties, the social tissue, that bound us
to Germany at the person-to-person level, have atrophied. I'm not sure
most Germans, or most Americans, now think the effort worthwhile. I was
writing the above journal entry while on a speaking tour at Ohio colleges,
just after the hopeful 1985 Carolina conference; yet when I tried to answer my own question, even then I could only say: "I'm not sure [we're
up to it] when I contemplate the clear trend here [in the U.S.] towards
'go-it-alone-ism' disdain for allies. Can we arouse Americans from their
complacency?"

The question today hovers over us even more insistently. When Donald Rumsfeld referred to the Germans and French as "old Europe" and the
Bush II administration ran roughshod into the Iraq quagmire with only a
few "new Europeans," such as Poles and Czechs, to help us and the British, the likely answer to my question appears grim. The glue that held the
West together has to a large extent begun to drain away.

The Bicentennial of the United States Constitution

Jack Hedges, an old buddy from my USIA days, phoned me early in 1985
to ask if I could help him, as a consultant, to formulate themes for the
public celebration of our U.S. Constitution's 200th birthday, coming up
in the summer of 1987. Congress and President Reagan had appointed a
Commission on the Bicentennial of the United States Constitution, and
Congress had provided an appropriation. Supreme Court Justice Warren
Burger was appointed Commission chairman (and retired soon from the
Court to devote full-time to the project). Hedges had been tapped to aid
Justice Berger as international coordinator for the celebration; this required
plans and a lot of suggestions for U.S. Information Service posts abroad,
for the USIA "home office" in Washington, and for nongovernmental bodies—largely foundations and educational organizations—that might be
enlisted. Most Americans and all but a few foreigners were aware of the
great importance of the 1787 Constitution, its impact on American life, especially its significant influence on what had happened around the world
to encourage and secure the foundations of freedom. Many abroad had
heard of the vaunted separation of powers and the ten-amendment Bill of
Rights, but few understood the significance of the *federal* character of our
basic law.

I leapt at the opportunity. Obviously, as a student of history and world politics, a protagonist of that protofederal enterprise that eventually became the European Union, and especially having had to explain the United States to foreigners at the Iron Curtain and elsewhere abroad, I already knew a good deal about the basic legal roots of my own country. But one can always learn more. It was a project made in heaven for USIA, my old stomping grounds, and for me personally. What Hedges needed was a wealth of carefully selected materials, and suggestions for ways to present these, that would illuminate the meaning of the Constitution for the past, present, and future of all humanity. The project took about a third of my time for the subsequent two years.

For me, the principal meaning of 1787 was the potential applicability of its principles and its tremendously ingenious provisions for individual nations wanting governmental systems that would give ethnic, geographic, and historical diversities their head while retaining national unity in managing problems that single states could not handle alone. This was the pervading principle behind the various 20th century schemes to unite Europe; today, for example, there are no internal barriers to trade within its single, common market, and most of its members now use a common currency. This problem was one of the original targets of the Continental Congress when it adopted the old Articles of Confederation (1777). By 1785, however, the Congress had begun to see that a much more radical and close-knit scheme would have to replace the rather loose arrangements under which the Revolutionary War had been fought.

As I began to read and think about what Catherine Drinker Bowen had called "the miracle at Philadelphia," I was constantly amazed at what the concentrated mental firepower of a small group of men, representing many different interests of the former colonies, had come up with in that sultry summer of 1787; with the remarkable durability and flexibility of the great new thing the Founding Fathers had wrought; and with what they had written about the spanking new system of government they were inventing. Only the Dutch and the Swiss had previously tried federalism; the former abandoned it; several centuries of tweaking and a short civil war were required for the Swiss to make it workable, finally, in 1848.

Such phrases as the majestic "We, the people of the United States, in order to form a more perfect union" came to have immense and sobering new meaning for me. The Constitution of 1787 could have been just one glorious historical accident; or perhaps the hand of Providence inspired these mostly normal, sometimes selfish and vainglorious, but on the whole rather amazing group to pull themselves up by their collective bootstraps. The import for the world's future was incalculable. In the event, Bicentennial lectures, conferences, cross-frontier visits by experts, and many new books and articles came forth around 1987, circling the globe during this celebratory period. Schools and universities were of course prime targets.

Radio and television (the Internet was not yet a general reality) were main elements in our 1985–87 campaign to show the relevance of the American Constitution to contemporary man in his attempts to arrange domestic and international order in the late 20th century. It was my job to work up some leading themes for the enterprise and to suggest materials (existing and yet to be created) to fuel the undertaking. Twenty years later, a good deal of the institutional memory created at Philadelphia, repackaged, remains for the inspiration of others seeking to create or improve federal systems.

At the outset of the project, I therefore proposed that Hedges add to the objectives of his Bicentennial information program something that to me is inherently the best, most ingenious, and almost universally applicable element to the situation of the nations, namely, *federalism*. He readily acquiesced, although his original ideas had focused on the Constitution in broad terms and on a chance to highlight a central page in American history. Federalism became a centerpiece of my proposals and of the story I outlined for USIS posts around the world.

In my judgment, our Constitution's truly major contribution to the history of government was the conception and fleshing out of the first workable federal system. True, it required another century and a bloody Civil War, fought not only on the slavery question but on the principle of the ultimate authority and indissolubility of the whole people, the federal glue that bound the American states together. The federal principle, I believed, could be applied and elaborated to meet the needs, for instance, of a developing and still-fragile European union. Since 2001, Europe has been transforming itself yet again with a proposed constitution that reached out for federal principles, despite recent setbacks. Other regions of the world were struggling in the same general direction, if even more fitfully.

World Federalists and other idealists would no doubt protest the inadequacy of contemporary international institutions more feebly than the European federalists—and with even less prospects for attainment of a world government—but the principles established by the U.S. Constitution of 1787, augmented by the national federal systems of several other countries established over the intervening years, are there as models when more nations and peoples feel ready and able to embrace and adapt them for local or regional use. As I write, the nation of Iraq is trying, with America as the principal midwife, to give birth to a workable new system of government. Federal principles that the United States and afterward many others have embodied in their systems are there for the taking, with obvious adaptations required to meet local needs. This Iraq experiment (and others) may not work, or work for very long, but at least the principles are known and endure. Meanwhile, such countries as Canada, Australia, Germany, Brazil, and India can give a measure of thanks to the 1787 Founders in Philadelphia.

In January 1987, as the Bicentennial Year began and after Colleen and I had finally returned to settle in Seattle, I wrote for a local newspaper, the *Seattle Post-Intelligencer*, an account of what I regarded as "the most pregnant meaning—if we can visualize it—of 1787, as the United States celebrates its 200th federal birthday""

> It is wildly utopian to think that the United Nations or any conceivable universal system could, within the foreseeable future, develop into an international federation. But it is not at all utopian to believe that a strong and free international community, based on the principles of 1787 and the experience of Europe since 1945 and coalescing among the genuinely democratic nations, could gradually develop into an effective world peace system. To help build— within nations and among them—the rule of law, civil rights and political liberties, self-government and, eventually, federal institutions, is the true American vocation.

The University of South Carolina at the Helm of the Known World— Briefly

At about the time Hedges enlisted me to help with the Constitution's bicentennial, I was approached by the University of South Carolina's "man in Washington" to help put some meat on the bones of a big idea: to convene fifty or sixty of the "free world's" chief thinkers and doers to project the future of the Western community some years ahead. Again, my old friend Walt Raymond, by 1985 an associate director of the U.S. Information Agency, came to my rescue. Walt had not only directed Jack Hedges to me but had brought me together with Jonathan Davidson, a fine young former British diplomat. Davidson had become an American and was representing the rather bumptious, revitalized University of South Carolina in the nation's capital. "Representing" meant, among other things, paving the way for congressional handouts to an important state university in all the diverse ways that this can be done, keeping in touch with the Beltway movers and shakers whom the university's president and staff might rely on for help in conceivable instances, and using national and international resources such as foreign embassies to enhance the university's public face and its curriculum.

The university's president, Dr. James B. Holderman, was one of the greatest political impresarios I have ever encountered. When I got to know Holderman, I felt he was a good and decent man who advanced himself and his own interests in dramatic and most effective ways, but he also advanced the best interests of his university and the public too. Under Holderman's brief tenure, there is little doubt that the university forged towards prominence statewide, nationally, and even internationally. Holderman, as the former No. 2 in a large U.S. foundation, was a master at securing foundation and federal grants. He relied on the South Carolina legislature to provide the basic educational funds but was able to flesh out the curriculum conspicuously with the private flows of money. In one year, for example, he enticed Henry Kissinger to the campus in Columbia for a series of lectures, enlisted Anwar Sadat's widow to lecture for a term on women's rights in the Arab world, and even attracted Pope John Paul II for a memorable weekend.

Enlisting such luminaries on a regular basis cost a good deal of money; Kissinger for example, required at least $25,000 for a lecture. To make it easy for Mme. Sadat to commute from her residence in Washington, D.C., to Columbia, Holderman sent his private jet weekly to pick her up and return her. Once I joined her and her huge Egyptian general–bodyguard on this flight. We had time to pass. I found her delightful and keen on her topic of women in Islam. Returning to Washington on the same plane, we three played Scrabble! On another occasion, I shared a flight from Washington to Columbia with the Japanese ambassador to the United States. We found a common bond in that both of us were in our respective countries' navies in World War II. When the ambassador explained, carefully, that he had trained to be a Kamikaze pilot but fortunately this career had been obviated by war's end, I thought we had pretty well exhausted old war stories.

Because President Holderman was so widely and favorably known in Washington, a memorable turnout of members of Congress and the Reagan administration, Supreme Court justices, K Street lobbyists, journalists, think-tankers, and other Beltway denizens came to a special birthday party for Holderman held in Washington in 1986.

I liked Jonathan Davidson immensely, and we became friends for life. When he told me Holderman wanted help in putting on the Conference on the Future of the Western Community—costs and other resources more or less no object—I responded quickly and positively, as both a consultant and a conferee. This, after all, was my special bailiwick—relations among the great democracies. Using Jonathan's contacts and my own, we recruited a glittering array of fifty-seven political, academic, media, and diplomatic stars to attend. Among these were:

Lord Carrington, the Secretary General of NATO and former UK foreign secretary and defence secretary

J. Malcolm Fraser, former Prime Minister of Australia

Lt. Gen. Brent Scowcroft, between administrations as national security adviser to the president

Ambassador Hisashi Owada, a specialist in international law then teaching at Harvard, later permanent undersecretary of the Japanese Foreign Ministry, and subsequently father-in-law to the Crown Prince of Japan and Justice of the World Court

Ambassador Lawrence S. Eagleburger, Chairman of the Conference and former Undersecretary of State (later Secretary of State) under President George H. W. Bush

Dr. Peter Corterier, former Minister for Foreign Affairs of West Germany, later Secretary-General of the North Atlantic Assembly

Admiral James Eberle, Director of the Royal Institute of International Affairs, London

Jim Hoagland, Assistant Managing Editor of the *Washington Post*

Thierry de Montbrial, Director, Institut Français des Relations Internationales, Paris

Guenter van Well, Germany's ambassador to the United States

Inger Lisa Skarstein, member of the Norwegian Parliament

Sir David Wills, founder of the Ditchley Foundation and the Atlantic Colleges, UK

Gerald Wright, President of the Canadian Atlantic Council and the Canadian Donner Foundation

John Richardson, former Assistant Secretary of State for Cultural and Educational Affairs, head of Youth for Understanding, and later President of the Council for a Community of Democracies and chairman of the National Endowment for Democracy.

Yoshio Okawara, Ambassador of Japan to the United States

David Abshire, U.S. Ambassador to NATO

U.S. Senator Malcolm Wallop

Alan Lee Williams, Director of the English-Speaking Union and the British Atlantic Committee and former MP

Charles Heck, director of the Trilateral Commission

Vice President George H. W. Bush addressed the conferees at a luncheon. He referred to the Western nations as the nucleus of "our community of democracies," at that time an unusual formulation from the highest levels of government. (Needless to say, as happened on a later White House occasion with President Reagan, Walt Raymond, Jonathan Davidson, and I had a hand in writing the most salient parts of Bush's speech.)

The words "community of democracies" had already been uttered in the papers and meetings of the original Committees for a Community of Democracies (November 1982 and April 1985). I later gave the idea a strong push in my book *Pax Democratica* (1998, 2001), and tried to flesh out the concept in terms of needed institutions. The expression resonated finally in Secretary of State Madeleine Albright's 1999 interview with the *Los Angeles Times* and was given practical form with the convening in 2000 of a real (if rather weak) global Community of Democracies in Warsaw (see chapter 18).

The Carolina conferees of 1985 also included a number of academics from both sides of the Atlantic, New Zealand, Japan, Australia, and Canada, in addition to heads of foundations and important nongovernmental associations and think tanks, including the early version of the CCDs, and the German political foundations. It was a representative and influential group, but sufficiently compact to enable considerable interaction for all present.

Lesson learned: Our Carolina conferees were notably, with few exceptions, stellar players in international relations whose personal predilections generally pointed in the same direction: the cohesion, consolidation, and expansion of what until this time had been the Atlantic, but was now the Western, Community, and the projection of an even larger democratic community in the future. We all agreed that Japan was a strong—indeed indispensable—member, even if not "Atlantic" geographically or culturally, in the West's pattern of security and economic alliances. The term "Atlantic-Pacific community" also surfaced, but "Western" was favored; after all, it was pointed out that Japanese Prime Minister Yasuhiro Nakasone had only recently said, "We [Japanese] are now in the West." For me, this meeting was an early inspiration to think about a concept of like-mindedness as a basis for a sound international order. I subsequently explored the concept at great length in my book, *Pax Democratica*.

Jonathan Davidson and I had had time to recruit most of the participants in personal interviews, or through tapping the long associations we had had with many of them. We arranged an agenda congenial to all, and particularly forward-looking for its day. I was tapped to write the main conference paper, which I entitled "The Once and Future West." This managed to sum up what our nations and peoples had done together in four decades, while setting forth a number of challenging aims (most later reflected in the Conference Report and Recommendations). These were in the main goals that I had offered to the Atlantic Council board of directors during my short tenure with them, but which for the most part appeared too expansive and futuristic to suit the traditionalists who dominated the ACUS political process.

Jonathan and I were able to recruit some new and fresh faces, as well as some of the tried-and-true, for a new "leap forward" to which we hoped the movers and shakers in and out of government could be attracted. In major part, we succeeded. Later, the first Bush administration, with Scowcroft and Eagleburger again in prominent official positions, was able to push the "South Carolina agenda" forward to a remarkable extent. Following are examples of the conference recommendations, with my commentary.

• **Defense in Europe should be "Europeanized," but only if it would make Europeans more responsible for their own security and not harm the cohesion of NATO.** It is interesting that one of the background papers for the 1985 conference, prepared by Professor Donald Puchala, surveyed elite and general public opinion in Europe and concluded that "the United States can't control [Atlantic defense] by hegemony anymore." At least until the 1991 demise of the Soviet Union and until after the first Gulf War, I believe the United States did continue to exercise this hegemony, although waveringly and usually benignly. The attempt to restore and greatly reinforce this unilateral leadership role, however, failed miserably prior to and during the Iraq War that began in 2003. Hegemony was never a sound basis for community. Joint leadership on many levels, I am convinced, is the only basis for an enduring relationship among the democracies, which is needed as much today as it was in the 1980s.

• **Western efforts should continue their "apparent political success in somewhat altering Soviet aspirations."** These efforts eventually led via real détente to the collapse of the USSR, although no one forecast this in 1985.

• **The security threat was seen as increasingly global**, not just Atlantic, and NATO informal consultations with non-NATO members not formally part of the Alliance, such as Japan, should be stepped up. Consideration of security interests in both the Atlantic and Pacific areas should be considered jointly more often than at the time. NATO's 2002 intervention in Afghanistan is a recent example.

• **China was seen as not "presently a threat,"** but the "West should posture itself in such a way that it does not detract from China's sense of its own security."

For the most part, events in the Chinese sphere have developed even more positively than this cautious scenario suggested, and Western policy has patiently encouraged this.

• **Global relations in economic, cultural, and technological sectors change, but security relationships in the past have "changed only as a result of war." How could the West help adjust security relationships without war?** Some basic answers have been found in the intervening twenty years—the peaceful dismantling of the Soviet empire in Eastern Europe being the prime example, the NATO–UN campaigns in Yugoslavia another, although there combat proved necessary. In other parts of the world, although peacekeeping (and sometimes peacemaking) efforts have sometimes been successful, there have also been egregious examples of Western ineffectiveness or downright inaction, as in Rwanda and Congo.

• An **"improved consultative mechanism"** was considered "extremely urgent," especially to "cover [NATO] out-of-area questions, or bring in important nonmembers for certain discussions." This should be done "at a lower level than Summits, and on a more permanent level of dialogue." Some of this was subsequently done, but it was evident during the Iraq crisis that much more would be needed. Again, in *Pax Democratica* (1998) I urged the formation of such a "Democracies Planning Group"—hard to accomplish but even more urgent in 2005 than it was in 1985. Continuous and quiet consultation among at least the most powerful of the Western group, and eventually others, seems to me imperative.

• Although rarely discussed in such conferences, previously or since, the question of **"how to strengthen the psychological and social fabric of the Western Community"** was examined at length in a special working group. I had written a paper for them urging a consolidation of the information and cultural services of the main Western countries to stress for all the common ideals and interests of their peoples. Some members of the group could not go this far, but they did recommend **increased educational exchange programs—especially with non-Western countries—as well as "retraining leaders and publics to think of our community as more than the North Atlantic region" and bringing Pacific peoples in particular into increased dialogue.** Other recommendations were to confront the mutual hostilities of some alliance peoples (such as the Greeks and Turks) and seek actively "to remove or reduce these." Governments were urged to "strengthen mutual loyalties among their peoples" and in other ways to act "in the spirit of community." The subsequent actions of Sir David Wills and Lord Carrington and others in setting up the 21st Century Trust "young leaders" programs were undertaken largely in this spirit. A good deal has been done, yet not nearly enough.

• A major recommendation of the "psychosocial" panel was to propose that **"one or more large new international foundations be established privately** for the purpose of enhancing the cohesion, dynamism, and free way of life of the Western Community of nations and peoples, and strengthening mutual loyalties." Subsequent efforts, led by some of the conferees, to set up at least one such foundation succeeded in the United Kingdom. Most unfortunately, as discussed below, a comparable and perhaps overly ambitious effort to create such a body in the United States failed, although such Carolina luminaries as Lawrence Eagleburger, Brent Scowcroft, and John Richardson were among the strong and active proponents.

• The conference's economic panel confronted other questions that were just as tough but more readily defined. **Most economic problems cited by the Conference, cited below, remain virtually the same two decades later.** The accumulation of advanced governments' debts was deplored. U.S. budget and trade deficits were especially worrisome. In the developing world, the IMF was criticized for conditions it imposed in return for aid that posed "serious hardships" and "imperiled democratic government" in many countries. The poor parts of the world badly needed more private foreign investment. And the "stabilization of exchange rates . . . would not solve problems of unemployment." Even the EU's adoption of a common currency, the Euro, in 2001 suggested this would not be enough—the members probably would have to merge their economic, fiscal, and even their social benefits systems to pave the way for a common, high rate of economic growth.

• **The General Agreement on Tariffs and Trade (created in 1948) was clearly in need of updating,** the conferees agreed, and this in fact was later done (1995) when the World Trade Organization (WTO) superseded GATT, creating in particular a judicial mechanism to settle trade disputes. The management of the Japanese economy came in for a good deal of criticism; in twenty years, although the second largest economy in the world, it has until recently been one of the sickest by comparison with other advanced countries.

The conference decided to make itself permanent and empowered its chairman and the University of South Carolina to convene further sessions (although, somewhat tragically, this was not to be). Above all, the spirit of the conference was upbeat and convivial. President Holderman held glittering dinners and luncheons, bringing together South Carolina dignitaries, university faculty, and conferees who were tackling the problems outlined above and who worked seriously to suggest new orientations for the Western Community. A good many of the fresh approaches found their way into the policies of governments and international bodies such as NATO and the G-7. In short, we all went home with some justified pride of accomplishment and with many new personal links established and old ones strengthened, expecting to be reconvened for more talks. Subsequent events prevented this.

The momentum of "South Carolina" might still have been preserved, but local events three years later that had nothing to do with the conference or the conferees or the great changes in the world transpired to scuttle the University of South Carolina's support and sponsorship for the work of the conference. Suddenly, in 1988, a scandal broke in the newspapers of Columbia, South Carolina's capital and the University's home: President Holderman was accused of misusing both public and private university funds—not so much for his own purposes but mainly to cut bureaucratic and legal corners that hampered (or so he apparently thought) his ability to move the institution he had greatly revivified into the national and international spotlight. Eventually the law and the State Legislature came down hard on him. He lost his position and drifted into oblivion.

Knowing nothing of the details of his undoing, I could not help but feel of two minds about the president's disgrace. Activities such as the Conference on the Future of the Western Community had done a great deal of public good. The conferees were an extraordinary group with considerable influence abroad and in their own countries; the subjects they dealt with and the policy conclusions they addressed were perhaps of a broader, more forward-looking, and more incisive nature than those reached in any number of other international gatherings I had attended or knew about. The groundwork had been laid for important contributions—some quite strategic in nature—to the togetherness of the core nations of the West. A good many challenging thoughts had been sprinkled over the participants that were later to animate fresh initiatives. The university's faculty had been upgraded and sometimes inspired by their interaction with what the British have come to call "the great and the good"—and how many university students or faculty would see the pope on their campus?

The idea of new private foundations to buttress the community psychologically took firm root in at least one country—the United Kingdom—and flowered into a continuous string of seminars for emerging world leaders that by the 21st century had enveloped a large number of young people within a functioning network to develop and push new ideas.

Also, the CCD objective (1982 in London, and April 1985 at Wingspread) of a worldwide community of democracies as a means of strengthening peace and good government had been floated at the Columbia meetings, to crystallize by 2000 in an interministerial global grouping of more than 100 democracies. Part of the answer, I guess—in the words of a popular song—was "blowing in the wind." Ideas are like seeds, and sometimes the ground they fall on is fertile. The CCD, for a time, was folded into the Association for a Union of Democracies (AUD), which held a small conference in 1992 to plan a much larger one—which might have been a successor to the Carolina events of 1985. But the original CCD and AUD ran out of steam. The support of the university was a real loss; the movement perforce languished.

Some of the Carolina spirit and some of the personal links among the conferees nevertheless persisted. In 1993 a dozen leaders of the Carolina group met with other leaders at the Cosmos Club to try to recapture the forward thrust. But by this time, with the Cold War ended, the perspectives of elites and publics had diversified greatly, and a period of drift in Western affairs had ensued, as discussed in chapter 18.

I commended then—and still do—James Holderman for having had the vision in 1985 to convene such a gathering and for having amassed a glittering array of contacts around the Western world. If they could no longer coalesce around him and the university, they were still important to the success of future networking of many such persons within the world of high politics. The connections formed between Lord Carrington and Sir David Wills on the one hand and Brent Scowcroft and Larry Eagleburger on the other were to flower in various ways.

Still, it is hard to fathom what sort of mental and emotional wrinkles in the psyche of Holderman could have induced him to overreach so disastrously. The "Carolina process"—begun with great promise—could not fulfill its potential. In large measure, Holderman spoiled it for his university, his state, and especially the larger international policy networks he had begun to establish. His fate was tragic, and not only personally for himself and family.

The Holderman scandal did not break until nearly three years after the 1985 Columbia conference. In the intervening period, Jonathan Davidson, the university's man in Washington, and the university's prestigious law firm were nonetheless able to bring to life an offshoot of the 1985 conference—the 21st Century Foundation. This too collapsed, however, like so many initiatives in this waning period of the Cold War, but not before it had planted still broader ideas and closer ties among the initiators. I believe that the run-up to the 1985 conference and the meetings themselves also had an important impact on the outlook and plans of the university's scholars and academic departments, widening perspectives (for me, as well). It may also have indirectly influenced government policy, at the time and during the Bush I administration that followed Reagan's.

The 21st Century Trust (UK) and the 21st Century Foundation (USA)

In 1982, as noted earlier, I had undertaken a survey of the many NGOs and nonprofits that helped in various ways to strengthen the psychological bonds of community among the NATO and OECD countries. NATO, the U.S. Information Agency, and Battelle had footed the costs of my time and travel. The completed survey formed the basis for much discussion about the importance and future of such private groups and enabled me to make the plea at the Carolina conference for more financial support for

such educational bodies. The 1985 conference responded by recommend-
ing the establishment of new foundations in several countries to support
this kind of work; leaders in both the United Kingdom and the United
States took the idea to heart.

Shortly after the conference, I was in London and phoned Sir David
Wills (by that time, after more than two decades of mutual support, an old
and trusted friend.) "David," I said, "you recall our South Carolina resolution about the idea of a big new foundation? Have you thought about
it more?" Said he, "Indeed I have, and I've already been able to consult a
few people. It's not something I could finance alone, though I could give
it a few pennies." He was as good as his word, and within a year or so he
had asked other wealthy people around the world (including the sultan
of Brunei) to jump into a scheme to be established under British charities
law. But the sultan and others said, more or less, "Fine idea, but count me
out."

So David launched the plan on his own in 1986 with his own money
and a more focused program. His 21st Century Trust was to be overseen
by an eminent group of trustees, including Lord Carrington, who had also
caught the foundation microbe at the Carolina conference. Lord Home
and Lord Callaghan, both former prime ministers, joined Carrington
among the original trustees. The Trust continues into the 21st century.
The founders wisely decided that, inasmuch as Sir David was not able
to establish a vast endowment, they would undertake one major activity
only—the holding of seminars for younger leaders for the airing of major
world problems. They have not limited their participants to the Western
world, as global needs for modernization of thought have dictated that
their net be cast globally.

By 2001, the Trust had held more than 60 seminars in various countries, with more than 1,000 young professionals—journalists, politicians,
academics, business leaders, government officials, trade unionists, and
the like—who seemed marked out for leadership in 65 countries around
the globe. Subjects included security, independence, and liberty; what role
governments and business should play in the arts; the economic, political, and social implications of the internet; and human rights as collective
rights, their benefits and pitfalls.

What Americans would call an alumni association of Trust participants has resulted, with follow-up meetings, publications, and the gradual creation of an interpersonal network as important features. There are
a few other groupings similar to those of the Trust, largely in Europe, but
the Trust has become one of the most important. Even more are needed.
Who knows what seeds of intellect and friendship of this kind might generate over the years? Thus, one of my general aims has been advanced

substantially. In 2004, an informal cooperative link was formed between the Trust and the newer (1999) Council for a Community of Democracies in Washington; the potential synergies are obvious. I continued to serve on the Trust's Advisory Board until 2004.

Sir David Wills passed away in 2000 at age 82, secure I think in the knowledge that yet another of the major philanthropic works of his life would continue to knit the "silken bonds," as David once called them, between members of the generations succeeding those who, like David, fought the second World War and the Cold War. David Wills also founded the Ditchley Foundation to do for established international leaders what the Trust would later do for "rising stars"—strengthen interpersonal ties. He was also a major contributor and cofounder of the United World Colleges system (discussed in chapter 11), with ten such colleges by 2000 spanning the globe. He was thus perhaps unique in having laid the groundwork for international education and understanding among members of three generational groups—16-to-19-year-olds, those roughly 30 to 40, and the men and women already guiding the world's work in their mature years. The queen made David a Knight Commander of the British Empire a few years ago in recognition of his work, but I would hope that some more enduring public tribute might eventuate. Sir David Wills was one of just a few unsung heroes of the 20th century, always working quietly behind the scenes to fortify the bonds of our modern global community. They represent the small but vital number of such dedicated persons, virtually faceless and most not seeking glory but satisfied only with the knowledge that they had indeed made the world a somewhat better place because of their efforts.

Home Again

By the spring of 1986, Colleen and I had decided firmly that our future lay again at home, in the Pacific Northwest. I had completed the survey of the Congress-Bundestag Teenage Exchange Program; I was nearing completion of my proposals for the international celebration of the Bicentennial of the U.S. Constitution; and I was assured by President Holderman (before his unfortunate troubles began) that he could use my talents, such as they were, for his university even if it involved some "commuting" to South Carolina from the State of Washington rather than from the rather closer "other Washington."

I actually ached to go Home—to a degree I had never experienced before. On the eve of departure I wrote in my journal: "The idea of returning to Seattle is exhilarating to say the least. In a strange way, I have been released mentally and emotionally."

We shipped our effects and drove west in March, settling in a small condo for two years in downtown Seattle, with a nearby tiny office. I resumed my consulting career—some of it for free because I believed so strongly in the cause of freedom and peace that had animated me for more than thirty years. Sometimes I was compensated for the advice or temporary professional services I could provide. My retirement did not actually begin until sometime in the 1990s, when I began to write and to pursue my civic ends as a local volunteer. I got mildly involved in civic (bordering on the political) affairs in rural Bainbridge Island, where we lived for twelve years, a part of Kitsap County across Puget Sound from Seattle. I continued to serve on boards dealing with international affairs in Seattle, such as the World Affairs Council, and often lectured at my old University of Washington. Colleen and I became particularly interested in saving open land for the future. The Bainbridge Island Land Trust took a fair amount of our time as we helped preserve some 650 acres of forest and meadowland, in two big parcels, for future generations.

But despite these often satisfying local diversions, I never gave up my pursuit of an international community of democracies. If anything, I worked harder than ever towards this goal from 1986 and into the 21st century. To pick up these threads is the main theme of the next chapter.

18
Towards a Global Community of Democracies

9 November 1989: *With the East German government near collapse, jubilant Berliners begin to tear down the Berlin Wall. By 3 October 1990, the two Germanys are united, as the Federal Republic of Germany.*

30 June 2000: *Foreign ministers of 106 countries sign the Declaration of Warsaw establishing a Community of Democracies, a project of Secretary of State Madeleine Albright. and her Polish counterpart.*

Two Decades of Great Change: 1986 –2006

The first major fault line in world affairs in this period was the downfall of the Communist system, in 1989–91. This was followed by a decade of adjustment—or lack thereof—by the major powers to the new realities of a post-Soviet world. In large measure, this was a time of drift, punctuated by midlevel regional and world crises but no major changes in the way the United States and its allies viewed the world, or tried to transform it. The second upheaval—which elicited fateful U.S. action but no solid consensus among the Allies—was the 2001 airliner attack on the twin World Trade Towers in New York and the Pentagon, now known as "9/11," followed by invasions of Afghanistan and Iraq.

In this chapter, I shall try to put these changes into some sort of useful context and indicate what I and other multilateralists of an integrationist/ democratic stripe tried to do to insure that these earthquakes in international relations would lead to positive outcomes. As I write, early in the new millennium, one thing seems clear—great issues remain undecided and uncertainty is rife everywhere.

9

St. Donat's Castle, Wales, ca. 1800, home of the Atlantic College, first in a series of United World Colleges. The author went to England in 1967 to help prepare what eventually became a global series of ten international colleges for 16- to 19-year-old students.

GUILDFORD
SURREY   The High Street

10

For seven years, the author and his wife lived in the "county town" of Guildford, south of London. The drawing shows a portion of Guildford's High Street, which Dickens once called the "prettiest high street in all of England."

11
The Roosevelt Room in the White House, where President Ronald Reagan met on 25 September 1986 with international leaders of the effort to create 21st Century Foundations in London and Washington.

SEATTLE POST-INTELLIGENCER | FRIDAY, DECEMBER 20, 2002

12
War has been on the author's mind since the 1930s. David Horsey is an astute young Seattle cartoonist who has chronicled the world's ups and downs trenchantly for some years; this is his comment on the eve of the Iraq War that began in 2003.

The collapse of Communism might have been foretold in the early 1980s coincident with the Reagan presidency, although virtually no observers—seasoned or otherwise—predicted this major tremor in the international system. My 1983–85 incumbency at the Atlantic Council of the United States and the extra year or so of consulting in the nation's capital that followed had been a period of some ferment. The Cold War was still on, but changes inside the Communist system, especially the assumption of power by Mikhail Gorbachev, and Reagan's defense build-up, coupled with strong efforts to bring about disarmament—in words as well as in big arms deals—brought crises, such as the mideighties' missile-placement confrontation in Europe. At the subsequent eye-opening summit meeting in Reykjavik, President Reagan alarmed his seasoned arms control advisers by proposing drastic cuts in weapons and was met with warmth by the Soviet leader.

It was during this period, 1983–89, that some of us tried hard to propose adjustments in the U.S. and Allied outlook. These included linkages between the Pacific and Atlantic world theaters, the lack of common structures for their management, and a general upgrading of alliances and economic arrangements. In particular, we saw the period between the fall of the Wall and 9/11 as a chance to reaffirm and strengthen democracy and interdependence generally. My own additional view was that standing still we actually slip backward. Interdependence is constantly in need of updated structures and leadership that reflect changing global realities and provide momentum.

In the middle of this period, in March 1986, Colleen and I returned to Seattle. The years that followed were tumultuous for both of us in some ways but even more so for the world. In this penultimate chapter I shall try to map the topography of these great changes, with comments as to what colleagues and I tried to do and how we succeeded, if only in part and always insufficiently.

The Collapse of Communism

Most dramatic and moving for me was the shattering of the Berlin Wall in November 1989. Everyone agrees that this and the subsequent collapse of the Soviet Union in 1991 could not have been forecast. However, as October 1989 came, there was a feeling that something terribly important was in the air. East Germans by the thousands pressed to leave the country and had begun do so despite their government's objections. In New York on 5 October, I wrote in my diary:

I awoke with a vision the other night: Unter den Linden, filled with a million Germans singing "Deutschland über Alles," celebrating the tumbling down of the cursed Wall but also the birth of a reunified Germany. Is it yet time? Can we trust them? Will Europe again become a continent of contesting nationalisms? Again, the bad dream from which we thought we had awakened.

As it turned out, the changes in Germany were almost all for the better; the European Union became stronger and expanded eastward, and Communism itself fell apart. I can best catch the actual spirit of those extraordinary days by once again quoting my journal, this time for the 12th of November 1989:

> Yesterday [11 November 1989], more than any other day, will I think be remembered as a great hinge in history, the end of the Cold War, or at least the day when the Unthinkable occurred. 1989 is at least as important a year as 1848. Fortunately, I am not recording the beginning of World War III (as I often thought I might have to if I lived to do it), but the true beginning of the post-postwar era, and hopefully a much better era.
>
> Yesterday [actually, on the 9th] the Berlin Wall began to come down. The bulldozers and jackhammers have not yet begun in earnest, but the GDR announced free travel for its citizens—anywhere. The TV is full of shots of young people from both sides of the Wall, on top of it, cracking bottles of champagne, shouting, picking away at the wall with hammers and chisels, and of hordes of East Germans streaming through the checkpoints, unhindered, many with tears streaming down their faces.

The next day, a nice Canadian neighbor knocked on the door to ask, "Jim, is all this happening because the Russians are broke?" Yes I said, in the most profound, widest sense of broke. Now I began to think of all the wonderful things the West could do, unhindered by fear of a Soviet nuclear attack, and of the brighter future that lay ahead for the peoples of the Communist empire. Now we *really* had a chance to change the world.

Over the next two years, Colleen and I were to glimpse for ourselves what had gone on behind the Iron Curtain. In 1990 we explored by rail the old East Zone and its East Berlin capital, Czechoslovakia, and Hungary. We also revisited Hof to see remnants, if any, of the Iron Curtain. Between my years in Hof, 1954–55 and 1970, when Colleen and I had viewed the Wall near Hof in its most forbidding guise, the East German authorities had created a concrete barrier some twenty feet high, punctuated by guard towers with searchlights and flanked on the western side by plowed minefields overlain with barbed wire. The idea that such a wall separated not only East Berlin from West Berlin but ran all the way from the Czech-Bavarian border to Stettin on the Baltic was monstrous and little understood. Churchill's 1946 portrayal of a Soviet-made "Iron Curtain" in the middle of Europe had become indeed a visual reality by the 1970s.

In the autumn of 1990, we returned to Helmstedt, near Hof, where the north-south autobahn crossed the Saale River, and drove across the old border, now marked only by a symbolic path of earth and cobblestones. The autobahn kiosks where the Peoples' Police had let a chosen few trickle across in either direction for years stood empty; some had already been removed. The nearby *Volkspolizei* barracks were already crumbling. We drove through Thuringian villages we had never seen, though they were but a kilometer or three from us in Cold War days. The roads, the old houses and farm buildings, and the countryside looked as if nothing had been done since 1945; every structure needed a good coat of paint, just as in West Europe at the outset of the Marshall Plan.

Just a short distance away from the autobahn bridge, we crossed the now-imaginary border to a newish suburb of Hof, bright and shining and adorned with traditional geranium window boxes. The contrast was striking, the breath of fresh air on both sides of the old Curtain exhilarating. In Mödlareuth, I had often taken visitors in the 1950s to glimpse a village inhumanly bisected by the then temporary wooden wall. Those who tore away this barrier and the longer one of concrete in 1989 had left one 300-meter section standing as a *Denkmal* (monument, a bystander explained). On one side was a tattered, crude poster in German, reading:

> *17 juni, Day of German Unity, 1953. Gera* [a small suburb of Berlin]: Old Spade-Beard-Tummy-and-Glasses [Walter Ulbricht, then emerging as East Germany's strongman]—these do not represent the will of the people. Soviet tanks against civilians. Mass arrests.
>
> *Plauen, 7 Oktober 1989*: Stasi, People's Police, and paramilitaries, use helicopters, machine pistols, water cannon and rubber truncheons against peaceful demonstrators. *21 Oktober 1989:* [Egon] Krenz [interim East German head of state after the long-endured Honnecker] opens the borders, to freedom without frontiers. Krenzlosen Freiheit [play on words here=freedom without Krenz; German word for borders is Grenz].

I had never before heard of the Plauen incident, but there must have been many in the months and days preceding the Eastern collapse. Until nearly the very end, the East German authorities vacillated between mailed fist and velvet glove.

On 3 October 1990, a day after formal reunification—and the singing by massed choruses in the old Reichstag of the "Ode to Joy" from Beethoven's Ninth: "All men will become brothers"—we gloried in Berlin's boisterous and joyful crowds. The vestiges of the Berlin Wall were mostly down, but the landscape was more scarred than in Hof; people everywhere were still knocking off souvenir pieces of the Wall (we still have one). Under and around the Brandenburg Gate, ragged lines of rickety tables were laden with souvenirs for the tourists. We bought a tiny model Trabant, the East's ubiquitous equivalent of the Volkswagen, plus a few Soviet medals and cap insignia—for sale mostly by forlorn-looking Russian soldiers in remnant uniforms. A year later, my friend, former Bundestag Member Peter Corterier, gave me a Soviet officer's watch, which I treasure for its symbolism. It is a solid chrome "turnip" of the kind my grandfather had carried in his waistcoat pocket. The chrome was adorned with leafy patterns; inside the hinged cover was a similarly convoluted design, with Roman numerals for the twelve hours and a wind-up stem. It connected by a simple steel chain to the officer's tunic. It reminded me of the tale of an old friend who had visited Moscow for the first time in the late 1950s and found that the toilets in the Tupolev airliner were all porcelain. How were these Soviets able to scare us for so long?

At the Lichtenberg station in East Berlin, on 8 October, we entrained for two cities we had never seen, Prague and Budapest. On the eastern side of the old Berlin Wall, en route to the station, we saw sacks full of winter coal supplies laboriously unloaded from a truck and trundled by wheelbarrow to a cellar casement. It took three men to do what one using machines would do in the West. In one short year, many economic, technical, and political changes had not yet reached daily life for East Germans.

Our rail trip across and down the Elbe River and thence to Prague passed many forlorn factories, dead looking and blackened, and also wound through and around Soviet army bases, some already deserted. I recall big pools of yellowish liquids standing alongside the train tracks—unmistakable signs of the carelessness and headlong industrialization and militarization that had accompanied the building of the expanding Soviet empire after 1945. These sights made the spoliation of the environment in the West look like a bucolic Sunday school picnic. Germany had a modern economy by the lights of the 1930s, but the Soviets managed to pretty well ruin its eastern third by carting away whole factories as reparations and then "allowing" the East Zone authorities to rebuild what they thought would be essential to an integrated imperial Soviet economy.

A year later, I went alone into eastern Germany, again by rail, but this time taking a different route—from Forcheim in northwestern Unterfranken (part of Bavaria) on a northeastern trajectory to Berlin. I covered much more industrial wasteland then we had seen in 1990. My journal records parts of this journey:

> [Passed through] the Thuringian town of Probstzella, which for me was only a very foreign name in the 1950s. At its rwy. station, it looks pitiful, as does the land around it. Some station buildings are very old and ill-painted, a few are newer and ill-painted. . . . On the western side, small fields mown with modern mechanical equipment—east, all by hand. Eastern villages—all shabby, with almost no exceptions. Like most of Europe in 1948 [when I first saw it]. . . . Coal/steam driven plants, making something; all rusty and rundown, still many Trabis, some abandoned, others still driven, for lack I suppose of wherewithal to replace them.
>
> [Near Halle] Leunewerke, an immense complex of chemical factories—all "dead"—filthy air, decay everywhere. hopelessly outdated industrial plant, but built on a vast scale with no thought for health of nearby inhabitants. At the end of the 20th century, this reproduces worst evils of Dickensian-era English industrialism. Halle also terribly blighted.

It was clear that the Soviets had imported their own type of hellbent-for-leather industrialization to East Germany, which in 1945—although terribly battered—still mirrored much of Western Europe. But four and a half decades later, while the Marshall Plan and mainly Western know-how had transformed lives in the Common Market countries, east of the Iron Curtain desolation ruled. We know that for most ordinary people in East Germany, there was an upside. For example, as our American Communist friends on their 1991 visit to Seattle never let us forget, all working mothers could leave their little ones in state-supported day-care centers, free of charge. In Berlin and major towns, some of the arts (opera, symphony, museums) thrived at a certain level and entry tickets were dirt-cheap. Rent was inexpensive, but building could not keep up with the demand. Some older industries such as the Leica factories were built up, and export sales could be brisk. A large common market in the whole Soviet empire supported transborder trade.

But, as Colleen and I found out when we visited Prague for a few days in 1990, there had been little building under the Communists—even of minimal workers' housing—and little retail trade had been encouraged. The few large tourist hotels in Prague were all full when we arrived; a Czech friend of a friend in Oregon met us at the rail station and took us proudly to a B&B he had arranged: one smallish bedroom down a long corridor in an old *fin de siècle* apartment that had been chopped up for families. The single toilet for five households was 70 feet down the corridor. Our landlady, a struggling divorced nurse, gave up her own bedroom for tourists—us—and slept on a couch in a tiny living-dining room. Off the kitchenette was a curtained bathtub. When we went out in the morning to locate a restaurant for breakfast, none was to be found. Finally, we joined a queue at a ramshackle grocery store, where a few apples, some carrots, a mound of cabbages, and some stingy slices of cheese were the only comestibles available. Some soft drinks or bottled water? "Down the street, in the State store." It was only when our old Czech-born friend from Oregon turned up a few days later that we could enjoy one of the few decent restaurants in Prague—supposedly for the political elite in the old days. We were aghast, our views of life under Communism (even a year after the Fall) almost uniformly gray.

Budapest was a good deal different, much gayer and more open to foreign tourists and vacationing Magyars from the countryside. Hungary had been given substantial latitude by the Soviet overlords since the Revolution of 1956. It was either loosen the economic bonds, ever so slowly but still visibly, or risk another political explosion. After 1968, the Czechs came in for more inexorable suppression, and the Soviet troops that throttled the Prague Spring stayed. Hungary had been cannier.

All in all, these two visits to three countries newly liberated from Communism provided us with sobering thoughts on the past, but with bright hopes for the future. Our new perspectives helped greatly in focusing on tasks for the West that remained undone. I tentatively entitled the new book manuscript I started to write in 1992 "Unfinished Business," but after a hiatus of writing from 1993–95, I began to call it "Pax Democratica," a title suggested by my old CCD comrade, Bob Foulon. I felt compelled, as most of my initiatives between 1984 and 1993 had been throttled at birth or soon after (in an organizational sense), to set down in print my views as to the situation in the world and the West, plus what I thought should be done about it. Of these manuscripts, more later.

On 13 March 1992, on the occasion of the departure of the U.S. VII Corps from its Stuttgart base, Manfred Rommel, longtime *Oberbuergermeister* of Stuttgart and son of the famous field marshal, told the press: "No other victorious nation has helped the defeated one so much. God bless you." I felt downright good. The next decade I spent trying to build more concepts for interdependence, more structures to enshrine the concepts, and better leaders who could understand what needed doing.

The Foundation That Couldn't Get Airborne

Beginning in 1963, one of the persistent ideas that I couldn't get out of my head was the need for a *big* pot of money to endow a foundation dedicated squarely to the continued unification of the West, maintaining—not slackening, as was already happening—the efforts to build ever-stronger social tissue among the peoples and a new set of updated institutions for tasks that no single nation could any longer manage alone. Joe Slater, my colleague at the Ford Foundation, had the same idea. We tried in 1965 to convince our masters that Ford should bankroll such a major philanthropy spinoff, in a way already understood by the Ford Trustees. But this could not be done; Ford began to face a large drain on its reserves due to overoptimistic plunges into the stock market. More important, the overall mood changed with the advent of McGeorge Bundy as president; he was a refugee from the Lyndon Johnson White House, from whence stemmed a general disillusion with the rest of the West and the world, based mostly on the impending fiasco in Vietnam. Besides, Bundy made it pretty clear— so said the newspapers—that he wanted to use Ford as a springboard for a possible political career; there were many domestic wants Ford could try to meet, but its overseas activities would be cut to do this.

I persisted in looking for ways to launch such a big Foundation for the West, as I then called it. Once, in 1975, I had written a proposal for such a foundation and laid it on the desk of the Norwegian ambassador in Washington. My reasoning was that (1) Norway had been one of the earliest advocates (1941) of what eventually became NATO; and (2) Norway had recently fallen heir to enormous riches under the North Sea—oil—and would need to find a way to dispose of some of the income constructively. I worked on a few of my Norwegian friends in Oslo as well. But none of this availed.

I told Ted Achilles about the foundation idea in 1963 and, always an activist, he instructed his lawyers to create such a philanthropy. I believe he also asked some of his wealthy friends to join him, but few were interested. In the end his North Atlantic Community Foundation never disposed of more than a few million in its endowment, and almost all of it came from Ted's family fortune. It earned enough to supply the Atlantic Council with frequent small grants—sometimes at strategic moments— but it was never a major source for the many other Atlantic ventures that needed help just to stay alive. In 1982–83, I made a survey of NGOs in the Atlantic countries that pointed out the great need for new sources of funds. Many were in desperate straits.

In 1984 while president of the Atlantic Council, I proposed to David Packard, one of the pioneers of the electronics/computer revolution and a former secretary of defense, that he put a couple of his liquid billions into a major endowment for mostly Atlantic purposes. He asked many questions, but in the end declined. (A few years later he unveiled, just before his death, a general purpose Packard Foundation that, among other things, created one of the world's top oceanographic teaching and research museums—of which his daughter was the first director.)

As may be noted from the account in chapter 17 of the University of South Carolina conference on the Western Community in 1985, I was able to wangle a ringing endorsement of the idea of some major new foundations from the worthies present. This led to the university's embrace of the idea and a major effort to review the concept, flesh it out, and then to try to enlist some extremely rich people who had not yet made their big philanthropic moves to back the idea of what we came to call the 21st Century Foundation. For the next couple of years, the university underwrote efforts by its Washington office and the law firm that housed it, and by me, to try to bring about a major new philanthropy. We created a legal 501(c)(3) entity (tax-exempt under the IRS code) and invited a number of truly distinguished people to sit on the board and help plan. I was amazed that some of them would give this project the necessary time. Jonathan Davidson, the university's Washington man, and I worked extremely hard to do the needed research, mainly on which rich people to target and how. We wrote up some careful prospectuses, astutely vetted by our board, and even got some of these onto the desks of the targets. Among the 21st Century board members were:

Lt. Gen. Brent Scowcroft, soon to be President Bush I's national security adviser

Lawrence S. Eagleburger, retired career diplomat, later Secretary of State

Cyrus Vance, President Jimmy Carter's Secretary of State

Sol Linowitz, retired Chairman of Xerox and ambassador

Senator Charles McC. Mathias of the Senate Foreign Relations Committee

John Richardson, former Assistant Secretary of State and Chairman of the National Endowment for Democracy

Dr. Steven Muller, retired President of Johns Hopkins University

William E. Brock, former Senator and President Reagan's Secretary of Labor

Lane Kirkland, President of the AFL-CIO

J. Malcolm Fraser, former Australian Prime Minister, later world chairman of CARE

John Whitehead, chairman of Goldman Sachs; former Deputy Secretary of State

Walter Raymond, then still in the Reagan administration NSC (later Associate Director of USIA)

Jonathan Davidson and I staffed the operation.

A Boost from the President

Perhaps a high point in Foundation morale was reached on 25 September 1986, the date Walt Raymond had arranged for a White House meeting of the 21st Century Trust and Foundation principals with President Ronald Reagan. We worked hard to find a convenient time for all concerned, not easy in view of the distance from which some of our 25 participants would have to come—for instance, Peter Corterier from Germany, Jim Prior from London. Both had been cabinet ministers. Bill Brock, Lane Kirkland, Sir David Wills, Malcolm Fraser, John Whitehead, Senators Dan Evans, Malcolm Wallop, and Mark Hatfield, and other supporters of the 21st Century boards (British and American), were also present. Our purpose was to register the support of President Reagan for the 21st Century Trust idea, and thereby energize our supporters and prospective funders.

A few days before the meeting, the Oval Office asked Walt Raymond to supply a half dozen 3x5 cards, with talking points, from which the president could speak. Walt and I toiled for hours, finally deciding that we could not get the key points into the small compass demanded and supplied instead about ten 5x8 cards with what we felt was an adequate message. More phone calls to Walt from the Oval Office: Cut these back to 3x5 cards and make fewer of them. We tried but simply could not pare the thoughts down without destroying them. Walt simply—and purposely—dawdled. I chewed my nails.

Mirabile dictu! On the morning of the 23rd, a presidential secretary phoned Walt: the president, reviewing his schedule, asked for his "remarks" for the 25th; he had previously seen our "long" version and said, "Get me *those* cards. *That's* what I want to go with!"

Still more last-minute consternation: Also on the 23rd, the Oval Office announced to Walt that our meeting with the president would have to be rescheduled from 1:00 to 3:00 p.m. We replied that if we were to make this change, we were heading for disaster; our participants were terribly busy people. The president's staff reported back that the time would remain at 1 p.m. Sighs of relief.

We gathered in the White House Roosevelt Room at noon, around a table just the right size, and ate a sandwich lunch. At 1:00 p.m. sharp, the president entered, accompanied by Donald Regan, his chief of staff. Jim Holderman, president of the University of South Carolina (still providing material support for the foundation's efforts) introduced Bill Brock (then secretary of labor), who presented the 21st Century project to the president, using the script that Walt and I had prepared for *him*; I spoke, adding some further essentials. The president replied (using our card-notes!), beautifully and elegantly urging our group to redouble its efforts. Mr. Reagan called ours an "historic enterprise." Walt told me later that it was unlikely that in the past six years *any* first draft had been so employed without Oval Office changes. This was highly amusing to me; I recalled the time, in 1960, noted earlier, when I had drafted an endorsement of the Atlantic Institute for Vice President Nixon, to which I had then written a reply on my return to Brussels for the signature of Paul van Zeeland!

Two or three of our principals responded to the president, notably Jim Prior, who eloquently told the president how much his days as a university student in the United States had meant to him and how much he hoped that a major new private effort to support such interchanges and other activities could mean for European-American relations. Then the president asked if the group would like to hear the latest story from the Kremlin? Of course. He recounted how "an old peasant woman asked to see Chairman Gorbachev. After many rebuffs she finally was granted an audience. Gorbachev asked her, 'What can I do for you, Mother?' She replied, 'Well, I have a question. I often hear people ask whether Communism is an art or a science. Can you tell me?' The chairman responded, 'Why, of course, Mother. It is a *science!*' She spoke again, 'Well, if that's so, why didn't they try it out first on *rats*?'"

Charles Wick, the president's California friend and director of USIA, said, "Mr. President, let's put this Foundation project on the next Economic Summit (G-7) agenda." The president said, "Good idea, Charlie! We'll do it."

Regan, sitting in the shadows behind the president throughout, tapped Reagan on the shoulder; they rose and exited, with the president smiling and waving.

Our group remained for another 45 minutes, agreed on what to do next and how, then adjourned—elated, euphoric, and tired.

I thought at the time that we had engendered some formidable new momentum, but the later Iran-Contra scandal—plus a White House reluctance to help get some of Reagan's fat-cat supporters interested in the Foundation, on grounds that it might divert funds on which they counted for Reagan's projected presidential library—took some shine off Ronald Reagan's endorsement. Other factors also conspired to mire down our effort. I confided to my diary on New Year's Day 1987: "I am not quite as optimistic about this country or the world as I was 10 years ago. We seem to be more greedy, careless, self-centered, and mistrustful, as a people. . . .

Economically our country is in a kind of holding pattern; I believe great underlying changes are taking place, but gone is the "can-do" spirit of 20, or even 10, years ago." In the new millennium, nearly twenty years after I wrote those words, and after a good many upheavals in world and national affairs, I cannot say that our prospects are a lot better—just different, perhaps.

Targeting the Wealthy

I spent a great deal of time, from 1986 to 1991, researching the rich. Some, such as the Rockefellers, had already created their great philanthropies; we tried anyway. But others, such as the new mogul on the scene, Bill Gates, at that time had not. Some, like Nixon's confidant, Ambassador Walter Annenberg, had created foundations but not yet fully defined their missions. In fact, Mr. Annenberg appeared to toy seriously with the idea of throwing a large amount into our new kitty but finally declined. Others whom we importuned (and almost always, we staffers left the importuning to members of our Board) included:

James S. McDonnell, the aircraft magnate from St. Louis
Sandy Mactaggart of Edmonton, a Canadian tycoon whom I knew
    well
Thomas J. Watson, Jr.
Ross Perot
The Hewlett Foundation
Gordon Getty
The Mars Family
Leslie W. Wexner
An Wang

Late in 1986, we enlisted Dr. Steven Muller as working but unpaid chairman of the board. He had just retired from the presidency of Johns Hopkins University, had an office in Washington, and was enthusiastic about our proposals. He promised to do his best to raise money for the new foundation. At the same time, he became a member (as were Cyrus Vance and I) of the Advisory Board of the 21st Century Trust in London, our companion organization. Steven Muller made a great many good suggestions as to how to proceed and sounded out a few rich prospects. But by the summer of 1990, he visited me on Bainbridge Island and confessed that he had been unable to do what he wanted with the Foundation idea. He explained that this kind of fund-raising (of which he had done much for Johns Hopkins) required a great deal of patience and time, and above all the long-term cultivation of the individual "targets." Unfortunately, he had found other demands coming at him, and he could never find the time to do the kind of cultivation of the likely sources that the rest of us had put on the table. Needless to say, I was greatly disappointed; he had been with us for more than four years and now we seemed back at Square One.

The British, however, plowed ahead with their 21st Century Trust and began their active (but more limited) program of international seminars for promising young leaders. Sir David Wills, with both the money and the conviction necessary, saw to it that the Trust would succeed. On 9–10 December 1986, I attended the first organizing conference of the 21st Century Trust at Ditchley in Oxfordshire. David Wills had capitalized the operating fund with £3 million. Lord Home and Lord Callaghan were present, as were Sir Michael Palliser, Sir Oliver Wright, and Guenter von Hase (all former ambassadors), MPs David Owen and John Gilbert, and other worthies also there as members of the Trustees or Advisory Council.

But afterwards the U.S. board, disillusioned with the departure in 1989 of Messrs. Eagleburger and Scowcroft to the new Bush I administration, the evaporation of the administrative support from the University of South Carolina, also in 1989, and the collapse in 1990 of Steven Muller's offer to raise money, took note of the impasse in our work. Generally disheartened by the lack of progress, we had pretty well decided by the end of December 1991 to disband. However our foundation had spawned one hopeful demonstration project—hands-on work to create an Action Committee for the Western Community along the lines of Jean Monnet's Action Committee for a United States of Europe, which had played an indispensable role in the private efforts to "make Europe" in the 1950s and 1960s. We believed that Monnet's aphorism "To make Europe is to make peace" could be eminently well applied in a broad transatlantic/transpacific context.

The Airlie House and Cosmos Club Conferences, 1992 and 1993

My story now becomes more complicated: The 21st Century Foundation was able to collect relatively small amounts for this Action Committee project and made grants for the purpose to the Association to Unite the Democracies. AUD (originally Clarence Streit's Federal Union) had changed its focus in May 1992, hired Dr. Charles Patrick as its CEO, and begun planning events we hoped could lead to creation of an Action Committee with an agenda of practical and pragmatic steps for remaking the West sufficiently exciting to attract the participation of top Western leaders of thought and action.

In September 1992, under the chairmanship of Bill Brock, AUD spon-sored a conference at Airlie House in Virginia, one of the capital region's splendid retreat facilities. Our conference title was "Rethinking Interde-pendence." The written introduction to the conference agenda character-ized "a world in transition, but nobody knows what to do" and urged the conferees to "fill the gap in ideas" and produce "a new organizing concept for the West." The overall rubric for the meeting, and subsequently for the entire project, was "The Next Century Initiative."

By 1992, the old Committees for a Community of Democracies had also pretty well petered out for lack of funds and, after thirteen years, the advancing age of their members. In 1991, the U.S. CCD had given National Security Adviser Scowcroft a statement setting out some national policy progress we hoped for; he had responded positively. But these small private CCD groups, whether in the United States or abroad, could not survive as entities without some central coordinating mechanism and modest funding. After the Airlie Conference (to which some of the CCD Old Guard came, from France, Britain, Germany, Canada, The Netherlands, and Australia as well as the United States), the 21st Century Foundation, the AUD–Next Century Initiative, and the first CCD incarnation all began to blend into a single entity, smaller but still resolute. The majority of those who had been committed to CCD's central organizing principle of a growing, vibrant community of democracies remained committed. However, the modest institutional frameworks that had housed these successive efforts had fallen apart. It was time for a new start.

The Airlie House Conference had called for a further meeting in 1993 of "major players" in international affairs. Charles Patrick and I toured Europe, while Raymond Gastil visited Japan, to enlist participants for a large public meeting to create the Action Committee for the Western Com-munity. We found moral support and willingness to participate, but no new sources of money abroad.

In spring 1993, John Richardson began the search for a chairman for the Action Committee. We tried, successively, Dick Cheney (then more or less a hero of the Gulf War), Paul Volcker, former head of the Federal Re-serve, and George Shultz, Reagan's able secretary of state. None could be persuaded.

To see if a good locale could be found for a large public conference, Bill Brock journeyed to Seattle to address a group of Northwest worthies that I convened on 4 October 1993. Though they did not say they would finance such a major conference, they were keen on moving ahead and hoped the conference could be held in Seattle to publicly launch the Action Committee. The consensus on the dire world situation and what ought to be done was not, however, reflected later in the month when we consulted a different group of U.S. and foreign leaders in Washington, D.C.

We needed a small critical mass of "top dogs" who would agree to launch an Action Committee, even if we didn't yet have a chairman. Based on the Airlie Conference and Brock's Seattle soundings, the little New Century Initiative (explained later) called together the nucleus of the Action Committee we wanted, who convened in Washington at the Cosmos Club on 29 October 1993, a year after Airlie. Bill Brock was in the chair. Most of the twenty participants were well informed beforehand. Charles Patrick and I had visited them earlier in Europe and in the States to brief them on the idea of an Action Committee, and we had circulated carefully drafted papers. Also, some were alumni of the 1985 South Carolina conference, of the old CCDs, of the Airlie Conference of 1992, and of the 21st Century Foundation and Trust efforts. I worked always in these years to try to create informal networks and bind them together if I could. In the Cosmos case, the intersecting networks inspired cordiality but also "frank exchanges of views" (as the taciturn communiqués from near-failed international summits usually say). There was no sufficient meeting of the minds.

One reason the Cosmos Conference failed was that, in order to capitalize on the presence in Washington of some of its principals (people such as Lord Carrington and John Whitehead), we had arranged our meeting for the afternoon—a Friday afternoon at that—just on the heels of a two-day meeting of the Bilderberg Group. Those participants in particular were tired and ready to head home. The time left for a serious discussion by our conferees—two short hours—was obviously insufficient. Another reason was that our principal energizer, John Richardson, who was scheduled to present our case to the conferees, was hung up on a fogbound airliner in Prague, en route from a dangerous visit to Bosnia, now in open civil war. Bill Brock opened our meeting splendidly; I pinch-hit for John, but the effect was not the same. Finally (and I believe this to have been the most crucial reason for our failure) was the fact that these movers and shakers of the Western world were seeing the post–Cold War era through substantially different lenses. No amount of preparatory papers we had sent them (and these had been pretty cogent) nor arguments by Brock and a few others would sway them. The shape of interdependence was no longer clear to leaders such as this. How could this be?

From the beginning in the 1950s, I had seen the challenge to the West as less a need to contain the Soviet Union than as an opportunity to promote a more democratic world and to unite the democracies for long-term good. "Victory" in the Cold War would follow, but most leaders and especially the publics thought of containment as the first priority, with a certain amount of political unity needed but never pursued to its logical ends. Many of the top people of the 1980s and 1990s, however, proved somehow unable to switch mental gears; the challenges to the West were seen as multiform, not always closely related, and calling for responses on which there was now little consensus. Our Cosmos participants, for example, did not seem to agree on the need to redouble the effort to achieve much closer political unity among the Western powers. Indeed, there were strong signs of willingness to simply drift . . . and wait.

In a paper sent to the Cosmos conferees beforehand, I had urged as our purpose the fashioning of a "new guiding concept" for the democracies, so that we would be able to face crises as they arose with strengthened unity. But in two short hours on a Friday afternoon, we could not clarify our thinking, and resolve our preoccupations (plural, as these differed) with present-day knotty and sometimes dangerous problems. Lord Carrington, a man of great wisdom and experience, observed that "the nations today appear to be more selfish and self-centered than in the earlier era," and "it is extremely difficult now to get them to see their common interest, let alone do important things together." Lane Kirkland, head of the AFL-CIO, was especially pessimistic; the institutions we had, such as the OECD, were not doing their jobs, he opined. Why create more? George Russell thought that whatever we proposed doing, China—a growing economic powerhouse—should be included. The setbacks in the Balkans and in Somalia were examples of the crises the conferees faced, and on which they differed substantially.

In short, no meeting of the minds was possible that day, or for some time to come.

This drift reflected the policy of governments as well. George H. W. Bush called for a "new world order," but his administration never defined what that should be or what long-range choices the Allies faced.

Bill Brock and I pointed out to the Cosmos group that the small ad hoc staff that had prepared the meeting (and the earlier Airlie conference) was running out of money. George Russell, a little-known but powerful financier from Tacoma, Washington, spoke up and pledged $5,000 if others would join him. John Whitehead and Bill Brock promised $5,000 each. There was thus just enough money to bolster the small NCI kitty for another month or two, so that the problems could be "better studied" and, as Whitehead put it, the group could possibly agree on a "mission statement." Such statements were then all the rage; "objectives" and "goals" were replaced by "missions" (and later by "visions"), and our little staff, pros and volunteers, went to work again.

In short, we had lost precious time in the eight years since the South Carolina conference and, once again, after the Airlie conclave. To be sure, the 21st Century Foundation group had thought that substantial funds would be needed but also available (if we tried astutely and hard enough) to continue efforts like the proposed Action Committee and reinvigorate many existing NGOs. We had of necessity thus taken time to try to raise a major fund. But none of this was working.

It was clear to our innermost circle, by the end of 1993, that we must somehow regroup and wait for a better time. I was especially downcast and frustrated by these roadblocks, but Walt Raymond, John Richardson, Albert "Ab" Hamilton, and Dick Olson were determined somehow to "mush on." Could I do otherwise? We embarked on a different and less costly exercise to try to maintain momentum and move toward our goals, for the time being without money.

Regrouping after the Cosmos Conference

A rump of the Airlie-Cosmos group, in a new approach (which later became the New Century Initiative), met at the Carnegie Endowment offices on 28 April 1994 to consider what might be done to improve the efficacy of the G-7 meetings, which the major Western powers had been holding since 1975. This time, we convened not the major figures of a Cosmos meeting, but scholars and doers who knew the G-7 effort in some detail. They produced a smart little pamphlet with strong recommendations for substantial reform of the G-7. We distributed copies around Washington and—lo and behold!—David Gergen of the White House staff gave one to President Clinton. He made our chief proposal a point in his agenda at the G-7 Summit that July. As we had recommended, it was agreed among other things that in preparation for the 1995 Summit a "full review of Western institutions" would be drawn up. We were elated.

Most unfortunately, this was never done, but the thought of the need had been planted. Some years later, our G-7 pamphlet popped up in other important meetings. In this way, ideas often drop below the horizon of public discussion, only to reappear later from the recesses of someone's mind.

A few years earlier, Dick Olson and I had together decided that we should legally set up as a new NGO an empty vessel that would be ready when and if the various enterprises, such as the AUD–Next Century Initiative or the 21st Century Foundation effort, ran out of steam. Dick found the lawyers to prepare the papers and secure a tax exemption; and in 1993 he and I quietly launched the New Century Initiative." Its founding officers were John Richardson, Dick Olson, Ab Hamilton, and I. We obtained tax-free IRS status in 1996. In 1999, we changed the name of the new corporation to the Council for a Community of Democracies.

Nudging the World towards a Community of Democracies

To show how these streams of effort and people later came together, I must now back up and characterize one of the other streams, the earlier Committees for a Community of Democracies. In chapter 16, I recounted the founding of the CCDs at a Washington cocktail party in 1979. An entirely volunteer effort, with small sums drawn from the National Endowment for Democracy and USIA to hold international meetings, the CCDs had developed a substantial network of dedicated persons in several countries. Once I had left the Atlantic Council, in January 1985, I spent more time with the CCDs.

In April 1985 I attended the CCD conference at the Wingspread center in Racine, Wisconsin, that, according to my journal entry of the time, "may have a considerable impact, I could say potentially historic." These words would turn out to be prophetic indeed by the year 2000. My journal in 1985 provided further background:

> [This] was the first time, to my knowledge, that a group of people, representing private or public interests, from a representative spread of democracies from around the globe (some developing countries, some "overdeveloped") got together to talk about the democracies of the world making common cause together, as democracies, for democracy, and in the name of democracy. The idea grew in part out of my [1980] book, *Uniting the Democracies*, in which I "proposed that the 'club' of the rich, essentially white countries . . . be opened up to democracies wherever they might be" The chief point of the discussion of the conference was a [prior] proposal, in 1982, to the CCDs, meeting in London, by John Wheeldon of Australia that an "association" of democracies be created by governments. His idea . . . was accepted with enthusiasm by this disparate group, more than half of whom had never met one another before.

The Wingspread conference was put on by the CCD–USA (Mark I), chaired by its president, Sam De Palma, and funded by the National Endowment for Democracy. The global theme was carried on by the twenty or more CCDs then extant and maintained until the committees met their demise, ultimately for lack of funds, in the mid-1990s. In the meantime Benazir Bhutto, then prime minister of Pakistan, had called for an Association of Democracies in a Harvard speech, 8 June 1989. I've never been able to find out where she picked up the idea—but as in many such cases, it was by then "in the air" and she grabbed it. Perhaps some

Pakistani intellectuals tossed it to her after CCD contact? In any case, no governments responded to her plea.

Leap over now for a moment the rest of the 1980s until June 1997, when Secretary of State Madeleine Albright spoke at a Harvard commencement, fifty years after George Marshall's historic speech heralding the Marshall Plan. Albright began to lay the groundwork for her own unprecedented initiative, the Community of Democracies, by telling the Harvard graduates:

> Let every nation acknowledge [that] the opportunity to be part of an international system based on democratic principles is available to all. This was not the case 50 years ago. . . . Last week in The Netherlands, President Clinton said that no democratic nation in Europe would be left out of the transatlantic community. Today I say that no nation in the world need be left out of the global system we are constructing.

Secretary Albright must have had this theme squarely on her mind during the next two years. In a 17 January 1999 interview with a correspondent for the *Los Angeles Times* Albright said that her number one priority for leaving a lasting legacy when she quit office was to see a global Community of Democracies created. This was accomplished in June 2000, when the Polish Government convened 107 democracies in Warsaw to do just that.

Later in 1999, I addressed U.S. Foreign Service officers and civil servants in the Acheson Auditorium of the State Department to support Secretary Albright's plans for Warsaw and to present my new book, *Pax Democratica*. How had we gotten to this point?

✄

The 1985 Wingspread Conference was also notable in that it called for the creation of an International Institute for Democracy and for a caucus of democracies at the United Nations.

A special CCD conference was held in July 1987 at the Canadian Parliament, hosted by MP David Kilgour, to flesh out the Institute idea; I provided a draft for the meeting, which was improved and adopted. Half a dozen study and training centers were created in the decade that followed, a few of them later to fade away. At the end of September 1987, the Council of Europe's parliamentary assembly invited a large number of parliaments outside Europe—in Latin America and Asia in particular—to send delegates to this assembly. Walt Raymond and I attended with a U.S.

congressional delegation. Though nothing much happened, some serious talk and personal networks are almost always good byproducts. Nor do a little *choucroute garnie* and some Riesling, Alsatian culinary mainstays, hurt the process. (One of the American delegates was a feisty but realistic former major general, elected to Congress from Guam. He seemed to appreciate the thrust of the conference, but said to me privately: "A lot of this talk is just bull***t!")

Francis Rosenstiel of the Council of Europe's secretariat took this opportunity to float the idea (which he had picked up at our Ottawa meeting a few months earlier) of a European Democracy Institute as an adjunct of the Council. This was ultimately done, as were similar efforts mounted in several places. Another Institute called I.D.E.A. was later set up in Stockholm; the NED itself established an in-house Democracy Forum and a *Journal of Democracy* to encourage research and development on new ideas about self-government.

After this conference, Walt and I journeyed around Europe to try to nail down plans in various places for new CCDs. The British (already well organized) and the Germans were especially responsive. We also found top people in France, some of whom we already knew, who were personally interested but—and this has unfortunately been true in France over the years—who did not particularly want to "coagulate" into a French committee with others.

The Ann Arbor Conference

In December 1988, under the leadership again of CCD–DC, an important international conference took place in former president Ford's Library at Ann Arbor, Michigan. Former president Carter was also present. Both presidents spoke to more than 100 delegates from around 50 countries. The French gadfly Jean-François Revel spoke trenchantly, calling for a "Democracy International." David Kilgour, in a special working group, guided through a resolution calling for more Institutes of Democracy. Some delegates were especially impressive: a young South Korean delegate in particular. During the conference, I noted in my journal: "A splendid day, an end of the beginning and a start on my dream of a world order built around *democracy*, not only around trade and international security. . . . Kudos to Sam De Palma, Bob Foulon, and the other old duffers who have pulled this off." This last "kudos" could not have been more heartfelt. There were at least two dozen key Americans, some from academia and most of them alumni of the Foreign Service, whose brains, experience, connections, and dedication had made the incipient "movement" a budding force in the world. Years later, their ideas were to bear fruit in NED's eventual World

Forum for Democracy, Madeleine Albright's Community of Democracies, and the UN's Democracies' Caucus. CCD (Mark I) had a strong hand in all of these concepts.

The CCDs had advocated the UN Democracy Caucus idea since their inception in the early 1980s; and on 1 April 2004, the UN announced in Geneva that such a caucus was in the process of formation. Dr. Raymond Gastil (who became the last president of the CCD–DC) had, I think, written the first paper on the caucus idea in 1982. By 2000, UN Secretary General Kofi Annan was backing the democracy idea strongly; he and other UN staffers and heads of UN affiliates such as the World Bank and the UN Development Program were saying that social and economic development plans would not mean much for many countries unless there was at least a beginning for a democratic base—"good governance" was all the rage.

What is the future of the UN and the democracy movement? Either the UN will be greatly changed, or the Community of Democracies will eventually supplant it, in my view. The process may take decades, but the underlying trends are mostly in the right direction.

The CCD movement kept growing, even though none of the committees ever had solid funding. At one point, around 1989, there were CCDs in Washington, New York, London, Seattle, Paris, Bonn, Ottawa, Montreal, San Francisco, Stockholm, Tokyo, Mauritius, Fiji, Côte d'Ivoire, Sydney, and Melbourne. Some faded away, others persisted—mainly through forming solid links among dedicated groups of individuals. CCD–DC managed to get a few more NED grants for small regional conferences in Stockholm, London, Africa, and Australia. As in so many cases in which I have been involved, excellent volunteers all over the world could be found to organize conferences, committees, and other activities—but if these groups could not find the money to fund the professional leadership plus small offices to carry on and coordinate their activities, they would come to an end, sooner or later. Good ideas and good people are not too hard to find, but some money is always needed, especially if the efforts are to be perpetuated. The London CCD endured longest—to 1993.

But the CCD (Mark I) "box score," over more than 20 years, was not bad. We had accomplished at least the following:

> The Community of Democracies (CD) created, which took from the early 1980s to 2000 for fruition;
> International Institute(s) for Democracy, from 1985; six created by 1990; and
> A Caucus of the Democracies at the UN—broached in 1980, launched in 2004, nearly a quarter century from conception to birth.

Fortunately, a few of the original adherents remained active when CCD (Mark 2) emerged into firm being in 1999.

Lesson learned: Don't be too impatient with big but good ideas. They usually take years to flesh out, publicize, float through the ether before some important person or institution sees that the time is ripe and energizes the process. Sometimes the energizers may not acknowledge—or even know—where the idea originally came from. And sometimes the originators may not know that someone *else* may indeed have stumbled on the idea before they did! Imaginative thinking helps, but persistence is even more important.

A corollary lesson: Don't be fussy about who gets the credit. Ultimately, a large number of people will be involved; who cares so long as the good thing is done? When an idea is "in the air," it has a good chance of materializing. (This I learned years earlier, from a YMCA secretary in Seattle—it's the ideas, not the people, that matter.)

Some NGOs Never Die—They Just Fade Away

By 1994, the old CCDs were effectively moribund. It is simply impossible to hold a group of volunteers together, infusing some newer blood as one goes along (our average age at this point was around 75) and maintaining morale, unless one has an office and professional and clerical help to insure some continuity and the requisite amount of coordination. The computer age had dawned and many of our adherents had e-mail facility; but without continuing program support or office funds our activity finally ground to a halt. The personal ties in many cases had been forged securely, so that ad hoc cooperation on the common goal was still sometimes possible. But we had gone through four chairmen—myself, Bill Olson, Sam De Palma, and David Popper. Raymond Gastil served for CCD's last two years as its president and CEO. De Palma and Popper were former ambassadors and senior State Department officials; Gastil was a world expert on democracy. We had floated some new ideas; some were promising. But we lacked the collective steam to work much more in the same loose organizational and funding framework.

The European committees and those outside the developed world more or less atrophied, except for the British, which maintained cohesion longer than any other, thanks to a splendid chairman, Maj. Gen. Tony Younger (retired), and top volunteers, all retired as well. These included Walter Lessing, who had chaired the Mid-Atlantic Club of London (he had begun life in Bamberg and then fled Germany for a fine career in British business); John Leech, an executive of the British overseas aid program; David Barton, a chartered accountant who chaired a European committee to standardize accounting systems and who had given all his off-hours to NGOs such as Federal Union, the European Movement, and the Charlemagne Trust; and Alan Lee Williams, former MP and head of the Atlantic Council of the UK, later chairman of the NATO-wide Atlantic Treaty Association. They were as stalwart and congenial a group of people as any I have ever worked with. And quite representative of what the British elites can do when they wish—this kind of organizing is "as easy as falling off a log" for them, as we used to say in Northwest timber country.

Preparing Yet Another Launch

The legal vessel Dick Olson and I had created in 1993, the New Century Initiative, was ready for use in a new incarnation. The original incorporators were Dick, John Richardson, Albert Hamilton, and I. This Initiative lay pretty well dormant until such time as we needed it. Over the 1990s, we made occasional use of the body and. as noted, eventually renamed it the Council for a Community of Democracies, fully activated in 1999.

Somewhat reluctantly in the early nineties, I turned my attention to other pursuits. As both the 21st Century Foundation and the CCDs (Mark I) had disintegrated, I determined to begin writing down my ideas, perhaps for publication, on the things that I believed about world peace, democracy, community, and related matters, so that a draft "creed for discussion" would be ready when needed. But I never took my eyes entirely off the linkage between bringing about an intergovernmental community of democracies and financing of the pushing of the idea. And I focused a good deal, in this connection, on my own Pacific Northwest.

By this time, Colleen and I had lived on Bainbridge Island for several years. I had a good place to work, thanks to the carpentry wizardry of my son David and the magic of an architect friend, Douglas Denkers, who designed a large study plus a cathedral-ceiling library—and even a home swimming pool for arthritis therapy. I also hired the first of a series of very smart high school students, Adrienne Janus, to help with archives and correspondence related to my research.

I was thus reasonably well equipped to dive into authorship, plus—as ever—a few extracurricular civic activities. These included membership on the Board of Directors of the Bainbridge Island Land Trust—a new kind of nonprofit, citizen-sponsored activity that was helping our small community to plan its land management for the future wisely and acquire chunks of land for parks, wildlife preserves, and just plain timbered and bucolic patches to separate rapidly expanding patches of urbanization. This movement has been stemming the headlong sprawl in many counties across the United States. For Colleen and me, the Land Trust provided an immensely satisfying ten-year experience: We manned booths at town and county fairs and parades, sold T-shirts emblazoned with "Save Gazzam Lake," and in the process made long friendships with the cream of the county's crop of young and old civic activists. Such grassroots experiences have restored my confidence in the future of the United States; so long as we can do these kinds of things well, our civic faith and political system will endure.

Money and a Creed

At the outset of 1992, I started the manuscript I'd tentatively entitled "Unfinished Business"; that title expressed my take at the time on the dangerous drift of the West and world affairs. We had come far in nearly fifty years in organizing an effective peace system for the world, but the follow-up was now lacking. The short, sharp Gulf War of 1990–91 showed what the West and congenial allies could do if a clear threat to world peace flared up in a far-off place. But President George H. W. Bush and his staff did not follow through to ride that wave to what he several times called a "new world order." For the most part, the steam was out of the World War II generation. I wanted to write something that would show how far we had come and why, and how far we still needed to go. Raymond Gastil and I had been thinking in 1990 about a joint book of this sort, which we at the time called "Beyond Containment." I wrote a paper with that title for an international colloquium at the University of Washington in April 1990. (I sent a copy of the paper to Brent Scowcroft—then President Bush I's national security adviser; he replied cordially, saying there were good new ideas in it, they were already trying some, and he had sent it to his staff to read.) These ideas finally morphed into what eventually became my next book, *Pax Democratica*, published in 1998, with a paperback in 2001.

I also continued to probe sources of funds to do the institutional things still needed. To pave the way, I had written an article for the obscure *Journal of Philanthropy* on the occasion of the centenary in 1989 of Andrew Carnegie's famous "Gospel of Wealth" article, wherein he had written, "The man who dies rich, dies disgraced." I pounded on this theme, sent many reprints to friends and some wealthy people. One day while traveling the ferry to Seattle with the Rev. Dale Turner of Seattle, whom I had known slightly, the two of us chatted for half an hour, and afterwards lunched together every few months. Dale had been the pastor of the Congregational Church the Gates family attended. I had had my eye on young Bill as a possible donor to community of democracy causes and as a philanthropist in general. He had started Microsoft as a very young man, made not just millions but billions. I gave Dale a copy of my article on Carnegie and then, one day over lunch, I said, "Dale, Bill Gates is amassing such a fortune that he will have a hard time getting rid of it, and if he doesn't start some kind of a foundation, the government will end up getting the bulk of it when he and Melinda die." At that point, Bill was rapidly becoming the richest man in the world; his net worth was around $7 or $8 billion. Dale agreed, and said he'd pass on my article, plus some biographies of Carnegie I gave him, to young Bill. I never asked Dale, "What did the Gateses say? What do they plan to do?" We just chatted about everything in the world (as we were both concerned but positive about our planet); but every now and then I would revert to Gates.

One day, in 1996, young Bill gave a Seattle speech that was reported in the local press. "I haven't yet made my philanthropic move," he was reported to have said, "but I plan to one of these days." Then he quoted Carnegie on the plight of the rich man dying disgraced! It wasn't too long before the creation of the Bill and Melinda Gates Foundation was announced (January 2000), with a corpus—$26 billion—that far exceeded that of any previous philanthropic endowment. (Only one older, British philanthropic trust, the Wellcome Foundation, approaches Gates in assets.) Bill and his wife had decided to set fairly stern guidelines for their giving: Health and medicine, especially in developing countries; and education, in a very broad sense. Their record of giving in the first few years has been admirable.

When it was clear that the birth of the Gates Foundation was imminent, four of us—University of Washington president William Gerberding, the estimable professor Herbert Ellison, a principal in a Seattle firm, Bob Capeloto, and I—made another *démarche* to the Gateses. Why not, we said, buy the Battelle Seattle research center (where I had worked for ten years, and which was now for sale) and make it the headquarters of the Gates Foundation and also a new center for World Future Studies? It didn't work.

In 2001, I wrote to Bill's father, William Gates Sr., whom I knew slightly and who had been made cochair of the Gates Foundation. He is a brilliant, genial lawyer with strong roots in the Pacific Northwest and, I should think, an excellent choice to superintend his son's giving. But Bill Senior said their priorities were other than democracy, good governance, and so on, and he was sorry. In 2004, I approached Bill Senior again for a possible grant, pointing out that the many great schemes of the Foundation for improving health in Africa would oft go awry if enough attention were not paid to the "delivery systems" of recipient countries. We met for lunch, thanks to a mutual friend, John Davis, who had in the 1970s been on the CAPA Board and who, for a time, was chair of the Seattle CCD. We three had a great meal together, comparing notes on the international scene. I think I was able to give the senior Gates a few helpful thoughts about the world crisis. But in the end, he said that the scheme I had proposed (an independent institute to study the interface between the promotion of democracy and efforts to strengthen international community) simply was—still—outside the Gates Foundation's terms of reference. I had to acknowledge that Steve Muller had been right: It takes a long time to bring any philanthropic target to closure; and, my own caveat, if the target in mind cannot fit the requester's needs into its "guidelines," no amount of polite insistence will work anyway.

CCD II Begins Work

The new CCD (Mark II), then in gestation, had better luck with George Russell, a Tacoma financier and philanthropist of extraordinary vision and sense of purpose. A Seattle friend had brought us together in March 1993; we had several subsequent meetings, one with a group of top Puget Sound business executives representing Boeing, Weyerhaeuser timber, the main Tacoma newspaper, and others. Even though that meeting brought interest (and some sour grapes from one family scion whose company had given $10,000 to help explore the CAPA project in 1978 and wondered "where the money had gone"), nobody—except George Russell—had the vision to understand our program to buttress the interdependence of the West and the world. George attended the October 1993 meeting at the Cosmos Club and began giving small but strategic sums to help a new CCD get started. He attended the CCD II "launch" at the Army-Navy Club in the fall of 1999 and gave generously once we had started operations.

One day I joined George in his Tacoma office for lunch. He told me he had just launched a new philanthropic venture, joining with other bigwigs at his instance in a new effort to remake Russian civic and democratic life. He said his inspiration was an article he had read in the *International Herald Tribune* in 1991, written by "Herb Ellison and someone else" on the crying need to back up the weak but real democratic forces in the new Russia and to undertake what the writers termed "a new Marshall Plan of ideas." I said softly, "George, Herb's coauthor was *me!*" He laughed, and has gone on with this project and others—a remarkable man. But our canvas—though large enough—did not quite square, on sober reflection, with his own view of the world's priorities on which he could make a real impact.

But in late 1999, we managed to float the new Council for a Community of Democracies, with financial help from George Russell, Robert Borden, Henry Luce II, John Whitehead, and a few other wealthy individuals.

CCD II represents both the culmination of two decades of dogged persistence of ideas and individuals and the launch—finally—of an organization with proper (if small) professional and clerical staff. CCD's financial future has always been rocky, necessitating the employment of only temporary staff; this is doable when one counts (as we have) on retired executives who can afford to take a chance because they can always fall back on their retirement pay. But for junior and clerical staff, the inability to pay expected medical and other benefits, and provide tenure, means continuous turnover and reliance on green but eager interns and often great administrative people who, however, usually turn out to want a CCD perch so they can continue to search for more permanent jobs.

The CCD II launch, making use of the legal vehicle created by Dick Olson in 1993, plus a name change from NCI to CCD, took place at the Army-Navy Club in Washington on 17 December 1999, under John Richardson's chairmanship as CCD's interim president. A decision by the State Department and the Polish government had given us a wonderful new lease on life—finally a world conference was being called, for June 2000, to launch an intergovernmental Community of Democracies! We climbed aboard and helped to steer behind the scenes.

We began CCD's first board meeting at 9 a.m., worked on through lunch, and closed in late afternoon. Discussion was no-punches-pulled and hard questions asked, but in the end we had a consensus that operations should begin and that our main job was to help the United States and other nations to prepare for Warsaw and beyond. We had $50,000 in our "kitty" (through a lawyer friend of a friend in New York); both Russell and Borden made conditional pledges of $25,000 each. But we still had to get organized.

Over the holidays, John Richardson and I struggled hard to convince Walt Raymond, our great friend of many years and one of the key progenitors of CCD and its many antecedents, to become the paid president of the new nonprofit. Walt was perfect for the job. He was then 70 years old (both John and I were older still), had had a distinguished CIA career working on democracy development and the unification of Europe, had then been on Reagan's NSC staff to help launch the 1982–85 democracy initiatives (the NED was largely his creation), and had pursued—after two years as associate director of USIA—a part-time career promoting the international interests of the Association of Former Members of Congress. To culminate this extraordinary career, it was quite natural for Walt to take on the presidency of a new and prestigious (if poor) NGO that symbolized all that he had worked for. But this was a hard decision for him; he had a few grandchildren and a close-knit family that longed for his attention, and he longed to fully retire and enjoy life. But John and I knew that "enjoying life" for Walt also meant being in the thick of good works inside the Beltway. He was an adept and inveterate organizer, and his constant goodwill and good intentions shone through everything he did. He was an excellent manager, a man with contacts everywhere around the world, and was widely trusted. John and I could not do better; the new board was fully behind us. And finally Walt gave in.

CCD II began work on a fully staffed basis in February 2000, in one spacious room in the historic DACOR Bacon House at 18th and F Streets Northwest. Our office neighbors were two other internationally oriented NGOs. Diplomatic and Consular Officers, Retired (DACOR) is an old club of Foreign Service officers (I was proud to have been one of its early members). It offered decent lunches and snacks and was halfway between the Department of State on C Street and the White House—a perfect location. Walt hired a fine administrative officer, who did not remain long, and a retired USIA executive with long experience, Bob LaGamma. Gradually, we enlisted a string of gung-ho, smart young interns from the local universities—for pittances (we used to say, "for carfare") and good experience in a fascinating nonprofit enterprise. I imagine that some of these young people—plus a number who have worked for me for a little in the Pacific Northwest—will over their mature lives make their own contributions to world peace, building a little, at least, on what we old birds taught them. Many of our longtime proponents, such as Ab Hamilton, CCD's 73-year-old treasurer, volunteered for full-time service in the CCD office; Ab had retired in April 2000 and spent many days thereafter, until his death in 2004, going over the finances of CCD or licking stamps for envelopes, as the situation required. Dick Olson, an old congressional warhorse, also gave a great deal of time to CCD matters—everything from trying to figure out how to receive Canadian charitable donations to becoming temporary unpaid administrative officer, when the incumbent quit suddenly. Such people, and the eventual 35-member Board of Directors, have been invaluable—indeed irreplaceable—sources of wisdom and concentrated effort when needed.

I wrote in my journal around this time: "All dotards to the colors!" The average age of CCD's Board is around 65 to 75, not ideal, but it represents the collective, almost irrepressible urge of veterans of World War II and the Cold War to continue to serve their country, and humankind. We have strong gut feelings about the absolutely essential continuity of world-minded leadership and the necessity to strengthen and perpetuate the community of democracies—the core of the "overdeveloped" and the many new democracies emerging around the globe.

In February 2000 I went to London, partly to help encourage British elites to see that the forthcoming Warsaw Conference would be greatly advantageous to all transatlantic countries and their concerns for stability in the developing world. Alan Lee Williams, old Atlantic veteran and one of the founders of CCD I, convened a group at the Reform Club for lunch and talk. The head of planning for the Polish Foreign Ministry spoke, followed by one of his young historian-colleagues and me. Although a couple of the old British CCDers were backing me up from the audience, the meeting was hard going. The minister for overseas aid, Clare Short, for one, couldn't quite see the point. I later had a separate chat with the head of policy planning at the Foreign Office, who very much saw the point and promised cooperation. This trip was concluded with a conference, put on by Britain's trade union movement at their old country manor in Stoke Rochford—incidentally Margaret Thatcher's hometown. Robert Hunter, just elected chairman of CCD II, and I both spoke on the "new" idea of rallying the democracies worldwide; the conference organizer told us our talks made the conferees "not just happy, but enthusiastic."

The Community of Democracies Is Born: Warsaw, June 2000

Imagine my exhilaration when the Poles announced the first conference of the Community of Democracies (CD, as it is now referred to, after several years)—the first time that all the democracies of the world would convene to consider what they have in common and what they can do to help each other and countries still striving for democracy. A result of the Madeleine Albright initiative, this three-day meeting attracted 107 foreign ministers. Alongside the official conference, it had been decided to convene a large number of nongovernmental groups from around the world, to survey their own common interests and to second-guess the ministers (NGOs, like the press, always enjoy doing that).

It was not easy to determine which governments should attend (how does one objectively define democratic credentials?), so somewhat more than the 80 or so "free" and "partly free" nations (according to Freedom House's annual survey at the time) were invited. When the CD convened for a second time, in November 2002 in Seoul, some countries invited to Warsaw as full participants were asked only as "observers."

The idea that the democracies of the world should make common cause within one grand Community was one I had pushed hard in my book *Pax Democratica*, although I had thought that something of this sort (I had termed it an Intercontinental Community of Democracies) would be a culminating step, once regional communities along the lines of the EU had been firmly established elsewhere, and after special-purpose but global economic and defense alliances were in place. But Secretary Albright and the Poles and others had different ideas, and Warsaw 2000 was the true beginning of a global process for them.

One should not make the mistake of assuming that Albright and the other organizers—or I and my CCD colleagues—were "one-worlders" or "world federalists." I'm sure that Secretary Albright and the many high officials of the U.S. and other governments who have taken the CD idea seriously realize that it could not represent in any sense of the word a global government. There are many critical people of limited experience in the United States and abroad who scoff at the United Nations, the World Trade Organization, or any other body that attempts to be fully international. The naysayers see these as the heralds of "one socialistic world government," as some of their literature puts it. Whatever readers may think of the accuracy of this characterization, they may rest assured that these bodies and the puny CD created in Warsaw represent little more than weak, if worthy, attempts to gather the nations of the world together for important goals that they share. The CD idea is to make common cause around the objectives of achieving greater respect for human rights, instituting the rule of law, stopping armed conflicts, improving the framework for full and fair trade, and so on. The relative improvement of prosperity of the world since the 1950s, and the fact that we have not (so far, at least) suffered World War III, can be attributed to the patient work of some national governments and international civil servants. Rwanda, Somalia, Darfur, and Congo represent some of the places where the UN and individual nations have failed to stem serious "system failures," largely because of poor governance or inadequate mechanisms for heading off regional crises among weak or rogue states.

But the work of the UN and now of the CD, feeble as both may be, must go on. Otherwise the world will spin out of control. Even the United States, for a time at least the world's only superpower, cannot police or feed or otherwise help the entire world. Insofar as it can be done, these are jobs for groups of nations or for the whole international community, as it is sometimes hopefully called.

Enter the Community of Democracies, with the CCD and a few other NGOs in different parts of the world backing it up, trying to induce governments to make something of it. The Board of our CCD II was purposely composed, half and half, of Republicans and Democrats, some of whom considered themselves independents. In any case, we have worked as a unit, and agreed on almost all that we had to do. The first job, after November 2000, was to convince the new Bush II administration that they must honor Albright's commitments in Warsaw and continue the U.S. support for the Community of Democracies. We were fortunate that one of our Board, Paula Dobriansky, was appointed under secretary of state almost immediately; she had headed the Washington office of the Council on Foreign Relations and, among other things, had arranged a talk for me there in 1999. She and others were able to convince Secretary Colin Powell that the CD might be worth some extra effort. With money, ideas, and some diplomatic persuasion—and a great tour de force by CCD president Walt Raymond—the second CD conference in Seoul, November 2002, came off reasonably well. As one might expect, helping the South Koreans (government and NGOs) behind the scenes to insure success was essential; with help from other U.S. NGOs, Walt did this superbly. Plans for a third CD meeting, in Santiago de Chile, in February 2005, then went ahead, with CCD again helping mightily. We were instrumental, I believe, in persuading the new secretary of state, Condoleezza Rice, to attend. Preparations this time were a much more internationally shared effort, relying heavily on NGOs from around the world.

It remains to be seen whether the CD and the CCD can both survive as the new century wears on. That this was done at all is a tribute to Madeleine Albright, her staff, and the CCDers (I and II), plus Freedom House and other U.S. NGOs who helped, and especially Walt Raymond. The National Endowment for Democracy (in the creation of which Walt had been the principal *éminence grise*) also had a major hand, especially in helping to create a loose worldwide association of democracy support groups. CD was built on the shoulders of ideas that many of us had espoused since the early 1980s. Whether it will continue, become stronger, and be able to make a record of preserving and stimulating democracy remains to be seen. The press and television so far pay CD or CCD little, if any, attention.

After three years as CCD's first CEO, Walt Raymond suddenly became ill in early 2003 and died that April. This was a great loss indeed, not just to CCD but to the country and the world. He deserves the strongest accolades that a grateful nation can bestow on its fallen, as he labored for years most effectively to preserve freedom through networking good men and women everywhere who shared freedom's ideals, and to create institutions to insure that the work would continue.

CCD was fortunate that Board Member Richard Rowson was ready and willing to pick up the pieces where Walt had left them. As of this writing the little organization—with tasks far larger than its tiny size and ephemeral nature would suggest—is continuing to do its quiet work for a better future.

Coda

During the best years of CCD and its ideas, Colleen and I continued to live on the shores of Puget Sound, leading double lives—as officers of the condo association where we lived and voters in a small but exciting semirural community, Bainbridge Island and as quiet citizens of the world. I finished *Pax Democratica*, which was marketed throughout Europe and North America, but didn't take any best-seller prizes for nonfiction. It came out in paperback in 2001, before 9/11. I would rewrite it a bit if there were to be yet another edition, especially given the upheavals that began in late 2001 when President Bush II took the reins in a world effort to conquer terrorism.

In July 2004, I took a good deal of satisfaction from an e-mail sent by my old friend and comrade in the wars (Cold and otherwise), Alan Lee Williams, chairman of the Atlantic Treaty Association, composed of all the citizens groups backing NATO. He wrote: "I went to the lecture given by the Foreign Policy Centre in London in which Larry Diamond [Senior Fellow of the Hoover Institution at Stanford and coeditor of the *Journal of Democracy*] spoke about democracy and referred to your book, as did a number of people, including myself. . . . Your ideas are as important as ever and getting more important daily." That helps, and I hope Alan continues to be right.

What's next? In the concluding chapter I'll try to wrap it all up—past, present, and the future as I hope it will be.

19
The Bottom Line

God grant that not only the love of liberty, but a thorough knowl-edge of the rights of men may pervade all the nations of the earth, so that a philosopher may set his foot anywhere on its surface and say, this is my country.

Benjamin Franklin

The End of the Beginning: Tale of a Peacenik

A favorite cousin from Seattle died in 1998. He had lived in London many years, working for the U.S. Defense Department and enjoying life as a bachelor. Bob and I saw a lot of each other over the years; he would visit our family, or we would visit him in London when I lived in England and four other parts of Europe. Once, when I was posted to the new U.S. diplomatic mission to the European Economic Community in Brussels, Bob and I visited the World War I battlefield of Ypres in Flanders. It was eerie, threading our way through a section of the trenches that had been preserved. Bob's dad, a Canadian, had been wounded at Ypres, so it had a special meaning for him. My father had been luckier; as a sergeant at a replacement depot in the south of France, he was spared the trenches. Bob and I had both served in the armed forces during World War II. These ex-periences had a special meaning for us, and we both hated war intensely.

As Bob's executor, I had a sizeable job to do, a good deal of it in Lon-don going through the tiny flat in which he had squirreled away thou-sands of pounds worth of antiques of every sort—ancient swords, guns of many kinds and eras, a midshipman's dagger from Nelson's navy, much Sheffield silver plate, Japanese *netsuke* (carved ivory purse-clasps), some good maritime drawings, moldy old scientific books, an RAF officer's fly-ing jacket from the First World War, antique navigating instruments, part of the tail of a Messerschmitt fighter, and much more. This was a real rat's nest, but for the most part full of precious objects.

Sorting Bob's old correspondence and documents, I ran across a French map of the battlefields of Verdun, a place Bob had visited more than once, but I never. It is a meticulous guide for the special sort of tourist who tries to piece together what happened there, from February through December 1916. The Germans were determined to pierce the great French fortifications and break the Allied line; the French were equally determined to resist to the death. In the end, six hundred thousand men died there in less than a year of futile fighting. *Six hundred thousand!* Although there may have been even costlier battles in history (Stalingrad, for one, or the three-year siege of Leningrad), Verdun has always stood for me as the symbol of ultimate human folly. When I was a small boy, I didn't grasp the full meaning of Verdun, but my father, an intelligent, mainly self-schooled man, let me know—usually by indirection—what he thought of "the war to end all wars." My mother kept up on world affairs in the 1930s and turned me into a preteen news junkie and, among other things, an advocate of the League of Nations. In chapter 2, I recounted some of this early and lasting attachment to the ideal of a peaceful world.

Since 1933, when I was a mere decade old, I have become steadily more convinced that my own mission on earth is to push for a world of peace. In the eighties, in the midst of my career, when *Who's Who* editors invited me, as they did others, to add to my short biography a statement as to what I considered a "full life," I wrote this:

> For a full life, embrace a worthy cause. Mine is the unity of the democracies. America's most precious asset is its free political system. It can be successfully defended only if we merge our force, our hearts, and our fortune with like-minded peoples. Like-mindedness is not simply a gift of history; it must be cultivated. My life's aim has been to forge consensus among the democracies as a prelude to the creation of a free, just, and durable world order.

This has been no easy task, but I've tried hard to stick with it, sometimes turning down attractive job offers that would have diverted me from my course. Peace, as a general condition, is not yet with us—only in the North Atlantic area, to be exact. I have tended at times to think that a more general peace was within reach, but this was not to be. Unfortunately, new conflicts pop up every few weeks, some horrific as in Rwanda or Darfur, others smaller in loss of life yet momentous in their consequences, such as the current Iraq venture. Sometimes I believe that I have been able to do precious little to stanch the senseless bloodletting. But when I look calmly at the world and what has come about since I was 10 years old, I know that we have nonetheless made a great deal of progress.

The Positive Side of the Ledger

I had a small hand in this, sometimes in ways that eventually paid off with substantial results. Let me count some of the ways, my own bottom line for peace:

1. Despite the stretching of transatlantic bonds until at times we thought they would sunder, the network of intense personal relationships and mutual institutional commitments—some stretching back in memory to World War II, when the fate of world civilization hung in the balance—for the most part still holds together. In so many different incarnations and by so many different channels, I've had a hand in seeing that both the nongovernmental and governmental ties have prospered, on balance, compared with 1940 or 1950 or 1970. Will they continue to hold? That's another question, unanswerable in my lifetime.

2. Europe—the locus of the world's greatest wars and rumors of wars over centuries—has now become a zone of peace. To have seen the 1996 wirephoto of Chancellor Kohl and President Mitterrand silently hand-in-hand at the Verdun battlefield is all the vindication I need to know that my efforts to help the Europeans put together their Union and other institutions that make up the vital web of joint interests and joint action were worth it, a thousand times over. Literally thousands of us, in high places and low, worked to make this come about, but I am satisfied that I helped. I doubt now that there will ever be another great war in Europe—perhaps someday on the fringes, such as in unsettled Kosovo, or Moldova or Georgia—but for the most part internecine war in Europe is a thing of the past.

3. I cherish the thought that I have helped the public dialogue and some of the principal actors in world affairs to acknowledge the cardinal importance of democracy to the ever-broadening creation of peace zones. Late in my life, because my classical education had many gaps in it, I came to the works of Immanuel Kant and to modern thought about his dictum that *democracies (he called them republics) do not make war on one another*. I had already learned this through experience and observation, but Kant became my big ally. This is the main intellectual foundation on which I have helped to build most of the transnational institutions and domestic order arrangements that buttress and move forward the cause of peace, internally and externally, through democracy. Madeleine Albright came to the same practical conclusion and, with her colleagues and the Polish government, created the Community of Democracies in 2000. Will it endure? Will it make a big difference? I'll never know, but it has had a start and I've given a hand.

4. I'm happy too that some of the civic building blocks of democratic regimes around the world have been buttressed by the National Endowment for Democracy, the design for which I helped move forward in the 1980s, with and through the CCDs (Mark I) and on my own with Walt Raymond. As Albright's CD moved towards its third interministerial conference, in Santiago de Chile in 2005, I noted that its backers and decision-makers adopted at least one specific idea from my handbook for unifying democracies, *Pax Democratica*: In 2005, they were to receive reports from around 100 democracies. Each had been asked to do its own self-searching and characterize as honestly as possible the "state of democratic institutions" in its own country. This is unprecedented and will no doubt work imperfectly to start with. I had recommended such a periodic review, along the lines of the NATO annual defense reviews and the OECD country economic reports. But there are formidable obstacles to extending such self-searching to the sensitive area of civic and political life. How will the United States, for example, come out of such an exercise in a satisfying, uncontentious, and reasonably objective way? Nonetheless, it's important to start the process of international "comparative introspection." How are we doing, "democracywise"? In the summer of 2005, American University took an informal crack at this, with a group of Mexicans, Canadians, and Americans criticizing the practice of democracy in their own countries.

5. I've helped in Europe, North America, and the Far East to open the eyes of some present and many future leaders to the ineluctable facts of interdependence and to the best path to peace: democracy at home and ever-closer links with other democracies. Through countless public and university lectures in North America, Europe, Japan, and Australia over the years, plus assisting at the creation of and, in a few cases conceiving, many nongovernmental associations—the Mid-Atlantic Clubs, the 21st Century Trust, the Atlantic Institute, and the successor generation projects of the Ford Foundation and other bodies—I've done my bit to spread the word, further the growth of like-mindedness, and build networks.

6. Here and there I've helped to kick-start the growth of modern philanthropy, as a concept (in INTERPHIL—the International Standing Conference on Philanthropy—for example) and as an open invitation to wealthy people, such as the Gateses, to build their own foundations for the public good. Because of INTERPHIL, there is a sizeable growth since 1970 in voluntarism and the birth of new foundations and NGOs in Europe.

None of this has been an effort to achieve public approval or plaudits. Nonetheless, it's sometimes good to know that one's efforts are appreciated. On 12 November 1989, my old Foreign Service friend, Martin Ackerman, phoned from Paris to say, "What's happened [the fall of the Wall], *you* did!" That was ridiculous, of course, but it gave me a measure of satisfaction. On another occasion a few years ago, a friend in Belgium interviewed Pierre Harmel, one of the ageing founders of NATO and author of the 1957 Harmel Report, which urged increased efforts to create détente with the Soviets and still remain strong. The interviewer told Harmel about my efforts to create the Atlantic Institute in Paris; Harmel had served on its Board of Governors after I left for the United States and had not known of my early efforts; he wrote a profusely commendatory letter to me, addressing me as *"Monsieur le Fondateur."* That too touched me deeply—someone historically important recognized some hard work.

This recitation of what I think I've accomplished is enough to make me reasonably satisfied, but only "reasonably." I know that the job has just begun, and I hope and pray that my own progeny, plus those young interns and staff members of new institutions whom I have temporarily "adopted" at various points in our intersecting lives, will carry on, finding new ways to help people help each other.

Enduring Obstacles to Peace

Soon after I returned to my native Northwest in 1974, someone gave me a big cardboard cutout of a sad-looking bloodhound with a cartoon "balloon" over his puzzled head that read: "Just when I learned all the answers, they changed all the questions." I've lost that soulful dog, but the message, while amusing, still sobers and mystifies me. Perhaps 1963, with JFK's death, was the watershed that most changed the old questions. Until then, it had seemed to me that at least the Western democracies, and most particularly our own, had begun to resolve many of the burning issues that had consumed mankind for eons. Perhaps we had—as Churchill said—"moved into the broad uplands" of human existence.

The Cold War had seemed a monstrous necessity, filling people the world over with fear and uncertainty. Yet the very effort to gird ourselves for a cataclysmic conflict that—finally and thankfully—never came, was always a sobering guest at the table. Within their broad, seemingly fragile, mutual defense framework, the North Americans, the Europeans, the Japanese, and the Australasians had made measurable political, social, and economic progress at home and in the developing world. We now look back with nostalgia at the late fifties and early sixties as a golden age of civility and progressiveness. I often think that Lee Harvey Oswald, the psychotic loner who shot JFK, has almost as much to answer for to history as Hitler or Lenin.

In most of that Cold War era, I was abroad, doing the nation's international work; thus the signs of progress were acutely visible to us in Europe with the perspective of distance. What was happening at home and by extension in Europe was quite evident. By November 1963, I had returned to the United States, working to extend the reach of the Atlantic Institute in my own country. One day, recovering from a small operation and watching an old black and white TV, I suddenly learned the appalling news of President Kennedy's assassination in Dallas. I am often overwhelmed by instinct at such momentous events — this time was no different. I suddenly asked myself, "What will this mean?" and was consumed with foreboding. Knowing something about history, and especially what its frightful toll had been in Europe from the 1920s through the 1940s, I thought, "This death will dramatically change people's hopes and perceptions, and not for the better."

In the days that followed Dallas, messages from friends all over flooded in. I'll never forget what my great friend Professor Arnold Bergstraesser of Freiburg University wrote to me soon after Kennedy's murder. (Arnold was one of those non-Jewish Germans who were not personally in danger when Hitler came to power; but he saw the handwriting on the wall—a future of vile illiberalism—and left Germany for the University of Chicago. Out of conviction that his country needed him again in 1946, Professor Bergstraesser returned to Germany for a full and influential academic career, becoming a confidant of great men such as Adenauer. More than any other single academic, I believe he exerted a powerful influence on German political and civic life during the years until his death, in 1964.) In his letter to me he described the scene on that November day in his university town. The news burst on the streets during evening mealtime, as he supped with friends in the student quarter. They rose to see what the commotion was outside. Students and older people poured out of eateries and pubs and were milling around in the cobbled lanes. Virtually everyone, wrote Arnold, had tears streaming down their faces. They were remembering a young and apparently fearless president who had made common cause with all Germans when, standing at the Wall, he said, "*Ich bin ein Berliner!*" And now they were bewildered, virtually rudderless, in the professor's opinion. Similar expressions of grief and incomprehension were also sent to me from other parts of the world and the USA.

It matters little that in later years publics have learned of JFK's moral fallibility. Some serious observers have written that, had he lived, his record as president would not have been so rosy as its prospects appeared in 1963. He might not even have been reelected for a second term. But JFK represented a young and confident America to the world—large numbers of people felt they could trust him and, through him, America. After 1963, I believe it was almost inevitable that the "Free World" would lapse into a long period of cynicism, based on the reawakening of old fears. In spite of the many momentous events and positive achievements since that time, I do not think that the world has yet climbed fully out of that abyss of Dallas. Coupled with the new instincts and capabilities of the media to wield destructive power, pointing out the rottenness (ranging from wholly true to not at all) of many institutions and public figures, the academic world, the political world, the religious world, the world of youth, the business world, and all other segments of society—in the West at least—lost their compass. Thus most of our hopes for a continuingly progressive Zeitgeist were dashed. The old bugaboos of the post–World War I era and the fears of failure in and after World War II had returned with a vengeance. And all the civic washing, colored and discolored, was being laundered in the full gaze of publics everywhere. The Internet and cellphones have only recently compounded the problem of distinguishing what's important and what's true from the ephemeral, titillating, and destructive.

The Youth Revolt

A symbol of the changes underway caught my eye, indelibly, in 1964, when I visited the Berkeley campus of the University of California. It was one of those cloudless, meteorologically blessed days that Californians take for granted, and which the rest of us often yearn for. I sat in the outdoor restaurant of the student union building with some professor friends. On the broad grassy slopes below, college boys—who looked typical of a now-vanished age of fraternity pranks and old-fashioned dating—were playing touch football. Their haircuts and attire were conventional, short, and casual, and they yelled playfully at one another. In their manner, I could see myself twenty-plus years earlier as a freshman at the University of Washington.

At a corner of the porch on which we sat, a group of scruffy, long-haired protohippies of the soon-to-be-conquering generation lounged and smoked who-knew-what. This was during the time of the so-called Free Speech Movement on the Berkeley campus; Mario Savio was the new messiah of these inheritors of the tiny but influential Beat Generation, eventually to overwhelm the universities from Berkeley to the rest of the United States, and on to Paris and Berlin and all of Europe, even Japan. This revolt became a flood of protest and mindlessness, sometimes clothed in what many would think the virtuous concepts of "tell it like it is" and "if it feels good, do it." And, within a few years and the advent of the casualty lists and tortured warfare of the misbegotten Vietnam adventure, the undermining and collapse of much of the moral structure of the Western world would eventuate—more quickly than most of us could ever have imagined. And it was led by such people as Timothy O'Leary, a well-known Harvard professor, Jane Fonda, daughter of one of the most respected Hollywood figures, and Herbert Marcuse, a German socialist academic persecuted by Hitler but now oblivious to modern society's need for a balance between freedom on the one hand and self-discipline and civic responsibility on the other. Marcuse, who should have known better, egged on the students and hippies in their willy-nilly course of destruction.

This is not the time or place to recount the full dimensions of this tragic period's still-lingering impact on our lives. But this youth revolt of the sixties and seventies has had a tremendous effect—on balance overwhelmingly deleterious, I believe—on the societies within which those who work for true peace and understanding and other forms of human progress must work.

Although I clearly acknowledge a few virtues of the new "freedom" unleashed by this movement and its possibly beneficent effects on the stodginess and pretensions of institutions such as the university (especially in Europe) and political and economic life, I nevertheless feel unabashedly resentful of those figures of authority—many of them exceedingly honorable persons—who in the sixties crumbled in the face of the youthful onslaught on common sense and liberal thought. On balance—and I admit the "on the one hand, on the other" character of such a judgment—I believe that what happened was an unnecessary and harmful unleashing

of powerful negative forces. Always present beneath the surface of any society, these pressures would have been dealt with anyway, and in a positive and gradual manner, had Western civilization not been torched as it was in these decades. This period of licentiousness, not real liberty at all, has yet to run its course.

The Degradation of Intellectual Thought

Most unfortunately, the effect of this vast upheaval on academia and other social institutions has been especially corrosive, widespread, and long lasting. It is as hard today for a true liberal or moderate to get a hearing on most American campuses as it is for a rock-ribbed conservative to do so. I blame the leaders of academia who caved in to intimidation and the lords of the media, who for the most part have reveled in the civilizational destruction.

One day in 1996, a professor at the University of Washington and I debated the world political outlook before students. We both harked back to the Second World War, the Marshall Plan, and so on, sparred a lot on details and what should be done next. Later, in the nearby men's room, I saw graffiti on a stall door:

No more Old Boy network . . . no more World War II
No more . . . stuffy, lame old has-beens
Reelect Clinton '96
Abolish the republican party . . . or get young new leaders

Perhaps they were referring to Bob Dole, Clinton's older but worthy opponent, or maybe they reflected my just-completed debate. Dole had a war-crippled left arm; I walked with a cane. Goes with the territory, I mused.

Perhaps more harmful than any other fallout from this leftward movement have been the false prophets such as Noam Chomsky, Jean-Paul Sartre, and Jacques Derrida, who have striven through the "deconstructionist" and existential schools to literally take apart and debase our major languages. This has led to the recrudescence of nihilism and the erosion of hope, when we should have been learning better to express ourselves in the endless service of noble goals and inclusive philosophies.

The reader should understand that, critical as I am of what happened to still the engines of real progress by means of mass appeals to "lid's-off-the-id" behavior, abetted by a greedy and reckless media, I am just as critical of the forces of reaction that responded. I am by nature a centrist and a moderate (I once told my teenage kids, "I'm an extremist—from the extreme center"). In my judgment, Rightist forces just as powerful as those from what one might call the unthinking Left have positioned themselves in certain churches, in the bars of bikers and hoodlums, in the recording studios and press, in some corporate boardrooms, and in the halls of the political establishment to confront the new phenomena with powerful appeals to presumed Righteousness, or sometimes just to Right-ness. Whether such movements are from Right or Left, they are at the expense of the values of the Enlightenment, wherein lie the sound roots of all modern social arrangements, including tolerance—and that's where I position myself.

Some evangelical/fundamentalist Christian preachers in recent years have branded all those who do not believe in a literal and selective interpretation of the Bible as "humanists." In one tract, Tim LaHaye lists abhorrent institutions shot through and through with "humanism" (and by his definition all "humanists" are also atheists). He begins with the National Academy of Sciences, the United Nations, and the *New York Times* and includes three badges of my own eternal damnation: Harvard University (I hold an MA), the State Department (I was in its toils for a decade), and the Ford Foundation. At Ford I had spent two of the most satisfying years of my life seeing how one could do some good for the human condition with plenty of money, and in the process learning a great deal about the frontier movements and processes in contemporary life around the world. I am not an atheist, and I know precious few of Rev. LaHaye's "humanists, " probably because I can't categorize them with any precision.

The worst aspects of the corroding of public thought by the thoughtless Right can be seen in the appearance, in the 1980s and 1990s, of neo-Nazism, with bigotry and nihilism linked in the "militia" movements. These incipient forms of fascism are just as dangerous to the democratic way of life in America and abroad as is the mindless work of the anarchists, ecoterrorists, neo-Marxists, or other nihilists of the Left. None of these rallies around the "vital center" of American or Western life, but tend in any way they can to tear it down, from either side or both.

Actually, I believe the "political spectrum" is not left-to-right linear but circular. If you leave the vital center and go far enough Left, you meet those coming round from the Right. Both end up in extreme totalitarian concepts: "It's my way or the highway, and if you don't believe it, I'll force you to, if I get the chance." Sad to say, the bulk of the arguments of the authoritarian Right—including much of religious fundamentalism's apparent beliefs—are clearly recognizable today in the early Cold War pronouncements of the ultraconservative John Birch Society.

Among other great contemporary challenges that have been left half met is that of race relations in the United States. In the early sixties, at great human cost, noble people, black and white, made a huge dent in the institutionalized bigotry of American life, mainly but not exclusively in the South. But the ensuing illiberalism and extremism, on both sides of the political divide, plus the advent of cynical pop culture—a spinoff of the youth revolt—have made the steady but moderate progress of the early sixties difficult to resume. To cite three examples: the assassination of Martin Luther King, the rise of terrorist gangs such as the ecoanarchists and Black Panthers, and the rejuvenation of the vile Ku Klux Klan.

I cite these as massive social and political obstacles to the kind of work I have tried to do for nearly six decades of my life. Much of this, whether from the know-nothing Left or the know-nothing Right, has burgeoned since the 1960s. For myself and anyone sincerely concerned with bettering the human condition through rational thought and gradual change, these new currents of profound ignorance in modern life present powerful obstacles.

Ignorance and the Decline of Internationalism

To be specific about another web of difficulties that abound in impeding a sensible and forward-looking approach to our civic challenges internationally, but also domestically, one must look at a great many Americans' lack of appreciation or understanding of the outside world. I cite these elements of the problem:

1. The media need more strong voices favoring moderation and progress and full and fair coverage—especially in the United States—of foreign affairs. Much of the trashy greed should also be squeezed out of TV, the films, radio, and the press and magazines. How? I don't know.

Sixty years ago the international content, percentagewise, of U.S. radio and print media was much greater than today as I write, in 2006. When I was a young Foreign Service officer, the wise old overseas correspondents of U.S. newspapers were notable for their on-the-spot coverage of international matters. Today, reporters parachuted by an editor to cover a hot foreign trouble spot and return home may provide crisis coverage, but not nearly so well or so constantly as the American public needs and deserves.

2. There is a lack of continuing, intelligent intercultural dialogue. Since the death of the U.S. Information Agency in 1997, thanks to the Clinton administration's making unholy common cause with Senator Jesse Helms—the enemy in that era of intelligent discourse and unbiased information in our foreign affairs—there has been a great lacuna at the heart of our nation's international work. The Department of State is unable to concentrate on this discrete set of vital tasks in the way that an essentially independent USIA could and did.

In the early years of the 21st century, the National Endowment for Democracy has bankrolled an extremely well-balanced and effective new organization, the Center for the Study of Islam and Democracy, run by a moderate Muslim cleric, Radwan Masmoudi. The center sponsors discussions between Islamic and other thinkers, searching for a middle ground for humans of reason, in the cause of a sort of international civics to help guide us away from conflict as a means of resolving differences. It is emblematic of what should be done on a much larger scale, by all responsible governments and, mostly, person-to-person.

3. Sadly, the great American foundations and some abroad have missed their proper targets by miles in the past two or three decades. As a consequence, although much more money is spent than before, even on foreign affairs, the outlays are mainly on relatively second-ary and less consequential matters. The gut issues—such as peace or the fundamental rebuilding of an archaic world system still based on the 1648 Treaty of Westphalia—have been left relatively untouched. Much of this reflects the inability of our World War II and Cold War generations to pass on, through parenting and academia, a clear un-derstanding by emerging leaders of thought and action of the real forces influencing the course of international events, and of the means that might be employed to mitigate the worst and encourage the best international practices.

Partly as a result of the sixties–seventies turmoil, today's foundation executives or founders do not have the compasses that point to fundamental, as distinct from peripheral, causes of decay, chaos, bad governance, illiberalism, and armed conflict that define so much of the central challenges of our time. In the seventies, for example, one important German-American foundation, dedicated to supporting ever better relations between Europe and the United States, made a sizeable grant to city fathers in Tacoma, Washington, and Cologne, Germany, to study new methods of collecting garbage in both towns. Compare this to the efforts of many well-meaning groups and foundations to deal with the health problems of Africa—as just one example—without making comparable sums and expertise available to improve civic life and governance in that continent, which, unless reformed, may partially or completely block effective delivery systems for public health, treatment, and medicines.

Opportunities Missed

With the fall of the Berlin Wall and the collapse of the Communist sys-tem in 1989–91, Western leaders lost a golden opportunity to replace the anticommunist goals of the Cold War with what had been secondary but should have become primary: the retooling and strengthening of democ-racy and of cooperation leading to integration among democracies. The reader will recall, from the previous chapter, some eventually fruitless soundings on foreign policy that serious colleagues and I took in the late 1980s and early 1990s. A few of us in the United States and abroad pro-posed a new strategy and a joint Allied foreign policy to fill the lacunae left by the vanished Cold War. This time we foresaw what could have been a positive, unexceptionable drive for human rights and democratic governance, freed from most of the constraints and contradictions of the Cold War and at some distant day encompassing the world.

Most unfortunately, the first President Bush, his successor President Clinton, and, in the early years of the new century, the second President Bush dillied and dallied, called on old habits of balance-of-power diplomacy when their advisors told them they must, and under the second George Bush struck out on a naked new policy of trying to run the world with few, if any, allies. The drift was in the direction of a Pax Americana, when the most knowledgeable foreign affairs specialists knew that the world needed something like a Pax Democratica such as I had tried to articulate in 1998, building on the international institution-founding legacy of the Cold War years. The trauma of 9/11 provided a great excuse to slip into power-politics-as-more-than-usual, when the trend should have been in the other direction. The opportunity presented itself, but only briefly, in the wake of 9/11.

Targeting Afghanistan was a logical, if difficult response. Most people around the world understood the righteous anger of Americans and the need to shut down Osama bin Laden. The Paris Le Monde headlined, "Now we are all Americans." On the North Atlantic, during NATO maneuvers then in progress, the crew of a German destroyer flying Old Glory as well as its own flag lined the taffrail and saluted as the vessel sailed by an American warship. The North Atlantic Council, meeting in Brussels three days after 9/11, invoked Article V of the North Atlantic Treaty for the first time in its history: Member nations had in 1949 agreed that "an attack on one is an attack on all"; the United States had been attacked on its own soil, and all members were bound, now in 2001, to come to its aid. What did the administration in Washington do? Politely thanked NATO and said, in effect: "Don't call us, we'll call you." There was a calculated effort on the part of near-fatally misguided leaders in the Bush administration to "go it alone."

As of this writing, Afghanistan's fate hangs in the balance. U.S. calls for Allied help—finally—were late in the game and overshadowed by Bush's plight in the new imbroglio over Iraq that began in 2002. NATO was finally given limited security tasks in Afghanistan and some role in training new Iraqi police, but whereas the initial campaign against bin Laden and Islamist terror might have been a truly joint NATO operation, such rhetoric in 2001 as George Bush's "If you're not with us, you're against us" had a bad ring to it in Europe and the Middle East. Many patriotic Americans did not know enough about the situation—or indeed about geopolitics— to distinguish between efforts to defend their country at any cost and a reasoned approach that would have emphasized our interdependence and consensus with valued allies and had a better chance of success.

Between the fall of 2001 and the start of 2006, when this memoir closes, the United States just may have suffered irreparable damage to the structures and networks of peace, democracy, and, above all, ever-closer multinational collaboration—all that a host of colleagues and I had created between 1947 and 2003. From Roosevelt through Truman, Eisenhower, and their successors—until George W. Bush—the decisive emphases in U.S. foreign policy had usually been on setting the world on a course in which disputes between nations would eventually be settled without recourse to conflict and ways found gradually to repair the ill effects of colonialism, Communism, and underdevelopment.

During the Cold War years, I often chafed at the bald self-serving actions and pronouncements that sometimes emanated from Washington; these were the last gasps, in my view, of recourse to old-fashioned, zero-sum world politics. But Europe, and to a great extent the Atlantic community and Japan, usually managed to locate the common interest and work together in common cause. However, under the young George Bush, this course was not to be followed, at least until it was almost too late.

In 2006, President Bush and Secretary of State Rice announced new U.S. efforts to promote democracy worldwide. But these initiatives ignored the long-term intercultural approach to nurturing the daily civic habits of democracy while fully employing the regional and global ties between democracies. America's allies in Europe and other parts of the world are not blameless in this 21st century backward slide from the ways of mutual cooperation. Nations such as France, and Germany too (in its 2002 elections), should have known better than to publicly and indiscriminately slander Bush and the United States while standing in the way of what the president and his team, along with Tony Blair, wished to do in Iraq. A good deal of unnecessary bad blood bubbled up on all sides. And the Allies' indisposition to modernize defense establishments so that NATO could act multinationally with effectiveness was also notable. NATO's joint defense capabilities have sadly been allowed to run down.

This state of affairs must be repaired. If it is not, and if Europe and North America, the core of the sixty-year-old world democracy and peace movement, do not resume a forward trajectory, much of my life's accomplishment, bound inextricably with what so many more able and important people in dozens of countries have striven mightily to bring about, may have been for naught.

I pray this will not be so. There is always cause for hope. The E.U.–U.S. summit of 20 June 2005 issued a strong, surprising bit of rhetoric, ignored by the press, indicating a new, joint intention to promote democracy worldwide (see Appendix J). This may end up as "just rhetoric"; but it could suggest a new grasp of essential truths about coming together to foster a durable peace based on democracy and cooperation.

The American Mind and Internationalism

Since I entered the Foreign Service in 1952, the American people overall have become somewhat more acquainted with what one might call "the international facts of life," but not yet enough. It's true that as a result of tourism and interpersonal exchanges of students and selected community and professional leaders, Americans have become more knowledgeable about other countries—cuisine, languages, cultural differences, and so on. This wave of opening up to the "foreign" began with World War II—hundreds of thousands of GIs returned home with exposure to foreign ways, often with foreign brides. In the early 1950s, some of us at the European end of the intercultural pipeline could count on Americans' opening their hearts and homes to European exchange students and older travelers who came to the United States to learn. But this growing sensitivity and openness has not been seized as an opportunity to enlighten public opinion on the fundamentals of an international future. Rather, it has been more like scattering wildflower seeds than planting a carefully planned garden and tending it constantly.

My own current hometown, Sequim in the State of Washington, has a sister-city relationship with Yamasaki, Japan; the two-way visits and exchanges of gardens (yes, whole little parks and not just a few plants or trees!) and gifts are touching, and many Sequimites seem to take this seriously. A number of our high school students visit Japan and other countries every year; the local newspaper often has tales of kids from all over the world studying or making shorter visits here. People of Sequim, as in big cities, travel abroad a lot. Many Sequimites have gone on serious trips to help the indigent and afflicted in developing countries. The "service clubs" such as Kiwanis, Soroptimists, and Rotary actively promote goodwill towards the world. In short, just as in most other U.S. communities, there's plenty of interaction with other cultures. Most larger towns and cities have world affairs councils and other programs that dispense good information and often arrange personal contacts that enhance understanding of the international scene.

Yet somehow, all this activity—and I have personally promoted a good deal of it over the years—does not yet add up to a critical mass of citizenry that sees the world and its intricacies in a truly sophisticated, knowing way. I stress "critical mass" because it is obvious that perhaps only five to ten percent of the population cares enough to listen and learn about such things. Better TV and press coverage of matters foreign can help the general population; but what matters more is the critical mass of local, regional, and national leaders who listen carefully and know how to sift through the barrage of information and make sense of it for the purpose of casting their votes and enlightening the electorate.

A month spent in Nicaragua, say, helping to harvest the coffee crop and find out how peasants really live, does little to equip the intelligent voter with an understanding of the broad sweep of U.S. relations with Central and South America and how these fit into the global pattern. When the White House issues the call to invade Iraq, few are the intelligent, leading local citizens who understand the Middle East and what it means to all of us—economically, politically, socially, ethically. The great universities do a fair job in preparing some Americans for a world seen reasonably whole, as do many smaller colleges. The Seattle World Affairs Council tells me about important Americans and foreigners in the city to explain a particular aspect of foreign affairs. This keeps a good number of our citizens reasonably well informed. Yet even these informative activities, plus chances to visit with foreign exchangees, do not give the ordinary educated person grounding in the many factors that impinge on the conduct of foreign policy and the broad sweep of interaction among nations, nor on the work of important intergovernmental organizations, such as the UN, NATO, or the European Union.

For the ignorance or miseducation of some of today's college-educated, the professoriate is somewhat to blame, because so many of its members are narrow specialists in certain areas of the world or in certain aspects of world affairs, like international trade or the Middle East. There are precious few generalists. Furthermore, many current faculty were educated in the framework of the prejudices of the Youth Revolt of the sixties and seventies. But at all levels in the schools, the colleges and universities, and in what passes for adult education, there are still striking—and even dangerous—gaps in integrated knowledge to be filled. If we are to make interdependence work, this must above all be corrected. We Americans avoid this central task at our peril.

Some decent, concerned citizens in the smaller towns and rural areas lack most of the opportunities available in big cities. But somebody is providing ideas and "information" about our overseas involvements. Else, why would there be such widespread willingness to believe that the UN, for example, is a "vast global conspiracy to enslave Americans in a socialist world government"? What poppycock! What dangerous know-nothingism! Those who get their ideas about matters "foreign" are welcome to the likes of Rush Limbaugh, Al Franken, and other radio and TV commentators; but if so, they are dangerously ill informed. Unfortunately, some fundamentalist and evangelical movements also disseminate inaccurate and biased views.

A vast gulf in international understanding still exists and needs somehow to be filled to help Americans as a whole come up to speed, for one important example, with their European cousins, who themselves constitute no paragon. One possible solution might be providing intensive short courses on geopolitics and international affairs to large numbers of adults.

I sometimes feel desperate about the citizenry's broad ignorance of what makes the world go round. To try, as I have for years, to explain the concept of our ineluctable interdependence with other peoples and societies is to bump into a wall of ignorance, bias, and misconceptions based on false information and premises. No matter how well meaning some of the carriers of such inadequate messages (and I am giving many the benefit of the doubt), this misinformation—built around a vast pool of ignorance—is a great impediment to a sensible, effective U.S. foreign policy and, ultimately, to a world of peace. Intelligent, educable leaders of the community at the very least need better mental constructs, and accurate information with which to apply them.

I can only reiterate what I have suggested throughout this book: A great deal more time and money and effort must be spent in ways to properly educate the American public on international issues and factors. We really cannot stand a lot more wars. But to prepare for a better world, many more of our citizens (and this is true in most other countries as well) must be helped to understand the truth about the factors that are at work globally. Heads-in-the-sand will not do. And even though many good citizens concentrate on the important work of saving souls and attending to the moral dictates of religious teachers, trying to reform the world one soul at a time—in my judgment—will not save us in time. These tasks are vitally important, but to help citizens vote intelligently on international issues is just as important and even more urgent in these perilous times.

At the elite level—the relatively sophisticated people who represent us in Congress and their staffs, the top civil and foreign service in the relevant federal departments, the newscasters and network heads, the head offices of great corporations and banks, the military leaders, the serious think-tankers and academicians, the lobbyists and the religious leaders—we are also deficient. There are (thankfully) still enough wise and well-versed people spread around the Washington Beltway in particular and the country in general to provide some intelligent input to the conduct of foreign affairs. But the wise ones' voices are often drowned out by the special pleadings of interests or the armor plating of ideologies—to listen to the truth is often less pleasing or comforting than to hear someone who can reinforce your biases, even if you think you don't have any.

And while I exhort the brightest and best young people to enter the Foreign Service (or the Peace Corps for starters), I must register my profound disappointment in the moral turpitude revealed in recent cases—for example, the conviction of two U.S. diplomats, one in June and the other in November of 2002, for selling visas in U.S. consulates abroad. Our ethical standards seem to be endangered in this profession of foreign affairs, so central to our being as a nation. Such flawed younger career officers, if undetected, might have moved up the career ladder to deal with, and endanger, the more complex and important tasks of democracy-building or fence-mending with allies. In such positions of international trust, we desperately need men and women of great integrity, capable of transnational ways of thinking and acting.

Rebuilding Civil Society

In Harvard professor Robert Putnam's prescient book, *Bowling Alone*, he showed the erosion of those civic associations of all kinds that have been an American hallmark since our earliest days as a people. Tocqueville wrote admiringly about them in 1830. Today, television, the Internet, the automobile, the airplane, computerized games, and the entire vast array of "entertainments" with which we may amuse ourselves are among the social forces that have been chipping away at Americans' sense of community. As important bodies, such as the National Endowment for Democracy and its affiliates here and abroad, educate foreign peoples in the importance to mature democracy of "civil society," and work to help bring good governance to those who have never had enough of it, if at all, we need to look to our own present-day cultural patterns in America. We must make sure we don't lose the greatness of civil society just when we are exhorting others to develop it. Civic spirit in America is eroding, in some troubling ways, although we may be progressing in other ways at the same time. I admit the contradictions are great, and the effort to prepare a balance sheet on American democracy—as I feel I must, for my own peace of mind at least—is exceedingly difficult.

The reader may feel that, like Job, I see nothing but woe ahead. But that is not so. I recognize how the world and especially American society have been changing at a headlong pace. Not all the changes have been deleterious. And those that are can be replaced with changed behavior that will put us far ahead of where we were fifty years ago. American goodwill and helping hands are still in copious supply. When I look around me every day I see examples of our abiding tolerance and goodheartedness.

On balance, our instincts and our wishes to help each other and the down-trodden everywhere are proliferating in new ways. For instance, some of the charitable appeals my wife and I receive daily in the mail, on the telephone, or at the door are bogus or at the least questionable, but the majority are not. The local food banks and helping organizations are busy doing their jobs. Many, many individuals and civic and religious organizations are trying to fill the cracks through which so many people drop, here and abroad.

I am also encouraged that uncompromising hard truths crop up continuously. They confront our national political leaders, who—no matter how hard they struggle to create a deceptively comfortable unilateral framework for policy-making—find that the requirements of interdependence with others are inescapable. These truths include:

- the need for solid, like-minded allies who will make important decisions *with* us, not just because we say they ought to;
- the requirement for joint management and agreed rules to govern the global economy; and
- the chaos that ensues when nations fail to recognize today's absolute necessity to govern democratically, to create and respect the rule of law, and to protect civil rights, not just domestically but also internationally.

These are not just "nice things" to bring about when we can, but absolute requirements for a free, prosperous, peaceful world.

If I did not believe that the long-term balance favors the Brotherhood of Man, I would not bother to think and write in this vein, or to continue to work with the many others who have enriched my life. During the Hungarian Revolution of 1956, for example, a small east coast organization, the International Rescue Committee, began to perform a great service. They brought out of Hungary—and over the intervening years, out of many beleaguered countries—political refugees who faced persecution and often death at home. IRC's work continues today, thanks to the generosity of citizens who support their efforts. This is only one of countless examples of what generous and percipient people, banding together in small ways, can do to express the highest values of our society and of democracy in general. This trend grows.

So I continue to believe that the course I chose many years ago has borne enough fruit to justify, several times over, the time spent.

What's Next?

As I enter my ninth decade, I still have plans for self-improvement, for helping a bit with improvement for others, and for—as my wife constantly admonishes me—taking some time to "smell the flowers."

And what flowers we have! And animals. And general surroundings. I am lucky beyond words to live in the far northwest corner of what Americans call the "lower 48," in the valley of the Dungeness River. One mile away to the north is the sea, bearer of fresh salt winds, both wild and gentle. Five miles to the south rise the Olympic Mountains, the last great wilderness, a million and more acres of it, in the continental United States. We live surrounded by our own small conifer forest on the crest of a ridge that overlooks the Strait of Juan de Fuca, with Canada in the distance. If we want the 2,500-meter peaks, we can enter (but never cross, as roads are few) Olympic National Park and be in the alpine wilderness in less than an hour.

Deer, raccoons, and other beasts stop here to graze (on our flowers, thank you!). Now and then people see cougar; a bit farther away, bear. Not far from us, literally inside the borders of the small town of Sequim, two herds of elk descend from the mountains now and then into farmers' fields—and sometimes homeowners' lawns—to find the food occasionally lacking in their usual haunts. Our weather is agreeable. In short, we are fortunate.

In Dearborn, Michigan, I once visited Henry Ford's outdoor museum, where he collected historic structures from all over America. One can see there, for instance, the Wright Brothers' cycle shop from Dayton, or Noah Webster's home from Connecticut. I was particularly impressed with a tiny cabin tucked away in a wood next to a small stream; it was the retreat of Charles Steinmetz, the wizard physicist of the late 19th century. Though he had laboratories in a city, when he wanted to think about fundamental things he repaired to his cabin in the Adirondacks. It contained a rude cot, a small stove, a couple of cupboards, and a table and chair. No electricity. He got his water from the nearby creek. I like the idea—although such surroundings are not easily reproducible today. But my wife's and my large "cabin in the woods," which is nicely heated and accoutered with computers and TV and all the contemporary paraphernalia required, will do nicely, because we live largely uninterrupted here, except by friends or family who drop by occasionally and are warmly welcome. We can drive to the Big City, Seattle, replete with a ferry ride, in two or three short hours, if we want to sample the arts and more old friends and progeny. In short, this is about as close to Steinmetz's cabin as I can easily be—or want to be. We have our copious share of peace and quiet.

I have bought all the naturalists' handbooks necessary to delve into everything about us, plus local histories. I want to read all these carefully, and also read the 2,000 books out of our collection of around 4,500 that I've not had time for. European history (especially the Enlightenment), for example, is still a passionate interest. And today one must learn about an even wider world; books on Japan and Asia also line the shelves.

I was never by disposition a bureaucrat, but I recognize a continuing need for good ones in our complex age. So I shall continue as best I can to help guide and prepare the diplomats and other public servants of the future, as well as some who will go into international business, academe, or other pursuits. Seeing them individually—especially those who will go abroad or otherwise have careers in international relations—talking to groups, or writing things I hope they will read, is most satisfying. Based on encounters in recent years with those preparing for careers, I can attest to the advent of a new generation of superior young Americans. I have great confidence in them. When I sometimes lecture to today's students, I am often astounded by the breadth of their understanding and their motivation to do good. Every opportunity to know people of this kind "makes my day."

I worry about my country and the world, and about tasks I leave undone. I will do my duty as a voter and now and then write a letter to an editor or a public servant. But the occasions when I think I can reach indirectly into the seats of power with a good idea and get a hearing are now rare. Now and then, however, e-mail brings me a query from someone who wants me to do just that; and sometimes I think perhaps my reply might help a little.

It's been a good life, and it still is.

Appendices

Appendix A

Institutional Evolution of a Democratic World (1947-2004)

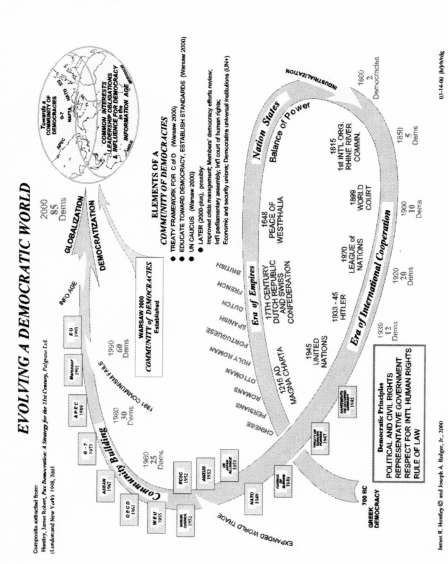

EVOLVING A DEMOCRATIC WORLD

Composite extracted from:

Huntley, James Robert, *Pax Democratica: A Strategy for the 21st Century*, Palgrave Ltd.
(London and New York) 1998, 2001

James R. Huntley © and Joseph A. Bulger, Jr., 2000

03-14-00 jb/rb/rdg

Notes to Chart: "Evolving a Democratic World"

1. *What is a democracy?* Definitions across the years have necessarily changed, and today, if strictly defined, a functioning democracy would securely establish political rights (alternating administrations, multiparty systems, periodic elections, universal suffrage, and so on); civil liberties (guarantees of significant personal and minority rights, such as freedom of speech, assembly, religion, education, etc.); and all this under an independent judiciary, i.e., the rule of law. Freedom House of New York, which for years tracked democratic progress, by individual countries and worldwide, ranks nations as "Free," "Partly Free," and "Not Free." (A 2000 FH report lists 85 "liberal democracies," representing 38 percent of the world's population.) Amnesty International, the Department of State, and others make independent assessments of human rights. Most tribal democracies, such as the early Swiss cantons and even Athens, lacked reliable civil rights—majority rule was close to absolute. In assuming there were *any* democracies before the 20th century, we also need to accept in the 19th century the lack of female suffrage almost everywhere, of black suffrage in the United States, etc. Standards for inclusion in a list of democracies should become higher as time goes on. The co-conveners of the Warsaw Conference in 2000 applied quite flexible criteria for those to be invited; the new "Community of Democracies" (see Appendix I) agreed on a declaration of democratic principles (to which members might later be held accountable). CCD's approximations in the accompanying chart of how many democracies existed at various dates in history represent only that—a general judgment for indicative purposes.

2. *What are international communities and intergovernmental organizations (IGOs)?* The first international institution with its own civil service was the Rhine River Commission (1815), followed by a number of special-purpose bodies promoting international cooperation, from unions for telegraphy and post to the League of Nations, the United Nations, and other bodies open to virtually all countries. In 1950, Robert Schuman and Jean Monnet proposed a new kind of international grouping, the *European Coal and Steel Community*, which was followed by other communities, now known collectively as the *European Union*. These and other institutions, Atlantic and European in scope, differ from classical IGOs in that they are composed only of democracies, and also involve a limited merging of powers so that qualified majorities can make some mutual decisions. In some cases (European Court of Human Rights in Strasbourg; European Community Court in Luxembourg), international community judiciaries make binding judgments on member-states or their nationals. *Communities are thus more than the sum of their individual national components.* This trend began only in the last half of the 20th century; it may be the wave of the future; it becomes possible when members share a high degree of common values (democracy, especially) and common interests, and recognize their mutuality. (For a detailed discussion of this development, see J. R. Huntley, Pax Democratica: A Strategy for the 21st Century [London and New Yoirk: Palgrave Ltd., 2001], especially Appendix B.)

INSTITUTION-BUILDING IN THE ATLANTIC / PACIFIC AREA

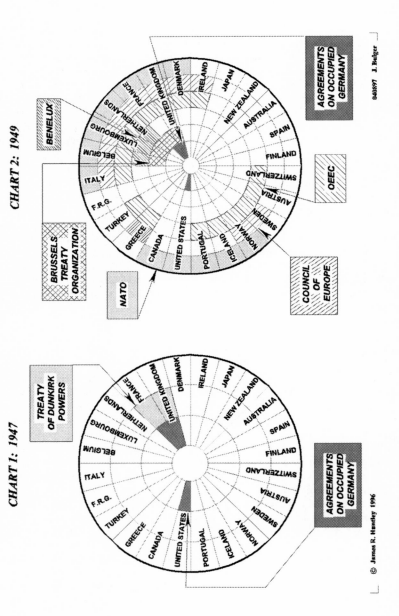

CHART 1: 1947

CHART 2: 1949

© James R. Huntley 1996

040897   J. Badger

INSTITUTION-BUILDING IN THE ATLANTIC / PACIFIC AREA

CHART 3: 1955

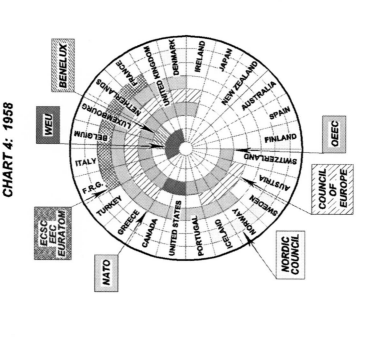

CHART 4: 1958

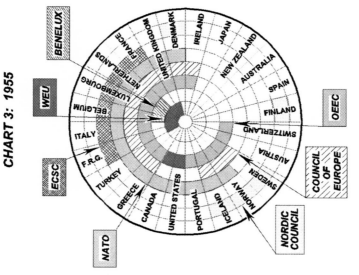

© James R. Huntley 1996

940897   J. Bulger

INSTITUTION-BUILDING IN THE ATLANTIC / PACIFIC AREA

CHART 6: 1975

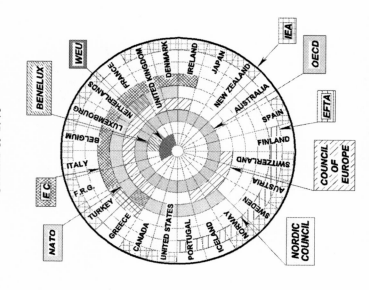

CHART 5: 1965

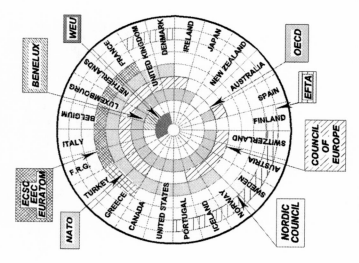

040897   J. Bulger

© James R. Huntley 1996

INSTITUTION-BUILDING IN THE ATLANTIC / PACIFIC AREA

CHART 7: 1984

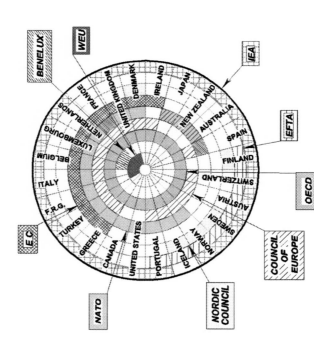

NOTE:
Japan, Australia, and New Zealand are
shown as informal associates of Western
security arrangements, based on ANZUS
and U.S. - Japan Mutual Security Treaty,
RIMPAC exercises, etc.

840897   J. Bulger

© James R. Huntley 1996

INSTITUTION BUILDING in the ATLANTIC / PACIFIC AREA

CHART 8: 1997

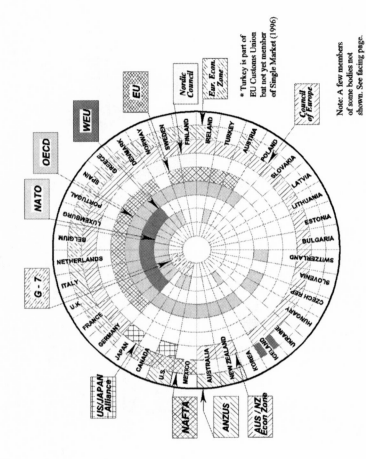

© James R. Huntley 1996

040997   J. Bulger

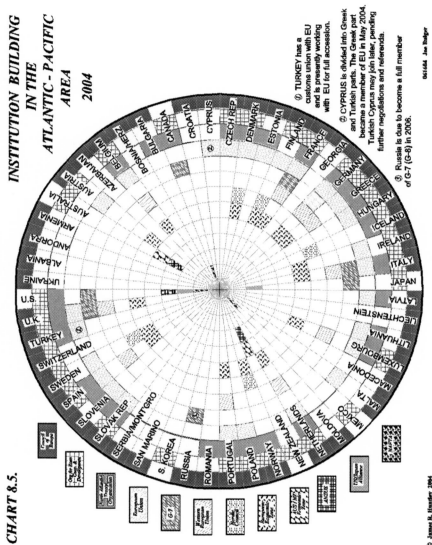

CHART 8.5.

INSTITUTION BUILDING IN THE ATLANTIC - PACIFIC AREA 2004

① TURKEY has a customs union with EU and is presently working with EU for full accession.

② CYPRUS is divided into Greek and Turkish parts. The Greek part became a member of EU in May 2004. Turkish Cyprus may join later, pending further negotiations and referenda.

③ Russia is due to become a full member of G-7 (G-8) in 2006.

© James R. Huntley 2004

Appendix B

Atlantic Congress: Declaration and Resolution on the Atlantic Institute (1959)

DECLARATION

prepared by the

CONGRESS DECLARATION COMMITTEE

under the chairmanship

of

Mr. Paul van Zeeland

and

Mr. Eric Johnston

I. PRINCIPLES

Six major principles have guided this Congress.

A.

1. The NATO military alliance has, in its first ten years, preserved the peace of Europe, although the threat of aggression is still present.

2. Great changes have taken place in this decade that make essential increased cooperation among Atlantic nations in all fields.

3. No military alliance can endure unless supported by close political and economic cooperation.

4. The time is ripe for these nations to build an Atlantic community with responsibilities extending to military, political, economic, social and scientific fields.

B.

5. The Atlantic nations are interdependent with other nations of the free world. All these nations want peace and the preservation of their own conception of life. All have a common interest in the development of economic activity and social improvement throughout the world; all people have a common stake and status in a free world.

6. The Atlantic community has a duty to help less developed countries to help themselves.

II. PROPOSALS

In order to apply these principles, the Congress has passed a number of important resolutions, attention being drawn particularly to the following:

A. *Political.*
1. That there should be increased consultation and cooperation among member states. Consultation should become a habit, not an occasional exercise.

2. That there should be broader and more frequent consultation among Parliamentarians of the Atlantic countries.

3. That the national governments should not take major decisions affecting NATO unity without previous consultation.

4. That the report of the "Three Wise Men" should be more fully implemented.

B. *Military.*
1. That the forces forming the European shield should be brought as soon as possible up to the minimum strength laid down in the agreed strategic concept of NATO.

2. That governments should give continual attention to improving the military structure of NATO, and in particular should foster increasing

interdependence throughout the military field.

C. *Economic*.
1. That governments should avoid restrictive economic measures, take all feasible actions to reduce tariff barriers and maintain monetary stability; and, in view of the services rendered by EEC and those one might expect from any other form of effective multilateral association, they should work especially for an increase of the benefits of closer economic integration.

2. That consideration be given to the possibility of transforming OEEC into an OAEC in which all Atlantic countries would hold full membership.

3. That the Atlantic countries should undertake policies which would encourage the expansion of economic activities and the raising of the standard of living in less developed areas.

D. *Cultural*.
1. That the most effective methods for countering ideological warfare should be further studied.

2. That a "Studies Centre for Atlantic Community" be set up, to serve as a clearing house and intellectual focus.

3. That there should be further integration of scientific research and in particular of pure research.

ATLANTIC INSTITUTE

A STUDIES CENTRE FOR THE ATLANTIC COMMUNITY

INTRODUCTION

The Atlantic Community: A Reality

The term "Atlantic Community" applies to a reality which has been the issue of a gradual historical development. Twenty centuries have extended the boundaries of the Mediterranean civilization of antique times, enriched it with much that is new, and finally given us our Western civilization, of which the fundamental principles have inspired our peoples and institutions on both sides of the Atlantic Ocean.

An historic reality may exist without the parties of which it is made up necessarily being aware of it. A threat from outside is the surest and (unhappily) the most frequent prod to awareness. The form which reaction then takes is commensurate with the form of the threat, and awareness is concentrated in that direction: in 1949, the North Atlantic Treaty Organization came into being.

A crystallization of this nature would however be very far from complete if it ended at this point. For a community of interests to become a force, its power of expression must extend into every field of which it is part and not merely the one imposed upon it by the urgency of a particularly visible danger. The geographical limits of the countries which make up the Atlantic Community are not the only frontiers of the Western civilization whose common values and the prolific diversity of which we have undertaken to defend and develop.

In such a spirit, the signatories to the North Atlantic Treaty of 1949 indicated the far wider concept in which they placed it when they referred in Article 2 to the need for a better understanding of the principles upon which the free institutions of the Community are founded.

Statement of Need

The achievements of Western civilization have come about through the effective utilization of a wealth of intellectual resources. An atmosphere of freedom has stimulated a process of growth and productive interchange in all fields of intellectual endeavour. Yet, today, when the nations of the West are confronted by a threat more serious than any danger in their past history, the diffuseness of Western thought has a paralyzing effect on policy and action. The Atlantic Community has not been able to articulate its views in such a way as to win support of many non-Western peoples of the Free World.

On both sides of the Atlantic, statesmen have forcefully affirmed the need for the West to stand united. NATO is a military response to the recognition of this need. But the efforts to bring about a closer community among thought leaders in the Atlantic world have been largely unrewarding. There is no rallying point, no common meeting ground, where leading minds in all fields of the arts and sciences can join together in seeking to resolve common problems.

While the cause of the West suffers from the inadequacy of the institutional framework for intellectual co-operation, there is a vast and confusing network of organizations in which governments and private groups on both sides of the Atlantic are associated. There is an urgent need to consolidate forces particularly among the many private groups working to promote closer Atlantic co-operation.

Strength may well be a product of the diversity of Western thought and expression. Certainly the Atlantic Community cannot embrace to any slightest degree the methods which have produced the monolith of Communist intellectual resources to bear on common problems. A wider area of freedom can be achieved only if the resources of scholarship are geared together with the talents of men of affairs in an effort to deal with questions of crucial import in the current world struggle.

Purpose

As a response to the needs outlined above, it is proposed to establish a Studies Centre for the Atlantic Community, which would encourage and support study by private individuals and organizations of those questions of politics, economics, and philosophy which the Centre judges to be of most vital interest to the nations of the Atlantic world. A constant guide in the determination of the program of the Centre activities would be the principle that unity is best achieved by working together to deal with common problems.

The functions of a Studies Centre for the Atlantic Community would be:

a. To stimulate study, either within the Centre framework or on the outside, of those subjects which it deems of greatest importance to the Atlantic Community.
b. To promote and support exchanges of persons among the Western nations as a means towards building closer understanding.
c. To provide facilities for bringing together not only academicians and so-called intellectuals but leaders from all fields and walks of life with a view towards evoking new insights into problems of common concern.
d. To serve as a clearinghouse and, upon request, as a co-coordinating agency for operations and projects related to its basic interest.
e. To promote and support educational activities designed to broaden the understanding and acceptance of the ideas of the Atlantic Community.

I. Role and Character of the Studies Centre for the Atlantic Community

To achieve the status of a community, the Atlantic alliance needs an intellectual rallying point for the constant and generating factors of this community, for promoting its awareness of the totalitarian menace, and for stressing its responsibility towards the uncommitted countries. In other words, it would be the purpose of the Studies Centre to explore joint attitudes and common tasks, and to undertake objectives, scientific and technical studies in the economic, fiscal, sociological, juristic and like professional fields of practical interest to the Atlantic community, and thus to harness the elements of both long- and short-term Atlantic policy.

So specific a programme can be carried to a successful conclusion neither by the national institutions at present in existence – however great their merit – nor by the universities, whose mission lies in an altogether different field.

This is why a recourse to other forms of organization and other methods of approach appear to be indispensable. These methods of work, far from excluding participation by qualified scholars (French text "savant") in universities and other appropriate institutions, do on the contrary involve sustained and extensive recourse to their experience and devotion.

Indeed, this Studies Centre would in principle operate first and foremost in the form of a scientific and administrative secretariat specially equipped to promote the study of problems that claim the attention of the Atlantic Community.

It would draw up and publish reports, conclusions and results of its work for the attention of the Atlantic Community leaders, of representatives of public opinion, and of the institutions and organizations concerned.

Only through intellectual independence – which is not only an integral part of the Western heritage, but is also one of the indispensable conditions for its success – can such a centre acquire and preserve the full authority it requires.

However necessary this authority may be, the Centre would always operate in close contact with both national and international authorities, and with any private organization working – in one form or another – for Atlantic co-operation.

(i) *The work of the Studies Centre*

There is no need to enumerate all the various activities to be undertaken by the Studies Centre. These are decisions which rest, of course,
with its directors, who in making these decisions will take into account requests both by governments of the Atlantic Community that
this or that specific problem should be more especially studied and by
the nongovernmental organizations that a more extensive and thorough knowledge should be gained of such nongovernmental factors
as would contribute to the strengthening and coherence of the Atlantic
Community. Further, there is a range of problems of vital practical importance for the Atlantic Community of an economic, fiscal, or migra-
tional character, etc, as well as problems connected with nationalism
in both the Atlantic and non-Atlantic world. These are issues, some of
them of a short range and technical character, on which economic and
other experts are capable of doing work, not yet undertaken, which
can result in unbiased, objective and scientific reports useful in the
shaping of policy and opinion. The Centre should also undertake the
preparation of a complete inventory of the resources of the Atlantic
countries, a study asked for by the Conference of NATO Parliamentarians.

Let us briefly quote, as examples, certain questions which have in the
past – or do at present – form the subject of the kind of work the Studies Centre would be called upon to undertake: studies of the ways in
which the Atlantic Community can help to solve problems concerning underdeveloped regions; studies of the elements in our traditional
values that unite us and the differences that may contribute to our
strength through a harmonious diversity of ways of life; an anthology
of major writings in the field of philosophy, politics, law, religion, history, and morals, such as have marked the progress of our civilization
through twenty-five centuries.

(ii) *Organisation of the tasks*

The Studies Centre leaders will draw on all those they consider possessed of outstanding knowledge or experience and who are outstanding in their various fields.

The Secretariat would therefore be called upon to secure the assistance
of authorities on each problem under study, to initiate brief exchanges
of view among experts on immediate problems of capital importance

for the future of the Community; to consider questions by governmental and nongovernmental organizations, etc.

By its flexibility, the quality and expeditiousness of its research, the extent of its contacts in the various quarters of the Atlantic world in the widest meaning of the term, by the scientific authority which it should lend to published works, the Secretariat would become the focal point for initiating, co-coordinating, and organizing the studies destined to foster a greater appreciation of the nature of the Atlantic community and of the amplitude of the struggle it is waging.

II. Organization

The Studies Centre for the Atlantic Community would be registered as a private non-profit corporation. Its Board of Governors would be composed of eminent men and women from Atlantic Community countries. An Executive Committee would supervise the affairs of the Centre and appoint an Executive Director to carry out the policies of the Board of Governors.

The headquarters of the Centre should be located in a NATO country. At the headquarters, comprising offices and conference rooms, a small staff would conduct the daily business of the Centre. Special branches would deal with research studies, education, international conferences, and organizational liaison. A joint program of work would be agreed on each year and approved by the Board of Governors of the Centre.

At the inception of its activities, the Centre would employ a small staff.

The work of the Centre would be organized flexibly. It could choose, in each instance, any of the following ways to carry out a given project:

a. The Centre could carry out these projects by itself;
b. It could initiate these projects and carry them out in co-operation with the appropriate international or professional organization; or
c. It could simply put forward an idea to be carried out by the appropriate existing organization.

The Institute would *not* engage in any of the following activities:

The organizing of propaganda or massive informational campaigns designed to promote any partisan view concerning Atlantic Community or co-operation.

The duplication of any program already being carried out by existing agencies, private or governmental.

The conduct of studies concerned with policy questions of such short range nature that they can be dealt with only by governmental agencies.

Therefore, a close liaison is necessary between the Studies Centre for the Atlantic Community and the existing national and international organizations concerned with the dissemination of information on the Atlantic Community. Close relations should also exist with other research centres and academic institutions concerned with international relations.

III. Finance

Because of the nature and scope of its activities, the Studies Centre for the Atlantic Community would require substantial funds. Preliminary studies suggest an average annual budget of at least $300,000 for the first five years. It must be emphasized that a mechanism capable of dealing with the broad tasks envisaged must dispose of resources commensurate with those tasks.

The Centre should be financed primarily by contributions or endowment from private sources. It could receive public funds as well. The form of such aid would vary according to national practices, but in all cases it must be "without strings."

It is anticipated that some of the activities of the Institute would be self-supporting.

IV. History

The formation of an Atlantic Institute or Studies Centre has been proposed by numerous international private groups and conferences on the Atlantic Community. All three international nongovernmental organizations testifying before the Committee of Three NATO Foreign Ministers in 1956 advocated this idea. A Conference on the Atlantic Community held in Bruges in September 1957 elaborated the idea still further. Subsequently, two annual meetings of the NATO Parliamentarians' Conference endorsed the idea of an Atlantic Institute.

V. The Atlantic Congress and the Studies Centre for the Atlantic Community

While some of the recommendations of the Atlantic Congress will go directly to governments, NATO, and to the NATO Parliamentarians' Conference, many of them will probably require additional study and follow-up. This work could be done by the Centre.

Appendix C

A Draft Declaration on Modern Philanthropy (1972)

Draft
June 1972

A DRAFT DECLARATION ON

MODERN PHILANTHROPY

Prepared by James R. Huntley

for INTERPHIL

Philanthropy and Human Behavior

1. The philanthropic impulse is rooted in the fundamental interdependence of all living creatures. The biological necessity for mutual aid is the creator and conditioner of all social institutions.

2. The alternative to living in isolation from one's fellow human beings is to communicate. And communication is more than simply talking—it consists of responses, both incoming and outgoing. The act of giving is one of the most satisfying forms of communication.

3. To give freely, spontaneously, and without calculation of cost or gain to the giver or merit on the part of the receiver is the highest form of giving. It lies at the heart of philanthropy.

4. Philanthropy is love for mankind. It is acceptance of responsibility for the condition of one's fellow men. It cannot be practiced without making choices. It is a fundamental human right, because it helps to assure to each

individual his liberty of action and his place in society. Philanthropy is a critically important human value; its practice builds the capillary system of a healthy community.

5. Philanthropy is an acquired habit. The development of one's philanthropic powers, offering opportunities for creativity, spontaneity, personal commitment, and human contact, fills spiritual gaps which are especially acute in a time of unsettling social change. To practice philanthropy is an essential part of a full life, and a sign of personal maturity.

6. A philanthropic act is most satisfying, to giver or receiver, when part of a chain of reciprocity. Philanthropy — in which receiving should be no less valued or important than giving — expresses fraternity, mutual aid, and human solidarity. A true gift is freely given, without thought of repayment; but the recipient acquires a moral obligation nonetheless: "to go forth and do likewise."

Society and Philanthropic Institutions

7. Philanthropic institutions are the instruments which men fashion voluntarily to give their time, talent, wealth, and concern collectively for the good of the community. They make possible those philanthropic acts which an individual alone cannot accomplish. They can set examples. They are especially valuable if they educate people to see philanthropy in themselves and to learn how to practice it. As expressions of human solidarity, philanthropic institutions can also help to counteract the stresses and strains of modern society and to dispel loneliness.

8. Philanthropic institutions have a duty to their supporters and to the community at large to be tough-minded and efficient in the management of their affairs.

9. In its essence, philanthropy can be practiced anywhere. An active love for mankind need not rely on any special political system for opportunity to express itself. But it is easier for such institutions to flourish under political systems which permit some creation of private wealth and which do not assume for the State an encompassing responsibility for all forms of human activity.

Three Pillars of Society: the State, Business, and Philanthropy

10. In countries which preserve an essentially free enterprise or mixed economy, the State, Business, and Philanthropy are distinct, separate social forces, which nevertheless complement and depend on one another. The State's concerns are wholly public; Philanthropy's concerns are public but its means are private; the concerns of Business are essentially private. Philanthropic institutions do not earn profits, but this is the principal aim of a business. Philanthropy deploys private wealth and services for public tasks which the State cannot or will not undertake, or which the State cannot do as well.

11. To ignore the presence of, or the opportunities for, philanthropy is to limit choice—to either laissez faire or an all-powerful State.

The State and Philanthropy

12. Everywhere, the State has far greater financial powers than Philanthropy, and it has a monopoly of legal power. In modern societies, it bears the chief responsibility for human security and welfare. But Philanthropy embodies forces of which the State, by its very nature, can never dispose. Philanthropy can neither be commanded nor legislated; it is always a product of individual volition. The State's reciprocal relationships with its citizens are legally binding; Philanthropy's practitioners are bound only by their own consciences. The State may express the moral obligations of a community, but it does so in legal form; its product is Justice. Philanthropy, in the form of voluntary action, expresses the moral obligations of individuals as each one sees them; its product is Love.

13. As charity alone can no longer discharge the social obligations which modern civilization has created, neither can the State do so single-handedly. Philanthropy provides a multiplicity of channels through which the conscience and goodwill of the community serve human needs which have not been recognized as the responsibility of every taxpayer. The State works from above; Philanthropy strengthens society at its base, from below.

14. The more complex society becomes, the more essential will it be to nourish pluralism and a de-concentration of social effort. Increasingly, the humane society will rely on a widespread and balanced interlocking of personal commitments, voluntary action, and judicious State support to accomplish its complex social tasks.

15. Philanthropy can act as a pilot for the State, identifying a human need and organizing voluntary action to fill it until a program has become a function of government. But in its essence, voluntary activity is not subordinate to what the State does. Although sometimes it can provide a stop-gap until the State steps in, that is not its basic significance.

16. Because the State represents all of society, and because voluntary bodies perform public functions, the State has both a right and a duty to establish rules for the practice of philanthropy.

17. Because philanthropy performs functions which benefit society, and which often relieve the burden on the State's finances, it is in the interest of the State to give philanthropy every reasonable incentive to flourish. The State should protect the intent of the donors of private funds set aside properly for public purposes. Philanthropic organizations should be exempt from most forms of taxation. The State is also justified in according preferential tax treatment in respect of philanthropic donations.

18. The State may also encourage philanthropic bodies by subsidizing their work. In such cases, the State must reserve the right to see that its money has been spent as agreed. But when the State's contributions become decisive in the life of the organization, and its control becomes substantial, then the work ceases to be voluntary.

Foundations and Philanthropy

19. A foundation is a special philanthropic instrument which transforms public wealth into an independent endowment to be used for public, non-profit purposes, and which is managed by its own trustees or board of directors. The source of a foundation's wealth might also be the State, but in this case it is not a true foundation unless its full independence of action is assured from the start.

20. Perhaps the most important function of foundations, given their independence, flexibility, and freedom of action, is to provide the venture capital for philanthropic action. But foundations have an equal responsibility to help established voluntary organizations find ways and means of financing their on-going costs.

Business and Philanthropy

a supplies

21. A firm's first duty is to its stockholders, its employees, and its clientele, but it also has a responsibility to the community over and above the goods or services it may provide. It may help the community, for example, by waiving economic considerations in part to hire and train the hard-core unemployed. It may also help the community by contributing to a wide variety of philanthropic enterprises. In so doing, it can provide examples for others, it can enhance its public reputation for far-sightedness, and it can do its part to enable independent institutions to survive and prosper. Business can also enhance the practice of philanthropy by lending its special talents to the improvement of management in voluntary organizations. *(ADM, THEORY)*

International Philanthropy

22. Philanthropy can and should make a major contribution to the process of social and economic development worldwide. For this reason, and because philanthropic action also increases general knowledge and goodwill among men, international organizations should encourage voluntary action which flows across national borders and individual states should grant to foreign and international philanthropies operating within their borders the same rights as they accord to their own, on condition of reciprocity.

Appendix D

Mid-Atlantic Clubs: What Are They? (1974)

March 1974
MID-ATLANTIC CLUBS:
WHAT ARE THEY?

The first Mid-Atlantic Club – a study group on transatlantic relations – started in London in 1970. There are now such Clubs in Washington, Paris, Brussels, New York, and San Francisco as well.

The rationale is this: Relations between the two sides of the Atlantic are probably in a more serious state than they have been for a generation. Responsible Europeans and Americans have a lot to talk about these days. Yet available channels of communication – especially for quiet, purposeful private dialogue – can hardly be regarded as sufficient. To remain vital, the transatlantic connection needs constant examination and attention by substantial numbers of concerned citizens. Those who started the prototype London Mid-Atlantic Club reasoned that if one were to bring together regularly, for systematic discussions on transatlantic affairs, citizens of countries from the North Atlantic basin who were resident in or near London, a modest contribution might be made indirectly to improved communication and consensus among the Atlantic partners.

There are now 80 Members in the London Club, a few more in New York and Washington, for example. Roughly half the membership of an M.A.C. is made up of local nationals, the remainder of foreign residents. There are younger as well as older people. There are lawyers, industrialists, politicians, diplomats, civil servants, journalists, bankers, and educators. The membership is thus multinational, multi-professional, and multi-generational.

An M.A.C. meets about once a month for a simple meal. After the meal, the Chairman introduces a "Discussion-Opener" – an expert with special knowledge of some "Atlantic" issue. He may or may not be a local Club Member; Mitchell Sharp, Robert Schaetzel, François Duchêne, Lord Shawcross, Kenneth Rush, Ralf Dahrendorf, Altiero Spinelli, and Pierre Uri are among those who have presented topics in the past. The "Opener" talks for twenty minutes (only), then an off-the-record discussion ensures. A written summary is later circulated to Members.

M.A.C. Members have found the exposure to different points of view stimulating, the opportunity to get to know others with a similar concern for the transatlantic tie useful. Mid-Atlantic Clubs are places to "float" ideas privately, to identify differences of view, and to search for common ground. The more such Clubs there are, in important cities around the Atlantic rim, the stronger will be our "citizen channels" of communication.

Mid-Atlantic Clubs have no preconceived ideological focus, but are devoted simply to a free exchange of serious points of view about the transatlantic connection. The adjective "Mid-Atlantic" refers to some mythical spot in the center of the Atlantic Ocean where certain vital interests of Europeans and North Americans may be presumed to meet and merge.

Appendix E

The Challenge of Building an International Community (1980)

August 1980

THE CHALLENGE OF BUILDING AN INTERNATIONAL
COMMUNITY

Introduction

This brief paper summarizes a unique approach to international community building developed by James R. Huntley over a period of three decades. The ideas set forth are based on his own research (under the aegis, at various times, of the Battelle Memorial Institute, the Foreign Policy Research Institute at the University of Pennsylvania, the Atlantic Institute for International Affairs [Paris], and Harvard University); on methods developed by the U.S. government and the Ford Foundation through funding nongovernmental activities in Europe; and on Mr. Huntley's own experience and insights.

The Case for Urgently Building an Atlantic-Pacific Community

This has been made by many distinguished individuals, over a period of many decades. Former ambassador and under-secretary of State Kenneth Rush recently stated: "The burning international issue of our times: How can the community of developed democracies streamline and modernize itself to face the still greater challenges of the near future and the long term?" In February 1917 Walter Lippmann wrote:

The safety of the Atlantic highway is something for which America should fight. Why? Because on the two shores of the Atlantic Ocean there has grown up a profound web of interest which joins together the Western world . . . if that community were destroyed we should then know what we had lost.

In the midst of the Second World War, Lippmann completed his formulation:

The Atlantic Ocean is not the frontier between Europe and the Americas. It is the inland sea of a community of nations allied with one another by geography, history, and vital necessity.

In 1980 it seems more evident than ever that the United States cannot face the perils of our times, world-encompassing as they now are, without trusted allies and partners, including Japan, Australia, and New Zealand in the Pacific. The energy crisis, the continuing conflict with the USSR, the problems of living harmoniously and constructively with a congeries of highly-diversified and generally conflict-ridden developing countries, and the successful management of a complex world economy all demand an irreducible minimum of joint decision-making and common action by the principal industrial democracies. The core of this group is the United States, the UK, France, Germany, and Japan. The next tier of vital states includes Italy, Canada, Australia, and the Benelux countries. Another group of the smaller but highly developed and strategic group of democracies brings the critical mass to about 24—the members of OECD (Organization for Economic Cooperation and Development), 15 of which are also in NATO, and three others of which have separate defense ties with the U.S.

The ties of community have begun to form among these countries over the past few decades; the record of success is impressive: World War III and another Great Depression have been avoided, and many other lesser but important world tasks accomplished. But the future nevertheless seems fraught with peril because the challenges are new and the stakes even greater. The only answer is for this community of nations to draw together even more closely. Alone, the United States cannot accept or discharge responsibility for world security and prosperity. A working community of the democratic nations, with borders and authority fairly shared, is therefore essential to the survival of the West and of the United States, at any rate in a form which we of today would recognize.

(The case for an "Atlantic-Pacific community" and the record of its accomplishments are set forth in detail in Mr. Huntley's recent book, *Uniting the Democracies: Institutions of the Emerging Atlantic-Pacific Community*, NYU Press, 1980.)

The Problem of Achieving an Effective Working Community

Why have the allied countries not recently moved faster to close ranks in the face of obvious danger? One reason is that the situation is new. Another is that all fear that in a "crunch" they will not be able to trust their allies, that "the Others" will in crisis each shift for itself. Within a federation such as the United States or Germany, it is inconceivable that Oregon or Virginia or New York would go its own way in a crisis, or that Bavaria could disassociate itself from the Federal Republic. The common political framework exists, the ideal of "America" or "Germany" is a reality in the minds and hearts of virtually all citizens. The nation is the last ditch hope.

But it is obvious in today's world that mutual trust and dependability of an irreducible number of allies it at least as important to the individual citizen's peace, security, and prosperity as is the safety and health of his own country. The two things are inextricably bound together. NATO is a prime symbol of this interdependence, an indispensable instrument for the protection of all its members. The guarantees of a treaty such as NATO's are crucially important; it has remained, to a great extent, a credible means of joint defense, a last line of security for Europe. But the NATO links will not be strong enough for tomorrow's worldwide challenges; more is now needed. To move beyond such historically valuable but increasingly obsolescent realities as NATO, three things are needed:

1. A *concept* of interdependence and community which is adequate to the common tasks of the members of the community, and also generally acceptable to them in both intellectual and emotional terms. The working out of the concept and the public acceptance of the concept are intertwined processes.
2. Better *institutions*, which provide for decisions in common and for joint action on an irreducible minimum number of common problems. One example: on the Soviet invasion of Afghanistan — there is not an agreed assessment of the nature of the problem, nor an agreed appraisal of the degree of danger, nor an agreed set of common measures to deal with the threat. Yet if this uncertainty and irresolution continue, and especially if the *next* major Soviet challenge to vital Western interests goes unmet, the West could indeed be on the slippery slope. In such a situation new and improved institutions can make a difference — e.g., new alliances with commitments similar to NATO's in the Indian and Pacific Ocean areas (or an enlargement of NATO's scope); a streamlined

"crisis cabinet" akin to the Churchill-Roosevelt arrangements and Combined Chiefs of Staff in World War II; a strong joint mechanism for dealing directly with OPEC in the purchase of oil, on behalf of all the industrial democracies. These are but examples, each not necessarily workable or desirable in itself, but each illustrating how one might take a step forward in the direction of pooling powers to meet urgent and vital common challenges related directly to Western survival. Institutions alone, of course, can be hollow shells; but, on the other hand, goodwill and purpose *without* institutions to give them effect are similarly of little use. There must be a commonly held concept of "togetherness," *plus* institutions which make common action possible and which, over time, mold the men who work them. This brings us to a third important element: the human factor.

3.   In order for concepts to be understood and made operative, and for institutions to emerge and work as they should, one must have *educated and committed manpower* in the right places. The people who operate the institutions, the leaders who make and implement the decisions, large and small, of an international community, must embrace the community idea, must possess a certain degree of empathy with their co-workers from other countries, must understand and accept the objective factors which make interdependence ineluctable. There must be a spirit which Ben Franklin called forth as the Continental Congress faced its problems: "We must all hang together—or assuredly we shall all hang separately." The *sine qua non* of such a community spirit is a feeling of common loyalty to still another level of polity, incorporating one's own nation, but—above and beyond it—in the case at hand, to a community of the developed democracies.

••••••

The foregoing analysis of the problem of international community-building embraces the key elements of Mr. Huntley's work over three decades. To summarize, he believes that an effective, working international community cannot be achieved unless:

1.   The *concepts* are sound;
2.   There are *institutions* to give practical effect to concepts;
3.   There are *leaders*, at all levels and in key places, who understand and embrace the concepts, who are committed to the institutions, and who have mutual trust in one another—i.e., an irreducible

set of common values which underlie the execution of the tasks at hand.

Now follows a brief discussion of each of these elements, concepts, institutions, and leadership, and how they can be created and strengthened.

Concepts

Much of the work of developing adequate concepts for the Atlantic Community, the ancillary European Community, and the more recent, larger community, which Mr. Huntley calls the "Atlantic-Pacific" system or community, has been done by diplomats, civil servants, and political leaders in times of crisis. They have been aided and abetted—sometimes pushed and inspired—by citizens outside government who understood the nature of the international situation better than they did, or who had extraordinary insight into the relevant lessons of history, or who were free to speak their minds.

One example of symbiosis between public and private men is Jean Monnet's work. He developed a concept of international community as a civil servant in World Wars I and II, then convinced American and European leaders that his principles should undergird a postwar "European Community." He served as head of the Coal and Steel Community which he invented, but retired to mobilize political, intellectual, and business forces on a private basis to press the governments to go even further and faster.

Others had come to somewhat the same conclusions as Monnet between the two World Wars and after; some were in, some outside, of government. A large number of these leaders of thought and action worked together, educating public opinion and elites, and fashioning together the concepts of how a European Community could and would work. Countless meetings, discussions, conferences, books, articles, pamphlets, and other forms of dialogue and intellectual intercourse—and argument—were necessary to get the concepts straight. Even today, the European part of the job remains unfinished, but the progress has been remarkable nevertheless, and without guiding concepts, would have been impossible. Monnet and others had ideas which were relatively simple to grasp, if often elaborate in their details. These ideas were refined and put forward forcefully to those who would have to make great decisions.

With respect to the broader Atlantic community, a case can be made that Clarence Streit's famous book, *Union Now*, first published in 1939, provided much of the intellectual underpinning and the forward thrust for NATO and other historic achievements in European-American cooperation during and immediately after World War II. Streit went further than others, calling for a "federation of the free." But his bold concept was at least a point of reference for those who said, "We can't go that far yet, but here are concepts which accomplish the most urgent of the tasks which his plan deems essential."

Concepts such as these are never the work of one person, although a single individual can have important insights and make powerful formulations that excite others. But essentially, concepts arise out of the symbiosis of great events and crises with extraordinary individuals and receptive elites. Scholars, practitioners of diplomacy and politics, international business leaders who have dealt with big problems of organization, publicists and journalists whose exposure to momentous events give them insight — these and others play roles at critical times in developing essential concepts for man's forward political movement.

The times and the necessary individuals do not necessarily always coincide. The situation after World War I cried out for a different set of international guiding principles and concepts, yet they were not there , or in any event, went unrecognized. After World War II, an extraordinary effort to *nurture and develop international concepts* was made, inspired by small groups of leading people outside government, and made usable and practical by small groups within government. A crucial role in the development of concepts was played by foundations and nongovernmental, non-profit organizations. The history of the Atlantic and European movements, post-1945, is to an important extent also the history of intellectual effort and consensus-building meetings of many kinds, which were sponsored under private auspices. Affairs such as the survival of the West are today too important to be left to the normal interplay of harassed politicians, government servants, military leaders, and others who must make day to day decisions and deal with immediate problems. Nor can they be left to the interplay of the largely irresponsible media and public opinion. If there is to be forward movement, ways and means must be found to get people with ideas, with commitment to international community, and with an understanding of the situation and the challenge working together to develop concepts that are adequate. A catalytic agent is absolutely indispensable in such efforts; small private organizations and unusual individuals can often play that role.

Institutions

Institutions must grow from the concepts, must be designed and fashioned by the people who appreciate and support the concepts and who are adept at giving "hands and feet to ideas." Institutions give continuity and body to the execution of international tasks.

Mr. Huntley thinks of two kinds of institutions in shaping international community:

1. major intergovernmental or supranational institutions (such as NATO or the European Economic Community), which make it possible to carry out essential international tasks and which in turn mold the actions and the attitudes of the people who operate them (learning through doing).
2. specialized nongovernmental institutions which can undertake such tasks as developing the concepts, designing new intergovernmental institutions, educating general publics as to the situation and the necessary steps, encouraging research on long-term problems, nurturing consensus among leaders and future leaders of the respective societies which make up the community.

Not all the tasks assigned above to nongovernmental bodies can be done by them alone; governments have in the past given important support for this kind of work and some of it they have done themselves. But in Western-type liberal democracies, it is evident that governments are not capable of leading in many of these matters, nor should they be allowed to do so in others. For example, the job of public education with respect to international community may well be left largely undone, if one expects governments to do it. Or the governments may do it, but do it wrongly — make the wrong case, urge the wrong steps, even misrepresent situations. Governments must have the capability of doing all these things, but it seems absolutely essential that the citizenry also analyze the problems, make the case, and work out the broad lines of solutions on its own — as the result of many independent and private initiatives.

Similarly, the job of conceiving, developing, and promoting new international institutions, while very much the proper province of governments, should not be left to them alone. Once more, governments can get it wrong. In democracies, it is not just safer, but it is *vital*, that private citizens and private groups also sift the issues, develop and refine concepts, and mobilize to affect the political process from outside.

One might argue that the traditional institutions of society which normally deal with such matters—the schools, the universities, the research institutes, the press and TV, the political parties—should be sufficient to get these jobs of public mobilization and public education done. But experience suggests that new and special nongovernmental mechanisms will always be important—even essential—to the task of international community building. The work of one lone Englishman, John Sewell of Devonshire, demonstrates this.

Assisted by a handful of volunteers, mostly retirees, Sewell for thirty years has prodded and pushed British education authorities to accept and teach the concepts of European and Atlantic community; he has organized almost single-handedly study tours for British teachers to see European and Atlantic institutions actually at work in Brussels, Paris, Luxembourg, and Strasbourg; he has gotten experts to meet with concerned laymen from virtually all parts of society, to discuss current international issues and the problems of community-building. He has had pittances of support, but with no strings, from his own government, from local education authorities, and occasionally from international institutions such as NATO and the European Communities. His work is literally a monument to what one man can do. Without his efforts, it is very likely that the support of the British public over the years for international community with its allies and partners would have been much less. Sewell, now 85, has been truly a "Johnny Appleseed" of ideas in our time.

John Sewell is only one of three- or four-score gifted individuals, Europeans, Americans, more recently Japanese, who have exercised this personal, private kind of leadership in the community-building process. Individuals and relatively modest organizations, in most cases, have been responsible for NGO institutional work and for its success.

Leadership and Manpower

People such as Sewell have worked on conceptual problems, have organized modest organizations of their own, and have on occasion promoted the development of large, intergovernmental institutions. But perhaps the most important work of NGOs has been education and development of leaders who in turn, in one way or another, will do the work of the emerging community, or—as multipliers—explain and interpret it to others.

In this connection, James Huntley has researched the operation of international institutions (such as General Eisenhower's SHAEF command in

World War II) in the past to try to draw lessons for the future. With the
assistance and advice of Professor Crane Brinton, of the history department at Harvard, Mr. Huntley went back to the role of elites in the Roman
"multinational state," as well as to more recent historical cases. He drew
in particular on the work of Professor Gaetano Mosca (*The Ruling Class*),
around the turn of this century, and to others who have studied the nature
and role of elites in society. Mr. Huntley has written at length on this subject. The essence of Mr. Huntley's "leadership" theory is:

That any human society which is coherent and organized depends on
leadership to set the tone of society, to propose and propound the society's
goals, to persuade and influence its citizenry. Elites evolve or are chosen in
many different ways; in modern democracies, leaders are not often thrust
into positions as the result of family or class associations, and if they are,
they rarely last unless they have leadership qualities. Modern leadership
in most of the West consists largely of people who rise through merit, determination, and other personal qualities. As it is these people, in a wide
variety of fields and occupations, who generally set society's goals and
tone, and to whom electorates usually listen, so any new kind of social
movement or institution must depend on a "critical mass" of leaders, in
order to take firm root.

With respect to the manning of the institutions of international community, and with respect to public support for alliances and the like, the role
of leaders of thought, opinion, and action is decisive. Thus, in international community building, one must seek first to identify leaders in fields
such as business, government, politics, religion, education, labor, law, and
the military; one must then try to reach and discuss with such leaders
the problems, needs, and concepts surrounding community building. Not
only must they recognize that there are important, urgent problems. But
there must eventually be a working consensus among a certain minimum
number of such persons—whatever number is required to move their
particular societies and, eventually, their governments. Thus *developing
consensus among leaders* is an indispensable part of the task of fashioning
international community.

The "Atlantic-Pacific Movement"

A methodology of international community building appears not to have
been articulated before. Many individuals with drive and conviction have
acted (usually instinctively) on various of these principles, to be sure.

There exists a fairly broad range of leading people and organizations, in the chief European countries, North America, Japan, and Australia, who in various ways are attempting to develop concepts, to build and promote institutions, and to educate both leaders and the general publics. Their efforts overall, however, and except in two or three very particular cases, are today badly underfunded, undermanned, and necessarily limited in scope and objectives. Mr. Huntley has several times in the past made analyses of these groups, individually and as a collectivity. He believes that their resources are currently grossly inadequate by comparison with the demands of community-building in the next decade or so; that a few organizations are not worth much and probably are not worth saving; that others could be reformed and re-funded and do a great deal; that probably some new mechanisms should be created; and that the overall effort needs a general, across-the-board expansion. Their contribution in the years ahead is potentially an indispensable one.

Why has this come to pass? One reason is that governments have not continued to assist private bodies to the extent they once did, if at all. Another is that the Ford Foundation, for several years by far the largest contributor to European and Atlantic NGOs, rather precipitately got out of the field around 1967. The international philanthropy of other foundations and of corporations, meanwhile, has also atrophied. Finally, as not enough attention was given, early on, to "bringing along" the newer generations, the field now has ageing leadership.

Appendix F

Excerpts from an Address to the British Parliament by President Ronald Reagan (1982)

Excerpts from an

ADDRESS TO MEMBERS OF THE BRITISH PARLIAMENT

President Ronald Reagan
June 8, 1982

My Lord Chancellor, Mr. Speaker:

The journey of which this visit forms a part is a long one. Already it has taken me to two great cities of the West, Rome and Paris, and to the economic summit at Versailles. And there, once again, our sister democracies have proved that even in a time of severe economic strain, free peoples can work together freely and voluntarily to address problems as serious as inflation, unemployment, trade, and economic development in a spirit of cooperation and solidarity . . .

If history teaches anything, it teaches self-delusion in the face of unpleasant facts is folly. We see around us today the marks of our terrible dilemma—predictions of doomsday, antinuclear demonstrations, an arms race in which the West must, for its own protection, be an unwilling participant. At the same time we see totalitarian forces in the world who seek subversion and conflict around the globe to further their barbarous assault on the human spirit. What, then, is our course? Must civilization perish in a hail of fiery atoms? Must freedom wither in a quiet, deadening accommodation with totalitarian evil? . . .

Around the world today, the democratic revolution is gathering new strength. In India a critical test has been passed with the peaceful change of governing political parties. In Africa, Nigeria is moving into remarkable and unmistakable ways to build and strengthen its democratic institutions. In the Caribbean and Central America, 16 of 24 countries have freely elected governments. And in the United Nations, eight of the 10 developing nations which have joined that body in the past five years are democracies.

In the Communist world as well, man's instinctive desire for freedom and self-determination surfaces again and again. To be sure, there are grim reminders of how brutally the police state attempts to snuff out this quest for self-rule—1953 in East Germany, 1956 in Hungary, 1968 in Czechoslovakia, 1981 in Poland. But the struggle continues in Poland. And we know that there are even those who strive and suffer for freedom within the confines of the Soviet Union itself. How we conduct ourselves here in the Western democracies will determine whether this trend continues.

No, democracy is not a fragile flower. Still it needs cultivating. If the rest of this century is to witness the gradual growth of freedom and democratic ideals, we must take actions to assist the campaign for democracy . . .

While we must be cautious about forcing the pace of change, we must not hesitate to declare our ultimate objectives and to take concrete actions to move toward them. We must be staunch in our conviction that freedom is not the sole prerogative of a lucky few, but the inalienable and universal right of all human beings. So states the United Nations Universal Declaration of Human Rights, which, among other things, guarantees free elections.

The objective I propose is quite simple to state: to foster the infrastructure of democracy, the system of a free press, unions, political parties, universities, which allows a people to choose their own way to develop their own culture, to reconcile their own differences through peaceful means.

This is not cultural imperialism, it is providing the means for genuine self-determination and protection for diversity. Democracy already flourishes in countries with very different cultures and historical experiences. It would be cultural condescension, or worse, to say that any people prefer dictatorship to democracy. Who would voluntarily choose not to have the right to vote, decide to purchase government propaganda handouts instead of independent newspapers, prefer government to worker-controlled unions, opt for land to be owned by the state instead of those who till it, want government repression of religious liberty, a single political party instead of a free choice, a rigid cultural orthodoxy instead of democratic tolerance and diversity?

Since 1917 the Soviet Union has given covert political training and assistance to Marxist-Leninists in many countries. Of course, it also has promoted the use of violence and subversion by these same forces. Over the past several decades, West European and other Social Democrats, Christian Democrats, and leaders have offered open assistance to fraternal, political, and social institutions to bring about peaceful and democratic progress. Appropriately, for a vigorous new democracy, the Federal Republic of Germany's political foundations have become a major force in this effort.

We in America now intend to take additional steps, as many of our allies have already done, toward realizing this same goal. The chairmen and other leaders of the national Republican and Democratic Party organizations are initiating a study with the bipartisan American political foundation to determine how the United States can best contribute as a nation to the global campaign for democracy now gathering force. They will have the cooperation of congressional leaders of both parties, along with representatives of business, labor, and other major institutions in our society. I look forward to receiving their recommendations and to working with these institutions and the Congress in the common task of strengthening democracy throughout the world.

It is time that we committed ourselves as a nation—in both the public and private sectors—to assisting democratic development.

Now, I don't wish to sound overly optimistic, yet the Soviet Union is not immune from the reality of what is going on in the world. It has happened in the past—a small ruling elite either mistakenly attempts to ease domestic unrest through greater repression and foreign adventure, or it chooses a wiser course. It begins to allow its people a voice in their own destiny. Even if this latter process is not realized soon, I believe the renewed strength of the democratic movement, complemented by a global campaign for freedom, will strengthen the prospects for arms control and a world at peace.

I have discussed on other occasions, including my address on May 9, the elements of Western policies toward the Soviet Union to safeguard our interests and protect the peace. What I am describing now is a plan and a hope for the long term—the march of freedom and democracy which will leave Marxism-Leninism on the ash-heap of history, as it has left other tyrannies which stifle the freedom and muzzle the self-expression of the people. . . .

The British people know that, given strong leadership, time and a little bit of hope, the forces of good ultimately rally and triumph over evil. Here among you is the cradle of self-government, the Mother of Parliaments. Here is the enduring greatness of the British contribution to mankind, the great civilized ideas: individual liberty, representative government, and the rule of law under God. . . .

Well, the task I've set forth will long outlive our own generation. But together, we too have come through the worst. Let us now begin a major effort to secure the best—a crusade for freedom that will engage the faith and fortitude of the next generation. For the sake of peace and justice, let us move toward a world in which all people are at last free to determine their own destiny.

Appendix G

Declaration of London: A Community of Democracies (1982)

DECLARATION OF LONDON – 7 November 1982

A Community of Democracies

The Committees for a Community of Democracies (CCD) advocate fundamental measures to strengthen relationships among the democracies of the world as a matter of the highest priority. In so doing they recognize democracy as the guiding and unifying principle, and community as the essential means for making their principles effective.

At a Founding Meeting in London on 5-7 November 1982 it was agreed that:

1. The Committees for a Community of Democracies will work to bring about the formation by those states who so wish of a community of democracies. By "democracies" we mean nation states characterized by political freedoms such as periodic elections, universal suffrage, plural party systems with majority votes leading to changes of government, elected free parliaments with the right of legislation, taxation, budgetary control, and deliberation of (including opposition to) the government's measures; by guaranteed civil rights, including freedom against arbitrary imprisonment, freedom of petition and association, freedom of movement, freedom of religion and education; and by an independent judiciary and courts to which everyone can have access

2. By "community" we mean a grouping of nation states acknowledging unity of purpose and common interests voluntarily coming together to undertake certain functions which they are better able to discharge jointly; and conferring on common institutions powers which go significantly beyond those of traditional intergovernmental

organizations. Such institutions would represent a "fusion of interests" of the democratic peoples, "not merely... an equilibrium of those interests through additional machinery of negotiation."

3. The Committee for a Community of Democracies will also work for the establishment of an Association of Democracies which will consist of those democracies which are prepared to confer with each other *as democracies* on matters relating to the advancement and preservation of democracy throughout the world.

4. It was agreed to set up an International Steering Group. Among its first tasks would be to advance the objectives of the CCD and the development and activation of a common program.

Appendix H

The Next Century Initiative: Building a New Democratic Order (1992)

THE NEXT CENTURY INITIATIVE

BUILDING A NEW DEMOCRATIC ORDER

Will international organizations such as NATO, the United Nations and the CSCE be able to prevent future ethnic conflicts?

How will human rights be fully extended into the next century?

Can today's international economic arrangements insure the development of free trade?

What will be the future of the world's environment if international organizations do not achieve global cooperation?

The Cold War produced an array of multinational organizations, each devoted to coping with specific "Cold War" issues. With the end of the Cold War, the world scene has dramatically changed and now we need to think again. Today, these organizations must be examined for their ability to handle the new economic, social and environmental issues of the next century.

Sponsored by:
The Association to Unite the Democracies
1506 Pennsylvania Ave., S.E. Washington, D.C. 20003
Tel: 202/544-5150 Fax: 202/544-3742

PROGRAM

The Initiative has been undertaken to promote the restructuring of international organizations to meet the challenges and opportunities that will face the next generation.

The end of the Cold War has necessitated a re-examination of international organizations. This examination Is urgent because new needs and dangers in the world are requiring new types of concerted action by governments. Today, because of the present state of International arrangements, needs are not being taken care of and dangers are increasing.

Therefore, these are the objectives of the Next Century Initiative:

1. Make the renewed case for organized cooperation among the developed democracies.

2. Review existing international ties, especially among the developed democracies. Appraise weaknesses and strengths of the present framework.

3. Propose the reform and possible inter-linkage of today's institutions. Consider the need for new institutions.

4. Consider how Institutional reforms among the developed democracies should relate to the United Nations and other international bodies

5. Form a non-governmental Action Committee at a high level that will carry on the work of the Next Century Initiative on a continuing basis

---

MAJOR ISSUE AREAS

International Trading and Monetary System
Development Aid
Security & Defense Relationships of the Developed Democracies
Global Security
Global and Developed Democracy Environmental Problems
Social & Political Security, Human Rights
Scientific and Technological Cooperation
The United Nations Structure
Emerging Democracies

A comprehensive non-governmental overview of international organizations has not been undertaken since the late forties and early fifties, when leaders in international affairs realized that an entirely new world situtation existed, and established new organizations to deal with the challenges of the Cold War.

Now, the world scene has dramatically changed once more, and we need to think again. The primary purpose of the Initiative Is to promote the restructuring of international organizations to cope with the challenges of the post-Cold War world. The first major undertaking is an international conference on **Building a New Democratic Order**.

SPONSORING COMMITTEE

The members of the Sponsoring Committee give authority, guidance and direction to the Initiative. Individuals who are committed to serve on the Committee include David Abshire, Senator William Brock, Dante Fascell, Rita Hauser, Lane Kirkland, Elliott Richardson and John Whitehead.

STEERING GROUPS

Steering groups in North America, Europe and the Pacific determine the issue areas which need to be addressed at the Conference and, with the help of the Sponsoring Committee, involve the best academics, business and political leaders in the issue areas under consideration.

STUDIES GROUP

Consisting of several working groups, the Studies Group provides the basis for the Conference's deliberations.

- Each working group will examine the case for developing or extending International Institutions in its area.
- In so far as it determines that there are problems that need to be addressed internationally and for which existing institutions are not adequate, the working group will then examine and develop specific proposals for international institutionalization in its area.
- Finally, each working group will consider how the strengthening of international governance and the revision of international regimes might support the achievement of desired changes in the working group's area of competence.

ACTION COMMITTEE FOR THE NEXT CENTURY INITIATIVE

The work of the above groups will culminate in a major International Conference. At this point, an Action Committee will be established for the Next Century Initiative. This Action Committee, composed of leaders in the international community, will start a process of high-level debate on proposals of the Conference, leading to further thought, public and governmental understanding, and constructive action.

The program and methods of the Action Committee may well be modeled on those of Jean Monnet's Action Committee for a United States of Europe, which played a major role in moving the European Community to develop closer unity among its members.

MEMBERS OF THE WASHINGTON, D.C. STEERING GROUP

Hon. John Richardson, Jr. (Chairman); Chairman Emeritus, National Endowment for Democracy and former Assistant Secretary of State for Educational and Cultural Affairs

Albert Hamilton (Secretary); Senior Associate, First Washington Associates, Ltd.

Richard Olson (founding Chairman of AUD's initiative); Proposal Manager, Dyncorp

Dr. Charles Patrick (Head of Secretariat for the Initiative), President, Association to Unite the Democracies

Dr. Raymond Gastil, (Director of Studies), Consultant to AID on democracy

Dr. Amelia Augustus, President and Co-Founder, Women's Economic Roundtable

Hon. Hodding Carter, Main Street TV Productions; former Assistant Secretary of State for Public Affairs

Robert Foulon, career Foreign Service Officer

Joseph Fromm, Chairman, U.S. Committee for International Institute of Strategic Studies

Dr. J. Allan Hovey, Senior Evaluator, US General Accounting Office

James Huntley, retired diplomat and former President of the Atlantic Council of the U.S.; member of AUD Board

Hon. Jed Johnson, Executive Director, Association of Former Members of Congress

Lawrence McQuade, President, Prudential Securities

Dr. Stephen Muller, Chairman, 21st Century Foundation; President Emeritus, Johns Hopkins University

Dr. Andrew Pierre, Senior Associate, Carnegie Endowment for International Peace

Walter R. Raymond, Jr., Project Director, 21st Century Foundation

Dr. John Saalberg, Consultant, Economic Planning and Business Development

Hon. Henry P. Smith III, former Member of Congress (NY)

Ted Van Dyk, President, Ted Van Dyk Associates

John N. Yochelson, Vice President, Economic and Business Policy, Center for Strategic and International Studies

---

We thank the following major donors:

Nicholas Doman
Halpern Associates
The Rita E. Hauser Foundation
Austin Lamont
The Henry Luce Foundation
Martha Politz
Jeanette Rohatyn
Nicolas Rohatyn
Hon. Adolph Schmidt
John C. Whitehead Foundation

The Secretariat for the Conference is sponsored by and under direction of The Association to Unite the Democracies, a [105(c)3] registered non-profit organization in Washington, D.C. Further information regarding The Next Century Initiative can be obtained from the Association.

Appendix I

Final Warsaw Declaration: Toward a Community of Democracies (2000)

Final Warsaw Declaration: Toward a Community of Democracies
Warsaw, Poland, June 27, 2000

We the participants from

Republic of Albania, People's Democratic Republic of Algeria, Argentine Republic, Republic of Armenia, Australia, Republic of Austria, Azerbaijani Republic, People's Republic of Bangladesh, Kingdom of Belgium, Belize, Republic of Benin, Republic of Bolivia, Bosnia and Herzegovina, Republic of Botswana, Federative Republic of Brazil, Republic of Bulgaria, Burkina Faso, Canada, Republic of Cape Verde, Republic of Chile, Republic of Colombia, Republic of Costa Rica, Republic of Croatia, Republic of Cyprus, Czech Republic, Kingdom of Denmark, Commonwealth of Dominica, Dominican Republic, Republic of Ecuador, Arab Republic of Egypt, Republic of El Salvador, Republic of Estonia, Republic of Finland, Georgia, Federal Republic of Germany, Republic of Guatemala, Republic of Haiti, Hellenic Republic, Republic of Hungary, Republic of Iceland, Republic of India, Republic of Indonesia, Ireland, State of Israel, Italian Republic, Japan, Hashemite Kingdom of Jordan, Republic of Kenya, Republic of Korea, State of Kuwait, Republic of Latvia, Kingdom of Lesotho, Principality of Liechtenstein, Republic of Lithuania, Grand Duchy of Luxembourg, former Yugoslav Republic of Macedonia, Republic of Madagascar, Republic of Malawi, Republic of Mali, Republic of Malta, Republic of Mauritius, Mexico, Republic of Moldova, Principality of Monaco, Mongolia, Kingdom of Morocco, Republic of Mozambique, Republic of Namibia, Kingdom of Nepal, Kingdom of the Netherlands, New Zealand, Republic of Nicaragua, Republic of the Niger, Federal Republic of Nigeria, Kingdom of Norway, Republic of Panama, Papua New Guinea, Republic of Paraguay, Republic of Peru, Republic of the Philippines, Republic of Poland,

Portuguese Republic, State of Qatar, Romania, Russian Federation, Saint Lucia, Democratic Republic of Sao Tome and Principe, Republic of Senegal, Republic of Seychelles, Slovak Republic, Republic of Slovenia, Republic of South Africa, Kingdom of Spain, Democratic Socialist Republic of Sri Lanka, Kingdom of Sweden, Swiss Confederation, United Republic of Tanzania, Kingdom of Thailand, Republic of Tunisia, Republic of Turkey, Ukraine, United Kingdom of Great Britain and Northern Ireland, United States of America, Eastern Republic of Uruguay, Bolivarian Republic of Venezuela, Republic of Yemen,
in the Community of Democracies Ministerial Meeting convened in Warsaw, 26–27 June 2000:

Expressing our common adherence to the purposes and principles set forth in the Charter of the United Nations and the Universal Declaration of Human Rights,

Reaffirming our commitment to respect relevant instruments of international law,

Emphasizing the interdependence between peace, development, human rights and democracy,

Recognizing the universality of democratic values,

Hereby agree to respect and uphold the following core democratic principles and practices:

- The will of the people shall be the basis of the authority of government, as expressed by exercise of the right and civic duties of citizens to choose their representatives through regular, free and fair elections with universal and equal suffrage, open to multiple parties, conducted by secret ballot, monitored by independent electoral authorities, and free of fraud and intimidation.

- The right of every person to equal access to public service and to take part in the conduct of public affairs, directly or through freely chosen representatives.

- The right of every person to equal protection of the law, without any discrimination as to race, color, sex, language, religion, political or other opinion, national or social origin, property, birth or other status.

- The right of every person to freedom of opinion and of expression, including to exchange and receive ideas and information through any media, regardless of frontiers.

- The right of every person to freedom of thought, conscience and religion.

- The right of every person to equal access to education.

- The right of the press to collect, report and disseminate information, news and opinions, subject only to restrictions necessary in a democratic society and prescribed by law, while bearing in mind evolving international practices in this field.

- The right of every person to respect for private family life, home, correspondence, including electronic communications, free of arbitrary or unlawful interference.

- The right of every person to freedom of peaceful assembly and association, including to establish or join their own political parties, civic groups, trade unions or other organizations with the necessary legal guarantees to allow them to operate freely on a basis of equal treatment before the law.

- The right of persons belonging to minorities or disadvantaged groups to equal protection of the law, and the freedom to enjoy their own culture, to profess and practice their own religion, and use their own language.

- The right of every person to be free from arbitrary arrest or detention; to be free from torture and other cruel, inhumane or degrading treatment or punishment; and to receive due process of law, including to be presumed innocent until proven guilty in a court of law.

- That the aforementioned rights, which are essential to full and effective participation in a democratic society, be enforced by a competent, independent and impartial judiciary open to the public, established and protected by law.

- That elected leaders uphold the law and function strictly in accordance with the constitution of the country concerned and procedures established by law.

- The right of those duly elected to form a government, assume office and fulfill the term of office as legally established.

- The obligation of an elected government to refrain from extraconstitutional actions, to allow the holding of periodic elections and to respect their results, and to relinquish power when its legal mandate ends.

- That government institutions be transparent, participatory and fully accountable to the citizenry of the country and take steps to combat corruption, which corrodes democracy.

- That the legislature be duly elected and transparent and accountable to the people.

- That civilian, democratic control over the military be established and preserved.

- That all human rights—civil, cultural, economic, political and social—be promoted and protected as set forth in the Universal Declaration of Human Rights and other relevant human rights instruments.

The Community of Democracies affirms our determination to work together to promote and strengthen democracy, recognizing that we are at differing stages in our democratic development. We will cooperate to consolidate and strengthen democratic institutions, with due respect for sovereignty and the principle of non-interference in internal affairs. Our goal is to support adherence to common democratic values and standards, as outlined above. To that end, our governments hereby agree to abide by these principles in practice, and to support one another in meeting these objectives which we set for ourselves today.

We will seek to strengthen institutions and processes of democracy. We appreciate the value of exchanging experiences in the consolidation of democracy and identifying best practices. We will promote discussions and, where appropriate, create forums on subjects relevant to democratic governance for the purpose of continuing and deepening our dialogue on democratization. We would focus our deliberations on our common principles and values rather than extraneous bilateral issues between members. We resolve jointly to cooperate to discourage and resist the threat to democracy posed by the overthrow of constitutionally elected governments. We resolve to strengthen cooperation to face the transnational challenges to democracy, such as state-sponsored, cross-border and other forms of terrorism; organized crime; corruption; drug trafficking; illegal arms trafficking; trafficking in human beings and money laundering, and to do so in accordance with respect for human rights of all persons and for the norms of international law.

We will encourage political leaders to uphold the values of tolerance and compromise that underpin effective democratic systems, and to promote respect for pluralism so as to enable societies to retain their multi-cultural character, and at the same time maintain stability and social cohesion. We reject ethnic and religious hatred, violence and other forms of extremism. We will also promote civil society, including women's organizations, nongovernmental organizations, labor and business associations, and independent media in their exercise of their democratic rights. Informed participation by all elements of society, men and women, in a country's economic and political life, including by persons belonging to minority groups, is fundamental to a vibrant and durable democracy.

We will help to promote government-to-government and people-to-people linkages and promote civic education and literacy, including education for democracy. In these ways we will strengthen democratic institutions and practices and support the diffusion of democratic norms and values.

We will work with relevant institutions and international organizations, civil society and governments to coordinate support for new and emerging democratic societies.

We recognize the importance our citizens place on the improvement of living conditions. We also recognize the mutually reinforcing benefits the democratic process offers to achieving sustained economic growth. To that end, we will seek to assist each other in economic and social development, including eradication of poverty, as an essential contributing factor to the promotion and preservation of democratic development.

We will collaborate on democracy-related issues in existing international and regional institutions, forming coalitions and caucuses to support resolutions and other international activities aimed at the promotion of democratic governance. This will help to create an external environment conducive to democratic development.

Final, June 27, 2 p.m.

Appendix J

EU-U.S. Summit Declaration on Democracy (2005)

**EU-U.S. SUMMIT DECLARATION
THE EUROPEAN UNION AND THE UNITED STATES
WORKING TOGETHER TO PROMOTE DEMOCRACY
AND SUPPORT FREEDOM, THE RULE OF LAW AND
HUMAN RIGHTS WORLDWIDE**

Washington & Brussels, 20 June 2005

1. The European Union and the United States believe that the spread of accountable and representative government, the rule of law, and respect for human rights as enshrined in the Universal Declaration of Human Rights, are a strategic priority as well as a moral necessity. We will continue to work together to advance these priorities around the world.

2. The work of the United Nations is central both to democracy and human rights. We welcome the proposals put forward by Kofi Annan to renew the UN's commitment and enhance its effectiveness in these areas. Specifically, we value the UN Secretary General's initiatives for reforming the UN human rights mechanisms and for creating a Peacebuilding Commission. We pledge to support the establishment of the UN Democracy Fund to assist countries in strengthening civil society and democratic institutions.

3. We express our admiration and pledge our support for all those engaged in the defence of freedom, democracy and human rights, in many cases at great personal risk.

4. We are encouraged by the efforts of many governments to open their societies and political systems. Recognizing that democratic reform is a process that deserves our support, we promise our solidarity and support

to those promoting democracy around the world, be it in Ukraine, Georgia, Kyrgyzstan, Lebanon, Iraq, Afghanistan, or elsewhere. We will continue to support pluralism and the development of civil society, and will encourage the political participation of women and minorities.

5. Free and fair elections are central to democracy. We congratulate the many thousands of citizens who have participated in organizing and observing elections in their own countries and abroad. We pledge to support the work of the United Nations in assisting in the organization of elections and will work together in multilateral fora to further strengthen international election standards and to spread the implementation of objective and fair election assessment mechanisms. We support the principles of impartially-conducted and transparent election administration and observation and commend the efforts undertaken by various regional organizations such as the OSCE or civil society in this context. We will continue to support the holding of free and fair elections in countries undergoing or desiring democratic transitions, including in Afghanistan, Haiti, DRC, Iraq, and in the Palestinian territories.

6. Democracy is not just a matter of elections; it must be anchored in democratic institutions, separation of powers, human rights, the rule of law, tolerance, good governance, and justice. Our assistance to third countries increasingly takes into account the need to sustain democracy in all these dimensions.

7. We have worked closely to create a Europe whole, free, and at peace; both the EU and NATO have played an important part in this, and continue to do so. We are confident that the reform process in the Balkans will further the region's successful integration into Europe. The European Neighbourhood Policy and U.S. support for democratic and economic transitions will contribute further to stability, prosperity and partnership. We will in particular continue to coordinate our efforts to promote democracy, the rule of law and respect for human rights in Belarus.

8. We are witnessing a growing desire for reform in the Middle East and welcome recent democratic developments. Democratic elections in the Palestinian territories, Iraq, and Lebanon have successfully taken place. We recognize the importance of transparent and fair elections and the need to expand freedom and opportunity across the region. We reaffirm our commitments made at Dromoland and Sea Island, and our support for the Forum for the Future and other elements of the G-8 BMENA Initiative. Recognizing that the threat of conflict can undermine democratic reforms,

we commit ourselves to support those who are working for the resolution of conflicts, in the Middle East and elsewhere.

9. We have both encouraged the growth of democratic institutions in many countries in Asia, Africa, and Latin America. **We acknowledge the important contributions by regional and multilateral organizations, as well as initiatives such as the Community of Democracies, to promote democracy and respect for fundamental human rights.**

10. We recognize that differences in history, culture and society mean that the paths taken towards democracy and the rule of law will be different and that the systems of government that result will be varied, reflecting local traditions and preferences. Democracy, while it is based on universal values, will not be uniform. However, the desire for justice, freedom, human rights, and accountable and representative government is universal. In the long term, only systems responsive to the wishes of the people they govern can achieve political stability.

Index

Printed in the United States
71754LV00004B/7